INTERPRETATIVE REPORTING

INTERPRETATIVE REPORTING

CURTIS D. MACDOUGALL, PH.D.

PROFESSOR OF JOURNALISM, *Northwestern University*

FOURTH EDITION

The Macmillan Company, New York
Collier-Macmillan Limited, London

Fourth Printing, 1965

Previous editions © copyright 1938, 1948, and 1957 by THE MACMILLAN COMPANY
Reporting for Beginners copyright 1932 by THE MACMILLAN COMPANY

Library of Congress catalog card number: 63-12136

The Macmillan Company, New York
Collier-Macmillan Canada, Ltd., Toronto, Ontario

PRINTED IN THE UNITED STATES OF AMERICA

ACKNOWLEDGEMENTS

MANY OF THE NEW IDEAS and most of the new examples in this edition came from practicing newspapermen and women who responded to the author's "cry for help." The following deserve to share whatever credit this book merits but, of course, are not to blame for any of its shortcomings:

Baden, Leon, Harrisburg (Pa.) *Patriot*
Beinhorn, Sherman, Middletown (Conn.) *Press*
Black, Creed, executive editor, Wilmington (Del.) *Journal-News*
Blade, Joseph, Toledo *Blade* (now diplomatic courier)
Blanchard, Robert O., Salt Lake City *Tribune* (now Syracuse University)
Block, Mervin, *Chicago's American* (now Columbia Broadcasting System, New York)
Botts, Jack C., Lincoln (Neb.) *Journal*
Cade, Dr. Dozier C., head, Department of Journalism, Georgia State College
Carty, Jr., James, Nashville *Tennessean* (now Bethany, W.Va. College)
Cockrell, James, financial editor, St. Louis *Globe-Democrat*
Croft, Duane E., Brush-Moore Newspapers, Canton (Ohio)
Driscoll, Thomas, city editor, Peoria *Journal-Star*
Eskey, Kenneth, Pittsburgh *Press*
Fisher, Prof. William, Kent State University
Francois, William, Dayton *Journal-Herald* (now Marshall University)
Full, Jerome, Salt Lake City *Tribune*
Garrison, Jerol, Little Rock *Gazette*
Geiselman, Jr., Arthur W., York (Pa.) *Gazette & Daily*
Gibson, Martin, Houston *Chronicle*
Hart, Ronald, Pittsburgh *Press*
Hayes, Charles, Paddock Publications, Arlington Heights (Ill.)
Hinson, Daniel, city editor, Orlando (Fla.) *Sentinel*
Kole, John, Milwaukee *Journal*
Little, William, Peoria *Journal-Star*
Littlewood, Tom, Springfield bureau, Chicago *Sun-Times*
Lunger, Phillip, Buffalo *Courier-Express*
MacDougall, A. Kent, Passaic (N.J.) *Herald-News* (now *Wall Street Journal*)
Mazzatenta, Ernest, city editor, Peru (Ind.) *Tribune* (now Omaha *World-Herald*)
Nofziger, Fred, Toledo *Blade*
Peeks, Edward, Washington *Afro-American* (now Charleston *Gazette*)
Perry, John, National Association of Broadcasters, Washington, D.C.
Price, Jo-Ann, New York *Herald Tribune*
Reynolds, Edward, San Francisco *Examiner*
Spaid, Ora, Louisville *Courier-Journal* (now Midwest Program of Airborne Television Instruction, Lafayette, Ind.)

v

Smart, Kenneth, assistant city editor, Dallas *Times Herald*

Spaid, Ora, Louisville *Courier-Journal*

Spiegler, William, Albany *Knickerbocker News* (now *Newsday*, Long Island, N.Y.)

Stanley, Robert, Dallas *Times Herald* (now North Texas State University, Denton, Texas)

Walz, Margaret, York (Pa.) *Gazette & Daily* (now Mrs. John Hyman, Toronto, Canada)

Watson, Harry, Milwaukee *Journal*

Werthimer, Prof. Jerrold, San Francisco State University

Williams, Edward, Milwaukee *Journal*

HISTORY AND PURPOSE

THE FIRST EDITION of this book appeared in 1932, entitled *Reporting for Beginners*.

In 1938 it was revised and given a new title, *Interpretative Reporting*. At the time few others had spoken up very loudly in favor of interpretation in the news, and reviews of the book were mostly critical essays on the idea.

The second revision of this book came out in 1948. It took cognizance of the fact that by then the debate over whether there should be interpretation had been won by the affirmative. The new edition predicted that the next issue to be discussed was specialization—how much and by whom. Today the need for specialization in journalism is generally recognized and only such practical matters as cost slow up its development.

In 1957 the third revision of this book took cognizance of the unfortunate misuse of the term "interpretation" to disguise editorializing and other bad news-writing practices. It stressed the fact that despite the trend throughout the past quarter century toward interpretation and specialization, the backbone of any editorial staff is the reporter thoroughly trained in newsgathering techniques and able to write a straightforward account of any routine occurrence. Such versatile reportorial experience is essential to all future activity in any branch of journalism. At the same time that he is mastering the fundamentals, however, the cub should be aware of the goal toward which he is striving—interpretative reporting and writing in a field of specialization.

The present revision is intended to make this book more serviceable than its predecessors in the attainment of this modern objective. It stresses methods of local reporting whereby the journalist can train himself to help readers understand the entire world in which they live.

TABLE OF CONTENTS

Part **I. Principles of News Writing**

1	The Modern Newsgatherer	3
2	Problems of Newsgathering	31
3	Organizing the Facts	49
4	Playing Up the Feature	65
5	Making It Attractive	85
6	Making It Readable	97
7	Saying It Right	121
8	Winning Reader Confidence	131
9	Keeping Up-to-Date	157
10	Giving It Substance	185

Part **II. Handling Important Assignments**

11	Persons and Personalities	211
12	Meetings, Conventions, Speeches	235
13	Illness and Death	255
14	Police, Crime, Criminal Law	285
15	Courts, Civil Law, Appeals	319
16	Politics, Elections	345
17	Government	369
18	Business, Finance, Labor	405
19	Religion, Science	441
20	Sports; Reviewing and Criticism; Features	461

Appendices

A	Style	493
B	Copy Reader's Symbols	505
C	Proof Reader's Symbols	507
D	Newspaper Terms	511
	INDEX	515

INTERPRETATIVE REPORTING

Part **I**

PRINCIPLES OF NEWS WRITING

A NEWSPAPERMAN'S CREDO

BY *Max Lerner*

1. *I believe in the integrity of the newspaperman to the facts and events with which he is dealing. He must give the event as it actually happened, the facts as they actually are, to the best of his descriptive power. His obligation to what actually happened is as exacting as the obligation of a historian, and his regard for evidence must be as scrupulous.*

2. *He has also the obligation, whenever the facts or events do not speak for themselves, to give the frame within which their meaning becomes clear. This may be a frame of history, or a broader interpretative frame of fact. In doing this he must make clear the distinction between fact and event on the one hand and his own opinion on the other.*

3. *In deciding what to include or omit he must use to the best of his ability the test of what is newsworthy in the minds of his readers, and what is of importance in the flow of events. He must resist the temptation of including or excluding on the basis of what will help or harm whatever team he is on and whatever crowd he runs with.*

4. *This means that he must give a hearing even to unpopular causes, including those which he may himself detest. He has the obligation to keep the channels of the press open for a competition of ideas, since only through such a competition will the people be able to arrive at their own decisions of what is right and good.*

5. *In any contest of opinion he has the obligation to state, as fairly as he knows how, the opposing viewpoints. At the same time, if he is presenting opinion in an editorial or a column, he has the obligation to set forth his own position honestly and forthrightly as his own, regardless of the consequences.*

6. *Beset as he inevitably will be by favor-seekers, special interests, press agents, public relations men, and operators of all kinds, he must keep himself scrupulously independent of their favors and pressures. This means that he must be strong enough to make himself unpopular with those who can smooth his path or make life pleasant for him.*

7. *He must resist all pressures from outside, whether they be from advertisers, government officials, businessmen, labor organizations, churches, ethnic groups, or any other source which has an effect on the circulation or revenue of his paper. This applies whether the newspaperman is a publisher, editor, reporter, reviewer, or columnist. Since the danger in many cases is that he will anticipate the pressures before they are exerted, and censor a news story, review, or opinion which may hurt circulation or revenue, he has the obligation to resist the voice from within himself which tells him to play it safe.*

8. *His responsibility is to his craft and to the integrity of his mind.*

Editor & Publisher

1

The Modern Newsgatherer

i. Journalism, Today and Tomorrow

ii. The Nature of Newspaper Work

iii. Reportorial Qualifications

1. *Valuable Traits*
2. *Nose for News*
3. *What Is News?*
4. *The Need for Interpretation*
5. *The Growth of Interpretation*

iv. How to Prepare

1. *Informational Background*
2. *Academic Preparation*
3. *Cub Reporting*
4. *Occupational Aids*

v. The Ethics of Journalism

1. *The Reporter's Prerogatives*
2. *Newspaper Policy*
3. *Invasion of Privacy*
4. *Reportorial Decision Making*
5. *Freedom of the Press*

ONE BIG HAPPY FAMILY

BY *Sydney J. Harris*

Journalism students are always writing in to ask if they can come up and look around a newspaper office, just to see how it runs. Since the weather may turn hot, I will spare them the trip, and explain some of the salient features of the editorial room.

This is the City Desk. The man sitting there with a scowl on his face is the City Editor. He is scowling because he wants more space for local news, and can't get it.

This is the Makeup Desk. The man sitting there with a scowl on his face is the Makeup Editor. He is scowling because he has to put 12,000 lines of type into 8,000 lines of space. This, as everyone knows, is impossible — but he will manage to do it.

This is the Copy Desk. The pale, haggard men lolling around the rim of the desk with scowls on their faces are Copyreaders. They are scowling because it is their job to read the stories the reporters have written. In their opinion, the reporters are stupid, incompetent, inaccurate and incoherent hacks who exist only to make life miserable for Copyreaders.

These are the Reporters' Desks. The reporters are scowling because the Copyreaders have butchered all their stories beyond recognition, and they are wondering how so many vicious and illiterate sadists managed to become Copyreaders on this particular newspaper.

This is the Rewrite Desk. The men leaning back on their chairs, with their feet on the desk, working the crossword puzzle, are Rewrite Men. They are scowling because they can't think of a three-letter word meaning a "domesticated feline."

This is a Feature Writer's Desk. The man sitting there with a scowl on his face is a Feature Writer. He is scowling because he hasn't had a juicy assignment in three days and is convinced there is a conspiracy to prevent him from getting a by-line for the rest of the year.

This is the Sports Desk. The man sitting there with a scowl on his face is a Sports Writer. He is scowling because all his relatives are pestering him for tickets to ball games and prize fights. Especially his wife's relatives.

This is the Editorial Writers' Desk. The man sitting there with a scowl on his face is an Editorial Writer. He is scowling because he has to write an editorial on the Foreign Ministers' Conference when he would rather be out fishing. Editorials in July sound like it, too.

This is a Columnist's Desk. The man sitting there with a scowl on his handsome face is a Columnist. He is scowling because everybody else on the paper hates him. The Editorial Writers would like to grab his space for more comment on the atomic bomb. The Feature Writers all know they could turn out a much better column with one hand. The Managing Editor is sure he is taking too much expense account money. The Publisher has a feeling nobody is reading his stuff. And his wife wants to know why he isn't getting more money for the wonderful job he's doing.

See that man across the room there? He's the only one who isn't scowling. He is the Window Washer.

Chicago Daily News

Regardless of whatever changes — social, economic, political, and other — that the future may bring, it is inconceivable that there ever will come a time when there will not be those whose full-time function it is to find out what is going on and to transmit that information to others, together with a proper explanation of its significance.

JOURNALISM, TODAY AND TOMORROW

As the world's population zooms and it becomes possible to visit all parts of the globe in a few hours, possibly even minutes, the problems and areas of interest with which the editor of the future must be concerned will multiply many times. The complexity and interdependence of all aspects of human living, furthermore, continue to enlarge both the opportunities and responsibilities of the newsgatherers and disseminators. And it will make no difference what the future medium of distribution is: slave runners, town criers, newsletters, carrier pigeons, telegraphs, telephones, printing presses, motion pictures, radio, television — or thought waves.

This also seems certain: It is going to take better men and women to report and edit the news of the world in the future than it has in the past. The qualifications required of those who enter journalism will continue to broaden as they have been doing steadily during the past quarter century. More and better education will be required and there will be an augmented need for those capable, after adequate preparation as general practitioners, to become specialists in a multitude of fields.

The improvement in the quality of the personnel engaged in journalism will continue to be both a business necessity and an essential to the future existence of democratic society. Only a competent and responsible journalism can provide the knowledge and understanding the masses of mankind need in order to maintain government of the people, by the people and for the people. From the standpoint of the young person choosing a career, this means that there is no other field of endeavor more likely to provide challenges and opportunities for personal development and service to mankind.

This book is for the benefit of beginners in this field who aspire some day to be newspaper publishers, magazine editors, radio or television commentators, foreign correspondents, editorial writers, syndicated columnists or authoritative journalistic experts on specialized subjects for any or all of the media. Just as the youngster who dreams of growing up to be a concert pianist begins with scales, finger exercises and Bach two-part inventions, so must the journalistic neophyte acquire the basic skills which he later can use regardless of the specific activity in which he is engaged.

No matter what electronic devices are developed for the use of the communicator, the need for a permanent record will persist. This means that there always is going to be something akin to the newspaper. This is so despite the fact that the huge expenditures involved in contemporary publishing have reduced the number of daily newspapers in the United States from approximately 2,600 to about 1,750 in a half century during which the population has more than doubled. Despite the decline in the number of newspapers, their total circulation reached an all-time high of close to 60 million at the end of the same period. About 150 million Americans read some newspaper every day.

Anyway, whatever the future may bring, as of today the daily newspaper still provides the best basic training for beginners in journalism, no matter what their lifetime ambitions may be. No other medium comes anywhere close to duplicating its efforts at speedy, accurate and thorough coverage of the news of the world. Acquiring the skills necessary for success as a newspaper reporter, therefore, is the smartest "first step" that anyone can take in the field of journalism. News magazines, television stations and other media prefer employes who have such experience.

Understandably, the young person considering a newspaper reportorial career asks himself:

1. How do I know I would like it?
2. How do I know I am qualified?
3. How should I prepare myself?
4. What about the ethics or morality of journalism?

THE NATURE OF NEWSPAPER
WORK

Old-time movies notwithstanding, newspaper reporters do not often emulate detectives in exposing murderers, kidnapers and subversives, nor do they shout "stop the presses" and compose headlines over the telephone after profanely "telling off" unreasonable superiors. Rather, they work regular eight-hour days in and out of remarkably quiet and orderly newsrooms, where they remove their hats.

In large cities, some reporters spend their entire working days on "beats" in the press rooms at police headquarters, city hall, the county building, the federal building and other places where it is certain important news will originate. They telephone their information to rewrite men in note form or they dictate it, composing as they go along. On smaller newspapers, beat men visit their news sources once or twice daily, returning to their offices to compose their own accounts. They also may double as "general assignment" reporters, covering news which occurs at places other than the familiar spots. In all instances they are under the careful direction and scrutiny of the city editor who in turn is responsible to the managing editor who has general charge of the entire news-editorial operation. How departmentalized a newspaper operation is and how split up the managerial and operational functions, depend upon its size. On even small papers the sports and society (or women's) departments usually are separate. Someone is in charge of handling news that reaches the office via the teletypesetters or leased wires of the press associations (Associated Press and United Press International) so there may be a telegraph or wire desk or, on larger papers, a foreign news department with a cable desk as a part of it. Large newspapers also have a central copy desk where most stories from whatever source are checked for style, accuracy, etc. and given headlines. Makeup (deciding where stories and other, mostly illustrative, material are to appear) may be handled by a separate makeup editor, by a news editor, or by someone else performing multiple duties. Perhaps no two newspapers are organized exactly alike, but the process of putting out a paper is the same no matter how the labor is divided. It is only by operating routinely on a predetermined schedule that it is possible to produce papers which appear daily at the same hour.

As for the reporter, despite the fact that he may consider himself haunted constantly by deadlines (the last minutes at which copy can be submitted to make editions), there is generally less monotony and consequently danger of "getting into a rut" in newspaper work than there is in almost anything else he could do today. This is the age of the Organization Man in which white-collar as well as blue-collar workers increasingly are becoming comparatively smaller and smaller cogs in huge industrial machines, the total operations (or even purposes) of which it is difficult for them to understand. Many recent authors have deplored the extent to which the contemporary economy puts a premium on conformity, stifles imagination and originality and, consequently, destroys initiative and even self-respect.

There is, of course, considerable sameness in the news from the same source day after day. Nevertheless, no two stories ever are exactly alike. The principals at least are different and so are their reactions to whatever befalls them: arrest, accident, honor, etc. And, even though the swash-buckling days of Richard Harding Davis are long since past, there is still a thrill, or at least a satisfied feeling, with every assignment successfully concluded. There is a greater pride of workmanship and sense of accomplishment than is possible for workers in most industries and offices in mid-twentieth century.

Even though he may consider himself low man on the press' totem pole, the cub reporter carries more prestige with the public than is true of apprentices in most other fields. At the scene of a fire or riot he flashes his press pass and is allowed across police lines. On the routine beat he is courted by those who want to get something in or to keep something out of the paper. From the very start of his journalistic career, by the very nature of his work, he "is somebody," and this fact cannot help but be gratifying to the human ego.

His is not a dream world or fool's paradise. The reporter actually *is* a responsible person. Several other persons will have a part in determining how whatever news he handles appears in the paper. Nevertheless, he has "first crack" at it. The original judgment which he exercises in determining whether and/or how something is to be reported is of the utmost importance. He, in other words, is the backbone of the news-gathering and disseminating operation. Truly, every reporter is also an editor and, conversely, the best editors continue throughout their future careers to maintain the attitudes of reporters.

The occupational disease that newspapermen must guard against is cynicism. Whereas skepticism is a journalistic asset, a hard-boiled or flippant attitude toward the so-called "realities" of life can lead not only to a flagrant disregard of the public interest but also to personal deterioration. Many of the public figures with whom he comes into diurnal contact, the reporter knows, do not deserve public adulation but are, to use the vernacular, stuffed shirts or phonies. Disillusionment comes also with discovery that the "rules of the game" — as the game actually is "played" in politics, business, and many other aspects of life — are often crass, mercenary and hypocritical. Overcoming gullibility and learning the "facts of life" can be valuable, provided they lead to intelligent sophistication.

Much superfluous effort has gone into the attempt to determine whether journalism is a profession, business or trade. What really counts is the attitude of the individual toward his work. Professionalism can be present or absent among carpenters, hotel clerks, nurses, doctors, lawyers, taxi drivers, newspapermen, and anybody or everybody else. As for journalism, there is no field which offers greater opportunities for the development of a professional point of view, idealism, public service and the like. It is the place for the starry-eyed youngster who wants to help "save the world." There is no better way for one who wants to help make democracy work more effectively to devote his talents. As in every other worthwhile endeavor, the road to the top is long and strewn with obstacles. At the summit, however, are the prestige and power which make the struggle worthwhile.

REPORTORIAL QUALIFICATIONS

As regards the myth that newspapermen are born and not made, Joseph Pulitzer, patriarch of the old New York *World*, and founder of the Pulitzer School of Journalism at Columbia University, said years ago:

> The only position that occurs to me that a man in our Republic can successfully fill by the simple fact of birth is that of an idiot. Is there any position for which a man does not demand and receive training — training at home, training in schools and colleges, training by master craftsmen, or training through bitter experience — through the burns that make the child dread the fire, through blunders costly to the aspirant?
>
> The "born editor" who has succeeded greatly without special preparation is simply a man with unusual ability and aptitude for his chosen profession, with great power of concentration and sustained effort. . . . Even in his case might it not be an advantage to have a system of instruction that would give him the same results at a saving of much time and labor?

Early in the century, Dr. John H. Finley, the scholarly editor of the New York *Times*, issued a challenge to those who own and operate newspapers, those who expect to work for them and those who prepare the latter for their life work when he said:

> If I were to make a plea to the colleges and universities on behalf of the press, it would be to prepare a few all-around men and women who should be competent to perform a planetary service, not only geographically but intelligently, to be in this democratic age what Democritus was in his day to his little world. Such men as one whom I knew who was prepared when the tomb of Tut-Ankh-Amen was opened to enter intelligently with the archaeologist; who when Einstein propounded his theory had some notion of what he was talking about; whom I found one day trying to find geometrically the area of a triangle in the terms of its sides; who in the midst of the last campaign wrote a two-column editorial on the new planet and yet who could tell you the baseball champions for the last ten years or the presidential returns for the last century.

A few years later a committee on schools of journalism of the American Society of Newspaper Editors reported:

We want the departments of journalism to turn out men . . . capable of appraising the changed and new world which will be theirs tomorrow. We want these boys — of course, they will start at the bottom — capable of rising to the posts of great newspaper power, equipped to wield that power intelligently. In other words, we wish them, while they are collecting police news and reporting banquets, to carry the mental equipment which, rightly directed, will one day invest them with editorial control. Each graduate ought to have in the knapsack of his mind the baton of the editor and publisher. . . . This society knows it is far more vital to the welfare of mankind that the men who make its journals of public opinion be culturally superior than it is that the surgeon or corporation lawyer be a man of manifold intellectual attainments.

Altogether too many college freshmen think training for journalism consists primarily in learning how to write. They are mostly students who did well in high school English and were inspired with literary ambitions by teachers who were surprised and grateful to find fewer than the average number of grammatical errors in their themes. Unfortunately, there is no such thing as "just writing," in journalism or any other field. William Shakespeare is immortal, not because of vocabulary or style but because of greatness of thought. He had an incomparable knowledge of history, psychology, geography, philosophy, and many other fields. He and other masters of past centuries are read today because they had something extraordinarily worthwhile to say.

Because great ideas rather than beautiful words and phrases make for superior writing, everything that a journalism student studies is of potential value to him. The subject matter of journalism includes all that is taught in courses in political science, history, economics, sociology, chemistry, physics and other subjects too numerous to mention. The student who recognizes this fact in his freshman year has a big advantage. By the time he takes his first journalism course in his sophomore, junior, or senior year, he will have more than the average liberal arts student's superficial interest in and knowledge of the contents of the innumerable textbooks he will have studied. He should have his head and files full of information on which to rely when he starts wandering on and off the campus in quest of news. It is the purpose of his journalism courses to make his textbook knowledge come alive, to show him how to utilize it in understanding and interpreting the contemporary scene. Through experience in hiring both liberal arts and journalism school graduates, editors have learned that a so-called "broad background" of general courses is not in itself adequate preparation for newspaper reporting. Liberal arts courses are mostly theoretical and purposeless; journalism courses are practical and purposeful. Since, however, the journalist deals mostly with news related to the subject matter of courses in the different social sciences, the student who discovers he has little or no interest in political science, economics and sociology should take stock to determine whether he really is wise to aspire to a career in journalism.

VALUABLE TRAITS

The young person who should be encouraged to go into journalism, therefore, is the one who wants very badly to spend his adulthood saying or writing worthwhile things. His chances of success may be judged by the extent to which at any early age he becomes interested in the world of affairs. There is no sense aspiring to a newspaper career unless one finds newspaper reading pleasurable as a youth. The more cosmopolitan the interests the better, as long as the news which will be mentioned in the political science, sociology and economics textbooks of the next few decades is included, for that is the kind of news with which the beginning reporter is most likely to come into contact.

Most of the personality traits usually listed as valuable for the journalist are ones which would be equally essential for success in most other professional fields: intelligence, friendliness, reliability, imagination, ingenuity, nerve, speed, accuracy, courage, endurance, ability to organize one's activities, perseverance, mental alertness, honesty, punctuality, cheerfulness, the power of observation, shrewdness, enterprise, optimism, humor, adaptability, initiative, and the like.

If there is any clue to be discovered in childhood by which to estimate journalistic capacity, it probably would be in the extent to which the boy or girl demonstrates curiosity and skepticism. A newsgatherer's stock in trade is his ability to keep on asking questions until he has exhausted all angles of an assignment. The youngster who wears out his parents by his querulousness may be worth encouraging as a potential journalistic great.

NOSE FOR NEWS

Usually listed first among the special qualifications which a newsgatherer needs is a "nose for news" which means the ability to recognize the news possibilities of an item of information and involves:

1. The ability to recognize that the information can be made of interest to readers.
2. The ability to recognize clues which may be very casual but which may lead to the discovery of important news.
3. The ability to recognize the relative importance of a number of facts concerning the same general subject.
4. The ability to recognize the possibility of other news related to the particular information at hand.

The anecdote often is told of a reporter assigned to cover a wedding who returned and dropped leisurely into his chair without turning in any story. Questioned by the editor, he replied, "Oh, there wasn't any wedding. The bride was there; so were the preacher, the attendants and all the guests. But the bridegroom didn't show up and so there isn't any story." Obviously, the nonappearance of the man was better (from the standpoint of interest) news than his appearance would have been. Intended bridegrooms usually are on time for their own weddings; and most weddings are much alike when it comes to writing them up.

Another reporter was given the story of a speech which an important man was to deliver. He was instructed to follow the speech with the advanced copy in his hands to see if the speaker deviated at all from the manuscript. The speech, in the meantime, had been written up and its publication awaited only the actual delivery.

The reporter strolled back to his editor's presence and reported that the speaker had cast aside his prepared manuscript and had talked extemporaneously. He said that it had been impossible to follow the speaker by means of the copy which he had. The reporter, however, had failed to take a single note on the speaker's impromptu remarks.

From these classical and possibly apocryphal examples it is clear that common sense is indispensable for the reporter. Especially in these days of public relations counsel and press releases, making news sources often difficult to see, the reporter must ask question after question to draw out whomever he does get to interview to learn about less obvious but important phases of the subject at hand. He must, in other words, be inquisitive, perceptive and healthfully skeptical.

The reporter with a cultivated nose for news realizes that, although the same elements may be present in similar stories, they invariably are there in different proportions as to importance. For instance, in an automobile accident story the reporter always must find out the names of all persons concerned, the extent of the injuries, details of the collision, etc. In Story A, however, the name of a person injured may be most important. In Story B the most important element may be the name of a prominent person who escaped injury. No two accidents ever result from exactly the same cause. In one case it may be a defective brake; in another, a drunken driver; and in a third, a billboard obstructing the view. Often the cause of an accident is very unusual — as when a bee makes a driver lose control of his machine.

In the same accident story there may be other important features which the reporter could not know without considerable questioning of the persons concerned. Perhaps the same two persons had been in accidents together before. Perhaps one of them recently left a hospital where he was recuperating from a previous accident. Perhaps one of them was on his way to an important engagement, a sick bed, or the scene of another accident.

The possibilities of a feature in a simple accident story have by no means been exhausted. Enough has been said, however, to indicate that to report a story "in depth" a reporter must be constantly "on his toes," as the expression goes. He has to think and think and think, and he has to ask and ask and ask. Good reporting consists in getting all the pertinent facts and then some more. Otherwise the story will not be complete and may be misleading because some of the important elements are left out. The reporter who learns to do a thorough job of delving into all of the potential angles of a simple "straight" news story is obtaining valuable training for interpretative reporting.

"Smelling a rat" is also an attribute of the straight news reporter and, especially, the interpretative reporter. For example, a reporter learned that a certain congressman was going to deliver a public address. He was sharp enough to inquire whether this meant that an important hearing over which the representative was to preside had been called off or postponed. Another reporter, unable to buy a certain game at several stores, investigated and learned that there was a new recreational fad in existence. Still another, noting that average school attendance in the elementary grades had gone up, investigated and came up with an article on the successful use of cold shots and other sickness preventatives.

WHAT IS NEWS?

Scholarly attempts to define news, for which the reporter is supposed to have a nose, correctly emphasize the fact that it is the account of an event, not the event itself. At any given moment millions of simultaneous events occur throughout the world. Someone dies, is born, gives a speech, attends a meeting, takes a trip, commits a crime, and so on ad infinitum. All of these occurrences are potentially news. They do not become so until some purveyor of news gives an account of them. The news, in other words, is the account of the event, not something intrinsic in the event itself.

Professional newsgatherers judge the potential interest and/or importance of an event before deciding whether to render an account of it, thus making it news. These newsgatherers are men, not deities. They possess no absolutistic yardstick by which to judge what to report and what to ignore. There is nothing that cannot be made interesting in the skilful telling; and only God Almighty is qualified to say what is important.

Understanding of the nature of news is not improved by adding such words as "timely," "concise," "accurate," or the like to definitions, as all such adjectives require explanations which differ with the editors or the circumstances.

THE NEED FOR INTERPRETATION

The successful journalist of the future is going to have to be more than a thoroughly trained journeyman if he is to climb the ladder of success. He must be capable of more than routine coverage and to interpret as well as report what is going on.

To interpret the news it is necessary to understand it, and understanding means more than just the ability to define the jargon used by persons in different walks of life. It involves recognizing the particular event as one of a series with both a cause and an effect. With their perspective the historians of the future may be better able to depict the trends and currents of the present, but if the gatherer of information is well informed, through his reading of history, his study of economics, sociology, political science and other academic subjects, and has acquaintance with the attempts of other observers to interpret the modern scene in books and magazine articles, he will at least be aware of the fact that an item of news is not an isolated incident but one inevitably linked to a chain of important events.

The interpretative reporter of the future should be as shock-proof as a psychoanalyst and a practical philosopher in his general outlook on life. He cannot succeed if he is hampered by prejudices and stereotyped attitudes which would bias his perception of human affairs. Modern psychiatry has proved that the first step in ridding a person of complexes is to make him aware of their bases. Hence, the newsgatherer should have a firm understanding of how men think and why, both to avoid pitfalls in his own search for so-called truth and to understand the behavior of those whose actions it is his responsibility to report.

What is this thing called public opinion which the newspaperman may think he is influencing? How explain a new political movement in terms of economic tendencies which give rise to such symptoms? What about the power which the demagogue of the moment seems to be able to exert? The interpreter of the news must see reasons where ordinary individuals observe only overt happenings. And he must study them as the scientist scrutinizes the specimen in his microscope, scientifically. He cannot be a participant in the events of which he writes or his viewpoint will be decidedly warped. Doing his best, he will err constantly; scientific method is nothing but being as approximately correct as possible. His mistakes, however, will be honest ones of an expert and not the blunders of an ignoramus. As Nathe P. Bagby, Texas newspaperman and journalism teacher, has said:

> Cultivation of the thinking habit will enable the reporter not only to handle his regular assignments in a manner more satisfactory and gratifying to his boss, but also make two stories grow where only one grew

before he took to thinking. The best stories are not generally found near the surface. Only the reporter who cultivates the habit of constant, thorough thoughtfulness finds them.

THE GROWTH OF INTERPRETATION

The first important impetus to interpretative handling of the news was provided by World War I. When it broke out most Americans were surprised — dumfounded in fact — and utterly unable to explain its causes. In his doctoral dissertation at the University of Wisconsin in the mid-'30s, the late Maynard Brown suggested the extent to which the newsgathering agencies were responsible for this phenomenon. Brown wrote in part:

> Where the Associated Press failed most was in preventing its reporters from sending background and informative articles based on politics and trends. It smugly adopted the attitude of permitting correspondents to report only what had definitely transpired. It wanted no interpretation of events but the mere factual reporting of the obvious. Some of its correspondents were trained in foreign affairs, but too few were able to interpret or discern significant events and tendencies.

Not only the Associated Press but other press associations and newspapers as well learned a great lesson from the experience of being totally unprepared either to understand the final steps which plunged the world into war or adequately to report the war once it started. During the '20s and '30s they peopled the capitals and other important news centers of the world with trained experts qualified not only to report but also to explain and interpret factual occurrences. Among the best of these journalistic scholars were Walter Duranty, John Gunther, Vincent Sheean, Edgar Ansel Mowrer, Quentin Reynolds, William Shirer and M. W. Fodor. In newspaper stories, magazine articles, authoritative books and radio commentaries, they and others did such a thoroughly competent job that, by contrast with 1914, for years before World War II began in 1939, an overwhelming majority of Americans expected it or at least knew it was possible if not probable.

Reader demand for more than mere drab objective reporting of domestic news grew tremendously after the stock-market crash of 1929 and during the depression years of the '30s and the period of New Deal experimentation which brought with it nationwide awareness of the increased importance in the life of every citizen of the federal government. Readership of the recently created weekly news magazines, *Time, Newsweek* and others, skyrocketed; so did the circulation of *Reader's Digest* and a multitude of other monthly digest magazines. So did the number and readership of how-to-do-it and other easily read books, allegedly compendious accounts of how to understand what was happening in a variety of fields of human interest and activity. So also did newsletters for general and specialized audiences.

Slow to modify their basic news formula, newspapers nevertheless expanded their contents to include signed columns by political analysts, most of which were syndicated at reasonable cost so as to be available for moderate and small-sized newspapers. In the mid-'30s newspapers also experimented with weekly news reviews, many of which (notably that of the New York *Times*) have survived. They also tried out various forms of daily reviews, expanded Sunday magazine or feature sections and increased the number of supplemental articles to provide historical, geographical, biographical and other background information to help make current news more understandable and meaningful. A whole new vocabulary developed to categorize these writings. Instead of lumping them all under the general heading of "think pieces" as in the past, newsmen now talk of sidebars, explainers, situationers, wrap-ups, button-ups, blockbusters and other types of explanatory, enterprise, offbeat, background, subsurface, creative, speculative or interpretative reporting and writing.

Since shortly after the end of World War II, no subject has received greater attention at the meetings of the American Society of Newspaper Editors and similar organizations than has that of interpretation, no matter what it is called. Since 1947, when they were formed, a number of the Continuing Study committees of the Associated Press Managing Editors have stimulated heated discussions of the problem annually.

Especially at first, a considerable amount of attention was devoted to definitions to determine what difference, if any, there is between interpretation and explanatory material, background facts, editorializing and opinion. Fundamental, however, was the question of policy: whether to permit AP writers leeway to go beyond the mere objective reporting of the news. Typical of many strong committee statements was that of the Business and Financial Report committee as follows:

> There is a tidal wave of demands for more interpretative writing. The average American is worried. He is worried as a producer and he is worried as a consumer. He doesn't know or understand what is happening to him, or to the world he lives in. But he is aware that tremendous events are occurring. He wonders how the United States is going to make its postwar comeback. He wants to read about new products, new methods and new leaders.

Today, the debate is virtually over with only a few still arguing against the necessity for interpretative reporting. This means that to become more than a humdrum journeyman the future reporter must prepare himself to help meet the increasing need and demand for "subsurface" or "depth" reporting, to "take the reader behind the scenes of the day's action," "relate the news to the reader's own framework and experience,"

"make sense out of the facts," "put factual news in perspective," "put meaning into the news," "point up the significance of current events," and so on, to use the expressions of various authorities. As Marquis W. Childs has written:

> The interpretive reporter expands the horizon of the news. He explains, he amplifies, he clarifies. . . .
>
> As contrasted with the sensationalist, the interpretive reporter must have a mature understanding of the importance and the responsibility of his function. . . .
>
> One of the most important tasks of the interpretive reporter is to expand the peripheries of the news . . . it is the special duty of the interpretive reporter to go behind the handout and the press conference. . . .
>
> You will ask where these interpretive reporters are going to be found. They come out of growth and experience. They come out of the city hall and the state capital. They grow in knowledge and experience and in confidence.

Foremost defender of interpretative reporting against its critics has been Lester Markel, Sunday editor of the New York *Times,* who has written:

> Those who object to interpretation say that a story should be confined to the "facts." I ask, "What facts?" And I discover that there is in reality no such thing as an "objective" article in the sense these objectors use it — or in any sense, for that matter.
>
> Take the most "objective" of reporters. He collects fifty facts; out of these fifty he selects twelve which he considers important enough to include in his piece, leaving out thirty-eight. This is the first exercise of judgment.
>
> Then the reporter decides which of these twelve facts shall constitute the lead of the story. The particular fact he chooses gets the emphasis — which is important because often the reader does not go beyond the first paragraph. This is the second exercise of judgment.
>
> Then the editor reads the so-called objective story and makes a decision as to whether it is to be played on page 1 or on page 29. If it is played on page 1 it may have considerable impact on opinion. If it is put on page 29 it has no such emphasis. The most important editorial decision on any paper, I believe, is what goes on page 1. This is the third exercise of judgment.
>
> In brief, this "objective" news is, in its exponents' own terms, very unobjective, and the kind of judgment required for interpretation is no different from the kind of judgment involved in the selection of the facts for a so-called factual story and in the display of that story.

In other words, just as the Constitution is said to mean what the Supreme Court says it means, so is news what newspapers and other media of communication decide it is to be.

HOW TO PREPARE

INFORMATIONAL BACKGROUND

The rule to follow in preparing for a career in journalism is: learn as much about as many things as possible and stay intellectually alert. The ignorant reporter is at a tremendous disadvantage. He annoys news sources, doesn't obtain all of the essential facts, and may make gross errors of fact as well as emphasis when he writes his story.

To cover intelligently a police station, criminal court, city hall, county, state or federal office, or political headquarters, one must understand the setups of government, the nature and functions of various offices. The reporter must be able to read and quickly digest the contents of legal documents. He must know the meanings of such terms as "corpus delicti," "habeas corpus," "injunction" and "certiorari." He cannot say "divorce" when he means "separate maintenance," or "parole" when he means "probation." He must be able to read a bank-balance sheet, know when a financial market is bullish and when bearish and what it means to sell short, hedge and stockpile. He must understand what it means to refinance a bond issue or liquidate the assets of a corporation. He doesn't confuse craft unions with industrial unions.

It is impossible for an interpretative reporter to write that the last obstacle to beginning a slum-clearance program has been removed unless he knows the procedure by which such projects are developed. He can't explain the status of a pending city ordinance unless he understands what the rules provide for future consideration of it. It is impossible for him to interview a prosecuting attorney regarding the course of action he may take in a particular case unless he knows what the alternatives are.

Although most editorial offices today are equipped with good libraries, or morgues as they often still are called, the reporter has to know which reference books and clipping files to consult to obtain historical and other explanatory information to "round out" a story. As he gathers experience he becomes a veritable storehouse of knowledge himself. Aware of the nature of different organizations, public and private, he knows which ones to consult on which occasion and what each group's slant or interest is likely to be.

Without background knowledge in a field a reporter cannot fill out an account by declaring that the home run was the longest ever hit in the park; that this was the first time a certain ward gave a voting majority to the candidates of a particular party; that a fatal accident occurred at an intersection where the city council once refused to permit the erection of stop signs; that what seems to be a new proposal for civic reform really was resurrected from a decade-old report by an elder statesman.

At a recent Associated Press Managing Editors meeting, Robert Paine of the Memphis *Commercial Appeal* cited the following story:

> Grand Junction, Tenn., Feb. 19. — (AP) — A smooth-working hound flushed seven bevies of quail in a three-hour trial yesterday for the top performance of the national championship.

Commented Paine:

> I imagine that every bird-dog owner in the country shuddered in horror at the word HOUND. That would be about the same as saying a cow won the Kentucky derby. They are strictly different kinds of dogs and bird-dog fanciers have a habit of shooting from the hip when one of their dogs is called a hound.
> Secondly, the word FLUSH is the exact opposite of the word that should have been used. That would be about like saying Babe Ruth won the game by striking out. Flush means to frighten the birds into flying away. The correct word is point.

It was not too many years ago that a journalistic ignoramus asked the Nobel prize-winning physicist, Dr. Robert Millikan, what cosmic rays were "good for." Those were the days when science was treated more or less as a joke in editorial offices and reporters assigned to science news stories were capable of little more than asking when the scholars expected to fly to Mars, find the missing link, or take the smell out of the onion. No wonder that many scientists still are reluctant to talk to reporters.

The interpretative reporter "reads the fine print" of a news story in order to answer the reader's query, "What does it mean?" To keep a particular news event "in focus," the interpretative reporter shows its comparative importance. Darrell Huff began his *How to Lie with Statistics*, a book every journalist of whatever kind would find valuable reading, with a warning that widespread reporting of a particular type of news, such as crime, easily can create a distorted impression as regards a social situation.

"Statistical methods and statistical terms," Huff wrote in his introduction, "are necessary in reporting the mass data of social and economic trends, business conditions, 'opinion' polls, the census. But without writers who use the words with honesty and understanding and readers who know what they mean, the result can only be semantic nonsense."

Mere figures showing total numbers of different types of crime committed in two or more areas only suggest the real story. Explanations of why styles in lawbreaking differ in different places at the same time and at the same place at different times, are to be found in such variable factors as size and complexion of population, police policies and activities and many others.

To present anywhere near a true picture of the housing situation in any community, a reporter must consider the age of the community and of the dwelling units; the adequacy of zoning and building codes and their enforcement; the influx of newcomers and the effect, including that caused by prejudice against certain types of persons because of race, national origin, religion or other reasons; the extent of overpopulation; transportation and parking facilities; educational, cultural and recreational advantages; the income and cost of living indices; nearby urban and suburban growth and similar factors. With such data he can provide readers with an understanding of the situation and enable them properly to evaluate proposals for change.

Mere announcement that consumer credit outstanding at any given time is such-and-such means little or nothing unless the reader knows how the figures given compare with similar ones for comparable periods in other months or years. Tables, graphs and charts help show trends; the news magazine, *U.S. News & World Report,* makes very effective use of them. For a broader picture of the state of the economy as a whole, more than comparative figures in any one economic category is necessary. In addition to installment buying, price indices, extent and kind (savings or checking) of bank deposits and withdrawals, a breakdown of the types of depositors (by size of deposits), purchase and cancellation of government securities (with comparable breakdown), bank loans, mortgages, new businesses, business failures, growth of chains and monopolies and other similar factors must be considered.

Often the motives of persons in the news must be known to make their actions understandable. The more a spectator knows about the strategy involved in an athletic contest, for instance, the more enjoyment he derives from it and the better able he is to second guess the manager or be a Monday morning quarterback. If, on the other hand, he knows little or nothing about such strategy, he won't understand why a weak hitter was given an intentional base on balls in order to pitch to a weaker one, possibly one batting from the same side as that from which the pitcher throws and supposedly more likely to hit into a double play. Or he will not understand why a quarterback called for a play which could not help but lose ground on the third down in order to put the ball in better position to try for a field goal on fourth down.

Just as sports writers explain the strategy of coaches, managers and contestants, so could reporters dealing with political affairs explain that precinct captains who rival the positions of ward committeemen often are made candidates for judgeships in order to remove them from active politics. Often the interpretative reporter seeks and easily obtains attribution in such situations but, after he has "been around" long enough, he knows the "tricks of the trade" and can at least suggest probable causes for the behavior of many newsworthy persons. If he fails to do so readers are in the position of just not knowing "what's going on."

To write with the perspective of the cultural anthropologist or historian of a century means to be aware of "schools of thought," "climates of opinion" and social, economic and political trends. A journalistic scholar should know when the views of an educator are consistent with those of an outstanding scholar or organization or with what has been attempted elsewhere. He should know what "progressive versus traditional" in pedagogical methods means. If he covers social welfare he should know the difference between the missonary (settlement house, boys club, etc.) and the self-help (area or community project) approaches.

There is a correlation between the extent of a feeling of insecurity and attacks upon civil liberties. Quite naturally the "curves" fluctuate with periods of war and depression, although it always is dangerous to draw historical parallels without thorough consideration of all possible factors.

Of this the studious interpretative reporter is certain: nothing just happens. A wave of intolerance has a cause. So has a revival movement, excessive hero worship, a bullish stock market, an increase in superstition, or any fad, fashion, craze or mass movement. Sometimes what seem to be isolated phenomena in several different fields really stem from the same causal roots. At any rate, there always is an explanation for how we "got that way." At an Associated Press Managing Editors meeting, John L. Morrison of the Greenville (Pennsylvania) *Record-Argus* adversely criticized the press association's handling of the trial of Hungarian Cardinal Mindszenty. He said:

> There was likely a great deal of background involving two or three centuries of religious struggle and complications, and even without Soviet interference, there could have been a high tension requiring only a small thing to ignite it. There was a wide field for speculation and an exceedingly small supply of factual information.

ACADEMIC PREPARATION

Although there probably always will be exceptions, present trends indicate that future journalists will be college trained. Such, in fact, is already the case on most metropolitan newspapers and, except for old timers, most of the degree holders went to schools of journalism. The proportion of those with master's and other higher degrees also is increasing.

Modern journalism schools are not trade schools. From two-thirds to four-fifths of a student's class work is taken in the liberal arts or other divisions. Anything and everything that a future journalist studies has potential future value for him and it is frustrating not to be able to take the entire curriculum in the humanities, natural and physical sciences. Those who are ambitious to specialize ultimately in particular fields should do so, but the majority should strive for a thorough and well-rounded background in the social sciences: political science, sociology and economics in particular. The student should try to get in courses in public finance, criminology and labor problems among others. History courses give him perspective and psychology enables him to come closer to understanding both individual and crowd behavior.

In his advanced journalism courses the student should expect to be taught how to utilize the background and theoretical knowledge acquired all over the rest of the campus in reporting and interpreting the contemporary scene. On assignments, he observes "theory becoming action," and if he takes some philosophy he will be better able to comprehend and evaluate the immediate incident in terms of the general and eternal.

A strict journalism instructor, simulating the exactness of a hard-boiled city editor, can teach sound methods of research. The journalistic fact finder does not begin with a hypothesis for which he seeks factual proof. Rather, he is an open-minded seeker after truth who explores every possible avenue of investigation; and only after he has exhausted every chance to obtain additional information does he attempt to draw conclusions regarding the accumulated data. This objective approach to knowledge is much sounder than that practiced by many researchers in other academic fields. In the process, the student-reporter becomes familiar with the nature of reference or source material; he may learn how to read and understand a county board's budget or the complicated declaration filed to begin a civil law action.

Since World War II, a number of social scientists have become interested in quantitative analysis of various aspects of social behavior and in communication theory. They use the tools of the statistician and the language of the sociologist to examine the effects of various ways to influence human thought and behavior. Many of their findings are of value to the propagandist, advertiser, public relations counsel and others who have ideas or products to sell. Knowledge of what they are up to is important for the true journalist who is a protector of their potential victims.

CUB REPORTING

Fortunate is the school of journalism graduate whose first job enables him to write as well as report. He should avoid being "buried" in a press room on a beat where he merely phones in the news, or on a copy desk or in a radio or television newsroom where press association and newspaper leads are rewritten so as to be suitable for broadcast.

There is no better vantage point from which to observe a cross section of life "in the raw" than police headquarters or courts. There the reporter will meet novelists, playwrights and magazine-article writers as well as sociology, law, and other scholars and students observing and gathering authentic information for their own understanding and usage. It is the place to "get your nose rubbed in it," meaning to come face to face with the squalid side of life, social problems, human frailties and personality types. Few would care to remain on the police beat indefinitely but anyone who skips the experience is shortchanged.

Thorough preliminary journalistic training also should include some contact with politics and government as well as the mine run of general assignments: meetings, speeches, obituaries, accidents, interviews, routine business, society and similar news. After a few years of such varied experience the beginner is able to start thinking about settling down to specialize. Thereafter, however, he will be wise to arrange for "change-of-pace" interludes such as those which discerning publishers and editors provide editorial writers, columnists, foreign news editors and others when they send them on trips of observation and fact-finding and encourage them to stay out of the rut or ivory tower.

OCCUPATIONAL AIDS

Ability to use a typewriter is essential. Usually a short evening or summer course provides adequate training, provided one has not already taught himself too many bad habits to be corrected. Until recently, few reporters felt the need of shorthand since the task of translating notes, of which there was temptation to take too many, slowed rather than hastened the process of reporting and writing. Today, however, when it often is necessary to interview news sources in the company of other reporters or to attend news conferences at which only a few get to ask questions, a verbatim record of what transpired often is valuable. Testimony in court or at committee hearings also can best be taken down in shorthand; thus more and more newsgatherers who specialize in such kind of work are learning it.

Those who have not done so usually develop their own system of short longhand, and may know some of the commercialized systems which are based primarily upon abbreviations for common syllables and combinations of letters. The reporter who develops his own system uses abbreviations for frequently used words and phrases. For instance, "2" is used for "to," "too," and "two," and "c" for "see," "u" for "you," "r" for "are," etc. The reporter can use simplified spelling in note taking if not in actual copy and can make use of such common abbreviations as "rr" for "railroad," "inc" for "incomplete," etc. He may even use foreign words which are shorter than English, as the French "selon" instead of "according to." Instead of "capital punishment" he may jot down "cp" and instead of "labor union" he may write "lu."

Wire or tape recorders are coming into greater use at news conferences and public functions and even during some interviews as a means of protecting both interviewer and interviewee as to the accuracy of subsequent quotation. There is the danger, however, that such interviews can become too formal and stilted and that the presence of the electronic device causes the interviewee to become overly cautious in his remarks. The same is true if motion pictures or television recordings are made. In such cases, of course, the reporter does not have to know how to operate the gadgets. On some small and medium-sized papers, however, he may be expected, on occasion at least, to be able to use a camera when a staff photographer is unable to accompany him on assignment. Labor union contracts may forbid his doing so in other places. In any case, it is unlikely that he will have to know more than how to take the pictures; the development and printing will be the task of others.

THE ETHICS OF JOURNALISM

In considering a possible life work, any young person with an adequate social conscience asks himself, "How much of my soul would I have to sell?" As regards journalism, he wants clarification of the accusations he has heard that the media are owned and run by conservative or reactionary businessmen whose interest is profit making rather than public service; that news and editorial policy is influenced too much by advertisers and powerful pressure groups, and that the individual reporter, to survive, must suppress, exaggerate, sensationalize and distort the news which he often gathers by means of dishonest practices, unjustly invading the privacy and betraying the confidences of those with whom he deals.

THE REPORTER'S PREROGATIVES

Flat denial of these and similar charges is impossible. Bad journalistic practices *do* exist in some places and it may not be much solace to know that a review of history reveals that the worst offenders ultimately succumb. There is a decided limit, however, to which the rank-and-file journalist deserves sympathy when he rationalizes his own sins and shortcomings by blaming his superiors. No editor worth working for requires any member of his staff to violate his moral standards or conscience. Any "dirty" assignments go to those who give evidence early in their careers that they are easy or perhaps eager to be pushed around. In few other occupations is it possible for hirelings to "talk up" to their bosses as much as in journalism. A careful fact-gatherer has a better-than-even chance on most publications if he undertakes to persuade his superiors to publish what he has found to be true. No matter how money-minded his publisher may be, the reporter on assignment is not so motivated. By contrast, a clerk or salesman is constantly aware of his responsibility to make a sale and even the smiles and courtesies with which he greets customers may be feigned. Lawyers cynically "cut corners" in the interest of clients. It is difficult to find the person who is qualified to "cast the first stone" at the working journalist.

NEWSPAPER POLICY

It is true that newspapers and other journalistic media are big business enterprises which means they are owned and operated by wealthy persons whose natural and sincere outlook is generally what is called conservative. Many of these publishers deserve more credit than they receive for their efforts to prevent their personal biases from distorting the fairness of basic news coverage. It is not true that on larger publications the advertisers dictate news and editorial policies. Especially as regards larger publications, the advertisers need the good will of the publication more than the publication needs them. Granting favors in the form of publicity stories for "sacred cows" or soft-pedaling unfavorable news is a decidedly shortsighted policy. The press' conservatism, which reflects itself mostly in endorsement of presidential candidates and attitudes toward national political issues, is derived honestly, no matter how unwisely, from the sincere beliefs of owners and publishers. They also are sensitive to reader and other criticisms as, witness the fact, that investigations of the handling of the 1960 campaign indicate extraordinary fairness following some bitter charges of bias in 1952 and 1956.

The American press is a patriotic one which means that often it is duped itself and misleads readers by rushing into print with statements by prominent public officials which later have to be modified or counteracted. Since the end of World War II, the overwhelming majority of American newspapers, magazines, radio and television networks and stations, and other journalistic media have been almost completely uncritical supporters of United States foreign policy. Any reader who peruses more than the streamer-headlined news, however, knows that American journalism has not succumbed to suggestions that it censor "the other side" of the news. Usually, when misinformation is disseminated, the original and most important offender is the news source, not the medium.

Certainly, at the beginners' level, newsgatherers are not instructed to fake or commit hoaxes. One beneficial by-product of the decline of competition, perhaps, has been the reduction of temptation to use unethical practices to obtain scoops. Few reporters any longer engage in picture stealing or misrepresent themselves as policemen or coroners' deputies. If they fail to give their readers more "inside dope" it usually is because they don't possess it themselves. A reporter is the last person to whom someone wishing to conceal facts unburdens himself. On the other hand, newspapers have expended huge sums of money, involving great expenditures of time and energy, to expose corruption or to verify or discover facts in the public interest.

INVASION OF PRIVACY

No legal or judicial clarification ever has been made of the extent to which any person possesses a right to privacy. Generally accepted is the fact that anyone who courts public attention, as the politician or entertainer, sacrifices much or most of his privacy. Others, such as witnesses to accidents, crimes and the like, lose it temporarily through no fault of their own. Few persons like gossip about themselves but fewer still fail to enjoy it when it involves someone else. Many newspapers suppress the names of juvenile first offenders, relatives of persons unfavorably in the news, innocent victims of rape, and other offenses and the like. Such policies are determined at the journalistic summit and should be made clear to all newsgatherers who then know they will be supported by their superiors in their grass-roots decision-making.

REPORTORIAL DECISION-MAKING

The same is true as regards many other ethical or policy matters, as whether to play up or down an outbreak of interracial violence, sensationalism in the handling of news of sex or crime, the details or even the facts of suicide, identification as to race, nationality or religion, and the like. The reporter can "pass the buck" to his superior when he knows he has operated in accordance with publication policy.

A troublesome decision which the reporter sometimes has to make for himself is whether to listen to "off-the-record" statements; that is, whether to receive information in confidence. Sometimes, by promising not to quote a news source, he can obtain facts which the public has a right to know, or he may get tips which he can follow up without implicating the tipster. At other times, however, he may find that he has allowed himself to be "conned" into suppressing something. It is difficult to set a rule which applies to all situations. One thing is certain, however: once given, a promise must be kept. Many journalists have gone to jail for refusal to betray a confidential news source.

FREEDOM OF THE PRESS

Properly to evaluate any journalistic performance, the original purpose of the freedom of the press clause in the first amendment to the Constitution must be borne in mind. On one hand, the founding fathers wanted to prevent any governmental interference with or censorship prior to publication of news in the public interest, as they recalled the centuries of struggle which it took in England to obtain such rights. On the other hand, freedom of the press also was intended as a positive instrument to bolster the chances of success for an experimental government of, by, and for the people. It really was the "right to be informed" that was being protected. If the founding fathers had thought some form of governmental regulation would best serve that purpose, undoubtedly they would have prescribed it. However, they felt the opposite: that wide-open freedom for any and all to publish or speak as they chose, even untruthfully and unfairly, would, in the long run, serve the public interest best. Thus, freedom of the press is a means to an end, not primarily an end in itself.

In the light of this purpose, it is discouraging to read the results of Gallup and other public-opinion polls which show gross and widespread ignorance regarding names and events in the news. The blame, however, is hardly primarily that of the journalistic media which are there for the public to use. Rather, superficiality of interest in public affairs must be traced to failures in the homes, schools, churches, and other places. Perhaps it is caused by the complexities and insecurities of our contemporary society. If the increasingly monopolistic press furthermore gives only one point of view on major issues, there nevertheless exists a quantity of liberal and iconoclastic magazines, newsletters and other periodicals to which it is possible to subscribe. It is not necessary to be uninformed or befuddled in the United States, the most literate nation in the world; and it is unfair to scapegoat the press, despite its shortcomings, for any public apathy. Possibly, a more enlightened and vigorous defense of civil liberties and civil rights by journalistic media would help, but it would only go so far in combating undemocratic forces. Anything that the idealistic newcomer to the ranks of journalism can contribute to the improvement of the rule of the news media in this respect is in the public interest. The opportunities for such service are greater than the young person would find most other places. He could, in fact, do no better than to attempt to live up to the code of the American Society of Newspaper Editors adopted in April, 1923 as follows:

> The primary function of newspapers is to communicate to the human race what its members do, feel and think. Journalism, therefore, demands of its practitioners the widest range of intelligence, of knowledge, and of

experience, as well as natural and trained powers of observation and reasoning. To its opportunities as a chronicle are indissolubly linked its obligations as teacher and interpreter.

To the end of finding some means of codifying sound practice and just aspirations of American journalism, these canons are set forth:

I

Responsibility. The right of a newspaper to attract and hold readers is restricted by nothing but consideration of public welfare. The use a newspaper makes of the share of public attention it gains serves to determine its sense of responsibility, which it shares with every member of its staff. A journalist who uses his power for any selfish or otherwise unworthy purpose is faithless to a high trust.

II

Freedom of the Press. Freedom of the press is to be guarded as a vital right of mankind. It is the unquestionable right to discuss whatever is not explicitly forbidden by law, including the wisdom of any restrictive statute.

III

Independence. Freedom from all obligations except that of fidelity to the public interest is vital.

1. Promotion of any private interest contrary to the general welfare, for whatever reason, is not compatible with honest journalism. So-called news communications from private sources should not be published without public notice of their source or else substantiation of their claims to value as news, both in form and substance.

2. Partisanship in editorial comment which knowingly departs from the truth does violence to the best spirit of American journalism; in the news columns it is subversive of a fundamental principle of the profession.

IV

Sincerity, Truthfulness, Accuracy. Good faith with the reader is the foundation of all journalism worthy of the name.

1. By every consideration of good faith a newspaper is constrained to be truthful. It is not to be excused for lack of thoroughness or accuracy within its control or failure to obtain command of these essential qualities.

2. Headlines should be fully warranted by the contents of the articles which they surmount.

V

Impartiality. Sound practice makes clear distinction between news reports and expressions of opinion. News reports should be free from opinion or bias of any kind.

1. This rule does not apply to so-called special articles unmistakably devoted to advocacy or characterized by a signature authorizing the writer's own conclusions and interpretations.

VI

Fair Play. A newspaper should not publish unofficial charges affecting reputation or moral character without opportunity given to the accused to be heard; right practice demands the giving of such opportunity in all cases of serious accusation outside judicial proceedings.

1. A newspaper should not invade private rights or feelings without sure warrant of public right as distinguished from public curiosity.

2. It is the privilege, as it is the duty, of a newspaper to make prompt and complete correction of its own serious mistakes of fact or opinion, whatever their origin.

VII

Decency. A newspaper cannot escape conviction of insincerity if while professing high moral purposes it supplies incentives to base conduct, such as are to be found in details of crime and vice, publication of which is not demonstrably for the general good. Lacking authority to enforce its canons, the journalism here represented can but express the hope that deliberate pandering to vicious instincts will encounter effective public disapproval or yield to the influence of a preponderant professional condemnation.

2

Problems of Newsgathering

I. Interviewing

1. *Resourcefulness*
2. *Perseverance*
3. *Friendships on Beats*
4. *Publicity Seekers*
5. *Formal Interviews*
6. *Denials*

II. The Interviewer

III. Public Relations

1. *Adverse Criticism*
2. *In Defense*
3. *Dangers*

IV. Government Secrecy

V. The Interpretative Viewpoint

JOURNALISM'S ADOLESCENCE

BY *Newbold Noyes, Jr.,* Washington *Evening Star*

In 1900, when my grandfather, Frank Noyes, helped found the modern Associated Press and embarked on 38 years of service as first president of that news agency, he and his associates were pretty sure they knew the answer to our question, how to tell the truth. Their answer was a thing called "objectivity." It was a very good answer, too.

Up to then, newspapers had been quite personal in their approach to the news. Most reporters fancied themselves as so many 19th century Westbrook Peglers. What they wrote was vastly entertaining, but they were not nearly so concerned with telling people the truth as with telling people off. They faithfully promoted their own ends, and cudgelled their enemies with gusto, and a good time was had by all. But the truth, somehow, tended to get lost in the shuffle.

The Associated Press realized at the start that it couldn't possibly cater to the opinion whims of all the different publishers receiving its service. It set out to correct the situation by instituting the principle and practice of "objective" news coverage. Gradually, as time went by, this revolutionary principle became accepted as the Number 1 item in the creed of the responsible press all over the country. It wholly changed the face of the newspaper world, and it set the pattern for a full half-century of journalistic growth and progress.

The idea of objective reporting is second nature to all of us today — so much so that we have to stop and think when it comes to defining it. Fundamentally, however, to the men who first preached it, objectivity meant that the only safe thing in a newspaper — outside of the editorial page — was a fact. The reporter's duty was to supply his readers with the cold, hard barren details of what had happened — and with nothing more. If he did try to give them something more, he was moving into dangerous ground — for he was interfering with the reader's right to make up his mind on the basis of the facts alone.

In the early decades of this century, in short, our responsible press operated under the theory that it was better to take a chance on not informing its readers than it was to take a chance on misinforming them. It tried, as we try today, to tell the public the truth. But it was afraid of trying to tell the whole truth. Its overriding concern was making sure that what it dispensed was nothing but the truth. It operated on the assumption that it simply was not feasible for a newspaper to attempt to tell the truth, the whole truth and nothing but the truth — all three at the same time.

The principle of strictly objective reporting was eminently sound. It provided an atmosphere in which the newspaper of this country could grow up out of its lusty and carefree youth into something like responsible maturity. The cult of objectivity, in other words, supplied the ground rules of a safe adolescence for American journalism.

But the day inevitably comes when an ex-adolescent must test for himself the forbidden fruits he has been taught are so dangerous. That time is hard upon us now.

Sometimes a reporter is present at a news event of which he writes, as a meeting, speech, court trial or athletic contest. More often he obtains his information second-hand, through interviewing eyewitnesses, authorities, and others, or from press releases, reports and documents. Even when the newsgatherer is at the scene he has to check facts and details with firemen, policemen, convention chairmen and the like.

INTERVIEWING

RESOURCEFULNESS

Newspaper reporters not only have risked and lost their lives in the front lines during warfare, but they have braved danger in peacetime to cover floods, hurricanes, fires, strikes, crimes and many other kinds of stories. No editor expects a reporter to place himself in unreasonable jeopardy, but he does drill into every cub the fact that there always is more than one way to get any story. Resourcefulness by the reporter is imperative; the editor miles away cannot do his most important thinking for him.

Consider an experience with which the beginning reporter is likely to meet — arrival at the scene of an automobile accident after the crowd has disappeared, the injured persons have been removed and the wreckage has been cleared away. The unresourceful reporter probably would phone his office that he is unable to get the story. The resourceful reporter, however, makes inquiries at the stores and residences nearby. He tries to find the policeman on the beat who probably has the names of the persons who were involved. Unsuccessful in these attempts he hastens to the nearest garages to find the damaged automobiles. Succeeding in that, he makes a notation of the license numbers in case the garage proprietor is unable to give him names. He phones police headquarters to discover the owners' names and addresses. He also phones the nearest hospitals. From one of these sources surely he learns the identity and whereabouts of the individuals whom he wishes to see. If he knows that someone was killed, he investigates at the morgue or calls the coroner.

The experienced reporter possesses the knowledge of all the possible channels through which he can obtain the information that he desires. Unidentified persons can be traced by means of laundry and other marks on their clothing, by dental work, even by bodily scars and deformities. A suicide may be explained by friends of the dead person who recall conversations which at the time seemed unimportant to them but which later cast light on the deceased's motive in taking his own life. Often the reporter may recall some news story printed in his paper weeks or months previously which suggests a solution to the mystery at hand. The wise reporter makes a practice of reading his own and rival newspapers daily, and he preserves news items which may be of value to him later. When in doubt whether to clip a certain article, he follows the safer policy and clips.

PERSEVERANCE

When he has established contact with someone able to give him information, the reporter may be chagrined to discover that the news source is reluctant to cooperate to the desired extent. Maybe he just doesn't want to "get mixed up" in some matter, for fear of being summoned as a witness in court or of arousing the displeasure of public officials, gangsters and others whom he fears. Possibly he does not want to reveal his ignorance or to tip his hand regarding business or personal plans. The reasons why a news source slams the telephone or door or "clams up" may be many and diverse, but the obligation of the reporter is the same. It is his duty to discover any facts that it is in the public interest be made known.

In many situations perseverance usually is rewarded. If a person deliberately evades the press by refusing to answer the telephone or by locking himself in his office or home, he plays a losing game. If he is a person whose information or opinion the newspaper has a right to request, his refusal to grant an interview does not make him appear in a very favorable light to readers. The reporter must be careful in stating that a man has disappeared to avoid being interviewed or facing charges, but he can say that a person could not be reached. In fact, he should include such a statement in his story to let his readers know that he has made the effort. If a person grants an interview but still refuses to talk, his silence may be even more important news than any statement would have been. Once the reporter has questioned a person and has received a noncommittal answer or no answer at all, he can say that Mr. So-and-So refused to make any comment. Then readers can draw their own conclusions as to why Mr. So-and-So would not talk.

Mayor Alvin R. Potter had nothing to say today regarding the accusation that city employes, including himself, obtain free gasoline from the city yards.

The charge was made yesterday by Ald. Leonard Ball, chairman of the streets committee. The chief executive's only reply to inquiring reporters was: "I have no statement to make at this time."

Sometimes the reporter may be able to convince his subject that it is to his advantage to make some statement. If a person knows that the paper will run a story of his refusal to comment, he may be frightened into speaking against his previous resolution not to do so.

A person who becomes involved in the news in a way distasteful to him may hesitate to speak for publication for fear of being misquoted or misrepresented. The personality and sincerity of a reporter may suffice to cause such a person to talk. Everything depends upon the approach which the reporter makes and upon his own attitude during the interview. His purpose should be to convince his subject that he bears no malice, and that he is seeking an accurate and fair quotation. If the reporter can convince his subject of this fact, he may find the person grateful for the opportunity of at last being able to talk to someone who is sympathetic and who affords him the chance of making his version of a story understood.

Fortunate is the reporter who possesses some bit of information which his subject does not expect him to know. Skillful interjection into the interview of this information may bring to an end any attempt at bluffing or fabrication. If he does not possess knowledge with which to intimidate his subject, the reporter may himself start bluffing. It often is necessary to put on a bold front and to challenge statement with statement.

The reporter should realize at all times that he has a powerful organization, his newspaper, in back of him. If he "curls up" and permits himself to be browbeaten, he fails in his duty to his editor. If he is treading on ground where he has a perfect right to tread, he never should be humble. Men who have been in public life for any length of time realize the power of the press and respect it. This does not mean that the reporter should be overbearing or that he should resort to threats, except in extreme cases where such measures are justified. The reporter must be guided by his common sense and his understanding of what constitutes public interest in determining when to threaten and when to cajole.

The best kind of interview is that which proceeds in a natural, friendly, informal way. The reporter may inspire confidence and make himself attractive by not coming to the point of his visit at once, but by beginning the conversation with some general comment. If he can get his subject chatting about another matter, he may be able to lead the interview easily into the channel that he wishes it to take.

It is wise to take as few notes as possible during an interview of this kind. Often it is disastrous to take a single note. If the reporter can get his subject to forget that he is speaking for publication, he will obtain much more than if the person is constantly reminded that the interviewer is taking down verbatim what he is saying.

Sometimes the interviewee requests the reporter to take verbatim notes. Or the reporter at the end of an interview may remark, "By the way, would you mind spelling that name for me?" Or he may ask for exact figures, addresses, etc., which the interviewee will be glad to have him get correctly. The reporter must be careful in asking for such information, however, that he does not suggest to the interviewee that he had better start designating which of his remarks were for publication and which not.

The reporter must train his memory to recall, an hour or so afterward, all the important remarks of the interviewee. He should make immediate mental note of any startling statement which he will want to use verbatim, and should keep turning it over in his mind during the rest of the interview. He should seize the first opportunity after leaving the scene of the interview to write down such statements and to make any other necessary notes. If he has an hour or so before he must write his story, he will be surprised to find that, bit by bit, virtually the entire interview will come back to him.

Few editors today encourage deception on the part of reporters in obtaining interviews. Frankness and fairness are recognized as the best standards of conduct. The reporter should let the person know who he is and the nature of his visit, and then should attempt by any legitimate means within his power, or by more drastic means if forced to them, to obtain the information that he desires.

In writing an opinion interview, it often is wise, for the sake of authority, to mention that the statements were made during an interview. If so, "Mr. White stated in an interview today," is better than, "Mr. White told a News reporter today." The newspaper should not boast of an exclusive interview unless it has shown ingenuity in outwitting opponents.

FRIENDSHIPS ON BEATS

Because nobody is as grammatically correct while speaking as while writing, it is common practice to "fix up" unprepared oral statements of persons in the news so as not to embarrass them or create a wrong impression. The sense of any quotation must, of course, be retained. On occasion, it may not be in the public interest to protect a source. If, for instance, despite overwhelming evidence to the contrary, a public official declares that he "knows nothing" of a scandalous situation with which he should be familiar, it is not unfair to quote him verbatim. When such necessity arises, the beat reporter who has daily contact with the news source would be pleased to have a "special" or general assignment reporter sent over to handle that particular story. Often the beat man finds it wise to warn someone with whom he has made friendly contact that an unfavorable story is going to appear. In other words, a reporter cannot be effective if he makes enemies of those on whom he must depend for information. How to maintain personal relationships of friendship and at the same time fulfill his newsgathering obligations is one of the most vexatious problems with which the beat reporter has to contend. As one of them put it:

A newspaper reporter, especially if he is assigned to a particular beat, enters into a very personal relationship with his news sources after a while. It can't be avoided, for these are the people you are talking with every day. In contrast, the public for which a reporter is writing, and to which he is responsible, is always a very impersonal and nebulous thing. There is a constant danger of giving the human being the benefit of the doubt at the expense of some quite abstract body of readers. For example, the superintendent of schools gets himself into a bad situation. Knowing him, you understand that he had the best motives in the world, but simply made a mistake of judgment. You know he recognizes it is your duty to advise the public of his action. Or, a situation I actually ran into: a cop had been suspended for striking a prisoner. I found out about it. The cop was a guy I had talked with every day for nearly a year. He'd told me all about himself, his family, and his ambitions. The suspension had been ordered promptly and there was no doubt that he was being properly punished for his action. I wondered at the time what possible good it would do the public to know of the suspension. Who was the public, anyway? Of course, I wrote the story and spent much time trying to explain to the cop and to his superior why it was necessary that the public be advised. But the point is that the reporter is called upon often to make that kind of decision, and unless he is very careful, he will unconsciously find himself giving in to the very human appeal of his news sources. I think I've found this the toughest temptation to guard against in the business.

PUBLICITY SEEKERS

By no means are all persons reticent in granting interviews. The person who attempts to bulldoze reporters or to "hand out" statements to further his own interests, is ubiquitous. The reporter constantly must be on his guard against him. He must sift every statement and try to determine its truth. Entertainers or lecturers filling engagements in the community value any publicity they can obtain. They may, however, be reluctant to grant interviews. They take secretaries with them to receive reporters and to inquire the subject on which an interview is sought. Then stock answers to stock questions are produced, often in typewritten or mimeographed form. The reporter who asks a question to which the interviewee has a standard, prepared answer ought to and does feel foolish.

It may not be so easy to get to see other types of celebrities who are attending conventions or engaged in business. Often the reporter can obtain an interview with a person difficult to approach, by means of a letter of introduction from some other prominent person. Or he may wait out his party, accosting him in the lobby of the hotel or behind the scenes during a dramatic performance, concert or lecture.

In the majority of cases the interview can be obtained by the reporter's simply sending up his name or by phoning the person's room from the hotel office. If he has called at an inconvenient hour, he can request an appointment later. Usually he will get it, for the person will recognize the value of the publicity he may receive if he sees the reporter. Anyway, he will not want to offend an important newspaper.

A musician, scientist, writer, politician or any person who has become prominent, despises the reporter who betrays ignorance of his activities and reputation. Anyone with a specialty, furthermore, is bored to have to talk to another who is utterly uninformed concerning that field of interest. There are numerous biographical reference books which the reporter may consult to learn the outstanding facts about a person's life and achievements. The newspaper's reference department usually can supply clippings telling of what the person has done recently.

Without some knowledge of his subject, the reporter may fail in his interview. A famous person accustomed to being interviewed may become sympathetic toward the cub and may give him a few stock statements. But familiar, often-used material is not what the editor wants the reporter to get.

The reporter should go to his interview with a number of possible questions memorized. These should be related to the interviewee's field of interest and yet should not be too elementary or questions which it is reasonable to suppose the person has been asked time and time again. The reporter should try to find some new angle of approach, some fresh subject upon which the person interviewed will be able to speak.

FORMAL INTERVIEWS

Persons who know that they are to be interviewed by the press often arrange for formal interviews at which representatives of all the newspapers in the community are present. From the standpoint of the reporter, such an interview is undesirable because none of the information he obtains is exclusive.

An advantage of the formal interview, however, lies in the fact that there are several minds thinking up questions to ask. Frequently the person to be interviewed announces in advance that these questions must be prepared in writing and submitted some time before the hour of the interview. This procedure permits the reporter to know exactly what the subject matter of the interview is to be, but it also allows the interviewee to prepare guarded answers to questions which, if presented spontaneously, might bring forth answers more to the reporter's liking.

Even when interviewing a person in the company of other reporters, it is possible to obtain material on which to write a different story from those which the others will write. The keenest listener and the sharpest wit present writes the best story. Comparison of several write-ups based on a joint interview often discloses several different methods of handling the subject. One reporter plays up one statement and another reporter picks an entirely different one for his feature. Still a third writer concentrates on the personality of the interviewee rather than upon his remarks.

Sometimes it is possible to loiter for a minute or two at the end of a group interview to get a quick answer to an exclusive question.

DENIALS

Sometimes a person quoted in an interview as having made a certain statement, issues a denial. He may even aver that he never saw the reporter who wrote the story. This happens when a reporter plays up some extemporaneous remark of an interviewee's which the person would not have made in a formal interview.

A denial of the facts of an interview, of course, can be avoided by presenting the copy of the write-up to the subject, but few newspapers favor such a practice. To do so means that the interviewee will delete everything the least bit unfavorable to himself. It also means delay which a newspaper may not be able to afford, and a surrender of the newspaper's privilege to gather its information and write up its stories as it sees fit.

If the reporter is not guilty of misquotation he may "stick to his guns" and, if his newspaper stands back of him, defy the interviewee who has denied making a statement. In another story he reaffirms that his original story was correct. Then the public can believe whomever it pleases. Too often it chooses to believe the person interviewed when the reporter really was right.

Reporters frequently do not use remarks which they suspect the interviewee would deny. If he wishes to make sure that the interview will not be denied, the reporter can phone or call upon the interviewee again to obtain verification of whatever he wishes to write. When he does so, or even when he obtains his original interview, he may take a third person with him as a witness to the interview. This, however, seldom is feasible as the presence of a third person may prevent informality.

THE INTERVIEWER

The scientist in his laboratory and the author in his den can be as shy as a mouse in the presence of a cat, uncommunicative, embarrassed by the company of others, incapable of either social conversation or formal speech making — can be, in fact, an anthrophobe (one who fears people) and still be considered a personal success and a benefactor of mankind; the newspaper reporter must be an entirely different kind of person.

It is conceivable that the newsgatherer secretly may dislike most of those with whom his work brings him into contact, but he is forced to learn how to conceal any such feeling and to be able to meet people, all sorts of people, and to get them to feel so easy in his presence that he can obtain what he wants from them.

Because they are unaccustomed to dealing with them, many persons are suspicious of newspapermen, regarding them almost as some strange species of animal life not to be trusted or treated with the courtesy customarily shown those with other ways of earning a livelihood. Says Henry F. Pringle, veteran reporter: "The novice about to be interviewed for the first time assumes that all reporters are ghouls waiting for the emergence of the family skeleton." Such people think nothing of using methods of evasion and prevarication to hinder a reporter in his legitimate quest for information which they condemn in obstreperous terms if he himself tries.

What this amounts to is that the newspaperman must be an expert salesman. Good salesmanship is the basis of all good reporting, and fundamental to successful salesmanship are personality and tact. Although the timid, awkward cub may get what he wants by creating pity, it is the person who gives the impression of self-confidence, self-assurance, and self-respect whose success is enduring. It is in the presence of such persons that others feel most at ease.

It is impossible to lay down general rules on how to develop personality and tact. There are many types of newspapermen, all equally successful. On the whole, however, newspapermen are extroverts or compensated introverts with poise, self-assurance, and self-respect. Caspar Milquetoasts don't succeed in newspaper or any other kind of work calling for daily contact with the public.

A few specific suggestions to beginners are the following:

1. Don't conceal your identity. Begin an interview with a frank acknowledgment of who you are and of the purpose of your visit.

Give the impression that you have an absolute right to obtain the information wanted and have no doubt of your ability to get it. Thus, it is wise to avoid negative questions, as, "You wouldn't care to say anything on this matter, would you?"

2. Inspire confidence and even awe by directness in speech. Don't "beat around the bush" by informing a person, "We'd like to know if you will give us a statement —" Rather, ask, "What do you think about it?"

3. Be particularly careful in telephone conversations when the other party has the power to end the interview simply by hanging up the receiver. Don't say, "I wonder if —" "I'd like to ask you —" A good beginning is, "This is — of the *Daily News*. I'm calling to ask your opinion about —" and don't end a telephone conversation with "All righty" or "Oky doke" or some similar moronic expression.

4. Always give the impression of knowing more about a story than you really do or that you have other ways of obtaining information if the immediate source fails to cooperate. At the same time, don't make threats except as a last resort in special cases. Often a person can be induced to give facts by questions which make him believe the reporter has wrong information which he'll use if not corrected. From fear of having a wrong impression broadcast, he may open up and tell the truth.

5. Often, if a person is reluctant to talk, it is advisable to engage him in conversation about some unrelated subject, as an object in the room, his wife's picture, or an extraneous bit of gossip. After the "ice has been broken" and an attitude of friendship has been created, it is possible cautiously to bring up the real subject occasioning the visit.

6. Don't stop questioning until you have all the facts you want or flat refusals on the part of the news source to give them. Often a person's refusal to make a statement is better news than if he were to become voluble.

PUBLIC RELATIONS

Most persons who quit newspapers or other journalistic media go into public relations work. Often this is because of the lure of a fatter paycheck, in which case the more basic reportorial experience the better. Others have been cynical failures in their attempt to find adequate means of self-expression where they were. Still others seek opportunities to promote causes in which they believe.

ADVERSE CRITICISM

Until recently, practicing journalists were almost unanimous in condemning public relations men as brazen if not unscrupulous space-grabbers and fakers. Today, this harsh judgment has been considerably modified, partly because of the impossibility of covering the wide range of potential news without assistance, and partly because of the considerable elevation of standards within the public relations field. Once they were mostly press agents, whose forte was the manufacturing of stunts and, more recently, they were mere publicity men whose success was determined largely by the amount of space their clients got in the legitimate news columns of the media. Now the best of them are skillful participants in top-level policy making who have the total "image" of their clients in mind. Instead of courting publicity they may, in fact, advise against seeking any journalistic mention. They concern themselves with internal problems of personnel and morale, advertising, product, salesmanship and total behavior. In their exalted positions they may be considered by some to be even more "dangerous" as hidden persuaders, pressure boys, masters of the invisible sell, space-grabbers, ballyhoo boys, hucksters, or malicious engineers of public consent, to use some of the titles by which they are known to their detractors.

IN DEFENSE

In their own defense, the hundreds of thousands, if not millions, of persons who perform public relations functions contend that their activities are of great social benefit. To quote from an article, "A Working Concept of Public Relations," which the author wrote for the October 1958 *Library Trends:*

> They take credit for having converted business and industry completely away from the "public-be-damned" attitude and say that they have humanized business, helped give it good manners and, most important, a conscience; and that they have taught it that he profits most who serves best. They define public relations as simply doing the right thing and letting people know about it, applying the Golden Rule in everyday activities while not letting one's light shine unnoticed under a basket. To them, sound public relations means the daily application of common sense, common courtesy, and common decency in accordance with a continuous program of enlightened self-interest through good works which not only earn one a good reputation but cause him to deserve it as a good neighbor.

In further defense of public relations as it relates to news media, it is indisputable that almost every legitimate news item which appears in public print has publicity value for someone. Even unfavorable mention or scandal doesn't seem to be fatal to national heroes, especially in the entertainment world. Readers' memories are short and inaccurate and when they go to the polls the familiar name has advantage, no matter how unsavory the situation in connection with which it was publicized. Organized baseball and other professional sports are commercial enterprises which have thrived on free publicity, through good-sized sports sections, for generations. The same is true of the theater, book publishing, concert stage and other artistic enterprises which are not entirely philanthropies.

Since John D. Rockefeller I hired Ivy Lee early in the century, the policy of the public relations profession has been increasingly toward more cooperation with the newsgathering media rather than agencies to suppress unfavorable news or retard newsgatherers in their efforts to obtain it. Public relations departments of railroads, airlines and industries today are a great asset to reporters at times of fires, accidents and other disasters, whereas a generation ago exactly the opposite was the case.

The news or publicity division of a public relations department provides a quantity of legitimate news handouts, full texts of speeches by important people, notices of meetings and conventions, plans for changes in policies and operations of both private and public institutions, and other services which no newspaper or magazine could afford to obtain by means of its own paid employes. To some extent, the media are today at the mercy of the public relations people to keep them informed of what is going on in large segments of society.

DANGERS

The great danger is the extent to which public relations men erect a barrier between the reporter and original news sources. If all news is obtained through carefully prepared news releases, the reporter becomes little more than a glorified messenger boy. Good newspapers and magazines consist of more than such handouts with proper headlines and picture captions added by the editors. No matter how cooperative and sensible, the public relations man never can lose sight of the fact that his primary obligation is to his employer. The reporter, on the other hand, is a public servant in a democracy. There are bound to be at least occasional clashes of interest. News releases today are usually well written and reliable but often there are omissions and obscurities which can be corrected only by personal contact between newsgatherer and news source.

Large news conferences, especially with the President and other prominent public figures, can be extremely frustrating as no reporter present has the opportunity to probe deeply into any matter. Too often a reporter is limited to a single question so that as many as possible can have a turn. It's impossible under such circumstances to be thorough in one's fact-finding. Even if better conditions prevail, a public relations man may hover over the shoulder of the interviewee to advise, augment and correct his statements. Reporters often are infuriated and feel that their dignity has been insulted. Serving one's editor and the public is extremely difficult under such circumstances.

From their standpoint, public relations men recognize the value of good will on the part of reporters. Hence, they not only try to create the impression at least of the best cooperation possible, but they also make life easier in other ways. At meetings and conventions there are usually press tables and press rooms with ample refreshments, desks, telephones and other equipment. Media differ in the extent to which they allow staff members to accept favors from public relations men, public officials and others. Some even forbid the acceptance of free books to review, of passes to athletic, dramatic, and other performances, or of gifts on Christmas or other holidays. Others, however, allow and even welcome large favors such as trips and tours, even to foreign lands. The beginning reporter does well to learn what his superiors' attitude regarding all forms of what is opprobriously called "payola" happens to be.

A more subtle way of influencing news judgment is the awards which are given in recognition of stellar performance in a particular field. The decision in such a case as to what constitutes good journalism is that of the donor of the prize. Some newspapers are eager to wallpaper their offices with plaques and certificates, and some keep a careful tab on announcements of such honors-in-the-offing. Too much ambition, however, may develop into exaggerated emphasis on news of a certain character rather than unprejudiced evaluation of the happenings of the day. In other words, conscious efforts to please donors of prizes can badly warp good editorial performance.

GOVERNMENTAL SECRECY

From the standpoint of the public's right to know, even more serious than the censorship exerted by private public relations men, is that which exists at all levels of government. Beginning with the Truman administration, federal administrators were instructed to classify potential information as to its secrecy. The uproar this system caused among members of the American Newspaper Publishers Association, American Society of Newpaper Editors, Sigma Delta Chi, and other journalistic groups, encouraged a House committee chaired by Representative John Moss of California to hold extensive hearings and to propose legislation intended to prevent unreasonable withholding of information. The results have been substantial but far from a complete victory for those who believe in complete freedom of the press.

Under the impetus created by the Washington furor, inquiries revealed that various elements in state and local governmental units also practice censorship. Under goading from the journalistic organizations mentioned and state press associations, some states have passed new laws requiring city council, boards of education, and similar bodies to hold only open meetings. Legislation also has been drafted to broaden the rights of reporters to inspect and use public records of all sorts. Since conditions vary so greatly from place to place, the beginning reporter must be certain to learn what his rights and privileges are as regards such matters and to get his information from official sources rather than taking the word of some bureaucrat. As he ferrets out the news and the news behind the news, he is truly an agent of democracy, a crusader for the right without which a free society cannot long exist — the right of the people to know.

THE INTERPRETATIVE VIEWPOINT

In gathering information about a news event, the reporter seeks answers to the *who, what, where, when, why,* and *how* of whatever happened. Of these, the first four are basic to virtually any account. The emphasis that they should receive under different circumstances will be discussed in Chapter 3. Offhand, it might be held that not all stories have a *why* or *how* element important enough to engage much of the newsgatherer's attention. Actually, exactly the contrary is the case. In delving into the *what* of most stories, the reporter really is asking "why?" even though the answers he receives may become part of the *what*.

The beginning journalist who aspires to the heights mentioned in the preceding chapter should be aware of this fact. Whenever he does a thorough job of interviewing for what may seem to be a minor or simple story, he is training himself for more penetrating assignments in the future. He is developing an attitude or frame of mind toward newsgathering. To illustrate:

Police arrested Carter Davis, 14, son of Mr. and Mrs. George Davis, 4513 W. Coral street.

Why?

Because he used a knife to stab his eighth-grade teacher at Tyler Junior high school, 1216 N. Marshall street. She is Mrs. Vivian Heller, 48, 5141 W. Falconer avenue.

Why did he do it?

The assault occurred just after she had told the boy that he would fail his course in English.

But other teenagers fail in their school work without committing violence against their teachers. *Why is this boy different?* The Behavior Clinic psychiatrist is examining him now in an attempt to find out. While waiting for the report, further facts can be obtained: the circumstances and sequences of the events, the victim's condition, police activities and so forth. Questioning of school authorities reveals Carter's academic and deportment records. Classmates tell of his behavior toward and reputation with his peers, expressing either surprise or the opposite as regards the immediate situation.

Further clues as to the answer to the *why* are obtained by a visit to Carter's home and neighborhood, by talks with parents and other relatives, neighbors and friends, and recreational and other workers with whom the boy has had contact.

The reporter is able to ask penetrating questions to a considerable extent because of his knowledge of modern thinking in the fields of psychology, social psychology, psychiatry and sociology. Not too many decades ago he would presume, with most everyone else, that there is a dichotomy of good boys and bad boys, determined largely by the individual's exercise of free will. A more lenient attitude would be to consider the social misfit a victim of some sort of demoniacal possession. In any case, harshness of punishment was the only known corrective. Police operated on the "catch 'em and kill 'em" philosophy and were goaded on by journalists who reflected the indignation of most of their readers whenever a particularly heinous example of misbehavior occurred.

Within a generation, the attitude of a majority of enforcement officers, judges, educators, journalists and others has changed. Today it is recognized that there is "something wrong" with a boy who commits an act like Carter's. Psychiatrists still are reluctant to discuss cases with news-gatherers until they have made their formal reports to whatever public authorities are involved. In the meantime, reporters must refrain from making medical diagnoses on the basis of their own investigations. They can, however, publicize such pertinent facts as that a misbehaving child comes from an underprivileged, broken slum home, or from a wealthy family where everything was lavished upon him except the most important ingredient of all — parental attention.

Why do some youngsters reared in the same neighborhood "go bad" whereas others do not? The answer concerns the behavior clinician who may conclude that the boy who does not act in accordance with group standards is the problem child rather than others who "go along" with the gang in committing antisocial acts. Human motivation is an extremely complex subject for scientific research, with multitudinous influences in and out of the home and other primary institutions affecting different children differently. The journalist should be warned against acceptance of "panacea" explanations such as broken homes, poverty, slum environments, and especially television, comic books, the movies and so forth, as providing easy answers to explain intricate situations.

Even if a reasonably clear picture emerges as regards an individual case, the probing reporter can continue to ask "why?" at several different levels of inquiry. If social statistics indicate that there are correlations between various factors, as slum conditions, racial, religious or nationality backgrounds, economic status, and so forth, for understanding it is necessary to ask "why?" as regards each item. What are the cause-and-effect relationships? And how explain the type of behavior which results? Why violence instead of suicide or something else? Because of the extreme frustration or sense of insecurity in the individual from whatever cause — an organic or biological reflex? Or because violence is an accepted or admired form of behavior in a group whose respect is desired? Or because there is violence in other aspects of the environment, including the international scene? These are matters which concern many different specialists in the social sciences whose erudition and research the newsgatherer cannot hope to duplicate. He can, however, solicit their information, assistance and advice. Most important, he can "get more" out of his assignments, both for immediate journalistic usage and for promotion of his general understanding, if he recognizes that the isolated news event is not really isolated.

It would be impossible and superfluous to attempt extensive probing into the broader aspects of every incident such as the hypothetical one of Carter Davis. Space will not permit usage of exhaustive analyses of every vagrant, jack roller, tough juvenile, prostitute, or others of society's "problem children." There is no beat to compare with police, however, to provide an opportunity to begin cultivation of a querying attitude toward life. When he later attempts to fathom the causes of a depression, war or major issue of any kind, the experienced newsgatherer utilizes the habits of mind that he cultivated back in his cubhood. If he doesn't take advantage of the opportunities provided to him at the beginning of his journalistic career, his grandchildren will still be visiting him in the same press room where he got his start.

A quarter-century ago, Sidney Kobre wrote in the September 1938 *Journalism Quarterly:*

> What are the next steps in American journalism, if the newspapers are to be made an effective up-to-date social institution? Certain lines of development can be pursued.
>
> The materials with which the newspaper deals are fundamentally of a psychological, economic and sociological character. It is an oversimplifica-

tion to handle this material as if it were ordinary routine stuff. All aspects of human life are being methodically investigated, instead of being viewed in the usual "common-sense" traditional manner. The human body is a complicated and intricate nervous and physical system. When it breaks down, only trained men can rehabilitate it. The stuff of which news is made is just as highly complicated because it relates to human behavior. Only specialized reporters with eyes sharpened in the social sciences can handle and interpret the facts intelligibly.

The expert has been quietly emerging up to now from university halls and entering every field affecting industry and politics. Why not journalism?

3

Organizing the Facts

I. Contemporary Trends

II. The Inverted Pyramid
Form

III. The Lead

IV. The Body
  1. *Spiraling*
  2. *Unity*
  3. *Block Paragraphing*
  4. *Themes*
  5. *Chronological*

V. The Reporter's Notes

STAFF MEETING

BY *B. F. Sylvester*

Mr. Edgeworth, publisher: "Well, the Meteor has done it again. What's the matter, Hoops?"

Hoops, managing editor: "I thought the Star was pretty fair today, Chief."

Mr. Edgeworth: "Why didn't we have the interview with Mr. Doddle on his trip to California?"

Hoops: "Isn't news. Millions of people have been to California."

Mr. Edgeworth: "But he said he was glad to be home, to the garden spot of the country. That's constructive."

Hoops: "Our readers would call it boloney."

Mr. Edgeworth: "I notice the Meteor is getting ahead by just such 'boloney.' Get it out of your head that we are publishing a New York city paper. We can't high-hat people like Mr. Doddle. People want the paper that prints the news about their friends."

Hoops: "If we printed all the Doddle items there wouldn't be room for Gandhi. We had some big exclusive news today —"

Mr. Edgeworth: "Of course, Hoops, you're supposed to use judgment. I don't want a small town sheet. But don't let the Meteor get ahead of us."

Hoops: "The Meteor didn't have a word about the elopement of Jerry Gold and the Evergreen club dancer."

Mr. Edgeworth: "An unsavory article, Hoops. The marriage was to have been annulled. Nobody would have been the wiser and there would have been no embarrassment. I'm sure the best people don't care for such news. Sorry it was in our paper. It will give the Meteor standing. And another thing, we had very little on Lindbergh."

Hoops: "We try to keep stories short, Mr. Edgeworth."

Mr. Edgeworth: "You have to use judgment, Hoops. There is a time to keep stories short and a time to give details. Well, gentlemen, that's all. Good day."

At the Meteor office:

Mr. Hawkins, publisher: "The Star has done it again. What's the matter, Watts?"

Watts, managing editor: "I thought the Meteor was pretty fair today, Chief."

Mr. Hawkins: "What about this elopement story?"

Watts: "It wasn't constructive. We'll gain in standing among the best people because we didn't use it."

Mr. Hawkins: "The best people! We want circulation. The Star could print it. That's the way the Star gets ahead. And another thing, why this tripe about Old Man Doddle?"

Watts: "He has lots of friends."

Mr. Hawkins: "He'll ask us to give him six copies of the paper and his friends will buy the Star to get the news. We've got to be more metropolitan. And will you tell me why we have to print 800 words on Lindbergh?"

Watts: "The public wants details."

Mr. Hawkins: "I see the Star was able to tell it in 200. Well, gentlemen, that's all. Good day."

Editor & Publisher

$\mathbf{E}$VEN BEFORE HE HAS COMPLETED THE TASK OF GATHERING the facts concerning a particular news event, the reporter starts thinking of how he will organize them into a news story. The more experienced he is, the more automatic or unconscious this habit becomes. As new information is obtained he may modify earlier ideas regarding the "theme" or "central idea" coming out of the assignment.

CONTEMPORARY TRENDS

Since World War II, there have been numerous studies of the traditional methods of organizing a news story. At several annual conventions the Associated Press Managing Editors devoted considerable attention to ways of making news writing more readable. In part, they were motivated by the success of news magazines in presenting the news in brighter and livelier ways. Also, and perhaps more important, radio and television newscasters demonstrated how the gist of a story often could be presented in fewer words than were contained in the usual traditional newspaper story lead.

The press associations and some large newspapers employed experts in readability to analyze their practices. A few journalistic higher-ups became so enthusiastic over some readability formulas that they blamed widespread reader ignorance and indifference upon traditional styles of journalistic composition. Some others thought the answer was to be found in greater understanding by journalists of the philosophical and statistical aspects of the communication process.

Because they have been taught to journalistic novitiates for several generations, the five *w's* often seem to be trite and academic. Nevertheless, no matter what writing or speaking style is used, the reader or listener's curiosity has to be satisfied as regards the *who, what, when, where* and *why*, as well as the *how* of a newsworthy occurrence. What has happened, largely as a result of the blandishments of the readability conscious and statistically conscious communication researchers, is a considerable loosening of the rigid rules regarding the structure of a news story. Whereas a generation ago it was virtually mandatory that as many as possible of the five *w's* and *h* be mentioned in the first paragraph of a news story, today considerably greater freedom is permitted in presenting them.

THE INVERTED PYRAMID FORM

Despite the extensive experimentation that has taken place, the great majority of news stories still are written in accordance with the traditional rule that the first part — whether it be a conventionally written single paragraph or a half-dozen or more one-sentence paragraphs — contain a succinct résumé of the story as a whole.

The striking difference between news writing in the United States and other forms of written composition, such as the essay, poetry, drama, novel, short story, etc., continues to be this: whereas the authors of these other forms of composition usually begin with minor or incidental details and work to a climax near or at the end of their compositions, the news writer reverses this plan of organization. That is, he begins with the climax or end of the story. Given a schedule of facts to arrange in the form of a newspaper article, he selects the most important fact or climax of the story he has to tell and puts it at the beginning. The second most important fact comes second, the third most important fact third and so on.

The traditional form of news writing is called the *inverted pyramid form*. It is said to have originated in Civil War days when correspondents used the telegraph for the first time. From fear that their accounts would not be transmitted all at one time, the war correspondents crowded as much information as possible into their first paragraphs.

Throughout the decades since that time, press associations, which transmit stories by telegraph, have perfected the system. Before the teletypesetter was introduced about mid-century, few leading stories ever were transmitted in one piece. Instead, a few paragraphs of several important stories were sent first and then the later paragraphs. Throughout a day's sending, there were numerous new or substitute first paragraphs (leads), inserts and additions.

Locally written news followed the press association pattern. The inverted pyramid form of organization was defended in several different ways, namely:

1. *To facilitate reading.* The reading matter of the average newspaper, if printed in book form, would fill a large volume. The American newspaper reader hasn't time to read that much daily. Neither is he interested in all the articles appearing in any newspaper. If the climax of each story is at the beginning, the reader can learn the gist of the news shortly, and if interested, can continue to the details of stories which attract him. He should not have to read any article to its conclusion to learn what it is **about.**

2. *To satisfy curiosity.* This is the natural way of telling an important item of news. If someone drowns while swimming, the average person would not begin telling of the incident by narrating the dead person's preparations for a visit to the beach with a group of friends. Rather he would tell the important news first — John was drowned while swimming. Then he would relate the supplementary details of how, when, and where it happened.

3. *To facilitate makeup.* In rectifying a page, the makeup editor often finds it necessary to cut the length of some articles. If the least important details are at the end of a story, he can do this without harming the story. The makeup editor should feel free to cut ordinary articles without consulting other editors.

4. *To facilitate headline writing.* The headline consists of the "key" words or their synonyms necessary to give an idea of what a story contains. If the story is well written, the headline writer should not have to look beyond the first paragraph or two to find these words.

A few years ago the Writing Committee of the Associated Press Managing Editors cited the story in the right-hand column below as one of the best examples of news writing of the year. It was written in the traditional inverted pyramid style. In the left-hand column below the same facts, using the identical phraseology as much as possible, are rearranged in chronological order.

Chronological Style

About 1 A.M. today, Mrs. Harry Rosenberg was awakened by the sound of a car roaring out of the driveway of her home. She rushed to the living room where she discovered that her granddaughter, Judith Ann Roberts, 7, no longer was sleeping on the studio couch and that the front door was standing open.

Mrs. Rosenberg called her daughter, Mrs. Shirley Roberts, wife of a Baltimore attorney and labor leader, who was visiting her parents. Mrs. Roberts, the missing child's mother, notified police of her daughter's kidnaping at 1:10 A.M.

Police said the kidnaper sneaked into the home of the grandparents, stole the keys to the

Newspaper Style

Judith Ann Roberts, blue-eyed, 7-year-old daughter of a Baltimore attorney and labor leader, was kidnaped from the home of her grandparents here today, raped and beaten to death.

Police found the child's nude and brutally battered body in a clump of bushes off fashionable Bayshore drive five hours after her mother, Mrs. Shirley Roberts, reported her missing.

She had been beaten on the head with a heavy instrument and a piece of gauze was knotted about her throat. Her flimsy seersucker nightgown, white with red polka dots, lay eight feet from the body.

Judith Ann's little body was caked with blood and dirt, indi-

Chronological Style

Newspaper Style

Rosenbergs' car from the grandfather's trousers pocket and took the child away.

Four hours and ten minutes after they were called, police found the Rosenberg car abandoned in the strip of sandy land between Bayshore drive and the shore of Biscayne Bay. Its wheels were mired in the sand and the tire marks showed the driver tried frantically to get it out.

Judith Ann's nude and brutally battered body was found a block from the car in a clump of bushes off fashionable Bayshore drive. It was caked with blood and dirt, indicating she put up a brave fight for her life. The blue-eyed child had been raped and beaten on the head with a heavy instrument and a piece of gauze was knotted about her throat. Her flimsy seersucker nightgown, white with red polka dots, lay eight feet from her body.

cating she put up a brave fight for her life.

Police said the killer sneaked into the home of the grandparents, Mr. and Mrs. Harry Rosenberg, about 1 A.M., stole the keys to Rosenberg's car from his trousers pocket and took the child from the studio couch in the living room where she was sleeping.

Mrs. Rosenberg was awakened by the sound of the car roaring out of the driveway. She found the child missing and the front door standing open.

Police were called at 1:10 A.M. Four hours and ten minutes later, they found the Rosenberg car abandoned in the strip of sandy land between Bayshore drive and the shore of Biscayne Bay. Its wheels were mired in the sand and the tire marks showed the driver tried frantically to get it out.

Judith's body was found a block from the car.

"Note, please," the A.P.M.E. Writing committee asked, "the many fine points . . . 'the seersucker nightgown, white and red polka dots, lay eight feet from the body.'

"How many little nightgowns like that are all over this land? And *eight feet* . . . no guess-work there; the reporter was *seeing* it for you Too, the killer sneaked in about 1 A.M. and 'police were called at 1:10 A.M.' The car was found *four hours and ten minutes later* . . . not simply later in the day."

Although few would argue with an unnamed telegraph editor with more than forty years' experience, whom the committee quoted as saying, "That Miami story is one of the finest writing jobs I've ever seen," the points cited by the committee indicate that the story's strength derived primarily from the fact that an extraordinary job of reporting, involving keen observation, had preceded its composition. In other words, *the most important step in communication is obtaining something worthwhile to communicate.* Stated still another way, the basis of all good journalism is thorough reporting. Shorter words, sentences, and paragraphs, desirable as they may be for clarity, cannot add important details to a journalistic account. *There is no substitute for good reporting no matter what writing style is used.*

THE LEAD

The Miami story was written in traditional inverted pyramid style. That is, the first paragraph contained the gist or skeleton outline of the entire story in a minimum of words. Subsequent paragraphs elaborated upon various aspects of the lead, making them more definite; or they supplied additional details in the order of their importance as the reporter judged them.

Since, for more than a half-century, this has been the orthodox form of news writing, the *lead* of a straight news story came to be defined as the first paragraph which contained all of the elements (five *w's* and *h*) necessary for the complete telling of the essential facts.

This practice often led to long and crowded first paragraphs. The lead of the Miami story, for instance, might have read something like this:

> The nude and brutally beaten body of Judith Ann Roberts, blue-eyed, 7-year-old daughter of a Baltimore attorney and labor leader, was found by police in a clump of bushes off fashionable Bayshore drive here at 1 A.M. today after she had been kidnaped from the home of her grandparents, Mr. and Mrs. Harry Rosenberg, and raped.

In the effort to avoid such cumbersome lead paragraphs, and to increase readability, some newspapers have gone to the opposite extreme of invoking the "one-fact sentence" rule which would lead to something like the following:

> A 7-year-old girl has been kidnaped, raped and beaten to death.
> She was blue-eyed Judith Ann Roberts of Baltimore. Her father is a lawyer and labor leader.
> Police found the child's body in a clump of bushes off fashionable Bayshore drive.
> The body was nude and brutally battered.
> The child's mother, Mrs. Shirley Roberts, reported her daughter missing at 1:10 A.M.
> That was four hours and ten minutes before the body was found by police.

It is difficult to determine just exactly how many of the one- or two-sentence paragraphs of a story written in this manner constitute the lead, or first unit of the story. Each sentence relates to some word or fact in a preceding sentence, and it takes a half-dozen or more of them to present all of the information which once would have been crowded into half the space or less. This form of writing says less in more words but is scored as more readable. The original version of the Miami story was a compromise between the new and old extremes.

Since the inverted pyramid form still is adhered to, even in the staccato type of paragraphing illustrated above, in that facts are arranged in the order of their supposed importance, the traditional definition of a news story lead holds: the first unit of the story which performs the function of telling the entire story in epitomized form.

A good lead, no matter how much it is strung out, has the following qualities:

1. Answers all of the questions that a reader wants to have answered when hearing of a particular incident. These include: the cause and result (the *how* or *why* and the *what*), the *who* and often the *where* and the *when*. These elements are called the five *w's* and the *h*. Not all of these must be present in every lead, but no important one should be omitted. (See Chapter 4.)
2. Plays up the feature of the story if there is one. (See Chapter 5.)
3. Is attractive and induces the reader to continue with the rest of the story. (See Chapter 6.)
4. Observes the canons of good news writing. (See Chapter 6.)
5. Suggests or gives the authority on which the news is printed. (See Chapter 8.)
6. Identifies the individuals mentioned in the story (or the story itself) by relating them (or it) to previous or contemporaneous news. (See Chapter 9.)

The Miami story fulfilled these requirements in this way:

Who — Judith Ann Roberts
What — Killed
When — July 7; time of day (1 A.M.) given later
Where — Miami, Florida
How — Kidnaped, raped and beaten to death
Authority — Police and relatives obvious sources of information
Identification — Seven-year-old daughter of a Baltimore lawyer and labor leader
Feature — Kidnaped from home of grandparents

THE BODY

In view of the tendency to reduce the first sentence of a news story to the fewest possible words, the function of the sentences and paragraphs which immediately follow is clearly to restate the facts of the first sentence so as to make them more definite. Loosening of the rule that the lead contain all of the five *w's* and the *h* means that succeeding paragraphs often must supply some additional pertinent facts crowded out of the lead in the interest of brevity.

It doesn't make any difference what academic labels are placed on units of a news story, and it is difficult or impossible to chart news stories so that units do not overlap. If you wish, you can consider the extreme attempt at epitomized writing ("A 7-year-old girl has been kidnaped, raped and beaten to death") as the lead and call all the rest of the story by its traditional name, *body*. Or you can insist that the lead proper include as many sentences as are necessary to make the basic elements (five *w's* and *h*) definite.

In either case, there often remain a number of additional paragraphs which can be labeled either "body" or "second part of body." If new details are added in the same sentences or paragraphs in which there is further amplification of the lead, telling exactly where the last unit of the story begins isn't easy.

SPIRALING

Perhaps a spiral with the broad part at the top would be a better simile than inverted pyramid to describe how a well-constructed news story today may unfold. Either by definite grammatical reference or linkage of thought, each well-written succeeding paragraph "flows" from the preceding one.

In the following example observe how each succeeding paragraph makes more definite an element of the preceding paragraph (words in *italics*) and in addition contains some new information.

Aaron L. Engstrand, who recently completed a study of previously made civil service surveys for the city administration, will get a full-time city *job* July 1.

He will become consultant to the city Civil Service commission, empowered to put into effect *recommendations* he submitted.

They include "more realistic examinations" in the *selection of city employes*, and improvements in personnel relations.

John S. Christopher, commission president, announced the appointment Friday. He said that one of Engstrand's first jobs will be to hire a *director of personnel* for the city.

Engstrand, a veteran in public administration and social-service work, refused the personnel director job when it was offered him recently.

UNITY

A method of obtaining rhetorical unity as one short paragraph follows another is by use of *linkage* words. Note in the following example how their skillful use creates "flow" and, at the same time, enables the writer to introduce new facts. This story could be cut at the end of almost any paragraph and there still would be a rhetorically complete account.

BY *Associated Press*

Mighty rivers on a late winter rampage surged through south central sections of Alabama, Georgia and Mississippi Wednesday, leaving wide trails of muddy ruin amounting to millions.

Except around Jackson, Miss., the highest levels of the flooding rivers were spread largely across rural areas as they continued toward their common draining point, the Gulf of Mexico.

However, more flood menace lies ahead for downstate residents, and even in ravaged mid-state sections where the worst is over, it will be days before the rampant rivers fall within their banks.

Alabama at Crest

At Selma in central Alabama, *for example*, the Alabama River reached its crest of 58.3 feet Tuesday night, but the muddy waters are not expected to creep back to the 45-foot flood level until March 9.

In hard-hit Selma and Montgomery and Demopolis, Ala., *as well as* Jackson, Miss., and West Point and Columbus, Ga., thousands in evacuation centers looked to more days of waiting for water to seep out of their homes.

To relieve the tension of Montgomery refugees, many facing their fifth night in shelters, the Red Cross put on recreation programs.

Damage to Alabama's public facilities *has already topped* $10 million in preliminary estimates. That includes only roads and bridges and county and municipal places — not homes, businesses, farmland and livestock.

Cattle Drowned

In central Alabama's Montgomery and Elmore Counties alone, a livestock broker estimates that about 2,500 head of cattle worth $500,000 have drowned *during the current flood.*

As the swollen Pearl River swirled around the Jackson, Miss., area Tuesday night and Wednesday, cutting a three-mile swath in some places, about 850 residents left their low-lying homes and most flocked to refuge centers.

Tampa *Tribune*

BLOCK PARAGRAPHING

In longer stories, regardless of whether the lead was one or several paragraphs long, or "straight" or spiraling, paragraphs are so written as to include a single subtopic each.

This type of paragraphing differs from the type which English composition students are taught is best. Because newspaper paragraphs of necessity (appearance) must be short, they do not follow the orthodox rule of rhetoric that each paragraph should include a complete thought or topic. Rather, in newspaper paragraphing the idea-unit is broken up into subtopics. In other words, news writers paragraph their paragraphs.

This type of paragraphing, called *block paragraphing*, is distinctly advantageous for news writing. It permits the insertion or deletion of paragraphs without disarranging a story. Frequently it is necessary, in the light of new information, to recast certain paragraphs, to add additional paragraphs, and to remove others. For example, note in the following story how additional information might be added without serious trouble. The paragraphs in italics quite conceivably could have been added after the story was written. Furthermore, several of them could have been inserted at other places in the story. Quite a few of the paragraphs, italicized or not, could be shifted around without destroying the effectiveness of the story. Often, different inserts are written by different reporters.

A five-alarm fire last night wrecked a big grain elevator in the 700 block West Jerome avenue, just west of Fort Alston.

Thirty-five pieces of fire equipment fought the blaze for three hours at the Northern Manufacturing company.

Damage was estimated at $225,000.

Flames and thick billows of smoke leaped high above the burning building as the blaze lighted the western sky. Periodically, a galaxy of sparks would burst from the roof, illuminating the entire area.

The wood-and-sheet metal building was still standing shortly before 1 A.M. but Patrick L. O'Hara, chief engineer of the Fire department, said the structure was a total loss.

One fireman was slightly injured when he ran a nail through his boot, but he was treated at the scene and returned to duty. No one else was reported hurt.

The blaze was discovered at 9:50 P.M. by Waldo Wozniak of the 2700 block Hazel avenue who was driving his children along Jerome avenue after showing them where he worked — the Key highway yards of the Keystone Steel company.

Mr. Wozniak said he saw flames through one of the elevator's windows.

He hurried west on Jerome avenue to Hurlburd street, the location of the No. 16 Engine company and the No. 18 Truck company. Mr. Wozniak told Firefighter Emerson Hudnutt what he had seen and led the first pieces of equipment to the scene.

The Police department sent sixteen motorcycle men and two radio cars to handle the traffic.

The fireboats *Mayo* and *Stirrup* quickly pulled into one of the Marble Point piers on the opposite side of Jerome avenue to supply additional water pressure for the land equipment's hoses.

Chief Mott and his men surrounded the burning elevator, which is about five stories high, and ordered them to direct their high pressure hoses against the building to keep the flames confined to as small an area as possible.

Three nearby tanks were scorched by the flames but received no further damage. Fire fighters watered down adjacent buildings to prevent them catching fire.

THEMES

Some stories can be written around a central theme which is perceivable although not bluntly stated or restated throughout. The following story was written to explain the importance to the community of the news it concerns. This purpose is achieved in successive paragraphs which introduce and elaborate upon various aspects of the story as a whole.

J. R. MacDonald, president and chairman of the board of General Cable Corp., announced yesterday that the Tampa plant will manufacture a $4.8 million order of telephone cable to be shipped to Israel.

The order was believed by MacDonald to be the largest manufacturing order destined for export trade ever to be handled in Florida.

He saw it as a "harbinger" of Florida becoming a state doing an extensive manufacturing business in export trade.

To Add to Pay Roll

Fulfilling the order will mean the hiring of about 120 additional persons who will be kept busy for a year at the plant on E. Hanna St. Additional equipment is being installed in the Tampa plant and the hiring and training of the added personnel is underway.

All material going into the order will come to Tampa through its port and the finished product will be shipped from the port.

MacDonald said the quality of workmanship available at the Tampa plant and lower manufacturing costs here were reasons for Tampa facility making up the order.

Enough wire will be produced for the order that, if wrapped around the world, would circle the globe 10 times.

The order was negotiated jointly by General Cable and Automatic Electric International Inc., a wholly owned subsidiary of the General Telephone and Electronics Corp.

Tampa *Tribune*

CHRONOLOGICAL

Still another widely used method of organizing the material after the lead is chronological, at least for a number of paragraphs, after which new facts can be added in block paragraph style. This type of organization is effective in stories in which action is described, as in the following example:

A gunman yesterday robbed the Eastwood Federal Savings and Loan association of about $7,000 while scores of noonday shoppers walked past the building at 118 S. Jeffrey street.

The bandit walked in at 12:45 P.M., normally the busiest time of day, and found the office empty of customers. A teller, Miss Virginia Kole, one of four employes present, asked the man if she could help him.

"Yeah. There's a lot you can do to help me," the man answered as he leaped up on the 4-foot high counter and pulled out an old rusty revolver.

"Get back, get back," he ordered from his perch. "I'm not fooling. I'll shoot the lady first. Don't step on the alarm."

Jospeh L. Dierks, vice president, said he was sitting in the back of the office and did not move, waiting to see what the man would do next.

The bandit jumped down on the floor behind the counter and ordered the four to a rest room in the rear. The other two workers were Howard K. Jacobs, secretary-treasurer of the association, and Robertson Evans, a teller.

As the holdup man was directing the group to the rear room, a customer came in. He was Walter Mather, 2130 W. Otis avenue, who also was ordered to the back room.

The robber closed the door on the five and went back to the front of the office where he rifled three cash drawers and the open safe.

When Mr. Evans heard the front door close, he hurried from the back room and ran to the front door hoping to see which way the bandit fled. The man apparently became quickly lost in the crowd and Mr. Evans could not see him.

Mr. Dierks said an early count indicated the stolen money totaled $6,829.15, but he thought the final tally would be higher, perhaps as much as $8,500.

The vice president considered the holdup man an extremely lucky amateur. He pointed out that an experienced robber probably would have looked over the office several days in advance and would have realized that the association usually was busiest between 12:15 and 1:15 P.M. when many customers come in on their lunch hours.

Mr. Dierks said the gunman was probably a very athletic person, judging from the way he hopped about the office. He appeared to be in his early twenties, about 5 feet 6 inches tall, and weighed about 140 pounds. He wore a blue cap, green shirt, and khaki trousers.

What must be avoided is making the lead sentence merely a "peg line." For example, "Alderman John F. Gates today called Mayor Henry R. Penrose a liar" is superior to "An alderman today called the mayor a liar." It is inferior to "Alderman John R. Gates today charged that Mayor Henry R. Penrose lied when he said he never owned any west-side real estate." If by some grotesque error the former lead sentence were to appear alone, there would be considerable embarrassment if not worse. There is, in other words, a limit beyond which it is wise to be brief. Too often brevity necessitates being vague or indefinite, which requires more rather than less effort on the part of the reader who seeks the facts of a news story.

THE REPORTER'S NOTES

Prerequisite to a well-organized news story is a careful rearrangement of the reporter's notes. For the experienced reporter, the task of dictating a story over the telephone to a rewrite man from a handful of notes scribbled on copy paper while standing in a stuffy booth is an everyday matter. While he's learning, however, the cub reporter profits by an outline of the facts he has gathered. He has, first of all, to pick the feature to go into his lead; next, to be certain he has answered all of the essential questions which need to be answered and has sufficient identification and authority; then, to decide which phases of the lead need amplification in the first part of the body of the story and how it is to be provided and, finally, to arrange the other facts which he wishes to include.

Seldom, if ever, does the reporter jot down facts in the order in which he will use them in his story. As he learns more and more about the incident he is reporting, one or more lead possibilities strike his attention. There are few if any reporters, regardless of experience, who fail to profit by a study of all notes taken and an outlining of them, if only in the head, before beginning to write or dictate. The young reporter frequently finds it profitable to number the facts included in his notes in the order of importance.

The necessity for rearranging and discarding notes can be seen by imagining how the reporter who covered the Judith Ann Roberts case gathered his facts. If he were stationed at police headquarters, the first information he obtained was: Mrs. Shirley Roberts called to report that her child had been kidnaped from the home of her parents whose address was given. Either then or when policemen, accompanied by reporters, arrived at the residence, the mother gave a complete description of the child's appearance and habits. She and her parents told how the child's disappearance was discovered and the condition of the room, including the empty couch and open door. Mr. or Mrs. Rosenberg provided a description of their automobile: its make, model, color, license number, mileage and distinguishing features.

In the search for clues, police and reporters asked the three adults and other residents about the visit of the mother and child to Miami. They wanted to know how the family and child spent the preceding day, especially what they did during the evening. They asked about Mr. Roberts and whether either he or any of the others had any enemies who might wish them ill. They wanted to know whom Judith had met, talked with, played with, where she had gone, etc.

Before the body was found, reporters made notes on the activities of the police: how many and who were assigned to the search, where they went and whom they questioned, what alarms were sent out, what clues, if any, they considered important, and the like. They inquired carefully into how discovery of the body was made — as part of a careful plan of investigation or by accident and so on.

Bear in mind that the example given was written for a press association which means it was intended for publication in cities other than Miami. In that city the story received much longer treatment with many additional details of interest to local readers.

To summarize, the first step in good news writing is good reporting. No story writes itself. The factual material must be gathered first. The person who doesn't know how to observe and gather facts never will be able to write a good news account.

4

Playing Up the Feature

I. News Values

    1. Timeliness
    2. Proximity
    3. Prominence
    4. Consequence
    5. Human Interest

II. The 5 W's and the H

    1. The Who
    2. The What
    3. The Why
    4. The Where
    5. The When
    6. The How

III. Rhetorical Devices

    1. The Summary Statement
    2. Conditional Clauses
    3. The Substantive Clause
    4. Phrases
    5. The Cartridge Lead
    6. The Punch Lead
    7. The Astonisher Lead

IV. More Than One Feature

    1. Separate Stories
    2. The Crowded Lead
    3. The "Shirttail" Method
    4. Boxes
    5. The 1-2-3-4-Lead

THE CITY EDITOR AT HOME

BY *B. F. Sylvester*

"You had a good paper tonight, Dad."

"Thanks, Junior. It was just fair. Not enough local."

"Isn't national and world news good news?"

"You have to have a certain amount. But what people want to read is what is happening to their neighbors."

"If anything happened to Mr. Wilkins, would that be news?"

"Wilkins, the janitor? It would have to be important; the mayor's car run over him, or something."

"Why don't you put in the paper that Mr. Thomas is painting his house?"

"The necktie manufacturer? That wouldn't be news."

"Was that chorus girl suing the former millionaire important news?"

"Not important, exactly. It was the story of a woman — "

"We'll let that one go, Dad. Tell me about this interview with Senator Loke. He says the country needs real patriots. What does he mean?"

"I suppose he means real leaders."

"Why didn't your reporter ask him what he meant?"

"It might have sounded impertinent."

"The reporter didn't know what he meant, did he?"

"Oh, he must have had an idea."

"Let's get back to Mr. Thomas' house, Dad. Why isn't painting his house important?"

"It doesn't mean anything except to Thomas. Things must be looking up for him."

"Then, Dad, maybe it means something to others. If business is better, perhaps the 1,000 men he laid off in January are going back to work. That would mean business stimulation in our city, grocery bills paid, home installments paid up, new cars sold. And look, Dad, if people have begun to buy neckties, it might mean a new spirit throughout the country. It might be the turning of the tide."

"Now, Junior, run along. You talk like an editorial writer."

"Junior, I want to thank you for that tip on Thomas painting his house."

"Then it was important? Did he put the men back to work? Is there an upturn in business?"

"Sorry, Junior, we didn't get around to that. Our story is that Mr. and Mrs. Thomas couldn't agree on the color so she's painting her side blue and he's painting his orange. It's a pip."

Editor & Publisher

THERE IS NO EXACT "ONE WAY" TO WRITE ANY NEWS STORY. Given the same schedule of facts, equally competent writers will compose accounts which read differently, and an impartial judge might find it impossible to choose the best.

The first and most important step in news writing is selection of the lead. That requires the exercise of editorial judgment to determine what angle or phase of the total information available is to receive emphasis. It is not enough that the first part of a story answer as many of the questions, Who? What? When? Where? Why? and How? as the story demands be answered. These elements must be so arranged as to give proper emphasis to those which are most important.

The entire tone of a news story is determined by the feature which is emphasized in the lead, often in the first sentence or even the first clause or phrase of the first sentence. Giving proper emphasis to the different ingredients of a news story is a simple, standard *method of interpretation* which was practiced long before words were used to describe it. The reporter who develops facility in this regard is training himself well for the future.

NEWS VALUES

Disregarding considerations of policy as a determinant of news judgment, newspapers and other media of communication, despite their differences, have similar criteria by which to determine the potential newsworthiness of the thousands or millions of occurrences from which they make their selection each day. Psychologically these criteria may be superficial or erroneous, but they have been tested by years of experience and, rightly or wrongly, are in vogue in all but a negligible number of news rooms.

Differing in arrangement, nomenclature and emphasis, the main determinants of news values, textbook writers and editors in the main agree, are these:

1. Timeliness
2. Proximity
3. Prominence
4. Consequence
5. Human interest

TIMELINESS

Familiar to every newsman of the past half-century is the axiom that "nothing is so dead as yesterday's newspaper." Today, possibly, should be added, "or the radio or television newscast of an hour ago." Certainly the increased speed by which news is transmitted has increased the zeal of all who are engaged in the communication business to obtain and stress "latest developments first." The rule is always to bring a story up-to-date as much as possible before going to press or on the air and, if at all possible, to avoid using "yesterday" except in early morning reports.

This "last minute" effect often can be obtained by omitting the "when" from the lead, as in the following:

A Circuit court judge has given the owners of a slum tenement 60 days to repair their building or face losing the property to the city.

The action was taken Thursday by Judge Ernest L. Eberholtz in a case involving the five-story brick building at 2122 W. Ashberry street.

In reporting speeches, announcements and the like, this form can be used:

Elimination of all overnight street parking is necessary to reduce Milltown's traffic accident rate in the opinion of Traffic Engineer L. Scott Updike.

"Many pedestrians are being injured at night because parked cars obstruct the vision of drivers," Updike told the Milltown Executive club last night.

PROXIMITY

An event occurring within the territory of a newspaper's circulation is of greater interest than a similar event outside that area. It takes a very important foreign story to crowd out a fairly important local story. Readers have a primary interest in names of persons and places with which they are familiar and in situations and trends which may affect them. They want, first of all, to know what is going on in their own community. Examination of the front pages of newspapers published the same day in different cities shows that editors believe that the local story should be given first place. Metropolitan newspapers, however, feel the necessity of printing more national and international news than formerly. One result has been a rapid increase in the size and number of community and suburban papers devoted primarily to local news coverage.

Not only do readers like to read of happenings in their vicinity of which they have no previous knowledge, but also, perhaps especially, do they look for accounts of events with which they are familiar. They like to see their own names in print and to read what the paper has to say about situations about which they already know something. When a person expects that his name, or the name of someone whom he knows well, is to appear in the newspaper, he looks first of all for the item containing it. He is eager to read the newspaper's account of a meeting that he has attended, an accident that he has seen, or an athletic contest at which he has been present. Logically, the contrary should be true: he should read first that which he already does not know. But he doesn't, and editors know that he doesn't. This being so, newspapers try to please as many readers as possible. If they feel that there is any chance of an appreciable number of readers being interested in an item, no matter how trivial it may be, they print the item.

This statement contradicts the supercilious attitude that it is only rural folk who delight in gossip. Just the opposite is true. We do not read in a New York paper that Mary Smith is spending the weekend with relatives in New Haven merely because not enough people are acquainted with Miss Smith. Those who do know her are interested in the item of her visit; if the name happens to be Kate Smith there is a strong possibility that the item will be published. There is no gossip about celebrities too trivial for publication in a metropolitan newspaper. No city reader has any right to laugh at readers of country weeklies who are interested to learn that Henry Jones has painted his barn red.

Writers are enjoined to play up the local as well as the latest angles of stories. For instance:

> Robert A. Brown Post No. 89 of the American Legion will be represented at the tenth annual convention of the state American Legion Monday, Tuesday and Wednesday at Neillsville, by a delegation of approximately 50 members, including 35 members of the fife and drum corps.

This is better than:

> The tenth annual convention of American Legion posts of the state will be held Monday, Tuesday and Wednesday at Neillsville. The local post, etc.

Newspapers rewrite or supplement the stories of press associations and correspondents which carry general leads, such as the second, in order to meet the interests of local readers. They "localize" national stories, as illustrated by the following:

> Hundreds of Wisconsin employes of the postal department, including 1,500 in the Milwaukee office and 1,200 rural carriers throughout the state, Wednesday faced a payless payday as Congress dallied on the post office and treasury department appropriations bill.
>
> Postmaster John A. Fleissner said that all checks due employes Thursday were being made out Wednesday and would be held in the vault until

word for their release is received from Washington, D.C. The Milwaukee office handles the paychecks for all the state's rural carriers, in addition to the local payrolls.

PROMINENCE

All men may be created equal, but some are more newsworthy than others. This may be because of the positions they hold, their entertainment value, or because they have behaved so unusually in the past that they have created interest in whatever else they may do.

What is true of persons also is true of places and organizations. All other elements being equal, a newsworthy event, such as a fire or crime, is more important if it occurs in one's home town. The reader, however, does not have the same interest in all other places. Such large population centers as New York, Chicago and Los Angeles rate ahead of most small cities and towns. Among the latter, however, there are some considered more newsworthy than others, often because they have become associated with a particular kind of news. Among such places are Reno, Las Vegas, Hollywood, Tia Juana and Monte Carlo.

To the home-town editor, news of all potential subscribers is important, and he tries to use the names of as many of them as space permits. Newspapers often print long lists of delegates to conventions, guests at weddings and social events, committee memberships, and so forth. Reporters are instructed to obtain as many names as possible and are cautioned to get complete names and their correct spellings. Last names seldom are enough. News media should use a person's name as he himself uses it in business and society generally. Sometimes a telephone book or city directory may give a full name whereas the person uses one or more initials or even a nickname. The only safe way is to ask the person.

If a widely known person figures in a news event, that fact may become the feature of a story, as in the following:

> State Sen. Lyle G. Fitzhugh and six other persons were injured last night when a row of temporary bleacher seats collapsed during the Milltown-Rushville basketball game.

CONSEQUENCE

Not only the prominence of persons, places, and things mentioned in news stories originating outside the community which a newspaper serves causes them to be published in place of local news; an equal or perhaps more important factor is the importance of the item.

To illustrate: news from Washington, D.C. is front-page copy in Chicago and San Francisco not primarily because it contains the widely known names of a senator or cabinet member, but because the problem with which those figures are connected vitally concerns the best interests of readers all over the country. Every American citizen is directly affected by an important piece of legislation before Congress. National or state political news often is more important than local political news. In a nuclear age one-world-mindedness is a necessity.

Stories concerning changes in the weather or fashions, and stories of epidemics and pestilences, are important because the immediate community may be affected indirectly if not directly. A coal strike in a distant state may lead to a local shortage of fuel; a new model of automobile will be on sale locally within a short space of time; an important scientific discovery may change a reader's way of thinking on a metaphysical problem. The interest in such stories is very personal and very real.

In addition to localizing nationally important stories, newspapers emphasize the consequence of news by seeking the *tomorrow* angle on strictly local stories. This device serves to make the item seem timely and to point up significance. Emphasis is on results rather than causes, on explaining what the present continuing or probable future effect will be.

> Policemen, firemen and other city service employes would be allowed to live in the suburbs under an ordinance introduced Wednesday in the City Council.

> Milltown taxpayers who are short of breath or in a hurry when they make their annual visit to the city hall will experience relief if Mayor R. O. Bushnell's plan to move the city treasurer's office from the third to the first floor of the Municipal Building is approved tonight by the City Council.

HUMAN INTEREST

Interest in human beings as such, and in events because they concern men and women in situations which might confront anyone else, is called human interest.

It is human interest, interest in the lives and welfare of others and in the well-being and progress of mankind as a whole, that causes us to read, with interest and sympathy, of loss of life and property in communities far removed from our own. When an earthquake destroys homes and takes lives in southern Italy or in Japan, there is little likelihood of our being affected directly, except perhaps as we are asked to contribute to the Red Cross relief fund; but we are interested in learning of such "acts of God" because other human beings like ourselves are involved.

It is this personal appeal which editors mean when they say that an item of news has "reader interest" even though it may not possess any of the other elements of news value: timeliness, proximity, prominence and consequence.

Strictly speaking, all reader interest is human interest. Because readers differ in their occupational, recreational, and other interests, some news which has a *personal appeal* to one reader fails to interest another. Any reader, however, no matter how cynical or self-centered, has some *sympathetic interest* in the lives and well-being of other humans. This interest includes both extremes of the pathetic and humorous in everyday life, whatever causes a reader to feel sorry for or to laugh with or at some other fellow being.

Interest in accounts of disasters involving loss of life and property is sympathetic. There may be other elements of interest in stories of fires, wrecks, accidents and other catastrophes; but when individuals are mentioned in unfortunate situations, there also is sympathetic interest. Sickness, near death, suffering of any kind, loss of wealth, etc., create attitudes of sympathy in readers.

At the other extreme, ludicrous accounts of typical men and women touch a sympathetic vein also. Americans like to laugh and are amused at almost anything in any way incongruous. In most humorous stories there is someone who suffers some inconvenience, but this does not detract from the humor of the situation any more than does knowledge of injury to a person who has slipped on a banana peel and fallen suffice to suppress the smile which comes to one's lips.

Such incidents also involve *unusualness*. People everywhere, and perhaps Americans in particular, love thrills and anything with an "-est" to it. Unusual people, quaint and picturesque places, exciting adventures, all appeal to us. And when we cannot meet these individuals, see those places, experience romance ourselves, we like to read of them all the more. We take vicarious pleasure from stories of adventure and romance.

Once news of new theories and discoveries in the field of science was considered unusual. In the present nuclear age the element of surprise has disappeared, but the interest in *progress* continues. Likewise, unfortunately, the element of reader interest which probably outweighs all others — that in *combat* — also continues. Critical examination of the lists of "biggest" news stories of any year indicates that there is no other single element of reader interest which is present more frequently. Americans, it must be, like a good fight and consider life as a whole to be a struggle. The element of combat is found most prominently in stories of athletic contests, crime, politics, adventure, disaster and heroism. Man against man or man against nature always draws a big crowd, which usually roots for the underdog.

If there is *suspense* in the story of combat, or any other story for that matter, the interest is heightened. Frequently, the attention of an entire nation is centered upon a single news event, as in the case of a mine disaster when rescuers work frantically to save human lives. Illness, especially of a prominent person or from an unusual cause, may be reported so as to emphasize the element of suspense. There is suspense in political campaigns, in law cases, and in athletic contests.

The so-called human interest in any kind of story is enhanced if the principals include a *child*, *animal* or *woman*, preferably a good-looking young woman. Hieroglyphic warnings against the increasing immorality of youth have been discovered by excavators, proving that adolescence always has been a problem. Furthermore, since before the days of chivalry, the female sex has caused more worry than the male.

Times haven't changed much and "flaming youth" still is having its inning, with debutantes, co-eds, waitresses, and heiresses flaming perhaps a bit more brightly than ever before. The growth of newspapers and of newspaper photography has helped satisfy the desire for accurate information of just what our allegedly wayward sons and daughters are doing, and how they look.

So-called middle age is, from the news standpoint, the drabbest of man's several stages. Precocious infancy and childhood and virile old age vie with hilarious adolescence in front-page importance. The little girl who calls on the mayor to let her doggie out of the pound, and the grandma who gets her hair bobbed are good copy. The thirties, forties, and fifties are the trying years if one is a publicity seeker. At those ages he really has to do something to get by the copy desk; or else he must employ an adroit public relations counsel.

Interest in animals is similar to interest in children and old age. Sometimes the reader is sympathetic, as in the case of a dog who refuses to leave his master's grave; sometimes he is resentful, as when a tame animal turns on someone and hurts him.

Stories of unusual intelligence in animals always are good copy, especially if the well-being of humans thereby is fostered. Also, anecdotes of admirable qualities, as faithfulness, have an appeal. Any freak from the animal kingdom attracts attention as Barnum knew, and there is plentiful interest remaining in the disappearing sport of hunting, especially of big game.

The beginning reporter must learn to recognize the human interest possibilities of stories and to brighten up what he writes by giving it the "twist" which turns a drab into a bright yarn without, of course, exaggeration or distortion.

The following are sprightly leads to factual news stories made so by adroitness on the part of their authors in picking and playing up phases lending themselves to human interest treatment or emphasis:

Toronto — (UP) — John Brock, 32, began serving a two-year penitentiary term Tuesday because he hates women.

He was convicted of assault for breaking into the ladies' room of a downtown tavern and mussing up a young housewife who was fixing her makeup. The housewife told police that Brock crashed in and shouted, "I hate women and you're one."

Duluth News-Tribune

Roars and snarls of protest raged around the Denver zoo Friday, but the noise was emanating from the city and county building, not City park.

The hubbub concerns the plans of Mayor Nicholson's administration to sign over management of the zoo to the Denver Zoological Foundation, a group of citizens long interested in the zoo's problems who believe they can operate it better than the city.

Denver Post

These examples illustrate that it is possible to adhere to the rules regarding the news story form and at the same time avoid "wooden" leads.

THE FIVE W'S AND THE H

The *who* or the *what* usually is the feature of a short one-incident (simple) news story. It often is difficult to determine which is more important, as most news concerns people and what they do. For instance, in the following short item many readers will be interested primarily in the young man mentioned as a friend or acquaintance. Others, however, will be interested chiefly because of the extent to which the local schools will be affected by the news. When the news is about a definite person the name usually comes first, as:

> Peter L. Clay has resigned his position as instructor in history in the local high school to accept a teaching fellowship in history at Booster college.

THE WHO

The *who* is unmistakably the feature in the following story:

> George L. Rose has been elected ninth vice president of the American Council of Civil Service Employes.

Often the interest in the *who* comes from the kind of person involved (judged by his occupation, religion, sex, age, etc., or by the circumstances in which he figures in the particular story), or from the number of persons involved, as:

> A private watchman shot a safecracker Tuesday when he and his accomplice resisted arrest.

The indefinite *who* is used increasingly as cities become larger and persons in the news are known to fewer other persons in proportion to the population as a whole.

THE WHAT

The *what* is more important than the *who* when the circumstance would be significant no matter who the persons involved, as:

One man was shot and another was beaten today in an outbreak of violence as strikers tried to prevent operation of the Johnson-Smith corporation.

A youth who went berserk with a butcher knife was captured and held by police tonight as a suspect in two recent murders in Milltown.

Press associations usually write their stories in this way, as names may not mean anything outside the immediate vicinity in which the event occurred. The writer of a news story always must decide which is more important, the name or the event.

Often a *what* lead begins with the *who* as an easier rhetorical method or to emphasize authority. Note in the following example that, although the *who* comes first, the *what* is more important.

President Joseph E. Jennings today announced that the county board is able to pay off current expenditures as they arise, despite the fact that it has retired $568,910 in outstanding debts since he assumed office three years ago.

In the following example the *what* is unmistakably predominant:

Vandalism against cars was reported in Southside Milltown Friday.
Vice squad detectives began an investigation after auto windshields and windows were reported smashed on Haberkorn road, Lakeside drive, Alcott drive and Norton road, SW.

In action stories readers usually are interested in results rather than causes, as:

A street-car bandit was killed and two others and a boy were captured in a robbery and raid early today. The boy was wounded when he got in line of fire.

THE WHY

Sometimes, however, it is the cause rather than the result that is the feature of the story, as:

Trying to pass another car while traveling at high speed brought serious injury to two men last night when their automobile overturned twice on Washington boulevard at Potter avenue.

THE WHERE

In advance stories of meetings, speeches, athletic events, accidents, etc., the *where* must be very definite. Room numbers, street addresses, etc., should be given. In local stories, it is not always necessary to mention the name of the city or a street address. The immediate community is understood, as:

Eight testing lanes on which motorists must submit their automobiles and trucks to examination for safe driving qualifications will be opened tomorrow.

The *where* may be the featurized element, as:

In her 400-year-old ancestral home, the only daughter of an English general recently became the wife of a gypsy, who worked as a handyman on the estate.

In each of the following examples, the *where* definitely was the feature although, in the second example, the *when* rhetorically came first.

A tract of approximately 30 acres at Forest boulevard and Kerwood avenue, assessed at $90,000, has been sold by Herschel Steel, represented by the Wray-Graw Co., to John L. Finch.

Beginning today, parking will be permitted in the Underground Lakeside Exhibition hall of Citizen's hall by patrons of events at the hall and the Civic auditorium, at a rate of 40 cents per car.

When a place is more familiar than the names of those associated with it, the following style may be used:

The operator of a candy store at 717 S. Ninth street pleaded guilty Monday in U.S. District court of the purchase, possession, and sale of 5 ounces of heroin.
He is Andrew Solberg, 41, of 141 Oak street, who was arrested by narcotics agents last month.

THE WHEN

About the same may be said of the *when* as of the *where*. It ordinarily is included inconspicuously in the lead, as:

Fur thieves hit two Milltown stores early Wednesday and got away with a total loot estimated at $230,000.

Frequently the *when* may be left until the second paragraph, as:

Commissioner William Wheat has appointed a seven-man hospital committee to look into the situation surrounding construction of a countywide hospital for pay patients.

The members were appointed at a Monday afternoon session with the commissioner.

Such omission of the *when* from the first paragraph is common practice with press associations, especially when preparing news of one day for use in morning newspapers the following day.

The *when* may be a matter of "continuous action," as:

A couple of perky oldsters who defied the wilderness for ten days on a can of beans, a bit of jelly and a small packet of powdered milk are recovering from exhaustion and hunger in Milltown hospital.

The *when* may be the featured element, as:

Midnight tonight is the deadline for 1962 automobile license plates and vehicles in use after 12:01 A.M. tomorrow must carry 1963 plates, the Bureau of Motor Vehicles reminded automobile owners yesterday.

A type of *when* lead is the "duration of time" lead, as:

After deliberating five hours last night, a Superior court jury returned a verdict of guilty in the steel purchase fraud trial of four Gruner county highway employes.

A similar type of *when* lead is the "since when" lead, as:

After being gone for two weeks, "Duke," a wistful looking Collie-Spitz hybrid, decided he liked his old home better and trudged 40 miles to return to the residence of his former owner, Humane Officer Thompson Meredith.

THE HOW

By definition the *how* means details to explain how something occurred. Consequently, when the feature unmistakably consists in such details, care must be exercised to avoid wordiness.

Madison, Wis., July 25. — (AP) — An Air Force jet plane returned to its home base today — the hard way.
The fighter crash-landed in a corn field, mowed a path and popped out of the field, skittered across a busy highway beside Truax Air Force Base and slid home on a familiar runway.
The pilot, Lieut. John P. Curchill, 25, of Madison, N.J., was unhurt. His plane developed engine trouble and he was returning to base when the engine quit.

Sports stories frequently are given *how* leads, as:

Crossinger, N.Y., June 18. — (UP) — Louise Suggs of Atlanta, Ga., sank a 25-foot putt for a birdie three on the 18th hole today to win the triangle round robin golf tournament with a total of 44 points.

RHETORICAL DEVICES

Skillful use of the ordinary rhetorical devices enables the news writer to play up a feature.

THE SUMMARY STATEMENT

Most news leads are mere summary statements consisting of simple sentences or of compound or complex sentences with the principal clauses first. Many examples given so far in this chapter illustrate how the feature of a story can be emphasized by means of such simple straightforward writing. Observe, in addition, the following example:

> The body of an elderly Groversville man was found floating face down in the Saginaw canal near 34th street and Countyline road yesterday.
> It was identified as that of Maurice Broadstreet, believed to be more than 80 years old.

CONDITIONAL CLAUSES

Often, however, it is difficult to get the feature into a main clause. This is so when the feature is present in addition to the main news idea which the writer must include in his lead. Features to be found in accompanying circumstances, conditions, coincidences in the *when*, *where*, etc., often can best be played up by beginning the lead with a complex or complex-compound sentence with the conditional clause first.

In the following examples note how the conditional clause contains the feature, whereas the main idea which is the excuse for the story still is in the main clause.

> Because Paul Gregg, 17-year-old high school boy, was caught as a stowaway and locked in the infirmary of the liner *Justice*, he started to burn the ship to seek his freedom, he admitted to steamship authorities here today.

This emphasizes the feature much more than would inversion of the clause order, as:

> Paul Gregg, 17-year-old high school boy, today admitted to steamship authorities here that he set fire to the liner *Justice* to obtain his freedom after being caught as a stowaway and locked in the infirmary.

THE SUBSTANTIVE CLAUSE

The substantive clause usually takes the form of a "that" clause which has been much overworked by news writers because it is easy

to write and is consequently taboo in many offices. Occasionally the sub-
tantive is forceful, as:

> That the present legislative appropriation must be doubled if mini-
> mum essentials are to be provided relief clients, is the warning con-
> tained in the monthly report made today by Harold G. Todd, local relief
> administrator, to the State Department of Public Welfare.

> Return to the pioneer days, when youths in their early teens could as-
> semble a muzzle-loader and pick off game 50 yards away, was sought in
> a bill before the state legislature today.

PHRASES

Infinitive, participial, prepositional and gerund phrases and
absolute constructions also may be used to emphasize a feature when it
happens to be one of the minor *w's* or *h*. In such constructions, the main
clause contains the *who* and *what*, one of which is modified by the phrase.

Inverted sentence structure may be used to identify (tie-back) the
news with previous news (see Chapter 9) and to identify persons, places
and events. Use of phrases and of the absolute construction for different
purposes is illustrated in the following examples:

WHEN

After a three-hour search by police and relatives, James Fillmore, 30,
his wife and four children who had been missing since Saturday, were
found early yesterday in a friend's home.

WHERE

Beside the Ring river, which he made famous in song and verse, the
body of Feodor Vladik today was buried with only a handful of close
relatives present.

WHY

Delayed somewhat by recent hurricane alerts, work to complete Harris
Civil Defense Headquarters in the basement of the Carnegie Free Library
was pressed anew last week.

HOW

Citing a permissive 1867 ordinance which never has been repealed,
Henry Bucher today won the right to raise geese in his backyard at 10
Cheery lane.

TIE-BACK

Disregarding three previous failures, Grace Slawson, 21-year-old grocery clerk, tomorrow will attempt to set a new record for swimming across
Lake Malthusia.

THE CARTRIDGE LEAD

When war is declared or ends, a president or some other widely known figure dies, and on similarly important occasions, it is customary to tell the gist of the news in the fewest possible words, as:

Galvania has declared war on Powry.
Mayor Charles A. Brinshaw is dead.
The Maroons are conference champions.

Stories written entirely in such staccato fashion have a breath-taking quality. Consequently, the style should not be used too extensively but reserved for occasions of particular importance.

THE PUNCH LEAD

What has traditionally been called a punch lead performs a function similar to that of the cartridge lead, but it is not so short, abrupt or definite. Since World War II, it has grown in popularity and on some newspapers is used for almost any kind of story, not just stories of presumed extra newsworthiness. It has been called the "blind" lead because of its emphasis upon situations rather than specific persons and details. It is a form of writing easily open to misuse: (1) on stories whose importance is thereby exaggerated, (2) by being excessively indefinite or "empty," an example being "Politics had a different look in Congress today," a sentence which tells exactly nothing. Paragraphs two and three of a well-written story with a punch lead should supply definite details.

A policeman has been suspended on charges that he deserted his school-crossing post.
Placed on indefinite suspension by Police Chief Patrick C. O'Brien Tuesday was Albert Murchison, 27, of 885 W. Strong avenue, attached to the Vickers station, 1412 E. Vickers avenue.
Lieut. Ira Walters of the Vickers district said a routine check at noon Monday disclosed that Murchison was absent from his post at Bristol and Sacramento roads.

THE ASTONISHER LEAD

Beginning writers are discouraged in their use of superlatives and expressions of opinion. When deserved, however, superlatives should be used, as:

One of the nation's most wanted fugitives was seized today while allegedly staging a $75 robbery of a chance tavern acquaintance.
He is Emil Littlejohn, 28, wanted by the F.B.I. in the kidnaping and rape of a middle-aged Milltown woman, an attack so savage it nearly killed her.

MORE THAN ONE FEATURE

So far, only stories containing simple features relatively easy to pick even though related to important events have been considered. Not infrequently, an item of news presents so many angles that the rhetorical devices described in this chapter are inadequate. There are several ways out of this difficulty.

SEPARATE STORIES

The easiest way is to write more than one story. When there are "sidelights" or interviews of opinion or features connected with a news event, the assignment usually is divided between two or more reporters. Some repetition usually occurs but is not discouraged; in fact, in some cases it is encouraged, and a paper may run several stories of the same event written by different reporters.

THE CROWDED LEAD

When the various elements of interest are of nearly equal value, a number of facts may be crowded into a single lead, as:

Standing committees were appointed, the street-lighting contract was continued for one year and a proposed new ordinance regulating business licenses was referred to the Finance committee last night at the weekly meeting of the Board of Aldermen.

Succeeding paragraphs naturally would take up each item mentioned in the lead, providing full details.

THE "SHIRTTAIL" METHOD

To avoid crowded and vague leads, one item deemed the most important can be played up. Paragraphs containing mention of other items then can be introduced by such expressions as, "In other actions the City Council . . ." or "In a similar accident . . ." and so forth.

Ald. Val G. Grauer (17th ward) has been elected chairman of the powerful Finance committee of the Board of Aldermen.

Other standing committee chairmen, named at last night's board meeting, follow . . .

The board also voted to continue for one year its contract with the Republic Light company for street lighting . . .

In other actions, the board referred a proposed new ordinance regulating business licenses to the Finance committee and rejected a request by Front street property owners that all-night parking be permitted in the 400 block.

BOXES

Often, statements, tabulations, data, side features, etc., can best be presented by means of a "box" set either ahead of the lead, within the main article or in an adjoining column. There are many other uses for the box, most of them connected with makeup. Material most frequently boxed includes:

1. Lists of dead and injured in accidents
2. Telling statements from speeches, reports, testimony, etc.
3. Statistics
4. Summaries of facts included in the story itself or in two or more related stories
5. Brief histories of events connected with the story
6. Local angles on press association stories

> After requiring 12 employes and six customers to lie face downward on the floor, three armed and masked bandits shortly after 8 A.M. today removed approximately $75,000 in currency from the cashiers' cages of the First National bank, 109 N. Main street, and escaped in a waiting automobile driven by a fourth man.

FOURTH IN TWO YEARS

Today's burglary of the First National bank was the fourth in two years in Milltown. Others, together with losses and outcomes, were:

March 3, 1960 — First National bank, $17,451 cash, recovered upon arrest of Abe Mason, now serving a ten-year term in the state penitentiary.

Sept. 21, 1961 — Milltown State bank, $41,150 cash and bonds, recovered when sheriff's posse killed John "Gunman" Hays three miles south of town the same day.

July 15, 1962 — Citizen's National bank, $50,000 removed by blowing open safe at night. Still unsolved.

The men were described by Wilmer Asher, head cashier, as all apparently under 25 years of age. They wore blue overalls and caps which were drawn down just above the eyes.

THE 1-2-3-4-LEAD

After a short summary statement of the situation constituting the news, the different features can be emphasized by tabulation and numbering, as:

The wishes of Mayor Louis T. Tupper were ignored by the new Board of Aldermen in several votes at its organizing meeting last night. Most importantly the board did the following:

1. Elected Ald. Val G. Grauer (17th ward), political rival of the mayor's, chairman of the powerful Finance committee.

2. Referred a proposed new ordinance regulating business licenses to Ald. Grauer's committee. The mayor has called the new ordinance unnecessary.

3. Continued for one year the contract with the Republic Light company for street lighting. The mayor opposed the renewal in campaign speeches last month.

4. Rejected a property owners' petition for all-night parking in the 400 block on Front street which the mayor had approved.

The preceding lead, of course, is interpretative. It plays up the significance of the board's actions rather than merely reporting them "deadpan." It does not editorialize for or against the board's insurgency, and the treatment probably could be adversely criticized only if it could be shown that each board action was taken despite rather than because of any attitude toward Mayor Tupper.

The article as written does not say the four actions indicated hostility by the board toward the mayor. Nevertheless, there is no mistaking the fact that such an impression is given. If, at a subsequent meeting, the board were to vote in favor of a number of measures sponsored by the mayor, the facts as they existed after the earlier meeting would have to be re-examined. If, however, the facts as stated in the first story are accurate, the reporter could not be accused of coloring his account. Certainly he provided his readers with background information whereby it would be possible for them to draw conclusions, whereas a strictly factual account of the actions of the Board of Aldermen, without attempt at any perspective, might have created a wrong impression.

It cannot be pointed out too often that essential for this kind of interpretative reporting is knowledge. Without it, the newsgatherer will consider as new something that is very old and will have news sources "revealing" and "disclosing" information that is common knowledge among a wide circle of readers.

In other words, you can't play up a feature unless you have brains enough to pick it.

5

Making It Attractive

I. The News Peg

II. The Contrast Lead

III. The Question Lead

IV. The Descriptive Lead

V. The Staccato Lead

VI. The Figurative Lead

VII. The Epigram Lead

VIII. The Literary Allusion Lead

IX. The Parody Lead

X. The Quotation Lead

XI. The Dialogue Lead

XII. Cumulative Interest

XIII. Suspended Interest

XIV. Sequence

XV. Direct Address

XVI. Freaks

DEEP THINKING IS ESSENTIAL
TO GOOD REPORTING TODAY

Depth journalism is an important phrase today. It is important because we live in a fast-moving world, where a great many significant events are constantly taking place.

And, more than ever, people want to know about and understand these events. They look to their mass media, and particularly their newspapers, to do the reporting, the explaining and the interpretation.

This can make reporting a pretty tough job. In some areas it calls for more than an ability to observe. An expert in the field he is writing about is often required.

However, the average newspaper cannot hire many specialists. But they can hire well educated, alert men and women who have a good background in political science, economics and the liberal arts.

With these tools, and a continuing hunger for more learning, they can practice depth journalism too.

Because it isn't only Geneva conferences and presidential campaigns that are complicated. City government can be a pretty complex affair too, and it takes a good, hard-working reporter to do the best job of explaining it to the public.

Publishers' Auxiliary

SPOT NEWS ISN'T ENOUGH

BY *Erwin D. Canham*

Mere publication of spot news in newspapers is not enough, and most newspapers have acted on that assumption for some time. The news must be clarified, explained, interpreted and integrated with other news. The commentators do that on the radio too. But people still demand the printed word. They still can't quite depend on what they hear.

Also, today's news is increasingly complicated. Therefore newspaper writers must be increasingly expert. They must be specialists in various subjects. Big news stories of the world can no longer be covered by a bright boy just off the police beat. Joseph Pulitzer recognized this fact half a century ago when he projected his post-graduate journalism school. This trend will greatly intensify. It takes a good man to explain to the lay reader the workings of the atomic bomb.

The Christian Science Monitor

If THE FIRST PART OF A NEWS STORY ANSWERS AS MANY OF THE five *w*'s and *h* as necessary (see Chapter 3) and gives the proper emphasis to the one which constitutes the feature (see Chapter 4), it is a good lead. If, in addition, the beginning of the news story is so interestingly written that the reader continues for that reason alone, it is a superior lead. No one reader is interested in a majority of the news items contained in any single newspaper edition; it is the purpose of headlines to direct him to those stories in which he does have an interest. The lead of a story authenticates and supplements its headline and is sufficient for a large proportion of readers who get that far.

Each news story, however, is composed for the minority of readers who peruse it to its very end. Both its content and the way it is written determine its interest value. In Part II, the emphasis is upon how to obtain completeness of detail in gathering information regarding a number of different kinds of events. The purpose of this chapter is to offer assistance to the beginning writer in how to attain rhetorical excellence without sacrificing news interest.

THE NEWS PEG

When a lead is written in feature or semifeature style, either to play up a feature angle or for rhetorical attractiveness, the part which contains the kernel or more of news regarding the event which is the story's excuse for being, is called the *news peg*. The extent to which it can be made secondary to featured fact or language depends upon its importance. If it is of vital public interest, it must be given emphasis. If, on the other hand, the feature interest of the story outweighs its importance as public information, the news peg can be played down. In the following examples, however, despite the feature treatment, the news pegs are present in the leads:

> After dressing her three small daughters in their Easter finery and taking them to church where they were baptized, Mrs. Nora MacMahon returned yesterday to her Pineville home and strangled them.

> Milltown area police are in a race against death — and may already be too late — in their feverish search for Harold A. Dunraven, 58.
> They know what he has in mind — suicide.

They hope to find him in time to prevent it.

Dunraven is the Crestwood Community Chest director who disappeared a week ago.

THE CONTRAST LEAD

Sometimes the feature of a news story consists in the contrast between the immediate and a former situation or between the event at hand and another of which, for any of a number of reasons, it is a reminder. Note that the news peg is retained in the following lead though not so definitely, the emphasis being upon the unusual situation:

Behind the same walnut desk which he used to dust 25 years ago as an office boy, Virgil N. Stimson yesterday received congratulations upon becoming president of Andalia Trucking company.

THE QUESTION LEAD

Ordinarily the reporter should answer, not ask, questions in his news stories. To do otherwise, merely delays telling the news, as in the case of a lead beginning "What causes delinquency?" followed by a summary of a new idea advanced by some authority. It would be much better to start: "Failure of teenagers to obtain jobs causes them to become delinquent in the opinion of . . ."

When the story concerns a problem of public interest or a matter likely to provoke debate among readers, however, it may be possible to obtain interest by means of a question lead, as:

How does it feel to be buried alive?

Edward Turner, 27-year-old laborer of 541 Green street can tell you. He learned first-hand when a bank of earth caved in on him at a construction project on W. Harmon avenue yesterday.

What is there to keeping Milltown's 2,500 parking meters in tip-top shape?

That will be debated Wednesday when a city council finance subcommittee starts wrestling with making a choice on next year's meter maintenance contract.

THE DESCRIPTIVE LEAD

The feature or "key to the spirit" of a story may be in its setting, the physical appearance of some person or object involved, or in an unusual phase of the action with which it deals. In such cases, a graphic or descriptive lead may be the most effective to give the tone or feeling necessary to proper understanding and appreciation. Before he can describe, the reporter must know how to observe; the best descriptive leads are written by eyewitnesses. To be avoided are superfluous and inapplicable adjectives, extraneous matter serving no purpose except, perhaps, to prove the writer's possession of an extensive vocabulary of trite and hackneyed expressions — clichés. The following leads to important stories avoid these hazards:

A fusillade of gunfire shattered the quiet of a Milltown street shortly before midnight, and when it was over a young man lay dead.

For more than a minute today the sun hung over central Minnesota like a twinkling, slate-blue Christmas ornament as the moon moved between it and the earth.

In the awesome half-light that covered the area, hundreds of scientists and thousands of other persons had a perfect view of the total solar eclipse.
The New York *Times*

THE STACCATO LEAD

When the time element — either fast action or the intervals separating a series of related events — is to be emphasized, the staccato lead occasionally suffices. It consists in a series of phrases, punctuated either by periods or dashes and usually is a form of descriptive lead. The style suggests the "tone" of the story, its feeling.

Hanover, June 23. — An ear-wracking roar followed by a series of cloudburst demonstrations. A serpent's tongue of flame. Dense billows of black smoke thinning gradually into white. Movement made almost invisible by velocity.

Thus the observer's brain recorded the spectacle of Fritz von Opel's rocket car blazing along the railroad tracks in the environs of this city today at a speed of 254 kilometers an hour — 39 faster than has ever been achieved before by a vehicle running on rails.

Thirty years ago — back in 1932 — in a different era, in a different life, after 40 years of happiness in her simple home, the light went out for Mrs. Hattie Downs, of Gregoryville and she became blind — stone blind.

Years passed — thirty of them — long and tortuous — and suddenly her prayers were answered, and Mrs. Hattie Downs could see.

THE FIGURATIVE LEAD

Triteness must be avoided in the use of metaphors, similes, and other figures of speech, either in the lead or any other part of a news story. Many expressions have become so common through usage that they are hardly noticed by casual readers as figurative. Among them are "plucked bare," "shoe on the wrong foot," "attach his wagon to a star," "put all its eggs in one basket" and many more. If the writer uses such expressions naturally, without strain, possibly even without awareness that they are figurative, the result is more likely to be good than if he deliberately tries for effect:

> Knocked on the ropes by a wet and windy one-two punch, Milltown's July heat wave refused to call it quits Friday.

> Washington, June 27. — (AP) — The army is putting teeth into the new defense department directive which authorized a secrecy cloak for information when it bears the stamp "for official use only."

THE EPIGRAM LEAD

The tone or moral of a story also may be emphasized by means of an epigram lead, in the writing of which bromides and platitudes must be avoided. The epigram is a concise and pointed expression, usually witty. The epigram lead may be either a familiar saying or a moral applicable to the story at hand, as:

> Silence can be golden in more ways than one, Shortstop Tommy Jacobs of the Maroons has discovered.
> After striking out three times against Bristol Aug. 12, Jacobs complained to his manager, Bucky Johnson, that he had been the victim of several debatable strike decisions.
> "The trouble with you," said Johnson, "is that you spend so much time turning around to squawk that you're not ready to hit the ball. Just for the fun of it, forget to turn around and look at the umpire for any reason and concentrate on hitting the ball."
> Tommy followed the advice and compiled the following record . . .

THE LITERARY ALLUSION LEAD

The writer with a normal background of knowledge in literature or history will have frequent chances to use it to advantage. Care must be taken to limit references to fictional or historical characters and to literary passages familiar to the average reader. The following examples illustrate how it is possible effectively to make use of one's general knowledge to improve his writing:

> A motorist who thought he was performing a Good Samaritan act today almost went to jail for aiding a criminal to escape.

The mountain wouldn't come to Mahomet, so a chewing-gum maker is going to the false teeth manufacturers.

Philip K. Wrigley, president of the William Wrigley, Jr., Co., announced this milestone in scientific research Tuesday at its annual stockholders' meeting.

Ever since the advent of plastic dentures 12 years ago, he said, the company's laboratories have sought to develop gum that won't stick to them. . . .   Chicago *Sun-Times*

THE PARODY LEAD

Popular song hits, bon mots by famous persons, titles of best-selling books or of motion pictures or new-coined phrases or expressions of any sort may be used while still fresh, usually in parodied form, to brighten an occasional news story lead. Well-established expressions may be used similarly. The following leads avoid the ever-lurking danger of triteness in such writing:

Sheridan, Wyo., Jan. 29. — Maybe it's a case of absence of water makes the heart grow fonder, but citizens of this northern Wyoming city have risen nobly to the call to help the flood-stricken dwellers along the Ohio River Valley.

Actor Charles Keller says you can't take it with you because the government takes it first.

The 77-year-old stage-and-screen star Tuesday urged outright repeal of the federal income tax, which he called an "economic cancer."

THE QUOTATION LEAD

In reporting speeches, public statements, and the like, it almost always is better to epitomize the feature in the reporter's own words rather than by means of a direct quotation.

Weak

"A sharp decrease in maternal mortality, medical progress, and greater economic prosperity have enabled welfare agencies to solve most of their problems except that of the emotionally disturbed child," Morace V. Updike, Council of Social Welfare director, said yesterday.

Strong

The emotionally disturbed child is the "No. 1 problem" facing welfare agencies today, Horace V. Updike, Council of Social Welfare director, said yesterday.

In news stories which are not accounts of speeches or documents, however, it sometimes is effective to begin with a direct quotation, as in the following examples:

"I just wanted to do something bad."

That, police said, was the only explanation 17-year-old Walter O'Malley could give for shooting and wounding two girls in a woodland ambush.

"Don't be an old grouch on the road!"

This advice for those who wish to stay alive although they drive in Labor Day weekend traffic comes from Francis Carroway, 18, judged Milltown's best teenage driver.

The partial or broken quote often can be used to add authenticity without making the lead unwieldly, as:

The city manager of Cresswood refused today to "commit myself" on revoking the liquor license of a saloon raided five times by sheriff's police in a year.

THE DIALOGUE LEAD

It is difficult, if not impossible, to begin a serious news story of an important event with dialogue. Minor court stories, with strong human interest, and occasionally stories of a more significant nature, however, can be handled effectively by means of a dialogue lead, as:

"Wouldn't it be terrible," asked Hazel Muller, 22, of 1864 E. Payne avenue, "if I got locked in that record vault and couldn't get out?"

"Ho, ho," replied Thomas Keyes, production manager of the Majestic Foundry company at 146 E. Belmont avenue, where Miss Muller is a secretary, "It couldn't happen."

But it DID happen Tuesday and it WAS terrible.

Here's a play-by-play account . . .

CUMULATIVE INTEREST

Most of the examples so far given have been leads to news stories which otherwise conform to the standard rule that they be written to make possible the cutting of at least a few paragraphs from the bottom up, without sacrificing completeness.

There are three principal types, rhetorically speaking, of news feature stories which must be printed in their entirety to preserve the news interest. One is the cumulative interest story, the lead of which differs from those of the other two types because it contains some sort of news peg. In addition to emphasizing the "tone" or "situation" of the story as it progresses, this kind of story incites reader interest which "cumulates" as each succeeding sentence and paragraph makes for greater definiteness:

Salt Lake City — (UP) — A 19-year-old salesgirl wants to wish a Merry Christmas to a Chicago soldier who provided an early holiday present when it was most needed.

The girl, Barbara Swindle, Farmington, Utah, had left a department store where she worked when she found her purse had been robbed of $50, almost all her week's earnings.

* * *

Next she found a tire on her car was flat. She couldn't find anyone to fix it.

She walked into a nearby bus station and was trying vainly to keep back tears when a soldier from Chicago persuaded her to tell him her troubles.

He handed her a $10 bill and told her to get some change so she could telephone home for help.

When she returned the soldier had boarded a bus for Chicago.

She does not know the soldier's name, but Barbara said, "I certainly wish that soldier, whoever he is, a Merry Christmas."

Chicago *Daily News*

SUSPENDED INTEREST

This name is given to the news feature in which the writer "strings along" the reader to the very end before giving him the news peg on which the item is based. Such stories resemble magazine short stories in that they must be read in their entirety. Frequently, the climax may be a surprise; in any case, it satisfies the reader's interest which has been suspended because of the indefiniteness of early details. The lead of a suspended interest story is not so definite as that of a cumulative interest story:

An ice-cream cone failed to have a cooling effect Saturday night on Patrolman Harry O'Brien.

O'Brien, assigned to the burglary detail, was parking his car on Auburn street near Wilson avenue, when a man approached the car, mumbling incoherently.

"What did you say?" O'Brien asked.

Without another word, the man suddenly jammed an ice-cream cone into the policeman's face.

O'Brien alighted, drew his gun, seized the man and was told, "You'll have to fight to take me in."

With that, the prisoner slugged O'Brien in the mouth with his fist. O'Brien countered with an uppercut which knocked the man flat.

At the Kenton Avenue Station the arrested man identified himself as Willis C. Solano of 1768 W. Tree street and said he thought policemen were "too hot" and he wanted to "cool one off."

SEQUENCE

The sequence story differs from both the cumulative and suspended interest stories only in arrangement of material, the object in all three cases being to postpone the climax or satisfaction of the reader's curiosity until near the end. The distinguishing feature of a story written in sequence style is that the facts are arranged in strictly chronological order, as:

Three-year-old Byron Halpert, being an inquisitive little fellow, opened a second-story window Tuesday a few minutes after his mother had left to take her daughter to school.

Byron leaned out to see what he could see. But he leaned so far that he lost his balance, fell through the opening and wound up hanging from the window sill by his finger tips, 20 feet above a concrete walk.

Just then a police car came by. Officer William Watson, sizing up the situation, ran to the spot below the window just as little Byron let go. The boy landed squarely in the policeman's arms, unhurt but tearfully scared.

DIRECT ADDRESS

Beginning reporters are admonished to keep out of their own stories, only an occasional reference to the fact that a reporter asked a certain question or made an unsuccessful effort to obtain an important fact being permitted. Use of either the first or second person is discouraged. Columnists, special writers who sign their articles and writers of feature stories are exempt from this rule when effectiveness cannot be obtained otherwise. The following are examples to show how the first or second person occasionally may be used in an ordinary news or news feature story such as a beginning reporter might write:

Kids, when Ma and Pa take a look at your report card then start the sermon about how smart they were in high school, do you see red? Do you want to chew nails?

Relax, kids, you've got a friend.

He is Dr. F. H. Finch of the University of Illinois, and he takes your side today in a monograph of the American Psychological Association.

Chicago *Daily News*

If you haven't heard of it, and wouldn't believe it if you had, it probably will be on display today at the National Inventors' Congress in the Hotel LaSalle.

Window glass that can't be seen through, lamps that give invisible light and solid water pipes that have no hollow space for the water — those are some of the things you may expect to find.

FREAKS

There isn't a rhetorical device which can't be used on occasion in writing for newspapers. The following are examples of unconventional leads which proved effective:

For sale: One college.

The board of directors of Pleasant View college, at Fairview announced today that the school, consisting of four buildings and several acres of land, is looking for a purchaser.

Financial difficulties forced its closing at the end of the 1962 school year.

> The turtle is a strange old bird,
> He's often seen and never heard
> He's best in soup, the taste is swell,
> But when he bites, he raises hell.
> — Apologies to Otto Werkmeister

The sentiment in the jingle expresses the firm belief of Gustave Riebow, 3225 S. Illinois ave.

The other day, according to a traffic accident report by the police department to the safety commission, Riebow was driving on S. Illinois ave. near his home.

His only passenger was a snapping turtle which Riebow believed to be safely stowed away in a box on the front seat. Riebow whistled gaily at the thought of fresh turtle soup. It was not recorded what the turtle thought.

Anyhow, the turtle climbed out of the box, and, with mayhem in his heart, went after the first object in his path. That object was Riebow's leg and the snapper snapped his jaws down hard.

The pain threw Riebow into confusion. He yelled, swung the wheel and rammed into a tree.

"That," mused Dr. B. L. Corbett, executive secretary of the commission, "is the first time a turtle got 'in the soup' with the law in a traffic accident in Milwaukee." Milwaukee *Journal*

6

Making It Readable

I. Readability Formulas

II. Objections to Formulas

III. Newspaper Style

IV. Conciseness

   1. *Superfluous Details*
   2. *Superfluous Words*
   3. *Superfluous Phrases*
   4. *Superfluous Clauses*
   5. *Simplicity*
   6. *Passive and Active Voice*
   7. *Proper Emphasis*

V. Avoiding Banality

   1. *Figures of Speech*
   2. *Bromides*
   3. *Shopworn Personifications*
   4. *Journalese*

VI. Correct Usage

   1. *Grammatical Faults*
   2. *Parts of Speech*
   3. *Troublesome Words*

BREAK THAT CLICHÉ!

BY *Marcia Winn*

Some of the heavy thinkers out at the University of Chicago are making a study of the freedom of the press. Is it free? If not, why not and what can be done to free it? Well, that's fine, but unless the gentlemen can find ways to free the press of the cliché (and our latest intelligence is that they are blandly ignoring it as an instrument of woe), their work is three-fourths lost.

But perhaps you don't read the newspapers as carefully as those who write them. Perhaps you don't realize how pervasive the cliché has become. The following questions and answers, an exercise in rote, should refresh your memory. Score yourself at will:

Q. How did the guests flee the hotel?   A. In scanty attire.
Q. What are police doing to the city?   A. Combing it.
Q. What are squad cars doing?   A. Cruising.
Q. What is any town that welcomes tourists?   A. A garden spot.
Q. What kind of a stare did he have?   A. A glassy stare.
Q. What kind of characteristic calm did he have?   A. Characteristic oriental calm.
Q. What were the passengers?   A. Badly shaken up.
Q. What was there?   A. There was a dull thud.
Q. The what young bandid committed the holdup?   A. The dapper young bandit.
Q. What do the blood splattered walls and bullet riddled chairs bear?   A. Mute testimony to the tragedy.
Q. What fell on the room?   A. Dead silence.
Q. How did the bride look?   A. Radiant.
Q. The bridegroom was the what of a wealthy family?   A. Scion.
Q. Who were late to their offices?   A. Scores of loop workers.
Q. What did the city do in the icy blast?   A. Shivered.
Q. What are expected in 24 hours?   A. Arrests.
Q. He was arrested in what through the city?   A. A mad chase.
Q. What swept the building?   A. A flash fire of unknown origin.
Q. What did bystanders do?   A. Fled for shelter.
Q. For what kind of effort was the chairman thanked?   A. Untiring.
Q. What did the introduction give the speaker?   A. Great pleasure.
Q. What was the courtroom packed with?   A. Interested onlookers.
Q. According to what from Washington?   A. Advices.
Q. What kind of sources?   A. Informed.
Q. What was the killer described as?   A. A man of 5 feet 10.
Q. The alderman was a man of what?   A. Unquestioned honesty and courage.
Q. Chief Corrigan did what?   A. Estimated the loss at $5,000.
Q. What did the suspect do when questioned?   A. Maintained a stony silence.

Well, that gives you a rough idea of the problem. You don't think it as grave as all that? Indeed, it is. It once even prompted a Chicago managing editor, an optimistic fellow, to send word to his writers, "give us some new platitudes. The old ones are worn out."

"FRONT VIEWS AND PROFILES," Chicago Tribune

MOST OF THE CHANGES IN NEWSPAPER STORY FORM AND STRUC-
ture since World War II have been made upon the advice of experts in
readability employed to make surveys by some newspapers and press
associations.

The changes all have been made to achieve brevity — shorter words,
shorter sentences and shorter paragraphs — in the belief that thereby the
average American, who has only a ninth grade education, will find the
result easier to read and comprehend.

READABILITY FORMULAS

To test the ease with which a given piece of writing can be
read and understood there exist numerous formulas. Among the best
known are those of Rudolf Flesch of New York University and Robert
Gunning, director of Readable News Reports of Columbus, Ohio. Following the recommendations of the former, the Associated Press reduced
its average lead sentence length from 27 to 23 words and its average lead
word sentence length from 1.74 to 1.55 syllables. Upon the advice of the
latter, the United Press simplified its writing style so as to be suitable
for readers with 11.7 years of education, whereas formerly it presumably
was writing for those who had gone to school 16.7 years.

For the Associated Press Managing Editors, Flesch explained as
follows:

> The formula is a statistical tool to estimate roughly the ease and in-
> terest with which a typical American newspaper reader will read the
> tested piece of writing. It was developed on the basis of reading compre-
> hension tests and has been checked against numerous readership studies of
> newspaper and magazine material, as well as audience studies of news
> broadcasts.
>
> The formula estimates "reading ease" and "human interest." "Reading
> ease" is measured by the average length of words and sentences — the
> shorter, the easier to read. My studies have shown that an average word
> length of 1.5 syllables and an average sentence length of 19 words is a
> good standard for newspaper material.
>
> "Human interest" is measured by the percentage of "personal words"
> and "personal sentences." These include names, pronouns, and certain
> other words referring to people, and direct quotes, questions, "you" sen-

tences, and other sentences indirectly addressed to another person. The more of these "personal" elements, the more interesting for the average reader. My studies have shown that 6 per cent "personal words" and 12 per cent "personal sentences" make a good standard for news writing.

On another occasion, Flesch told the same group how to use the formula:

1. *The length of the average word.*   This is measured by figuring the number of syllables per hundred words. You can do these easily for yourself: just read aloud and count. (What make words hard to read are prefixes and suffixes like –ation and –osity; counting syllables is just an easy shortcut for counting prefixes and suffixes.) Naturally, the higher this count, the poorer the readability.

2. *The length of the average sentence.*   This is measured by counting the number of words and dividing by the number of sentences. Again, long sentences make for hard reading. So the higher the count, the lower the readability score.

3. *The percentage of words that have human interest.*   What counts here is names, personal pronouns that refer to people, the word people itself, and all words that have masculine or feminine gender. (Words that may be masculine or feminine, like teacher, do not count here.) The more of these "personal words" per 100 words, the better the readability.

4. *The percentage of sentences that have human interest.*   Here I count all sentences that are addressed to the reader (questions, commands, requests) and all sentences that are addressed to one or more listeners and quoted in the text. If a quoted sentence is part of a large one, I count that one. To figure the percentage, I divide the number of these "personal sentences" by the total number of sentences. Quotations from written or printed stuff don't count, of course.

Gunning considers three factors:

1. *Sentence pattern.*   It was found that difficulty begins when the average number of words per sentence exceeds twenty. *Time,* the news magazine, averages 16 to 18 words per sentence and *Reader's Digest* sentences average 18, suggesting that their popularity may depend more on the way they are written than upon what they contain. *Atlantic Monthly* averages 24 words per sentence and appeals to so-called "high brows."

2. *Fog Index.*   This is a measure of complex or abstract words, as "prodigious expenditure" for "big expense," "undoubtedly" for "no doubt," "rendezvous" for "meeting," etc.

3. *Human interest factor.*   This means that frequent use of names of people, referents to those names, and other human interest words increases readability.

In *The Technique of Clear Writing,* Gunning enumerated the steps to find the Fog Index as follows:

1. Jot down the number of words in successive sentences. If the piece is long, you may wish to take several samples of 100 words, spaced evenly through it. If you do, stop the sentence count with the sentence which ends nearest the 100-word mark. Divide the total number of words in the passage by the number of sentences. This gives the average sentence length of the passage.

2. Count the number of words of three syllables or more per 100 words. Don't count the words (1) that are capitalized, (2) that are combinations of short easy words (like "bookkeeper" and "butterfly"), (3) that are verb forms made into three syllables by adding –ed or –es (like "created" or "trespasses"). This gives you the per cent of hard words.

3. To get the Fog Index, total the two factors just counted and multiply by .4.

Gunning presented the following "key" for practical judgment of Fog Index results:

R E A D I N G   L E V E L

Fog Index	By Grade	By Magazine
17	College graduate	(No popular magazine
16	College senior	this difficult)
15	College junior	
14	College sophomore	
13	College freshman	
DANGER LINE		
12	High school senior	*Atlantic Monthly*
11	High school junior	*Harper's*
10	High school sophomore	*Time*
9	High school freshman	*Reader's Digest*
8	Eighth grade	*Ladies' Home Journal*
7	Seventh grade	*True Confessions*
6	Sixth grade	*Comics*

OBJECTIONS TO FORMULAS

As an A.P.M.E. Readability committee once reported: "The virtue of the Flesch experiment is that it *has* made writers think more of their writing."

The same, of course, could be said of the Gunning and several other formulas. The principal effect of them has been a loosening of the rule that all five *w*'s and *h* should be included in the first paragraph or lead of a news story. Most newspapers now achieve brevity by playing up only the most important of these elements (usually the *who* and *what*), leaving the others for succeeding paragraphs or even omitting them. Furthermore, the *who* or *what* may be indefinite in the lead, being made more specific later in the story.

That these and other techniques to obtain brevity can be overdone is obvious. After what they considered fair trial, some newspapermen concluded that a new rigid formula merely was being substituted for another. One of the most outspoken of rewrite men who considered the new "strait jacket" worse than the old was Robert Faherty of the Chicago *Daily News* who wrote on "Cutting Paper Dolls on a Typewriter" for the Jan. 13, 1950 *Guild Reporter:*

> The formula wastes writer-time, which costs money. It wastes writer-skill. It wastes writer-strength, cutting efficiency. It kills writer-creativeness, which some editors regard as desirable.
>
> It is often difficult to achieve a 14-word lead that expresses the news element and properly identifies a principal. It is often necessary to discard two or three attempts. A Formula 14W story about anything more complex than a warehouse fire requires double or triple the time of a story written in normal-sentence flow.
>
> The formula wastes space. A 14-word sentence very often becomes a 14-word paragraph. . . . Meager paragraphs waste space.
>
> There is waste in the unavoidable use of surplus words. Subordinate clauses must be turned into full sentences by the use of introductory words such as "But Mr. Jones also was . . ." rather than the use of comma or conjunction.
>
> The structural faults of sentences that have been cut abruptly to the formula give structural faults to the stories. Abnormality and artificiality are instantly evident.

A typical example cited by Faherty of how the craze for brevity in sentence length actually makes for more rather than fewer total words was "Swindler Sigmund Engel, 74, was sentenced Wednesday to two to ten years in prison. It was the penalty for wooing Reseda Corrigan and winning her money." Faherty argued that one sentence would have simplified the writing and eliminated "It was the penalty."

Faherty called the new style of writing bumpy and without parallel except in first-grade school primers. He and others contend that simplification often is achieved by avoiding or evading controversy and that "worship at the altar of color" can lower the reading habits and thinking ability of newspaper readers. These critics charge that slavish adherence to brevity formulas only adds "fluff" to the news columns.

In an article, "Literature by Slide Rule," in *The Saturday Review* for Feb. 14, 1953, Stephen E. Fitzgerald pointed out that many of the classics had a high Fog Index but managed to communicate. Of the "readability boys," this author wrote, "They threaten to put our words in a literary strait jacket, leaving us only the solace of an illusion . . . that by shortening our sentences, we have somehow clarified our thought."

Brevity, this and other critics contend, does not necessarily equate with clarity. A short word can be as vague as a long one, and a short sentence can be as misleading as a book. To strip writing down to the "lowest levels of understanding." Fitzgerald wrote, "is as though we were to insist on reducing all music to the primitive rhythm of a jungle beat, thus hoping to widen the audience."

Using the syllable-length criterion advanced by Flesch, such words as *beautiful, patriotism, vacation, prearrange, improbable, candlestick, bracelet, watermelon,* and other familiar ones would be considered difficult whereas use of *ohm, joule, watt, erg, baize, arn, tweak, volt* and *tort* would contribute to a high readability score.

Different from either the Flesch or Gunning system, in that it takes account of the reader's probable familiarity with words, is the system devised by Professor Edgar Dale and Mrs. Jeanne S. Chall of the Bureau of Educational Research of Ohio State University. The Dale-Chall system takes into account average sentence length but also uses a list of 3,000 words familiar to fourth graders.

Dr. Dale discounts the value of counting affixes, suffixes and prefixes, as advocated by Flesch, by declaring that no two skilled judges ever get the same count. He also rejects Flesch's personal referent principle and is fond of citing a quotation from Koffka's *Principles of Gestalt Psychology* which contains personal pronouns equal to 5.8 per cent as follows:

> In the first case, real moving objects present in the field, the shift of the retinal pattern leads to behavioral motion of objects, whether I fixate a nonmoving object or follow a moving one with my regard; in the second case, when my eyes roam stationary objects, such a shift will not have this result. . . .

That would be considered very readable by both the Flesch and Gunning systems.

Proper names, other critics of these formulas have pointed out, do not necessarily lead to greater understanding unless the reader knows the persons mentioned and understands the references to them. "He was as mad as Hamlet," for instance, is about as readable as you can get; but if the reader never has heard of Hamlet, its meaning is lost on him.

In reviewing Flesch's book, *The Art of Readable Writing*, Lester Markel, New York *Times* Sunday editor, wrote, "The basic problem is not to humanize or to technicolor the news; it is to make the news understandable." According to Markel and his ilk, good writing is not mathematical or mechanical. Ease of reading depends, not on sentence length but on thought. It is his paucity of ideas and factual background information that gives a reader difficulty, not polysyllabic words. Popular magazines are read, not because the words and sentences are shorter but rather because the thought is simple. Even when news stories were written in allegedly ponderous style, readers devoured the sensational accounts and ignored the serious, each written in the same style. The problem, therefore, becomes one of supplying the reader with the necessary information to comprehend the immediate news account. Today, even the most erudite specialist, such as a scientist, needs to have the vocabulary of a fellow specialist in another field translated for him. In writing for the masses, newsmen long have adhered to the rule that they should not overestimate a reader's information nor underestimate his intelligence. It still is a good rule, and writing "A rose is a rose is a rose" merely because it scores high on a readability scale is futile if readers don't know what in thunder you're driving at.

NEWSPAPER STYLE

Long before readability became a cult, newspapers strived for many of the objectives which the researchers since have advocated. Disregarding criticism from literary purists, they developed an economical style well suited to the purposes for which it was intended. Characteristics of effective newspaper English in virtually every newsroom in the United States include the following:

1. Compact, usually short, sentences, each word selected and placed for maximum effect.
2. Short, terse paragraphs, each complete in itself and generally capable of being removed without destroying the sense of a story.
3. Conciseness, directness and simplicity, through elimination of superfluous words, phrases and clauses and through proper emphasis.
4. Factualness, without editorial opinion, puffs and boosts, unwise superlatives, adjectives, nouns, or other dogmatic words.
5. Avoidance of "fine" writing, strong verbs and nouns being preferred to trite, hackneyed and obsolete words and expressions.
6. Observance of the rules of good grammatical and word usage.

What the readability experts did was shock many newspapers into the realization that they were not living up to their own rules. That a few should go to extremes to find new ways of doing so probably was to be expected. The readability fans placed too much emphasis on brevity without considering adequately other aspects of good writing.

CONCISENESS

The objective of effective journalistic writing should be to avoid cumbersomeness without becoming choppy or repetitious through the excessive use of referents.

SUPERFLUOUS DETAILS

Relaxing of the rule that all of the five *w*'s and *h* must be included in the first paragraph of a news story generally achieves the objective of uncluttering the lead.

Cluttered

Clifford Britt, 38, 1459 Grove street, and another passenger on an eastbound Mitchell boulevard street car were injured about 8 A.M. today when the car jumped the track and collided with a westbound car at Mitchell boulevard and Perkins street.

Scores of other passengers en route to work who filled both cars were heavily jostled and shaken up as the two cars came together, according to Mitchell boulevard police who also said another man was injured but disappeared from the scene of the accident.

Britt was taken to Municipal hospital with cuts and bruises on the head and hands.

Uncluttered

Two men were injured and scores shaken when two street cars collided at Mitchell boulevard and Perkins street about 8 A.M. today.

One car was going west and the other east on Mitchell boulevard.

Hitting an open electric switch, the eastbound car jumped the tracks, struck the other, and derailed it.

One of the injured men was Clifford Britt, 38, 1459 Grove street. Police said another man was injured but disappeared from the scene of the accident.

Britt received cut and bruises on the head and hands. He was taken to Municipal hospital.

Both cars were filled with passengers en route to work. They were heavily jostled as the two cars came together.

SUPERFLUOUS WORDS

The articles *the, a* and *an* often can be eliminated, as:

WEAK: The Booster students who heard the talk —
BETTER: Booster students who heard the —

WEAK: It is a part of a title.
BETTER: It is part of a title.

WEAK: It is for the men who make good.
BETTER: It is for men who make good.

In an article, "Write the Way You Talk and People May Read It," in the February 1956 *Quill*, Erling H. Erlandson warned against excess in adherence to this rule. Otherwise the result might be "nonsensical writing," as: "Cause of the dispute was the overtime clause. Union had demanded time and a half for work after 5 P.M." Summarized Erlandson:

"Two words saved at the expense of communication."

Sentences may be shortened and made more forceful by making verbs more direct, as:

WEAK: The committee arrived at a conclusion.
BETTER: The committee concluded.

WEAK: The society held a discussion on the matter.
BETTER: The society discussed the matter.

WEAK: He put in an appearance.
BETTER: He appeared.

WEAK: They did away with the old building.
BETTER: They razed the old building.

WEAK: When he got through with his work —
BETTER: When he finished his work —

Some words are unnecessary and even incorrect, as:

WEAK: She fell off of the roof.
BETTER: She fell off the roof.

WEAK: The case is a difficult one.
BETTER: The case is difficult.

WEAK: The man fell a distance of 50 feet.
BETTER: The man fell 50 feet.

WRONG: The actual fact is —
RIGHT: The fact is —

WRONG: The building was completely destroyed.
RIGHT: The building was destroyed.

WEAK: There is no vacancy at the present time.
BETTER: There is no vacancy at present.

WEAK: It reverts back to the former subject.
BETTER: It reverts to the former subject.

WRONG: It was plainly obvious.
RIGHT: It was obvious.

WEAK: He didn't know whether or not to go.
BETTER: He didn't know whether to go.

It is not necessary to include the state with the names of large cities, or to mention the state with the name of a city in the same state as that in which the newspaper is published.

WEAK: He lives in Los Angeles, Calif.
BETTER: He lives in Los Angeles.

But:

VAGUE: He lives in Springfield.
CLEAR: He lives in Springfield, Mass.

Don't waste words in giving dates, as:

WEAK: The Chemical society will meet on Saturday.
BETTER: The Chemical society will meet Saturday.

WEAK: The meeting will be held this coming Friday.
BETTER: The meeting will be held Friday.

WEAK: The meeting was held at 12 o'clock noon.
BETTER: The meeting was held at noon.

WEAK: It occurred the other Friday.
BETTER: It occurred Friday before last.

Sometimes a series of related facts can be presented in *series* form, in chronological order, as a word saver. In an article, "Condensation: A Check List of Current Techniques," in the Summer 1951 *Journalism Quarterly*, Robert G. Martin gave the following example:

> He was born in Russia, reared in Austria, graduated in 1914 from the University of Vienna, and then served throughout World War I as an Austrian artillery officer on the Italian and Russian fronts.

Erlandson, on the other hand, correctly warns against misuse of this style, as "Born in Tennessee, he served on the Los Angeles Board of Education from 1935 to 1941." Wrote Erlandson: "When two unrelated facts are jammed together, it may be bright writing but it's also faulty subordination."

SUPERFLUOUS PHRASES

WEAK: The meeting was held for the purpose of discussing the matter.
BETTER: The meeting was held to discuss the matter.

WEAK: We met at the corner of Spring and High streets.
BETTER: We met at Spring and High streets.

WEAK: He was a man by the name of Jones.
BETTER: He was a man named Jones.

WEAK: We reached him by the use of telephone.
BETTER: We reached him by telephone.

WEAK: The color of the cart was red.
BETTER: The cart was red.

WEAK: He will be here for a period of three weeks.
BETTER: He will be here for three weeks.

Often a strong verb, adjective, adverb or possessive form can be substituted for a phrase.

WEAK: A baby with brown eyes.
BETTER: A brown-eyed baby.

WEAK: The arguments of Brown.
BETTER: Brown's arguments.

WEAK: They assembled with little commotion.
BETTER: They assembled quietly.

WEAK: The howitzer went off with a boom.
BETTER: The howitzer boomed.

Before emulating the last preceding example, which was given by Martin, the writer must be certain that he has not distorted meaning. There is great temptation to use shorter action verbs which create a feeling of excitement not justified by the facts of the story. Some newspapers have been accused of offending considerably in this respect through frequent use of such words as *hits, slaps, traps, raps, rips, flays, slays, breaks, looms, dooms, lashes, kills, fires, cracks, nabs, grabs, quizzes, grills, curbs, blocks* and *foils*, to use a list compiled by Sydney J. Harris in the Jan. 3, 1956 Chicago *Daily News*.

SUPERFLUOUS CLAUSES

WEAK: All citizens who are interested should come.
BETTER: All interested citizens should come.

WEAK: He will speak at the meeting which will be held Monday.
BETTER: He will speak at the meeting Monday.

WEAK: John Farrell, who is secretary of the Engineers' club, will be there.
BETTER: John Farrell, secretary of the Engineers' club, will be there.

On the other hand, clauses can be used effectively for word-preserving interpolations, as in the following example given by Martin:

Even though he lost them both, 8–6 and 9–7, he outscored Sedgman in earned points, 46–43, and his passing shots, often executed while he was running full tilt, were beautiful to watch.

SIMPLICITY

This quality is obtained in large part by avoiding "elegant" words when simple ones would do better.

about is better than *with reference to*

agreement is better than *concordance*

although is better than *despite the fact that*

before is better than *prior to*

body is better than *remains*

buried is better than *interred*

burned is better than *destroyed by fire*

city people is better than *urban people*

clear is better than *obvious*

coffin is better than *casket*

danger is better than *precariousness*

died is better than *passed away* or *succumbed*

dog is better than *canine*

farming is better than *agriculture*

fear is better than *apprehension*

fire is better than *conflagration*

forced is better than *compelled*

funeral is better than *obsequies*

horse is better than *domesticated quadruped*

if is better than *in the event of*

leg is better than *limb*

man is better than *gentleman*

marriage is better than *nuptials*

meeting is better than *rendezvous*

money is better than *lucre*

nearness is better than *contiguity*

normal is better than *traditional*

since is better than *inasmuch as*

theft is better than *larceny*

truth is better than *veracity*

understand is better than *comprehend*

well paying is better than *lucrative*

woman is better than *lady*

When two words are synonyms, brevity can be obtained by using the shorter, as

after for *following*

ask for *request*

buy for *purchase*

car for *automobile*

expect for *anticipate*

get for *obtain*

try for *attempt*

use for *utilize*

PASSIVE AND ACTIVE VOICE

The active voice usually is more emphatic than the passive. The passive should be used, however, when warranted by the importance of the grammatical object of a sentence. In the following sentences, for example, the passive voice is preferable to the active:

Henry Binger has been appointed chairman of the County Republican campaign committee.

Earl Kromer, prominent local merchant, was killed instantly early today when a bolt of lightning struck his home, 34 E. Wilson street.

Increased rates for the Middletown municipal water works were ordered by the public service commission in an order issued Thursday.

In other cases the feature can better be played up by use of the active voice, as:

WEAK: The accident was witnessed by ten boys.
BETTER: Ten boys witnessed the accident.

WEAK: The report was received by the mayor.
BETTER: The mayor received the report.

WEAK: The result was announced by the clerk.
BETTER: The clerk announced the result.

WEAK: The keynote address was delivered by Governor Furman.
BETTER: Governor Furman delivered the keynote address.

PROPER EMPHASIS

Vagueness and indefiniteness are avoided, and clarity obtained, by placing important ideas at the beginnings of sentences. Also by playing up the action, significance, result or feature of the paragraph or story, by avoiding vague and indefinite words and eliminating superfluous details, words, phrases and clauses.

VAGUE: Some 50 persons were present.
BETTER: About 50 were present.

WORDY: People of Chester will be asked to contribute $4,000 to the National Red Cross campaign to relieve suffering in the drought area of the United States, according to announcements made yesterday by John Doe, local chairman.
CONCISE: Chester's quota in the National Red Cross campaign for drought relief is $4,000, John Doe, local chairman, said yesterday.

WEAK: When asked what he thought of the compromise plan of unemployment relief, Senator Sapo today said that —
DEFINITE: Senator Sapo today condemned the compromise plan for unemployment relief as demagogic, unconstitutional and inadequate.

WEAK: The purpose of the Student Council meeting at 7 P.M. Monday in Swift hall is to discuss the proposal to limit student activities.
BETTER: The Student Council will discuss limitation of student activities at 7 P.M. Monday in Swift hall.

WEAK: It was decided by the Men's club at its meeting last evening to hold a smoker next Monday evening in the club room.
BETTER: The Men's club will hold a smoker Monday evening in the club room, it was decided at last evening's meeting.

Newspaper style books and journalism texts once admonished reporters never to begin a story with an article or indefinite pronoun. Like every other rule, this one could and should be broken on occasion. Such a lead as "There will be a meeting, etc." ordinarily should be avoided. Such effective writing as the following, however, should be encouraged.

There was to have been a birthday party Saturday in the Ken Rose Rest Home, 6255 N. Kenmore. But instead there was quiet sadness.

The party was to have celebrated the 102d birthday of Miss Frances Benson, a resident of the home.

Miss Benson, a retired Chicago schoolteacher, died Friday after suffering a sudden stroke.

Chicago *Daily News*

AVOIDING BANALITY

The day of the grammatical purist is gone. Contemporary authorities recognize that language makes dictionaries and not vice versa. Many words in common use today were once frowned upon as slang or vulgarisms. Each year prominent writers coin new words or resurrect archaic ones which meet with popular acceptance. The fault of young writers as regards word choice is not so much selection of what might be called undignified words but tactless use of bromides, platitudes and clichés. What constitutes tactfulness in using slang, trite and hackneyed expressions is for the English department, not the school of journalism, to teach. Nevertheless, the journalism teacher and certainly the newspaper copyreader can spot a threadbare word or phrase used in a threadbare way.

There isn't a word listed below, as one to be used cautiously, which can't be used effectively on occasion. This is decidedly not a don't section, merely one of precaution.

FIGURES OF SPEECH

The following figures of speech generally should be avoided because they are likely to be misused. They are whiskered with age and mark their innocent user as callow.

a checkered career
acid test
buffeted by defeat
busy as a bee
clutches of the law
cool as a cucumber
cool his heels
departed this Vale of tears
devouring elements
hail of bullets
hangs in the balance
heart of the business district
Herculean strength

hungry as bears
in the limelight
long hours of the night
loomed like sentinels
met his Waterloo
never rains but it pours
nipped in the bud
picture of health
pillar of the church
point with pride
police combing the city
rains cats and dogs
sea of upturned faces
silver lining
smell a rat

stalked the spector
stormy session
stuck to the banner
the crying need
the great beyond
the wings of disaster
threw a monkey wrench
to swing the pendulum
unscramble the situation
view with alarm
watery grave
white as a sheet
won his spurs
worked like Trojans

BROMIDES

Generally considered too trite or hackneyed for effective use are the following:

all-out effort
almost fatally injured
any way, shape or form
as luck would have it
augurs well
bated breath
better half
bids fair
bigger and better
blushing bride
bright and fair
bright and smiling
burly Negro
crisp bill
dances divinely
departed this life
doing as well as can be expected
doomed to disappointment
dull thud
each and every

easy prey
fair maidens
favor with a selection
feature
few and far between
green-eyed monster
hale and hearty
head over heels
hectic
he-man
host of friends
in the offing
internal fury
laid at rest
last but not least
last sad rites
leering ghost
light fantastic toe
loomed on the horizon
many and various
method in his madness
music hath charms, etc.

no uncertain terms
order out of chaos
powder keg
present day and generation
received an ovation
red-blooded
render a solo
resting comfortably
scintillating
sigh of relief
signs of the times
smashed to smithereens
thick and fast
trend of public sentiment
variety is the spice of life
vital stake
weather permitting
wild and woolly

SHOPWORN PERSONIFICATIONS

The following mythical characters have been introduced into all kinds of writing so often that they have lost their ability to impress or amuse:

Betty Coed
Dame Fashion
Dame Rumor
Dan Cupid
Father Neptune
Father Time

G.I. Joe
Grim Reaper
Jack Frost
Joe College
John Q. Public
Jupiter Pluvius

Lady Luck
Man in the Street
Mother Earth
Mr. Average Citizen
Old Sol

JOURNALESE

Newspapers have not contributed so much as one might expect to the coinage of new words, but they have helped exhaust the effectiveness of a large number through indiscriminate repetition. Among these are the following:

blunt instrument	gruesome find	sleuths
bolt from a clear sky	grilled by police	smoke-filled room
brutal crime	hot seat	smoking revolver
brutally murdered	infuriated mob	solon
cannon fodder	man hunt	speculation is rife
cheered to the echo	moron	swoop down
clubber	mystery surrounds	thug
crime wave	news leaked out	war clouds
cynosure of all eyes	police drag nets	while thousands cheer
death car	political pot boiling	whirlwind tour
fatal noose	probe	will be staged
feeling ran high	quiz	
focus attention	rush	

CORRECT USAGE

It is presumed that the student has completed a course in English grammar and composition and, therefore, that he knows the rudiments of good English. Although some reputable writers still split their infinitives without losing effect, few misuse "lay" and "lie," use "none" as a plural, get "don't" and "doesn't" twisted, misplace "only," or use "like" when they mean "as if." If the student of this book is deficient in his knowledge of grammar, he had better concentrate on it constantly. Cubs who cannot make their subjects and predicates agree and who can't spell ordinary words don't last long.

In every newspaper office there are some rules of grammar, word usage, punctuation, etc., which are emphasized more than others. Most newspapers issue style sheets for the guidance of new staff members as to what kind of writing is preferred. A sample style sheet is given in Appendix A, and the student should study it at this time.

GRAMMATICAL FAULTS

Several years of correcting journalism students' papers have convinced the writer that the following are among the most common grammatical errors about which aspiring reporters need caution.

WRONG: Neither the mayor nor the city clerk are willing to talk.
RIGHT: Neither the mayor nor the city clerk is willing to talk.

WRONG: The Chamber of Commerce will begin their annual membership drive Monday.
RIGHT: The Chamber of Commerce will begin its annual membership drive Monday.

WRONG: Howard is not as tall as Harold.
RIGHT: Howard is not so tall as Harold.

The next two examples do not illustrate infallible rules; in other cases these constructions may be better:

WEAK: He has always wanted to go.
BETTER: He always has wanted to go.

WEAK: He was ordered to immediately arrest Jones.
BETTER: He was ordered to arrest Jones immediately.

WRONG: Having arrived an hour late, the audience had begun to disperse before Smith began to speak.
RIGHT: Having arrived an hour late, Smith found his audience had begun to disperse.

WRONG: After Graham and Mitchell had shaken hands he turned to greet the senator.
RIGHT: After Graham and Mitchell had shaken hands the former turned to greet the senator.
STRONGER: After Graham shook hands with Mitchell he greeted the senator.

PARTS OF SPEECH

To obtain originality of expression, writers (not all of them journalists) sometimes change the part of speech of a word. In many cases the dictionaries have caught up with popular usage. For instance, it is proper to say "chair a meeting," "jail a prisoner," "hospitalize a sick person" or "table a resolution." Even such words as "alibi," "probe" and "torpedo," to whose use as verbs objection often is heard, are listed as such.

In view of the dynamic character of the language, one hesitates to become crotchety when a newspaper columnist says someone "week ended" or "house guested" another or that a dowager "lorgnetted" a stranger. Usually, however, it is left to special writers who sign their stories, sports reporters and feature writers to invent new usages. Authors of formal stories are more conservative and wait until the dictionaries have sanctioned an innovation before using it casually.

TROUBLESOME WORDS

The following are some words and expressions which often cause difficulty:

Above Should not be used for *over* or *more than.*

Accord Do not use in the sense of *award. Give* is better.

Act A single incident. An *action* consists of several acts.

Actual facts All facts are actual.

Administer Used with reference to medicine, governments or oaths. Blows are not *administered,* but *dealt.*

Adopt Not synonymous with *decide* or *assume.*

Affect; effect *Affect* means to have an influence on; *effect* means to cause, to produce, to result in.

Aggravate Means *to increase;* not synonymous with *irritate.*

Aggregate Not synonymous with *total.*

Allege Not synonymous with *assert.* Say the *alleged* crime, but "He *said* he is innocent."

Allow; permit The former means *not to forbid;* the latter means *to grant leave.*

Allude Do not confuse with *refer.*

Almost; nearly *Almost* regards the ending of an act; *nearly* the beginning.

Alternative Indicates a choice of two things. Incorrect to speak of *two alternatives* or *one alternative.*

Among Use when more than two is meant; for two only, use *between.*

Antecedents Do not use in the sense of *ancestors, forefathers, history* or *origin.*

A number of Indefinite. Specify.

Anxious Implies worry. Not synonymous with *eager* which implies anticipation or desire.

Anyone or none Use in speaking of more than two. *Either* and *neither* are used when speaking of only two. All take singular verbs.

Appears, looks, smells, seems, etc. Take an adjective complement.

As the result of an operation Avoid this expression. Usually incorrect and libelous.

At Use *in* before the names of large cities: He is *in* New York, but the meeting was held *at* Greenville.

Audience An *audience* hears, *spectators* see.

Autopsy An *autopsy* is *performed,* not *held.*

Avocation A man's pleasure, while *vocation* is his business or profession.

Awful Means *to fill with awe;* not synonymous with *very* or *extremely.*

Balance Not synonymous with *rest* or *remainder.*

Banquet Only a few dinners are worth the name. Use *dinner* or *supper.*

Because Better than *due to* in, "They fought because of a misunderstanding."

Beside; besides The first means *by the side of*; the second, *in addition to*.

By Use instead of *with* in such sentences as, "The effect was gained by colored lights."

Call attention Do not use it for *direct attention*.

Canon; cannon The former is a *law*; the latter is a large *gun*.

Canvas; canvass The former is a *cloth*; the latter means *to solicit*.

Capitol The building is the *capitol*; the city is the *capital*.

Casualty Should not be confused with *disaster, accident, mishap*.

Childish Not synonymous with *childlike*.

Chinese Don't use *Chinaman*.

Claim A transitive verb. One may "claim a dog" but not that "Boston is larger than Portland."

Cold facts (or statistics). When is a fact hot?

Collide To collide both objects must be in motion.

Commence Usually *begin* or *start* is better.

Compared with Use *compared with* in speaking of two things coming under the same classification; use *compared to* if the classes are different.

Comprise Do not use for *compose*.

Confess A man confesses a crime to the police, but he does not confess to a crime.

Conscious Not synonymous with *aware*.

Consensus Don't say *consensus of opinion*; simply say *consensus*.

Consequence Sometimes misused in the sense of "importance" and "of moment," as "They are all persons of consequence" (importance); "A matter of no consequence" (moment).

Consists in Distinguish between *consists in* and *consists of*.

Consummation Look up in the dictionary. Do not use in reference to marriage.

Continual; continuous That is *–al* which either is always going on or recurs at short intervals and never comes (or is regarded as never coming) to an end. That is *–ous* in which no break occurs between the beginning and the end.

Convene Delegates, not a convention, convene.

Correspondent; co-respondent The former *communicates in writing*; the latter *answers jointly* with another.

Council; counsel The former is a meeting for deliberation. The latter is advice or one who gives advice.

Couple Used only when two things are joined, not of separate things.

Crime Do not confuse with *sin* or *vice*. *Crime* is a violation of the law of the state; *vice* refers to a violation of moral law; *sin* is a violation of religious law.

Cultured Don't use for *cultivated*.

Cyclone Distinguish from *hurricane, typhoon, tornado, gale* and *storm*.

Dangerously Not *dangerously* but *critically* or *alarmingly* ill.

Data Plural. *Datum* is singular.

Date from Not *date back to*.

Depot Don't use for *station*. A *depot* is a storehouse for freight or supplies; railway passengers arrive at a *station*.

Die of Not *die from*.

Different from Not *different than*.

Dimensions; proportions The former pertains to *magnitude*; the latter to *form*.

Divide Don't say, "The money was divided between Smith, Jones and Brown." Use *among* when more than two are concerned.

Dove Should not be used for *dived*.

Drops dead *Falls dead* is what is meant.

During Do not confuse with *in*. *During* answers the question, "How long?" *in* the question, "When? At what time?" as, "We were in Princeton *during* the winter"; "We received the letter *in* the morning."

Each other; one another The former pertains to *two*; the latter to *three* or *more*.

Either; neither Use when speaking of two only.

Elicit Means to "draw out against the will."

Emigrant Do not confuse with *immigrant*. An *emigrant* leaves, and an *immigrant* comes in.

Envelop; envelope The former means to *surround*; the latter is a *covering* or *wrapper*.

Event Do not confuse with *incident, affair, occurrence* or *happening*.

Experiment Don't say *try* an experiment. Experiments are *made*.

Fail To *fail* one must try. Usually what is meant is *did not*.

Fakir; faker The former is an Oriental ascetic; the latter is a street peddler.

Farther Denotes distance; *further* denotes time.

Final; finale The former means *last*; the latter is a *concluding act* or *number*.

From A person dies *of*, not *from*, a disease.

Graduate, as a verb. Colleges graduate; students *are graduated*.

Gun Don't confuse with *revolver* and *pistol*.

Had Implies volition. Don't say, "Had his arm cut off."

Healthy A person is *healthy*, but climate is *healthful* and food *wholesome*.

Heart failure Everyone dies of heart failure. There is a disease known as *heart disease*.

Hectic "Hectic flush" is the feverish blush of consumption. Not to be used in the sense of *excited, impassioned, intense, rapturous, uncontrolled, wild,* etc., except when a jocosity is intended.

High Distinguish from *large.*

Hoi polloi "The many." Do not use "the" before it.

Hold Use advisedly. The Supreme Court *holds* a law constitutional, but one *asserts* that one man is a better boxer than another.

Hung A criminal is *hanged.* Clothes are *hung* on a line.

Inaugurate Does not mean *begin.*

Incumbent It is redundant to write *present incumbent.*

Indorse Not synonymous with *approve.*

Infer; imply The former means to *deduce;* the latter to *signify.*

Initial A man may sign his initial, but he does not make an *initial payment.* He makes the *first payment.*

Innumerable Not synonymous with *endless.*

Invited guests Most guests are invited; omit the adjective.

Last Not synonymous with *latest* or *past.*

Leave Don't confuse with *let.*

Leaves a widow Impossible. He leaves a *wife.*

Less Use *less* money but *fewer* coins.

Like Avoid using as a conjunction. The idiomatic form is "I should like," not "I would like."

Locate A building is *located* when its site is picked; thereafter it is *situated.* A person is *found,* not *located.*

Majority The lead over *all* others; a plurality is a lead over *one* other.

Mathematics Singular.

Memorandum Singular. *Memoranda,* plural.

Mend You *mend* a dress but *repair* a street.

Minister Distinguish between *minister,* a term used in Protestant churches, and *priest,* used in Catholic churches. Every *preacher* is not a *pastor;* a *pastor* has a church, a *minister* may not.

Musical; musicale The former means *rhythmic;* the latter is a *recital* or *concert.*

Name after The correct form is *name for.*

Near accident There is no such thing.

Nee Give only last name, "Mrs. Helen Kuenzel, nee Bauman."

Nice Means *exact,* not *agreeable* or *pleasant.*

Notorious Different from *famous.*

Occur Accidents *occur* rather than *happen,* but weddings *take place.*

Old adages There are no *new adages.*

Over Means *above; more than* means *in excess of.*

Partly completed Has no meaning. The words are contradictory.

Past Not synonymous with *last.*

People Refers to population. Do not confuse with *persons.*

Per cent Do not say "large per cent" when you mean "large proportion."

Politics Singular.

Practically Not synonymous with *virtually*. Different from *almost*.

Principle Always a noun. *Principal* is generally an adjective.

Prone on the back. Impossible. The word means "lying on the face." *Supine* is "lying on the back."

Provided Not *providing* he will go.

Public Singular.

Put in You *occupy, devote* or *spend* time, never *put in* time.

Quite Means *fully* or *wholly*. Do not, for example, write, "He is *quite* wealthy," but, "He is *rather* wealthy."

Raised Animals are *raised*; children are *reared*.

Render You *render* lard or a judgment, but you *sing* a song.

Rumor It is redundant to write *unverified rumor*.

Secure Means *to make fast*. Don't use it for *obtain, procure* or *acquire*.

Sensation; emotion The former is *physical*; the latter is *mental*.

Ship Cattle are *shipped* but corpses are *sent*.

So Use in a negative comparison instead of *as*.

Someone, somebody, etc. Take singular verbs.

Suicide Do not use as a verb.

Sustain Injuries are not *sustained* but *received*.

To the nth An unspecified number, not necessarily infinite or large. Do not use for *to the utmost possible extent*.

Transpire Means *to emerge from secrecy into knowledge, to become gradually known*. Not to be used in the senses of *happen, occur*, etc.; must not be followed by an infinitive.

Treble; triple The former means *three times*; the latter means *three kinds*.

True facts Facts never are false.

Try and Use *try to*.

Two first Say *first two*.

Unique Its adverbs are *absolutely, almost, in some respects, nearly, perhaps, quite, really* and *surely*. It does not admit of comparison. There are no degrees of uniqueness. It means *alone of its kind*. *Different* means *out of the ordinary*.

Unknown, unidentified The former means *not recognizable by* anyone; the latter means *not yet recognized*.

Various Not synonymous with *different*.

Vender; vendor The former is a *seller*; the latter is a legal term.

Want; wish The former means *need and desire*; the latter means only *desire*.

We Don't use the editorial *we*. Name the paper.

Well-known Usually *widely known* is meant.

Whether Do not use for *if*. Don't add *or not*.

Widow Never use *widow woman*.

Yacht Do not say *private yacht*. There are no *public* ones.

7

Saying It Right

             I. Definitions

          II. Unfamiliar Words

        III. Editorializing

            1. Connotations
            2. Puffs and Boosts

IV. Evaluative Words

    1. Nouns
    2. Adjectives
    3. Verbs
    4. Adverbs
    5. Phrases

V. Impressionistic Reporting

MORE "ANTICS WITH SEMANTICS"

BY *Sydney J. Harris*

Why is it that Our secret agents are "patriots," while Their secret agents are nothing but "spies"?

When I have one over the limit, I become "the life of the party"; when you have one over the limit, you become a "loudmouth."

I am "strongminded," but you are "opinionated."

My candidate's plan for the future shows he has "vision," but your candidate's plan for the future makes him a "wild-eyed dreamer."

I am about the only capable and careful driver on the road; all other motorists are either "stick-in-the-muds" or "reckless maniacs."

My failure to laugh at your dirty jokes shows my "good breeding," but your failure to laugh at my dirty joke shows "stuffiness."

* * *

The British are too "reserved," and the French are too "effusive"; the Italians are too "impulsive," and the Scandinavians are too "cold"; the Germans are too "arrogant," and the Japanese are too "diffident"—surely God must be an American.

My new two-tone car is "gay," but your new two-tone car is just "loud."

I give an inexpensive present because "it's the spirit behind it that counts," but you give an inexpensive present because you're cheap.

My son hit yours over the head with a block because he is "playful," but yours hit mine over the head because he is "vicious."

A "sound" man is a man who sounds like me.

When I spread gossip, it is always a "harmless tidbit," but when you spread gossip, it is "malicious rumor-mongering."

A "realistic" novel is a novel that agrees with the idea of reality I held before I even opened the book.

* * *

My family, which is poor, lost its tremendous fortune during the Depression; but your family, which is rich, made all its money profiteering during the War.

Why is it that "modern" is an approving adjective for plumbing, but a disapproving adjective for art?

My wife's dress is "simple," but your wife's dress is "dowdy."

Likewise, my summer wardrobe is "casual," but yours is "sloppy."

Our relatives may "get into trouble," but your relatives have illegitimate babies, go to jail and take up dope. (Ours are, of course, "unfortunate," but yours are "bad.")

Chicago Daily News

$\mathbf{D}$ESPITE ITS LENGTH, THE FOLLOWING SENTENCE PROBABLY would be considered readable by the experts:

Many boys and girls are working at too young an age, for too long hours, too late at night, in dangerous and other undesirable conditions.

A general semanticist, however, would be quick to point out that no matter how clear the sentence may be, the information it conveys is vague and biased. How many is "many"? When you say "boys and girls" do you mean little children, such as worked in sweatshops a half-century ago, or do you mean teenagers? What determines when one is too young to deliver newspapers, set pins in a bowling alley, run errands for a grocer, sew buttons or work on a lathe? How long is "too long" and how late is "too late"? What is a "dangerous" condition? Especially, what are "other undesirable" conditions?

DEFINITIONS

No experienced newsgatherer would fail to ask these questions if such a statement were made during the course of an interview. Often, however, such "glittering generalities," as the Institute for Propaganda Analysis (1937–1942) would have called them, appear in publicity releases and in public addresses, especially by politicians. They need amplification to convey important meaning to others, and it will be a happy day when editors toss them into the wastebasket unless it is possible to obtain such amplification.

On assignment, the interpretative reporter must be sharp enough to ask the proper questions to clarify vague statements and define "virtue" or "smear" words. Often, if not always, this requires more than the usual amount of knowledge on the reporter's part regarding the field of interest. In other words, the more one knows about a subject, the better able he is to interview someone regarding it. All the readability formulas and other aids to good writing cannot substitute for thorough fact-gathering.

"Pin the man down" should be the newsgatherer's first rule. If his subject talks about "progress," the reporter should ask him what he means by the term and for the facts and figures that justify its use. If the person being interviewed mentions "special circumstances," he should be asked what he means by "circumstances" and what makes them "special" and to give specific examples of what he's talking about.

UNFAMILIAR WORDS

If the words an interviewee uses are specific but nevertheless unfamiliar, the reporter had best overcome any sheepishness and ask for a little elementary shop talk from his subject. Otherwise, he might neglect to probe deeply enough into the potential facts of the story at hand. Lacking such an opportunity for "depth" reporting, the reporter should consult dictionaries, encyclopedias and other reference works to fill the gaps in his own knowledge.

If a reporter has to ask or look up the meaning of an expression, he can be fairly certain that a goodly number of his readers will need explanation of it. Perhaps he can even avoid use of the unfamiliar word in his story. He can, for instance, say, "Union A is attempting to persuade members of Union B to change their membership from B to A." Then he can explain, "This is called 'raiding' in labor circles." Or, if he uses "raiding" in his principal statement, he can define it, perhaps in an italicized parenthetical insert.

"Jurisdictional strike," "mass picketing" and "secondary boycott" are among the other terms in a story of a labor dispute which may need explanation. In weather stories, it probably is wise to make clear the difference between hurricanes, tornadoes, cyclones, and just plain gales or wind storms. Few readers probably remember what a nautical knot is or a French kilometer or an English mile. With the world becoming more complex daily and the areas of specialization growing, the need for such explanatory journalism is increasing.

EDITORIALIZING

Thorough reporting is the best safeguard against the misuse of words.

CONNOTATIONS

"The workers *won* a wage boost" has one connotation. "The workers *were given* a wage boost" has quite another. Only painstaking reporting can determine which is correct in any particular case. There can be no laziness or carelessness when the public interest is involved, as it usually is in stories pertaining to labor relations, governmental activities and the like.

Perhaps a news source condemns government "interference" when he really means he opposes government "regulation" in a particular area. Such words are loaded. Reportorial questioning should lead to specific details rather than vague charges or mere name calling. If loaded words are used from some necessity, they probably should be included in quotation marks or some explanatory matter should be added to indicate the alternative words for the same thought.

Newspapers propagandize if they use the labels of those with whom they agree editorially to describe pending legislation or situations. Examples of such editorializing would be "slave labor bill" for a measure regulating the mobility of the labor force in time of emergency; "dictator bill" for a proposal to increase the power of an executive; "goon" for labor-union pickets, and the like. It makes a great deal of difference whether you write:

crop relief *or* farm dictatorship
foreign *or* alien
labor organizer *or* labor agitator
nonstriker *or* loyal worker
picketing *or* mass picketing
regulation *or* regimentation
U.A.W. chieftain *or* U.A.W. dictator

PUFFS AND BOOSTS

Against one type of editorializing most newspapers are sufficiently on the alert. That is the practice of making gratuitous complimentary remarks regarding a person or event rather than stating the facts and allowing them to speak for themselves. Some such expressions, obsolete in most newsrooms, are the following:

A big success	Happy pair
A good time was had by all	In a very entertaining manner
A stellar performance	It beggars description
An enjoyable occasion	It bids fair
An impressive sight	Likable personality
An interesting program was offered	Prospects are bright
Attractive decorations	Proud possessor
Charming hostess	Replete with interest
Everything went along nicely	Talented young man
Fills a long-felt need	The trip was the most popular ever taken

Such expressions are taboo if for no other reason than that they have been overworked.

EVALUATIVE WORDS

In quite a different category are attempts to improve the reader's understanding by the use of qualifying adjectives, other parts of speech and expressions. Even some editors who have been outspoken in adverse criticism of interpretative reporting have for years allowed and encouraged their reporters to write, "One of America's *leading composers* will play his own compositions," "The two *top contenders* for the championship will meet in the first round," "An *unusual* workshop class in creative writing for talented children will be organized," "The court will hear arguments on the *complex, controversial and crucial questions,*" and the like.

There is no denying that such expressions involve judgment and, to be socially responsible, the judgment must be based on adequate information. When a sports writer, for instance, writes that the outcome of a contest was "a stunning upset," he must know that leaders in the sports world and fans expected it to be different. No competent reporter uses superlatives without investigating to determine whether they are justified: *most devastating fire, largest audience, longest report,* etc.

NOUNS

When, however, can you call a disturbance a *panic* or *riot*? When can you use such words as *catastrophe, fiasco, disaster, climax, zenith* or *debacle*? All you can say is that such terms should be used judiciously. To make common use of them would be to devitalize them. It would be like crying "wolf" when there was no wolf.

What, therefore, is "judicious" use? The experienced reporter who has covered many similar stories has a basis for comparison, and his own experience usually is better than that of most everyone else, especially ax-grinders with motives for hoping he uses this word instead of that. Competent reporting and integrity are more likely to give readers correct information than writing formulas are.

ADJECTIVES

When is a girl pretty or beautiful? Not every time she gets into a newsworthy situation certainly. Since the development of photography, reporters have become more cautious over indiscriminate use of such descriptive adjectives. Since there is no similar restraining influence in other areas, the best that can be done is to advise caution in the use of such words as the following:

brave	ferocious	popular
brilliant	gigantic	remarkable
clever	happy-go-lucky	successful
cowardly	huge	tasteful
eloquent	illimitable	unpatriotic
enjoyable	impressive	valiant
exciting	nice	widely known

VERBS

Verbs must be exact. If a news source answers "yes" to a reporter's question, it is not always proper to say he "admitted" something. When he makes an announcement, he cannot be said to have "revealed" or "disclosed" something unless the matter previously had been kept secret intentionally. "Charge" is a strong word implying an accusation which the news source might have had no intention of making. "Claim" suggests that someone is trying to correct a wrong impression or obtain possession of something which he considers rightfully his. "Probe" implies detectives of some sort are afoot.

Since very few words are exact synonyms for each other, a good dictionary or thesaurus is a better companion for the writer seeking to impart correct information than Gunning's formula to determine the Fog Index. The practice of intentionally using a strong synonym for maximum visceral effect on readers instead of the word which comes closer to stating the situation correctly cannot be condoned.

Here is a list of verbs which the reporter should be hesitant about using:

allege	laugh	sneer
beg	object	squeak
confess	plead	threaten
flee	prowl	urge
grimace	roar	whine
implore	shout	whisper
insult	sneak	

ADVERBS

A properly placed adverb can change the entire meaning of a news story. Consider the potential power of the following:

accidentally	calmly	facetiously
angrily	carelessly	grimly
boastfully	casually	immodestly

inadvertently	jokingly	seriously
intentionally	laughingly	stupidly
ironically	mockingly	viciously

PHRASES

Evaluational phrases can "make or break" a news story and also, perhaps, some of the principals mentioned in it. Consider the potency of the following:

angry response	pale with anger
in an arrogant manner	shaking with grief
in an unprecedented personal state- ment	showing great dignity under duress
in top oratorical form	with profound feeling

IMPRESSIONISTIC REPORTING

In an address at the University of Missouri, Newbold Noyes Jr. of the Washington *Evening Star* advocated "impressionistic reporting." By it, he explained, he meant attempts by skilled and impartial reporters to create in the reader the same feeling about an important event as the reporter had as an eyewitness of it. In an article, "War, Peace and Journalism," in the April 16, 1949, *Nation*, Thomas Sancton pleaded for "gestalt journalism," which he defined as "journalism which seeks the whole truth in any given field of politics, deeming the whole truth, or even the mere effort to discover it, greater and qualitatively different than piecemeal, selective reporting of its parts — gestalt journalism in this sense describes only what serious reporters have tried to do since writing began."

Sancton cited several news situations when "my on-the-scene notes contained, as a reporter's notes invariably do, more of the total mood and meaning . . . came closer to its 'gestalt' than their ultimate rewriting would ever have done."

To be impressionistic or to achieve a gestalt or to give correctly the "atmosphere" or "essential reality" concerning a news situation is primarily a task of fact-gathering. What the actual words shall be is dependent upon what needs to be written. After he cross-examined Senator Joseph R. McCarthy during the Army-McCarthy hearings, Chief Counsel Joseph N. Welch "went outside into the hallway where he broke down and wept," the Associated Press reported. Some managing editors objected to inclusion of this fact in the AP report. Others didn't like the statements, "Stevens bowed to the demands of McCarthy," and "Many spectators in the jam-packed steaming hearing room broke into loud unchecked applause after Welch denounced McCarthy." Still others thought it was bad to report during the subsequent Senate committee hearing that Senator Francis Case slammed down a report "with a force that scattered papers." A majority of those who expressed opinions, however, favored inclusion of such details in the interest of completeness and accuracy.

In the same edition of the A.P.M.E. *Red Book* in which appears the report of the discussion of the service's handling of the McCarthy hearings, there is also included a résumé of other parts of the Managing Editors' conference. The first few paragraphs of one section were as follows:

> Mary Margaret McBride, AP Newsfeature columnist, stole the show and the hearts of many of the editors when she matched them quip for quip in an hour of verbal sparring touched off by her contention that it is wrong to departmentalize all women's news under a "woman's page" label.
>
> This widely known writer, wearing a mink stole and a colorful orchid, beamed beneath an upswept hair-do as she prodded, argued, baited and cajoled while appearing at the two-part session on Newsfeatures, directed by Roderick J. Watts, of the Houston *Chronicle*, chairman of the Newsfeatures committee.
>
> On one occasion, Miss McBride even shouted. And the editors loved it. Some were seen to wipe tears of laughter from their eyes as their colleagues sought to match wits with Miss McBride in an unsuccessful attempt to beat her at her own game — the art of interviewing.

This obviously violated the Associated Press' own rules for proper sentence length, but everyone who read it probably caught the spirit of the occasion.

That the account includes "value" judgments there can be no doubt. The writer thought Miss McBride "prodded, argued, baited and cajoled," for instance. Quite possibly another observer might have thought she was becoming histrionic in the attempt to conceal inadequacy in the face of a barrage of questions.

The clever writer who attempts to convey his impressions of an occasion substantiates such statements as, "And the editors loved it," by reporting that "Some were seen to wipe tears of laughter from their eyes." Not always, of course, is there such tangible reportable evidence available. In such cases the reporter's experience, informational background, record of past achievement and, most of all, integrity are his weapons and his readers' protection.

The future unquestionably will bring increased recognition of the necessity to develop newsgatherers of such high quality. The alternative is despairingly to retreat to so-called objective reporting which leaves the reader completely in the cold as to the meaning or significance of much of the news.

As the late Elmer Davis wrote in an article, "News and the Whole Truth," in the August 1952 *Atlantic*, later reprinted in his book, *But We Were Born Free:*

But objectivity often leans over backward so far that it makes the news business merely a transmission belt for pretentious phonies. . . .

There was not much objectivity in the American press through most of the nineteenth century; if a story touched on the political or economic interest of the editor or owner, it was usually written so as to make his side look good. Some papers still follow that practice, but most of them, for some decades past, have accepted the principle that they ought to try to be objective in the news columns, leaving arguments to the editorial page. Publish everything that is said on both sides of a controversial issue, and let the reader make up his mind. A noble theory; but suppose that men who talk on one side (or on both) are known to be lying to serve their own personal interest; or suppose they don't know what they are talking about. To call attention to these facts, except on the editorial page, would not, according to most newspaper practice, be objective. Yet in the complex news of today, how many readers have enough personal knowledge to distinguish fact from fiction, ignorance from knowledge, interest from partiality?

This practice is perhaps not quite so prevalent now as it was twenty-five years or so ago — in the golden age of Calvin Coolidge, when it was the general opinion that things are what they seem. In those days, if the Honorable John P. Hoozis was an important person, you were likely to see him quoted at length in the newspapers, on almost any subject, with no indication that he had a strong personal interest in getting people to believe what he said — even if the editor who printed the story happened to know it. He was an important man; he had made a statement; and it would not have been objective not to print it. We have been getting away from that dead-pan objectivity of late years — or were, till the rise of Senator McCarthy.

8

Winning Reader Confidence

I. How to Be Accurate
   1. *Second-Hand Informa-tion*
   2. *Verification*
   3. *Qualification*
   4. *Total Effect*
II. Authority in the News
   1. *Direct Quotation*
   2. *Indirect Reference*
   3. *When Unnecessary*

III. Persistence
IV. Obeying the Law
V. Copyright
VI. How to Avoid Libel?
   1. *What Is Libel?*
   2. *Dangerous Words*
   3. *Insinuations*
   4. *Damages*
   5. *Defenses*
   6. *Playing Safe*

HATH DIFFICULTIES?
BEHOLD THE EDITOR

Consider the editor. He weareth purple and fine linen. His abode is amongst the mansions of the rich. His wife hath her limousine and his first born sporteth a racing car that can hit her up in forty flat.

Lo! All the people breaketh their necks to hand him money. A child is born unto the wife of a merchant in the bazaar. The physician getteth 10 gold plunks. The editor writeth a stick and a half and telleth the multitude that the child tippeth the beam at nine pounds. Yea, he lieth even as a centurion. And the proud father giveth him a Cremo.

Behold, the young one groweth up and graduateth. And the editor putteth into his paper a swell notice. Yea, a peach of a notice. He telleth of the wisdom of the young woman, and of her exceeding comeliness. Like the roses of Sharon is she and her gown is played up to beat the band. And the dressmaker getteth two score and four iron men. And the editor getteth a note of thanks from the SGG.

The daughter goeth on a journey. And the editor throweth himself on the story of the farewell party. It runneth a column, solid. And the fair one remembreth him from afar off with a picture postal card that costeth six for a jitney.

Behold, she returneth and the youth of the city fall down and worship. She picketh one and Lo, she picketh a lemon. But the editor calleth him one of our most promising young men and getteth away with it. And they send unto him a bid to the wedding feast and behold, the bids are fashioned by Muntgummery Hawbuck, in a far city.

Flowery and long is the wedding notice which the editor printeth. The minister getteth 10 bones. The groom standeth the editor off for a twelve-month subscription.

All flesh is grass and in time the wife is gathered into the silo. The minister getteth his bit. The editor printeth a death notice, two columns of obituary, three lodge notices, a cubit of poetry and a card of thanks. And he forgetteth to read proof on the head, and the darned thing cometh out "Gone to Her Last Roasting Place."

And all that are akin to the deceased jumpeth on the editor with exceeding great jumps. And they pulleth out their ads and cancelleth their subscriptions and they swing the hammer unto the third and fourth generations.

Canst thou beat it?

Cowilitz County Advocate

The chief complaint of a newspaper's critics — that is, everybody who reads it — is not bias through distortion and suppression. Nor is it sensationalism with its by-product, violation of the right to privacy. On the contrary, the American reader prefers the newspaper which gives him a point of view coinciding with his own and complains of prejudice only when he disagrees. His patronage of newspapers which specialize in lurid details, discounts any feigned distaste for them.

What the average American newspaper reader considers the cardinal journalistic sin is inaccuracy. Suppress news favorable to the other fellow and play up news favorable to your side but score the point through use of facts. It is a terrible letdown to be faced with irrefragable proof that something one wants to believe is false. Likewise, if the juicy sex story or other sensational yarn is shown to be untrue, it ceases to entertain.

Readers don't mean it when they say they don't believe anything they read in the newspapers; actually most of what they know is learned in that way. They apply the opprobrious term, "just newspaper talk," to a story unpleasant to believe, regardless of its truth.

Because editors are aware of these aspects of man's social behavior, and because there is no reason why a newspaper should be anything but one hundred per cent accurate in a vast majority of the stories it publishes, one of the first lessons the beginning reporter must learn is how to avoid making mistakes. There are some newsrooms even in large cities where a certain amount of carelessness is condoned, but not many. A standard of accuracy way beyond anything to which the recent college graduate has been accustomed in his English composition classes is maintained by a large majority of those newspapers worthy of being called first-rate. Lucky is the cub who starts his reporting career under an editor or desk man prone to "raising the roof" whenever he detects a misspelled word or incorrect middle initial in a piece of copy.

HOW TO BE ACCURATE

Although no news writer commits errors for personal enjoyment, a study by Professor Mitchell Charnley of the University of Minnesota revealed that altogether too many occur in at least three average

American newspapers. Of 591 straight news stories which Charnley was able to verify through a questionnaire sent to persons either mentioned in them or in positions to know, only 319, or 54 per cent, contained no errors of any kind. Paper A was 52 per cent accurate, Paper B 53 per cent and Paper C 57 per cent. The inaccurate stories contained an average of 1.67 errors and, most revealing of all, only 34 per cent of the stories handled by reporters were correct whereas 62 per cent of the stories obtained from original sources, largely in the form of publicity releases, were without mistake.

Why this situation? Probably for several reasons which will be discussed in connection with suggestions of remedies.

SECOND-HAND INFORMATION

Most news is gathered by reporters second-hand. News sources unquestionably are responsible for as many if not more news story errors than reporters. Mistakes made by those giving out news may be intentional or unintentional. If intentional, the news source has reasons for wanting a half-truth or untruth to appear in print. If unintentional, the source was a faulty witness or has a poor memory. The errancy of testimony and the influences, including suggestion and what is popularly called "wishful thinking," which make for errors in observation and recall, have been examined by psychologists and proved in the experimental laboratory so often as to leave no element of doubt regarding the really small chance the reporter has to get accurate answers during interviews for facts.

The reporter's weapons against inaccuracy, as a result of a news source's inability or unwillingness to give reliable information, are verification and honesty of purpose. If he does not rely on one person's say-so but interviews as many as possible, he invariably is able to correct many mistakes made in the first stages of gathering material about a news event. If he approaches the task of both reporting and writing his story without prejudice, whatever errors he does make will be at least unintentional. Fairness and caution both require that, when two persons interviewed differ greatly as to the truth, the statements of both be included in the news story. To achieve this objective, newspapers go to extremes of which the general public hardly dreams. The sentence saying that Mr. Smith could not be reached for a statement may have been added to a story after hours of futile effort to attain either accuracy or fairness or both.

Newsgatherers increasingly are up against what has been called "hand-outitis," which means the refusal of many news sources to provide any more information than is contained in carefully prepared publicity releases. Between the reporter and a principal in the news is the public relations counsel, as publicity men and press agents like to call themselves today. On the whole, these intermediaries perform a useful function, as no newspaper could possibly employ staffs large enough to cover all a community's activities. They also can be helpful to the reporter who wants additional information not included in a press release or who is seeking an original story. It must not be lost sight of, however, that public relations men are employed to advance the best interests of their employers, which means that often ways to circumvent them must be sought. The reporter who is content with what is included in a mimeographed press release may become little more than a messenger boy.

VERIFICATION

Verifying a story means more than checking the statements of different news sources against each other. It also means making use of the standard books of reference to check spellings, addresses, middle initials and many similar details. In many newsrooms, reporters are required to write "All names verified" on their copy, and woe be it to them if such is not true. In many police and court stories more than the newspaper's reputation for accuracy may be at stake; innocence or carelessness is no defense against libel.

The newspaper takes a chance whenever it prints an unverified story. Mere rumor it generally can detect, but when a story contains something which seems improbable, it is safer to miss an edition than use the story before checking. Often men in public life say things to reporters which they later regret. It may seem to the layman that the newspaper should quote them regarding what they have let slip and then stand by its guns and insist upon its own accuracy. It is the same layman, however, who with few exceptions believes the important personage's denial even though it be a gross lie. For this reason many an editor has held up a story until he has had a chance to check on even a reliable reporter's work.

Telephone books, city directories, clippings in the newspaper's library and books of reference are available to the newspaper reporter for a purpose — so that they will be used. In interviews, it is possible to repeat information to be sure it has been heard correctly. Over the telephone, difficult words can be spelled in code: A as in Adam, B as in Boston, etc. If the reporter has profited by his high school and college education, he should avoid many errors which the uneducated might commit, such as giving a ship's speed as "knots per hour," the office as chief justice of the Supreme court instead of chief justice of the United States, the Court of St. James instead of the Court of St. Jameses, Noble instead of Nobel prizes, half-mast instead of half-staff, John Hopkins University instead of Johns Hopkins University, and many other "teasers," mastery of which is a journalistic prerequisite.

QUALIFICATION

When certain about the main facts of a story but doubtful about others, a way to make the earliest edition before complete verification is possible is to qualify what is written, as:

A man believed to be Hillyer Swanson, 30, of Salt Lake City, was found by police today wandering in Forest Park, apparently an amnesia victim. Partial identification was made by means of a billfold and checkbook found in his possession.

Fire thought to have resulted from faulty electric wiring in the coal cellar caused approximately $500 damage early today to the dwelling at 1514 Murphy place occupied by Mr. and Mrs. O. B. Ryan and their three small children.

Stories such as the following inspire the confidence in readers that newspapers attempt to give the truth as far as possible.

Mayor Ezra Hawkins today intimated that he will not be a candidate for reelection, but Corporation Counsel Fred Bacon, who managed the mayor's last campaign, declared that "when the time comes the proper announcement will be made" and that "friends of His Honor will be pleased by the announcement."

It is when the reporter guesses or takes a chance that he is most likely to err. Such careless habits not only are bad practice from the newspaper's selfish standpoint, but reprehensible ethically as well. The speed with which newspapers are produced and the other obstacles to accuracy in reporting make a minimum number of errors seem almost inevitable. If the newspaper is generous in publishing corrections of the most serious errors and if it gives evidence of striving to attain the ideal of absolute accuracy, the supercilious reader should not be "off" a newspaper for life because on one occasion it made a mistake in the middle initial of his great aunt's brother-in-law.

TOTAL EFFECT

An account can be devoid of errors in facts, spellings, and the like and still be inaccurate if the impression it gives as a whole is wrong. This, as has been pointed out several times already in earlier chapters, can happen when pertinent facts are omitted, when motivations are disregarded, when cause and effect relationships are not made clear, and in many other similar ways.

Thorough reporting is the best protection against unintentional distortion. For example, a story telling of an arrest for reckless driving could be error-free, but would it be accurate unless it were explained that the apparently careless motorist was trying to get to his injured child's side? Without the part after the "but" the following lead would have given an erroneous impression. The reporter obviously asked, "Why?"

> Chicago — The number of persons drawing unemployment conpensation declined by 5,154 during the second week of this month, but indications are that more than 3,000 of them were off the rolls because their eligibility expired. Peoria *Transcript*

Professor David Manning White of Boston University has warned the press against becoming "unwitting or unwilling accomplices in creating an atmosphere in which prejudice, half-truths and misinformation bloom with a noisome stench." He had in mind so-called "deadpan" reporting of unsupported charges by United States senators and others without attempt to allow simultaneous reply by persons affected by the charges.

The simple first step in avoidance of inaccuracy through total impression is to try to get "the other side" of every story that is in any way controversial. To print inaccurate statements merely because they were made by some newsworthy person is not accurate reporting. It can be irresponsible journalism.

The following example indicates a common method of "presenting both sides," even when the original story comes from a press association:

> Cairo, Ill., July 14. — (AP) — William P. McCauley of Olney, American Legion rehabilitation commission chairman for Illinois, charged in a speech here today that the removal of cancer patients from the Veterans Administration Hospital at Hines, to the Chicago Loop Medical Clinic was "for no other reason than to make guinea pigs of war-veteran cancer victims."
>
> McCauley told the 5th Division American Legion convention that the clinic at Hines had resulted from many years of Legion effort, that the Legion had spent $7,000 for the first radium used there and that its work was responsible for recent addition of 500 beds there.
>
> (Informed of McCauley's charges, Charles G. Beck, Veterans Administration deputy director for the Midwest region, declared in Chicago:
>
> ("I think the statement that we're going to make guinea pigs of these cancer patients is, to say the least, ridiculous. The removal of which McCauley speaks has not yet taken place. It will not take place for at least a year.
>
> ("When we move our cancer center, the men will receive treatment at least as good as they have received at Hines. The entire clinic, its doctors, nurses, and equipment will be moved. How can that mean any change for the worse?
>
> ### Idea Credited to Bradley
>
> ("It was the idea of Gen. Omar Bradley, head of the V.A., that these unfortunate veterans would be better served if they were located in the city, instead of 12 miles away from it.")

In another speech, Omar J. Mackin, Salem, State Legion commander, asked the state's 1,029 Legion posts to pass resolutions against the Ku Klux Klan, which he termed "un-American and contrary to the principles and the rights guaranteed under the Constitution."   Chicago *Sun*

AUTHORITY IN THE NEWS

Everything that has been said so far in this chapter goes to prove that the most convincing authority a newspaper can give to a particular story is its own general reputation for authenticity. If it has established itself as a publication ambitious to be accurate and fair, it doesn't have to resort to elaborate means to quote authority in every paragraph of every news story.

As a matter of fact, however, newspapers which are the most careful to relate every important fact in every story to someone enjoy reputations for coming closest to the truth. "Who said this?" bawls out the city editor of such a paper to the cub. "Why, Mr. Smith, whose name is in the lead as having given the speech," is no defense but merely provocation for a further remark such as, "You don't say he said this unquoted part down in the fifth paragraph. I know he made the statement in the lead, but the rest of your story reads like an editorial."

DIRECT QUOTATION

To avoid such reprimands, the smart reporter "documents" his stories. How to attain accuracy and authority in different types of news stories will be considered more fully in the chapters devoted to them in Part II. Including authority in the lead adds emphasis, satisfies the reader's curiosity, and partially protects the newspaper against criticism.

Promotion of W. C. Fairchild, 2308 S. 10th street, lieutenant of the Superior Railroad police in the Milltown division, to captain of police of the Logan division, was announced today by Ronald Weber, superintendent of the Milltown division.

When the news consists in the fact that an announcement or statement has been made, especially if it is one which has been expected for some time, authority should be given the greatest emphasis possible by beginning the lead with it, as:

Mayor Herbert G. Van Duesen announced today charges of irregularities in the collection of business licenses made by the Chamber of Commerce will be referred to the Board of Aldermen Friday evening.

When someone in public life makes an attack on another, the lead should begin with that person's name, as:

State Sen. Rollin A. Bishop today called Gov. Joseph B. Dilling a "crackpot" and described his plan to consolidate seven state departments as "the wild idea of a neophyte in public life."

This type of lead is much better than the following:

Gov. Joseph B. Dilling is a "crackpot" and his plan to consolidate seven state departments is "the wild idea of a neophyte in public life," State Sen. Rollin A. Bishop said today.

It is the fact that Senator Bishop attacked the governor that is news; what he said is opinion unless he was much more definite than either lead would indicate. If he did make specific charges, then what has been said regarding efforts to obtain "the other side" applies.

In stories growing out of public reports, statements or announcements, mention of the authority may be delayed until the second paragraph but seldom should be any later than that:

Milltown users of natural gas pay a higher rate than consumers in any other American city of comparable size, but local rates for electricity are among the lowest in the United States.

These facts were revealed by a Federal Power commission report released today. . . .

Care, however, must be exercised to avoid a "tag line" type of lead which, standing alone, is misleading, as:

Rep. Y. S. Owen could defeat Mayor L. L. Wood.

That is the opinion of Judge K. K. Wendell who spoke at noon today.

The extent to which a careful newspaper goes to give adequate authority throughout a controversial story is indicated in the following example:

All ships of the North German Lloyd and Hamburg-American lines may be placed on the strike list of the International Longshoremen's association along with the Cunard White Star and Furness-Withy lines, *it was announced today* by Joseph P. Ryan, president of the longshoremen, when he learned a North German liner was scheduled to arrive at Montreal today.

If the ship is unloaded at Montreal by members of a union not affiliated with the I.L.A., *Mr. Ryan said*, his union will strike all German ships on the Atlantic coast from Portland to Newport News.

Although peace efforts continued in a three-way conference among I.L.A. officers, steamship officials, and representatives of the Montreal independent unions, plans were made for a protracted fight if necessary, *Mr. Ryan said*.

Threats of delay failed to halt the sailing of the Furness-Withy liner, Queen of Bermuda, which left her pier at 55th street and the North river promptly at 3 P.M. without tugs. The ship left behind more than a hundred tons of freight, but officers arranged to have crew members carry aboard the baggage of passengers.

The presence of 700 travelers in Bermuda awaiting return to New York caused the company officials to proceed without waiting for freight. Before the Queen of Bermuda sailed *Mr. Ryan declared* that if crew members carried aboard the baggage "they can continue doing it from now on." *He also said* that if tugs were used it would be "a long time" before the tugs would again take any ships out of New York. Two tugs were ready, but were not required because of the favorable tide.

A peace conference between Mr. Ryan and his associates and officers of the National Independent Longshoremen's Union apparently made some headway. *Mr. Ryan said* that he "told them what terms they (the Canadians) could have."

There are 700 passengers awaiting return from Bermuda, *it was said.*

The steamship officials regard the trouble as largely out of their jurisdiction because it revolves about an inter-union dispute. *They expressed* the hope that a quick adjustment could be made, and offered to sit in at the union meetings as "observers."

That efforts of the C.I.O. to organize waterfront workers is behind the I.L.A. move to assert its claims was indicated by *Mr. Ryan in a statement* protesting against C.I.O. inroads.   New York *World-Telegram*

INDIRECT REFERENCE

Even the parts of the example just given which are not attached definitely to an authority imply that they were verified by a careful reporter. Note in paragraph 4, for instance, that the writer knew of "threats to delay" and that "officers arranged" to meet the situation. Possibly this paragraph and the first sentence of Paragraph 5 were guesswork, but the careful inclusion of both cause and effect regarding each incident, plus the adequate authority given in other parts of the story, give the reader confidence in the correctness of the story as a whole.

No reporter should write a story supplied by an anonymous source, which means that practical jokers and persons with grievances who telephone and write to newspapers in the hope of giving news without disclosing their identity seldom are successful. When taking, over the telephone, information about which any question may arise, the reporter should obtain the informant's number, hang up and call him back. This practice often will expose impersonators, provided the reporter also checks the telephone numbers in the directory. Sometimes, at the request of high public officials, newspapers thinly veil sources of information by referring to "sources close to — " "a source known to be reliable — " "an official spokesman," "a high official," etc.

Washington — (AP) — Trevor Gardner was reported Tuesday to be ready to resign as chief of Air Force research in protest against the way the guided missile program is being handled.

His detailed objections were not stated. But on the basis of reports from friends and his own past public statements, Gardner apparently wants more attention and money devoted to research and a more exact division of missile work among the three armed services.

He was in Miami Tuesday to lay his case before Defense Sec. Charles E. Wilson, who is vacationing there. . . . Chicago *Sun-Times*

It is irritating to any reputable reporter to have to write this way, and protests against the refusals of public officials to permit their names to be used as authorities are frequent. Such vagueness weakens the confidence of readers in any newspaper which practices it on its own volition.

Senator Joseph R. McCarthy once gave reporters a statement regarding monitored telephone calls, but insisted that it be used as emanating from "a person who declined to let his name be used publicly." Commented Russell Wiggins, Washington *Post* managing editor, "The press associations and the publishing newspapers allowed him to put out a transcript under conditions that it originated from an unprejudiced source." To this, Claude Ramsey of the Asheville *Citizen & Times* added: "Senatorial immunity is bad enough without being compounded with senatorial anonymity."

The President of the United States generally designates into which of four classes what he says at a press conference falls: (1) quotable directly as from the President, (2) quotable as from a reliable source in high governmental circles, (3) not quotable but valuable as background information for writers, (4) completely off the record. Reporters respect the President's wishes. In fact, newspapers guard jealously the identity of any news source who wishes his name concealed, provided they have agreed, before obtaining the information, that it is to be used anonymously. Editors and reporters have gone to jail for refusing to tell a judge where they obtained a particular item of news. Several states have passed laws protecting newspapers against being declared in contempt of court for so doing.

WHEN UNNECESSARY

In the average run of police, legislative and many other types of news it is possible to omit specific mention of the source of information. In such stories it is presumed that a reliable authority was interviewed, and the newspaper's general reputation for accuracy is the reader's safeguard, as in the following examples:

The Keeler polygraph gave the lie today to Henry (Hank) Munson's denial that he shot and killed his nephew, Arnold Munson, Sunday in the rooming house at 717 Victoria place where they both lived.

The 95 boys and girls who came to Milltown to participate in the state spelling bee finals Friday will attend a banquet at 6:15 P.M. today at the Hotel Bedford.

One way excessive attribution can be avoided is by being careful not to cite authority for old, especially widely known facts. You wouldn't, for instance, write: "The capital of Wyoming is Cheyenne, according to Senator Blimp." Neither, unless there was uncertainty regarding it, would you give authority when mentioning the capital of Tibet, Afghanistan, or any other place. Such facts, though probably unfamiliar to most people, are easily obtained from standard reference books.

To cite authority for old facts can be misleading. It is likely to create the impression that the information is new. For example:

> To be eligible for low-cost public housing a person must not earn more than $3,600 annually, Theodore McCoughna, economist for the Public Housing administration, said today.

would be bad if the $3,600 ceiling had been in effect for some time. The example would be worse if "revealed," "announced," "admitted," or some similar verb had been used. When a statement of fact is inserted in a story as part of the background to enable readers properly to evaluate some item of news, it should not be attributed to any authority unless, in the newsman's judgment, it might not be accepted as true otherwise. Then dictionaries, encyclopedias, public laws and other authoritative reference works can be mentioned. Never use such vague expression as "statistics prove" or "authorities agree."

A lead which must be handled with caution is the "opinion here today" type. Seldom is such a lead based on an exhaustive survey of the "trend of public sentiment." The danger, from the standpoint of ethics, is the creation of what social psychologists call the "illusion of universality." It may be a gross exaggeration to write that "the entire city today mourned the death of Mayor Bull," or that "the world of music lovers was turned topsy-turvy," or that "business leaders today feared . . ."

In sports stories, which are written with a recognized good nature and prejudice for the home club, such leads may be condoned, but when used in political writing they generally are misleading. If it actually can be established that a majority of public officials or of any other group believe a certain way, there should be some indication not too long delayed that the news writer knows what he's talking about.

PERSISTENCE

A case study in the difficulties encountered by a medium-sized daily in its efforts to serve its readers is provided by Sherman Beinhorn of the Middletown (Connecticut) *Press*.

The major portion of the story in the April 6, 1961, issue follows:

The presidential stop order on development of a nuclear aircraft engine brought the first notice of job layoffs and transfers at the Connecticut Aircraft Nuclear Engine Laboratory, it was learned today.

Mayor Clew said he had information that notices had gone out Wednesday and sources at Pratt and Whitney Aircraft in East Hartford later confirmed this fact.

Pratt and Whitney would not say what the number of first layoffs would be.

In addition to sending out the pink slips, P&WA also sent out job relocation offers to employes faced with layoff at CANAL.

No information was available from P&WA as to the number of workers in this group. Neither would the company say what places in the United Aircraft Corp., of which P&WA is a division, are being held out to the CANEL people.

UAC had no comment to make today when asked what its president, William Gwinn, thought about a statement made earlier this week by Sen. Prescott Bush.

Little Unemployment

". . . I've also talked with the president of the United Aircraft about the decision," Bush stated. "From the assurance given me, I believe alternate job opportunities will be offered, so that little if any unemployment will result. I devoutly hope this will be the case."

Public relations people at UAC and at P&WA said the policy of the corporation has always been to transfer and relocate where possible.

President Kennedy asked Congress to knock out the nuclear-powered plane program March 28. Three days later came information from Air Force Maj. Gen. Thomas E. Musgrave that cancellation of the program meant elimination of 735 Air Force-financed jobs at CANEL. General Electric, Convair and Lockheed, all working under the nuclear plane contract, also were notified of the numbers of job elimination each faced.

While the fate of 735 CANEL jobs was sealed by the Air Force notice, no decision was made on the employment of 1,665 other CANEL employes, those under contract let by the Atomic Energy Commission.

The key to the future of these 1,665 was in the hands of a fact-finding committee that reached CANEL yesterday to hold discussions with UAC management.

Decision Shortly

Dr. A. J. Vander Weyden, deputy director of the AEC's division on reactor development and leader of the team, said today that a decision will be made shortly on the future of the local nuclear research facility.

He declared that a smaller operation, if one is approved, was in sight for the project under the new AEC program. . . .

Meanwhile, sources close to the plant indicated confusion among employes and continued rumors of mass layoffs.

Seeks Information

Mayor Clew said this morning that he is attempting to get information on the situation from Cong. Frank Kowalski. He was in touch this morning with public relations at UAC but learned nothing about the numbers given notice Wednesday.

The Unemployment Compensation Office in Middletown reported no applications for jobless pay from CANEL employes as yet. A staffer said the office understood that the CANEL employes were being given two-week notices. No applications could be made until the final two weeks of employment ended.

John Sullivan, business manager of the International Association of Machinists, said his office had no knowledge of notice of layoffs. . . .

Regarding the difficulties of coverage, Beinhorn wrote:

This is an example of a story that will indicate a good deal made of nothing new. The story says several times that information to such and such question would not be given. In a sense, this is a story in frustration.

I have been on this Connecticut Aircraft Nuclear Engine Laboratory since 1956. The lab is owned by the Atomic Energy commission and the Air department but is operated by Pratt and Whitney Aircraft. CANEL is a city unto itself. It is closed to the press. It has no public relations man of its own. Its manager says nothing. And there is no way to open the place up.

Late in March, President Kennedy stopped work on the billion dollar nuclear aircraft engine program. This meant that the jobs of 8,400 people at CANEL were jeopardized. Naturally, the story was a big one for us.

Luckily we got the first break. Kennedy's announcement broke on our time. But on almost all the other stories we have had to follow the bigger papers in Hartford, whose Washington bureaus can follow through at AEC or at the Pentagon. We have to rely on UPI which has other things to do, or go to our area congressmen and ask them to get news for us. It is all very second-hand.

The very second-handedness of it made us blush badly when Kennedy made his announcement. Our Congressman Kowalski and Congressman Price of Illinois had assured us this program would go forward. They gave us a lead story one day only to have it come back in our faces. All this to tell you how difficult it is for the small city daily to handle stories that have an origin behind the federal curtain of secrecy.

The instant story is also an example of giving substance to very little. We want to keep this news before the public and we also want to show the reader we are doing our level best. I think this shows through. This I think is important. "No comment" doesn't say very much. But it does indicate a try, which I feel the public appreciates.

The difficulty in handling stories of this kind also has to do with standing fast against the rumor when there is nothing else. Everybody in town knows how many were laid off, from the barber on down to the street cleaner. On this story, I am convinced Pratt and Whitney public relations could have told us the number given notice on Wednesday, the number offered transfers, and where those transfers were to. This is all good information around here.

It's tough. But if you can't get to the core of the news today, at least shoot around it and get ready for tomorrow.

OBEYING THE LAW

Unless he is forewarned, one of the first big surprises that the young reporter may have in his quest for authority is the discovery that he can invoke the freedom-of-the-press clause in the Constitution from morn to night and still be denied access to some documents which his naïveté might lead him to believe are public records open to all. Should he be able to break down certain barriers, he still might run the risk of being cited for contempt of court or sued for libel were he to use information thereby obtained.

It is regrettable that there is no place to which the reporter, or the editor either, can be directed for a clearcut statement of what his rights and privileges in particular instances are. Not only are the laws of different states different, but the same law is likely to have been interpreted differently by two or more courts of law in what would seem to be cases involving identical issues. As regards a number of important legal problems involving newspapers, there is little or no law, either statute or common. For this, newspapers themselves are partly if not largely to blame because they prefer to settle law suits out of court.

The principle generally observed, regardless of the clarity of state or municipal law, is that the public — which includes the press — has the right to inspect public documents except when the public interest thereby would be harmed. The frequent clashes between newspapers and public officials result from differences of opinion as to what constitutes a public record and what constitutes public interest. Some states have been careful to define public documents; others haven't. In either case, and regardless of the fact that there have been few tests in court, newspapers do not expect to be allowed to cover grand jury proceedings, executive sessions of law-making bodies, or to be shown records of unsolved cases in the police detective bureau, the report of an autopsy before it is presented to a coroner's jury, the report of an examiner to either a fire marshal or public banking official, or a number of other similar documents. In fact, public officials probably would be sustained by most courts were they to refuse the press access to many records now available to it. Pleading "public interest," the county clerk who refuses to disclose the names of applicants for marriage licenses, so as to protect them from commercial salesmen, probably is on sound legal ground.

The cub reporter should learn what both the law and general practice are in the community where he is to work, and the policy of his paper as to defiance or circumvention of public officials seeking to conceal news. Some editors encourage reporters to search for "leaks" whereby grand jury and executive session news may be obtained and they have defied judges' orders with resultant citations for contempt. Several years ago, the United Press forced the United States Senate to modify its rule regarding secret sessions after Paul Mallon obtained a secret roll call on the confirmation of a presidential nominee for a cabinet position. The rights of the press to cover state legislatures and city council meetings never have been clearly defined, but there seems no question that legally a judge has the complete right to govern the conduct of everyone in his court, including the right of expulsion.

It is the persistent clamor on the part of newspapers that has forced public officials to be as liberal as they are in what they make accessible to reporters. Since the fall of 1951, that clamor has increased in volume in opposition to presidential executive orders requiring federal agencies to classify news. Under President Truman's original order the classifications were: top secret, secret, confidential, and restricted. Two years later President Eisenhower abolished the fourth class and greatly decreased the number of agencies permitted to withhold information. Neither order satisfied the American Society of Newspaper Editors, which established a vigorous Freedom of Information committee. Under its auspices, Harold L. Cross, prominent attorney, wrote *The People's Right to Know* which pointed out a considerable increase of information withheld at all levels of government. In late 1955, a subcommittee of the Committee on Government Operations of the House of Representatives, with Rep. John E. Moss of California as chairman, began hearings on federal government news secrecy policies. That the situation continued to be bad was explained by Clark Mollenhoff in his 1962 book, *Washington Coverup*.

COPYRIGHT

Facts (news) cannot be copyrighted. The actual wording of an account of those facts, however, can be. A Conference of Press Experts called by the League of Nations in 1927 at Geneva stated the principle as follows:

> The Conference of Press Experts lays down a fundamental principle that the publication of a piece of news is legitimate, subject to the condition that the news in question has reached the person who publishes it by regular and unobjectionable means, and not by an act of unfair competition. No one may acquire the right of suppressing news of public interest.

The Conference affirms the principle that newspapers, news agencies, and other news organizations are entitled after publication as well as before publication to the reward of their labor, enterprise and financial expenditure upon the production of news reports, but holds that this principle shall not be so interpreted as to result in the creation or the encouragement of any monopoly in news.

Although facts cannot be copyrighted, newspapers can seek redress for pirating of news as a violation of fair business practices. In the case of Associated Press vs. International News Service, the United States Supreme Court declared Dec. 23, 1918:

> . . . Except for matters improperly disclosed, or published in breach of trust or confidence, or in violation of law, none of which is involved in this branch of the case, the news of current events may be regarded as common property. . . . Regarding the news, therefore . . . it must be regarded as quasi-property, irrespective of the rights of either as against the public.

A newspaper which wishes to rewrite or quote a copyrighted article appearing in another publication, either buys the copyright privilege or requests permission to quote. In either case, credit must be given to the publication which originally printed the material. If the copyright privilege is purchased, this credit line appears at the top of the article, as:

Copyright, 1946, by The New York Times

> Honolulu, T. H., July 29. — Evidence of mounting animosity between the army air forces and the navy over the results of the atomic-bomb tests and their subsequent evaluation appeared here today as a high AAF officer attacked the "battleship mentality" of diehard naval officers and experts. . . .

Otherwise, if permission to quote is given, the newspaper which copyrighted the article is given credit in the story itself. Unless permission is received, the paper using material in this manner is in danger of being sued for violation of copyright laws.

> Detroit, Aug. 3. — (AP) — The Detroit *Times*, in a copyrighted story, said today that a Wyandotte, Mich., grandmother has identified "Little Miss 1565," hitherto unidentified victim of a Hartford, Conn., circus fire, as her granddaughter. . . .

Magazine articles and books usually are copyrighted, but a newspaper seldom cares to quote enough of such material to run the risk of violating copyright privileges. Often a magazine article or book contains an important fact which a newspaper wants to quote. Credit always is given to the original publication, as:

> How the United States Marines are helping to settle local disputes in China is told by The North China Marine, weekly Marine newspaper

published at Tientsin, in an article from Sgt. C. Ray Stokes in Chin Hsien, who tells how a Marine-staffed "truce team" in the forward area functions. . . .   New York *Times*

A copyright runs for 28 years and can be renewed for a second 28 years. After that the previously copyrighted material passes into the public domain and can be quoted with impunity.

HOW TO AVOID LIBEL

As important as how to obtain access to public records is how to report the news they contain, or any other kind of news for that matter, so as not to involve one's newspaper in a libel suit. This problem is of personal importance to the reporter because any newspaper employe who had any hand in the preparation of a libelous news story is as subject to suit as the newspaper itself. Actually, it is seldom that action is brought against a reporter, but the chance that such might happen provides an added incentive to carefulness.

WHAT IS LIBEL?

The confusion already mentioned as regards the right of the press to obtain access to public records is even greater as regards libel. Succinctly, a libel is a written defamation as distinguished from a slander which is oral defamation. A more adequate definition which at the same time defines defamation is that given in the *American and English Encyclopedia of Law* as follows:

> A libel is a malicious defamation expressed either by writing or printing or by signs, pictures, effigies or the like; tending to blacken the memory of one who is dead, or to impeach the honesty, integrity, virtue or reputation, or to publish the natural or alleged defects of one who is alive and thereby expose him to public hatred, contempt, ridicule or obloquy; or to cause him to be shunned or avoided, or to injure him in his office, business or occupation.

It will be seen from this definition that cartoons, photographs and other illustrations are included.

Commission of a libel is a graver offense than slander because the written statement appearing in a publication with a wide circulation has greater possibilities of injury. In conversation, one may call another an opprobrious name and the effect be short-lived and restricted to a small circle of bystanders. Such statements made in print, however, have a far-reaching and more important effect.

In *The Rights and Privileges of the Press*, Fredrick S. Siebert deplores the distinction which formerly it was customary to make between words which are libelous *per se* (that is, libelous in themselves without the necessity of proving that their utterance or publication actually caused injury) and those libelous *per quod* (otherwise legitimate statements, libelous because of the circumstances under which made, so as to cause particular loss, as through declaring diphtheria to be prevalent at a summer resort). Instead of the old distinction, which he accredits to confusion resulting from the fact that only certain types of detraction once were regarded as actionable in slander, Siebert suggests a three-fold classification of all questionable words as: (1) obviously innocent, (2) questionable, for the jury to decide, (3) obviously defamatory. It is the duty of the judge, he says, to indicate into which class the particular word, phrase or story falls.

That there is no reliable criterion by which to anticipate how either judge or jury will decide, Siebert indicates by many examples. So do others who have studied outcomes of libel actions. In their *Hold Your Tongue!* for instance, Morris L. Ernst and Alexander Lindey reveal the following absurd situation. It has been held libelous to call a man an "arch hypocrite," but not libelous to call him a "political hypocrite." In Tennessee one may, with impunity, call a woman a "hermaphrodite," but may not make the charge in Ohio. California holds "son of a bitch" not libelous and New York has legalized "God damn." On the other hand, however, while it is not libelous to say of a man that "he caught the pox," it is libelous to say that he "got the pox from a yellow-haired wench." In Minnesota, the statement, "You did rob the town of St. Cloud, you are a public robber," was held not libelous because the crime of robbery cannot be committed against a town; similarly, there was no redress for a church warden who was accused of stealing the bell ropes, because the warden is custodian of the ropes and cannot steal his own property. On the other hand, when it was said of a woman, "She did have pups," and when the accused sought to defend herself by alleging the inherent improbability of the accusation, an Indiana judge held that though the people are bound to know the law, they are not bound to know scientific facts and might therefore believe the charge a possible one. In New York, a similar statement, "She had a litter of pups," was held not libelous for exactly the reason that it could not be true.

These few examples should be sufficient to impress the young reporter as to the care he must exercise to avoid committing libel. While many of the cases to which reference has been made involved editorial comment rather than news stories, exactly the same inconsistencies are to be found in judicial decisions regarding other kinds of libel actions. It has been held both that the dead can and cannot be libeled, that a newspaper is and is not responsible for libelous statements in press association stories, and that a libelous headline alone is sufficient cause for action and that an article must be judged as a whole.

DANGEROUS WORDS

Despite this confusion, to be on the safe side, the reporter may expect that a court will consider defamatory statements that:

1. Charge that a person has committed or has attempted to commit a crime, or that he has been arrested for the commission of a crime, indicted for a crime, has confessed to committing a crime or has served a penitentiary sentence.
2. Impute that a person has committed an infamous offense, even though the words do not designate the particular offense.
3. Tend to diminish the respectability of a person and to expose him to disgrace and obloquy even though they do not impute commission of a crime.
4. Tend to disgrace, degrade or injure the character of a person, or to bring him into contempt, hatred or ridicule.
5. Tend to reduce the character or reputation of a person in the estimation of his friends or acquaintances or the public from a higher to a lower grade, or that tend to deprive him of the favor and esteem of his friends or acquaintances or the public.
6. Impute that one has a perverted sense of moral virtue, duty or obligation, or that he has been guilty of immoral conduct or has committed immoral acts.
7. Impute commission of fraud, breach of trust, want of chastity, drunkenness, gambling, cheating at play, violation of duties imposed by domestic relations, swindling, etc.
8. Impute weakness of understanding or insanity.
9. Impute a loathsome pestilential disease, as leprosy, plague or venereal disorders.
10. Tend to expose a person in his office, trade, profession, business or means of getting a livelihood, to the hazards of losing his office or charge him with fraud, indirect dealings or incapacity, and thereby tend to injure him in his trade, business or profession.

Words and expressions the use of which has led to libel suits and which, therefore, must be used with great care by news writers, include:

abductor	blasphemer	dago
abortionist	bribery	dead beat
adulterer	buggery	defaulter
anarchist	burglar	degenerate
arson	common drunk	deserter
bestiality	conspirator	drunkard
bigamist	counterfeiter	embezzler
blackguard	criminal	embracery
blackmailer	crook	eunuch

extortionist
false pretenses
false swearing
forger
fornication
fraud
fugitive from jus- tice
gambler
grafter
homicide
hoodlum
humbug
hypocrite
imp of the devil
incest
indecent exposure
informer
insane

kidnaping
larceny
leper
liar
libelous journalist
libertine
malicious mischief
mistress
murderer
nigger
perjury
pettifogger
prostitute
quack
rape
rascal
robber
rogue
scandal monger

sedition
seducer
shyster
skunk
slacker
smuggler
social leper
sodomist
spy
stock rustler
subornation
swindler
thief
traitor
villain
whore
wop

It has been held actionable to publish of a butcher that he used false weights; of a jeweler that he was a "cozening knave" who sold a sapphire for a diamond; of a brewer that he makes and sells unwholesome beer or uses filthy water in the malting of grain for brewing; of a tradesman that he adulterates the article he sells; of a schoolmaster that he is an "ignoramous" on the subject he pretends to teach; of a clergyman that he is immoral or "preaches lies" or is a "drunkard" or "perjurer"; of an attorney that he offered himself as a witness in order to divulge the secrets of his clients or that he "betrayed his client" or "would take a fee from both sides" or that he "deserves to be struck off the roll"; of a physician that he is "empiric" or "mountebank" or "quack" or "vends quack medi- cines"; of a mechanic that he is ignorant of his trade; of a judge that he lacks capacity and has abandoned the common principles of truth; and of anyone in public office a charge of malfeasance or want of capacity to fulfill its duties.

H. W. Sackett in *The Law of Libel* cites the following published charges as having been held to be actionable: want of chastity (as ap- plied to women, at all events) or adultery (charged upon either man or woman); the publication of the obituary of a person known to the writer to be living; a charge that a member of Congress was a "misrepresenta- tive" and a groveling office seeker; that a juror agreed with another juror to rest the determination of the damages in a case upon a game of checkers; characterizing a verdict of a jury as "infamous" and charging the jurors with having violated their oaths; stating in the criticism of a book that the motives of the author are dishonorable or disreputable; calling a white man a Negro.

INSINUATIONS

It will be seen that a libel may be committed by mere insinuations. It is necessary only that the insinuation contain the elements of libel and that the readers of the paper understand it in its derogatory sense.

Likewise, allegory and irony may be libelous, as imputing to a person the qualities of a "frozen snake in the fable" or heading an article in regard to a lawyer's sharp practices, "An Honest Lawyer."

DAMAGES

Damages resulting from libel suits may be of three kinds: (1) general, (2) special and (3) punitive or exemplary.

General damages are awarded in cases of proof of libel when injury is recognized as the natural consequence of such publication. No proof of actual injury need be submitted.

A plaintiff may receive special damages when he can prove particular loss. When special damages are asked, proof of specific injury must be established by the plaintiff. Special damages may, however, be awarded in addition to general damages.

Punitive damages are inflicted as punishment for malice on the part of the offending publication. Proof of malice must be established by the plaintiff. Punitive damages may be awarded upon proof of gross negligence or if a newspaper reiterates its libelous statement after being warned that it is untrue.

DEFENSES

There are five possible defenses against libel:

1. *Truth.* In civil actions the truth of a publication is a complete defense, even though natural inferences of a defamatory character might be drawn which would be untrue. If malicious intent can be proved, however, truth may not be a defense. In criminal prosecutions, unless the publication was made for the public benefit or with good motives and for justifiable ends, truth is not a defense. The law in this respect differs in different states.

A publication must not only know the truth of what it has printed, but it must be able to submit legal proof. It is not a defense to claim that the libelous matter was printed upon the authority of another person.

For example, publication of libelous statements made in a public address is not privileged, and the injured party can sue both the individual making the statement and all publications which reported it.

2. *Privilege.*   Publication of the contents or of extracts of public records and documents for justifiable purposes and without malice, even though they contain libelous matter, is privileged by law. Publication of the contents of complaints or petitions before a public hearing has been held on them is not privileged; neither are publication of the proceedings of a private hearing, the contents of a warrant before it is served, confessions to police, news of arrests unless by warrant, and many other exceptions.

The law on this subject reads as follows:

> An action, civil or criminal, cannot be maintained against a reporter, editor, publisher or proprietor of a newspaper, for the publication therein of a fair and true report of any judicial, legislative or other public official proceedings, without proving actual malice in making the report.

Another provision qualifies this as follows:

> The last section does not apply to a libel, contained in the heading of the report; or in any other matter, added by any person concerned in the publication; or in the report of anything said or done, at the time and place of the public and official proceedings, which was not a part thereof.

3. *Fair comment.*   Authors, playwrights, actors, office holders and other public characters who invite the attention of the public to their work are liable to fair comment and criticism. This privilege, however, extends only to an individual's work and not to his private life, and there must be no malice.

In the case of office holders, comment or criticism must be confined to official acts or actual qualifications, and there must be an honest purpose to enlighten the community upon the matter under discussion.

The language of such criticism cannot be so severe as to imply malice, and the statement or comment must, in fact, be comment and not an allegation of fact. It, furthermore, must be on a matter of public interest, such as comment on public affairs, the church, the administration of justice, pictures, moving pictures, architecture, public institutions of all kinds, other publications, etc.

4. *Absence of malice.*   Malice is an important element of all libel suits. Its presence leads to larger damages than its absence. Malice is either *in fact*, which means that it springs from ill will, intent, hatred, etc., or *in law*, which is disregard for the rights of the person without legal justification.

Absence of intent to libel is no defense, but proof of unintentional libel helps to mitigate damages. According to Sackett in proving absence of malice the defendant in a libel suit may show:

a. That the general conduct of the plaintiff gave the defendant "probable cause" for believing the charges to be true.

b. That rumors to the same effect as the libelous publication had long been prevalent and generally believed in the community and never contradicted by the accused or his friends.

c. That the libelous article was copied from another newspaper and believed to be true.

d. That the complainant's general character is bad.

e. That the publication was made in heat and passion, provoked by the acts of the plaintiff.

f. That the charge published had been made orally in the presence of the plaintiff before publication, and he had not denied it.

g. That the publication was made of a political antagonist in the heat of a political campaign.

h. That as soon as the defendant discovered that he was in error he published a retraction, correction or apology.

i. That the defamatory publication had reference not to the plaintiff, but to another person of a similar name, concerning whom the charges were true, and that readers understood this other person to be meant.

5. *Retraction.* Often a newspaper can avoid a suit by prompt publication of a retraction. If a suit does result, such retraction serves to mitigate damages, especially if it is given a position in the paper equally prominent to that given the previously published libelous statement.

PLAYING SAFE

Since truth is the best defense against a charge of libel, the primary responsibility of the reporter is clear; it is to be one hundred per cent accurate — which means carefulness and diligence of the type described earlier in this chapter. It is true that newspapers take many chances daily, especially in police news, but not in cases where the element of doubt is great. Among the precautions which the reporter should heed are the following:

1. Be sure that you have names and addresses correct.

2. Stop and think, "Will this defame anyone's character or hurt his business?"

3. Never call a man a crook, bootlegger, thief, forger or any other kind of criminal unless he is so proved in court. Don't anticipate what the court will do. Remember that an accused person is not

a prisoner until after he is sentenced, and that he is innocent until proven guilty.

4. Only formal charges by proper authorities warrant their unqualified use by a newspaper.

5. The news of an arrest and the charge may be printed, but the reporter should obtain his information from the official police blotter and not from any other source. Testimony of witnesses also must be printed cautiously until made under oath.

6. "Police say," "it is alleged," "it is reported," and similar expressions are absolutely no protection, although insertion of such "softeners" may result in mitigation of damages.

7. Don't say someone is wanted "for the murder." Rather that he is wanted for questioning in connection with the murder or to answer a charge of murder.

8. Be careful to avoid imputing blame. It is better to say two automobiles collided than that one struck the other, unless, of course, one was stationary.

9. Verify all rumors, hearsay and comment.

10. Questionable statements always should be attached to an authority.

11. Remember that eyewitness testimony has been proven time and time again to err. Always interview as many eyewitnesses as you can.

12. If you doubt that a person has given his right name or address, write " — who gave his name as John Smith — " or "John Smith who gave his address as — " etc.

13. Be careful to say exactly what you mean. Avoid, for instance, saying that a man died "from" an operation when you mean "after" an operation.

14. Be careful of photographs gathered for the city desk. Many suits have resulted from improperly identified pictures.

15. Republication of a libelous statement from another medium is libelous. A newspaper is responsible for everything that it prints regardless of the source of its information or the authority upon which it prints it.

16. Never write anything when in a heat of passion or with the intention of injuring anyone, even though the statements that you make are true.

17. Forget your enthusiasm and personal opinions when writing a news story.

18. Avoid insinuations, innuendoes and irony.

19. Remember that a retraction is no defense.

20. Copyread what you have written before turning it in.

21. When in doubt, leave it out.

9

Keeping Up-to-date

I. Identification

   1. Persons

     a. Making It Attractive
     b. Picking the Identification
     c. Double Identification
     d. Synonyms
     e. Identification as the Feature
     f. Indefinite "Who"
     g. Delayed Identification
     h. Biographical Sidebars

   2. Organizations

     a. By Type
     b. By Purpose
     c. By Achievement
     d. By Reputation

   3. Places

   4. Events

     a. Occasions
     b. Comprehensive Leads and Stories
     c. Predictions
     d. The Tie-back
     e. Coincidences

   5. Words

II. The Follow-up

   1. The Second-day Story
   2. Featuring the Follow-up
   3. Second-day Comment
   4. Localization
   5. Reminiscences
   6. The Running Story
   7. The Revived Story
   8. Investigations
   9. The Resurrected Story

III. Rewrite

   1. The Nature of Rewrite
   2. Picking the Feature

     a. Buried Feature
     b. Secondary Feature
     c. Follow-up Feature
     d. Comprehensive Lead
     e. Combined Stories
     f. Local Angle

THE REWARDS OF A REPORTER

BY *Philip Kinsley*, Chicago *Daily Tribune*

The last fifty years have brought so much of invention, discovery, and knowledge regarding man and his universe that we have not had time to assimilate the new ideas. Here lies a unique opportunity for the reporter, one which emphasizes the need of all the so-called education that he can muster. Where human activities tend to become more and more specialized, it needs someone to look over the fence and see what is going on in the next yard and tell his neighbors about it. In scientific conventions, I have noticed, the terminology of specialists becomes so abstruse that one group does not know what the other is talking about. The reporter should have just enough education to understand and appreciate these groups, and yet not too much to become warped.

It would be impossible to draw a line here. People never know when they are insane or their judgment is bad. It is safe to say that we can never know enough. Our blind sides correspond with those of this insect and lower animal world.

In the course of thirty years I have probably written five million words about human affairs, living men and living problems. It may be mere rationalization for not having gone into something more important, but I cannot think of a greater responsibility than that of historian of current events. The words may be leaden or winged, but they certainly carry their reactions into future events of some sort. The ripples widen and touch far shores. I think that if I should meet De Lawd walking in some green pastures here that he would ask: "Did you tell the truth?" I might say, "Yes, Lawd, as I saw it," and he would say, "Go and learn some more."

Out of all this medley of good, bad and indifferent, I must conclude with John Burroughs in his Sundown Papers that the only fruit I can see is in fairer flowers, or a higher type of mind and life that follows in this world and to which our lives may contribute. This valley with its rocks and streams and trees seems eternal, but we know that it is constantly changing and shifting its component parts under major laws of cause and effect. The same is true of the human scene but where the mind enters this change may have a measure of direction. Beyond this we need not know.

THERE IS NOTHING SO SHORT AS A NEWSPAPER READER'S MEMory. No matter how carefully he reads a news story — and most newspaper purchasers read newspaper stories hurriedly if at all — when the next day's issue appears with news of later developments about any event, he finds that many if not most details of the first account have been forgotten.

As with events so also with persons in the news, no matter how prominent they may be. Results of current-events quizzes in which college students and other supposedly well-informed persons make bad "boners" are amusing, but instructions for such tests usually indicate that a very low score is "average." Names like faces may be familiar, but try to identify them! It is part of the interpretative reporter's responsibility to refresh readers' memories so that the immediate news account is more meaningful.

IDENTIFICATION

The obligation of the newspaper adequately to identify persons, groups, places and events in straight news stories is recognized in any efficient newsroom. The rule is never to presume that the reader has seen yesterday's story.

PERSONS

It is seldom that the name of a person is mentioned in a news story without some identification. Even the occupant of the White House is given his title, and other persons mentioned frequently in the news are identified by their news past or importance. Ordinary persons may be identified in several ways. The most common methods of identification include:

1. Address	8. News Past
2. Occupation	9. Achievement
3. Age	10. Life Span
4. Title	11. Reputation
5. Nicknames	12. Relationship
6. Race, nationality	13. Description
7. War Record	14. Occasion

Address. "Where do you live?" is one of the first questions asked any-one who is supplying information about himself. A man's address in a news story locates him, and the reader does not have to ask himself, "I wonder if that is the Newton Blue who lives in the next block?" Readers are interested in news pertaining to persons residing in their own or in a familiar neighborhood, even though not personally acquainted with them.

Great care must be taken to get correct addresses. Libel suits have been started by persons with names similar to those of others mentioned in news stories. Rare cases have been reported of two persons by the same name living at the same address. It is important to ascertain whether it is "street," "avenue," "place," "boulevard," "terrace," etc., as there may be both a Ridge avenue and a Ridge terrace. Whether it is East, North, West or South also must be mentioned.

> Peter R. Farrel, 159 E. Trembly place, was taken to Municipal hos-pital today after he accidentally cut his right foot while chopping wood.

Occupation. "What do you do?" also is high up in the list of questions asked when data are being sought about a person. The reader wonders if Harry Snow, 1516 Chestnut street, is the carpenter by that name who worked on his new garage.

> Donald C. Sorenson, 51, Edwardstown, district representative for the Common Laborers Union, Monday was sentenced to a two-year jail term and fined $1,500 for income tax evasion.

The occupation of a person mentioned in the news may be the feature, as:

> A butcher today used his knowledge of animal anatomy to save the life of his hunting dog, Romeo, accidentally caught in a bear trap.

Sometimes the feature is in the fact that a person in a particular posi-tion has done a certain thing whereas the same thing done by another would not be so newsworthy.

> An assistant postmaster general charged here today that Sen. Edwin F. Dietz has been talking out of both sides of his mouth in criticizing the Post Office department.

Age. It is customary to give the age of a person who is involved in a law suit or the victim of an accident. Otherwise, unless age has importance in the story, it may be omitted. Many persons do not like to have their ages known, but readers are eager to find out how old popular heroes and heroines are.

> William Murphy, 16-year-old Greenwich high school junior, today identified John Pratt, 21-year-old bootblack, as the armed bandit who robbed him of his clothing and $15 in cash Sunday night on W. Totze avenue.

Age frequently is the feature, as:

> An 18-year-old girl will marry a 73-year-old man on Saturday because "our common religious beliefs are of far more importance than the disparity in our ages."

Title. When a person has a title by which he is known, the news writer should use it. A short title is better placed before a name; a long title should be placed after a name, as:

> City Clerk George Johannsen will deliver the commencement address at 10 A.M. tomorrow at Craven Junior High School.
>
> James R. Wesley, commissioner of public works, will represent the city tonight at . . .

Nicknames. Nicknames seldom are used without first names; rather, they are inserted between the first name or initials and the surname. In sports stories and in feature articles, nicknames may be used alone. Often persons prominent in the news are better known by their nicknames than by their real names, as "Ike" Eisenhower, "Bing" Crosby, "Sugar Chile" Robinson, "Babe" Ruth, etc. When such nicknames become widely familiar, the quotation marks usually are omitted. It is a common practice with some newspapers to invent nicknames for persons mentioned in the news, frequently in crime stories. In doing so, care must be exercised so that the connotation given the nickname is not prejudicial to the proper administration of justice or otherwise socially harmful.

> William "Wee Willie" Doody, pint-sized killer-bandit of the 1920s, died Wednesday evening in the Stateville prison hospital. Death was attributed to a liver infection.
>
> The baby-faced killer, who got his nickname because he was only 5 feet 3 inches tall, was serving a life sentence for the slaying in 1929 of Berwyn's police chief. Chicago *Daily News*

Race, Nationality. Deciding when to pass copy containing "Negro," "Puerto Rican," "Polish-born," "of German descent," and similar identifications has caused many an editor many a headache. Members of racial and nationality minority groups understandably object to persistent use of such identifications in crime stories, especially in headlines: "Negro Rapist Sought," "Italian Gangster Shot," etc. There is a slow but steady drift away from such practices, but the rule remains that race or nationality shall be used when pertinent. Determining just when that is often is not easy. When someone is in the limelight — as a politician, athlete or entertainer, for instance — his fans are eager to learn every picayunish fact regarding him, including his ancestry; certainly no injustice is intended when such details are given. For some people, as musicians and artists, a foreign background may be considered as an asset.

Columbus, Ga. — (UP) — Dr. Thomas H. Brewer, 72-year-old Negro civil rights leader and state Republican Party member, was shot to death Saturday night.   Chicago *Sun-Times*

War Record.   Under pressure from veterans' organizations, many newspapers have ceased identifying veterans as such in crime stories. Often, however, veteran status is a legitimate, even necessary, identification. It may, in fact, be the feature.

Thomas Thomas, a former paratrooper, just couldn't get his training out of his head. He was sleeping in the apartment of a friend when he awoke and jumped out of a third floor window. He landed on a roof a few feet below the window sill. He was not hurt, and he explained that he had dreamed he was back in the army and had been given an order to jump.

News Past.   After having once appeared in the news in connection with an important event, a person continues to be potentially more newsworthy than others. Should he become "copy" again, his former exploits are a means of identification.

Miss Jane Boynton, 22, winner of a "most beautiful baby" contest 20 years ago, today filed suit against Dr. N. O. Holten, for $15,000, charging that his plastic surgery "disfigured her for life."

Leon L. Desmond, star witness in the Fox-Delaney murder case four years ago, today was appointed chief deputy inspector of Raymond county by Sheriff L. L. Tyler.

Achievement.   More than 30 years later, Charles A. Lindbergh still was being identified as "the first person to make a non-stop solo flight from New York to Paris." The achievement of one's early life may be his identification in later life or after death, as:

Dr. Hal Foster, first Kansas City physician and surgeon to specialize in the treatment of eye, ear, nose and throat, died at 6 o'clock this morning at his home at the Brookside hotel, Fifty-fourth street and Brookside boulevard. He was 88 years old.

Life Span.   Sometimes it is pertinent to identify a person in relation to the historical events or changes that have occurred during his lifetime, especially as they relate to the news at hand.

Julius C. Jacobsen, who joined the internal revenue staff 38 years ago, when relatively few persons paid income taxes, and stayed long enough to see virtually everyone pay, will retire Saturday.   Milwaukee *Journal*

Mrs. Eliza Addis, who was born in Philadelphia when City Council met in Independence Hall and City Hall was just a blueprint, is celebrating her 100th birthday today.   Philadelphia *Bulletin*

Reputation. When identifying a person by means of his reputation, it is necessary to be careful that the reputation is deserved. It is possible for a newspaper to make or break a person by referring to him constantly as the foremost authority on a certain subject, or as a mere pretender or charlatan.

> James (Jimmy) Eder, reputedly the wealthiest and most successful jockey in the history of the Latin American turf, yesterday was named defendant in a suit for divorce or separate maintenance filed in Superior court by Mrs. Ruth Eder.

Relationship. A person's news importance may depend upon the prominence of a relative or friend. How far the families of persons important in public life or in the news of the day should be written up and photographed is another problem for debate by a class in newspaper ethics. Relationship may be used as identification even when the members of the family referred to are not of particular importance. Minors often are identified by parentage.

Legitimate use of relationship in identification is illustrated in the following examples:

> Maj. James R. Garfield, II, training officer of the 107th Armored Cavalry Regiment, Ohio National Guard, and great-grandson of James Abram Garfield, 20th President of the United States, is taking summer training at Fort Knox. Louisville *Courier-Journal*

> Robert Campbell MacCombie Auld, 80, a descendant of Robert Burns and an authority on the Scottish poet's life and Scottish history, died yesterday after a five weeks' illness.

Description. Sometimes the writer brightens up his identification by a bit of personal description, without which it often would be impossible to obtain a true impression of the story's importance. In the following example, note the use of descriptive identification throughout:

> Their shoes didn't squeak. They didn't talk out of the sides of their mouths. They showed no inclination to clip anyone on the jaw.
>
> Yet the dozen plain-looking fellows who gathered at the Hotel Sherman last night were honest-to-goodness private detectives They were holding their first postwar meeting of International Investigators, Inc.
>
> Head man is Ray Schindler, world-famed New York detective. Other members include Leonarde Keeler, inventor of the lie detector; Dr. Le Moyne Snyder of Lansing, medical-legal director of the Michigan State Police, and Clark Sellers, Los Angeles handwriting expert and document ace who worked on the Lindbergh kidnapping case.
>
> Most of the men, unlike such movie detectives as Alan Ladd, Humphrey Bogart and Dick Powell, are in the 50s and 60s and are quite calm about their work.

But one, at least, was not without a kind word for their movie counterparts. Said Harry Lewis of Sioux City, Iowa: "Those boys talk pretty tough and seem to run into an awful lot of trouble. But they get their job done and that's what counts."   Chicago *Sun*

Occasion.   A person's part in a news story must be explained no matter how else he is identified.

Prince Albert of Belgium, who is on a two-month study tour of the United States, will visit Chicago Oct. 12–13.

A mother, burned in a street car-gasoline trailer crash which killed 31 persons Aug. 14, 1961, won a $30,000 out-of-court settlement Monday.

MAKING IT ATTRACTIVE

It is not necessary that the identification always be formal and dull. In stories with considerable feature interest, all formal rules may be stretched or violated, as:

Vienna, April 22 — (UP) — A beautiful 27-year-old widow named Aimona, of Mitrovitza, Yugoslavia, has lost all five of the suitors who made her the envy of the town's unmarried women, a dispatch to the newspaper Tagblatt said today.

In identifying persons prominent in the news, it is possible to brighten up the identification to avoid dullness, provided good taste does not forbid.

New York, April 21 — (AP) — Father Major J. Divine, the little Negro "Messiah," who descended on Harlem in a cloud of smoke — so say his followers — tonight appeared to have vanished in even less than that.
Behind him he left:
A group of somewhat belligerent "angels" who chanted "Peace, it's wonderful!" to no one in particular and "scram" to everyone who ventured to inquire about reports of discord in the West One Hundred and Fifteenth street heaven.
Also a group of mere mortals wearing police badges who wanted to question the missing "Messiah" about a stabbing affray in his main kingdom yesterday morning.
His terrestrial attorney, Arthur A. Madison, expressed the opinion that the father was off communing with the spirits somewhere in one of his branch heavens.

PICKING THE IDENTIFICATION

The proper method by which to identify a person must be decided in each case. The appropriate identification should be sought in the case of a person with a number of achievements or a considerable news past, as:

Harold Bank, president of the senior class, today announced committees for class day.

Harold "Bud" Bank, football captain, will not be a candidate for the basketball team this winter.

The Associated Press Managing Editors once debated the propriety of identifying former New York Governor Thomas E. Dewey as "a two-time failure as a Republican presidential candidate" years after his candidacies and in stories which did not deal with national politics. The consensus was that in many instances recalling that part of Dewey's "news past" was poor journalism.

Often the occasion calls for special identifications for prominent persons, identifications which would be inappropriate at most other times.

Washington, Dec. 11 — (UP) — President Eisenhower, who never voted before 1948, plans to transfer his voting residence from New York to Pennsylvania where he has a farm at historic Gettysburg.

New York *Herald Tribune*

Cleveland, July 25 — (AP) — Federal Judge Paul Jones, once a football player himself, will hear injunction suits against Bobby Freeman and Jack Locklear, who jumped contracts with a Canadian pro team to join the Cleveland Browns.

Baltimore *Sun*

DOUBLE IDENTIFICATION

Sometimes, especially in obituary stories, more than one identification may be crowded into the lead, as:

William Jay Schieffelin, retired chairman of the board of Schieffelin & Co., wholesale drug concern, and a crusader for government reform, education for Negroes and many other humanitarian causes, died Friday night at his home, 620 Park Avenue, after a long illness. He was 89 years old on April 14.

New York *Times*

SYNONYMS

It is impossible, however, to use more than two or three identifications without making the lead awkward. One way out of this difficulty is to use the points of identification as synonyms for the person's name after the name itself has been used once. In this way, nicknames, reputation, news past, various titles, etc., can be brought in and repetition of the name or of personal pronouns avoided, as:

Former Alderman Guy L. Millard today charged that the local Fair Employment Practices commission is failing to perform its functions.

Chief backer of the commission when he was a member of the City Council, Millard now believes the agency's work is being sabotaged. The 78-year-old president of the Royal Dye Works said he has personally interviewed 20 local workers who had sought the commission's help in vain.

IDENTIFICATION THE FEATURE

When the achievement, reputation, occasion, or news past by which a person may be identified, seems more important or better known than the person's name, the identification should precede the name, as:

Murray, Ky., July 28 — (AP) — The man who wrote the official history of General Dwight Eisenhower's unified European command will deliver the commencement address at Murray State college's summer exercises next Friday.

He is Dr. Forrest C. Pogue, commissioned by President Eisenhower to write a history of his World War II record, "Supreme Command."

INDEFINITE "WHO"

When the *what* of the story is more important than the *who*, the identification may be featured, names being delayed until the second paragraph, as:

A 32-year-old Congregational minister has been named director of Youth Inc., a new nondenominational religious research agency.

The Rev. Charles L. Burns Jr., minister of the Westchester Community Church since 1953, will take over direction of the agency in January at Wichita, Kas.   Chicago *Sun-Times*

DELAYED IDENTIFICATION

Similarly, overcrowding a lead already packed with important facts, can be avoided by postponing identification until the second paragraph, as:

Denver — The eloquence of Walter Reuther held a crowd of 1,200 farm delegates and their wives spellbound for an hour and 20 minutes here.

The sandy-haired president of the United Auto Workers amused and delighted his National Farmers Union audience Tuesday night with raps at big business, Wall Street and Secretary of Agriculture Benson.   Chicago *Daily News*

BIOGRAPHICAL SIDEBARS

A quarter-century ago the J. David Stern papers developed a much-imitated practice of box inserts to provide additional information about persons, places, things and events mentioned in the news. Longer sidebars and feature articles also can be used to satisfy curiosity as to "Who is this fellow?" and make current news more understandable. Under the heading, "In College — and in Jail," the Chicago *Sun* used the following box insert at the time independent India was coming into existence:

Pandit Jawaharlal Nehru, head of the newly formed Indian interim government, has had intimate contact with the British — first in college and then in jail.

The 57-year-old leader of the All-India Congress Party received his education at Harrow and at Cambridge University in England where he became a barrister-at-law.

Returning to India he joined the famous non-cooperation movement of Mohandas K. Gandhi in 1920 and became actively associated with native independence and peasant movements.

He was president of the Indian National Congress in 1929 and 1936–37.

He has been repeatedly imprisoned by the British for his political activities and his anti-war speeches.

For many years, Nehru was sympathetic with the aims of the Soviet Union, although in political doctrine he was regarded as a Marxian Socialist rather than a Communist. In recent years, however, his leftism has become somewhat diluted.

ORGANIZATIONS

Organizations as well as persons must be identified adequately:

BY TYPE

Directors of the Monument Builders of America, Inc., a national association of the retail monument dealers, today condemned as "a national disgrace" the unkempt condition of the Statue of Liberty.

Chicago *Daily News*

BY PURPOSE

Milltown's Transit Authority, set up to bring order out of the city's long existent transportation muddle, has ended a year of operation with a record of substantial accomplishments although difficulties still lie ahead.

The eight-man board held its first meeting July 29, 1962, in offices at 35 Elm street, beginning operations with the backing of a $200,000 fund made up of two equal contributions from the city and state, joint sponsors of the enterprise.

As a municipal authority, it has the power, fixed by state law, to acquire and operate transportation lines in and around Milltown.

BY ACHIEVEMENT

Pleasanton, June 19 — The Alameda County Fair, which has been America's "jockey incubator" since the close of World War II, has a record crop of apprentices on hand for its 12-day race meeting opening here Friday.

BY REPUTATION

The Milltown Associates, which for 23 years was the leader in promoting city beautification, will disband Jan. 1.

In stories related to important public issues — controversial matters — brief identification of an organization usually is not enough. The interpretative reporter may have to write a parenthetical paragraph, side-bar, or full-length feature to provide proper understanding of what is involved. Readers cannot judge the true nature of a group by a high-sounding title. Typical situations in which full-length identification of an organization may be necessary include the following:

1. When the name resembles closely that of another group whose outlook is different. Example: the National Council of the Churches of Christ in the United States of America and the American Council of Christian Churches.

2. When a powerful group takes a stand on a public issue, pending piece of legislation, etc. In such cases it may be wise to point out whether the immediate action is consistent with previous activities by the same group. It may be possible to throw light on any selfish motives by revealing the business or other connections of the group's leadership or the general nature of its membership.

3. When a new group is organized, especially when its aims are expressed in semantically vague terms or it seems interested in only a single measure or matter of public interest. In such cases it may be a "front" organization for some other older interest group. Identification of the leadership may cast more light on the organization's real purposes than a quotation from its charter or constitution.

4. When an organization is involved in an act of force or violence. In such cases it may be necessary to seek reasons for the group's very existence in the social, economic or political conditions that brought it into being. Such was done extensively as regards the Puerto Rican Nationalist party after some of its members attempted to assassinate President Truman in 1950 and shot several members of Congress in 1954. Otherwise the incidents would have seemed to be isolated ones by individual fanatics.

PLACES

Places must be identified when they are not widely known or when significant or the feature of the story, as:

Purchase of the 1600 block on Palmer road for a new junior high school was announced today by the Board of Education. Twenty-three private dwellings, almost all of them condemned by the Department of Health, now occupy the site.

A place's news past or its proximity to another place previously in the news may be the best identification; often it is the feature:

Within a few feet of the spot where once grew the elm under which George Washington accepted command of the Continental Army, 25

Boston University students yesterday organized the Army of American Liberation. Its purpose is to "wage incessant warfare against forces which are destroying American democracy."

Places, as individuals, have reputations which may be used to identify them, as:

Sauk City, Minn., the "Gopher Prairie" of native son Sinclair Lewis' "Main Street" . . .

Reno, Nev., divorce capital of the United States . . .

Tarrytown, near which Rip Van Winkle allegedly took his long nap . . .

EVENTS

Events may be identified and explained:
1. By their significance (the occasion).
2. By their importance in relation to other events (comprehensive leads and stories).
3. By relating them to the "atmosphere" in the light of which they must be understood (the situation).
4. By their probable consequence (prediction).
5. By definite reference to preceding events to which they are related (tie-backs).
6. By the coincidence between them and other events.

OCCASIONS

Circumstances of a news event — purpose, importance, significance, etc. — must be made clear, as:

The annual appeal for the Catholic Charities, which opened last Monday, will be extended into next week, Msgr. Robert F. Keegan, secretary of charities in the archdiocese of New York, announced today.

Often the feature of the story may be found in the purpose or importance of the occasion which is the subject of the story, as:

Fort Washakie, Wyo. — (UP) — An age-old tradition was broken here when an Indian woman with white blood in her veins became a "chief" of the Arapahoe tribe.

The comparison between the immediate event and preceding similar events may be pointed out, either in the lead paragraph or shortly thereafter, as:

For the first time in memory, neither political party has a contest for any office in Crow county in the April 8 election.

COMPREHENSIVE LEADS AND STORIES

The comprehensive lead is correlative and explanatory. Used in straight news writing, it is not opinionated, however, because it deals with the incontrovertible.

One kind of comprehensive lead attempts to interpret the immediate news in the light of previous events, as:

> Six more witnesses Friday were called before the federal grand jury investigating the distribution of juke boxes in Farwell township.

> Further evidence that the voters of this city really elected a "reform" administration last month was provided by today's order by Mayor L. O. Oliver closing all amusement places in violation of municipal health ordinances.

A comprehensive lead emphasizes situations. When several stories related to the same general news event are received, they may be combined into one story and a general round-up or comprehensive lead be written. This type of lead is suitable particularly for election stories, stories of wrecks and other disasters, accidents, weather stories, etc. Facts on which a comprehensive lead and story of this sort are written usually are gathered by more than one reporter or correspondent.

PREDICTIONS

The significance of an event may be explained by pointing out the probable consequences or likely "next steps."

> The City Council's Big 10 crime commission starts five days of public hearings Wednesday — probably the last hearings the committee will hold.

> Drastic revision of the curriculum of Serena Junior High School will result if the Board of Education approves the unanimous recommendation of its Educational Policies committee.

> Among the changes which Mrs. Rose Blakely's committee says should be made are the following . . .

THE TIE-BACK

The tie-back is the part of the lead of a story which shows the relation between the immediate news and some previous news event. In the following examples, the tie-backs are in italics:

> Miss Colista Connor, 20, reputed heiress to a $500,000 fortune, *who disappeared mysteriously a week ago and returned Wednesday night to explain she was "on vacation,"* was gone again yesterday.

> Five hundred and fifty-two *additional* influenza cases were quarantined in Will county today, *a slight increase over yesterday's figures,* while six deaths were recorded from flu and 14 *more* from pneumonia.

COINCIDENCES

The tie-back to a previous story may be made by emphasizing coincidence. In many cases, the immediate incident may be newsworthy primarily or solely because of the coincidence, and the prior event may have received no publicity.

A second tragedy within two months today deepened the sorrow of Mrs. Mary McKinley, 26.

On June 1, her husband, Thomas, 35, a tuckpointer, was killed in a 12-foot fall. Yesterday her son, Robert, 4, was crushed to death by a truck.

WORDS

Parenthetical sentences or paragraphs sometimes are necessary to define or explain the context in which unusual words or expressions appear. Representative Clarence Brown of Ohio, for instance, sent reporters to the thesaurus when he accused the president of "ingannation." At that time, the Louisville *Courier-Journal* interjected the following in a United Press account:

(The word is not in *Webster's New International Dictionary*. The United Press said it meant to confuse or bewilder, and the Associated Press reported solemnly, "On consulting a thesaurus, reporters found the word ingannation listed as a synonym for deception.")

When President Truman accused a senator of raising many "Macedonian cries or yells," the Chicago *Daily News* used the following italicized parenthetical paragraph:

(A Macedonian cry is a cry for help, so called from Act XVI, 9, "Come over into Macedonia and help us.")

When the president told the nation that it could achieve a production goal of $500 billion a year within ten years, the same newspaper explained as follows:

(Five hundred billion dollars is half a trillion. A trillion is a 1 with 12 zeros behind it.)

Sometimes it is a legal term that needs explaining or a diplomatic proceeding, as the following which was once used when the United Nations received a plea for the application of sanctions:

(Sanctions are positive measures that may be taken against aggressor governments under the U.N. charter, such as cutting off trade, communications, etc.)

THE FOLLOW-UP

Most of the news in any edition of a newspaper is related in some way to other news. It usually takes more than a single article to tell any story. After the first account has appeared, there may be new developments.

Ability to sense phases of a news story which must be investigated further (followed up) is a valuable asset to a reporter or editor. Newspapers are read carefully for stories which in their original form are incomplete or which should be watched for further developments.

THE SECOND-DAY STORY

The second-day story of any event may include: (1) new information not available when the first story was written, (2) causes and motives not included in the first story, (3) more recent developments, results and consequences since the first story, (4) opinions regarding the event.

Latest developments always are emphasized in follow-up stories, and the use of a tie-back is a rigid rule. Never should the writer of a news story presume that a reader has seen the previous story or stories. Just as each installment of a serial story is prefaced by a brief summary of what has gone before, so each news story related to a single event has a short reference to previous news stories.

The tie-back usually is inserted in the lead in the form of a phrase or dependent clause, but any grammatical device may be used; sometimes the tie-back is delayed until the second paragraph.

New Information

A 44-year-old Ardmore woman who was found unconscious on Coulter street near Sibley avenue, a block from her home, is in serious condition at Bryn Mawr hospital today while police searched for an unidentified man believed to have attacked her without motive.

Philadelphia *Daily News*

Cause: Motive

Four firemen who perished in a flaming back-draft that surged through the Backstage night club early Tuesday morning died while fighting a fire which was deliberately, criminally set.

That flat charge came yesterday from Fire Marshal Frank Kelly, chief of the San Francisco fire prevention and investigation bureau.

"The fire was not accidental," Chief Kelly declared following more than 24 hours of investigation. . . .

San Francisco *Chronicle*

New Development

State officials took over the Englewood Industrial Bank yesterday as forgery charges were filed against its president, 42-year-old Homer H. Owen, widely-known Denver banker and loan company executive.

Owen, who was the object of a nationwide search in 1941 when he disappeared for 10 days with a large sum of money, was jailed Sunday after bank examiners discovered a $43,921.90 discrepancy in bank records, District Attorney Richard H. Simon reported.

Denver *Rocky Mountain News*

Opinion

BY *Art Stewart*

Angry parents today charged the "L" system with neglect in the crossing death of an 8-year-old boy.

A system whereby one man controls two crossings at Flournoy and Lexington at Long endangers the lives of children in three schools, the parents declared.

Donald Kieft, 5227 Lexington, was crushed to death Monday when he attempted to cross the tracks at Flournoy on a bicycle.

The crossings are protected by gates. So many trains traveling at a high rate of speed pass the intersections in the residential district that the lone gateman keeps the gates lowered even when trains are not approaching. . . .

Metropolitan morning newspapers frequently use the follow-up technique on stories which "broke" for the afternoon papers the day before; afternoon papers do the same for stories the first news of which appeared in morning papers.

FEATURIZING THE FOLLOW-UP

An important news story "breaks" too fast to permit investigation of its feature possibilities. By a later edition or the next day, however, the features are developed either in a rewritten story, or in supplementary stories (sidebars). If the reporter finds himself "stuck" with few new facts, he may simply retell the story in feature style:

Laramie *Boomerang*

A freak accident was investigated early this morning when an automobile belonging to Ralph Conwell, 803 Flint, crashed into a parked pickup belonging to C. H. Melvin, 657 North Eighth, and then crashed into the front of the Melvin home.

Laramie *Bulletin*

It was 4 A.M. Tuesday.

Mr. and Mrs. Ralph Conwell were parked in front of their home ready to leave for a vacation at their ranch near Daniel, Wyo.

Conwell started the car. Mrs. Conwell was secure in a new

Laramie *Boomerang*

Police said apparently the Conwells were starting on a trip and after taking the car out of his garage, Mr. Conwell got out of the car to check if the garage was locked and the lights were out inside.

The car started creeping forward headed west on Flint. Mrs. Conwell, who was in the car and had on a safety belt, attempted to halt the car by applying the foot brake and inadvertently applied pressure to the accelerator.

The car surged forward hitting the curb and climbing it at the corner of Flint and Eighth and then headed north, striking glancingly on the outside of the Melvin pickup, also headed north, which was parked next to the curb, knocking the pickup upon the parking.

The Conwell car continued and jumped the curb to the right and came to a stop after uprooting a large lilac bush and smashing into the front of the Melvin home.

The impact of the car was just beneath the window of the bedroom where Mr. and Mrs. Melvin were sleeping. Although the wall was driven in about ten inches from the impact, the window pane remained intact.

Police said there were no injuries reported to them.

Laramie *Bulletin*

safety belt next to the driver's seat.

Conwell remembered he left the garage door open and left the car to close it.

The car began rolling.

Mrs. Conwell struggled to get out of her "secure" position, gave up the idea and reached for the steering wheel and the brake.

She got the wheel, but hit the accelerator with her foot.

Around the corner she went, her husband running after her, the horn honking.

The car struck a parked ton truck, threw it 40 feet, jumped the curb, hit a 25-year-old lilac bush, threw it several feet, and smashed into the bedroom of Conwell's next door neighbor — Mr. and Mrs. C. H. Melvin.

Said Mrs. Conwell:

"It was the safety belt that saved me. You can never tell when an accident is going to happen."

Said Mrs. Melvin: "I thought it was a drunken driver."

Said Mr. Melvin: "My mother-in-law planted that bush here 25 years ago. I never thought it'd save our lives."

Mr. Conwell wasn't available for comment — he went back to the ranch, leaving his wife behind.

SECOND-DAY COMMENT

Whenever the President delivers an important message, the Supreme Court hands down a significant decision, a new scientific discovery is announced, or any one of a number of unusual events occurs, newspapers and press associations scour the country to obtain opinions from persons qualified to comment cogently. The inquiring reporter technique also can be used for matters of a nonpolitical nature, as in the following illustration:

BY *James Ullman*

Adolphe Menjou, take note.

Chicagoans don't think your estimate of what a man should spend to be well groomed is worth an old pair of spats.

The dapper Menjou, one of Hollywood's best-dressed men, told the United Press that in order to be smartly dressed, a man should put out "at least" $6,500 for a starting wardrobe and be prepared to spend from $10,000 to $12,000 to keep it up. For instance, he said, a man can't be really well tailored for less than $250 a suit.

He also generalized to the effect that politicians don't dress as well as businessmen and actors do, and added:

"I'm dedicated to improving the appearance of male attire. Right now, I'm trying to bring back spats, derbies and walking sticks."

In Chicago, Joel Goldblatt, president of Goldblatt's department stores, said he "certainly did not agree" with Menjou.

"Taste has more to do with it than dollars," Goldblatt said. "There's a difference between being neat and well dressed and being fancy. We're living in the 20th Century and we don't need striped pants unless we're diplomats or we're going to a wedding." Chicago *Sun-Times*

LOCALIZATION

A news item originating in a faraway place may have a local "angle," or it may cause readers to ask, "Could it happen here?"

Local parents need have no fear that babies in local hospitals will become confused and cause another Pittman-Garner baby mix-up a generation or so hence.

So thorough is the identification system employed in this community's three hospitals that their authorities consider mix-ups like Madeline Louise Garner-Pittman's in Georgia last month an impossibility.

Although many hospitals throughout the country supplement foot and palm printing as an added precaution, adequate supervision is the only real safeguard, in the opinion of H. James Baxter, superintendent of General Hospital since 1921. . . .

REMINISCENCES

Similarly, readers may ask, "Has anything like that ever happened before?" Old timers draw parallels between the present and the past and relate anecdotes brought to mind by the immediate news item.

Washington, Feb. 27 – (AP) – There was another woman doctor in the White House 80 years ago, records show.

Dr. Susan Ann Edson, one of the early women physicians, helped care for President James Garfield from the time an assassin shot him until his death two and one-half months later, on Sept. 19, 1881.

President John F. Kennedy still gets credit officially for appointment of the first full-time woman White House physician, Dr. Janet Travell.

Washington relatives of Dr. Edson have discovered she had the distinction of serving as head nurse to the dying President Garfield and also attended his ailing wife.

An Edson family genealogy notes she was Garfield's "family physician and longtime friend."   Tampa *Tribune*

THE RUNNING STORY

Newspapers continue to follow up stories as long as there are new angles or developments to investigate or until reader interest lags. Each succeeding story is written to bring the situation up-to-date.

In case of a flood, war, important court trial or political contest (to mention only a few of the possibilities), daily, almost hourly, stories are written to give the latest developments. A murder story frequently occupies the front page for weeks.

Note how the following story developed day by day, as shown by three successive leads from the Kansas City *Star*:

About 124,000 women here today are being given the opportunity to state whether they desire to serve as jurors. The ballots should be returned to the Jackson County courthouse by June 10.

Eighty-six ballots on jury service for women had been received this afternoon at the jury commission office in the Jackson County courthouse. Twenty-nine indicated a desire to serve on juries here. Fifty-seven declined to serve.

The number of women desiring jury service was increasing this afternoon when 314 of the 1,440 ballots received by the jury commission indicated that more than one in four women responding to the poll were willing to be jurors. The remaining 1,136 do not desire to serve on Jackson County juries other than federal.

THE REVIVED STORY

Days, weeks or months later a reporter may be assigned to find out "what ever happened to so-and-so" or regarding "such-and-such."

Five years ago Wednesday Dorothy Mae Stevens was brought to Michael Reese hospital, frozen stiff and brittle as an icicle.

Her body temperature was an unbelievable 64 degrees — so low, physicians had to use a chemical thermometer because regular clinical thermometers record only as low as 93. Normal body temperature is 98.6.

The 23-year-old woman had been found in an areaway at 3108 Vernon. She had been there about 11 hours.

When doctors examined Mrs. Stevens they found:

Her blood had congealed into a mud-like sludge.

Her breathing rate was three to five times a minute compared to a normal 18 to 22.

Pulse was 12 (normal is 70–80).

Blood pressure could not be recorded.

Her deep frozen condition attracted the attention of physicians everywhere. She was called the "human icicle," "deep-freeze girl," "frozen woman," and "human hibernater."

* * *

Mrs. Stevens was back in Michael Reese hospital Tuesday where she helped write medical history.

"She has been undergoing treatment in connection with her artificial limbs," a spokesman said. "She'll be here about two more weeks."

Physicians, about a month after she was brought to the hospital amputated both of her legs below the knee; all of the fingers on her right hand and all but one finger on the left.

* * *

Still in good spirits, Mrs. Stevens is keeping busy in the hospital reading and doing leathercraft. Now 28, she lives in a flat at 3800 Lake Park.

"I'm still a young woman and I have my whole life to live yet," she says. Chicago *Daily News*

INVESTIGATIONS

Often such assignments are for "policy" purposes, but the disclosures from the resultant investigations may be definitely in the public interest. Newspapers frequently "keep after" someone, particularly a public official, to correct an evil brought to light by some news event.

BY *Curtis Fuller*

Doors still swing inward at Niles Center and Morton Grove taverns a year after seven persons, two of them Northwestern university students, burned to death in the Club Rendezvous. Doors still swing inward for bodies to pile up against, and do not even have exit signs to mark them.

Last year a week after the Rendezvous tragedy, two Daily News-Index reporters visited more than 15 taverns in the Howard street, Morton Grove, and Niles Center districts to discover if conditions existed which might cause other Rendezvous tragedies some day. They found fire hazards frequent. Sunday night the reporters visited the same taverns again, found the same conditions.

In three of a dozen Morton Grove and Niles Center taverns, doors comply with county fire regulations by opening out. In two of the three, exit signs direct customers to the doors.

The Cook county board April 4 passed a new fire ordinance to take effect April 30, ordering all taverns to have at least two exit doors that open outward, progress through which is unimpeded. Electrically operated catches for exit doors are prohibited by the ordinance. Other provisions included use of fireproof or slow-burning construction.

These regulations are not enforced. They are violated by more than half the taverns visited Sunday night.

Nowhere did we see fire extinguishers in plain sight. One of the ironies of the evening came as we sat in the Paris Gardens talking to the bartender. A man dashed in yelling that his car was on fire. There was no fire extinguisher handy, and the bartender handed him a seltzer bottle which the man took and dashed out.   Evanston (Ill.) *News-Index*

THE RESURRECTED STORY

Sometimes a mystery is years in the solving, or a new fact is discovered which casts new light on some historical event or personage. In writing such a story the "tie-back" rule must be observed, although the lead seldom is adequate to supply all of the "resurrected" facts which must be told. For instance, if a criminal who has long evaded capture is arrested, the story may include a recapitulation of his crime and may even be accompanied by pictures and diagrams taken or made at the time of the crime. Later, when the person is brought to trial, the story may be repeated, and again if the criminal is put to death legally.

In every news office there are notations of stories which are said to be "hanging fire," and which may "break" at any time. Verdicts are withheld, a committee delays its report, there is a postponement in the filing of a suit, or an important person does not make an announcement of which he has hinted.

In the following examples, note the tie-backs to events of some time previous:

Ten cases of typhoid fever — one resulting in death — have been traced to a church wedding reception in suburban Rosehill last Nov. 1, Dr. R. L. Edmonson, director of the Rosehill Health Department, disclosed today.

North Manchester, July 4. — Midnight lights burned by a Dr. Elies Ohmart prior to 1885 were explained here when Tom Richardson came across an ancient, handwritten record book in the attic of the John W. Ulrey home which he recently purchased.

The book contained notes of scientific inventions including a telephone patented by Bell in 1876, an electric arc lamp, the separation of aluminum from clay, a mechanical table of logarithms and an electric sign board.
                                                    Fort Wayne (Ind.) *News-Sentinel*

REWRITE

The day of the major newspaper "scoop" is gone. In the first place, except in a small and dwindling number of large cities, there is no competitor for the one surviving daily newspaper to scoop. Furthermore, the important day-by-day news of the world is gathered mostly by two press associations (Associated Press and United Press International) and transmitted simultaneously to all subscribers. Most important, radio and television have made it impossible for any periodical to be first with such news.

Newspapers and magazines amplify, explain and interpret the news, sometimes shortly after its occurrence; but often, weeks, months, or years later when new information becomes available or the passage of time gives new perspective. Newspapers today often are competitors of magazines in the attempt to obtain first rights to the memoirs of persons able to cast new light on old events.

THE NATURE OF REWRITE

Within newspaper offices the title rewrite man now is used to designate a person who spends his time in the office taking news over the telephone, mostly from the paper's own reporters. There persists, however, a considerable amount of rewriting in the old sense: "borrowed," with little or no attempt to obtain additional facts, from other printed sources.

Such sources include press releases, community newspapers, trade journals, house organs, public and private reports and announcements, newsletters intended for special interest groups and out-of-town newspapers (exchanges). Some papers run a column of news briefs or oddities from the exchanges or the day's wire report. Stories in the earlier editions of one's own newspaper may be rewritten for later editions, when new facts are obtained or for reasons of space, clarity, etc.

Usually, the rewrite man attempts to compose an item which will read as though it had been written up on original information. In his attempt to play up a new fresh angle he must avoid killing a good lead and burying an undoubted feature. Awareness of the extent to which radio and television have taken the edge off some of the news may lead to this error unless there is conscious effort to avoid it.

PICKING THE FEATURE

The rewrite man must obey the rules of good news writing which, among other things, means that the lead of his story must play up the feature of the item. The difficulty of the rewrite man is obvious when it is realized that this feature probably already was played up in the original story. The poorer the first story, the easier the task of the rewrite man who must do more than merely restate or reword the original lead.

The rewrite man, with no facts in addition to those of the original story, therefore, asks himself several questions, including:

1. Did the writer play up the real feature of the story or is it buried some place in the article?
2. Is there another feature of equal or almost equal importance as the one which the writer used, that might be played up?
3. Can I make my story read like a follow-up story by emphasizing the latest developments mentioned in the first story, or by suggesting the next probable consequence?
4. Can I write a comprehensive lead which will interpret this item of news in the light of other news?
5. Is there any other news today with which I can combine this story?
6. In the case of stories appearing in publications outside of the immediate community, is there a local angle that can be played up?

BURIED FEATURE

If the writer of the original story has missed the feature, the task of the rewrite man is simple, as:

Original Story

The question of submitting to the voters of Milltown at a special election Mayor A. L. Hunter's proposal to issue $400,000 worth of street improvement bonds again was the major "bone of contention" at last night's City Council meeting.

Ald. Joel Oldberg, 15th ward, presented a list of streets which he said are badly in need of repair and urged the holding of the special election. Opposing him was Ald. Arthur West, 21st ward, who said the city already has too large a bonded indebtedness.

After three hours of debate the Council voted 21 to 17 in favor of Alderman Oldberg's motion to call a special election Sept. 14.

Rewritten Story

Milltown voters will decide Sept. 14 at a special election whether the city's bonded indebtedness shall be increased $400,000 to finance Mayor A. L. Hunter's street improvement program.

Decision to submit the matter to voters was made by the City Council last night after three hours' debate. The vote was 21 to 17.

The motion was passed over the opposition of Ald. Arthur West, 21st ward, who argued that the city already is heavily indebted. Maker and chief supporter of the motion was Ald. Joel Oldberg, 15th ward, who presented a list of streets which he says need repairs.

SECONDARY FEATURE

Note in the following example how the rewrite man found a second feature equally as important as the one played up in the original story:

Original Story

Loss of between $75,000 and $100,000 resulted from a fire which raged for three hours early today in the Central Chemical

Rewritten Story

Firemen of Hammond and Calumet City braved the dangers of huge stores of highly inflammable nitric acid yesterday to company plant at Calumet City. The plant, which manufactured nitric acid, was a subsidiary of Wilson & Co., packing firm.

Spontaneous combustion is believed to have been the cause of the fire which was noticed about 2:30 A.M. by two workmen, only occupants of the building at the time. In the attempt to save acid valued at about $50,000 in storage tanks, the two men, Abel Puffer and Jared Bean, shut off safety valves to the tanks.

Exact loss cannot be determined until the tanks are opened today and tests made as to whether water reached their contents. Because nitric acid is highly inflammable, Hammond and Calumet City firemen were in constant danger as they fought the fire.

battle a fire which destroyed the Central Chemical company plant at Calumet City. The loss was estimated at $75,000 to $100,000.

The plant, a subsidiary of the packing firm of Wilson & Co., is devoted entirely to the manufacture of the acid. Quantities of acid valued at $50,000 were in storage tanks.

The blaze raged for three hours. The acid tanks will be opened today to determine whether water seeped into them and spoiled the stores.

Two workmen, the only persons in the plant, shut off safety valves to the tanks when the fire began, apparently from spontaneous combustion.

FOLLOW-UP FEATURE

In rewriting the following story, the writer certainly was safe in assuming the next probable consequence. Note how this story contains a tie-back and reads as a follow-up story, although no new information is included:

Original Story

After strangling her three baby daughters with a clothesline, Mrs. Gilda Heyda last night hanged herself in her home at 423 S. Reba street.

The bodies of the three girls, Roberta, 4, Ruth, 2, and Hazel, four months, were discovered by Mrs. Sylvia Priem, mother of Mrs. Heyda when she arrived about 8 P.M. for a visit. The children were lying on a bed with the body of their mother nearby.

The father and husband is Wilfred A. Heyda, unemployed carpenter, believed to be somewhere in the middle west on his way to Texas to seek employment.

Chief piece of evidence at the inquest which was to open this

Rewritten Story

Somewhere in the middle west today tragic news followed a father who is in pursuit of employment to support his wife and three small daughters.

The young husband and father, Wilfred Heyda, unemployed carpenter, was sought by authorities who were to inform him his wife, Mrs. Gilda Heyda, strangled their three baby girls and then committed suicide last night in their home at 423 S. Reba street.

As an inquest opened into the deaths this morning, police expressed the belief that Mrs. Heyda had become despondent from loneliness. She left a note to her mother, Mrs. Sylvia Priem, saying:

"It's pretty good! Wilfred has

Original Story

morning will be a note to her mother left by Mrs. Heyda, reading:

"It's pretty good! Wilfred has kids and can't even send them a card while on a trip."

Heyda left three weeks ago and was last heard from in Cincinnati from where he expected to go to Indianapolis, Chicago, Springfield, Ill., and St. Louis before heading for the southwest.

Police believe Mrs. Heyda's act resulted from loneliness because of her husband's absence and failure to write more frequently.

Rewritten Story

kids and can't even send them a card while on a trip."

The last word from the father, who left home three weeks ago, was from Cincinnati. From there he wrote he was on his way to Texas by way of Indianapolis, Springfield, Ill., Chicago, and St. Louis.

The slain children were Roberta, 4, Ruth, 2, and Hazel, four months. Their bodies were discovered by Mrs. Priem lying on a bed when she came to visit. Nearby was the body of Mrs. Heyda who apparently had used a clothesline to strangle her daughters and then take her own life.

COMPREHENSIVE LEAD

The rewrite man's knowledge of recent news events is valuable. In the following example, the writer was able to supply additional information out of his memory. If time permits and the story merits the trouble, the rewrite man may consult the newspaper's library and reference department to obtain information of this kind.

Original Story

Virgil Miner, 17, son of Mr. and Mrs. Charlton Miner, 386 Coates street, last night won first place in the annual state high school extemporaneous speaking contest. Speakers from 11 other high schools competed at Beardstown Municipal auditorium.

Representing the local high school, Virgil drew "Neutrality" as his subject. All contestants were given 30 minutes in which to prepare and each spoke ten minutes. Judges were . . .

Rewritten Story

For the second time in five years, the Milltown high school entry won first honors in the annual state high school extemporaneous speaking contest when Virgil Miner last night was declared the winner at Beardstown Municipal auditorium.

Three years ago, Leland West, now a student at Booster college, won the contest which was held at Lincoln. By an odd coincidence, both boys drew the same topic, "Neutrality."

Virgil is the 17-year-old son of Mr. and Mrs. Charlton Miner, 386 Coates street, and a senior at the high school.

Rules of the contest give each entrant 30 minutes in which to prepare to give a ten minute speech. Twelve students competed last night. Judges were . . .

COMBINED STORIES

The following example shows how one rewrite man combined two items into a single story.

Original Stories

Losing control of his automobile when a butterfly flew against his face, Edgar Lewis, 33, 1301 Sherman street, crashed into a fire hydrant about 6:30 P.M. yesterday at the northwest corner of Simpson and Michigan streets. He was taken to Municipal hospital with only minor bruises.

Sylvester Finger, 28, 1428 Grove street, is in Municipal hospital today with two fractured ribs as the result of an automobile accident about 7 P.M. yesterday. Finger's car struck a telephone pole at the southeast corner of Michigan and Central streets after he took his hands off the steering wheel to drive away ants which were crawling on his ankles.

Combined Story

Insects were responsible for two odd automobile mishaps in Milltown early last evening.

Ants crawling on the ankles of one driver led to a smashup which sent him to Municipal hospital with two fractured ribs. In the other accident, a butterfly flew against the driver's face and caused him to lose control of his machine.

The injured man is . . .

LOCAL ANGLE

The rewrite man who reads newspapers from other cities, official reports and documents, press agent material, and the like, should look for a local angle to feature, as:

Original Story

PEORIA NEWSPAPER

A state-wide membership drive of the Fraternal Order of Leopards will be planned here next Thusday at a meeting of representatives of the eight original chapters in as many cities.

Goal of the campaign will be 25 chapters and 2,000 members before July 1, according to J. S. Kienlen, Peoria, state commander, who called the meeting.

Cities to be represented at Thursday's meeting and delegates

Rewritten Story

FREEPORT
NEWSPAPER

Lowell Watson, 34 W. Bushnell place, commander of the local chapter of the Fraternal Order of Leopards, will attend an organization meeting next Thursday at Peoria to help plan a state-wide membership campaign for the order.

Representatives from all eight original Leopards chapters in the state will take part in the meeting called by J. S. Kienlen, Peoria, state commander.

Original Story

are: Wayne Lueck, Danville; R. S. Kirschten, Cairo; Lowell Watson, Freeport; S. O. McNeil, Aurora; Silas Layman, Springfield; Richard Yates, Elgin; O. L. Moss, Bloomington; and Mr. Kienlen.

Rewritten Story

Objectives of the proposed campaign are a membership of 2,000 and 25 Illinois chapters. To attend Thursday's meeting, in addition to Watson and Kienlen, are . . .

10

Giving It Substance

---

i. Completing the Account

    1. Factual Background
    2. Eyewitness Accounts
    3. Sidebars
    4. Localization
    5. "The Other Side"

ii. Interpretations

    1. Causes and Motives
    2. Significance
    3. Analysis
    4. Comparisons
    5. Forecasts

iii. Providing Perspective

    1. Résumés
    2. Surveys
    3. Investigations
    4. Stunts
    5. Situations and Trends

THE CASE FOR INTERPRETATION

Foremost among those who advocated and campaigned for interpretation is Lester Markel, Sunday editor of the New York *Times*. The following extract from his article, "The Case for Interpretation," in the April 1, 1953, *Bulletin* of the A.S.N.E., is typical of his numerous comments on the subject:

Interpretation, as I see it, is the deeper sense of the news. It places a particular event in the larger flow of events. It is the color, the atmosphere, the human element that give meaning to a fact. It is, in short, setting, sequence, and, above all, significance.

There is a vast difference between interpretation and opinion. And the distinction is of the utmost importance. Three elements, not two, are involved in this debate: first, news; second, interpretation; third, opinion. To take a primitive example:

To say that Senator McThing is investigating the teaching of Patagonian in the schools is news.

To explain why Senator McThing is carrying on this investigation is interpretation.

To remark that Senator McThing should be ashamed of himself is opinion.

Interpretation is an objective judgment based on background knowledge of a situation, appraisal of an event. Editorial judgment, on the other hand, is a subjective judgment; it may include an appraisal of the facts but there is an additional and distinctive element, namely, emotional impact.

Opinion should be confined, almost religiously, to the editorial page; interpretation is an essential part of the news. This is vital and it cannot have too much emphasis.

I see no difference between "interpretation" and "background." Of course, part of interpretation may be the setting out of some antecedent facts — and this many editors consider "background" as distinguished from "interpretation." But interpretation is much more than shirttail material; it is in addition to the presentation of the pertinent facts, present and past, an effort to assay the meaning of those facts.

Experienced reporters who develop specialties often become recognized experts. They write not only authoritative newspaper articles but magazine pieces and books as well. Their vast amount of background knowledge enables them to give meaning to current happenings. More than that, they become critics in their fields and can warn and forecast and even give advice to policy leaders, including heads of state. They may have a powerful effect upon public opinion.

Later journalistic success is determined by early experience. Nobody, that is, is catapulted into a top position of prestige and influence without having served a long apprenticeship during which he learned correct work habits and attitudes. Local reporting provides the first and best opportunity for the development of such essential traits as thoroughness, accuracy, resourcefulness and the like. The aspirant for future fame and fortune as an interpretative reporter and writer begins by becoming a superior gatherer of so-called "straight" news which he writes objectively. He "gets around" more than his competitors and digs deeper in his fact-finding. In other words, he does whatever is required and then a bit more, the key to success in most any area of endeavor.

The reporter who deals first-hand with the events which make news lays the foundation for a future as interpreter as well as chronicler of current affairs by conditioning himself to inquire regarding each assignment:

1. What happened? That is, what *really* happened — the complete story, not just the end results of a series of incidents.
2. Why (or how) did it happen? That is, what is the explanation?
3. What does it mean? That is, how interpret it?
4. What next? In the light of today's news, what may be expected to happen tomorrow?
5. What's beneath the surface? What are the trends, ideologies, situations, etc., of which one should be aware so that an overt news incident will "make sense"?

COMPLETING THE ACCOUNT

FACTUAL BACKGROUND

When an event of major significance occurs, because of the mass of detailed information involved and from lack of time and space, first news stories may be in the straight news-writing tradition, leaving the interpretation for another edition or day. If, however, the reporter has an adequate knowledge and understanding of preceding events related to the one at hand, even his first story, prepared in haste, will have greater substance.

If there are both a morning and an afternoon newspaper, any news story inevitably "breaks" to the comparative advantage of one over the other. The publication with the earlier deadline will be able to print the story first, but the other paper should be able to prepare a more detailed account. For instance, the Peoria (Illinois) *Journal-Star*, a morning newspaper, once reported that an attempt by an alderman to have a painting contract awarded to the second lowest bidder was defeated when the mayor cast the deciding vote. The Peoria *Transcript*, that afternoon, with more time, cast new light on the incident by revealing that the alderman and contractor were brothers-in-law, that the alderman was attending his first meeting following election and that the mayor's vote brought about a tie, not a majority.

The knowledgeable reporter will recall the history of a bill or ordinance and of previous attempts to promote similar legislation. He knows whether lawmakers are behaving consistently, the identity of individuals and groups in support or opposition, and other facts of the same sort which enable readers to come to a better understanding of the immediate occurrence.

EYEWITNESS ACCOUNTS

To supplement the formal stories, it is common practice to ask victims of disasters (train wrecks, floods, fires, etc.) to relate their personal experiences. Often, such accounts are ghost written or are printed under the by-lines of the principals "as told to" some staff writer. Reporters themselves write eyewitness accounts of important scenes they have witnessed. Such stories are more informal than straight news accounts and usually provide graphic word pictures of what happened.

Photography, including motion pictures, has not yet made written description obsolete, nor is it likely to do so for some time, if for no other reason than that cameramen are not always present at news events about which it is necessary to answer, "What did it look like?" in order to present a complete account. Before he can describe well, a reporter must be able to observe. Careful observation means noting features which escape the untrained spectator. A bizarre vocabulary containing innumerable adjectives is not essential. The reader, in fact, will "see" best what the writer is describing if the words are familiar; ambiguous qualitative adjectives such as "handsome," "delicate," etc., are omitted and figures of speech, historical and literary allusions, and other rhetorical devices used are easily understood.

In selecting anecdotes to relate and persons to describe, caution must be exercised so that they are either important in their own right or typical of a general situation. Otherwise a distorted impression can be created. A typical situation in which this might occur is a mine cave-in or flood or similar disaster. At the scene, probably accompanying rescue workers, the reporter is attempting to describe the reaction of victims and others so the reader can get the "feel" of the story. He must realize that one sobbing woman does not constitute an hysterical mob. The reader must be able to depend upon the integrity of the reporter.

That the best-intentioned newsgatherers will differ in their observations and impressions is inevitable. Carl Lindstrom, who quit the executive editorship of the Hartford (Connecticut) *Times*, after a quarter-century, and wrote *The Fading American Newspaper*, and others point up the danger of permitting reporters to attempt to be interpretative. They cite the example of widespread differences in reports of a press conference with Dr. Otto John after he fled from West to East Germany in 1954. According to the Associated Press:

> He spoke nervously at first. Then he got over his first mild stage fright and was completely at ease. Pink-cheeked, he was the picture of German health. His low modulated voice was pleasing to hear, regardless of how one would react to the sentiments involved. He made many wisecracks that brought laughter, wisecracks appreciated only in his native German tongue which lost much of their salt in translation. Not all of the laughs came from the Communist press either.

What the United Press reporter saw was as follows:

> His press conference statement today was recited grimly and hurriedly, much in the manner of confessions made by the victims of numerous Red Purge trials.
>
> He gave the tell-tale evidence of Communist brainwashing tactics: He was wooden-faced and nervous at the conference. He never smiled, although some of his comments brought laughter from newsmen.

An International News Service writer in Washington, using material purported to be supplied by Allied counter-intelligence sources, wrote:

> These sources are convinced that, through use of a highly developed combination of hypnosis and hypodermic needles, Dr. John became a virtual "zombie" without a will of his own, capable of acting and speaking only at the dictates of his Communist masters.

Over the National Broadcasting company airways, Robert McCormick commented as follows:

John handled himself with self-confidence and assurance. He definitely showed no signs of being drugged, beaten or tortured and, in fact, seemed quite happy. If anything, he looked more content than he looked in Bonn.

It is impossible to argue with the importance of attempting to describe Dr. John's attitude after his sensational act. No deadpan recording of whatever words he spoke would have sufficed to give readers a hint of the motives for his act. Equally obvious is the fact that at least one (which?) of those who attended the press conference was a thoroughly incompetent reporter. The example does not disprove the value or necessity of interpretative reporting. Rather, it provides argument for the fact that journalists, whether they report and write objectively or interpretatively, must be highly ethical.

SIDEBARS

Whenever an important story occurs, reporters often use sidebars to "round out" the complete account. A sidebar deals with phases of a story as a whole which conceivably could be included in the main account but not without either lengthening it too much or sacrificing some details. When an office building in Chicago's Loop exploded, among the anecdotal sidebars were the following: (1) 105,000 feet of new glass being rushed to city to replace show-window glass broken, (2) analysis of city ordinances covering gas leakage which allegedly caused the blast, (3) description of army of glaziers at work in area, (4) police pass system to admit workers employed in area, (5) refusal of pass to a window washer, obviously because there were no windows left to wash, (6) symposium of eyewitness accounts, (7) narrow escape of nearby elevated tower operator, (8) instructions on how to enter area, (9) Red Cross activities, (10) list of buildings whose windows were blown out.

In such sidebars, the reader finds the answers to questions which naturally occur to him while reading the main story. A common rhetorical device is to pose the question presumably in the reader's mind and then supply the information necessary for formation of an answer.

When the news relates to a scheduled event, several reporters may be assigned to cover different "angles." A woman reporter, for instance, may stay close to the wife of a visiting celebrity; at the same time, another reporter may concentrate his attention on the crowd, noting its size and nature, ever watchful for unusual personalities and incidents. Still another may observe the behavior of the police, marshals, secret-service men and the like, or he may interview members of the party of either the guest or the host or both. Someone else, who might not even need to be present, can compare the occasion with similar ones in the past, here and/or elsewhere. Some of the information obtained by members of a reportorial team may be used by whoever writes the main story of the event but each probably will have enough left for a separate piece.

LOCALIZATION

The effects of some news events are felt at considerable distances. Without mention of some of the repercussions, the original story is not complete. For instance, whenever the President of the United States or some other leader of government makes an important announcement, there are reverberations on Capitol Hill, where congressional leaders abandon or alter old tactics or institute new ones. The stock market may be influenced by mere rumor. A Supreme Court decision may affect governmental practices and legal procedures in the states and cities.

In all such and similar cases, the reader wants to know, "How will this affect me?" That is the perspective from which the interpretative reporter should approach his task. In that spirit, the Evanston (Illinois) *Review* figured out the average cost for every man, woman, and child in Illinois of a newly announced federal budget. Similarly, when the United States Supreme Court upheld the blue laws of some eastern states, the United Press International bureau in Topeka compiled a list of laws still on the books in Kansas regulating behavior on the Sabbath. The Baltimore *Sun* used a similar story to explain how a Supreme Court decision regarding motion-picture censorship would affect Baltimore and Maryland.

Many a newspaper has investigated to determine how long the local supply of coal or steel or some other commodity would last in the event a strike continued affecting the faraway source of supply. How a new federal or state law will affect the community specifically, probably always should be explained by the public-spirited local press.

"THE OTHER SIDE"

Deadpan reporting of the contents of a report, speech or the like, even when the source is reputable, may be misleading in that it does not give readers the "whole" or "essential" truth. When the news source is irresponsible, grave disservice may be done the reading public. It certainly is newsworthy when someone important in public life attacks another person. Such news often cannot be ignored. It can, however, be put in better perspective if there is simultaneous opportunity for reply by the otherwise injured party. Readers want to know how those most affected by any news event react to it. Unless their curiosity is satisfied, the account is incomplete.

How "real objectivity" was attained by an interpretative reporter for the Memphis *Press-Scimitar* who merely filled in background and, without drawing conclusions, gave readers additional information by which to judge a current news story, was related by the editors of the April 1950 *Nieman Reports* special issue. The incident occurred during the campaign of B. Carroll Reece, Republican candidate for United States senator from Tennessee.

In a Memphis speech, Reece lambasted the "motley crowd" of Democrats in charge of the federal government for speaking "with such a variety of accents, all of them un-American, that they sound like the tongues of Babel." Continued Reece:

> These mixed tongues are chanting many themes that are utterly offensive to our American instincts. None is more offensive than their chant that "States' Rights might give way to human rights." Under this sweet-sounding slogan is a snake in the grass as vicious as any reptile we have ever encountered. Herein lies the efforts of men who are either recent immigrants to our shore or whose ideas of government are immigrant to our shore — to move in on our system of States' Rights for the kill. . . . We of the South shall throw the pretty phrases back in their teeth. We say to them that the South has always preserved human rights. . . .

Straight-laced reporting of this speech, the Nieman writers declared, would have appeared under some such headline as, "ALIENS CONTROL U.S. GOVERNMENT, WARNS REECE." However, the Memphis reporter included in his interpretative article the fact that in an earlier speech in Buffalo (New York) Reece said:

> This element [the Southern Democrats] which of course stemmed from the slave-holding oligarchy which once plunged this nation into a bloody war to preserve the institution of slavery, is the group which still maintains itself in power in a large section of this country by the practice of outrageous racial discrimination, preventing millions of American citizens from exercising the right to vote. It is the element of the party which inaugurated Jim Crow laws; the element which had pushed discrimination into the North. . . .

The interpretative article was headed, "REECE VERSUS REECE."

Many American editors came to wish they had accorded the late Senator Joseph McCarthy of Wisconsin similar treatment.

There are, of course, a pro and a con regarding every public issue. The ethical newspaper considers itself a public forum for the airing of diverse opinions. The obligation, however, is not just to the person who wishes to express himself, but primarily to readers so that they can be fully informed. When a new curfew law for adolescents is under consideration, for instance, the paper should seek out persons who are in positions to have intelligent opinions on the subject. This is not the inquiring-reporter technique which often results in obtaining uninformed and unrepresentative viewpoints. Rather, it is a search for the best opinion available.

An example of how an experienced reporter can supply objective facts to make an important news story interpretative in spirit is provided by John W. Kole of the Milwaukee *Journal*. Its author does not consider it exceptional. "Instead," he writes, "it is what we strive for each day in the presentation of public affairs." Kole further explains: "We feel that the problems of local government, like those of our national government, become more complex each year. Interpretation is absolutely necessary to keep readers informed. In my mind, interpretative reporting of public affairs is simply the use of facts and the opinions of informed people to make a point."

The story, together with marginal notes by Kole, follows:

Switching more than three million dollars in street and sewer construction from cash to bond financing, the Milwaukee common council Thursday afternoon adopted a record city and school budget for 1960 of $142,554,153.

The budget, combined with the county budget, will require a tax of $58.20 per $1,000 of assessed valuation, which will mean a $35 higher tax bill for a typical Milwaukee home owner.

Obviously, huge financial figures mean little to a reader unless he knows what it will cost him. Thus, the $35 figure for the typical home owner.

The council reversed its finance committee by approving five controversial amendments. The actions so angered Ald. John H. Budzien, committee vice chairman, that he resigned from the committee immediately after the wild three-hour meeting.

Mayor Zeidler said Friday he was "seriously considering" a veto of some of the council budget actions, especially the one switching the cash items to bonds.

"I am also disturbed by the impression left by the council that a group can get something out of line if it has a special pleader," Zeidler said.

He said he would confer with finance committee members and other city officials Friday afternoon before making his decision.

The $58.20 tax rate actually is lower than the $59.37 rate for 1959 purposes, but is based on 10% higher property assessments. Based on last year's assessments, the 1960 rate would be $64.02.

With an obvious eye toward next spring's election, aldermen cut the $50.08 combined rate proposed by the finance committee by $1.88, a move which will save a typical home owner $14.50 in 1960.

But because the cuts were made by slashing $3,250,000 from the cash program for streets and sewers and authorizing instead $4,250,000 for these items through bond financing, the typical home owner eventually will pay far more than the $14.50.

In contrast, county supervisors transferred more than three million dollars from the bond to the cash program during their budget hearings and recent budget adoption. This move will reduce their debt service costs in future years.

The city's budget examining committee had recommended the cash financing as a start in reversing a 10 year program of bond financing which has put the city more than 120 million dollars in debt. The committee was overruled by a 15 to 5 vote.

A disconcerting factor to some city officials was the lobbying success of two employe groups in getting special wage raises for city workers who the city personnel director said were no more deserving than others.

In four amendments, the council:

By a 17 to 3 vote, authorized a fourth week of vacation for 778 city workers with 25 years or more of service.

The aldermen were particularly careful to keep the tax rate down by cutting the cash program and increasing the bonds. We felt the reader should be told that this move would cost him more in the long run.

By a 19 to 1 vote, gave extra $25 a month pay increases to about 100 civil engineers who are college graduates and registered by special examinations.

By a 12 to 8 vote, gave extra $5 a month wage boosts to most of 1,084 workers in pay range 5, which includes ash collectors, forestry workers, janitors and others.

By an 11 to 9 vote, eliminated the position of the mayor's urban renewal coordinator, a job held recently by Sol Ackerman, now in private business.

The extra wage increases were on top of a 4% across the board boost given to all general city employes in the budget.

"The two extra wage increases amounted to succumbing to special pressure groups," Zeidler commented. "The actions create inequities which will create many problems in the near future."

[*Then followed 11 paragraphs mostly comparing the new with old budgets and with other details.*]

Only Budzien, Mortier and Richard B. Nowakowski voted against the fourth week of vacation after 25 years, an amendment proposed by Bernard B. Kroenke.

But Meyers pointed out that the finance committee had granted a 4% instead of a 3½% increase while deciding to eliminate the fourth week proposal. Most of this new fringe benefit will be absorbed by various departments. The estimated additional cost for 1960 is $25,000.

Robert C. Garnier, city personnel director, said that although the county board granted a fourth week after 20 years of service, it was not general practice in either industry or government service.

Extra wage increases were won by disturbing lobbying tactics. We used a statement by Mayor Zeidler (Milwaukee's mayor does not preside at council meetings; the executive branch is entirely separate) to bring this out.

A fourth week of vacation was tossed in — contrary to the practice in most of private industry and despite the fact that city employes get twice as many holidays as most other workers.

General city employes next year will get 14½ paid holidays. Added to four weeks vacation, those with 25 years or more of service in effect will get one-half day short of seven weeks vacation, plus sick leave benefits. Firemen and policemen get less than half the holidays of general city employes.

The most curious action was the one granting most of the 1,084 workers in pay range 5 an extra $5 a month raise. This amendment also was sponsored by Kroenke.

Several hundred of the pay range 5 employes are represented by John C. Zinos, executive director of district council 48 of the American Federation of State, County and Municipal Employes.

Zinos and two of his staff members were busy buttonholing aldermen in the council chambers right up to the start of the meeting.

Typical of the argument in favor of the amendment was that of Ald. Clarence A. Heiden, who pleaded with his colleagues to "give the poor little scrubwoman a break."

(Actually, city scrubwomen will not benefit from the amendment because they are in a lower pay range.)

[Then followed 4 paragraphs of direct quotations on the amendment.]

The $25 extra a month for graduate registered civil engineers was boomed by Atty. John J. Fleming, a former alderman and a leading city hall lobbyist. He represented the Association of Graduate and Registered Engineers.

The finance committee last June committed itself to special adjustments for engineers, but found as the wage hearings progressed

Some more lobbying for pay raises. We point out that the lobbyists were at work right in the council chambers. And a parenthetical insert is used to show up an alderman who pleads, "Give the poor little scrubwoman a break."

An individual lobbying effort by an attorney who has powerful friends in the council, plus a comment by the city personnel director that the civil engineers were no more deserving of an extra pay increase than other groups.

that all of the higher income city ranges needed special attention.

But a motion to give extra raises in the higher brackets was defeated in committee, with only Mortier supporting it.

The result of Thursday's action, Garnier said, would be to give extra raises to 100 persons who deserved them no more than several hundred other persons in higher ranges.

"In fact, there are several other groups that need special attention far more than the civil engineers," Garnier said.

[*Then followed 5 paragraphs to explain what the amendment would cost and to give a few additional details.*]

The switch from cash to bonds was sponsored by Schmit, Heiden, Valentine V. Kujawa and Ralph F. Kelly, all of whom represent outlying wards where constituents pay comparatively high tax bills because they have newer houses.

Most of the improvements financed by the street and sewer bonds will be in those four wards.

All finance committee members except Mrs. Vel R. Phillips voted against the amendment. They were joined only by Hass.

A couple of paragraphs showing that the force behind switching cash improvements to bonds was especially concerned about property taxes, yet represented wards which get most of the improvements.

INTERPRETATIONS

It decidedly is not true that "what you don't know won't hurt you." On the contrary, in a democracy it is essential that everyone have access to as many facts as possible so that he can form proper judgments and influence public affairs. Increasingly since the end of World War II, journalistic organizations have been alarmed at the extent to which secrecy *de facto* and *de jure* has led to distortions in the news. Sometimes it has taken days, weeks, months or longer to ascertain the truth regarding some major political decision or action. By then it may be too late to undo considerable harm.

At a recent meeting of the A.P.M.E., the veteran New York *Times* political writer, James B. Reston, declared:

> The whole future of reporting depends on telling intelligently what is going on in the world. The world is getting more complicated every year.
> Explanatory writing is the field in which we can excel. You cannot merely report the literal truth. You have to explain it.
> But you have to pay a price for explanatory writing. You pay first in the length of stories. You can't say stories should be brief and explanatory too.
> Explanatory writing is a matter of judgment. The judgment may be wrong from time to time. You have to give the interpretive writer leeway. You also have to pay in more time. If a man is tired by a day of work, he won't be in the mood to write an analytical piece late in the evening.
> The explanatory writer is the lens through which you see what is not obvious. He reads the "fine print" for you.

At the same session John Hightower, AP diplomatic writer, said:

> We have a terrific responsiblity in writing the essential truth. I think that the AP must always stick to certain fundamentals. Our basic job is to tell people what happens. But there has been an increasing feeling that isn't all.

CAUSES AND MOTIVES

The probing reporter keeps on asking "why?" as he seeks the "news behind the news." He knows that official proclamations and carefully prepared press releases may conceal causes and motives which preceded the spot or "end result" news of the moment. So he digs "beneath the surface."

Sometimes it is possible to conjecture. For instance, if a mayor and corporation counsel have disagreed frequently in public, the reasons for the latter's impending resignation would seem to be obvious. Too often, however, newspaper columnists and others, acting on rumors and tips from "persons close to" or "usually reliable sources," may be wrong. If, for instance, the mayor and corporation counsel announce after a conference that they have settled their differences and, in fact, now "see eye to eye," only a naïve journalist would accept the announcement on its face value. To obtain the "real lowdown," however, may be difficult or impossible. Perhaps the counsel threatened to make a public statement which would be embarrassing to the mayor. Perhaps he agreed to "go along" on some current matter in exchange for a promise of political support at some future date. Perhaps the mayor indicated he would withdraw some patronage from the counsel's followers. The possibilities are many and the responsible journalist must be careful not to give currency to gossip, rumor and surmise.

Once a large company with plants in several cities announced it intended to close its factory in City A and shift operations to City B. The announcement included a strong statement of regret by management, praise for City A and the like but explained that it had become necessary to retrench, operate closer to its supply of raw materials and avoid the necessity of investing in costly new machinery. This sounded reasonable but an experienced reporter "smelled a rat" and started snooping. Before long he learned that months earlier the company had negotiated a contract with a union local in City B at a wage rate much lower than that which prevailed in City A. The City B union accepted the deal as it would mean jobs for several thousand unemployed members. Further probing revealed that this act was considered by City A unionists to be a "sell-out" and was part of the campaign of a certain national labor leader to increase his strength. The City B union consisted mainly of his followers whereas those in City A belonged to a rival faction within the national organization. Facts such as these are necessary for a proper understanding of the news. The free press has been called a watchdog on government. It can perform no more worthwhile function than to scrutinize carefully everything which affects the public interest.

SIGNIFICANCE

Referring a proposal to a committee may mean either that its enactment into law is being accelerated or that it is being killed. The perspicacious newsgatherer should know which and should so inform his readers. The same for all other acts of all branches of government. Readers are able to understand the significance of parliamentary and diplomatic maneuvering, but it must be pointed out to them by someone who keeps close check.

When a convicted person is sentenced to a long term of imprisonment, it is customary to point out the minimum time that he would have to serve before being eligible for release on parole. When a deadline passes for filing or withdrawing a petition, it should be pointed out what thereby becomes possible or impossible. If a diplomat attends one function and boycotts another, there may or may not be significant repercussions. In some cases, in other words, it is not difficult to explain consequences objectively. In others, a certain amount of guesswork may be necessary, in which case the rule of caution must be invoked.

ANALYSIS

Long and/or complicated documents, including ordinances and statutes, must be analyzed so that they can be understood. This often is merely a job of tedious objective reporting to explain what now is forbidden, allowed or required and who will be affected in what way. Often the analyst will discover ramifications and repercussions which escaped even the lawmakers.

Speeches by important persons are analyzed almost immediately by journalists and later by scholars. What the speaker emphasizes, the number of times he mentions a particular matter, and what he omits are noted. Qualitative judgment enters into evaluating the importance of gestures, facial expressions, tone of voice, pauses in delivery and the like and also in estimating the reaction of a visible audience. It is not difficult to note the amount and duration of applause, of course, but the intangibles are so many that great restraint is needed by the reporter. The audience, for instance, may be easily identifiable as partisan to begin with. Nevertheless, how it reacts is part of the complete coverage.

Often explanation is needed for proper analysis. This is often true of crime records. Changes in the frequency of certain types of offenses may be seasonal. The population complexion of areas may change during a reporting period. Police departments have been known to alter their methods of reporting, even with the intention of making the results seem better than they should. An example would be to list automobiles as missing instead of stolen.

COMPARISONS

As with crime statistics, so with the budgets of public and private bodies, achievements of athletes, votes received by candidates and numerous other matters, the reader wants to know how the present compares with the past. Is something more or less, higher or lower, better or worse? Answers to such questions must be given with all possible influencing factors considered so as not to be deceptive. It would, for instance, be misleading to cite an expenditure as twice that for a comparable item some time in the past without taking into consideration changes in the value of the dollar, population increases, changing needs and demands and so forth.

Political party platforms can be compared with each other and with those of previous years. Faced with a vexatious local problem, public officials and newspapers may send representatives to other communities to study what steps were taken there by way of solution. Whenever a disaster of importance occurs, it is common journalistic practice to prepare sidebars, often in the form of charts or tabulations, to show how the immediate catastrophe compares in intensity with others of the past.

Old-timers are prone to draw historical parallels, to feel that some contemporary event is "just like" one they recall from years before; they feel they have "lived through this before," possibly when they observe a widespread practice which they consider undersirable, as excessive installment buying, stock market speculation, real estate booms and the like. There is no gainsaying the fact that history teaches many valuable lessons, but what may seem to be history repeating itself may not be that at all. Numerous cities previously tried and abandoned services which today are orthodox, as parking meters, traffic signals, one-way streets and off-street parking, to mention only examples in one area. Increasing populations and automobile ownership created new conditions for which new remedies no longer were premature.

Reform movements come and go in many communities. One reason for their failure to last often is the tendency of many supporters to become lackadaisical after the immediate first objective has been attained. History does prove that eternal vigilance is a prerequisite for a properly functioning democracy.

FORECASTS

Giving a news story a "tomorrow" angle often is a form of interpretation. Based on his analysis of an action by the city council, a reporter can predict new employment, building, police activities and the like. He can see "trouble ahead" for certain groups as the result of a sweeping court decision and business advantages to others. A drastic price cut by one retail establishment usually results in a price "war" among competitors. Tightening child labor laws may have the immediate effect of throwing a certain number of miners out of work.

When it comes to predicting beyond the immediate effect, as that the unemployed juveniles will become delinquent, the reporter may be merely speculating. He should draw on expert opinion and historical example and still be slow about making deductions. The death of a prominent figure may or may not clear the way toward a reconciliation between disputing factions, lead to a struggle for succession to a position of power or destroy the chances for achieving a certain goal. The expert can point out the possibilities but he should not forget that some pundits have lost the confidence of their audiences by excessive smugness which the future exposed as such.

PROVIDING PERSPECTIVE

News does not consist only in specific incidents which can be written up with clearcut inclusion of all of the five *w's*. Ideas are news. So are ideologies, trends of thought, psychological situations and similar "intangibles." It is not highbrow to believe that it would be a better world if more newspaper readers were aware of social, political, economic and other "stresses and strains" which often must be written about without definite news pegs. The "think piece" is a comparatively old journalistic device, but its use constantly is being broadened to include areas previously reserved for research scholars.

As Robert E. Garst, assistant managing editor of the New York *Times*, wrote in the *Nieman Reports:*

> Too much of past reporting has dealt only with the surface facts — the spot news — and too rarely has dug into the reasons for them.
>
> A race riot, a prison outbreak, a bad slum condition — even a murder — has a social background, deeply rooted perhaps in the customs, traditions, and economic conditions of a region or community; but it is there and discoverable. It's the newspaper's job, it seems to me, to discover it. Only with that knowledge can a remedy be found for many of the ills that affect us.

RÉSUMÉS

News weeklies, monthly digest magazines and weekly newspaper news reviews got their start during the depression years and appealed to persons in all walks of life who sought understanding in the midst of confusion. They have continued as an adjunct to quick spot-news reporting to provide recapitulations or résumés of series of fast-happening events. Few occurrences are treated as isolated happenings but as related to other events preceding and following them.

In addition to weekly news reviews, newspapers use "wrap-up" articles on running stories such as legislative assemblies, court trials, political campaigns and the like. In such stories, the expert reporter treats the events of a number of days, usually a week, as constituting material for a single story. Readers' memories are refreshed and relationships are pointed out. Often a condensed chronological recapitulation of the news is sufficient. In other cases, interpretation is added. This week, the observant reviewer may write, a certain objective came closer to realization because of this or that train of events. Defense strategy, another may explain, became clearer as cross-examination of prosecution witnesses continued in a court trial. A public official took two steps forward and one backward under observation by a knowledgeable journalist. And so on, all in the attempt to round up the events of a period into a comprehensive single story with proper perspective.

At the end of any session of the state legislature, a résumé of its activities is a journalistic must. Annual or semi-annual appraisals of the handling of his official acts by a public official are in the same category. The news reviewer often takes "a second look" at the cumulative record about each part of which he previously has composed separate accounts.

SURVEYS

When similar news occurs in a number of places, a journalistic medium may conduct a survey to find out what the over-all situation happens to be. Perhaps attempts to enact similar legislation were made in a number of states, in which case a compilation of the results is significant. Let disaster of any kind occur in one place and a follow-up survey reveals how widespread are conditions believed to have been its cause.

Newspapers have conducted surveys to determine the death rates on transcontinental highways, the outcomes of referenda on school bond issues, the use of prison labor on private projects, the attitude of condemned prisoners toward capital punishment, the extent of racial and religious discrimination in housing, schooling and job opportunities, the increase in the ownership of yachts, and on many and many other matters. Some of the material, though not quite so up-to-the-minute, might have been obtained from public and private research agencies.

In drawing conclusions from any kind of data, the press must avoid the error which professional researchers and pollsters also must avoid, that of inadequacy or lack of representativeness of the sample. It is incorrect to write, "Public opinion today here is that or that" unless one has exhaustively questioned persons in all walks of life, something it is rarely possible for a newspaperman to do. Even an impressive group of interviewees within a given area may not be typical. There is no field in which unanimity exists among experts. Quoting leaders is good journalism but minorities also should be contacted and exaggeration always avoided.

INVESTIGATIONS

Any newspaper with standing in its community is constantly being importuned to "look into" this or that, which usually means to uncover facts which it allegedly is in the public interest be known but which someone is attempting to conceal. The annals of American journalism are replete with examples of successful ventures of this sort. Many of them, in fact, have resulted in Pulitzer or other prizes for community service.

Annoying and time consuming as it may become to observe the rule, it is unsafe to ignore tipsters, no matter how unreliable or "crackpot" they may seem to be. Maybe the policeman whose neighbor cannot understand how he is able to afford an expensive car, *did* inherit a large sum of money. On the other hand, his affluence may be the clue to scandal involving others as well as himself.

No special attributes are required of the investigative reporter except a sharp inquisitive mind and familiarity with the area of his investigation. The investigative reporter seldom plays detective in the sense of shadowing persons. Rather, his quest more often takes him to public records where he uncovers information about which to query interviewees. In print, these facts usually speak for themselves. This was true as regards the assignment given Edward R. Cony, *Wall Street Journal* news editor, for which he was awarded the Pultizer prize for reporting of national affairs. As the paper summarized it:

> In his prize-winning story, Mr. Cony disclosed that Carrol Shanks, then president of Prudential Insurance Co. of America, was in position to make a substantial saving in his income taxes as a result of a personal transaction with Georgia-Pacific. At the time, Mr. Shanks was a director of Georgia-Pacific, which had received over $50 million of loans from Prudential over a five-year period.
>
> The article told how Mr. Shanks had purchased 13,000 acres of Oregon timberland and then immediately sold it to Georgia-Pacific for the same price he paid for it, plus costs of financing the transaction. Mr. Shanks financed the purchase with a $3.9 million bank loan. Since interest on this loan would be tax deductible, it was estimated that Mr. Shanks might save as much as $400,000 on his tax bill over the five-year life of the loan.
>
> Mr. Shanks, while maintaining there was nothing unethical about the transaction, subsequently disposed of his interest in the financing and resigned from Prudential, citing as a reason "my highly publicized personal transaction" with Georgia-Pacific.
>
> The story also revealed the personal dealings which Owen Cheatham, chairman, and John Brandis, senior vice president, of Georgia-Pacific, had had with the company.
>
> Shortly after the story appeared, Georgia-Pacific announced it had acquired Plywood Products Corp., a plywood concern which had been owned principally by Mr. Brandis, trusts settled by him, and members of his family. The Wall Street Journal story had detailed Plywood Products' extensive business dealings with Georgia-Pacific. Georgia-Pacific is currently facing a stockholder suit which charges, among other things, that when Georgia-Pacific acquired Plywood Products it paid Mr. Brandis and his associates a price excessive "by at least $2 million."
>
> Mr. Cony, in addition to interviewing Mr. Shanks in New Jersey and Georgia-Pacific officials in Oregon, spent many hours probing records in New York and numerous county seats in Oregon. Ray Schrick, manager of The Wall Street Journal's Portland bureau, aided Mr. Cony with research and reporting on the Oregon phase of the story.

Not all journalist investigations result in exposes or crusades. Sometimes exactly the opposite occurs and the public interest is served by revealing that rumors and charges are groundless. To avoid merely white-

washing, however, the reporter must not be so naive as to accept uncritically whatever he may be told by interested parties. He must observe
first-hand and check conflicting statements of fact and opinion against
each other. At the same time, he must also avoid a chip-on-the-shoulder
attitude so as not to give anyone the impression that he is out to "get"
him regardless of the truth.

All of which just adds up to the advice: be thorough, be open-minded,
be fair. There is no better advice which can be given to a newsgatherer
whatever the assignment.

STUNTS

Often the best, perhaps the only way to investigate a situation
is from the inside. Edgar May of the Buffalo *Evening News* won a Pulitzer
prize for his series of articles after working for three months as a case-
worker for the Erie County Department of Social Welfare. Ted Smart
of the Chicago *Daily News* won several citations for his exposé of conditions in the Chicago Bridewell to which he got himself committed as
a common drunk. Several official investigations resulted after Edward
Williams, Milwaukee *Journal* reporter, spent ten days in the House of
Correction posing as a vagrant.

Other reporters have obtained employment as guards or attendants
in prisons, mental hospitals and other public institutions. The existence
of illegal gambling has been exposed by investigative reporters who were
supplied with money and told to find bookmakers with whom to place
bets. Because of the growing complaint by teachers that students are
unruly, reporters with the proper credentials have obtained teaching positions or have acted as substitutes in the classroom to observe first-hand.

The opportunities for such "undercover" journalism are boundless.
Usually, some properly qualified official, as a judge or social worker, is
"in" on the stunt, often to legalize it and, in any case, to soften adverse
criticisms of entrapment or other unethical conduct. Certainly the responsibility is great not to yield to the temptation to merely "make a
case" in the interest of a sensational story. It is easy to find that for which
one earnestly is looking. The reporter and newspaper are vulnerable unless
the highest principles of ethical journalism are observed.

SITUATIONS AND TRENDS

Getting his idea from an article on the subject in a national
magazine, a city editor assigned a reporter to "find out how much moon-
lighting there is in this community." Other editors have sought the answers to such questions as, "What do we do for the mentally retarded

in our town?" "What about juvenile delinquency among girls?" "Are there any independent grocers left?" "What's happening to our wild life?" and many others.

Often such assignments result in feature articles concerning little-known or off-the-beaten-path persons or groups. In other cases, there may be forthcoming broader expositions of current situations to which the journalistic limelight is applied. The net result is a better acquaintance with all aspects of the life of the community and possibly an arousal of civic interest in improvement where needed.

No reporter should start on an assignment of this sort without adequate preparation which should include, not merely examination of the publication's own clipping files but also the reading of books, magazine articles and other material to acquaint himself with the aspects of the situation which he should bear in mind during his fact-finding. When the reporter encounters someone with views contrary to those which he believes to be orthodox, he should avoid altercation. Instead, he should tactfully request his news source to comment on the viewpoint of "the other side" as he understands it.

Fortified with information from a number of other places, the perceptive reporter may conclude that what he is studying is not just a local phenomenon but part of a widespread trend. Farmers on the fringes of suburban areas, for instance, may be keeping land out of cultivation in expectation of selling their property to urban developers. "Blockbusting" to circumvent racial prejudice by real-estate interests, sit-in demonstrations, sympathetic picketing, panty raids by college boys, fads in games, dress, music, and the like may be national or international in extent. The locally written feature can stress home-town manifestations but would be inadequate if it did not mention the broader aspects.

Ora Spaid did a colossally successful job for the Louisville *Courier-Journal* when he investigated post-basketball game fights between rival gangs of high school boys. The following extracts, approximately the middle-third of the first of three articles, indicate how Spaid tackled the assignment, writing as the careful reporter and specialist-expert that he is, having been a social worker before he turned to journalism:

Athletics

One of those not-new conditions is overemphasis of athletics.

A high-school basketball game has become an orgy of emotionalism closely resembling a voodoo ritual. Big crowds pack into small gyms. Drums pound a savage throb, and pretty little girls whip up frenzied partisan spirit that doesn't let up even when play begins.

Sportsmanship is usually evident — as in the exchange of "Hello" yells at the beginning. But it breaks down easily, as when a player from the other team steps to the line for a crucial free throw and the crowd jeers and shouts to distract him.

Coaches talk of the "home-court advantage" — the fact that the crowd is so partisan you can't expect a fair contest.

Emotions Stirred

Emotional pitch is built before the game in school-wide "pep assemblies," a practice that teachers consider "a necessary evil." A psychology teacher says pointedly that pep assemblies "are a real study in mass psychology sometimes."

The question is: Where does school spirit leave off and hysteria begin?

The concept of high-school sports for participation long ago lost out to the necessity of winning. Coaches build the equivalent of farm systems to produce material for winning teams. A coach becomes as much a victim of "ratings" as a television show; there's a tendency to enlarge the point spread over a defeated opponent to gain a higher rating.

Utterly lost is the grace of losing. High-school girls weep as if death had descended when their teams lose. Fathers grumble about ineffective coaches.

But gainsaying overemphasis of athletics is not enough. Why are athletics overemphasized?

It's a result, some say, of "urbanization." The exodus of people from the cities of recent decades and attendant flight to the suburbs produces a lonely-in-the-crowd society.

It also produces the big school, a factor that men like Richard Van Hoose, superintendent of Jefferson County schools, and Sam V. Noe, his counterpart in Louisville schools, hold as the root cause of many problems.

The Big School

Today's suburban high school of 2,500 or more students is almost what yesterday's college was.

Let Earl Duncan, principal of the 2,600-student Waggener High School, tell of some of the problems.

"In a school of 2,600, only 12 boys can play basketball, but certainly a lot more would like to," he said. "Only five youngsters can be elected to offices in a graduating class of 350. Think how many that leaves out."

It's a case of being lost in a big school.

A bright boy in a big suburban school came home last week with failing grades. He told his mother, "I'm not good at sports; I'm not in the band; I can't get on the school paper. I've just lost all interest in school."

Most young people don't lose interest — they plunge. If they can't find something they can participate in actively, they participate vicariously. The school is something they can belong to, something to "give them identity," as the psychologists say. So they become rabid fans, fanatic followers.

May Boil Over

But nonparticipation isn't too satisfying; there's not much opportunity to blow off steam, unless in violent rooting. And it's always possible that this pent-up steam may boil over into violence, particularly if there is some way to rationalize it, like defending the school's honor or avenging a lost game.

Big schools build up tension in ways other than pep assemblies — subtler ways, often overlooked.

Principal Duncan points out that when you have only one gymnasium and it is given over to varsity teams, there is no place for other youngsters to play. To "make the best use of facilities," in gym periods or after school, the play must be scheduled and organized. Regimentation is another word for it — constant supervision, no opportunity to just horse around.

Drop in at one of these big schools at noon hour and you will see long lines of students in the cafeteria. The sheer impossibility of feeding all students at once means they eat in shifts. And mark this: lunch hour usually lasts only 20 minutes. Not only that, but by the time a student gets his food, he may have only 10 minutes to eat it. Of necessity, he must "bolt his food" or miss his next class.

Difference Is Great

Compare this with the paper-sack days when pupils brought their lunches, ate leisurely and spent the rest of a long lunch hour dozing under a tree or breaking the tension of long hours at a desk in a make-up ball game.

This means that today's school children put in a 7-hour day with little let-up, seldom released from supervision. Even recess is now a matter of "supervised play," and in some schools, children are given a grade for lunchroom conduct.

Then there is homework. There always has been homework, but it seems to a lot of students that teachers are trying to close up the missile gap with Russia by the sheer bulk of homework they assign. The youngsters respond, not by learning from homework, but merely by "getting it done."

Getting it done means more hours under supervision, this time from a Mom or Dad anxious to see a good report card.

All this adds up to this: youngsters today are under greater tension than ever before but have less opportunity to dissipate it.

Part **II**

HANDLING IMPORTANT
ASSIGNMENTS

THE MISSION OF THE PRESS

BY *Wayne Rea*

Managing Editor, The Urbana, Ill., *Daily Courier*

> The press has a mission; and what is it, pray?
> The clergyman claims 'tis to preach,
> 'Tis to sway voters, the ward heelers say,
> And the pedagogue thinks 'tis to teach.
>
> The women declare 'tis to publish the styles,
> The card parties, socials and hops,
> While the man on the street just quietly smiles,
> As he scans the sport pages and stops.
>
> The broker wants figures in his reading stuff,
> The farmer wants prices of hogs,
> And some think that crime news is reading enough,
> Then wail that we've gone to the dogs.
>
> The kids want the "funnies" and then they are through,
> Unless there's a column of jokes,
> But some of their elders like comic strips, too,
> And police news reads great to the soaks.
>
> There are some folks who revel in carnage and death;
> They want their stuff gruesome, with gore;
> They like to read "yellows" that fair take their breath —
> If there's none in the paper they're sore.
>
> Some like it heavy, but most like it light;
> They don't like deep delving in thought,
> They want it served clearly, tersely and bright,
> So they won't have to think as they ought.
>
> The press has a mission, or rather a job —
> 'Tis to humor each hobby or whim,
> With news of variety, hot for the mob —
> The same that cried, "Crucify Him!"

Reprinted from *Quill*

11

Persons and Personalities

I. Gossip Is News

  1. *The Personal Element*
  2. *Sources of Brevities*
  3. *Faults to Avoid*

II. Types of Personal News

  1. *Births*
  2. *Guests*
  3. *Newcomers*
  4. *Employment*
  5. *Trips*
  6. *Vacations*
  7. *College Students*

III. The Society Page

  1. *Types of Society News*
  2. *Elements in Society News*

IV. Covering Society News

  1. *Style*
  2. *Receptions*
  3. *Coming-out Parties*
  4. *Engagements*
  5. *Showers*
  6. *Weddings*
  7. *Picking the Feature*
  8. *Style*

V. Gossip Columns

  1. *Anecdotes*
  2. *Night Life*
  3. *Entertainment Places*
  4. *Society*

VI. Personality Interviews

VII. Ethics

IT HAPPENS EVERY DAY

"Hello, is this the reporter?"

"This is one of the reporters."

"Well, I want the reporter who writes the articles for the paper."

"This is one of the reporters who writes news for the paper."

"Are you the reporter who puts in all those articles?'

"I'm one of them. What can I do for you?"

"Well, I want to put an article in the paper. Have you got your pencil ready?"

"Yes, I'm all ready."

"Well, here it is. Take it down just as I give it to you. Mrs. J. J. Whuzzis, W-H-U-Z-Z-I-S, and her charming and talented daughter, Euphrasia, will leave their palatial home, 9999 W. 38th street today, for a motor trip through the East where they will visit her aunt Lucy in the metropolis of New York City. She has a fine home there and is very rich. These two prominent Wichita ladies will return in three months to their mansion. Now read that back to me."

"I just took down notes. I didn't take it verbatim."

"I didn't want it verbatim. I wanted you to take it the way I read it. That's the way I want it in the paper."

"I'll put it in with all the facts correct."

"That ain't the idea. I want it put in the way I gave it to you, if I have to pay for it. How much will I have to pay to get it put in the way I gave it to you?"

"You'll have to talk to the advertising department about that."

"Well, I'll take it to the other paper. I never was so insulted in my life."

Wichita Beacon

"The question of who rates mention in the society columns is still a matter between the newspaper's policy and the society editor's seventh sense — a special function enabling the born society reporter to evaluate on the instant the importance of a name to readers."

Helen M. Staunton in
Editor & Publisher

EVERYONE LIKES TO SEE HIS NAME OR THAT OF A FRIEND OR acquaintance in print. This is as true of the city dweller as of anyone who resides in a small town or on a farm. Large newspapers do not refrain from publishing more items concerning births, newcomers to the community, trips, parties, engagements, weddings, illnesses, and deaths, etc., because they fail to recognize the reader interest in such events but merely because of lack of space. Gossip among urbanites still largely concerns such occurrences as they involve relatives, friends and acquaintances. Community newspapers within the large cities and suburban newspapers are capitalizing increasingly on the metropolitan press' inability any longer to devote much space to such news.

GOSSIP IS NEWS

THE PERSONAL ELEMENT

In the country weekly, serving a community in which acquaintanceships are proportionately greater, the "personals" column never has ceased to be the chief reader attention-getter. Larger papers are using more and more news briefs after a short period during which there was a feeling that these were "hickish." Today, small and medium-sized newspapers are ceasing in the attempt to emulate their metropolitan betters and are concerned with how to serve better the needs of their own readers. Reader interest in gossip about "big shots" in the national field having been proved through the popular reception of syndicated columns from New York, Washington, and Hollywood, local "It Happened in — " "Heard about — " and similar columns are growing in frequency.

SOURCES OF BREVITIES

Haunting the waiting rooms of railroad stations, hotel lobbies, clubrooms, floral shops, delicatessen stores, and stopping to chat with friends on street corners or at their places of business still is excellent "breaking in" for the cub reporter. Not only does he receive items or tips for the "local happenings" or "news in brief" column but, while ostensibly in search for such comparatively trivial information, he comes across numerous first-rate stories.

Typical of the one-paragraph personals which the reporter may obtain just by "hanging around" or by telephone conversations with his friends, are the following:

> Mrs. Edwin P. Morrow of Washington, D.C., is visiting at the home of her son, Charles R. Morrow, 636 Sherman avenue. Mrs. Morrow is the widow of the late Edwin P. Morrow, former governor of Kentucky.

> Miss Eva Rathbone entertained her fellow members in the Puella Sunday school class of First Presbyterian church at dinner Friday night at her home, 133 N. Prairie avenue. During the evening, the girls worked on patch quilts to be distributed by the Women's Missionary society of the church.

> Five Milltown students at Augustana college will spend the Thanksgiving weekend with their parents here. They are . . .

Some papers which do not have a special column for short items of this sort use them as fillers; others restrict their use to the society page. In the country and rural town weeklies such items concern purchases of new farm equipment, planting and harvesting, unusual crops, etc. Large city dwellers may laugh at such news, but if they move to the city from the country or a small place, it is what they look for when the home-town paper arrives each week. And it's what they want to know about their friends in the big city.

FAULTS TO AVOID

The three most serious errors to avoid in writing short personals or brevities are: (1) underwriting, (2) overwriting, (3) stylistic banality.

Underwriting means writing as a brief what should have been a longer news or feature story, or not getting all the essentials into the brevity itself. The properly written personal really is a news lead. As such, it is good if it fulfills the requirements of a good lead and bad if it doesn't. Note how the following barren brevities might have been made more nearly complete and interesting while still remaining brevities:

Insufficient	Sufficient
A. L. Scobey, 1434 Ellis street, has returned from a two-week trip to San Francisco.	A. L. Scobey, 1434 Ellis street, returned today from San Francisco with the prize given the delegate traveling the farthest distance to attend the annual convention of the Fraternal Order of Leopards there last week. Mr. Scobey represented the local Leopards lodge of which he is commander. The prize was a traveling bag.

Insufficient	*Sufficient*
Mr. and Mrs. Edward L. Parkhouse, 683 Pulliam avenue, entertained 16 guests Monday night at a theater party.	To celebrate their 25th wedding anniversary, Mr. and Mrs. Edward L. Parkhouse, 683 Pulliam avenue, entertained 16 guests Monday night at a theater party. Formerly it was believed the Parkhouses had been married only 15 years, but they chose this belated occasion to reveal that they had been secretly wed for ten years before making an announcement.

It easily can be imagined how either of these, especially the second, could have been elaborated into a much longer story with considerable reader interest. Unfortunately, it is not presumptuous to imagine a beginning reporter's getting no more than the original items cited. Articles have been written by despairing state or county editors on the inability of rural correspondents to sense news values. Reporters may be able to pick important names out of hotel registers, but they may miss the fact that the out-of-town visitor listed inconspicuously among those "in town for the day" is negotiating with the directors of a bank for its purchase, consulting with Chamber of Commerce officials about the establishment of a new industry, or applying for a position in the local schools or for the pastorate of a local church.

Overwriting, on the other hand, means going to the opposite extreme of including irrelevant and unimportant details of little or no interest even to residents of a small community. Such "padding" may be for the purpose of pleasing a friend or an advertiser, but too much of it alienates more general readers than it attracts. It should be paid for at regular advertising rates.

> Employment of an agronomist of high repute by the Ohio Sugar company is an innovation that will meet hearty appreciation by Henry county farmers.
>
> Mr. McLaughlin, an O.S.U. graduate, who has had supervision of the State Experiment station at Holgate for the past six years, and prior to that gained valuable experience at the Wooster experiment station, will have charge of this new department beginning Jan. 1.
>
> Mr. McLaughlin's advice to farmers and beet growers will be of incalculable benefit and every farmer is urged to avail himself of his wise counsel. There are so many perplexing problems that confront the farmer that no doubt this new department will be most heartily welcomed. Adaptability of the different Henry county soils to the various crops is one thing where Mr. McLaughlin's knowledge of agronomy will serve the farmer who seeks his advice most beneficially.
>
> While Mr. McLaughlin may, to a certain degree, specialize in beet cul-

ture, he is equally well informed on every phase of agriculture and his advice is free for the asking. The Ohio Sugar company is maintaining this almost solely for the benefit of growers and it hopes every farmer will avail himself of this service which is proffered free.

The most frequent criticism of personals, as used in country weeklies and small-town newspapers, is excessive informality and maudlin rhetoric. A chatty column is one thing; a banal one is another. Too much opinion, the extension of too many good wishes and insipid predictions are sickening to even the uneducated reader, although it is a remarkable fact that many persons who submit unsolicited personal items to large city papers often write them in such a manner. The following illustrative examples of misdirected energy were taken from small-town newspapers:

W. P. Nelson is again on the job at the bank following a siege with chicken pox. Walt had a real mixup with this "kid" disease and he says he was sure sick. Aside from being "well marked" he is okay.

The new band leader, Don Walters, put his Hubbard group through its paces last Saturday and again Tuesday and Wednesday of this week. The youngsters are all eager and ready to go to Iowa City this coming Saturday and do themselves and their community proud. Everything points to a good chance for them to come through with shining colors. The group expects to leave town about 7 o'clock in the morning so as to give the performers time to get some of the kinks from riding out of their system.

So let's cheer them on with three big rahs. All right, here we go — rah! Rah! RAH!

We extend congratulations to Mr. and Mrs. Dave Heden, who were recently united in marriage. We are not acquainted with the groom, but his bride, formerly Agnes Attleson, is well known here as this was her former home though she has been working in Chicago for several years. She has hosts of friends who wish her much joy, for she was a very nice young lady. They expect to make their home in Chicago, where the groom has employment.

TYPES OF PERSONAL NEWS

BIRTHS

Characteristic of the growing frankness of newspapers in recent years is the prominence now given to announcements of impending parenthood on the part of prominent persons. The gossip columns, notably Walter Winchell's, were a large factor in breaking down the scrupulous rule against mentioning "blessed events" until they had occurred. Pregnancy, once a tabooed topic, is even recognized today by motion pictures and television.

For the routine birth notice the reporter should obtain:

1. Names and address of parents
2. Time and place of birth
3. Weight of the baby
4. Sex of the baby
5. The name, if chosen

The mother's maiden name may be included if she has not been married more than a few years, if the couple is living in another city and the girl's married name is unfamiliar locally, or if she uses her maiden name professionally. If the date of the marriage is mentioned, care must be taken to give it correctly. Libel suits have resulted from mistakes of this sort.

Since all parents are "proud," that fact is of no news value. And it never has been proved scientifically that newly born babies bounce. A baby's rosy cheeks, lusty lungs, dimpled chin, etc., may be taken for granted. "Daughter" or "son" is better than "baby girl" or "baby boy." Do not use "cherub" or "the new arrival to bless the home," etc.

The name of the attending physician should not be included in a birth notice or, in fact, in any story of illness or death. This rule is broken in the case of a person of great prominence and in stories in which the physician himself plays a part, as a participant in an accident, etc. Ordinarily, however, the name of the physician is left out, frequently at the request of the local medical society.

Whether the fact that "mother and baby are both doing nicely" is to be included probably is debatable. Ordinarily, however, it seems as though good health should be assumed; if either child or mother is in danger that fact may be included. Likewise, the number, names and ages of other children of the parents of a newly born baby may or may not be mentioned.

Mr. and Mrs. Ralph Elsasser, 711 Renrose ave., became the parents of a daughter in Swedish-American hospital on Monday. Named Marie Lynette, the infant weighed 5 pounds, 5 ounces at birth. She joins a brother, Terry Lee, 12; and a sister, Vicki Lynn, 8. Rockford *Star*

Mr. and Mrs. Jimmie Collins, Stonington, welcomed their first child, a son, at 4:56 (CST) o'clock Friday night in the St. Vincent Memorial Hospital. He weighed 6 pounds and 6 ounces. The mother is the former Anna Marie Jones. Taylorville (Illinois) *Breeze-Courier*

A frequent temptation to a beat reporter is to turn in a story telling of how some new father on his beat acted or announced the event to his co-workers. Such items must be adroitly handled to avoid the common fault of banality.

It was cigars for everybody today in the office of Mitchell C. Robin, clerk of the Probate court. He explained that his wife, Mrs. Dorothy Robin, had given birth to their first child, a girl, at the Michael Reese hospital.

> Menlo Park, Calif. — (AP) — Sammy Yates showed up in the eighth grade at Central school with a cigar box.
>
> He opened it and passed out all-day suckers, explaining: "I'm a brother."
>
> Chicago Daily News

Siamese twins, triplets and quadruplets are unusual enough to rate considerably more than routine treatment. Quintuplets are the news story of the year! Unusual weight or size, physical deformity or the circumstances under which birth took place may elevate the event above the level of the routine birth notice, as was the case in each of the following stories:

> Wenatchee, Wash. — (UP) — Mr. and Mrs. W. E. Robinson of Entiat Valley claim to be parents of the first baby born in an auto trailer in the Pacific northwest. A daughter, Kay, was born to them in March.
>
> The fire department ambulance crew in charge of Lieut. Irvin Martin aided the stork early Wednesday and a baby was presented to Mrs. Callie Burns, 21, 1216 Freeman avenue. Mother and infant were then taken to the general hospital.

Some newspapers "play" births more prominently than others. One way is to obtain pictures of the newly born together with short feature stories in which source of the name, brothers and sisters, date of birth or some feature angle may be emphasized. The following is a typical entry from such a column:

> Even if she is a girl, the first child of Mr. and Mrs. William Clifford Richards Jr., 1415 Ashland avenue, was named for her father and is called Billie Mae. Her second name is the first name of her maternal grandmother. Weighing 8 pounds 14 ounces the addition who has made the Richards family a threesome, was born Dec. 2 at Evanston hospital.

GUESTS

Whenever a visiting dignitary is entertained at the White House it is news from coast to coast. There is nationwide interest also in the travels of celebrities of all sorts. Just as important are the comings and goings of "ordinary" folk within the circle of one's acquaintance.

> Mr. and Mrs. Ralph J. Peterson and daughter Linda are visiting here from North Hollywood, Calif. They are sharing their stay with Mr. Peterson's brother-in-law and sister in Salt Lake City, Mr. and Mrs. Cleon Anderson, 1851 Harrison Ave., and Mrs. Peterson's mother in Ogden, Mrs. Fred King. The coast matron is the former Phyllis King of Ogden.
>
> Among those entertaining for them during their visit are Mr. and Mrs. Ferdinand Peterson, 1370 E. 9th South; Mr. and Mrs. Jess R. Jensen, 1621 Princeton Ave.; and Mrs. Ray Whitmeyer of Ogden.

The Californians will visit with their son Scott in Army training at Grand Junction, Colo., before returning to Hollywood.

Salt Lake City *Tribune*

NEWCOMERS

Even in crowded city apartments, a new family in the building or neighborhood is an event, especially if both households have children through which some of the adults are bound to become acquainted if only for the purpose of discussing discipline. The habit of calling on newcomers virtually has disappeared in the larger cities but is still proper etiquette in the small town. In places of all sizes, curiosity at least must be satisfied. The newspaper is in the best position to appease it.

A one-sentence brevity announcing the change of residence on the real estate page or telling of a newcomer to the community may be all a newspaper feels it can afford. On the other hand, some newspapers are subscribing to commercial services which collect data on new residents in the community and are using the information for editorial as well as business purposes.

A newcomers' column serves the purpose both of extending a welcome and of acquainting old-timers with the special interests of the arrivals. Organizations similar to those with which members of the new families were affiliated in their former cities of residence can follow such a column to learn of possible additions to their own rolls.

Newcomer to Phoenix is Ballerina Eileen Colgrove, native of London, England.

She and her husband, Michael Thoday, live at 35 W. Enconto Blvd.

Among Miss Colgrove's diplomas she holds a fellowship, or top degree, from the Imperial Society of Teacher of Dancing in London. This includes degrees in national, ballet, and stage branches. She is a graduate of teachers' course of Sadler's Wells ballet company, and also holds diplomas from the National Association and Midland Association.

Miss Colgrove has done radio and television work on ballet education programs in both England and Canada. She was recently a teacher at the National Ballet Co. summer school session in Toronto. At the summer session she taught children, professional ballerinas, and teachers of ballet.

During her career she has taught some children from the royal family, including the Earl of Uxbridge and Lady Henrietta Paget.

In Phoenix she will instruct at the Ruth Freethy School of Dancing, 16 W. Cypress, beginning Sept. 19.   Phoenix *Arizona Republic*

EMPLOYMENT

It is difficult to enforce any rule against "free publicity" connected with new jobs. It is news when a large corporation elects a new president or chairman of its board of directors. Similarly it is news when a friend or acquaintance changes his employment.

> Franklin R. Raynor today resigned his position as office manager of the Grayson Real Estate company to accept a similar position with the South Side Realtors. In his new position he succeeds Vincent L. Coke who died recently.

> Miss Sylvia Waters, 574 W. Sequoia place, left today for Minocqua, Wis., where she will become director of a Girl Scouts summer camp.

TRIPS

Friends are interested when anyone takes a trip but may be bored when he returns and insists on relating the commonplace. Nevertheless, a skillful reporter should be able to keep a returned traveler off a textbookish account of the glories of Niagara, the Lincoln Memorial or Yellowstone and find something in the peregrinations of most everyone, regardless of how well traveled the road taken may have been.

When a person goes away, the purpose of his trip may be news, as he may be combining business with pleasure, attending a convention, or returning to the scene of an interesting former experience. If the journey is a short one, to be completed in a day, emphasis should not be on the fact that the traveler left but that he is in the other city.

WEAK: Carol Winters left Jefferson City today to visit relatives in Columbia.
BETTER: Carol Winters is spending the weekend with relatives in Columbia.

The shortest type of brevity regarding a trip resembles the following:

> Mr. and Mrs. Fred N. Sigman, 1415 N. Cherry street, have returned from a two weeks' visit with their son, Fred, Jr., an intern in General hospital, Boston.

Often a returned traveler has experiences to relate or opinions to express which are newsworthy.

BY Marjorie McCabe

Instead of dining on such delicacies of the French provinces as matelot sparnassienne in Champagne or poularde truffe along the Rhone this spring, Mrs. Frank Timberlake was partaking of Madrid's unattractive oranges or indescribable squid in thick black sauce.

This is what came of the projected gourmet tour of France planned by Camille Timberlake and Mrs. Anne Cope Moulder.

But let there be no misimpression of the edibility of Spain's oranges and squid. Mrs. Timberlake, who is an epicure as well as a sterling cook, found the loss of the matelot sparnassienne and the poularde truffe more than compensated for by the oranges ("magnificent, despite their appearance") and the squid (called "calamares en su tinta, and very tasty").

The mis-meshing of schedules that were to have taken the two attractive matrons on their provincial motor tour served to send them off instead to the discovery of Spain holding hypothetical rain-checks for the gourmet tour.　　　　　　　　　　　　　　San Francisco *Chronicle*

VACATIONS

Resorts and other vacation places maintain publicity departments to keep faraway newspapers informed of the arrivals and departures of persons from their communities. They also provide articles and pictures (bathing, tennis, skiing, etc.) of the social notables enjoying themselves. Newspapers send their own society page columnists to report the activities of vacationing colonists. The following paragraphs from one such column are typical:

Making the most of their vacation days are Misses Virginia Barrett and Joan Chandler (Carl Walden photo), pictured here at Macfadden-Deauville Cabana club, where they take part in water sports. . . . Tennis also is included in their summer recreation program. . . . Joan, daughter of the Everett W. Chandlers, Miami Shores, is a student at Stephens college, and Virginia's parents are Mr. and Mrs. William Barrett, Miami Shores.

A trip through the Canadian Rockies then on to Alaska is included in the vacation itinerary of Mr. and Mrs. Frank E. Ellis, Miami Beach, who plan to leave next Monday.

They will sail from Vancouver, B.C., and after they return from Alaska they will go to New York. They also plan a sojourn at Hot Springs, Ark., before they return home.

Joining vacation travelers on Monday, Miss Phyllis Brettell left by plane for New York. . . . Phyllis, a daughter of Mr. and Mrs. Clinton Brettell, 1355 Biaritz dr., Normany Isles, will visit her aunt, Mrs. William Hafer, in New York and later will be the guest of Mrs. William N. Guthrie in Woodmont, Conn. . . . Also, she will visit Miss Maeve O'Toole, a Miami Beach winter resident, at her home in Forest Hills, L.I., and will go to Larchmont, N.Y., to visit other friends before she returns home in September.　　　　　　　　　　　　　　　　Miami *Herald*

Another typical handling of news of vacations follows:

BY *Marie McNair*

Looking forward to an opportunity to "get away from it all," Mrs. Mitchell Palmer is leaving Sunday for Lake Racquet in the Adirondacks and Mrs. Francis P. Garvan's luxurious camp, open again for the first time since the war.

Train service being what it is to that rather remote section of northern New York, Mrs. Palmer will try a plane from New York to Utica this time and motor the 60 miles from there to camp. It's that or land there by train and arouse the family at 4 A.M.

For almost a score of years Peggy Palmer has been a summer visitor to the Garvan camp. She has known the three boys, Francis, jr., Peter and Anthony, and their sister, Marcia, as enchanting small fry; said goodby to the young Garvans as they went off to war and will be present at Marcia's marriage to Frank Coyle in September.

Wednesday, Francis, jr. — better known as Pat — will celebrate his birthday and a big party's planned. Francis, you may remember, married the lovely Hope Jackson, so well known in Washington. While her husband served in the Air Intelligence, U.S.N., Mrs. Garvan was studying voice, made her debut as an opera singer in the leading role in Tosca in Hartford, Conn., last spring, and according to critics, is definitely slated for greater heights. Washington *Post*

COLLEGE STUDENTS

Directors of publicity at the nation's colleges and universities won't believe it, but to the average newspaper of any size a news item telling of the selection for a homecoming committee of some student from the city has greater news value than the commencement speaker's name, an addition to the curriculum, a solemn pronouncement by the dean of women or even a routine football victory. When the boys and girls return for vacations, win scholastic honors, and approach graduation and on many other occasions, the news gets prominent play and pictures are used.

Jack Perry, son of Mr. and Mrs. S. L. Perry, is playing the co-lead part in the Cornell Summer theater's production of "Under Canvas," comedy-drama of tent-show days. The story concerns the hectic lives of a typical tent-show group. "Under Canvas" will be presented to the public on Friday and Saturday nights, July 5 and 6.

Mr. Perry, a freshman at Cornell, is studying journalism and dramatic art. Clarion (Iowa) *Wright County Monitor*

As much a puzzle to Booster college regulars as for four years it was to members of the Suburban Football league is the passing attack of Wayne "Bossy" Wilbur, half-back on the Booster freshman team.

Wilbur, the son of Nellie Wilbur, 148 W. Jackson street, was the mainstay of the Milltown high school football team for three years, two of which he served as captain. . . .

THE SOCIETY PAGE

When New York newspapers near the end of the last century began printing the guest lists of parties attended by members of the so-called 400, they made journalistic history. At first this "invasion of privacy" was resented, but through "leaks" and gate-crashing, the news continued to be obtained. Today the problem of most society editors is not how to get news but how to satisfy everyone wanting "nice" notices on the page.

The original and enduring appeal of the society page has been two-fold: (1) to the vanity of those considered important enough to receive mention, (2) to the curiosity of all others regarding the glamorous way of life of their social superiors. In recent years, an increasingly large number of newspapers have come to regard these values as fictitious and to criticize the undemocratic "snob appeal" of the society page. For this and other reasons — including the headaches entailed in arbitrarily deciding who is and who is not socially important — the society page is waning. Much of the space formerly devoted to it is being given to news of the activities of clubs and to news of interest to women at all economic levels. Whereas such news formerly was sandwiched in on the society page, the trend now is to squeeze society news in on the club page or women's page. The glamour appeal now is provided by movie stars and other entertainers who get full treatment on other pages. They are the modern public heroines or goddesses, not the society matron.

TYPES OF SOCIETY NEWS

The typical society page or section consists mainly of the following kinds of news:

Parties: birthday, reunions, anniversary, coming-out, announcement, showers, weekend, house, theater, card and miscellaneous
Teas, luncheons, dinners, banquets, suppers, cocktail parties and picnics
Meetings and announcements of meetings of women's organizations if there is no club page
Receptions
Dances and balls
Benefits, bazaars, etc.
Personal items if not used in another part of the paper
Engagements and weddings

As this list suggests, the society page is written principally for women although men are interested in many stories of engagements, weddings, parties and personal activities. A majority of society editors are women who have social rank themselves although many large papers have male society editors. Of whichever sex, the editor should be able to attend major social events on an equal footing with other guests, although only a few occasions require the presence of a reporter. A large majority of society page items are contributed by persons concerned or by social secretaries, either in writing or by telephone. The society editor must be ever on the alert for practical jokers sending or phoning in bogus announcements of engagements, weddings and other social events. Nothing should be used without verification. If the society editor needs pipelines, such people as chefs, florists, hairdressers and delicatessen store operators are among the best to utilize.

ELEMENTS IN SOCIETY NEWS

Most society events of any importance have elements in common which include:

Names. Host and hostess; guests of honor; members of the receiving line in order of importance; assistants to hostess in the parlor and dining room; members of committees; entertainers; musicians and their selections; prominent guests; relation of guest of honor to hostess or of assistants to either.

Decorations. Color scheme, its significance and how it was carried out: flowers, palms and ferns to make room resemble tropical garden, an outdoor scene, etc.

Refreshments. Distinguish between luncheon and tea and between supper, dinner and banquet. At receptions, always learn who poured and who served and ask if these assistants were selected for any particular reason (relatives, sorority sisters, officers of an organization, etc.).

Occasion. Is it an anniversary or an annual event? what will be done with any proceeds? does the place have any significance?

It is difficult to achieve variety in writing similar accounts of social events. Consequently, the society editor welcomes any possible feature.

COVERING SOCIETY NEWS

STYLE

In writing routine society news, restraint should be exercised. Every hostess would like to see her party or luncheon mentioned as the "loveliest affair of the season." To avoid offending anyone, such superlatives must be subdued.

There is a tendency, however, toward more informality in longer feature stories concerning important social events. Much of the material on the society or club page is signed. Functions, the proceeds of which go to charity, frequently are given better writeups than private affairs.

The capable writer does not need to use hackneyed adjectives such as "gorgeous," "exquisite," etc. An accurate, impartial description of an object or an event conveys its beauty much better than does an article which makes indiscriminate use of adjectives. Only the writer who is not able to write better descriptions falls back on the "old standbys."

A few additional words should be said about some of the more important kinds of stories classifiable as society news.

RECEPTIONS

The reception story should emphasize the name of the guest of honor, the occasion for the reception and the receiving line. Likewise, those who assist the hostess, entertainers, and musicians and decorations.

COMING-OUT PARTIES

A debutante is presented to society by her parents, or, if they are dead, by a near relative. Some biographical data concerning the girl should be included, as well as a description of her dress. A possible feature may be found in the date or place or in the number or names of guests. In some coming-out party stories, the gowns of all the prominent women guests are described.

ENGAGEMENTS

Usually the parents of the bride-to-be announce their daughter's engagement. Sometimes the announcement merely takes the form of a newspaper notice. Often, however, an announcement is made at a social function. If such is the case, the manner of the announcement constitutes the feature. Especially if a girl chooses to announce her own engagement, the attempt is made to invent some novel method. For instance, the intended wife of a bank clerk uses as place cards or favors imitation bank books containing her fiancé's picture.

In the announcement story, the names of the bride- and bridegroom-to-be must be mentioned, and also their parents' names and addresses. Also the probable date of the wedding and the city in which the couple will live. The principals should be identified by their occupations and education. Sometimes the way in which the two met is interesting, as when a war veteran marries the nurse who cared for him in a hospital.

SHOWERS

Female relatives and friends of a bride-to-be are hostesses at showers. Guests are expected to bring gifts. Often the type of gift to be brought is designated. If it is, the shower should be referred to as a kitchen shower, linen shower, etc. Otherwise, it should be called miscellaneous.

WEDDINGS

The backbone of the society page is the wedding story. It is the longest and most difficult to write. Since most weddings are planned, it is possible for the society editor to obtain information about them and even to write them up in advance. In a majority of states a couple contemplating marriage must make application at least five days before the day set for the wedding. The city hall reporter gets the names of couples who apply for marriage licenses and, after including them in a short news item, gives them to the society editor.

The society editor writes an advanced story of the approaching wedding of a young woman who is prominent socially, often using a picture with the story. Many papers do not run such stories or pictures without charge. Ordinarily, the advanced story of a wedding is brief unless the principals are prominent.

After receiving the names of intended brides, the society editor of an average-sized newspaper sends a wedding blank to each bride about whose marriage she will want a story. This blank contains spaces for the girl to insert answers to the questions suggested. Use of the wedding blank eliminates the necessity of personal reporting and insures accuracy. Seldom does the society editor attend a wedding. Most wedding stories are written upon the facts provided by the bride. A sample wedding blank follows:

WEDDING REPORT

Full name of bride ....

Address of bride ....

Full names of bride's parents or guardians ....

Address of bride's parents ....

Full name of bridegroom ....

Address of bridegroom ....

Full names of bridegroom's parents ....

Address of bridegroom's parents ....

Date of wedding .... Time ....

Place of ceremony ....

Who will perform ceremony? ....

Will bride wear a gown or suit? .... Describe ....

....

Will she wear a veil? .... Is it an heirloom? ....

Describe the veil ....

Will she carry a prayer book? ....

Will she carry or wear flowers? .... Describe ....

....

Who will give the bride away? (name, address and relationship) ......

....

Name of maid or matron of honor and relationship ....

Describe her gown and flowers ....

Names and addresses of bridesmaids ....

....

Describe their gowns and flowers ....

Ribbon, ring or flower bearers ....

Describe their gowns and flowers ....

Name and address of best man ....

Groomsmen ....

Ushers ....

Will ceremony be formal or informal? ....

Musicians ....

Musical selections:

    Before ceremony ....

    As bridal party enters ....

    During ceremony ....

    As bridal party leaves ....

Order in which bridal party will enter ....

....

Decorations (color scheme and how carried out; significance) ....

....

Number of invitations sent out ...... Probable attendance ....

Will a reception follow? .... Where? ....

How many will attend reception? ....

Decorations ....

Hostesses:

    In parlor ....

    In dining room ....

Will breakfast, luncheon, or dinner be served? ...... Where? ....

Will couple take a trip? ...... Where? .... When? ....

When and where will couple be at home? ....

Bridegroom's occupation and business address ....

Former occupation of the bride ....

Bridegroom's education and degrees ....

Bridegroom's fraternal connections ....

Bride's education and degrees ....

Bride's sorority connections ....

Bridegroom's war record: service, rank, area in which served and duration,

    citations, unusual experiences, etc. ....

....

Bride's war record ....

Guests from away, names, initials and addresses ....

....

Other information ....

....

PICKING THE FEATURE

The society editor welcomes any possible feature with which to lead off the wedding story. Possible features include:

1. *The romance.* The manner of meeting or the length of the engagement if unusual. Sometimes childhood sweethearts are united after years of separation. Or there may be an Evangeline or Enoch Arden complication. Ordinarily, unless the bride is a widow, the fact of any previous marriage is omitted. Exceptions to this rule are persons prominent in the news, especially motion picture actors and actresses. In their cases it is common practice to write: "It is her third marriage and his fourth."

2. *The place.* Perhaps some relative of either party was married in the same church. Maybe an outdoor ceremony is performed on the spot where the betrothal took place. Often a couple selects an unusual site for its nuptials, as an airship, beneath the water in diving suits, etc. Wedding ceremonies have been performed in hospitals, prisons and by long-distance telephone or radio.

3. *The date or hour.* It may be the anniversary of the engagement. Perhaps the bride's mother or some other relative was married on the same date. In an effort to make its wedding the first of the year or month, a couple may be married shortly after midnight.

4. *Bride's costume.* Often a bride wears her mother's dress or veil or some other family heirloom. There is an old superstition that a bride always should wear something old and something new, something borrowed and something blue; many modern brides adhere to this, and some article of a bride's costume may be unusual.

5. *Relationship.* If the scions of two old and prominent families are married, their family connections may constitute the feature. If either is descended from Revolutionary or Colonial ancestry that fact should be played up.

The feature, of course, may be found in any one of a number of other elements. Perhaps the bridegroom wears a military uniform or the bride cuts the wedding cake with her husband's sword. Maybe the minister is a relative. The attendants may be sorority sisters or representatives of some organization. Whatever it is, the society editor tries to find it and to feature it. Anything to drive off the monotony of the stereotyped wedding lead.

STYLE

The trite and hackneyed style of the "country" wedding story must be avoided. To this end, avoid use of such expressions as "blushing bride," "plighted their troth," "holy wedlock," "linked in matrimony," etc. The word "nuptials" should not be overworked.

The easiest lead sentence is the straightforward: "A and B were married — " For variety, other possibilities include:

— exchanged (spoke) nuptial (marriage) vows
Miss A became the bride of B —
Miss A was married to B —
First church was the scene of the marriage of —
A simple ceremony united in marriage Miss A and B —
The marriage of A and B took place —
— attended the nuptials of A and B
Nuptial vows were spoken by A and B —
The marriage of A and B was solemnized —
Chaplain C read the service which joined A and B in marriage —
Chaplain C officiated at —

Some of these phrases may be appropriate in other parts of the story. When a page includes a half-dozen or more wedding stories, it is desirable to obtain variety. However worded, the lead of the wedding story should contain the feature, if there is one, the names of the principals with the bride's name ordinarily mentioned first and the time and place of the wedding. The principals usually are identified by addresses and parentage.

Writers vary the order of details in the body of the story. Most frequently, perhaps, the bride's costume is described right after the lead, and then the costumes of her attendants. The decorations or order of march, however, may come first. If there is a procession, the order in which it entered the church or home should be described.

The account of any wedding dinner or reception follows the account of the service proper. More nearly complete identification of the principals, the wedding trip and future residence and the list of guests come at the very end. Other elements which enter into the account are included in the sample wedding blank in this chapter.

Note in the following examples of well-written leads to wedding stories how the writers were able to find and play up unusual features. The leads are all from the Fort Wayne *News-Sentinel*:

The Rev. Val Hennig, minister of St. John's Lutheran Church on the South Whitley Road, read the nuptial service, at which his youngest daughter, Katharine Alice, and Clarence Bade, son of Mrs. Chester Bade, 1721 South Hanna St., were united in marriage at 6 P.M. Saturday, June 29. Edwin Meitzler, organist, accompanied Howard Ropa, vocalist, who gave the musicale before the ceremony.

Gold vases of white larkspur and Madonna lilies and palms decked the sanctuary of St. John the Baptist Catholic Church where Miss Eileen McGary and Robert John Wiltshire exchanged marriage vows this morning at 10 o'clock. The Rev. Leo Pursley officiated at the double ring ceremony and nuptial mass after a musicale of bridal airs given by Miss Frieda Winegart, organist, and Miss Mary Jo Kohl, who sang "Panis Angelicus" and "On This Day O Beautiful Mother."

The bride is the daughter of Mr. and Mrs. William James McGary, 117 McKinnie Ave., and her husband the son of Mr. and Mrs. L. Wallace Wiltshire, 4225 South Calhoun St.

In a quiet ceremony read in the presence of a few intimate friends, Miss Betty Ruth Beard, 2214 Winter St., and Lester Green, of Edgerton, O., were married last Saturday in the rectory of St. Peter's Catholic Church.

GOSSIP COLUMNS

The avidity of readers for "inside dope" — intimate though perhaps inconsequential humorous, pathetic, unusual or anecdotal items — about friends and acquaintances and popular heroes worshipped at a distance, has resulted, not only in Washington, New York, and Hollywood personal columns but also in a recrudescence of local "Around the Town," "On the Square," and similar columns.

The unusual new neon sign in front of a restaurant, the abnormally high sunflower, the skilfully sculptured snow man, the practical joke played upon a dignified prominent citizen — many of these and other items which give substance to the local gossip column might be developed into separate brevity features. Collected and presented in the individualized style of a particular writer, however, their attention-getting value may be enhanced. Permitted greater stylistic freedom and a bit of friendly editorializing, the gossip columnist also can use a quantity of material which it would be difficult to work up into even an informal news feature.

ANECDOTES

After the Chicago *Sun* included in its "Chicago Briefs" column an item telling of the long eyelashes of one of the city's children, mothers actually fought with each other in the newspaper office for the privilege of having their offsprings' lashes measured and photographed. One subsequent item in the series was as follows:

> Move over, Mickey Cribben, Maureen Fitzpatrick, Dolores Wenk, Patricia Capetta and all you other lucky people with those long eyelashes!
>
> Make room for a newcomer — Patsy Ann Doyle, 5, who lives at 5149 Enerald av. Her mother claims Patsy's blond lashes are a mite over ⅝ inches long, which is longer than Mickey's, Maureen's, etc. etc.
>
> Chicago *Sun*

Columns of anecdotes may be called "Chatter," "It Happened In — " "Evening Chat," "Informing You," "It's News to Me," "Front Row," "Personally Speaking," or the like. The Wakefield (Massachusetts) *Daily Item* heads its column "The Item Hears" and begins each paragraph anecdote with "that." Typical items follow:

> That visitors to Wakefield from the West ran into what they described as a "gold mine" this week when they were permitted to visit a huge field of corn and select their own, fresh-picked ears for the unusually low price of 50 cents a dozen.
>
> That a youngster 9 years old and his younger sister of Yale avenue, appeared at the police station Tuesday with a wallet they had found which contained $8. It was discovered at the station that the wallet belonged to a Melrose man.

NIGHT LIFE

In metropolitan centers the frequenter of night clubs has superseded the Social Registerite as copy for columnists who make the rounds after dark.

The following are extracts from a typical "It Happened Last Night" column by Earl Wilson in the New York *Post*.*

> When Jackie Gleason played Santa at the Lighthouse, he cracked, "I'm the only Santa Claus that didn't have to use a pillow" . . . Comedienne Patsy Shaw reports this New England dialogue: "I hear you had an operation on your nose" . . . "Yup, it was getting so I could hardly talk through it."

ENTERTAINMENT PLACES

Similarly, the night clubs themselves and other amusement places often are reviewed in the same manner as dramatic or musical events.

* Reprinted by permission from the New York *Post*. Copyright 1955, New York Post Corporation.

BY *Elizabeth Rannells*

Soft lights, beautiful decor, hors d'oeuvres with the individual touch and solicitous service are the reasons the Town and Country room has become one of the town's quick-clicks. It is the spot for that pre-dinner, pre-show appointment, equally the place for the post-prandial, post-show meeting.

Not for heavy appetites is this addition to the Palmer House. It is just for that lull in the late afternoon, or for that after-the-show session, where every table has its coterie of critics.

And what is almost as important — the feminine guests feel like Powers' models, thanks to the bland and gentle illumination and the flattering colors of the room. They blend with all make-ups, thus putting the distaff customers in the cheerful mood. Chicago *Sun*

SOCIETY

To brighten the society page there is the society column, usually signed which, while newsy, is in keeping with the trend toward interpretative writing to give and explain the news behind the news.

Effective formals seen recently include Nancy Wilmanns' (Mrs. Fred) strapless kelly green silk faille gown accented with a large pink rose at the waistline . . . Carol Herzfeld in a gown of her own design with a high neckline black lace bodice atop a bouffant white organdy skirt with inserts of the black lace . . . the strapless white dotted swiss dress of Carolyn Rowe (Mrs. Charles) . . . Nancy Inbusch (Mrs. Ralph) in a black crepe creation featuring a peplum edged with white lace . . . Betty Wright (Mrs. David) in a floral printed crepe gown in a patriotic motif — red, white and blue.

Was Helen Ely's face red when she "gracefully" tripped over the full skirt of her formal at a recent affair and landed in a horizontal position! Milwaukee *Journal*

PERSONALITY INTERVIEWS

The growth of magazines, radio and television has made it more difficult for newspapers to obtain this type of interview. Celebrities and persons prominent in the news for the moment are offered such attractive prices for their life stories or opinions, by syndicates, that they hesitate to grant gratis interviews with newspaper reporters.

When a prominent person returns from abroad or is a visitor in the community, however, he hardly can avoid granting some kind of interview with the press. Such interviews often resemble interviews for opinion, although the subject matter may not be of immediate importance.

When a member of Congress returns from foreign shores, of course, the statement which he gives out may be important. When an actress, athlete or public lecturer passes through the city, however, the reporter may be "hard put to it" to find questions to ask for a "between-trains" interview. The importance of knowing something about one's subject was impressed upon the Atlanta reporter who asked Vivien Leigh what part she had played in the motion picture version of *Gone with the Wind* when the actress showed up for the première of the re-issue of the 1939 Academy Award winner. Miss Leigh simply informed the reporter that she did not care to be interviewed by such an ignorant person.

Not only national celebrities but local persons who have won honors, taken new positions of importance, or been in the news prominently are the frequent subjects of reportorial inquiry. Reporters follow candidates for public office around during a day of campaigning to make a full report on their activities. Articles written after interviews with newly appointed school superintendents, bank presidents, chairmen of civic organizations, and the like may resemble the profiles (combined biography, character sketch and description) originally made popular by *The New Yorker*. The object is to give readers the "feel" of the person, not just statistical facts regarding him and his activities.

When a person is being written up primarily because of his information or opinions regarding a matter, personality traits and description should be kept to a minimum or ignored. If a man shouts, bangs on the table, hesitates before giving an answer or in some other way behaves so that proper understanding of his comments requires mention of such circumstances, they may be included. Unless such is the case, references to "the balding professor" or "the slight soft-spoken man" may be inconsistent and out of place.

Entirely the opposite is true when the object is to make readers thoroughly acquainted with the subject of the interview as a person. In such cases, the subject's opinions are secondary and are used to help build a total word picture. How a person appears, talks and behaves during the interview may be pertinent, especially if the reporter elects to write in the first person.

These rules are applicable to all kinds of subjects including the off-the-beaten-path "characters" who may be the subjects of feature articles: retiring lifeguards, octogenarians, persons with unusual hobbies or reminiscences, and the like. Pictures supplement and confirm written accounts in such cases, not the contrary.

ETHICS

One of the most frequently heard criticisms of newspapers

is that they unnecessarily invade the privacy of persons in the news. Sometimes, of course, the charge has validity. Increasingly, in a public relations-conscious society, however, the apparent victim of the invasion is getting exactly what he asked — or at least hoped — for. Acting in the belief that any publicity is valuable, persons in the public eye, especially entertainers, have been known to promote disturbances or engage in other kinds of behavior which the press could not ignore.

Reputable newspapermen gag at having to report the antics of publicity seekers who operate on the principle, "I don't care what they say as long as they say something" and whose only concern is that their names be spelled correctly. Readers get a distorted impression when there is deadpan reporting of something which should properly be exposed as manufactured news.

During the '50s a rash of magazines appeared to traffic in "inside dope" about public celebrities, mostly motion picture stars. Much of it verged on the scandalous and scurrilous and numerous libel suits resulted. This revival of "town topics" journalism became the object of widespread debate regarding the extent to which persons in public life are entitled to privacy. Admittedly, facts related to the character and capacities of public officials and other civic leaders are important for voters and patrons to know. No law ever has been written or probably could be written to draw a fine line between what is and is not permissible. The interpretative reporter knows that a person's actions frequently are understandable only when much is known regarding his background. On the other hand, a person's achievements, especially in the arts, often can be judged on their own merits. Pending the miracle of a legal definition in this matter, the ethical journalist must maintain a high consciousness of social responsibility and realize that a gossip-ridden society in which personal freedoms are minimized is not a good society.

12

Meetings, Conventions, Speeches

I. Meetings
  1. *The Preliminary Story*
  2. *The Follow-up*
  3. *Style*
II. Conventions
  1. *The Preliminary No-tice*
  2. *The First-day Story*
  3. *The Follow-up*

III. Speeches
  1. *The Preliminary Story*
  2. *The Follow-up*
    a. The Lead
    b. The Body

BANQUETS

Every reporter worth his salt has, at one time or another, yearned to write two stories without worrying about the laws of libel and the canons of good taste — first, a frank interview with a pompous politician, and second, an objective account of a typical banquet. We're saving the first of these for the next time our pet senator comes to town, and today we present the parody story that ought to be — but never is — written, on a banquet we had the profound misfortune to attend the other night:

"Four hundred members of the Do Nothing Club, who had quarreled with their wives last night and didn't want to stay home, were guests at a banquet in honor of the club's retiring president, George Spelvin, who is probably the emptiest windbag in the Northwest Territory.

"Great quantities of inferior liquor were served before the dinner (to deaden the taste of the unpalatable food) and each guest was so spifflicated by speechmaking time that the talks were even more subnormal than their usual paleolithic level.

"The toastmaster, Bert Blowhard, was an insufferable bore, with a burleycue sense of humor and an irritating habit of roaring loudly at his own half-witticisms — which periodically woke up at least 200 of the postprandial snoozers.

"Principal speaker of the evening was Judge Joseph 'Vestpocket' Jones, who came out in favor of motherhood, the American flag and the inalienable right of every citizen to breathe. He rose to the heights of eloquent incoherence at one point, when he dramatically stated that "if the Redcoats ever dare to attack Concord again, we will seize our muskets and repel them as valiantly as our forefathers at Thermopylae!' This bold challenge was greeted with fervent applause by 116 grubby wardheelers whom the judge had packed into the balcony.

"After the speeches, an interminable song recital was given by Miss Hortense Flab, a 300-pound off-pitch basso who possesses the most raucous set of pipes this side of Mars. Miss Flab almost strangled herself to death while singing the 'Valkyrie Song' with gestures. Four Valkyries later shot themselves in protest.

"The banquet ended at 6 A.M. when the bartenders were forced to call for a rush-order of wheel barrows to cart off the remaining guests. It was subsequently discovered that Spelvin had absconded with the proceeds of the affair, and police have been instructed to send searching-parties after him and three other club officers who were found to have embezzled charity funds. The club's next meeting has been indefinitely canceled."

Chicago Sun

MEETINGS, CONVENTIONS AND SPEECHES OCCUPY THE ATTENtion of the women's organizations mentioned on the society and club pages and of other organizations whose news is printed in other parts of the newspaper. It is impossible for any newspaper to give adequate coverage to any sizable proportion of the total number of groups seeking publicity. Those considered the most newsworthy are of the following types:

1. Those which take an active part in local, state or national political and governmental affairs, as the League of Women Voters, Chamber of Commerce, Daughters of the American Revolution, American Legion, etc.
2. Those which have programs including widely known speakers, musicians, artists, etc.
3. Those with large, nationwide memberships which hold elaborate conventions annually. Of this type are most fraternal lodges, routine news of which may be ignored but whose yearly meetings are first-rate shows.

In small city dailies, community and suburban newspapers, almost any organization is newsworthy. The initiative may be left to the group to send in its notices voluntarily, or the publication may follow a sounder policy of attempting to have complete coverage, especially of such organizations as the P.T.A., church groups, Boy Scouts, Girl Scouts, Y.M.C.A., Y.W.C.A., and so forth.

MEETINGS

THE PRELIMINARY STORY

Every meeting is held for a purpose and this purpose should be the feature of the preliminary or advanced notice. From the secretary or some other officer of the group which is to meet, the reporter should learn the nature of important business to be discussed, of committees which will report, speakers, entertainment, etc.

Note how the second of the following leads emphasizes purpose:

WEAK: The Cosmos club will hold a meeting at 7:30 o'clock Thursday evening in Swift hall for the purpose of discussing the question of whether or not undergraduate students should own automobiles.

better: Undergraduate ownership of automobiles will be discussed by the Cosmos club at its meeting at 7:30 Thursday evening in Swift hall.

Other vague beginnings to avoid include:

There will be a meeting —
The purpose of the meeting —
At 7:30 o'clock —
The first meeting of the year —

The reporter should ask if the meeting is regular or special, business or social. He should inquire if a dinner or refreshments will precede or follow, whether any entertainment, dramatic, musical, or otherwise, is planned. The main attraction of the meeting may be some special program. A meeting to elect or install officers, initiate candidates, hear a particular committee report or a speaker, or to celebrate an anniversary, etc., has an obvious feature from the news standpoint.

The reporter must be sure to obtain the following data:

1. *The organization.* Its exact name, and the name and number of the post or chapter. "Local Odd Fellows" is not enough; instead, write, "Keystone Lodge No. 14, I. O. O. F." That is the usual form: name of the local chapter first, then the number and finally the name or usual abbreviation of the national organization.

2. *Time and place.* In the preliminary story this information must be definite and accurate. A meeting scheduled for 8 o'clock should not be mentioned in the news story as to begin at 8:15. "Friday evening" is not enough; the exact hour should be given. Both the building and room should be given in stating the place.

3. *The program.* If there is a program of entertainment, the reporter should obtain it in detail. He must get names of musicians and their selections, names of casts and dramatic coaches, decorations, orchestras, committees in charge, etc. Only the "highlights" of a program need be mentioned, and in order of importance, rather than in the order included in the program.

Note how purpose is emphasized in the following examples:

The American Legion Auxiliary's 5th District will meet at 8 p.m. Saturday in the Community club rooms, 1600 South Grand avenue, to hear annual reports by district chairmen and to elect delegates to the state and national conventions. Mrs. Martha Watkins, district director, will preside.

A score of California law-enforcement officials gathered here yesterday to discuss ways of living up to the new rule excluding illegally obtained evidence from criminal trials.

It was the first meeting of Attorney General Edmund G. Brown's committee on arrests, searches and seizures.

Brown announced that he would seek an immediate hearing before the State Supreme Court on five Los Angeles narcotics cases that were dismissed as a result of the new rule, announced by the high court on April 27.   San Francisco *Chronicle*

Sometimes the preliminary note may be the excuse for a historical sketch of the organization, as:

Having enjoyed a vigorous life for 80 years, the United Charities is pausing next week to give itself a birthday party. With a program as impressive as the occasion demands, the celebration will take place at the Palmer House the afternoon of the 16th.

Dr. James Rowland Angell is coming out from Yale to make the principal address of the party, and a pageant and tea will supplement the speeches.

As president of the group, Merle Trees will be chief host. Mrs. Gordon Lang heads the committee in charge of the event, and is drafting a corps of her young friends who will act as ushers and hostesses in costumes their mothers used to wear as members of the organization. . . .

Since 1857, when 23 Chicago business men founded the organization, it has been run largely by the same families. Joseph T. Ryerson, William H. Brown, John H. Dunham, Mark Skinner, John Kinzie, Philo Carpenter, and Wirt Dexter were some of the founders who named themselves the Chicago Relief and Aid society and obtained a state charter still in use.

They confronted the first big test of their efficiency in 1871 when Mayor Roswell B. Mason turned over to them the job of looking after the thousands of Chicagoans whose homes were burned down in the October fire. Until then their chief means of relief had been money, but that fall, with T. M. Avery as chairman of their shelter committee, they bought timber to build 8,000 houses, one of which still stands on the near northwest side.

Henry King, the father of Mrs. Cyrus Bentley and Henry King, was president of the society that year and wrote letters of thanks to people in the Sandwich Islands, in China and Guatemala, and in more familiar places, for their contributions to Chicago's rebuilding fund.

It was Mr. Avery's task to distribute building materials, food and clothes that came in from all parts of the country, and files in the present headquarters on N. Wabash avenue still contain requests made to the shelter committee. . . .   Chicago *Daily News*

THE FOLLOW-UP

In the follow-up or story after the meeting has been held, the outcome or result should be featured, and the writer should look to the future. For instance, avoid:

Keystone Lodge No. 14, I.O.O.F. last evening voted to build a new million dollar lodge hall.

Rather, emphasize the future, as:

Keystone Lodge No. 14, I.O.O.F. will build a million dollar lodge hall, it was decided at last evening's meeting.

Or, better still:

A new lodge hall to cost one million dollars will be erected by Keystone Lodge No. 14, I.O.O.F., as the result of last evening's meeting.

Other beginnings to avoid include:

The Cosmos club met last evening —
At a meeting of —
There was a meeting —
The purpose of the meeting was —
One of the most interesting —
The outcome of the meeting —

The reporter should learn the disposition of each item of business. Some matters will be laid on the table or referred to committees. Others will be defeated outright. Some business, of course, will be concluded. If the meeting or business is important, the writer should include in his story, not only the result of balloting, but also the arguments presented by both supporters and opponents of each measure, both those that passed and those that were defeated.

The account of a meeting which has been held never should read as the secretary's minutes. The items of business are mentioned in the order of their importance, rather than chronologically as considered at the meeting.

It is important to obtain the exact wording of resolutions and the memberships of committees. It is not necessary to mention the presiding officer unless someone other than the president or usual chairman was in charge.

In the follow-up story, the time and place need not be stated so definitely. "Last evening" is sufficient as the exact moment at which the chairman sounded his gavel is immaterial. The name of the building in which the meeting was held is enough, especially if the organization has a regular meeting place. If the time of the next meeting is not fixed by custom it should be mentioned.

Names of everyone who took part in the program should be obtained if a complete account is desired. If a ladies' auxiliary serves a meal or refreshments, the names of the women who helped should be mentioned.

Note in the following example how the writer caught the spirit or importance of the occasion which he interpreted interestingly:

The so-called conservative element in the labor union movement was successful in the annual election held Wednesday night by the Milwaukee Federated Trades' council.

Herman Seide was reelected secretary by a vote of 458 to 169 over Al Benson, former sheriff and now organizer for the United Textile Workers of America, a C.I.O. affiliate.

Anton Sterner, nominated to oppose J. F. Friedrick for the post of general organizer, withdrew. Friedrick was reelected by 624 votes.

For secretary-treasurer, Emil Brodde was reelected with 458 to 164 for Severino Pollo. Frank Wietzke, sergeant-at-arms for more than 40 years, was reelected without opposition.

In the contest between conservative and liberal slates for the nine places on the executive board, the same division was apparent. Those elected and their votes are . . .   Milwaukee *Journal*

STYLE

Expressions such as, "Members are urged to attend," and "The public is cordially invited," should be avoided. If the purpose of the meeting is stated correctly, the former expression is superfluous. The latter expression is poor because of the "cordially." If an invitation is not cordial, it should not be extended.

Other expressions to avoid include:

— was the most important happening —
— was the main business transacted —
— was the topic of discussion —
— featured the meeting —
— was the principal transaction —

CONVENTIONS

Some organizations, such as the American Legion, W.C.T.U. and the D.A.R., are influential in state and national affairs. Consequently, when one of these organizations meets, what it does is of general interest. Such conventions frequently pass resolutions concerning vital political and business situations and recommend passage of certain laws by state legislatures and Congress. They even send lobbyists to state capitals and to Washington.

Conventions of other organizations which ordinarily are nonpolitical may be of widespread interest because of their large membership. Fraternal orders such as the Masons, Elks and Moose have chapters in all parts of the country, and their conventions attract thousands of delegates from all states. Church groups, businessmen's organizations, scientific and educational bodies, etc., consider matters of general interest. Frequently the first announcement of a new scientific discovery or theory is made in a paper presented at a convention of some scientific group.

Aside from the general interest which an important convention creates, there also is local interest, provided the locality is to be represented by delegates. If any local person is an officer or has a part in the program, the local interest is heightened. Many fraternal organizations hold drill team, band, fife and drum corps, and other contests at conventions, and the local chapter may compete.

THE PRELIMINARY NOTICE

The first story of a convention usually appears a week or two before the opening session. Almost every important organization has a secretary or official who prepares notices for the press. The advanced notice emphasizes the business of the convention and the important speeches or papers to be given or read. Sometimes the nature of a report which a special committee will make is disclosed in advance.

Note in the following examples of leads of preliminary notices of conventions that the writer in each case emphasizes the most important plans from the standpoint of general interest:

> College training for women interested in the field of commerce and business administration will be studied and discussed at the 10th annual convention of Gamma Theta Phi, national professional sorority of commerce and business administration, tomorrow through Sunday in the Windmere hotel.

> The National Federation of Women's Republican Clubs will make congressional campaign issues the principal theme of the organization's third biennial convention in Philadelphia Sept. 26 and 27. Mrs. W. Glenn Suthers of Chicago, president since 1952, will direct the sessions at the Bellevue-Stratford hotel. Several hundred delegates from 42 states and the District of Columbia are expected.

In addition to the general story of a convention, or even instead of it, a local newspaper may print a story playing up the "local" angle — the part that local delegates will play, as:

> With the hope and expectation of bringing next year's state convention to Milltown, 58 members of Keystone Lodge No. 14, I.O.O.F., accompanied by wives and families, are in Petersburgh today.

> Occasion is the 27th annual convention of the state I.O.O.F. in which several members of the local lodge will play prominent parts.

THE FIRST-DAY STORY

The story which appears just before the convention begins may emphasize the purpose and main business of the meeting, or it may play up the arrival of delegates, the probable attendance and the first day's program. Often a meeting of the officers or executive committee precedes the convention proper.

Some matter related exclusively to the internal organization of the group may be of sufficient general interest to be the feature, as when a rule changing the requirements for membership, or union with another organization is to be debated. Frequently an internal political fight is anticipated in the election of officers or selection of the next convention city.

> The leaders of the nation's banking fraternity, 8,500 strong, are arriving for the four-day annual American Bankers Association convention.
>
> The meeting, largest since the 1920s, will focus on the perplexing problem of the banker's role in curbing, while not blighting, the boom.
>
> The program at the Conrad Hilton hotel will also include speeches on the farm price problem and the task of building the free world's strength through NATO and the nation's strength through a strong free enterprise economy.
>
> In addition, a wide range of subjects, some of interest chiefly to bankers, others with a general scope, will be discussed.
>
> While thousands of bankers and their wives flock to a private showing of the General Motors Corp. Powerama Sunday, other bankers on 22 special committees — such as those on credit policy and federal legislation — will buckle down to work.
>
> But the committee which may prove to be the most controversial does not meet until Monday. That is the 50-member nominating committee, representing each state.
>
> There's no doubt, short of catastrophe, who the next president will be. He's the vice president, Fred F. Florence, president, Republic National Bank of Dallas. He'll take over automatically from Homer J. Livingston, president, the First National Bank of Chicago.
>
> The rub will come when a successor vice president to Florence is named.
>
> Observers think that for the first time in a generation there may be an open fight for control of the ABA, with the issue being state versus national banks.
>
> The "state's righters" argue that they haven't had a president for the last seven years. Because they can't name one directly this year, their strategy is to name the vice president who will move up to the presidency.
>
> Chicago *Sun-Times*

A newspaper printed in the city entertaining a convention joins with the rest of the community in welcoming delegates. Reporters are assigned to gather side features and anecdotes unrelated to the serious business of the convention. Statistics may be included of the oldest delegate, the delegate who has come the longest distance, the delegate who has attended the most conventions, the delegate who flew to the convention by private airplane or arrived in some other unusual manner, the tallest delegate, the shortest, etc.

The newspaper may take advantage of the opportunity to obtain feature interviews with important or picturesque delegates and speakers. At a gathering of editors of college newspapers, a reporter obtained numerous interviews regarding drinking in colleges, a subject entirely different from the business of the convention.

The following is a well-written first-day convention story which "catches" the spirit of the occasion:

Cleveland, July 13 — (AP) — The Shrine brought its big show to town today and made Cleveland an oriental oasis of parades, concerts, ceremonies and funmaking.

Delegates were arriving by the thousands, by special trains, by automobile, by plane and by boat, and tomorrow between 60,000 and 100,000 nobles are expected here for the 57th annual convention of the Ancient and Arabic Order of the Nobles of the Mystic Shrine of North America.

Today was listed on the program as all-Ohio day, with 750 members of the six Ohio temples initiated into the order, but the arrival of delegations from all parts of the country came in for equal attention.

One thousand members of Medinah temple of Chicago, the largest in the order, arrived in spectacular fashion, on the Lake Steamer Seeandbee. The Chicagoans, bedecked in red, green and yellow uniforms and bright red fezzes, paraded from the dock behind Al Koran patrol of Cleveland, and tied up downtown traffic for a half hour.

Medinah sent a brass band, an oriental band, 500 uniformed men, and a headquarters company from its 23,000 members. This year a Chicago man, Thomas J. Houston, is to be elected imperial potentate and the windy city is a contender for next year's convention.

Lulu temple of Philadelphia sent the next largest delegation — 900 — and presented a quarter-mile long march of sound and color. Moolah temple, St. Louis, with 500 nobles, arrived on the Steamer Eastern States, while Iram temple of Wilkes-Barre, Pa., also came by boat, via Buffalo.

Abu Bekr, Sioux City, attracted attention with its white Arabian mounted patrol of 30 pure white horses. Syria temple, Pittsburgh, was represented by 700 nobles campaigning for the election of J. Milton Ryall for outer guard.

Band concerts, a lake cruise to Put-in Bay, patrol drills and the annual meetings of the recorders and the royal order of jesters, composed of men high in shrinedom, completed the day's program. Tonight was given over to a Mardi Gras and carnival, with Lakeside avenue roped off for the merrymakers.

San Francisco was unexpectedly put forward as a candidate for the next convention of the Shrine of North America. Pacific coast delegates got behind the move at a breakfast given by Leo Youngsworth, Los Angeles, past potentate of Islam temple. Previously Chicago had been the only city mentioned for next year's gathering.

Fourteen nobles of Hella temple, Dallas, came by airplane. Another long distance air delegate was Gerald Biles, postmaster of the Canal Zone, who flew from Panama to Cleveland.

Lou B. Windsor of Grand Rapids, Mich. is the oldest member of the imperial council present and is attending his 44th annual convention. He was imperial potentate in 1900. Another veteran in attendance is John A. Morrison of Kismet temple, Brooklyn, N.Y., known as the "grand old man of New York Masonry," who says he has attended every convention since "way back when."

Robert B. Kennan of Carnegie, Pa., the tallest delegate attending the Shrine convention, was listed by police today as the first "convention casualty."

Kennan, seven feet tall, was cut on the neck when a bottle of stench fluid was tossed in the lobby of the Hotel Winton. More than 100 persons were routed by the incident, which police blamed on hotel labor troubles.

THE FOLLOW-UP

After a convention begins, newspapers report its progress. Important speeches and debates are reported, and the outcomes of votes watched. Minor speeches, such as the address of welcome and the response and the humorous after-dinner talks at the banquet, may be ignored by press associations and correspondents, unless someone disregards custom and selects such an occasion for an important statement. Scientific papers and speeches must be written up so as to be understandable to the average reader.

Entertainment provided for delegates and their wives, the convention parade and minor business matters pertaining to the organization only, are not given much space. If the organization awards prizes of any sort, the names of the winners are desired by various outside papers whose readers are likely to be interested. Such prizes may be for the best showing in the parade, for the largest delegation, for the delegation coming the longest distance, for drill team, band, or fife and drum corps competition, for the chapter which has increased its membership the most during the year, for the chapter which has contributed most to a certain fund, and so on.

The results of the election of officers and selection of the next convention city usually are of general news interest. Papers in cities which bid for the convention or whose chapters have candidates for offices, frequently arrange for prompt coverage of elections, depending upon the importance of the convention.

SPEECHES

THE PRELIMINARY STORY

In obtaining information for a story about a speech to be given, the reporter must pay special attention to the following:

1. Adequate identification of the speaker
2. The occasion for the speech
3. The exact time and place
4. The exact title of the speech

Identification of the speaker in the lead may not be lengthy, but the body of the story should contain those facts about the man which indicate that he is qualified to discuss his subject. The opinions of other persons may be obtained and quoted to emphasize the speaker's ability, but the reporter himself should not say that "he is well qualified," "is an authority on his subject," etc. It is better to give an adequate account of the speaker's experience and let it speak for itself.

The speaker's name usually is more important than his subject and, therefore, should come first in the lead. Sometimes, however, the subject may be more important, but it rarely is advisable to begin with the exact title in quotation marks. Note in the second example below how the writer emphasizes the subject and at the same time the importance of the speaker:

WEAK: "Commercial Aviation" will be the subject of a speech to be given . . .

BETTER: The causes of several recent commercial airline accidents will be analyzed by . . .

Sometimes the occasion is more important than either the speaker or his topic, as:

The 55th anniversary of the Milltown Salvation Army will be celebrated at 3 P.M. Sunday at the Municipal Opera house with Commander A. K. Asp delivering the principal address, a résumé of the Army's rise to second position among local charities.

In addition to a further identification of the speaker, the body of a preliminary speech story should contain the program of the meeting at which the speech will be given and additional details about the occasion.

In the following example of a well-written preliminary speech story, the lead emphasizes the speaker's name, and the body explains his importance and also the occasion on which he is to speak.

State Sen. Charles H. Bradfield, Rushville, will speak on the state parole system at the monthly meeting of the Council of Social Agencies at 12:15 P.M. Thursday at Hotel Wolseley.

A member of the joint legislative committee which recently recommended a complete overhauling of the existent parole system, Senator Bradfield has been a severe critic of Gov. Herbert Crowe for his failure to make a public statement on the committee's report.

"It was Senator Bradfield, more than any other member, who was responsible for the recommendation that a board of alienists be substituted for the present board," declared Maurice S. Honig, president of the council, in announcing Thursday's meeting.

The council's committee on legislation, of which Mrs. Arne Oswald is chairman, will report on the results of its study of the legislative committee's recommendations.

THE FOLLOW-UP

After the speech has been given, the emphasis should be upon what the speaker said, rather than upon the fact that he spoke. Never write:

Bruce Paddock, Prescott city manager, gave a lecture Thursday on "Municipal Government" to the Kiwanis club of Greensboro.

Such a lead is vague and indefinite. It is only a preliminary story lead put into the past tense. It misses the feature entirely.

The feature should be found in something that the speaker said. The reporter must follow the orthodox rule of important details first and must disregard the chronological order of a person's remarks. No good speaker ever makes his most important point in his introduction. The reporter should play up the speaker's most startling or important remark, which may come at the very end of his speech. Such expressions as "The speaker continued . . ." "In conclusion the speaker said . . ." etc., do not appear in a well-written story.

Every speaker tries to make a point, and the news writer should play up the speaker's attitude toward his subject as a whole. This is not a hard and fast rule, however, as frequently it is better to pick for the lead some casual statement or remark that has strong local interest. In playing up an aside or incidental remark, however, care must be taken not to give a wrong impression. It is easy to misrepresent a speaker's attitude by picking a single sentence which, when printed alone, has a very different meaning than when considered as a part of the complete text.

The timeliness of a speaker's remarks may determine selection of the feature. If he refers to some vital public problem of the moment, his opinion regarding it may be more important than anything else he says. This, of course, is contingent upon his importance as an authority on whatever he may be discussing.

During political campaigns, it is difficult for a reporter who travels with a candidate to write a different story daily, because the aspirant for office gives nearly the same speech day after day. The same difficulty is met with in reporting public lectures by persons who speak frequently on the same subject. If the write-up of the speech is for local consumption only, the feature may be selected on its face value, provided an account of a similar speech by the same person has not been printed recently. The reporter, however, should not play up as something new and startling, a remark which actually is "old stuff" to both speaker and auditors.

As preparation for speech reporting, there is no substitute for adequate knowledge of both the speaker and his field of interest. A reporter with little or no background in science, for instance, would be completely unable to evaluate the relative importance of points made by a nuclear physicist, some of which might be of great potential general interest. An uninformed reporter in any field might write that a speaker "revealed" or "made known" something that could be found in elementary textbooks on the subject.

To localize the appeal of a speech means to play up any reference which the speaker makes to the immediate locality. Thus, if in the course of a lecture on geology, the speaker declares that the vicinity in which he is visiting is a very fertile field for research, that remark may be the most interesting, from the standpoint of his audience, of any he makes. The same speech, written up for a press association, might have an entirely different lead.

The time and place need not be stated so definitely in the follow-up as in the preliminary story, and the identification of the speaker should be brief.

THE LEAD

Possible rhetoric leads for a follow-up speech story include:
1. The speaker's name
2. The title
3. A direct quotation
4. A summary statement of the main point or keynote
5. The occasion or circumstances

If there is reason for emphasizing the authority of the speaker, the story may begin with the name, as:

> Chief of Police Arthur O. Shanesy last night told members of the Chamber of Commerce at their monthly meeting that traffic accidents in the downtown business district are largely the fault of merchants.

> A prosecuting attorney today advocated the abolition of capital punishment.

> Instead of the death penalty, District Attorney Howard Crossman of Bristol county told a luncheon meeting of the Rotary club, the law should provide mandatory life imprisonment for convicted murderers.

Ordinarily, it is weak to begin with the speaker's name, because by so doing the importance of his remarks is minimized. For the same reason, the lead seldom should begin with the exact title unless it is stated in an unusual way or in a way which makes a title lead effective, as:

> "America's Weakness" is her failure to realize that the frontier has disappeared, according to Prof. Arnold L. Magnus of Booster college's political science department, who spoke on the subject last evening to the Milltown Lions club.

Opinion differs regarding the direct quotation lead. Jackson S. Elliott, of the Associated Press, once said, "Show me a news story that begins with a direct quotation, no matter how striking it is, and I will show you how it could be improved by taking the quoted statement out of the lead and placing it in the body of the story."

Other editors condone the direct quotation lead when the intention of the writer is to play up some startling statement rather than to epitomize the speaker's general attitude. Obviously, it is seldom that a speaker himself summarizes his entire speech in any one sentence contained in the speech itself.

The following is a fairly good use of the direct quotation lead:

> "World War III is inevitable within five years," Harold E. Paulson, professor of political science at Booster college, told the World Affairs club last night in Memorial hall.

The "partial-quotation" lead is a way to avoid lengthy direct quotations which would lack definiteness, as:

> Schools, by failing to develop to the full the "creativeness" of all their students, are responsible in large measure for "countless not fully developed humans," Dr. John L. Tildsley, retiring assistant superintendent of schools, told 1,800 art teachers and students yesterday. He spoke at the opening session at the Hotel Pennsylvania of the 28th annual convention of the Eastern Arts association.

The best lead for a speech story is one which summarizes the speaker's general attitude toward his subject or which gives the "keynote" of the speech. The following are good examples of this type of indirect quotation lead:

> Kindergarten reading is out of place in high school and college, even if the students are coping with a foreign language.
>
> So a University of Illinois professor told his fellow teachers of French, Friday, in a national meeting in the Palmer House.
>
> "The books we're reading with our students in the first few years of French are far below their intellectual level, and below the seriousness of

things they are reading in other classrooms," declared Prof. Charles A. Knudson, head of romance language at Urbana.

"In short, in French classes we are reading tripe."

Chicago *Daily News*

The lead may emphasize the occasion or the ovation given the speaker, the crowd or some unexpected circumstance which occurs during delivery of a speech, as in the following examples:

> Just six weeks after he was arrested for having in his possession a pamphlet of the American Workers' party, A. J. Muste, executive chairman of the party, last night explained its tenets to an audience of about 100 in the auditorium of Belleville city hall.

> A well-organized group of about 50 hecklers last night failed to persuade State Sen. Roger Parnell to discuss loyalty oaths for public employes.

> Instead, the Republican candidate for reelection stuck to his announced topic, "The State's Proposed Highway Program," and police evicted the troublemakers from an audience of about 500 in Masonic hall.

> The Vernon County Republican club sponsored the meeting.

If several speech stories are to appear on the same page, as a page in a Monday edition including stories of Sunday's sermons, there should be variety in the use of leads. The average sermon is difficult to report because there seldom is a well-defined feature or keynote. A "title" or "speaker's name" lead may be used for a sermon story.

Beginnings to avoid in writing a speech story include:

> The feature of the Chemical society meeting last evening in Swift hall was a speech by . . .

> Lieut. Amos Andrews spoke to members of the Chemical Society in Swift hall on the subject . . .

> "Shakespeare" was the topic of an address given last evening in Swift hall by . . .

> Speaking at a meeting of the Chemical society last evening in Swift hall, Lieut. Amos Andrews declared that . . .

> Pennsylvania limestone was discussed last evening at a Geology society meeting in Swift hall by . . .

All of these leads are vague and indefinite. They do not satisfy the reader's curiosity as to what the speaker thinks about his subject.

THE BODY

Prominent persons, as public officials, usually speak from prepared manuscripts, copies of which often are distributed to newspapermen before actual delivery. This enables a reporter to write part or all of his account in advance. The danger of going to press prematurely is obvious, as the speaker may make last-minute changes or digress from his text.

The safe way is never to publish a speech account until word has been received that delivery actually has begun. Even in such cases, and especially if it is impossible to obey the rule of delay, it is wise to use the identification, "in a speech prepared for delivery" on such and such an occasion in the first or second paragraph. This offers protection in case there are unexpected developments. If there are none, the reporter, manuscript in hand, can follow the speaker and make note of any modifications necessary in the story he already has written.

The second paragraph of a speech story ordinarily should explain the occasion on which the speech was given, if the lead does not do so. The rest of the body should consist of paragraphs of alternating direct and indirect quotation. The first paragraph of direct quotation well may be an elaboration of the indirect quotation lead.

If, as often happens, the reporter has an advanced copy of the speech, he has no difficulty in obtaining direct quotations. Otherwise, he must develop facility in taking notes.

The reporter needs to exercise his best judgment in selecting the parts of a speech to quote directly. Ordinarily he should quote directly:

1. Statements representing a strong point of view, especially if related to a newsworthy controversial matter. Often it is more forceful to use the material in indirect quotation first, possibly in the lead, as "Mayor Brinton will not be a candidate for reelection." Readers, however, like to know the exact words which a speaker used and they should be given in the body of the story even though a verbatim account appears elsewhere in the paper.
2. Uniquely worded statements, including ones which might become aphorisms or slogans, as "Lafayette, we are here," "I do not choose to run," etc.
3. Statements of facts not generally known, perhaps in statistical terms.

Ordinarily, statements which are merely ones of evaluative opinion or which contain old or easily ascertained information can be summarized in a reporter's own words if they are newsworthy at all. It would be foolish, for instance, to quote a labor leader as saying, "Unions are the hope of America." If, however, the president of the National Association of Manufacturers were to say so, it would be a sensational news story lead.

Instead of quoting directly a statement containing an old fact, the reporter can say, "The speaker reminded the audience that white-collar workers are the most difficult to organize," or, "He recalled that the governor vetoed the measure two years ago."

How often a "he said" or synonym should be inserted in the body of a speech story depends on the length of the article. In paragraphs of indirect quotation a "he said" should be used as often as needed to make it clear that the ideas expressed are those of the speaker rather than of the writer. Direct quotations should be preceded, broken or followed by a "he said" or its equivalent.

The writer should try to use the most forceful synonym for the verb "to say." Any good dictionary of synonyms or a thesaurus includes many score. Since no two verbs have exactly the same meaning, great care must be exercised in their selection. If a speaker "roared," the interpretative reporter owes it to his readers to say so. If, however, the speaker merely raised his voice normally, grave injustice can be done by a reportorial magnavox.

Substance can be given to the speech story only by the reporter who knows something about the speaker and his subject. Otherwise it is impossible to comprehend the speech as a whole, to digest it with proper emphasis, or to convey the proper impression of the occasion on which it was delivered. A speech is an event and the superior reporter comprehends its significance. The factual material of a series of phrases in a sentence or paragraph may come from a half-dozen widely separated portions of the speech as a whole, yet be properly grouped so as to give a complete and accurate summary of the speaker's point of view. Note the understanding displayed by the writer of the following story:

> A brave new world is dawning in the United States today, "a world in which people will believe all other people are people."
>
> But this new desegregated world poses a tremendous problem for the teachers of America:
>
> How do you educate children to live in a world that no American has ever known?
>
> That problem and some suggested approaches to it formed the essence of a talk given here yesterday by Dr. Margaret Mead, New York anthropologist. Dr. Mead addressed the final general session of the Kentucky Teachers Association at Central High School.
>
> "A lot of the children you are teaching now," she said, "aren't living — in their minds — in the present world. They're off living in a 'galactic civilization' — which no girl and few boys over 16 can understand. (A galactic civilization in modern science fiction is one existing among all planets in a galaxy.)
>
> "They have already gone into outer space in their minds.
>
> "We must develop in ourselves a state of mind that realizes they are going into a new world right here. And we must convince our students that they can live in this new world that has never existed before."
>
> The first handicap teachers must shake off, she said, is the traditional American pattern of bringing up children to be "just like me" in preparation for "living in my world." That pattern of training, she said, will not prepare them for the new world.
>
> All through American history, she went on, the two major groups in

the U.S. population (Negroes and white) have thought of each other as "something different."

"How then," she asked, "are we to prepare them to think people they didn't think were people are really people?"

She suggested three lines of approach for teachers:

1. Think enough in terms of this new world so that "we don't pin our children down to our own world."

2. Seek out actively and find those children who believe they can do things that have never been done before. "Find one child who can do something no one in his grade has done before, and you can insult them all into doing it too."

3. Hunt for those individuals "who luckily already live in the world we're moving into, and let them lead the way."

"One of the tasks of teachers and superintendents is to identify individual children and parents who will have the trust to move into the new world. Trust is as contagious as fear. They will spread the trust to their groups and lead others."

People frequently ask her, Dr. Mead said, what it is that makes Dr. Ralph Bunche, famous Negro diplomat and scholar, so outstanding.

The main thing, she said, besides "his great brain and great character, is that he thinks white people are people. When I sit across a table from him at a committee meeting, I forget I'm white. With him, one feels like a human being."

She Takes Swipe at 'Mixed Snobbery'

During a question period after her address, Dr. Mead took a healthy swipe at the "mixed snobbery" of many teachers who snap, "Junior, put that comic book away!" and then the teachers "read all the comic books they confiscate."

"We must realize this is the way the ideas of the present are reaching our children. Teachers ought to know what is in comic books, they ought to watch the TV programs their pupils watch and listen to the radio programs, and maybe most of all read the backs of cereal boxes.

"We're teaching them about calories, the metric system, and letting them paper rooms (with pictures), and the new ideas are reaching them through all these other things.

"Sometimes I think teachers should spend much more time remembering their own childhood and comparing it with the childhood of today's children. That will keep them shaken up. And we need to be kept shaken up." Louisville *Courier-Journal*

13

Illness and Death

I. Illness

II. Mental Health

III. Obituaries

1. *Basic Elements*
2. *Circumstances of Death*
3. *Reviewing a Life*
4. *Evaluating a Career*
5. *Morgue Stories*
6. *Localization*
7. *Side Features*
8. *The Second-day Story*
9. *The Funeral Story*
10. *Follow-ups*
11. *The Obituary Blank*
12. *Language and Style*

IV. Suicides

1. *The Motive*
2. *The Method*
3. *Inquests*

V. Accidents, Disasters

1. *Elements of Interest*
2. *Picking the Feature*
3. *Precautions*
4. *Side Features*
5. *Perspective*

IN A COUPLE OF YEARS

BY *Bob Sibley*

"Hey, Maguire! There's a four-alarm fire down in Western avenue and it's getting late for the story. Did you call up somebody on television to see what it looks like?"

"Well, I just tried to get a drug store on the corner there, but I didn't get a look-in. They didn't answer."

"Too bad. I hate to waste a reporter's time when we can do so well on the 'vision, but you'd better send someone."

"I did, boss; Kane called in and I told him to get going on it 15 minutes ago . . . here he is now on Mirror 24. . . . Hello, Kane! What in the world happened to you? You look like a drowned rat in that Mirror."

"Hello, Maguire; of course I do. A hose line just broke right next to me while I was starting to look for a television booth. Say, this is quite a fire; one dead and half a dozen hurt; apartment house, stores and warehouse."

"All right, Kane. I'll handle it while somebody throws a head together. Can you put the pictures on the wire first?"

"Oh, a couple, I guess; it's late, isn't it?"

"Sure, but we've got a few minutes; time enough."

"All right, put Joe on with a camera. . . . Step into the booth, you. . . . Hey, Joe! Can you see this cop here? Camera all set? Shoot! Don't grin at the office camera, you idiot! Hold it a minute. This is Officer Philmore O'Brien of Precinct 14, Maguire. He discovered the fire. A little too late to help much, but never mind that. You can say he's badly affected by smoke from warning occupants of the apartments . . . barely escaped with his own life. Beat it, Phil.

"Next! Step right in. Can you see, Joe? This guy here with his arm in a sling is Wallace Jones, who jumped into a net from the fourth floor . . . how's he look in your mirror, Joe? Hold it . . . shoot. . . . He bounced right into the net and bounced right out again . . . thanks, Wallace.

"I'll hold up this snapshot for you, Joe. See? This is Mrs. Fannie Fresco, who died from smoke and gas trying to save the family canary . . . suffocated . . . first floor back . . . hurry up, there's three other guys waiting for this picture.

"Say, Maguire, give the damage about a million, tons of water, brave fire laddies, threatened the district, tied up traffic, and now when I find a 'vision near the window I'll fix it up for Joe to make a picture of the blaze if you still want it."

Editor & Publisher

I**F HIS FRIEND, OR SOMEONE WITH WHOSE NAME HE IS FAMILIAR** because of its prominence in local or world affairs, is ill or dies, the newspaper reader is interested because of the personality involved. If an obscure person of whom he never before has heard has an unusual disease or makes a heroic struggle against affliction, millions of Americans "plug" for him mentally from edition to edition. If a new medical discovery is announced, everyone who may be affected beneficially as a result is pleased to learn of it. If a contagious disease threatens to become an epidemic, readers appreciate being warned of the danger.

ILLNESS

Although the illness story may seem to be routine, it frequently is one of the most difficult to report and write. This is because the medical profession is reluctant to give out information about the condition of patients or about their own discoveries, unusual surgical performances, etc. Physicians hold that they are duty bound to protect the privacy of those under their care, and the ethics of the profession forbids anything suggesting personal publicity. They may feel that knowledge of his condition, gained through a newspaper account, will be detrimental to a patient's recovery, and they do not trust the average reporter to report medical news accurately.

Relatives of a prominent person who is ill usually can be persuaded to authorize the physician in charge to release periodic bulletins regarding the patient's condition, but these may be in scientific language which must be translated. Until newspapers can employ reporters capable of handling medical news with the same understanding that baseball writers handle their specialty, the only safe way is to ask the doctors themselves for popular "translations," or to consult a medical dictionary. Because in many cases they have gone to extremes in refusing cooperation with the press, physicians and surgeons must share part of the blame for any inaccuracies which occur in news concerning them.

Chambers of commerce also are a handicap to adequate coverage of medical news because of the influence they often bring upon editors to play down news of epidemics. Fortunately, few newspapers listen to such requests, holding their social responsibility to be too great and the loss of prestige they would suffer if the contagion reached sizable proportions to be an offsetting consideration. The paper with a sense of responsibility, of course, must take care not to frighten readers unnecessarily.

The following are a few precautions to observe in avoiding some of the grossest mistakes which otherwise might occur in medical news:

1. Be cautious about announcing cures for important diseases. The hopes of millions of cancer victims have been raised cruelly through newspaper publicity to discoveries which turned out to be false alarms.

2. Be certain that a newly announced discovery actually is recent. Cases have been reported of some cure or method's being bally-hooed as a startling find when it has been familiar to medical men for years.

3. Go easy on accrediting dogmatic statements to any medical researcher. Few of them ever speak in positive terms. Their efforts may be directed toward a certain goal, but they are extremely cautious about claiming credit for having reached it. Often they report to their scientific brethren on the progress of work they are doing; the newspaper should not credit them with having completed something which they have only begun.

4. Do not use without verification stories of miraculous cures.

5. Do not ascribe a pestilential disease to a person without absolute authority, as such a story, if untrue, is libelous.

6. Do not say a person died "from" instead of "after" an operation, as such a statement may be libelous.

7. Everyone dies of "heart failure." There are diseases of the heart and such a thing as a heart attack.

8. A person does not "entertain" a sickness; and not everyone "suffers" while under a physician's care.

9. Very seldom does a person "have his arm cut off." Rather it is cut off contrary to his plans and wishes.

10. Injuries are not "sustained" but are "received."

11. The nature of a diagnosis ordinarily should be stated unless there is weighty reason for omitting it.

12. Scientific names of diseases may be used provided the popular name of a disease also is given.

13. Attach statements of diagnoses and of the seriousness of an epidemic to an authority.

14. Do not mention the name of a physician except in stories of the illness of a prominent individual.

15. Avoid stories of medical freaks unless authorized by a medical association. Expectant mothers can be frightened dangerously by accounts which advance public understanding little or not at all.

MENTAL HEALTH

The fastest growing field of medical knowledge probably is that of mental health. Although the supply of competent psychiatrists still is woefully inadequate, during the past few decades the thinking of many, within and without the medical profession, has been profoundly affected by discoveries and theories regarding the motivations of human behavior.

Among those most influenced by developments in the mental health field have been journalists. They have helped expose bad conditions in many hospitals for the mentally ill and have assisted psychiatrists, social workers, probation and parole officers, educators, judges and others in enlightening the public regarding the many ramifications of the newer knowledge. In its reporting of crime, juvenile delinquency, school problems and similar matters, the press has become much more understanding and consequently more intelligent in its exercise of news judgment.

For "depth" reporting in this field, considerable specialized knowledge is necessary. For a quarter-century, Dr. Sidney Kobre, of Florida State University, has advocated this form of journalistic specialization and greater knowledge by all newspapermen and newspaper readers. He did so in his first book, *Backgrounding the News*, in 1937 and in *Psychology and the News* and *News Behind the News* in 1955.

The following example shows how a well-informed reporter can make understandable a phase of the attack on mental illness.

BY *Ruth Dunbar*

Tommy, 6 years old and sick with a peptic ulcer, takes no medicine and eats enough spicy foods to make many doctors shudder.

Yet he is steadily improving during his stay in a children's ward at the University of Illinois' Neuropsychiatric Institute.

Doctors are concentrating on the emotional roots of his trouble. As he is helped to achieve a more healthy adjustment to life, Tommy's ulcer is healing.

Ward in Second Year

Now in its second year, the ward is a center for studying children with psychosomatic illnesses — those physical disorders which have an emotional base.

Patients admitted to the 12-bed ward are seriously ill with such disorders as rheumatoid arthritis, ulcerative colitis or ulcers.

They also have personality problems, deep-seated and closely related to their physical illness.

An unusual feature of treatment in the center is the absence of medication or special diets, according to Dr. John Kenward, one of two psychiatrists working in the ward.

Some Exceptions

Exceptions to the no-medicine rule are made for colds, pain or unusual circumstances. Children with ulcerative colitis receive blood transfusions as needed.

Youngsters eat what they like and as often as they wish between meals. This is often the only way they'll eat, Dr. Kenward said.

Intensive psychotherapy sessions and 24-hour-a-day controlled environment help the young patients regain emotional stability.

Seek to Win Confidence

Much time and patience are needed to win the confidence of these youngsters, who are typically suspicious and withdrawn.

Playing with them at their own level, whether it means rough-housing or making cowboy suits, psychiatrists not only gain the child's confidence, they also are learning something about the child's problems.

At first most patients are docile. As they gain confidence in an atmosphere of affection and acceptance, they often become aggressive and openly express the hostility and greed bottled up inside them.

Gradually they learn to behave in more socially accepted ways, and with the personality changes, the child's physical disorders cease or tend to diminish.

Children have ranged in age from 2 to 14 years. Their stays average between six months and a year.

The research is financed by a grant from Field Foundation, Inc.

As yet, the researchers are cautious about conclusions. One thing they are sure of: There is no one simple cause of psychosomatic illness, said Mrs. Ann Magaret Garner, professor of psychology, who leads the research.

Chicago *Sun-Times*

OBITUARIES

BASIC ELEMENTS

The size obituary a person gets depends upon his importance as news. Even the shortest, however, must include these basic facts:

1. Name of deceased
2. Identification
3. Time of death
4. Place of death

Two other facts really are essential for even a one- or two-sentence notice:

5. Cause of death
6. Age of deceased

Unless death occurs in some unusual way the name (*who*) always is the feature of an obituary. Identification in the brief notice may be by address or occupation only. No authority need be stated unless the dispatch comes from an obscure place or is third- or fourth-hand. Then "it was learned here today" or some similar statement should be used. The paper must be on guard against false rumors of a man's death started by enemies.

In giving the age of a dead person some papers permit the form "Henry Baxter, 61, died today, etc.," whereas others object to this form on the ground that placing the age after the name indicates the present tense. Papers with this attitude prefer a phrase "at the age of 61 years" or a second sentence, "He was 61 years old."

> Rutherford Regal, 414 Oates street, a City Yards employe, died at 3 A.M. today at his home following a week's illness from pneumonia. He was 43 years old.

A man's importance or the achievement by which he will longest be remembered ordinarily should be used in identifying him, as:

> Daytona Beach, Fla., March 2 — (AP) — Fred Merkle, former major league baseball player who was best remembered for a "boner" that cost the New York Giants the pennant in 1908, died today. He was 67 years old. New York *Times*

Sometimes a reporter discovers an interesting circumstance in the life of a relatively unimportant person who has died. Perhaps, for instance, he was present at the assassination of a president, was a pioneer of the locality, a former millionaire or in some other way a romantic figure, as:

> William Dickinson, 81, lifelong Milan resident whose grandfather laid out the village and founded and built the Presbyterian church here, died at 6 P.M. yesterday in his home on Dickson street.

> James Mauris, whose restaurant at 1464 E. 57th street has for many years been a rendezvous for faculty members and students of the University of Chicago, died suddenly of a heart attack last night. He was 70 years old.

CIRCUMSTANCES OF DEATH

When a person is known to a large number of readers, the circumstance of his death should be related as that is one of the first things about which a friend inquires when he hears of another's demise. Circumstances of death include:

7. Bedside scene
8. Last words, messages, etc.
9. Account of last illness

In a full-length obituary, according to the formula being developed, these facts usually follow the lead.

Allen E. Schoenlaub, 57, cashier of the First National bank, died suddenly about 8 P.M. yesterday at his home, 1146 Elm street, from a heart attack.

He was found in the kitchen by his wife after she heard him fall while in quest of a drink of water. About a half hour before the attack, Mr. Schoenlaub complained of feeling queer. He had spent a normal day at the bank and ate dinner with his wife, son, Robert, 22, and daughter, Flora, 18, apparently in excellent health. He had had no previous heart attacks nor any other recent illness.

A physician whom Mrs. Schoenlaub summoned declared death was due to coronary thrombosis and that Mr. Schoenlaub probably died instantly.

In addition to his wife and two children, he is survived by a brother, Herbert, Kansas City, Mo., and a sister, Mrs. R. S. Bostrum, Chicago.

Mr. Schoenlaub was connected with the First National bank for 26 years, the last 18 of which he was cashier. He was born Jan. 30, 1896, at Ann Arbor, Mich., and was graduated from the University of Michigan in 1918. He moved here in 1927 after nine years as teller and cashier of the State Bank & Trust Co., of Dowagiac, Mich.

Mr. Schoenlaub was an active member of the First Baptist church, having been president of the Men's club from 1941–50. He also was a member of Keystone Lodge No. 14, B.P.O.E., and of Milltown Lodge No. 150 F. & A.M.

Funeral arrangements have not yet been made.

Note in the above the presence of three other important elements:
10. Surviving relatives
11. Funeral plans
12. Biographical highlights

Sometimes the circumstances of death constitute the feature, especially in the case of an obscure person:

Cleveland, April 22 — (UP) — In a dingy one-room attic they shared, three men were found dead today amid evidence of a last struggle against either poisoning or coal gas fumes.

The room was the same in which two of the victims were overcome by natural gas fumes and a third man was killed a year ago.

The victims . . .

REVIEWING A LIFE

Often the news interest in a death is in the events in the life just ended which the occasion recalls. This is as true of a comparatively obscure person as of a prominent person. Note the emphasis upon the biographical in the following example:

Special to The New York Times

Chicago, Feb. 8 — Robert Morss Lovett, stormy figure in education and government for nearly sixty years, died today in St. Joseph's Hospital. He was 85 years old on Christmas Day.

Dr. Lovett came to the University of Chicago as an instructor in English in 1893 under its first president, William Rainey Harper. He taught there continuously until 1939, when he retired. He was held there deliberately three years after the compulsory retirement age of 65 in defiance of a state legislative committee, which had recommended that he be retired.

Throughout his life, from the time he arrived in Chicago as a young Harvard graduate, Dr. Lovett was embroiled in the forefront of the radical movement. He was often on the picket lines where strike violence was worst, and was a friend and confidant of most of the leaders of the radical movement.

Denied He Was Communist

Government witnesses accused him of belonging to as many as fifty-six "Communist fronts." Dr. Lovett denied he ever was a Communist.

He was proud of his early work as editor of the old Dial, the literary magazine, and his association with Harriet Monroe in Poetry magazine. Both publications brought many young authors to prominence. Among the writers whose careers Dr. Lovett helped to start were John Dos Passos, Vardis Fisher and James T. Farrell.

After his retirement from the University of Chicago, Dr. Lovett was appointed Government Secretary to the Virgin Islands by his friend and old-time associate, the late Harold Ickes, who was Secretary of the Interior. Professor Lovett's record of affiliations aroused the ire of the House Appropriations Committee in the spring of 1943.

Soon thereafter the House and Senate passed a bill discharging Professor Lovett and two others, William E. Dodd and Goodwin B. Watson, both Federal Communications Commission employes. They were barred forever from the Federal payroll.

Won in Supreme Court

Dr. Lovett went to the University of Puerto Rico, then governed by his old associate, Prof. Rexford Tugwell, formerly of the Franklin D. Roosevelt "Brain Trust." Dr. Lovett and the other two men fought the dismissal as a "bill of attainder." They won a victory in the Supreme Court, which ordered Congress to pay them their back salary.

Congress failed to appropriate the money for many years, but Dr. Lovett's relatives say he eventually got the $1,996 owed to him.

After leaving the University of Puerto Rico Dr. Lovett taught for a year at Fisk University, Nashville, Tenn., and then returned to Chicago.

His wife, Ida, who survives, was a close friend and associate of Jane Addams, founder of Hull House in Chicago. In recent years the couple resided at Hull House.

EVALUATING A CAREER

The death of a nationally or world-famous person, one whom history will remember, is the occasion for an interpretative piece of writing which blends the details of death with attempts to evaluate the person's importance. Its purpose is to "place" the dead person in history with emphasis upon his importance and contributions. The interpretative obituary is not an editorial although it is impossible for a writer, qualified to pass judgment upon his subject, to avoid evaluation.

BY *Herman Kogan*

Henry L. Mencken's long, turbulent life came to an end Sunday when he died in his sleep in his native Baltimore. He was 75.

Since suffering a stroke in 1948, he had been inactive, although only last week the "sage of Baltimore" had announced that next May a book titled "Minority Report" — a collection of typically acrid opinions he compiled before his illness — would be published.

Long ago, Mr. Mencken penned his own epitaph: "If after I depart this vale, you ever remember me and have thought to please my ghost, forgive some sinner and wink your eye at some homely girl."

Whatever else he was or became in his lifetime, Mr. Mencken possessed a crackling wit, the skeptic's fine distrust of stuffed shirtism in all its forms and the genius touch for annihilating — or at least wounding — his foes with his caustic attacks.

Certainly this intellectual gadfly, who irritated, amused, provoked, stimulated, annoyed, angered and titillated America for half a century, was never a "popular" literary hero.

One Memory

And he was too complex to be understood, his actions often too contradictory to be condoned even by those who respected his talents and cherished him as a friend.

There are, for instance, many whose sole memory of Mr. Mencken will be that he was severely critical of the late President Roosevelt and many New Deal measures.

And there will be those who bridle at the mention of Mr. Mencken's name because he wasn't so sure — and said so — that the world really would be safe for democracy after World War I; or because he seemed to be pretty fond of Adolf Hitler at one time; or because he found himself allied in his bitter anti-New Deal days with assorted crackpots for whom the iconoclastic Mr. Mencken of the 1920s would have had only contemptuous cackles; or because he was a fierce foe of labor unions and "do-good" organizations; or because he jeered at Rotarians and, being an agnostic, at organized religion, or for a dozen other reasons, valid or not.

But there will be as many and more to whom Mr. Mencken will signify meanings and significance beside which these annoyances and disturbing aspects of his personality will fade.

This larger and happier group will recall Mr. Mencken the newspaperman, who was a reporter at 18, the country's youngest managing editor at 25 of the old Baltimore Herald, then on and off, an editor, columnist and consultant for the Baltimore Sunpapers.

Reminiscences Cited

They will read again his drama criticism, his book reviews, his scathing, brilliant indictments of literary censors and the Ku Klux Klan and southern and northern bigots.

They will dip again into his "Happy Days" and "Newspaper Days," collections of reminiscences he did in his mellowing years for the New Yorker magazine, and relive and relish an era that has vanished and, for better or worse, is not likely to be duplicated.

And there must surely remain the memory of the earlier astounding American Mercury, in those rip-roaring days of the 1920s when Mr. Mencken and his brilliant sidekick, George Jean Nathan, fashioned the magazine into a compendium of smooth scholarship and tradition-shattering challenges to the American mind and "jazz age" status quo.

Or the volumes that were banged out by Mr. Mencken in his Hollins St. study in Baltimore or his newspaper office from 1903 for nearly 50 years on.

The series of "Prejudices," witty, startling, provocative; "In Defense of Women," whose first paragraph reads, "A man's women folk, whatever their outward show of respect for his merit and authority, always regard him secretly as an ass, and with something akin to pity"; and the others — "Treatise on the Gods," "Notes on Democracy," "A Book of Burlesque," and "A Book of Prefaces."

And the one that may outlast all the others: the tremendous "American Language," which he began in 1908 and kept re-editing and revising until his death.

Attacks Superpatriots

There also will be memories of the 1920s when Mr. Mencken attacked the 110 per cent patriots who were seeking Reds in every nook of every home or editorial office; the super-Babbitts whose interests outside of their offices ran as far as the speed of their new cars; the price of bootleg gin; the blue-noses who sought, without letting the readers decide for themselves, to decree what should and should not be sold on newsstands or in bookstores; religious bigots who held narrow, fanatic, destructive views and sought to bar all others — and of the later days when Mr. Mencken, as if turning his back on his younger self, sounded like a doddering reactionary, blind to a changing world as his foes 15 years before had been blind to his efforts to bring light into the darkened climes.

Survivors include a brother, August, with whom Mr. Mencken lived; another brother, Charles, who resides in Pittsburgh, and a sister, Anna Gertrude, who lives in Baltimore. His wife, the former Sara Haardt of Montgomery, Ala., died in 1933, five years after they were married.

Funeral arrangements will be private, August Mencken said.

Chicago *Sun-Times*

MORGUE STORIES

The entire obituary of a famous person may be written after he has died. Newspapers have on file, however, biographical sketches of most prominent persons; it was because they once contained little else except such sketches that newspaper libraries came to be called morgues.

If it seems advisable, and if time permits, the morgue story is revised or edited to be a part of the obituary proper. More ordinary practice, however, is to add it at the end of the story of death with slight, if any, alterations. Events occurring in the man's life after the sketch was written are worked into the newly written first part.

The morgue story actually is an interpretative biographical sketch in which the writer attempts to evaluate the person and assign him his proper historical importance. In composing it, the reporter has an opportunity to do some of his best writing. The best source of material about the basic facts of a man's life is, of course, the man himself. Since the morgue sketch is prepared during its subject's lifetime, it usually is written following an interview. Also, the writer consults previously written material about the person and makes his own impartial estimate of the highlights of the career he is reviewing.

Emphasis in writing should be upon the outstanding characteristics, achievements and activities of the person. The temptation of the young writer is to begin with the fact of a person's birth and to continue with a chronological narrative of his life. In interviewing a person for material about himself it may be convenient to have him tell about himself in such a way but, in writing, the principle to be followed is the same as in all other news writing: most important facts first. The fact of birth seldom is the most important.

When only a short bulletin of an important person's death is received in time for an edition, the morgue part of the printed story may constitute almost the entire printed story as in the case of the Robert Morss Lovett obituary.

LOCALIZATION

When a famous person dies there is a chance for a localized feature based on the material in the morgue and interviews with local citizens. The following is the lead of a story telling of King Albert's visits to St. Louis. If this sort of story is not possible, an interview with someone in the community who had some contact with the dead celebrity could be written in almost any city, no matter how small.

Albert I, beloved wartime king of the Belgians, visited St. Louis twice during his lifetime. The first time, in May 1898, he attracted little attention as he was traveling incognito under the name of "John Banks." On his second visit, of five hours' duration Oct. 21, 1919, he was acclaimed by a crowd said at the time to exceed that which greeted President Woodrow Wilson the same year.

Many legends have arisen as the result of Albert's sojourn in America when he was crown prince. He is known to have denied a tale that he served as a newspaper reporter in New York, Minneapolis and other cities. In St. Louis he is said to have been entertained by the Belgian consul and other natives of his country.

In interviews with reporters here in 1919 the triumphant monarch asserted that the reception accorded him by St. Louisans exceeded in cordiality and enthusiasm any other in scores of cities on his itinerary in the United States.

Speaking of St. Louis, Albert I said, "One of the things I admire most is your wonderful activity, and the spirit of enterprise and the large scale of your industrial plants. This allows me to look for greater production. Without increased production, the world, I fear, will have a very difficult year."

The king was accompanied upon his American postwar trip by Queen Elizabeth and Crown Prince Leopold, soon to become his successor to the throne. Heading the St. Louis reception committee were the late Governor Gardner and Mayor Kiel. Ambassador David Francis also rode in the automobile parade to the principal parts of the city and attended a 1:30 P.M. luncheon by the Chamber of Commerce at Hotel Statler. . . .

St. Louis *Star-Times*

SIDE FEATURES

In addition to the obituary proper, a newspaper may print several other related items.

1. It is the habit of newspapers, for instance, to print encomiums of prominent individuals who die. Persons acquainted with the career and reputation of the dead man are solicited for statements which usually are included in a single story with a comprehensive lead. Many of these statements are prepared in writing by the persons quoted; others are written following interviews by reporters who express the interviewee's attitude if not his exact words. Expressions of appreciation of certain persons may be published as separate items. If the president of the United States makes a statement, it usually constitutes a separate item. Dispatches from foreign countries carry separate datelines.

2. Sometimes the death of a prominent person leads to an official proclamation by a public official, ordering flags to be flown at half staff or suggesting the cessation of business on the day or during the hours of the funeral.

3. When messages of condolence are received by members of the dead

person's family, a newspaper obtains them for publication, either in place of or in addition to the statements that it gathers itself.

4. Resolutions of sympathy passed by organizations with which the deceased was affiliated usually are given to the press for immediate publication.

5. When a businessman dies, especially in a small community, those who had any dealings with him are interested to know whether the establishment will remain open. Newspapers print notices of how long, if at all, the business will be suspended, and whether other business places will close for any length of time as a gesture of respect.

6. The death of a prominent person is the excuse for a recitation of anecdotes of his life. Persons who were close to the deceased frequently write first-person reminiscences. In smaller communities, newspapers try to find citizens who were acquainted in some way with a prominent person who dies. In after years, on the anniversary of the famous person's death or birth or of some outstanding event in his career, more anecdotes are sought.

THE SECOND-DAY STORY

The second-day story is primarily the preliminary story of the funeral. When more than a day intervenes between death and the funeral, there may be two follow-up stories.

Details to look for in the funeral arrangements include:

Time and place
Who will officiate?
Will services be public or private?
How many will attend?
Arrangements for handling a crowd
Names of relatives
Names of notables who will attend
Will any club, lodge, etc. have a part?
Organizations to attend in a body or to be represented
Names of musicians and selections
Who will preach a sermon or deliver a eulogy?
Pallbearers, active and honorary
Where will burial take place?
What will be the program of the services?

The second-day story also may include additional details of the last illness and death, additional panegyrics, letters of sympathy received by the family, resolutions, memorial services, and the floral offerings. If the family requests that friends omit flowers, the newspaper should include the request. If floral offerings are sent, the newspaper should obtain a list and description of the important pieces and the names of the individuals or organizations sending them. Sometimes potential senders of flowers are asked instead to contribute to some worthy cause.

In virtually every case of death, friends of the dead person are given an opportunity to view the body before the time of the funeral. The newspaper should find out when and where the body will lie in state. Organizations which will not be formally represented at the funeral may view the body as a group.

When a member of Congress dies while in Washington, both houses pass resolutions and appoint committees to accompany the body home. Sometimes they adjourn out of respect. The practice of holding a separate memorial service for each deceased congressman has been dispensed with, and only one memorial service now is held each year at which all members of Congress who have died during the year are eulogized. Many clubs and lodges have a similar custom.

A few long-time friends of H. L. Mencken will join members of his family today at a funeral establishment to "speed him on his way."

Mr. Mencken, who died early Sunday, wanted no religious service.

His brother, August Mencken, said the gathering would be at 1 P.M. at an "unnamed mortician's place."

"One of the crying needs of the time in this incomparable republic is for a suitable burial service for the admittedly damned," H. L. Mencken wrote nearly 30 years ago.

Suggestion to Poets

He called on poets to concoct a service for the "doubting dead," saying: "What is needed, and what I bawl for politely, is a service that is free from the pious but unsupported asseverations that revolt so many of our best minds, and yet remains happily graceful and consoling . . . a suitable funeral for doubters, full of lovely poetry, but devoid of any specific pronouncement on the subject of a future life . . .

"Such a libretto for the inescapable last act would be humane and valuable. I renew my suggestion that the poets spit upon their hands and confect it at once."

Mr. Mencken's bawling apparently produced nothing to his taste.

Either August Mencken or Hamilton Owens, editor-in-chief of the Sunpapers, will address today's assembly briefly.

"Harry Left Instructions"

"We'll simply tell them Harry left instructions there was to be no religious service but he did want a few old friends around to speed him on his way," Mr. Mencken said.

Friends of the world-famous newspaperman and critic who are expected to be there include W. Edwin Moffett, who was a member of the old Saturday Night Club; Siegfried Weisberger, who ran the Peabody Bookshop; James M. Cain, novelist, of Hyattsville; Frank R. Kent, political columnist for The Sun and Mr. and Mrs. Louis Cheslock.

Mr. Cheslock, of the Peabody Institute, was another member of the Saturday Night Club and spent Saturday evening at the Mencken house at 1524 Hollins street.

Mr. Mencken died at home in his sleep.

His body will be cremated, and the ashes will be buried in the family plot at Loudon Park Cemetery next to those of his wife, who was Sara Powell Haardt. Mrs. Mencken died in 1933.

Mr. Mencken's survivors include August Mencken, the brother with whom he lived; Charles E. Mencken, another brother, of Pittsburgh; and Anna Gertrude Mencken, a sister, of 5110 Gwynn Oak avenue.

Mr. Mencken, closely associated with the Sunpapers during his long career, left a box in the newspaper office with orders that it remain locked until he died. Managing editors of The Sun and the Evening Sun had keys to it.

When it was opened Sunday morning, it yielded a brief note requesting that news of his death receive as scanty coverage as possible.

Baltimore *Sun*

THE FUNERAL STORY

When a collection is made of outstanding newspaper stories of history, there will be included more than one account of a funeral. The story of the burial of the unknown soldier by Kirke L. Simpson of the Associated Press has become a classic, as have stories of the funerals of most of the presidents of the United States. The following is a straight-forward account of an important funeral:

BY *Keith Shelton, Staff Writer*

Bonham — Sam Rayburn was buried Saturday in the combination of greatness, simplicity and dignity that characterized his life.

As a Primitive Baptist country preacher compared him to the Apostle Paul, the great men of the nation sat and mourned.

Only three persons took part in the service — the elder of the church in which he was baptized, the chaplain of the U.S. House of Representatives and an organist.

His grave in the family plot at Willow Wild Cemetery between his beloved home and his proud library was marked only by a simple, two-by-one-foot stone just as those for other family members.

A large monument with only the word "Rayburn" has marked the family plot for years.

On the front row of the left section of the First Baptist Church, President John F. Kennedy sat on the aisle. Beside him down the pew were Vice President Lyndon B. Johnson, former President Dwight D. Eisenhower and former President Harry S. Truman.

A good portion of the United States Congress sat behind them.

Tom Clark Present

Members of the Rayburn family occupied the middle tier of pews directly in front of the pulpit.

Justice Tom Clark of the U.S. Supreme Court, Defense Secretary Robert S. McNamara, Secretary of Health, Education and Welfare Abraham A. Ribicoff, Air Force Secretary Eugene M. Zuckert, Navy Secretary John Connally, and Army Secretary Elvis J. Stahr were in the congregation.

Chairman of the Joint Chiefs of Staff, Gen. Lyman L. Lemnitzer, represented the military.

Daniel on Hand

Consul General Alvaro Beltrain of St. Louis represented the Italian government.

Gov. Price Daniel attended for the State of Texas.

Fannin County and Bonham were represented by hundreds.

Mrs. J. C. Christian Jr. began the service at 1:15 P.M. by playing Bach and Mendelssohn. After 15 minutes, she began to play familiar hymns — "How Firm a Foundation," "Jesus, Lover of My Soul," "Lead, Kindly Light" and "The Lord is My Shepherd."

Recites 23rd Psalm

As a television camera plied the aisle, Dr. Bernard Braskamp, Chaplain of the House, recited the 23rd Psalm, "The Lord Is My Shepherd, I Shall Not Want . . ."

"Thou dost give and thou dost take away," he said.

Then he prayed: "We thank Thee for the life of him. We shall miss him because his place will be empty . . . His soul is at home with the Lord."

Dr. Braskamp called Mr. Rayburn a man "dedicated and devoted to duty, a man with genius and skill in the business of statecraft."

Text from John

"We are not saying farewell," he said, "but only good night."

Elder H. Grady Ball, who baptized the speaker into the Tioga, Tex., Primitive Baptist Church three years ago, took his text from the 14th Chapter of the Book of John:

"In my Father's house are many mansions: If it were not so, I would have told you. I go to prepare a place for you. And if I go and prepare a place for you, I will come again, and receive you unto myself; that where I am, there ye may be also."

Personal Friend

Elder Ball referred repeatedly to "our good friend," reflecting the very personal nature of Mr. Rayburn to the people of his home area.

"The poor, the lowly, the less fortunate were objects of his consideration and compassion," he said of the speaker. "Many the time they have felt the touch of his kindness."

Such men, he said, are made, not born.

The Apostle Paul was such a man, able to meet the great of the earth or the poor, the noble or the ignoble, he said.

To comfort the family, he gave 2 Timothy 4:7, "I have fought a good fight, I have finished my course, I have kept the faith."

Fairness Recalled

Mr. Rayburn fought the good fight for liberty and freedom and for his Bonham friends, he said. "He was fair. He was loyal."

Then the elder gave a short prayer, the organist played, "America the Beautiful," and the body was carried from the church.

Somber, ashen clouds hung low as the procession moved out the dirt road to the cemetery. But as the burial rites began at the graveside, the sun broke out of a thick haze and beamed down.

"The sunshine of God's eternal love has lighted his pathway into glory," Elder Ball had said at the church.

Flowers Plentiful

On a gentle rise up to the cemetery, an abundance of flowers was arranged for the graveside service. Other floral offerings were placed in and around the family plot.

Mr. Sam is the ninth of his family to be buried there. He was placed to rest between a brother, Abner, who died July 26, 1914, and a sister, Lucinda, who helped him in office many years and who died July 26, 1956, of cancer.

Others buried there are the Speaker's father and mother, brothers Tom, William, and John Franklin Rayburn; and a sister-in-law, Nina Jackson Rayburn.

Staff Serve

Among the 23 floral tributes were those from Tennessee, his native state, the U.S. House of Representatives and, characteristically, one from the City of Ladonia, Texas.

Pallbearers were members of the speaker's staff and longtime friends, Buster Cole, John Holton, Choice Moore, Dr. Joe Risser, H. G. Dulaney and Robert West.

The President, vice president and the two former presidents entered the church by a side door. Mr. Truman nodded to the President and President Kennedy talked to Gen. Eisenhower in an ante room before the service.

Church Jammed

Only 1,000 could be crowded into the modernistic, new church auditorium and Sunday school classes, where loudspeakers had been set up.

Thousands more stood outside the church. They had started to gather early Saturday morning for the 1:30 P.M. services. Some were there to see the celebrities. Others were Bonham friends of Mr. Rayburn who only wanted to pay their last respects.

The farm boy who served twice as long as any man as the House's presiding officer died peacefully in his sleep at 6:20 A.M. Thursday.

He had given half a century of public service in the times of eight U.S. presidents. Mr. Rayburn was elected to the Texas Legislature in 1906 and became the youngest speaker of the Texas House in 1911.

He had served in the Congress since 1912 and was speaker when the Democrats were in power since 1940.　　　　　Dallas *Times Herald*

FOLLOW-UPS

A number of other stories may grow out of that of a death. Virtually everyone who is worthy of an obituary has held some position which will have to be filled. Before a speaker of the house is buried, newspapers print stories speculating as to who will be his successor. Frequently there are changes in business organizations after the death of an executive. A smart editor reads the account of a man's death and notes the organizations, business, fraternal, and otherwise, in which he held an office, and assigns reporters to learn how the man's place will be filled in each case.

The courthouse reporter watches for the filing of wills and follows carefully each legal step up to and including the final settlement and discharge.

Memorial services may be held weeks or months after a person's death, schools and clubs may be named for him, monuments and tablets erected to his memory.

THE OBITUARY BLANK

The obituary may seem an important assignment, yet it is one of the first that a cub reporter receives. He is as likely to be sent out to gather facts about a death as to frequent a railroad station or hotel in quest of brevities. This is because few obituaries approach in importance those given as examples in this chapter, and because the elements of all stories of death are similar.

Most newspapers have an obituary blank for reporters who gather facts about deaths. These printed forms also are given to undertakers who cooperate in obtaining information for newspapers. A sample blank follows:

OBITUARY REPORT

Full name ....

Residence ....

Place of death .... Time ....

Cause of death ....

Duration of illness ....

Present at deathbed ....

Circumstances of death ....

....

Date of birth .... Place ....

Surviving relatives: Wife or husband ....

Parents .... Address ....

Brothers .... Address ....

.... Address ....

 and

Sisters .... Address ....

.... Address ....

Children .... Address ....

.... Address ....

.... Address ....

Date of marriage .... Place ....

Came to this country .... Naturalized ....

Residence here since ....

Previous residence and duration ....

Last occupation ....

Previous occupations ....

Education, with degrees and dates ....

Fraternal orders, clubs, etc. ....

Distinguished service, fraternal, educational, industrial, political, etc. .....

....

....

....

Church affiliations ....

War record: Division, war ....

When discharged .... Rank ....

Honors ....

Time of funeral .... Place ....

Who will officiate ....

Organizations to attend in a body ....

Body will lie in state: When .... Where ....

Active pallbearers ....

....

Honorary pallbearers ....

....

Music ....

....

Burial place ....

Prominent floral pieces . . . .
. . . .
Attending from away . . . .
. . . .
Additional information . . . .
. . . .
. . . .
. . . .
. . . .

No blank can include every question which a reporter may want answered, and so it is better not to rely entirely upon an undertaker but to interview the nearest living relative.

If he relies upon another to obtain his facts for him, the reporter may miss the feature of his story, especially if death resulted from violence or an accident. Possible features not suggested by the questions on the blank include: failure of a close relative to reach the bedside in time, a letter written by the dead person containing instructions for his own funeral, the last words of the deceased, some request made shortly before death, any coincidence in the date, place, or manner of death, and some other event in the history of the individual or his family, etc.

LANGUAGE AND STYLE

The language of the obituary should be simple and dignified. The verb "to die" is the safest to use. No religious group can take offense at it but can interpret it to suit its own tenets. "Passed away," "passed on," "called home," "the great beyond," "gone to his reward," "the angel of death," "the grim reaper," "departed this life," and similar expressions should be avoided. Also, let it be repeated, attempts at "fine" writing may be only maudlin.

SUICIDES

In covering a suicide, the reporter seeks the same information about a man's career, funeral arrangements, when the body will lie in state, etc., as in the case of an ordinary obituary. Elements peculiar to the suicide story, however, include:

1. The motive
2. The method
3. The probable circumstances leading up to the act
4. The coroner's inquest

THE MOTIVE

A person who commits suicide usually is despondent because of financial difficulties, ill health, marital unhappiness, a mental disorder, or a philosophic attitude of discouragement toward life in general.

If the person does not leave a letter explaining his motive, the reporter must investigate whichever motives seem most probable. A man's banker or doctor, his business associates, and his friends and relatives should be interviewed. The reporter should ask if the person made any previous attempts at suicide, if he ever mentioned suicide, if he appeared to be in good health recently, especially the day before he took his life. How did he take leave of his family and friends? Was there anything at all suspicious about his actions or remarks recently? If he had not consulted a physician recently, others who knew him can pass judgment upon his state of health. His appetite, sleep, recreation, hours of work, etc., may have been affected noticeably.

When there is no apparent motive, the news writer should say so and should quote those whom he has interviewed to that effect. He should not attempt to concoct a motive and must be particularly careful not to ascribe a suicidal motive when none was present. Legally, no suicide is a suicide until so called by a coroner's jury. If there is a doubt, the account of death should be qualified by a statement as, "thought to be suicide."

Even when the suicidal motive is present beyond a doubt, some newspapers hesitate to use the word. The editor of a paper in a small community may attempt to protect the feelings of surviving relatives by covering up the suicidal intent. Seldom is such an attempt successful, as an unprejudiced statement of the facts surrounding death indicates either suicide or murder. Only by deliberate fabrication is it possible really to "protect" the widow and other survivors.

It is doubtful, furthermore, whether the paper does as much good as harm in "hushing up" a suicide story. Anyone who knew the dead person will become acquainted with the facts anyway, and if he encounters an effort to deceive him as to what actually happened, he conjectures. The rumors which circulate as to the motive of a suicide usually are much more damaging to a person's reputation than the simple truth would have been. A frank newspaper account puts an end to rumors.

THE METHOD

The method by which suicide was accomplished usually is obvious. A newspaper should not dramatize the means of a suicide or print a story that might encourage another to take his life. A poison used for suicidal purpose should not be mentioned by name, and if suicide by any other method is prevalent, newspapers should cooperate with authorities by omitting the method.

The coroner or physician summoned to examine the body can estimate the length of time the person has been dead. Members of the family and friends can provide clues as to what actions preceded the accomplishment of the act. The reporter should try to find the person who last saw the deceased alive.

In the following story the suicides are "placed" in relation to other pertinent events, the effect being interpretative:

Elizabeth, N.J., May 10 — (AP) — Two Elizabeth officials, who testified before a Union County grand jury probing alleged laxity in connection with gambling, committed suicide yesterday.

A bullet in the head ended the life of 65-year-old Police Captain August F. Winkelmann, who had been on terminal leave and was due to retire next month.

Fire Commissioner Francis De Stephan, 39, waded fully clothed into Raritan Bay and drowned.

Both deaths were listed officially by authorities as suicides. Both men were found in Monmouth County. De Stephan's body was removed from marshland in Matawan Township. Winkelmann was still alive when found near the Manasquan River inlet. He died later in Point Pleasant Hospital.

Uncertain About Connection

Union County Prosecutor H. Russell Morss, Jr., told newsmen he "couldn't say whether there was any connection" between the deaths of Winkelmann and De Stephan. Morss also declined to say whether either man had been scheduled to appear again before the grand jury.

Winkelmann had refused to honor one grand jury subpoena, but finally testified April 26. De Stephan had been called before the panel March 2 but didn't testify until 19 days later.

Received Questionnaires

The fire commissioner's brother, Dr. Joseph L. De Stephan, a dentist, said Francis had been worried about his appearance before the grand jury and also was concerned over debts.

Winkelmann was among 68 law enforcement officers who received questionnaires from the panel concerning their financial affairs.

In a recent action, Superior Court Judge Richard J. Hughes declined to order the recipients to fill out the forms. However, the judge did rule that each Elizabeth and Union County police officer may be called before the grand jury, be handed the questionnaire, and be asked to answer the questions.

Prosecutor Morss said his staff would work along with state and county police in an investigation of the suicides.

The grand jury probe began 11 weeks ago, and indictments have been returned against three persons. Philadelphia *Bulletin*

INQUESTS

The coroner, a county official whose duty it is to investigate cases of unusual death, usually orders an inquest into a case believed to be suicide. Sometimes this is delayed until an autopsy is performed on the body and until circumstances of the death are fully determined. The coroner's jury may determine the motive as well as the manner of death. If in doubt, it returns an open verdict.

ACCIDENTS, DISASTERS

Part of the price which modern man pays for the benefits of a highly industrialized society is the danger he runs of sudden, violent injury or death. Automobile accidents result annually in about 40,000 deaths and many times that number of injuries. Wrecks of common carriers — railroads, street cars, buses, airplanes, airships, boats, etc. — are fewer but are more destructive than in the days of slower speed and less delicate mechanics. Homes, public buildings, industrial plants, mines, etc., are better protected against fire and explosions, but an undetected minor flaw may result in a catastrophe without warning. Because of lack of foresight on the part of our grandfathers, we who live in the United States today are facing a national crisis as to how to control floods, dust storms, and soil erosion which cause tremendous losses of life and property and, some say, are turning our country into a desert. Other "acts of God," such as hurricanes, tornadoes, earthquakes, cyclones, etc., continue to occur with their same frequency, and man has not yet learned how to protect himself adequately against them.

ELEMENTS OF INTEREST

Although they differ from each other by types, and although no two disasters of any kind are alike from the standpoint of news interest, news events pertaining to loss of life and property have in common numerous aspects which a reporter must bear in mind. Among the possible angles which no reporter can overlook are the following:
  1. Casualties (dead and injured)
     a. Number killed and injured
     b. Number who escaped
     c. Nature of injuries and how received
     d. Care given injured
     e. Disposition made of the dead

    f. Prominence of anyone who was killed, injured or who escaped

    g. How escape was handicapped or cut off

2. Property damage
   a. Estimated loss in value
   b. Description (kind of building, etc.)
   c. Importance of property (historical significance, etc.)
   d. Other property threatened
   e. Insurance protection
   f. Previous disasters in vicinity

3. Cause of disaster
   a. Testimony of participants
   b. Testimony of witnesses
   c. Testimony of others: fire chief, property owner, relief workers, etc.
   d. How was accident discovered?
   e. Who sounded alarm or summoned aid?
   f. Previous intimation of danger: ship or building condemned, etc.

4. Rescue and relief work
   a. Number engaged in rescue work, fire fighting, etc.
   b. Are any prominent persons among the relief workers?
   c. Equipment used: number of water lines, chemicals, etc.
   d. Handicaps: wind, inadequate water supply or pressure, etc.
   e. Care of destitute and homeless
   f. How disaster was prevented from spreading: adjacent buildings soaked, counter forest fire, etc.
   g. How much property was saved? How?
   h. Heroism in rescue work

5. Description
   a. Spread of fire, flood, hurricane, etc.
   b. Blasts and explosions
   c. Attempts at escape and rescue
   d. Duration
   e. Collapsing walls, etc.
   f. Extent and color of flames

6. Accompanying incidents
   a. Spectators: number and attitude, how controlled, etc.
   b. Unusual happenings: room or article untouched, etc.
   c. Anxiety of relatives

7. Legal action as result
   a. Inquests, post mortems, autopsies
   b. Search for arsonist, hit-and-run driver, etc.
   c. Protest of insurance company
   d. Negligence of fire fighters, police, etc.
   e. Investigation of cause

In all stories of disaster there is human interest. In most of them, there also are suspense and a recognition of combat between man and the elements. Disaster stories, furthermore, are action stories and contain considerable details as to exactly what happened. If these details are not present in chronological order, they at least are so arranged as to leave no doubt in the reader's mind regarding the sequence of the most important of them.

Few other types of stories offer the writer greater opportunity for descriptive writing. Although major disaster stories are illustrated, the writer does not rely upon a photograph to do the work of 1,000 or even 100 or ten words.

PICKING THE FEATURE

No formula for writing a disaster story — or any other type of story for that matter — should be accepted as absolute. In general, however, the lead of the disaster story should follow the orthodox rule of playing up the five *w*'s, giving identification and authority and playing up the feature. Any one of the elements listed may be the feature of the story at hand. Regardless of what is played up, the occasion must be identified in the lead by the amount of loss, either in lives or property. The reader judges the importance of the disaster by the size of the casualty list or the number of digits after the dollar sign. When the casualty list or inventory of property is long, it is impossible to be specific in the lead. Names, however, must be high in the story. If their number is not prohibitive, they should come immediately after the lead; otherwise, they should be included in a box either within or next to the story proper. If included in the story itself, they should be followed by explanations as to how each casualty or item of damage occurred.

PRECAUTIONS

The reporter must be careful not to assign blame in an automobile accident, the type of disaster story which he has most frequent occasion to write. Police reports are not adequate protection against libel in such a story as the following:

> Disregarding a traffic signal and a policeman's whistle, Alex Winser, 1421 Talcott street, crashed into an automobile driven by Miss Ruth Hazelhurst, 1191 W. Vilas court, at 11 o'clock this morning at Third and Hamilton streets.

The following is a much safer way:

> Two automobiles, one driven by Miss Ruth Hazelhurst, 1191 W. Vilas court, and the other by Alex Winser, 1421 Talcott street, collided at 11

o'clock this morning at Third and Hamilton streets. Neither driver was injured.

Some editors insist on the form, "the automobile driven by" or "the automobile in which the couple was riding," etc., instead of "his automobile" or "the couple's machine." This is a precaution against possible libel action when the driver or occupant of a car is not the owner. Other editors consider the precaution unnecessary.

Care must be exercised in using "crashed," "demolished," "destroyed," and other descriptive verbs. The reporter should study the definitions of such words to avoid misapplying them. The makes of automobiles should not be mentioned.

It must be remembered that to collide two bodies must be in motion. Thus, if a moving automobile hits one which is parked at the curbing, there is no collision; rather, the car in motion strikes the other.

In the attempt to make drivers more careful and thus reduce accidents, many newspapers print daily tables or charts to show the total number of accidents and casualties by comparison with the preceding year. Likewise, since a magazine campaign against automobile accidents a few years ago, newspapers have been more inclined to include frank details of such mishaps to emphasize their horror. Much more gruesome pictures also are being used than formerly.

In the belief that they are performing a public service as well as fostering both reader interest and friendship, some newspapers undisguisedly editorialize in accident stories, as:

> The danger of bicycle riding on public streets again was illustrated about 7 P.M. yesterday when Harold, 13-year-old son of Mr. and Mrs. Emil J. Bornstein, 636 Cabany street, was seriously injured in the 1200 block of Chicksaw avenue. He was struck by an automobile driven by O. S. Patrick, 802 Lunt avenue.

SIDE FEATURES

Any one of the elements which go to make up a complete disaster story conceivably could be played up in a sidebar: acts of heroism, miraculous escapes, rescue and relief work, coincidences, etc. It is customary to use boxes or separate stories for long tabulations of casualties or damages and for lists of previous catastrophes of a similar nature. Eyewitness accounts are provided by victims who had narrow escapes and by bystanders, rescue workers, reporters and others. When the disaster occurs outside the circulation area of the publication, it is customary to use a sidebar or in some other way play up the names of any local persons who were involved.

PERSPECTIVE

Many disasters can be prevented by such obvious precautions as straightening highways, repairing defective electrical wiring and posting warning signals. Others cannot be controlled without scientific study and analysis and action on a much broader scale. The media of communication can help the public understand why a certain type of disaster is prevalent in a community, area, state, or nation by "digging deeper" than the facts related to a specific news event.

Rufus Terral, St. Louis *Post-Dispatch* editorial writer, for instance, began an article, "In the Wake of the Floods," in the October, 1951 *Survey* as follows:

> Behind last summer's great natural catastrophe, the devastating floods in Kansas and Missouri, is a simple story. The sweeping tragedy of 44 persons killed, 500,000 persons displaced, 2,000,000 acres flooded, 45,000 houses damaged or destroyed, the teeming Kansas Citys gutted by water and flame, and a $2.5 billion loss is only an effect. Underlying it all is the tale of three dams that became lost in politics in Kansas and the District of Columbia, and never got built.

Sociological phenomena are interrelated. Why flood control projects are not constructed involves consideration of more than selfish political interests. The stories of the depletion of natural resources, chiefly forests and grazing lands, and of soil erosion and other bad consequences of unscientific methods of farming are intricate ones.

Slum area fires usually can be blamed on faulty building codes and/or their improper enforcement. Probing deeper, to obtain perspective, however, the interpretative reporter may discover the origin of overcrowded housing in the heavy migration of Negroes, Puerto Ricans or others into areas where segregation is enforced and programs for integrating newcomers into the economic and social life of the community are inadequate. The machinations of some real estate operators to reap personal profit by playing race against race or nationality group against nationality group may be revealed. Tracing the ownership of tenement property, often concealed by "dummy" title holders, may be enlightening and a first step toward removal of fire hazards.

At a different level, newspapers can lead the way in educating home owners and tenants in how to preserve and renovate property so as to remove hazards. The famous Baltimore Plan of urban renewal could not have succeeded without the vigorous support of the *Sunpapers*.

Those concerned with safety on the streets and highways still stress the *three E's*: engineering, education and enforcement. Increasingly, however, researchers are paying more attention to so-called human factors.

The psychology of the automobile driver is being studied with remarkable results. The causes of "accident proneness" often are deep seated within the individual and, for proper understanding, may require study of social factors external to the individual. Only a start has been made toward understanding the interrelationships in this field.

The same is true of most other aspects of the problem as a whole. Too many explanations of why teenagers are more reckless drivers than adults are superficial and contradictory. Simple explanations and answers should be avoided until much more study has been completed. In the meantime, the interpretative journalist can help keep the public informed as to the status of that research.

14

Police, Crime, Criminal Law

I. Learning the Ropes
  1. *The Police System*
  2. *What Constitutes Crime*

II. Elements of Crime News
  1. *The Police Blotter*
  2. *Picking the Feature*
  3. *Juveniles*
  4. *Human Interest*
  5. *Other Police News*
  6. *Crime Statistics*
  7. *Situation Stories*

III. Criminal Procedure
  1. *Arraignment*
  2. *Preliminary Hearing*
  3. *The Grand Jury*
  4. *Pleas and Motions*
  5. *Other Preliminaries*

IV. Criminal Trials
  1. *First Stories*
  2. *Picking the Jury*
  3. *Opening Statements*
  4. *Evidence*
  5. *Closing Statements*
  6. *Reporting Trials*
  7. *Verdicts*
  8. *Sentences*
  9. *Punishments*

V. The Ethics of Crime News

MIRRORS OF LIFE

Newspapers are often castigated for printing crime news, for printing sordid things, for telling about human conduct as it really exists.

Newspapers — and the reference here is to those in the United States and the British Empire which operate without coercion or intimidation by the government — perform the function of telling what has happened, what will take place, and of commenting and interpreting. They have other functions, too, but the main duties are those cited.

At Owensboro, Ky., one morning last week, 15,000 persons crowded into a small enclosure to see a man hanged. Here are a few sentences from the story of that Roman holiday:

"Souvenir hunters ripped the hangman's hood from the face of Bethea immediately after the convicted attacker of a 70-year-old white woman was hanged.

"Bethea still breathed when a few persons from the crowd rushed the four-foot wire enclosure about the scaffold and scrambled for fragments as mementoes of the spectacle.

"The crowd came in automobiles, wagons and by hundreds on freight trains.

"Throughout the night the spectators pushed into choice positions to watch Bethea die. Thousands milled about the streets converging upon the scene.

"About half of those who fought and shoved to get closer to the enclosure were women, young girls, and children. Babies in arms and toddlers by the score clung to their mothers.

"People stood on roofs of nearby buildings, hung from telephone poles, leaned out of windows, stood on automobiles, to witness the execution."

This is not a report of cruel Saracen nomads anxious for the lives of Christian martyrs, nor of the cries of a Mayan priest screaming for a human sacrifice, nor of a band of Voodoo worshipping savages in darkest Africa.

It is a report on the behavior of a part of those people who choose to call themselves the most civilized race of human beings in the world.

Newspapers are but the mirror of life. Details of the Owensboro hanging were printed after the event took place, not before, and therefore were a reflection of what took place, not a textbook on a future course of action.

No, human nature will have to change before crime, horror, scandal, and lust can be eliminated from the pages of the honest newspaper.

When these things cease to be, newspapers will not have to report them.

Des Moines Register

IF FOR SOME UNIMAGINABLE REASON A NEWSPAPER WERE COM-pelled to remove all of its beat reporters but one, it would be the man at police headquarters who would remain at his post. This is so, not because crime news is considered so overpoweringly important, but because in addition to learning of homes that have been broken into, checks that have been forged and murders that have been committed, the police reporter usually is the first to turn in tips of accidents, attempted suicides, missing persons, rabid dogs, strikes and many other events about which newspapers carry stories.

Because the police are in close touch with more phases of everyday life than any other news source, the police beat affords excellent training for the beginning reporter and, fortunately, is one which he is likely to get. In the small community, covering police means visiting the police station two or three or more times a day, visiting the scenes of the infrequent important crimes which occur, verifying and amplifying the comparatively meager reports contained on the official police blotter or bulletin and writing all police news worth mention. In a large city, covering police means to remain all day at headquarters or at a district station, watching the steadily growing day's report and phoning tips of the most important items (perhaps 25 per cent of the total) to the city desk. When anything happens about which the paper wants more than the beat man can obtain from the police bulletin or by interviewing members of the force or witnesses brought to the station, an assignment man is sent out; the writing is done by rewrite men.

Neither the life of the police reporter nor of the average police detective resembles very closely that which the continuity strips and magazine short stories depict. After he has seen one sobbing mother, one hardboiled harlot, one repentant gunman, and one of each of the other types which frequent police headquarters, the reporter has seen them all. When this fact dawns upon him, and as he becomes accustomed to the intransigence of all parties concerned in the diurnal police drama, he may have to struggle against both cynicism and discouragement. A good turn at police reporting is the best hazing possible for the callow graduate and aspiring author of the world's greatest novel. There are few newspapermen of importance who did not take the test and pass. An attitude of detached studiousness will enable the beginning reporter to make his police reporting experience what it should be: the most valuable of his entire journalistic career.

LEARNING THE ROPES

THE POLICE SYSTEM

The police reporter has got to know who's who and why at headquarters or at the district station which is his to cover. On the opposite page is shown the setup of the police department in an average-sized American city. In other cities, the organization may differ in details but not fundamentally. At the top is always a chief of police, superintendent of police, police commissioner or some other individual appointed either by the mayor with the approval of the lawmaking body or by a police commission so appointed. Whatever its title, this office is a political one, and its holder may have little or nothing to say about the formation of general policies. If the higher-ups decide that certain "places" are to be allowed to remain open, they remain open until the word comes from above, either as a result of public pressure or for other reasons. Whenever any change in policy is made it is, of course, the chief who "fronts," making the announcements and receiving the credit; likewise, when something goes wrong, he is the scapegoat unless it is possible to "pass the buck" down the line to some underling.

This realistic picture of how the law enforcement system operates may be disturbing to young reporters with an idealistic or reformist nature, but until the public insists on an extension of the civil service system to include heads of police departments and upon strict observance of discipline and honesty throughout the entire system, the situation will not change. The trouble is that the element in the population which might favor an improvement either is unaware of the true state of affairs or is too indolent to do anything about it. The irate citizen who fulminates against the patrolman who looks the other way for a slight consideration or because of orders from above, is the same who, when he receives a ticket for parking his automobile overtime, starts on a hunt for someone who knows someone who knows someone. The practice of frightening children into proper behavior by threatening to call a policeman also is not conducive to a helpful attitude on the part of the same children when they become adults.

Despite modern training methods, many if not most policemen adhere to the "catch 'em and lock 'em up" school of criminology. Understandably, they want every arrest they make to lead to a conviction in court. They find it difficult to accept the principle of everyone's being considered innocent until proved guilty. They chafe under court restrictions regarding the gathering of evidence which forbid entering a place or searching a suspect without a proper warrant. They believe some eavesdropping, wire tapping and even entrapment to be necessary. They also want more

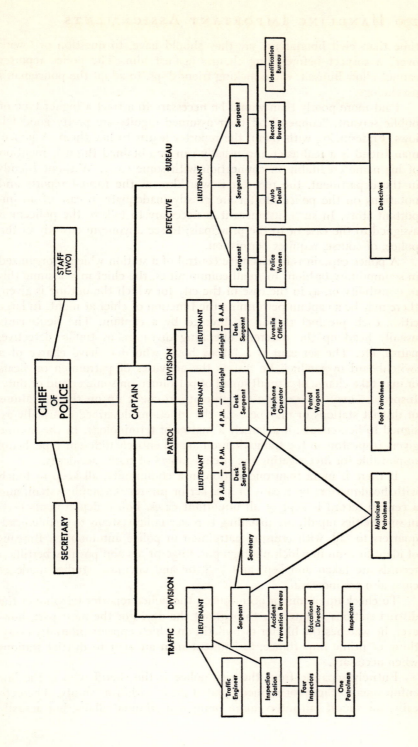

time than civil libertarians say they should have, to question or "work over" a suspect before filing charges against him. The police reporter cannot allow himself, while making friendships, to adopt the policeman's psychology.

Paid more poorly than would be necessary to attract a higher type of public servant, "coppers" off their assumed dignity are pretty good fellows. Fraternizing with them, the reporter learns to like them. A policeman friend is a real asset and usually can be obtained through mention of his name creditably in connection with some story. Without friends in the department, the reporter is worthless as the formal reports and notations on the police blotter are grossly inadequate in case of an important story. In such instances it is necessary to talk to the policemen assigned to the case or to the principals; to see anyone in custody of the police, of course, requires permission.

A police captain is in executive control of a station which is organized in semimilitary fashion. In small communities, the chief may assume this responsibility or, as in the case of the city for which the outline is given, there may be a captain performing the function of chief at night. In large cities, each precinct station is directed by a captain. The lieutenants usually head up the different operating divisions, as traffic, detective, patrol, etc. The sergeant is a "straw boss" who may have charge of a switchboard over which he directs the activities of patrolmen on beats or may take charge of a small squad of patrolmen on some errand or duty. Inspectors may have roving assignments to check up on the operations of district stations or may perform the functions described as usually assigned to lieutenants; it is largely a matter of terminology. In the outline given, inspectors in the traffic division are an entirely different type, being responsible for investigating the circumstances of traffic accidents.

If there is more than one station in a community, all keep in touch with headquarters by means of a ticker or printer telegraph system, and a central record is kept of all important cases. Police departments even in small cities rapidly are installing two-way radio systems to enable headquarters to talk with cruising patrolmen in police automobiles. Bureaus of identification in which photographs, fingerprints and possibly bertillion records are taken and kept and ballistic and chemical studies made of clues also are increasing.

To check up on minor occurrences, the police reporter telephones the district stations at intervals throughout the day. For the most part, however, he watches the blotter or bulletin on which appears promptly everything of prime importance; assignment men are sent to district stations when necessary.

Entirely separate from the city police is the sheriff who is the law enforcement officer for unincorporated areas within a county. Theoretically, the sheriff can intervene in municipal criminal affairs, but actually he seldom does so except when invited or when local law enforcement breaks down. When such happens, it is extremely newsworthy and someone inevitably charges "politics."

Sheriff's raids are made mostly to break up illegal gambling establishments outside city limits. Sheriff traffic police also patrol the highways along with a limited number of state police. In states where the township unit of government persists, the law enforcement officer is the constable and the local judicial officer is the justice of the peace.

County prosecuting attorneys are called circuit or district attorneys or state's attorneys. They are elected locally but are responsible to the state attorney general in the enforcement of state law. Federal prosecutors are district attorneys, federal law enforcement officers are marshals, and preliminary hearings are conducted by commissioners.

WHAT CONSTITUTES CRIME

As important to the reporter as knowing police procedure is a knowledge of what constitutes crime. A breach of the law may be either a felony or misdemeanor. Since the law differs in different states the same offense may be a felony in one state and a misdemeanor in another; and a felony or misdemeanor in one state may not be considered a crime at all in another. A felony always is a serious offense such as murder, whereas a misdemeanor is a minor offense such as breaking the speed law. Felonies are punishable by death or imprisonment, whereas a misdemeanor usually results in a fine or confinement in a local jail. A *capital* crime is one punishable by death; an *infamous* crime is one punishable by a prison sentence.

Crimes may be classified as follows:

1. Against the person
   a. Simple assault: threatening, doubling the fist, etc.
   b. Aggravated assault: threat violent enough to cause flight
   c. Battery: actually striking a person, a rider's horse, spitting on another, etc.
   d. False imprisonment: liberty unlawfully restrained by anyone
   e. Kidnaping: stealing away a person; may use abduction for women or children
   f. Rape: unlawful carnal knowledge of a woman forcibly detained; statutory rape occurs when girl is minor even though she consents
   g. Maim (mayhem): the attacker disables or dismembers his victim
   h. Homicide: killing when the victim dies within a year and a day
      (1) Matricide: killing one's mother
      (2) Patricide: killing one's father

       (3) Fratricide: killing one's brother or sister

       (4) Uxoricide: killing one's wife or husband

       (5) Justified: in self-defense or in line of duty

       (6) Felonious: either murder or manslaughter

    i. Manslaughter

       (1) Voluntary: intentionally in the heat of passion or as the result of extreme provocation

       (2) Involuntary: unintentional but with criminal negligence

    j. Murder

       (1) First degree: with expressed malice and premeditation

       (2) Second degree: no premeditation but intent to kill or inflict injury regardless of outcome

    k. Abortion: interfering with pregnancy

2. Against habitation

    a. Burglary: entering another's dwelling with intent to commit a felony therein; often extended to include any building

    b. Arson: malicious burning of another's real estate

3. Against property

    a. Larceny: taking and converting to use with felonious intent the the property of another

    b. Robbery: larceny with intimidation or violence against the person

    c. Embezzlement: larceny by means of a breach of confidence

    d. False pretenses: confidence games, impostures, swindles

    e. Receiving stolen goods: for sale or concealment; recipient called "fence"

    f. Forgery: altering or falsely marking a piece of writing for private profit or deception of another

    g. Malicious mischief: killing animals, mutilating or defacing property

    h. Extortion: blackmail; obtaining illegal compensation to do or not to do any act

4. Against morality and decency

    a. Adultery: sexual relations between a married and unmarried person

    b. Fornication: sexual relations between unmarried persons

    c. Bigamy: second marriage without dissolving the first

    d. Incest: sexual relations between persons so closely related that they are forbidden to marry

    e. Miscegenation: marriage between races forbidden to intermarry

    f. Seduction: inducing an unmarried girl to engage in sexual relations by false promises or deception

    g. Prostitution: promiscuous indulgence in sexual relations by women for profit

    h. Sodomy: homosexual relations between men

    i. Obscenity: anything offensive to one's sense of chastity

    j. Indecency: anything outrageously disgusting

    k. Contributing to delinquency of a minor: encouraging or permitting any waywardness in youths

    l. Sabbath laws: restrict commercial and other activities on Sundays

5. Against the public peace

    a. Breach of the peace: may cover disorderly conduct and a variety of nuisances

    b. Affray: fighting in a public place to the terror of the public

    c. Unlawful assembly: for purpose of planning or committing illegal act

    d. Rout: occurs when unlawful assembly begins to move

    e. Riot: occurs when assembly or rout becomes tumultuous or violent

    f. Disturbance of public assembly: interference with legal meeting

    g. Disorderly conduct: statutes stipulate acts forbidden

    h. Forcible entry and detainer: illegal seizure or holding of property

    i. Defamation: written is libel; spoken is slander

    j. Concealed weapons: may be listed as disorderly conduct

    k. Gaming: playing games for money or games of chance

    l. Gambling: betting on outcomes of events over which bettors have no control

6. Against justice and authority

    a. Treason: breach of allegiance to country; giving enemy aid

    b. Perjury: false testimony under oath in judicial proceedings

    c. Bribery: attempt to influence public official in his duties

    d. Embracery: attempt to influence a juror

    e. Counterfeiting: making false money which is passed as genuine

    f. Misconduct in office: extortion, breach of trust, neglect, etc.

    g. Obstructing justice: resisting arrest; refusing to aid arresting officer

    h. Obstructing punishment: escape; prison breach

    i. Compounding a felony: agreeing not to prosecute felon or assisting him in evading justice

    j. Exciting litigation: stirring up lawsuits for profit; barratry; maintenance; champerty

    k. Election laws: fraud or illegal interference with voting

    l. Conspiracy: planning or plotting to commit crime

    m. Contempt: improper respect for court

7. Against public safety, health and comfort

    a. Nuisances: annoyances

b. Traffic regulations
c. Food and drug acts
d. Health regulations
e. Safety laws for common carriers, use of explosives, etc.

The police reporter must understand these popular definitions of criminal offenses, the names of which may or may not correspond to the statutory titles which differ somewhat by states.

ELEMENTS OF CRIME NEWS

THE POLICE BLOTTER

Despite the quantity of news emanating from police headquarters which gets into print, much more that appears on the blotter or bulletin is disregarded by the police reporter. Whereas it is possible to give feature treatment to almost everything that is reported to police, there is so much sameness in most of the routine of law enforcement that such entries on the bulletin as complaints against peddlers, small boys or dogs, notices from the police of other cities to be on the outlook for a certain person or automobile and reports of suspicious characters, lost and found articles, etc., go unheeded. What follows is an almost verbatim copy of the entries covering several hours on the police bulletin in an average-sized city, together with the use made of the material by the police reporter:

BULLETIN	NEWSPAPER TREATMENT
The following were injured in auto accident at McCabe and Dunmore and taken to Municipal hospital: Joseph Muenter, 623 Center street, Massillion, Ohio, laceration to hand; Mrs. Ollie Richter, Peru, Ill., age 51, laceration to scalp.	Not used because minor and occurred outside city limits; no local citizens in any way involved. Reporter talked to traffic inspectors who investigated.
L. D. Donaldson, 117 Forest avenue, reports the loss of a male bull dog.	Ignored as trivial.
Grover Mack (c), 1835 Grey avenue, arrested for passing a red light on complaint of Robert A. Kirkhope, 118 N. Park avenue, Waukegan, in connection with accident. Case set for 9/23 and defendant locked up awaiting bond.	Combined with other report; see below.

BULLETIN

Attempts made to burglarize Royal Cafe, 1248 Chicago avenue, between 2 A.M. and 6:45 A.M. Used a one-inch drill on rear door. Entrance not gained.

Attempt made to burglarize Helen's Cafe, 523 Dempster street, between 2 A.M. and 6 A.M. Used a one-inch drill on rear door. Entrance not gained.

John C. Scale, 826 Sherman avenue, driving a Chevrolet coupe eastbound on Dempster street, at McCormick boulevard, backed into a Studebaker sedan driven by Lawrence G. Briggs, 1238 Oak avenue, and then continued east on Dempster street into city.

John C. Scale, 826 Sherman avenue, was arrested for driving while intoxicated on Dempster street. Locked up and case set for 9/23.

Hugh C. Collins, 809 Washington street, driving a Chevrolet coupe east-bound on Washington street, west of Elmwood avenue, collided with a Ford coupe parked in front of 910 Washington street, owned by Richard Steele, 4730¼ Woodlawn avenue, Chicago.

NEWSPAPER TREATMENT

Two-paragraph story, as follows:

Burglars early today failed in their attempt to enter and burglarize two Evanston restaurants.

A screen over the rear window at the Royal Cafe, 1248 Chicago avenue, was torn but no entrance gained. The burglars also failed to gain entrance at Helen's Cafe, 523 Dempster street, after using a drill on the rear door, police say.

The following are paragraphs near the end of a general accident story, the lead for which was a serious accident, occurring after the reporter left police headquarters:

Two men were arrested on charges of driving under the influence of liquor yesterday after the car in which both of them drove was in two collisions. The men are: Hugh C. Collins, 809 Washington Street, and John C. Scale, 826 Sherman avenue.

Scale was driving the car when it was involved in an accident with one driven by Lawrence G. Briggs, 1238 Oak avenue, at Dempster street and McCormick boulevard, police say. He left the scene of the accident, police report, but was arrested a few blocks away.

His companion, Collins, drove the car toward his home, but it hit one owned by Richard Steele, 4730½ Woodlawn avenue, Chicago, parked at the curb in front of 910 Washington street, police say. He continued to his home and was arrested by police on charges of driving while intoxicated and leaving the scene of an accident.

BULLETIN

NEWSPAPER
TREATMENT

Grover Mark (c), 1835 Grey avenue, driving a Pontiac sedan eastbound on Emerson street, at McCormick boulevard, collided with a Dodge sedan driven north by Robert Kirkhope, 118 S. Park avenue, Waukegan. Dorothy Brush, 1926 Noyes street, received a broken collar bone and was attended at St. Francis hospital.

Both drivers in a two-car collision yesterday were arrested by police on charges of passing a red light when police were unable to ascertain which of the drivers passed the light. Grover Mack, 1835 Grey avenue, asserted he had the green light at the intersection at Emerson Street and McCormick road. Robert Kirkhope, 118 N. Park avenue, Waukegan, driving at right angles to Mack, said he had the green light. The cars collided causing approximately $300 damages.

Dorothy Brush, 1926 Noyes street, was attended at St. Francis hospital for a fractured collar bone.

Stephen Blake, 330 N. Kerr street, picked up around garage at 837 Dale avenue. Held for investigation.

Ignored as trivial.

Citizen reported someone in the St. Cloud Hat Shop, 106 Sherwin street. No one found. Store locked up.

Ignored as trivial.

More nearly complete records are turned in on regulation forms in all such cases, and these blanks may be consulted by the police reporter. Usually, however, he prefers to talk to the policemen involved if he can find them, or with the principals. It is not safe practice to rely upon the police bulletin as authentic because policemen are notoriously bad spellers and make numerous mistakes in names and addresses, some of which may be noted in the examples given. If attempts at verification fail, the reporter should accredit his story to the police bulletin. It is presumed, of course, that he knows the law of libel which offers him no protection if he uses the expression, "police say." It is not safe to print news of an arrest until a person has been taken into custody and booked on a certain charge; then the newspaper can relate only what has happened. It is impossible to say without risk that a person is "wanted for having fled the scene of an accident." Rather, the reporter should write the person is wanted "in connection with the accident . . ." Every item of police news should be verified before being used. As is seen from the examples given, for an adequate account of any item appearing on the police bulletin, more details than given there are needed.

PICKING THE FEATURE

All crime stories involve action. They relate to incidents which are potentially exciting when read about provided the reporter has been resourceful and thorough in his newsgathering. Until a case reaches court, knowledge of law is secondary to ability to observe, describe and imagine all of the angles needing investigation and the sources from which information may be obtainable. The crime reporter, in other words, must possess some of the qualities of a good detective although his purpose is entirely different. He is not out to solve the crime but to learn all that it is possible to find out about it.

Because anything can and constantly does happen, the following list of potential elements of interest in news of crime cannot possibly be complete. It is only suggestive.

1. Casualties
   a. Lives lost or threatened
   b. Injuries and how received
   c. Description of any gun play or fighting
   d. Disposition of dead and injured
   e. Prominent names among dead and injured
2. Property loss
   a. Value of loss
   b. Nature of property stolen or destroyed
   c. Other property threatened
3. Method of crime
   a. How entrance was effected
   b. Weapons or instruments used
   c. Treatment of victims
   d. Description of unusual circumstances
   e. Similarity to previous crimes
4. Cause or motive
   a. Confessions
   b. Statements of victims
   c. Statements of police, witnesses and others
   d. Threats
5. Arrests
   a. Names of persons arrested
   b. Complaint or policeman making arrest
   c. Charges entered on police blotter
   d. Police ingenuity
   e. Danger incurred by police
   f. Arraignment
6. Clues as to identity of criminals
   a. Evidence at scene of crime
   b. Testimony of witnesses

    c. Statement of police
    d. Statements of victim and others
    e. Connection with other crimes
7. Search for offender
    a. Probability of arrest
    b. Description of missing persons
    c. Value of clues
    d. Contact with criminal through ransom notes, etc.

JUVENILES

Until the immediate past, most newspapers followed a policy of not using the names of juvenile offenders except in cases of major crimes, such as homicide. Since juvenile delinquency began to increase markedly in the post-World War II years, some modifications in this rule have been made in numerous newsrooms. The Peru (Indiana) *Tribune*, for instance, adopted a new policy after extensive consultations with the chief of police, state police, city police juvenile officers, the county welfare director and Circuit Court judges. The pertinent part of the statement of policy follows:

The *Tribune* will publish the names, ages, and addresses of all youthful offenders thirteen years of age or older provided:
    1. in the opinion of the court there is no valid reason for such information to be withheld from publication
    2. the offenses are not of an extremely minor nature
    3. the offenders are actually charged with a specific offense
These facts will appear, along with all other pertinent facts of the case released by the proper authority.

The *Tribune* will follow up with stories which tell whether or not the youth charged has been found guilty or not guilty.

No names will be published unless and until charges are actually filed in juvenile court.

The *Tribune* will work closely with all law enforcing officials to make sure a consistent application of policy is adhered to at all times.

HUMAN INTEREST

In every community, no matter how small, there occur minor brushes with the law or situations reported to police which, in the hands of a skilled writer, can be made into extremely bright copy. In writing brevities originating on the police beat, the rewrite man is permitted considerable stylistic leeway as the emotional appeal outweighs the news interest.

The dire possibilities of equipping residential structures with an inadequate number of baths was demonstrated here today when two indoor bathers were arrested for causing a riot through the too-prolonged use of the only bathtub in the rooming establishment of which they were tenants.

Unfortunately, the two offenders chose Saturday night for a general overhauling. The operation consumed so much time that the regular weekly indulgence of the other ten guests, awaiting their turn outside the bathroom door, seemed in jeopardy. After a long wait, during which epithets of an uncomplimentary nature were hissed through the keyhole, disorder broke out among the would-be bathers, and soon took on such proportions that a riot call was sent into police headquarters.

When a sufficient number of patrolmen who were not at the moment taking their Saturday night baths could be corralled and sent to the scene, the two bath monopolists were taken into custody, charged with inciting riot and fined the goodly sum of $3, plus costs.

Leonard Rawlings, 45, of 1968 Winthrop avenue, stepped into a saloon Friday and, between beers, told a fellow he'd sure like to have a new car. And as a result, Leonard's $1,070 poorer.

The fellow, a character in a snappy sports jacket, said that it so happened he had a car to sell. If Leonard would meet him the next day at Division street and Wilmette avenue, he'd accommodate him.

Yesterday, Leonard showed up with his $1,070. The other showed up too, saying, "Let me have the money and I'll be back in a jiffy with the car."

That was at 6 P.M. By 10 P.M. Leonard got tired of waiting and trudged to the Central police station. He reported his loss to Sgt. Michael Thomason, who promptly informed Leonard that he undoubtedly had been swindled by a confidence man.

OTHER POLICE NEWS

Not all news originating in police headquarters has to do with lawbreaking. Police engage in a variety of noncriminal activities, many of which may be newsworthy. For instance, the missing persons bureau of any large department receives hundreds of calls weekly. Children who leave home in search of adventure, old people who wander off, and spouses and parents who desert their families often are news. The first intimation that a crime has been committed also may come from a report that a certain person is missing.

New traffic rules, warnings concerning dangerous intersections, demands that householders make better disposal of their garbage, and innumerable similar announcements come from police headquarters. Then there are additions to the staff, retirements, promotions, demotions, citations and social activities within the department itself. Monthly, annual and other reports contain statistics and other information of public interest.

CRIME STATISTICS

Since 1930, the Federal Bureau of Investigation, in cooperation with the International Association of Chiefs of Police, has published

Uniform Crime Reports. Great caution, however, must be exercised in using the statistics therein contained because they are submitted voluntarily by local police departments. As the F.B.I. itself warns, "In publishing the facts sent in by chiefs of police in different cities, the F.B.I. does not vouch for their accuracy. They are given out as current information which may throw some light on problems of crime and criminal-law enforcement."

For several years, the crime figures for New York City were so patently inaccurate that the F.B.I. refused to include them in its reports. After the Chicago police department was reorganized under a new commissioner, its improved reporting system indicated crime had increased 85 per cent in a year. Newspaper investigation, however, previously had supported the Chicago Crime commission's contention that the old department had been officially reporting only about one-third of the crimes it actually handled. Among the devices used to minimize the situation were listing automobiles and other objects as lost instead of stolen, making burglaries seem to be larcenies, making grand larcenies seem to be petty larcenies by "writing down" the amount of loss and so forth.

"With reference to the volume of crime — number of offenses — pressures are always present to keep the figures low," the Chicago Crime commission warns. In addition, the same source declares, numerous known crimes never are reported, including: (1) various types of sex offenses because the victims wish to avoid the embarrassment of publicity, (2) those which private citizens fail to report because of lack of confidence in the police, (3) those unreported by citizens who do not wish to become involved in extended court actions, and (4) matters which are handled largely by private police or protective agencies.

Negroes and members of other minority groups are especially reluctant to summon policemen to their neighborhoods. This fact counterbalances, in part at least, the greater avidity with which police often arrest members of minority groups.

All these and numerous other factors contribute to making the best crime statistics of questionable validity. They suggest the caution with which newspapers should handle such news and the opportunity that exists for investigative reporting to uncover the truth.

SITUATION STORIES

One type of interpretative writing open to the police reporter is that in which he describes, not one or a number of specific crimes, but a situation related to anti-social conduct or law enforcement of continuous public interest.

BY *Marjean Phillips*

A woman's handbag is the sleek complement to a costume, a necessary sack to carry half the paperwork of a household, and an object of convenience, responsible for money, keys, identification and quick aids to beauty. True, it's useful, but this cache is a threat to woman's peace of mind. Why? The thing is always disappearing! Half the trouble, women agree, is due to their own forgetfulness. Also, there is the real danger of a purse thief, particularly now when stores and busses are more crowded with holiday shoppers.

What often happens, according to Miss Betty Lou Martin, retail store buyer, is that women put their purses and coats on a counter and turn away to a mirror to try on a blouse.

"They might not even leave the floor," she said, "but someone sees the temptation, picks up the purse, and is away before anyone notices."

An Easy Mistake

Occasionally, a shopper thinks her purse is lost when it's really on her arm, Miss Martin pointed out.

"With a lot of packages you can't get the feeling of where each item is located," she said. "It's natural to think the purse was left behind. Just like looking for glasses on the forehead!"

Lieut. Ora Gregg of the police department cautions that shoulder-type bags are easy prey for the pickpocket.

"If a woman has that style she should be sure to keep her hand on top," he said. "A pickpocket could bump her and easily flip the purse flag and get the billfold. Bumping is to distract the person. If a thief sees he is failing in an attempt, he is likely to go on and say, 'excuse me.'"

Sometimes a woman takes out her money purse, lays it on the counter, and thinks about something else. Then, it is hard to tell whether this is a lost article or a real purse theft, he pointed out.

"The best thing is to always hold on to the purse, as well as packages," he urged.

Lock Packages in Car

Lieutenant Gregg, who commands the general assignment unit of the detective bureau, also advises women to lock their purchases in the trunk of a car, instead of leaving them out in the back seat or floor. That merely tempts a thief to take out a screw driver and go to work.

The street is the scene of other trouble. A purse thief may approach women walking home alone late at night. Miss Margaret F. Richardson, 3304 Wabash avenue, former policewoman, has this advice: "Scream or throw a fit if someone bothers you."

Miss Richardson recalled an incident when she was surprised by a teenage boy, who worked as a team with another youth. He pulled on her purse (a box type hanging over her arm), and failed to take it because she kept jerking and yelling at him. Then the partner came up and asked to help her pick up a package she dropped in the struggle. Suspicious, she warned, "You get away or I'll scream again!" The two-man system is a common tactic, she explained.

Troubles in Offices

Office workers, Miss Richardson says, invite disappointment by leaving pocketbooks out on desks. The purses are safer in a locked drawer. If there is no lock, a secretary can place the handbag in a large manila envelope in the desk farthest from the office entrance. The noise of the drawer opening might alert others.

Women have worked out their own safety rules for homes, such as pulling down window shades before counting money. Also garage doors are closed when the homemaker drives out to go downtown.

It's an achievement for young mothers to get out of a grocery store with a child in one arm, parcels in another and the purse, hopefully, someplace in between.

Mrs. J. M. Bills, 7902 Fairway drive, manages by using a shoulder bag; the safest way is to place its closing side against her body. At home, she doesn't leave her purse in the kitchen where it could be spotted by an intruder.

Mrs. Bills recalled that a friend who frequently lost her purse had the unusual habit of going to the movie and placing her purse on the seat next to her.

Another example of carelessness was cited by Mrs. Ed G. Freed, 5820 the Paseo, who observed that women hang large handbags on the backs of their chairs in restaurants. Mrs. Freed keeps her purse on her lap.

Left on Busses

Handbags are numerous in the thousands of articles left on busses and streetcars. Of course, some never reach their owners again. Proof of honesty, however, are the 10,000 to 12,000 items returned by the lost articles department of the Public Service company each year. The clerks at the main office are Mrs. Mary Knight and Mrs. Georgia Ashenfelter.

"Operators turn in lost articles at the car barns each day," Mrs. Knight explained. "A quadruple record is made there and the objects are brought to the general office at Eighth and Delaware for thirty days.

"If there is identification, letters are written asking persons to come in. If unclaimed after thirty days, the articles are sent back to the finder or the operator," she said.

Even Mrs. Knight has lost her purse . . . on a streetcar.

"Yes, I lost my purse and it beat me home. The person who found it on the street car took it to my home. I had gone back to look for it," she recalled.   Kansas City *Star*

CRIMINAL PROCEDURE

When a person is arrested and charged with a crime, he is taken immediately to a jail or police station where he is held pending arraignment. If the arrest is made upon the complaint of another person, the magistrate or judge already has provided the arresting officer with a *warrant* which commands him to bring the defendant to court. Anyone seeking the arrest of another must affirm under oath that he has reasonable grounds for belief in the guilt of the accused. A *search warrant* permits search of a premise where there is reason to believe evidence of a crime may be found. Unless police on raids have search warrants, their testimony is worthless in court. By a *motion to suppress* the evidence the defense obtains the right to question the arresting officer as to the means by which he gained admittance to the place where the arrest was made. Even though the entrance was legitimate, the case still may be dismissed if *entrapment* (inducing someone to commit a crime) is proved.

ARRAIGNMENT

A person has a constitutional right to be brought into court promptly to be confronted with the charge against him. When that is done, he gives his legal answer to the charge. If he remains mute, a not guilty plea is entered. Then the court proceeds according to its authority.

Andrew Konstans, 19, of 5700 Michigan avenue, stood mute on arraignment on a murder charge before Recorder's Judge W. L. Swanson. A plea of not guilty was entered for him and he was remanded without bond for examination Dec. 1.

The murder charge resulted from the death of Policeman Arthur Kendricks, 44, of 156 South Wells street. Kendricks died of three gunshot wounds suffered when he interrupted the holdup of a grocery store Nov. 15.

PRELIMINARY HEARING

If the offense is one over which the inferior court does not have jurisdiction, it holds a hearing to determine whether there is enough presumption of guilt to *bind over* the case for grand jury action in the higher court. If it decides differently, it dismisses the case and frees the suspect. In such a case, either on a coroner's jury verdict or on the initiative of the prosecuting attorney, the case still can be presented to the grand jury. Persons charged with indictable offenses frequently waive preliminary hearing.

Judge John A. Williams, sitting in Felony court, today ordered three women held to the grand jury under bonds of $15,000 each in the theft of checks from hallway mailboxes.

If the court in which the prisoner is arraigned has jurisdiction, it holds, not a preliminary hearing but, a trial. Inferior court trials provide abundant human interest material, more than a paper can use.

Frank Peterson, 30, of 2231 Wells street, was called "the lowest of criminals" today by City Judge Raymond C. Owens who sentenced him to a year in Bridewell for obtaining money under false pretenses.

Peterson was found guilty of taking $10 from Mrs. Sarah Thorton, 619 Clybourn avenue, on the promise that he would go to St. Louis to seek her missing husband.

Pending hearing, the prisoner may be released on *bail*, usually requiring a bond of cash or security. Sometimes a person is released on a *recognizance*, which is merely his written promise to appear when wanted or forfeit a stipulated sum.

THE GRAND JURY

The grand jury must be distinguished from the petit jury. It does not try a case but merely investigates crimes which have been committed and decides whether there is enough evidence to warrant the expense of bringing the accused persons to trial in the circuit or district court. The grand jury hears the evidence of the prosecution only, and, on the basis of that *ex parte* (one-sided) evidence, it may indict the accused.

An *indictment* may take the form of a *true bill* in case the evidence has been submitted by the prosecuting attorney. If the jury itself gathers evidence of a crime, the indictment is called a *presentment*. A grand jury is supposed to investigate the conduct of government in the territory served by the court and to consider conditions which it thinks should be remedied by law.

In some states, accused persons may be brought to trial upon *informations* submitted by the prosecuting attorney under oath and without a grand jury investigation.

Whenever a crime has been committed and the guilty person has not been ascertained, a *John Doe hearing* is held by the grand jury in the attempt to discover the identity of the person wanted. The prosecuting attorney has the power to summon witnesses to any grand jury hearing.

Grand jury proceedings are secret, but there frequently are leaks from which the reporter benefits. It is contempt of court, however, to publish the results of a grand jury action before it is reported in court. Often, newspapers withhold information even longer so that indicted persons not in custody of police can be arrested on a *bench warrant* (or *capias*) without tipoff.

The reporter should watch: (1) the number of indictments naming the same person, (2) the number of counts or charges in the same indictment, (3) the number of persons included in the same indictment. By standing outside the jury room, he can determine who the witnesses were and, on his past knowledge of the case, can speculate as to what their testimony must have been. The law under which indictments are returned and the punishment, in case of ultimate conviction, frequently should be obtained. The power of the prosecutor in determining what evidence shall be presented to a grand jury makes him a powerful political figure, and a trained reporter keeps an eye on his office as a public watchdog. In writing his story, the reporter must use great care to accredit every statement to the true bill.

Five police officers and six private citizens appeared before the special grand jury investigating police department activities in the jury's second consecutive meeting of the week, Tuesday night at East side court.

One of the first police officers to be called was Detective Sgt. Thomas Buzalka who remained closeted with the jury for more than an hour. While awaiting call, Buzalka chatted with Robert Hull, head of the police garage, and Patrolman R. L. Lincoln, who also appeared before the jury.

Emerging from the jury room, Buzalka left the building hurriedly with a brief "good night" thrown over his shoulder to those awaiting their turns.

Six indictments charging five companies and 14 individuals with illegally obtaining 800,000 gallons of cane syrup were returned by the federal grand jury yesterday before Judge Peter Ennis.

The indictments followed an investigation by the Agriculture and Justice departments to determine how the companies were complying with a supplement to the federal sugar rationing order.

PLEAS AND MOTIONS

When arraigned on an indictment, or at any time thereafter up to trial, there are numerous pleas and motions that may be made, chiefly by the defense. Those which merely seek delays are called *pleas in abatement*. One such is a *challenge of the panel* (or *to the array*) which contends that the grand jurors were selected or acted improperly. A motion for a *bill of particulars* asks that the charges be made more specific. A motion for a *continuance* is merely a request for a *postponement*. A *severance* may be asked so that a defendant will not have to stand trial with others named in the same indictment.

A *plea to the jurisdiction* challenges the authority of the court. A motion for a *change of venue* asks that the case be transferred to another court or locale or that a new judge be assigned to it. Motions which would stop all action are *pleas in bar*. One is a *demurrer* which contends that even though true, the acts alleged in the indictment do not indicate crime. A *plea of former jeopardy* is an assertion that the accused previously has been tried on the same charge.

The two common pleas, of course, are *guilty* and *not guilty*. A modified form of the former is *nolo contendere* by which the accused says he will not contest the charges. It is frequent after a test case when others awaiting trial realize they have no chance to "beat the rap." It keeps the defendant's record clear of an admission but otherwise is the equivalent of a guilty plea. If any civil action is brought against the defendant, this plea cannot be used against him.

There is no legal plea of "innocent," but some newspapers use the word instead of "not guilty" as a precautionary measure. They fear that the "not" might get lost in the composing room, thereby committing possible libel.

The one important plea that the prosecution can make is *nolle prosequi* (*nol pros*) which means "do not wish to prosecute." It is made when new evidence convinces the prosecutor of the accused's innocence or when there is insufficient evidence to convict. If it occurs under any other circumstances, an alert newspaper should expose the fact.

> Fifteen to 60 years' imprisonment was in prospect for Frankie Waters, 24-year-old fugitive from a Georgia chain gang, who pleaded guilty yesterday to a charge of robbery in the first degree to cover a 15-count indictment alleging robbery and assaults on women passengers in taxicabs he had stolen.
>
> Waters entered his plea before General Sessions Judge T. L. Bohn. After the plea had been made by Waters' court-assigned counsel, Charles Shueman, Judge Bohn asked:
>
> "Do you realize that if you plead guilty I can give you no less than 15 years and up to 60 years?" . . .

> Circuit Attorney Franklin Moore today dismissed in Circuit Judge Harry Jamieson's court, indictments against six precinct officials in the Fifteenth precinct of the Fourth ward, charged with fraudulent removal and secretion of ballots in the primary election, Aug. 7.
>
> The indictments were returned Nov. 3, but the cases have been continued from time to time by the defendants who said they were not ready for trial. The cases were originally assigned to Judge Charles R. Watson, but transferred to Judge Jamieson on a change of venue.
>
> The last continuance was sought Monday by the state, which said it was not ready for trial, in view of the fact that the State Supreme court had not yet acted on applications for permanent writs of prohibition to prevent the Madison grand jury from examining ballot boxes and other election records of the Fourth ward. Moore told a Journal reporter that the records were needed to prosecute the cases.
>
> Those indicted were . . .

OTHER PRELIMINARIES

When a fugitive from justice in one state is arrested in another, he may be returned to the jurisdiction where he must answer charges by *extradition*. The procedure is for the governor of the state seeking custody of the fugitive to request the governor of the state in which he is apprehended to return him. It is newsworthy when such a request is denied, as it sometimes is by a northern governor reluctant to send a prisoner back south; or in the case of an ex-convict who has lived an exemplary life for years since a prison break. In federal courts, the equivalent of extradition is *removal* from one jurisdiction to another following hearing before a commissioner.

> A description of torture allegedly inflicted upon him in the Georgia State penitentiary was given yesterday by an escaped prisoner as he opened a fight against extradition proceedings to return him to that prison.
> He is Leland Brothers, 35, who was released Tuesday from the Stateville penitentiary after serving a one-to-three-year sentence from Brown county for armed robbery.
> Yesterday he filed a petition for a writ of habeas corpus in the Wayne County Circuit court.

In both criminal and civil cases, *depositions* may be taken with court permission when there is a likelihood that a witness will be unavailable during trial. A deposition differs from an *affidavit* because it is conducted by a court appointee, both sides are notified, and the rules of evidence are followed. In other words, the witness testifies under the same conditions that he would in court; the transcript of his testimony may be introduced as evidence.

Witnesses who do appear in court usually are there as the result of *subpoenas* (court orders) which either side may obtain as a matter of right. A *subpoena duces tecum* orders a witness to produce certain real evidence, usually documents and records.

CRIMINAL TRIALS

Most criminal trials (same is true of civil trials) last only a few hours or minutes. Some, however, take days, weeks or months. The story the day before or on the day of trial may forecast its probable length, based on statements by attorneys for both sides and what the reporter knows of the probable evidence.

FIRST STORIES

The reporter should include in his story: (1) careful tie-back to the crime itself — time, place, names, events, (2) the charges as stated in the indictment, (3) the possible outcome, meaning the minimum and maximum penalties fixed by law for all of the possible verdicts in the case, (4) the probable evidence with names of witnesses and attorneys' statements, if obtainable, as to what they will attempt to establish, (5) any unusual angles, as possible difficulty in obtaining a jury; for instance, one side may be expected to favor persons of ages, occupations, religion or politics different from those favored by the other side. Maybe this is the first trial of its kind, or the first in a long time, or a new law may be applied to some part of the proceedings. The possibilities are limitless.

PICKING THE JURY

After the indictment has been read and the plea entered, and after any last-minute motions have been disposed of, selection of the jury begins. The jury of twelve is picked from a panel of *veniremen* prepared by the jury commissioners or its equivalent. They are questioned by attorneys of both sides and, if found unsatisfactory for reasons which are obvious, may be *challenged for cause*. In addition, each side has a stated number of *peremptory challenges* for which no reasons need be given; usually the defense has twice as many as the prosecution. Clues to future tactics may be obtained from the types of questions asked veniremen. If, for instance, the prosecutor does not inquire whether they are prejudiced against the death penalty, it is apparent he does not intend to ask for that punishment. If the original panel of veniremen is exhausted without a jury's being completed, additional persons are summoned; they are known as *talesmen* and in inferior courts may be brought in off the street or selected from courtroom spectators.

OPENING STATEMENTS

The state leads off with a statement of what it intends to prove and the nature of the evidence to be introduced. The prosecutor presents no evidence. The defense may make its reply immediately or may wait until after the prosecution's evidence has been presented.

EVIDENCE

First witnesses for the state are called for the purpose of establishing the *corpus delicti*, or proof that a crime was committed. All testimony is given in answer to questions by attorneys. After *direct examination* by attorneys for the side calling him, a witness is subjected to *cross-examination* by attorneys for the other side. They must restrict their questions to matters about which he already has testified and they often attempt to *impeach a witness* by catching him in contradictory statements. Objections to questions frequently are made by counsel; the judge is the arbiter. Occasionally, the jury is taken from the room while argument on admissibility of evidence is debated. A *jury view* is the taking of a jury to the scene of a crime or any other place outside the courtroom for the purpose of seeing anything pertinent to the case.

After it has presented all of its evidence, both through the testimony of witnesses and by exhibits, the state *rests*. Then the defense usually automatically makes a motion for a *directed verdict of acquittal* on the ground that the state has failed to prove its case. Most such motions are denied as automatically as they are made; when they are not, there is a news story. A *mistrial* can result in case of gross irregularity as an attempt to bribe a juror.

> The overzealous interest of a juror in a robbery case before County Judge Nova in Brooklyn caused a mistrial yesterday, and brought a reprimand from the court. The juror was William E. Rejall, 54 Tompkins place, Brooklyn, who had sat for two days in the trial of Joseph Fernandez, charged with holding up Felix Orrusti, 173 Washington street, Brooklyn.
>
> When the trial opened yesterday, Rejall stood up and asked if he might question the complainant.
>
> "I took the trouble to visit the scene and I want to ask the complaining witness how he could identify anyone in the dark," the juror explained. Judge Nova appeared surprised.
>
> "You are entitled only to the evidence that is submitted in court in the presence of the defendant," the court said. "You should not have gone to the scene. I must declare a mistrial."　　　New York *Times*

All motions having been denied, the defense presents its case, beginning with its opening statement if not already made. Direct and cross-examination proceed as before. There follow *rebuttal* witnesses by the state and frequently the recalling of witnesses by either side for further questioning.

CLOSING STATEMENTS

The prosecuting attorney usually has the right to go first and then to follow the attorney for the defense with a brief rebuttal; frequently he waives his right to speak twice and lets the defense go first. These final statements by attorneys are argumentative. Then the judge *charges* the jury, explaining the law in the case, the possible verdicts it can return, and the meaning of each. Often the law stipulates the exact wording a judge must use in at least part of his charge. Judges have little right to comment on the evidence itself but by facial expressions, gestures and verbal emphasis they often can prejudice a jury without the fact being evident in a written transcript.

REPORTING TRIALS

In reporting trials of long duration, the reporter bases each new lead on the most important new development since his last preceding story. Factors to consider are:

1. Does some new testimony or other evidence contradict or supplement some preceding evidence?
2. Do the questions asked by defense counsel on cross-examination portend what the constructive defense case will be?
3. Is any of the evidence surprising; that is, has it been unreported in connection with either the crime itself or the trial?
4. How do the versions of what happened as presented by both sides coincide or differ?
5. Is there consistency of purpose in the types of objections raised by counsel and in the judge's rulings on them? Is the defense laying the ground for possible future appeal?

Seeking answers to these and similar questions involves an interpretative approach to the assignment. Much of the reporting "on deadline," however, is likely to be strictly factual. Often testimony can be presented in Q and A (question and answer) form if there is space; otherwise, it can be summarized briefly or the important parts quoted. The courtroom scene, including the attitude of principals, witnesses, relatives, friends and spectators is newsworthy, especially if there are any disturbances. In capital cases, the way the defendant acts when the verdict is announced is of interest.

> While Vincent Cilenti, 32-year-old ex-convict was in County Jail awating trial on a first-degree murder charge, he allegedly attempted to "shakedown" Mrs. Mary Carmigiano a second time in connection with the bombing of Angelo Pappalardo's home.
>
> This was the testimony today of Albert P. Lauerhaus, alleged confederate of Cilenti, who is on trial for blackmail and bombing of the Pappalardo home.
>
> The trial was interrupted shortly before noon when John Draggo of 3861 Montevista Rd., Cleveland Heights, a state witness, repudiated a statement he made to police in 1942 accusing Cilenti of "shaking him down" for $100.
>
> Common Pleas Judge Alva R. Corlett excused the jury, summoned attorneys into his chamber and warned them he would not permit perjury in the courtroom.

Tells of Bulldozing

> After the noon recess, Draggo reluctantly told a story of being bulldozed by Cilenti into signing papers which Draggo thought made him cosigner for a loan for purchase of an auto. Later, he said, he learned that he had actually been the one to sign the papers and that Cilenti had placed both car and license in Draggo's name, forcing Draggo to make the payments.
>
> Lauerhaus, 32, said it was in November, 1942, while Cilenti was waiting trial in the murder of Peter Laduca (of which he was acquitted) that he sent for Lauerhaus to visit him at County Jail.

"I want you to see Mrs. Carmigiano," Lauerhaus said Cilenti told him. "She owes me some money. Go out and get it for me."

Q. What did you do then?

A. I went out and she said she didn't owe Cilenti any money. I didn't get any money from her.

Lauerhaus said he couldn't remember the exact amount of money Cilenti said she owed. Mrs. Carmigiano said in testimony yesterday that after paying Cilenti $300 she was approached for $600 more.

Lauerhaus confirmed Mrs. Carmigiano's testimony about how he drove her to see Cilenti in September after the Pappalardo home had been bombed.

Then James P. Hart, assistant county prosecutor, asked him: "Did you ever have any conversation with Cilenti about the bombing?" Lauerhaus said he did, talking to him about how Mrs. Carmigiano had complained that Cilenti had bombed the home without telling her about it or getting her approval.

"What does she think I am, a damn fool?" Lauerhaus said Cilenti told him. "Does she think I'd tell her when I'd be there so she could be in the window waiting for the explosion?"

Mrs. Carmigiano, 1392 SOM Center Rd., Mayfield Heights, yesterday told how Cilenti extorted $300 from her for bombing a neighbor's home without her knowledge or approval.

Mrs. Carmigiano, a real estate agent, said Cilenti first came to see her early in 1942, when she lived on Arrowhead Ave., about renting a house. Later, she related, he returned saying he understood she was having trouble with a neighbor.

Mrs. Carmigiano said she told him of arguments she had with the family of Angelo Pappalardo, 19408 Arrowhead Ave.

A. He said I should punish the people next door.

Q. What did you say?

A. Well, I don't know how to punish them. I'm only a widow. There's nothing I can do about it.

Q. What did Cilenti say to this?

A. He said: "I can take care of it for you." I asked him in what way. He replied: "Just leave it to me. We know how to take care of it for you." I told him I didn't want anybody hurt.

Mrs. Carmigiano moved from Arrowhead Ave. in May, 1942. The Pappalardo home was bombed July 8. She told DeMarco she read of the bombing in the newspapers. Then Lauerhaus came to see her several times, she said, telling her: "Cilenti wants to see you."

On the second or third visit he came at night and pushed his way into her house, Mrs. Carmigiano said.

Q. What happened, then?

A. He took me in his car to 82d St. and Quincy Ave. He left me in the car awhile. I waited about an hour, so I went into a cafe and asked for Cilenti. They said they didn't know where he was. I went back to the car and someone came out and took me to Cilenti. Cilenti said to me, "The job is done. The boys want their money."

Mrs. Carmigiano said she asked: "What money?"

"They want $300."

"For what?"

"For the Pappalardo job," she said Cilenti replied.

Asked for Receipt

The interview, she testified, closed with Cilenti driving her home and telling her to get him the money by 2 P.M. that day. She said she borrowed the money from a friend, took it to Cilenti's home, accompanied by one of her sons. She said she gave the money to Cilenti and when she asked for a receipt she testified he told her:

"Oh, no. We don't do business that way."

Mrs. Carmigiano denied she was operating a still in 1941, but added that Cilenti's purpose in wanting to rent a house from her was to establish a hideout for operation of a still. S. M. Lo Presti, defense attorney, sought to show that the money transaction between Mrs. Carmigiano and Cilenti involved a bootlegging deal rather than a bombing.   Cleveland *Press*

VERDICTS

The jury leaves the courtroom and deliberates, with the foreman presiding. After the case is over, the reporter may find out, by questioning jurors, how many ballots were taken and how the vote stood each time. The length of time it takes a jury to reach unanimity is newsworthy. If no decision ever is reached, the jury is said to be *hung*, and there is a *mistrial*. Some indication of how a jury is thinking may be obtained if it returns to the jury room to ask further instructions or to have part of the evidence read to it again. The reporter's best tipster as to what goes on in a jury room is the bailiff standing guard at the door.

The defendant must be in court when the verdict is read. If a verdict is reached late at night, it may be written and *sealed* and left with a court official, so that the jurors may leave. All, however, must be present when the verdict is opened. The losing side may demand a *poll* of the jury, which requires each juror to declare that he concurs. If any juror changes his mind during such a poll, it is "hot" copy.

A Criminal Court jury Wednesday night convicted James Kyler, 22, of the murder of a milkman and set his penalty at 14 years in prison.

The jury of nine men and three women deliberated 8 hours 55 minutes in reaching its verdict. The penalty it recommended is the minimum for murder under state law.

Three boys, 8, 10 and 11 years old, were the chief state witnesses who connected Kyler with the slaying of the milkman, Jerome Giza, 30, of 1740 N. Mason, last Oct. 15. Giza was shot to death during a holdup attempt at 117 S. Rockwell.

Kyler, of 2546 W. Monroe, testified at the trial presided over by

Judge Joseph J. Drucker that he was in a friend's home at the time of the slaying. His attorney said he would appeal the verdict.

Lennette Earl Brown, 35, of 2500 W. Warren, acused of participating with Kyler in the hold-up-slaying of Giza, will go on trial for murder April 3. Chicago *Sun-Times*

SENTENCES

A jury's verdict is advisory only; the judge accepts or rejects it. He may grant a defense motion to *set aside* the verdict and grant a *new trial* if there have been errors which he knows would cause an appellate court to reverse the verdict and *remand* the case. A motion for *arrest of judgment* accompanies such motions to postpone sentencing.

The leeway permitted a judge in pronouncing sentence is established by statute for each crime. In some cases, he may have no choice at all; convictions on a certain charge may mean an automatic sentence of a certain kind. A *suspended sentence* is one which the convicted person does not have to serve pending good behavior. It is rapidly being replaced by *probation* which gives the convicted person limited freedom of action under the supervision of probation officials; if anyone violates the conditions of his probation, he serves not only the original sentence but an additional one also because of the violation. Probation is most common for minors and first offenders. It should not be confused with *parole* which is the supervised conditional release of prisoners who already have served part of their prison terms.

If someone is convicted on more than one count, he may serve his several sentences *concurrently* or *consecutively*. If the former, he serves only the longest of the several sentences; if the latter, he serves the accumulated total of them all. An *indeterminate* sentence sends a convicted person to the penitentiary for "not less than" a designated number of years, and "not more than" another number of years. The exact time of his release is determined by the state board of paroles. Usually he is not eligible to apply for parole until after at least one-third of his time has been served, so judges often give maximum penalties to run consecutively to make release on parole unlikely.

Clarence Whittle, 20, of 187 South Water street, was sentenced by Judge John S. Anthony in Criminal court yesterday to serve a term of not less than 10 years to life in the penitentiary for armed robbery.

Judge Anthony overruled a motion for a new trial before pronouncing the sentence. Whittle was convicted by a jury Jan. 10 of holding up a tavern at 1700 Ashland avenue, on Sept. 1 and taking $190.

Whittle faces charges of murdering Michael Storms, 50, a tavern owner of 5800 Market street, on July 15. Four others have pleaded guilty to participating in the shooting of Storms and a fifth is under sentence of 20 years in prison.

Federal Judge John P. Altman today deferred a prison sentence for one of two men convicted of black market meat deals and reduced a fine against their company from $50,000 to $25,000.

He approved a stay of execution until March 15 for Martin Orton, president of the Orton Meat Packing company, on his penitentiary sentence of a year and a day.

Orton, who lives at 151 West Monroe street, and Walter Sherwood, of 989 Wells street, secretary-treasurer of the company, were given identical sentences by Judge Altman Sept. 1.

The government charged them and the company with filing false subsidy claims with the government to obtain $155,000, and having sold meat at overceiling prices and failure to set aside 1,300,000 pounds for the armed forces.

On motions of Oscar Nethercott, attorney for the defense, Judge Altman granted the stay to Orton today so another man can be found to head the company, and reduced the $50,000 fine against the company to $25,000. Sherwood will surrender Monday to the U.S. marshal.

Assistant U.S. Attorney Bernard Whiteman opposed the motions, asserting the two had "at least $150,000 in black market money," and had refused to cooperate with the government in a costly investigation of their activities.

"At the time I assessed the fine I wondered if it were not too drastic," Judge Altman said. "Now I think it was."

PUNISHMENTS

Despite the trend toward individualized treatment of law-breakers and the substitution of theories of reformation and protection of society for theories of retaliation and expiation, the criminal law still requires that a convicted person "pay his debt to society." To carry out any sentence is to *execute* it, although the popular connotation of the word limits it to cases in which capital punishment is inflicted. The death penalty rapidly is passing out because judges and juries are reluctant to impose it. It is within the power of a governor to *commute* any sentence: that is, to reduce it, as from death to life imprisonment. A governor also can issue a *reprieve* which, however, is merely a postponement of execution. A *pardon* is a granting of freedom. If absolute, it restores civil rights. If conditional, it prescribes limits to the ex-convict's behavior. Few states as yet have adequate systems for recompensing persons proved to have been imprisoned wrongly.

THE ETHICS OF CRIME NEWS

No ethical problem connected with newspaper publishing has been more thoroughly discussed by both newspapermen and laymen than the treatment of crime news. Upon his superiors' attitude toward the problem depends largely the type of occurrences to which the police reporter pays particular attention and the manner in which he writes his articles. A few papers, notably the *Christian Science Monitor*, generally ignore anti-social behavior; others have experimented with leaving crime news off the front page or of playing it down in the writing. Familiar, on the other hand, is the type of newspaper which considers a sensational crime story as second to few other types in potential reader interest.

It is not so much a question of the amount of crime news but of how it is presented. Contrary to popular opinion, only a small proportion of the total offering of the average newspaper relates to lawlessness. Several years ago, for instance, Henry Fairfield Osborn revealed that whereas readers guessed from 25 to 50 per cent of the contents of their newspapers was crime news, scientific study showed the average space devoted to such news to be only 3.5 per cent.

Some newspapers, magazines, and radio and television stations have been accused of inciting to crime by glorifying and making heroes of criminals; of assisting criminals to escape by relating detailed accounts of the activities of police; of interfering with the administration of justice by emphasizing the horrible aspects of brutal crimes, by quoting the prosecuting attorney as to the severe punishment he is going to demand and by editorial comment; of causing unfair suffering on the part of the relatives and friends of principals in a criminal case and of offending public taste by relating lurid details of crimes and scandals.

Regardless of the validity of any of these charges — and much can and has been said pro and con — none compares in importance with the contention that the media of communication have not taken sufficient cognizance of modern criminological and penological thought. By advocating harshness of treatment as the only corrective, by labeling every sex offender (even before apprehended) as a moron (a scientific term meaning high-grade feebleminded), by pointing to every paroled prisoner violating his parole as proof of the unsoundness of the parole principle, by ridiculing leading thinkers as maudlin sentimentalists, and in other ways, the media, it is charged, are a sizable obstacle in the movement to replace a barbaric philosophy and methods of curbing anti-sociability with a scientific approach.

Following a scientific study of the life history of Giuseppe Zangara, the psychopathic immigrant who attempted to assassinate President-elect Franklin D. Roosevelt in 1933, Sidney Kobre said in part regarding the manner in which the American press handled the story:

> Newspapers, in theory, print the news as it occurs, head it according to its significance, and comment on its important aspects. Here, certainly, was an opportunity for them to get at the root of a social evil — to insist, rather than on laws to prevent purchase of guns or enforce deportation of

aliens, on the essential nature of the problem. Zangara, had the influences under which he labored been understood (and they might have been discovered when he entered the Italian army, when he passed through the immigration bureau, when he was admitted to citizenship, when he was a patient in a hospital), might have been headed off, his physical and psychological ailments corrected. Suggestions for the isolation and treatment of the class from whom are "recruited the criminal types and cranks" might have been made, along with emphasis on the fact that the class is not composed exclusively of aliens. . . .

The newspapers had opportunity to examine the impulse behind the shooting at its root. . . . For the most part they did not do so. Instead they seized upon the "red" stereotype, or proposed police or legislative methods of dealing with the evil once it had arisen, rather than psychiatric or medical methods of preventing it from arising. . . . Most American editors handling this story chose stereotypes and superficialities rather than the more subtle but certainly more fundamental implications. . . .

The American newspaper is the only agency which adequately reports such a case to the public. Because the attempted shooting of Roosevelt was dramatic news, attention was centered on a vital social problem. The newspapers had, therefore, an extraordinary opportunity to present the important news behind the surface facts — to mold public thought and action in a social, constructive pattern, if you will. The facts recited above show that they failed. And it should be noted that the Zangara case is but a single instance of a blundering habit — a habit that will repeat itself time and again unless newspapers can learn from it where their machinery is defective.

Since Kobre wrote this article, later expanded for inclusion in his *Backgrounding the News*, there has been considerable improvement on many newspapers. World War II awakened interest in psychiatry and acquainted millions with the fact that abnormal behavior does not necessarily result from malicious willful choice. Sociological research, furthermore, has proved that what is considered criminal in one environment may be perfectly normal in another, and that, particularly in large cities, there are communities in which the incidence of crime remains virtually constant although the racial or nationality complexion of the population changes many times. Gone is belief in "born" criminals, feeblemindedness as a major cause of criminal behavior, and many other unscientific explanations. Today, psychiatry is throwing light on the peculiarities of the individual offender and sociologists are examining slums, economic status, marital relations and other social factors which breed misbehavior.

In tune with the times, few newspapers any longer consult phrenologists, handwriting experts, fortunetellers, and other quacks whenever a major crime occurs. Instead, they interview scientists and they steadily are adding to their own staffs specialists able to do more than invent "cute" headline-fitting nicknames for murderers and their victims.

After a gang of fourteen teen-aged boys participated in the murder of another boy, the Chicago *Sun-Times* assigned a team of six reporters to try to discover "what pent-up fury could turn seemingly normal boys into a pack of murderous avengers." What follows is one of a series of articles "aimed at the grass roots of juvenile crime — the backgrounds of the offenders." Its subject was the boy who pulled the trigger.

BY *Jack Olsen*

Stanley Macis sat in his darkened living room. His voice was flat, sob-wracked:

"I came home from work at 12:30. My wife said, 'Stan, your shotgun is gone.' I said, 'Oh, my God, honey, we gotta stop him before he kills somebody.'

"Cookie came in at 1. The cops came at 2. They said he killed a boy. I said to myself, 'Yeh, I know it. I knew it all the time.' "

Macis, 37, father of five boys, is a dejected, heartbroken man. He not only knows what hit him, but he also saw it coming.

His son, Clement, 14, was indicted for murder after the teen-gang slaying of 17-year-old Kenneth Sleboda July 1. Juvenile authorities have refused to discuss his case, on the ground that he is too young.

The Macis family lives in a drab, gray cottage at 3841 S. Union, a few blocks northeast of the stockyards, in a neighborhood which has produced more than its share of Chicago's civic and religious leaders.

If the family isn't prosperous, it isn't poverty stricken, either. Macis has worked as a mechanic for four years. Each week he gives his $79 pay-check to his wife, Ann, and whatever is left after essentials is put into the house — new tiles, wallpaper, a game room for the boys, a TV set.

"You can look all year," the sobbing Macis says, "and you'll never find anything in this house to explain what happened. Cookie had everything. He was happy. It's just that when his brother went into the Marines, everything changed."

The brother is Stanley Jr., 17. A handsome, strapping youth, he was young Clement's idol. "Wherever Junior went," his father says, "Cookie was with him. Seemed like his whole life was his brother."

In mid-1954, Stanley Jr. came home with half his teeth knocked out. "Cookie was white," Macis says. "He cried all night. He begged Junior, 'What happened to you, Junior?' Junior wouldn't snitch. But it was one of them gangs.

'All Beat Up'

"Junior came home a few more times all beat up. He said they wouldn't leave him alone. He asked me could he get in the Marines. I signed for him in January. Cookie? He was lost."

Before his brother's enlistment, Clement had been taking a general course at Tilden Technical High School, 4747 S. Union. Entering as an "R" student (needing remedial work in reading), the boy wound up the first term with marks of "good," "fair," "excellent" and "superior." His teachers were proud of him, and so noted on his report card.

Then Stanley Jr. went away. School records for the weeks after that note: "Clement Macis became a severe truant and showed virtually no interest in his work. He failed all of his subjects because of truancy."

Counselor Notes Change

A counselor at the Valentine branch of the Chicago Boys Club, 3400 S. Emerald, told The Sun-Times he also noticed a change after the brother's departure.

"Clement was around here less and less," the counselor reported. "Then we noticed him hanging with the street corner gangs, poking around parked cars. It was unlike the boy. But then — so was the shooting."

His father explains what had happened:

"When Junior went away, Cookie couldn't sit still. He had to get out. Then he started coming home all beat up, just like Junior. Week after week. Every time I'd ask him, he'd say he fell down the steps."

Tells Fear of Gang

On March 2, court records show, the boy was arrested for car theft. He claimed that the older boys made him take the car and deliver it to them, to prove he wasn't "chicken." He was put on probation in the care of his father.

"From then on," his father continues, "Cookie was more scared than ever. He looked like one of them zombies in the movies. Cars would keep pulling up in front, and Cookie, he'd say, 'Tell 'em I ain't home, Daddy.' Then he'd duck out the back door. Few hours later, he'd come back, all beat up, shaking. I'd ask him what happened. He'd just sit there with that pasty look on his face.

"One day I finally broke him down a little. He said, 'Daddy, get us away from here. Them boys, they won't leave me alone. They call me chicken.' I said, 'Son, we'll get outa here as soon as we can afford it.' "

Clement Macis couldn't wait. Using an assumed name and lying about his age, he bolted to Fort Riley, Kan., and became a paratrooper.

It took the family four months to run him down. On June 23, one week before the Sleboda killing, young Macis was ordered home.

The afternoon of the gang slaying, just before leaving for his night-shift job, Macis had one last talk with the boy. He promised his son they would move away from the gangs in a few months. Clement sobbed. "Couldn't it be sooner?" he asked his father.

"No, son," Macis answered. "We don't have the money yet."

Twelve hours from then, it was too late.

15

Courts, Civil Law, Appeals

I. Kinds of Law

II. The Court System

1. Inferior Courts
2. County and Probate Courts
3. Courts of First Instance
4. Appellate Courts
5. Federal Courts
6. Officers of the Court

III. Civil Law

1. Starting an Action
2. Defending an Action
3. Civil Trials
4. Enforcing Civil Law

IV. Civil Actions

1. Damage Suits
2. Divorce
3. Foreclosures
4. Evictions
5. Condemnation Suits
6. Receiverships
7. Bankruptcy
8. Injunctions

V. Extraordinary Remedies

1. Prohibition
2. Certiorari
3. Mandamus
4. Quo Warranto

VI. Probate Proceedings

1. Filing a Will
2. Admitting to Probate
3. Contesting a Will

VII. Rules of Evidence

1. Nature of Evidence
2. Burden of Proof
3. Presumptions
4. Judicial Notice
5. Qualifications of Witnesses
6. Privilege
7. Leading Questions
8. Hearsay Evidence
9. Opinion Evidence
10. Real Evidence
11. Circumstantial Evidence
12. Best Evidence

VIII. Appeals

JUDICIAL OPINIONS

There are times when judges need some plain speaking to, and upon such occasions an alert, fearless and vigorous press is a public godsend.

Editorial, Wheeling (W.Va.) News

To consent to the right of judges to punish criticism of their past ineptitudes would be to concur in the establishment of a judicial oligarchy such as has not afflicted us heretofore.

Editorial, Baltimore Sun

Gentlemen of the press, I have no control over your actions or speech, nor am I trying to run the newspapers, but the time has gone by when the merits of a case shall be tried in the papers. I must ask the press to express no opinions as to the merits or faults of things done in course of the trial, or the veracity of testimony of the different witnesses or alleged inconsistencies among the witnesses. It is not within the privilege of the press. As highly as this court regards the press, it will insist that the case be not tried in the newspapers. Please do not think this is censure.

Judge Joseph B. David,
Chicago Superior Court

Perhaps the most serious problem, so far as the punishment of criminals and the actual functioning of the courts are concerned, is the publication, before trial, and sometimes before capture of the person accused of crime, of testimony of witnesses, and of the actions, clues, surmises, and theories of the prosecuting officers.

Before arrest, this may interfere with and lessen the chances of apprehension and increase the criminal's chance of escape. One of the most serious problems in the administration of justice is detection. As our jurors are a cross section of our social life, it becomes difficult to secure jurors to try a case fairly. Many of them, having read the colored reports following the commission of the offense, have formed an opinion of the facts and if not actually disqualified will disqualify themselves.

Judge Leon R. Yankwich,
Los Angeles Superior Court

The most serious criticism of American criminal procedure today, is that the judges of the courts permit newspapers to usurp the court's own duties and functions.

Newspaper interference with criminal justice always appears most flagrantly in celebrated criminal cases. Those judicial proceedings, therefore, in which American criminal justice most needs to be a calm investigation of the truth are, on the contrary, most violently "hippodromed" and "panicked" by the press.

Not the least serious result of this interference in the business of the courts is the jeopardizing of the defendant's life or liberty if he is innocent, or the jeopardizing of the defendant's conviction, both in the trial court and the appellate court, if he is guilty.

American Bar Association
Committee on Criminal Procedure

J UST AS IT IS ESSENTIAL FOR A SPORTS REPORTER WHO COVERS baseball to understand the rules of the game, so is it necessary for the reporter assigned to the courts to know the basic structure of American law.

KINDS OF LAW

Roughly, all laws can be divided into *public* and *private* (usually called *civil*), the distinction being whether the state (organized society) is a party to the litigation. The dichotomy is not exact because government can be a party to certain types of civil actions. In general, however, the distinction holds. Branches of public law include: constitutional, administrative, international and criminal, with the ordinary reporter, of course, being most interested in the last.

The two major divisions of private, or civil law, are *common law* and *equity*. The former is that law which was developed through the centuries in judicial decisions in English courts, and — roughly again — it can be divided into *real* and *personal* law. Real law relates to the possession of and title to property whereas personal law relates to attempts to recover damages for injuries received, to enforce a contract, to bring about the return of property and to similar matters. The two major divisions of personal law relate to *contracts* and *torts* (all injuries received other than by violation of contract). Equity law, as developed in the equity (or *chancery*) courts of England, begins where law leaves off. One does not go to equity to recover damages for injuries to himself or his property, but to compel someone to do or to refrain from doing something. Modern equity courts handle such matters as injunctions, foreclosures, receiverships, partitions, etc.

The law administered in the courts originates either (1) in the acts of Congress, of a state legislature, or of some other lawmaking body, such law being known as *statutory*, or (2) in the accumulated decisions of courts both here and in England, such law being known as *common law*. Courts adhere to the principle of *stare decisis* (let the decision stand), which means that lawyers quote at length from decisions in earlier cases in the attempt to show that the case in hand should be decided similarly. When there has been a pertinent decision by the Supreme Court of the United

States or some state appellate court, the issue may seem clearcut. Usually, however, such is not the case. Either the matter at hand differs in some essential from the previously decided case, or the appellate court decision is limited in scope. Also, there may be conflicting decisions in apparently identical cases.

Young reporters should know that, despite the apparent inconsistencies in both the written (*basic*) law itself and common law decisions, and despite their ability to find citations to substantiate both or all sides of almost any argument, lawyers as a whole profess belief in the existence of absolute justice, and hold that the purpose of any court case is to find the abstract principle which applies. Such lawyers are not conscious rogues, whose main interest is to "play a game" and win a judgment for their clients at all costs. They have been trained to think in a precise specialized manner which makes it easy for them to rationalize their actions, even though to the layman the results may not seem tantamount to anything resembling common sense or justice.

THE COURT SYSTEM

A knowledge of the court system of the state in which he works is essential to the reporter assigned to cover the courts. If he moves from one state to another he will discover that even the names of generally similar courts may differ. For instance, what is known as a circuit court in Indiana is called a district court in Nebraska, a superior court in Massachusetts and a supreme court in New York.

The jurisdictions of courts also differ, even between counties of different sizes within the same state. For instance, there may be a separate probate court in one county or state whereas probate matters may be handled by the circuit court or its equivalent in another place. One court may handle both civil and criminal matters or there may be different courts (*common pleas* courts are civil courts; courts of *oyer and terminer* are criminal courts). Similarly, law and equity courts may be separate or combined. The practice is growing of establishing special branches of courts to handle particular kinds of cases, and these branches may be referred to in news stories by their specialized names, as Renters' Court, Juvenile Court, Traffic Court, Divorce Court, etc. To the reader, it makes little or no difference that such courts really are only branches of a circuit, municipal or county court, but the reporter should know their nature.

It is particularly important that the reporter know which are *courts of record*; that is, ones which keep a permanent record of their proceedings. What happens in *courts not of record* is not privileged and the newspaper which covers them must be careful to avoid committing libel.

Differences in both the *substantive law* (defines what is and is not proper behavior) and *adjective law* (defines legal rules and procedures) also provide potential snares for unwary newsmen. For instance, in one state grand larceny may be defined as stealing anything worth more than $15 whereas in another state stealing anything worth less than $100 or $1,000 may be petty larceny. Since inferior courts generally can handle petty larceny cases but not grand larceny cases, the same offense committed in one jurisdiction will be tried in one type of court whereas if it happens in another jurisdiction, it will be tried in a different type court. In one jurisdiction, a civil action may be considered to have begun with the filing of a complaint, whereupon the reporter is safe in reporting it; in another, however, the action is not considered to exist until the other party has been notified. Similar rules may affect all motions by attorneys and court rulings.

Fortunately, the similarities between the 50 court systems are greater than their differences. Roughly, the typical system is as follows:

INFERIOR COURTS

These are the courts with the least amount of jurisdiction. Generally they can handle criminal cases involving misdemeanors for which the punishment is a fine only. Their jurisdiction in civil matters generally is limited to cases in which the amount of money does not exceed a few hundred dollars. Among the most common of such courts are the following: *justice of the peace* (townships); *police magistrates* (limited to a city or a section of a city); and *city* and *municipal* courts, which, however, in some larger places may have much greater jurisdiction.

COUNTY AND PROBATE COURTS

The jurisdiction of a county court depends upon what other state courts exist. Thus, it may be an inferior court or a court of first instance, with unlimited jurisdiction in civil and criminal matters. In other cases, it may operate mostly as a probate or juvenile court or as overseer of the election machinery and county institutions and agencies concerned with poor relief, adoptions and similar matters. Probate courts supervise the disposition of the estates of deceased persons and may also handle adoptions, lunacy hearings, commitment of feebleminded and insane persons, and guardianships for minors and incompetents.

COURTS OF FIRST INSTANCE

The "backbone" courts are the circuit, superior, district, supreme, or whatever they are called. In them, all kinds of civil actions may be brought and, unless there are separate criminal courts, criminal matters as well. In some states, there are separate equity, divorce and other courts, but in a large majority of states the court of original jurisdiction either has separate calendars or branches for different kinds of civil actions. The criminal court may be set up separately or may be a branch of the circuit court. It may handle all kinds of criminal matters, or there may be separate courts for felonies (as the Court of General Sessions in New York). The number of circuit or district courts in a state is dependent upon the state's size and population. A large city or county may be a circuit in itself and may be permitted a large number of judges, the exact number being established by constitution or statute. Outside of thickly populated areas, a circuit may include two, three, ten or more counties and the judges may hold court at different times in different county seats. The number of terms annually and often their length is established by constitution or statute.

APPELLATE COURTS

These courts do not try cases originally, but only review decisions reached by courts of jurisdiction in the first instance when defeated parties, dissatisfied with lower court decisions, appeal to the higher courts. In smaller states, there is likely to be only one appellate court, usually called supreme, ranging in size from three to twenty-three judges, either appointed by the governor with the consent of the state legislature or elected (at large or by divisions). In larger states, there are intermediate courts of review, often called circuit courts of appeal, which, however, seldom if ever receive appeals involving constitutional or other important matters. Some of the decisions of the intermediate court may be appealed a second time to the highest appellate court, either as a matter of right or with that court's permission. The three, five, seven or more members of an intermediate appellate court may be appointed or elected, or they may be regularly elected circuit or district court judges assigned to appellate court duty by the supreme court. Appellate courts do not try cases as lower courts do; they merely pass on the arguments of attorneys in the case as presented to them in written form (*briefs*) and orally (at *hearings*). The practice is growing to permit new evidence not introduced in an original trial of a case to be presented to an appellate court, but this is not yet common practice. All appellate court decisions are by majority vote of the judges; there never is anything resembling a jury trial in an appellate court.

FEDERAL COURTS

Although it is growing in importance with the passage by Congress of an increasing number of laws defining as federal crimes certain offenses of which formerly only the states took cognizance, and with the establishment of additional federal court districts, the federal judicial system is outside the worries of the average small-city reporter. Anyone arrested in his territory for a federal offense is taken for arraignment to the nearest city in which a federal court is situated.

Despite the activities of the Federal Bureau of Investigation (G-men) in recent years, kidnaping is not a federal offense because Congress does not believe the Supreme Court would hold constitutional a law declaring it such. The so-called Lindbergh law makes the transportation of a kidnaped person across state lines a federal offense which, together with the federal law against sending ransom notes through the mails, allows the G-men to enter kidnaping cases.

Similar technicalities permit federal agents to participate in other criminal cases. For instance, automobile theft is not a federal crime but transporting stolen automobiles across state lines is prohibited by the Dyer act; seduction is not a federal offense but transporting a female across state lines for immoral purposes is prohibited by the Mann act. The notorious Al Capone was not convicted in a federal court for gangsterism but for failure to make a faithful federal income tax return.

In addition to those suggested, cases commonly handled by the federal courts include (1) frauds against the federal government, including embezzlements from national banks, (2) citizenship and denaturalization cases, (3) violations of federal income tax and other revenue laws, (4) violations of post office regulations, including sending threats and other improper material through the mail, rifling mailboxes, and other interferences with the mails, (5) violations of federal statutes as the food and drug acts, anti-trust act, Securities and Exchange act, Interstate Commerce acts, narcotics act, Railway Labor act, etc., (6) bankruptcy proceedings.

OFFICERS OF THE COURT

Officers of a circuit court or a court with similar jurisdiction are: (1) *judge*, who presides during trials, decides points of law, rules on the admissibility of evidence, instructs juries as to the law, pronounces final judgments and sentences, admits criminal defendants to probation, etc. In fact, the judge *is* the court and even his oral orders are authoritative and violations of them constitute contempt of court, (2) *clerk of court*, who receives applications and motions made formally to him for the record, preserves pleadings until used in a formal trial, prepares a court docket and trial calendar with the cooperation of the judge, during a trial records all motions and prepares records and orders of the judge, receives moneys paid to the court as fines, damages and judgments, etc., (3) *prosecuting attorney*, who prosecutes all civil and criminal actions in which the state is a party, defends actions brought against the county, examines all persons brought before any judge on habeas corpus, gives legal opinions to any county officer or justice of the peace and, in general, represents the constituency electing him in all legal matters. The prosecuting attorney usually is called *district attorney* or *state's attorney*, (4) *public defender*, paid by the state to defend persons unable to afford private counsel; where no such officer exists the court often appoints a member of the local bar to serve in that capacity, (5) *bailiff*, who acts as sergeant-at-arms, announces the opening of court ("Hear ye, hear ye," etc.), keeps order in the courtroom, calls witnesses, ushers jurors from the jury room, acts as messenger, etc. Many bailiffs really are *sheriff's deputies*, assigned to the courts. In justice of the peace courts the comparable officer is the *constable*; in federal courts it is the *marshal*, (6) *masters, referees* and *commissioners*, act as "assistant judges," in civil matters. They hear protracted testimony and make recommendations to the judge who has final authority. Masters act in *chancery* (equity) matters and referees in *common law* matters. Commissioners in state courts are appointed for particular tasks, mostly investigative; federal commissioners are examining magistrates in criminal matters, (7) *court reporter*, who is not an elected official but a licensed stenographer authorized to take verbatim testimony and prepare notes in a transcript as evidence called a record. The court reporter may sell copies of his transcript to parties engaged in a trial; in cases of appeal, several copies of a transcript are necessary, (8) *a friend of the court*, a temporarily appointed adviser to the judge who serves during the particular case for which he is selected, (9) *jury commissioners*, who make up a jury list or panel consisting of the names of a certain number of voters in the territory served by the court for each term of court. In smaller counties, the board of supervisors appoints the commissioners; in larger counties, they are appointed by the county judge.

CIVIL LAW

Through codification and/or passage of civil practices acts, many states have simplified both the substantive and adjective law. Whereas formerly it was necessary to bring parts of the same action in different courts, in the federal courts and many state courts it now is possible to ask for both legal and equitable relief in the same action. For instance, you can ask for *damages* (legal relief) and for an *injunction* (equitable relief) to prevent continuation of the cause of injury in the same complaint.

The reporter must be warned, however, that such is not universally true. Several Atlantic seaboard states in particular still adhere to old common law and equity definitions and procedures. In those states you would not bring a simple action to set aside a contract or to force compliance with it or to recover damages because of its breach. Rather, you would bring an action in *covenant* (to recover money damages), or *debt* (to recover specific sums), or *assumpsit* (for damages if the contract was not under seal), or *detinue* (to recover specific chattels). Similarly, a damage suit (tort action) would be one in *trespass* (for money damages), or *trespass on the case* (if injuries were not the direct result of the action complained of), or *detinue* (to recover specific chattels) or *replevin* (a statutory right to recover both property and damages) or *trover* (damages in case the property is lost, destroyed or otherwise incapable of return) or *deceit* (damages for a wrong committed deceitfully).

STARTING AN ACTION

In noncode states a common law action is an *action at law* whereas a case in equity is a *suit in equity*. In federal courts and states with civil practices acts, there is just one *civil action*. To start it the *plaintiff* (he who brings the action) files a *petition* (also called *declaration* or *complaint* or *statement of claim*) stating clearly the alleged cause for action and the relief which he wishes the court to grant. Each paragraph of the complaint is numbered and is called a *count*. When he files an *answer*, as he must do within a specified period to avoid the plaintiff's winning a *judgment by default*, the *defendant* (often called *respondent*, with any third parties mentioned as equally guilty, being *co-respondents*) must admit or deny each count. In the old days, litigants could continue arguing a case on paper almost indefinitely. Under simplified procedures, the *pleadings* — as all such written arguments are called — are limited to two or three by each party.

There follows a typical complaint:

STATE OF ILLINOIS } SS
COUNTY OF COOK }

IN THE SUPERIOR COURT OF COOK COUNTY

IRIS GARDNER,
    Plaintiff
    — vs —   NO. 43 S 10542
CHARLES W. WRIGLEY,
    Defendant

COMPLAINT AT LAW FOR
BREACH OF CONTRACT
JURY DEMANDED

Now comes IRIS GARDNER, plaintiff in the above entitled cause, and complains of the defendant, CHARLES W. WRIGLEY, as follows:

1. That the plaintiff was, on the 15th day of October A.D. 1937 temporarily sojourning in the City of Chicago, County of Cook and state of

Illinois; and, on the date aforesaid, she was about to depart from said city, county and state, and return to her domiciliary city and state, to-wit: St. Louis, Missouri.

2. That plaintiff had a long social acquaintance and friendship with the defendant, CHARLES W. WRIGLEY, prior to October 15, A.D., 1937, when, on the date aforesaid, she, the plaintiff, at the special instance and request of the defendant, CHARLES W. WRIGLEY, met the defendant, CHARLES W. WRIGLEY, in his offices, located at 400 North Michigan Avenue, in the City of Chicago, County of Cook and State of Illinois, and that at the place and on the date aforesaid, plaintiff entered into a verbal agreement with the defendant, CHARLES W. WRIGLEY, the substance of which agreement is hereinafter verbatim alleged.

3. That the defendant, CHARLES W. WRIGLEY, was then, and is now, engaged in the advertising business, and was then, and is now, reputed to have considerable material wealth.

4. That the plaintiff was then, and is now, a woman possessed of pulchritude, charm, and numerous other attributes and qualities to enchant, charm, and grace any person; or, in fact, any social circle.

5. That the defendant, CHARLES W. WRIGLEY, met the plaintiff, at the place and on the date aforesaid, at his special instance and request; and then and there the defendant, CHARLES W. WRIGLEY, was expressly charmed and enchanted by the plaintiff, because of plaintiff's charm, graciousness, and other womanly qualities and attributes and thereupon the defendant, CHARLES W. WRIGLEY, informed plaintiff that she was the person for whom he had been searching to assist him, socially and in his business. Whereupon, the parties entered into a verbal agreement, which, in words, figures and substance, is as follows:

a. The defendant, CHARLES W. WRIGLEY, verbally agreed with the plaintiff to pay plaintiff the sum of One Thousand Dollars ($1,000) per month, either in cash, or by letters of credit, or in any other mode or manner the plaintiff might see fit, provided the said sum was paid in full to the plaintiff, before the expiration of each and every month, commencing on the 1st day of November, A.D. 1937, during the rest of her natural life; and the defendant, CHARLES W. WRIGLEY, further agreed, in order to protect plaintiff, in the event he predeceased plaintiff, to create a trust in the sum of Two Hundred and Fifty Thousand Dollars ($250,000.00), said trust to be evidenced by a trust agreement, the provisions of which trust agreement were to provide that the plaintiff would be entitled to receive the proceeds, rents, profits, and emoluments accruing therefrom, during the plaintiff's natural life.

b. That in consideration of the said verbal agreement, the plaintiff was to cancel her then imminent departure, as aforesaid from the City of Chicago, County of Cook and State of Illinois; and it was further agreed that the plaintiff should reside and domicile continuously in the City of Chicago, County of Cook and State of Illinois, during the natural life of the defendant, CHARLES W. WRIGLEY, in order to assist the defendant, CHARLES W. WRIGLEY, in his social activities, as the defendant might, from time to time, direct, which social activities,

according to the defendant, CHARLES W. WRIGLEY, could be effica-
ciously performed only by the plaintiff, or by some other member of
the fair sex with abilities co-equal to those possessed by the plaintiff.

c. That in pursuance of said verbal agreement, the plaintiff remained,
resided and domiciled, and continues to remain, reside, and domicile,
in the City of Chicago, County of Cook, and State of Illinois; that the
defendant, CHARLES W. WRIGLEY, in pursuance of the terms of said
verbal agreement, obtained or rented an apartment on behalf of the
plaintiff, at the St. Clair Hotel, and paid plaintiff (in cash or by
check, or paid the expenditures of the plaintiff directly to plaintiff's
creditors) the stipulated consideration thereof to-wit: One Thousand
Dollars ($1,000.00) per month, including the rental for said apartment;
and that the defendant, CHARLES W. WRIGLEY, continued to comply
with the terms of said agreement until on or about the 30th day of
May, A.D. 1943, on which date the defendant, CHARLES W. WRIGLEY,
expressly repudiated the same, verbally informing and advising plaintiff
that he would no longer continue payment, thereof, in view of his
reduced financial status.

6. That in pursuance of the terms of said verbal agreement, the plaintiff heretofore has exerted much effort, and expended her youth, grace and
charm, to the end of ameliorating defendant's social as well as esthetic,
well-being.

7. That at the time the aforesaid agreement was entered into defendant was approximately twenty (20) years plaintiff's senior.

8. That the plaintiff has performed each and every condition of her
contract with the defendant, CHARLES W. WRIGLEY, whether precedent or
subsequent, and she is not in default thereof.

9. That the defendant, CHARLES W. WRIGLEY, has wilfully and mali-
ciously, and without any just cause, but merely whimsically, breached the
provisions of said verbal agreement.

10. That the plaintiff has sustained damages, by reason of the breach
of said agreement by the defendant, CHARLES W. WRIGLEY, in the sum of
Five Hundred Thousand Dollars ($500,000.00).

WHEREFORE, plaintiff brings her suit, and asks that a judgment be
entered in her behalf and against the defendant, CHARLES W. WRIGLEY, in
the sum of Five Hundred Thousand Dollars ($500,000.00) and costs.

This is how the Chicago *Sun* handled this news:

Suit for $500,000 charging breach of contract, was filed in Superior
Court yesterday against Charles W. Wrigley, 71, brother of the late
William Wrigley Jr., chewing-gum magnate, by a woman who described
herself as possessing "pulchritude, charm, and manner."

She is identified in the bill as Mrs. Iris Gardner, 41, of the St. Clair
Hotel.

Her complaint, according to the bill, alleges that Wrigley is not paying
her $1,000 a month. He agreed to do this back in 1937, she said, and kept
up the payments for six years before quitting.

Wrigley Indignant

Wrigley, head of an outdoor advertising firm, with offices at 400 N. Michigan av., indignantly denied the entire alleged transaction. Reached at his home, 10 Canterbury ct., Wilmette, he said:

"It's an outrage to file a suit like that. The lady's husband worked for me 15 years ago.

"She never worked for me. As to the payments of $1,000 a month, why, that's crazy! Where would I get the money? She started after me just after Charlie Chaplin's trouble."

Asserts Trust Fund Pledged

According to the bill, Wrigley, uncle of Philip K. Wrigley, owner of the Chicago Cubs, agreed to pay Mrs. Gardner $1,000 a month for life and, if he died first, leave a $250,000 trust fund to provide the income.

In return, the bill continued, Mrs. Gardner was to "assist him socially and in his business." The agreement, Mrs. Gardner said, was verbal.

Note: (1) the reporter obtained information other than that contained in the complaint, (2) he exercised great care in ascribing every fact based on the complaint to the complaint itself, by means of such phrases as "according to the bill," and "the bill continued." It is absolutely necessary never to allow any statement in a story based on a legal document to stand by itself, even at the risk of boring repetition of references.

During the course of his day the reporter watches for the filing of actions which are newsworthy either because of the persons or the amount of money involved or because of the unusualness of the charges. He should not be deceived, however, by exorbitant demands, especially in damage suits. Otherwise, he will be chagrined to learn that a $10,000 action was settled out of court for $250, as often happens.

A $18,000 damage suit was filed in Superior court yesterday by Mrs. Alice Allison, 50, of 179 North Shore drive, for injuries which she said she suffered when a truck collided with a car in which she was riding at McCormick boulevard and North Shore drive last May 1.

Eric Swanson, 55, of 2900 Milwaukee avenue, Mrs. Allison's nephew, was at the wheel of the car, the petition alleges, when a Petroleum Motor company truck violated traffic signals and smashed into it at high speed. The company and Ralph T. and Ernest J. Walton, its owners, are the defendants.

DEFENDING AN ACTION

A defendant who has been properly served by *summons* (law) or *subpoena* (equity) must answer within a prescribed time or at least file an *appearance*, which is an acknowledgment and indication that he will answer later. When the answer is filed the reporter scans it for its contents.

To avoid answering, the defendant may enter a *motion to dismiss* the action, contending that the plaintiff has no legal right to bring it. In such a motion, he may challenge the jurisdiction of the court or the sufficiency of the process by which he was notified of the beginning of the suit; or, most importantly, he may contend that the plaintiff has failed to state a ground for action. Under old procedures, he may enter a *demurrer*, which is a plea that, even if true, the facts alleged do not constitute a cause for action. He also may plead that the *statute of limitations*, setting the time limit within which such action can be brought, has been violated.

To delay or postpone the case, the defendant may resort to dilatory tactics by a *plea in abatement* which may: (1) *challenge the array*; that is, question the procedure by which the panel of veniremen (potential jurors) was selected as the case nears trial, (2) ask a *change of venue*, which is a transfer to another court or branch of the same court on the grounds that judge or jurors are prejudiced, (3) ask a *continuance*, or postponement for any of a variety of reasons, the merits of which the judge must decide, (4) be a *motion to quash* because the summons was defective.

A special kind of answer is one in *confession and avoidance* wherein the defendant admits the facts but declares he acted within his legal rights. A *counterclaim* is an answer in which the defendant not only denies liability but contends that the plaintiff is obligated to him. Counterclaims are frequent in damage cases involving automobile accidents; each driver blames the other.

When several actions related to the same incident are begun, the court may order that there be a *joinder of parties* or *joinder of causes*. On the other hand, on its own motion or that of one of the parties, the court may grant a *severance* when co-defendants make separate answers. A third party who believes his interests are affected by the action may petition the court for permission to file an *intervening* petition to become either a plaintiff or defendant.

> Complications in the divorce suit of Constantin Dantes against Mrs. Marie Busch Jones Dantes arose today with announcement by Carl Enger, attorney for Mrs. Gertrude Stuprich, Dantes' former wife, that he would file an intervening petition in the suit against Mrs. Marie Dantes.
>
> Basis for the intervening petition, Enger said, would be Dantes' failure to pay $7.50 a week for the support of his 17-year-old daughter, Bertha, as provided in the divorce obtained by Mrs. Stuprich in Circuit Judge James E. McLaughlin's court last Nov. 15. . . . St. Louis *Post-Dispatch*

So that he will understand what is going on, the reporter should be familiar with a few other types of motions: (1) a *bill of particulars* may be demanded by the defendant if the complaint is unclear or not sufficiently specific, (2) a *bill of discovery* may be asked if the defendant wishes to examine documents or other material in the plaintiff's possession, (3) either party may ask permission to submit an *interrogatory*, or set of questions, to the other to obtain necessary information, (4) scandalous, redundant, irrelevant or otherwise objectionable portions of any pleading may be eliminated if the court grants a *motion to strike*.

CIVIL TRIALS

Unless there is a *default judgment* (or *decree*) because of failure of the defendant to answer; or a *summary judgment* because the answer is inadequate; or a *judgment by confession* because the defendant admits the plaintiff's charges, the issue becomes joined and, upon motion of either party or the court itself, the case is placed on the trial calendar.

Most civil trials today are heard by a judge alone. In fact, it generally is necessary to make a formal request and pay a court fee at the time of filing a complaint or answer to obtain a civil trial by jury. Except for the preliminary step of selecting the jurors, theoretically the procedure is the same. The steps are as follows:

1. Opening statement by plaintiff, through his attorney, of what he expects to prove
2. Opening statement by defendant
3. Direct examination of plaintiff's witnesses
4. Cross-examination by defendant of plaintiff's witnesses
5. Direct and cross-examination of defendant's witnesses
6. Redirect or rebuttal witnesses for plaintiff
7. Closing statements by both sides, plaintiff speaking first, then the defendant, and, finally, rebuttal by plaintiff

In actual practice, a hearing before a judge usually is informal. With all of the principals and their attorneys and witnesses clustered about the bench, the judge may interrupt, change the usual order of procedure and take a hand at questioning. Then he either takes the case under *advisement* (meaning he wants to think it over before deciding) or he enters a *judgment* for either plaintiff or defendant, in a law action, or a *decree* if the case is one at equity. Even if there is a jury, it can only recommend what *damages* are to be assessed against the loser in a law action; the final decision is up to the judge and, upon motion of the losing party or on his own initiative, he can disregard the jury's findings and enter a *judgment notwithstanding the verdict*.

Damages may be: (1) *general*, meaning they are the same as might be expected to compensate anyone for the type of loss proved to have been incurred, (2) *special*, those peculiar to the particular case, (3) *nominal*, which are trifling and for the purpose of moral vindication only, or (4) *exemplary*, assessed in addition to the general or *compensatory* damages, to punish the other party.

A judgment for $119,358 against the Global Securities & Holding company as stockholders in the Acorn National bank, was ordered by Federal Judge Frick today in favor of Gerald Swayne, receiver of the bank. The amount of the judgment represented a double assessment against the company as holders of 1,101 shares of the bank's stock and $9,358 accrued interest.

A civil action may end in a *nonsuit* if at any time the plaintiff fails to continue; such a judgment naturally is for the defendant. So is a *dismissal*, the difference being, however, that in case of a nonsuit the plaintiff may begin another action whereas a dismissal is a final disposition of a case, unless it is a *dismissal without prejudice* which usually comes upon request of the plaintiff himself. A *consent* judgment is entered when the court approves an out-of-court agreement between the parties. A *declaratory* judgment, obtainable in federal courts and some state courts, is an informatory opinion in advance of any legal action; by means of it the court declares what its decision would be in the event action were brought. Its use prevents much expensive and useless litigation.

An ordinary judgment or decree is either: (1) *final*, or (2) *conditional*, which means certain acts (as exchange of property) must be performed before it becomes final, or (3) *nisi* (unless), which means it becomes final after a certain lapse of time if certain forbidden acts do not occur, or (4) *interlocutory*, in which case restrictions on behavior—as against remarriage—are designated.

ENFORCING CIVIL LAW

There is no imprisonment for debt in the United States, so a plaintiff may not be much better off after he receives a judgment against the defendant than before. By applying for a *writ of execution*, the judgment creditor can force sale of the judgment debtor's property to satisfy his claim, but if the debtor does not possess enough assets to meet the obligation, it is often better to allow the judgment to stand as a lien against what he does have until the day when it is wise to enforce it. To discover a debtor's assets, a creditor may obtain a court *citation* ordering the debtor to appear in court for questioning by a referee. Failure to comply means that one may be cited for *contempt of court* which, in some cases, may be punished by imprisonment. In such cases, however, the judgment creditor usually has to pay for the debtor's keep. The inmates of "alimony row" in the county jail are contemptuous divorcees.

Either at the beginning of a suit or after a judgment has been obtained, the plaintiff may obtain a *property attachment*, placing the defendant's assets under control of the court to prevent their conversion. A *body attachment* or execution is a court order to arrest a principal to prevent his untimely departure from its jurisdiction. A *ne exeat* decree is an order forbidding such departure. *Garnishment* proceedings are for the purpose of attaching a debtor's income, usually his salary, for the benefit of the creditor.

If a court becomes convinced that a supposedly closed case should be reopened, it can entertain a motion to *reinstate* a case which has been dismissed, to *set aside* a verdict, to *vacate* a judgment or to *review* a decree. A *writ of audita querela* stops execution of a judgment when new evidence is presented. A *writ of supersedeas* orders a court officer to stop execution which has not gone too far.

Many damage suits contain a *malice* count which means that the alleged injury was committed intentionally or because of gross negligence. If the court upholds the contention, the guilty defendant may be jailed if he fails to satisfy the judgment.

CIVIL ACTIONS

There is a semingly interminable number of kinds of actions. Judges and lawyers with years of experience pore over ponderous legal tomes for hours to refresh their memories regarding many of them. The lay reporter cannot be expected to master the intricacies of even an appreciable number of them. If he understands the basic differences between the major types of actions and can translate the most frequently used legal language, he can get along. There are several good law dictionaries which he can consult when he "encounters a new one." What follows are a few suggestions concerning some of the kinds of actions which are most newsworthy:

DAMAGE SUITS

The news interest usually is in the incident giving rise to the action: an automobile accident, surgeon's error, etc. If so, perhaps the paper carried a story at the time, which means the account of the filing of the complaint should contain a careful tie-back. The reporter should get: names and addresses of principals; the plaintiff's version of exactly what happened, all charges being carefully accredited to the complaint; the comments of the defendant on the charges; the amount of money demanded; is there a malice count?

DIVORCE

Distinguish between it and *annulment*, and between *separate maintenance* and *alimony*. What are the grounds (desertion, cruelty, etc.)? Watch out for libel when reporting specific incidents cited as grievances (beatings, criminal behavior, etc.). The reporter should obtain: names and addresses of both principals; date of marriage and of separation; names and ages of children and what bill requests regarding them; suggested disposition of property; whether alimony is requested; whether wife asks court to authorize use of her maiden name. When a case comes to hearing, testimony, of course, can be reported; state whether defendant contests case or allows decree to be obtained by default.

FORECLOSURES

A person who defaults in payments on a mortgage stands to lose the property through foreclosure proceedings. In most states, however, he has an *equity of redemption* — a period of time in which to pay up, even though a court has awarded the property to the mortgage holder.

EVICTIONS

The Renters' Court always is a fertile source for human interest stories. The legal name for actions to evict is *forcible entry and detainer*. During housing shortages, renters' courts are crowded. The reporter does well to examine the statutes of the state for sections pertaining to the rights of landlords to evict or refuse to rent to families with children or pets. He also should read up on statutes and court decisions related to *restrictive covenants* whereby property owners are forbidden to sell or lease to Negroes, Jews, or members of other minority groups, or are otherwise restricted in the use of property.

CONDEMNATION SUITS

When a new street or highway or public building is planned, the proper government agency uses its right of *eminent domain* to purchase — at a fair price — any privately owned land needed for the improvement. Property owners often resist such taking of their property or hold out for higher compensation. Public clamor may cause a change in official plans, as happened when property owners in Connecticut objected to the headquarters of the United Nations being established there.

RECEIVERSHIPS

Creditors or stockholders of a corporation or individuals in financial difficulties may apply to an equity court for appointment of a receiver to conserve assets and rescue the business. A chancery receivership, intended to put a going concern back on its feet, must be distinguished from a receiver in bankruptcy, who is in charge of liquidating a defunct institution. Many banks, hotels, transportation and other companies continue operating under receiverships for years. Often newspapers uncover scandals regarding political favoritism in appointment of receivers or companies with which they do business. Reporters should watch the periodic reports which receivers must make to the courts appointing them.

BANKRUPTCY

A financial failure may file a *voluntary petition* in bankruptcy, or his creditors may file an *involuntary petition* in his case. The reporter should examine the inventory filed with the petition, to obtain: total assets; total liabilities; nature of the assets (stocks, real estate, controlling interest in other companies, etc.); nature of liabilities, clues as to reasons for failure. Bankruptcy matters are handled by the federal courts. Each petition is referred to a *referee in bankruptcy*, a permanent court officer; the *trustee* is elected by the creditors and, if approved by the court, takes over the task of liquidating the assets and distributing them on a pro rata basis. Instead of dissolving a business, a company may undergo *reorganization* under a court-approved plan. Usually, some creditors are "frozen out" when such happens, and the legal jockeying between them to avoid that happening is newsworthy when the company is important. Since every action of a trustee must be approved by the court, the reporter can keep close to the situation.

INJUNCTIONS

Distinguish between a *preliminary restraining order*, which is issued by a judge on ex parte evidence only and without notice, and between *temporary* and *permanent* injunctions. The orthodox procedure is for the court to issue a temporary order to the defendant to appear in court and "show cause" why it should not become permanent. In the meantime, the alleged offensive conduct must cease. Injunctions are used to prohibit government agencies and officials from exceeding their authority; to test the constitutionality of a law; to restrain picketing and other activities by labor unions; to restrain corporations from acts injurious to stock- or bond-holders; to compel persons to keep the peace and not interfere with the civil liberties and other rights of others; to stop and prevent nuisances, and for other purposes.

EXTRAORDINARY REMEDIES

The equitable relief provided by an injunction originated as an extraordinary remedy, but has become so common it no longer is extraordinary. Almost the same is true of *habeas corpus*, whereby a jailer is required to produce a prisoner in court to answer charges against him. Dating from Magna Charta, it is one of the great Anglo-Saxon democratic protections.

Other so-called extraordinary remedies follow.

PROHIBITION

This is a writ issued by a superior court to one of inferior jurisdiction commanding it to desist in handling any matter beyond its authority to consider.

CERTIORARI

This also is an inquiry into the behavior of a lower court after it has taken some action. Thus, it usually operates as an appeal, to bring about a review of the lower court's action in the higher court. In granting a writ of certiorari or *writ of review*, as it is called, however, the higher court merely agrees to look into the matter. It may return the case later.

MANDAMUS

This writ is directed by a higher court to administrative officers, corporations or an inferior court ordering some action required by law. It does not specify what the action must be — as in a case where a required appointment is overdue — but it does demand that some action be taken.

QUO WARRANTO

By this writ, a higher court inquires into the right of a public official to hold office or of a corporation to exercise a franchise.

PROBATE PROCEEDINGS

When a person dies, the state supervises payment of his debts and distribution of his property. If he dies *testate* (that is, if he leaves a will), unless someone can prove that the contrary should be done, the court sees that its provisions are carried out. It usually appoints the *executor* named in the will to supervise settling the estate; that official, often a relative of the deceased, posts bond for about one-and-a-half times the estimated value of the estate and receives a commission when his work is done. If there is no will (deceased died *intestate*) the court appoints an *administrator*. In many states there now are public administrators. Either executor or administrator receives *letters testamentary* to authorize his work which includes notification of beneficiaries named in a will, or legal heirs if there is no will; advertising for bills against the estate; collecting money due the estate; preparing an inventory of the estate, etc.

FILING A WILL

The first step in probate proceedings is the filing of the will by whoever has it in custody or finds it. Reporters watch for such filings of wills of prominent persons recently deceased. In their case, it is news whether the estate is large or small. As a matter of fact, it usually is difficult or impossible to determine an estate's size from the will itself; it is not known with certainty until an appraisal is made months later. The first public information may come with the filing of an inheritance tax return.

> The estate of Henry B. Paschen, Chicago construction contractor, totaled $3,062,182, according to an inheritance tax return filed Thursday with the Cook County clerk.
>
> Paschen, uncle of former county treasurer Herbert C. Paschen, died Dec. 19, 1959, at the age of 77. He lived at 345 W. Fullerton.
>
> The estate was left in trust to the widow, Lillian, with a provision that upon her death one-half of it go to their children, Mrs. Marjorie O'Neil of 706 S. Sheridan, Evanston, and Henry Jr., of 12 E. Scott.
>
> The federal tax on the estate was $358,659 and the state levy, $117,-328.　　　　　　　　　　　　　　　　　　Chicago *Sun-Times*

An ingenious reporter in some cases can estimate value by determining the market value of securities, the assessor's valuations of real estate and by similar investigation. Frequently, the nature of an estate is newsworthy as a person may be revealed to be the owner of property which he was not known to possess. From the will, the beneficiaries can be determined and often they contain surprises. The first news story should mention when and where the will was drawn and possibly the witnesses. In small places, virtually every will is newsworthy; in larger places, only those of important persons or involving large estates receive mention.

ADMITTING TO PROBATE

The reporter must not confuse filing a will and admitting a will to probate which is done by court order upon petition of the executor or someone else. Before such a petition is granted it must be "proved" to be genuine and there also must be proof of heirship; usually referees supervise such matters which are routine. If anything happens to disturb the routine, it probably is newsworthy.

> The will of Richard W. Young, founder and chairman of the board of the Young corporation, who died March 1, at the age of 70, was admitted to probate today by County Judge Thomas Sullivan.

The executors are Thomas B. Young and R. L. Waters. Waters declined to place an estimate on the size of the estate, but it is generally understood to be in the millions.

Sets Up Trust Fund

The will sets up a trust fund on behalf of 11 relatives of the industrialist. The division is as follows:

One-sixth of the estate to Thomas B. Young, now president of the Young corporation, a nephew. One-eighth to Frank Young, a nephew. One-eight to Ruth Young Stoddard, a niece.

One-twelfth to Louise R. White, a niece. One-twelfth to Margaret Rolnick, a niece. One-twelfth to Nancy Young, a niece. One-twelfth to Mary Sheridan, a niece. One-twelfth to Robert Carpenter, a nephew. One-twelfth to Richard Sheridan, a nephew.

One-twenty-fourth to Patricia Young, a grand-niece and one-twenty-fourth to Kent Young, a grand-nephew.

May Be Liquidated

The will provides that the Young Investment company, established by Young, may be liquidated within 12 months of his death and the assets distributed to the stockholders, this with the approval of the executors. It also provides that the entire estate shall be liquidated within 20 years and may be liquidated, if the executors approve, in ten years.

CONTESTING A WILL

By law an interval, which varies from three months to two years, must elapse between the time a will is admitted to probate and a *final accounting*. During that period, suit may be brought to break the will, perhaps by a disgruntled relative who was disinherited. Common charges are that the deceased was unduly influenced when he made the will, or was not in full possession of his mental faculties. Sometimes it is charged that the will filed was not the most recent. Such suits usually are filed in courts other than that handling routine probate matters.

Suit to contest the will of Mrs. Margaret W. Miller, widow of Charles B. Miller, an official of Carson Pirie Scott & Co., whereby she left most of $100,000 to friends, was filed in Circuit Court yesterday by six relatives, including three sisters and a brother. Mrs. Miller plunged to her death from a room in the Palmer House last July 27 at the age of 68.

The suit charges she was "eccentric and peculiar" and "susceptible to influence and blandishments," and that undue influence was put upon her in making the will. Attorney Coram T. Davis, co-executor under the will, who was left a $20,000 bequest, was her close financial adviser, and Attorney Vernon E. Victorine, also left $20,000, was his associate, the bill points out.   Chicago *Sun*

RULES OF EVIDENCE

To "feel at home" as he should, whenever he steps into any courtroom, a reporter must understand the fundamental rules of evidence.

NATURE OF EVIDENCE

Most evidence is in the form of testimony by witnesses. Other forms of evidence include objects and written material introduced as exhibits. Together they constitute the *proof* whereby it is intended to influence the court's decision. All evidence must be: (1) *material* — have a direct relation to the case, (2) *relevant* — pertinent, and (3) *competent* — authoritative. Otherwise, the court will uphold an *objection* to its introduction.

BURDEN OF PROOF

In a civil action, it is *preponderance of evidence* that counts; in criminal cases, the state must prove guilt *beyond any reasonable doubt*. At all times, the burden of proof rests with the side which must refute evidence which, if allowed to stand, would be injurious to it.

PRESUMPTIONS

The law presumes that any situation known to exist at one time continues to exist unless proof to the contrary is provided. Thus good character and impeccable behavior on the part of all citizens is presumed until disproved.

JUDICIAL NOTICE

Common knowledge, such as the organization of government, size and location of cities and countries, business practices, etc., need not be proved in court. Instead, the court "takes notice" of them unless challenged for doing so.

QUALIFICATIONS OF WITNESSES

Children, wives, husbands, insane persons, felons, dependents, interested lawyers, and other parties once were barred from testifying. Today, the restrictions are much lighter. Almost anyone competent at the time of trial or hearing can be a witness; the credibility to be attached to his testimony is a different matter.

PRIVILEGE

The Fifth Amendment to the Constitution of the United States protects anyone from being compelled to testify against himself. In actual practice, refusal to testify because to do so might incriminate oneself often is a "dodge." No lawyer can be compelled to reveal what a client has told him in confidence. Similar protection is afforded physicians and clergymen in many cases and, in a few states, newspapermen.

LEADING QUESTIONS

Witnesses tell their stories in response to questions by attorneys. Those questions cannot be so worded as to suggest the answers desired.

HEARSAY EVIDENCE

A witness can testify only to that of which he has first-hand knowledge. He cannot draw inferences from the facts. Exceptions to the rule include dying declarations, spontaneous declarations, confessions, and admissions against one's interest.

OPINION EVIDENCE

Anyone is an authority on matters which he has witnessed or which are within the knowledge of an ordinary person. Experts must be qualified before their testimony is considered credible. An expert's opinion often is obtained by means of a *hypothetical question* in which a situation comparable to that at issue is described.

REAL EVIDENCE

Clothing, weapons and objects of all sorts are introduced as exhibits. So are models and photographs.

CIRCUMSTANTIAL EVIDENCE

Correct inferences often can be drawn from evidence pertaining to a person's behavior both before and after a crime is committed and from his known capacities and predilections. A great deal of the evidence in both civil and criminal cases is circumstantial rather than by eyewitnesses.

BEST EVIDENCE

Copies of documents are admissible only when there is proof that originals are unavailable. In every case, the court demands the best possible evidence regarding any point.

APPEALS

Since the trial judge passes on motions for new trials, not many are granted. Only in rare cases, however, does a judge refuse to grant a dissatisfied party the right to take his case to the appellate court. In criminal matters, no appeal is possible by the state in the event of acquittal, but a convicted defendant can appeal; and in civil matters either side can do so.

The distinction between *appeal* (of civil law origin) and *writ of error* (of common law origin) is virtually nonexistent today. Where it exists, it means that in the former instance a case is removed entirely from the lower to the higher court which then can review both the law and the evidence; a writ of error, by contrast, is an original proceeding, not a continuation of that in the lower court.

Appeals are either *as of right* or *by permission* of the upper court as the statutes designate. Common grounds on which an appeal can be made are: (1) irregularity of the submission of evidence, (2) new evidence discovered since the trial ended, (3) misconduct of the jury, (4) lack of jurisdiction of the court, (5) an error by the judge in instructing the jury, (6) incompetent witnesses, (7) excessive damages allowed (in civil cases), (8) influencing or packing of the jury by the adverse party.

A *bill of exceptions* (also called *statement of the case* or *certificate of reasonable doubt*) must set forth clearly and completely the grounds on which appeal is taken. It may be accompanied by a *brief* in which the details are made more elaborate and the case as a whole summarized, although the trend is toward simplification of procedure so that only one document is necessary. Certified copies of *transcripts* and *abstracts* of lower court records also are submitted.

The party taking the appeal is known as the *appellant* or *plaintiff in error* and the other party (usually the winner in the lower court) as the *appellee* or *defendant in error*. It is good practice for a reporter always to ask a defeated party in an important case whether he intends to appeal. Otherwise, he first learns of such action by a *notice of appeal* filed in the appellate court. Today, such notice acts as an automatic *stay of proceedings* or *supersedeas* to hold up execution of any lower court judgment or sentence. In some jurisdictions, however, it is necessary to petition for such writs.

If the higher court's permission is necessary, whatever the court decides regarding a petition is news. If it agrees to review a case, it sets a date for *oral arguments* by attorneys. Then it takes the case *under advisement*. Each justice studies the case independently before the court meets to discuss it. After a vote is taken, the chief justice assigns one justice to prepare the *majority opinion* supporting the court's *decision*. Other members may prepare *concurring opinions* or *dissenting opinions*. Any part of a decision which deals with background not directly pertinent to the case at hand is called *obiter dictum*; it explains the mental processes by which the justices formed their opinions.

By its decision, the appellate court *upholds* or *reverses* or *modifies* the lower court's decision. A *mandate* is an order to a lower court to take any kind of action, and the upper court *remands* the case to the lower so that it can act.

Only an experienced reporter is likely to be assigned to cover appellate court proceedings. By the time he has mastered the art of handling lower court news, he will be thoroughly qualified to do so.

> The United States Circuit Court of Appeals took under review yesterday the criminal conviction of Henry Lustig, millionaire restaurateur, and two others on charges of having defrauded the Federal Government of $2,872,766 in income taxes owed by the Longchamps Restaurant chain.
>
> Decision was reserved after arguments for three and a half hours by former Gov. Nathan L. Miller, attorney for the appellants, and Bruno Schachner, assistant United States Attorney.
>
> Convicted last June 20 on all 23 counts of an indictment were Lustig, who was sentenced to four years in jail, and fined $115,000; E. Allen Lustig, his nephew, secretary of the restaurants, who received a three-year sentence, and Joseph Sobol, an accountant, who was sentenced to two years.
>
> Mr. Miller pursued the argument presented at the trial that the defendants were entitled to immunity from criminal prosecution because of an alleged voluntary disclosure made to William J. Pedrick, collector of internal revenue for the Second District, by Allen Lustig on March 26, 1945.
>
> He told the court that the question to be decided was whether such immunity existed when a disclosure of delinquency had been made prior to the start of a government investigation and if such a self-incriminating disclosure could be used as a basis for criminal conviction.
>
> Mr. Miller said that at the trial the question of fraud was not contested and that the only question litigated was whether a voluntary disclosure had been made before a Treasury investigation started. He said that a ruling by the lower court judge, Harold Kennedy, that the Treasury Department was not morally bound to keep a promise of immunity from prosecution had the effect of virtually decimating the verdict. . . .
>
> New York *Times*

16

Politics, Elections

I. Political Philosophy

II. Political Public Opinion

III. Political Organization

   1. Local

   2. Precinct and Ward

   3. County

   4. State, National

IV. Pre-campaign Activities

   1. Petitions

   2. Registration

   3. Primaries

   4. Conventions

V. Campaigns

   1. Speeches

   2. Strategy

   3. Roorbacks

   4. Issues

VI. Elections

   1. Predictions

   2. Election Day

   3. Election Results

VII. "Post Mortems"

POLITICS IS SERIOUS BUSINESS

Is the candidate for city council telling the truth or is he fibbing? Does the party platform mean what it says or is it hokum? Does the corporation report, disclose or conceal the truth? Answers to these questions require accuracy of perspective, and how can you have this accuracy without solid background?

Sometimes I see ignorance and lack of understanding among journalists in their handling of subjects. Their ignorance, their misconception, their faulty appraisal of the importance or meaning of the facts which they present, are magnified a thousand times upon the public which reads their product.

I have seen political writers who write brightly of the superficial aspects of current politics, without a glimmer of an idea concerning the fundamental trends, or the meaning, or the economic foundation of politics. They treat politics as a vaudeville show. They miss the meaning, and thereby millions of voters also miss the meaning.

Willard M. Kiplinger

The press would be quick to criticize (and properly so) if I selected inexperienced officers to display judgment and exercise the discretionary powers necessary to the conduct of those administering the affairs of a great city. Yet this same press is not careful in selecting experienced men for the important job of reporting to our citizens the complex affairs of a city spending $2,000,000 a day.

Would they send the grand opera critic to the Army-Notre Dame game? You bet your life they wouldn't. Would they send the office boy to a first night at the theater?

Fiorello LaGuardia

THE AMERICAN POLITICIAN IS A PRACTICAL BUSINESSMAN. What he sells is his public service which the public purchases with its ballots. His remuneration is employment by the electorate with all the emoluments that the position entails. As a merchant, the politician is responsive to consumer demand and, in turn, attempts to influence that demand. Although independents in other lines of business have been able to withstand the competition of Big Business with its holding companies, chain stores, etc., the lone wolf in politics is virtually hopeless. Any success he attains is temporary; to get far he must align himself with one of the two large rival organizations which, since the Civil War have divided the nation's political profits with very little loss to third parties.

Since communism and fascism began to threaten democracy in Old World countries and since the American New Dealers introduced a new note in our political life, newspaper readers have become more conscious of the broader aspects or philosophic bases of world politics. This awareness, however, still is predominately academic; all that the defeat of candidates standing for principles which formerly were popular means to the practical politician-businessman is that consumer demand has changed. The professor or student of political theory may be aware of national and international social and economic trends which are reflected in overt political events, but neither candidate nor voter has such breadth of vision. Should an aspirant for office also be a scholar he nevertheless, to be successful (that is, get elected), has to play the game as it is played.

Despite the increase in serious articles, usually Sunday features or on the editorial page, discussing politics philosophically, the American newspaper remains as practical in its attitude toward the business of getting and staying elected as the politician himself. Because of consolidations, which have left few cities with fewer than 100,000 inhabitants with more than one newspaper, most newspapers today term themselves "independent" whereas formerly they prided themselves on being either Republican or Democratic. This change obviously was made for good business reasons so as not to alienate about 50 per cent of the potential subscribers. Political independence, however, is not tantamount to political indifference as to which party wins a particular election; rather, it means merely that the newspaper reserves the right to decide on which side it will be in each campaign. Theoretically, it is free to be Democratic one year and Republican the next or to support candidates of both parties for different offices in the same election. Once it has made its decision as to whom it will support, the allegedly independent newspaper may be as unfair in his behalf as the frankly aligned paper.

Truly interpretative political writing consists in explaining the immediate phenomenon in terms of long-range trends, national or international. Accepting the fact that practical politicians still do not operate with any appreciable awareness of such trends, pragmatic interpretative political writing consists in identifying leaders with movements and "seeing through" motives and actions to discover their probable meaning and effect upon political fortunes.

From whichever angle he regards the political scene, the political reporter, to "keep his feet on the ground," must see beyond the externals which the politician hopes, usually successfully, will be all of which the average voter is aware. What benefits this overcoming of naïveté will be to the reporter, outside of the extent to which it furthers his education, is dependent upon the attitude of his superiors. No matter what they profess, newspapers *are* involved in politics and, all the statistical evidence to the contrary, both candidates and voters act as though the press is an important factor. Any aspirant for any office welcomes the support of any newspaper, and any newspaper is glad to have a political friend in public office. As long as a newspaper attacks a politician it advertises him; the most effective journalistic weapon is to ignore a person. Although there have been numerous instances in which exactly that was done, it is not common practice if for no other reason than to avoid "one party press" criticisms which result when a newspaper does not seem to be giving rival candidates for an office equal treatment.

In small cities, the primary interest is local politics inasmuch as the small newspaper has little to gain directly from state or national politics. Local political news is written by staff members whereas material regarding state or national politics is obtained from press associations, syndicates and political headquarters. That all of this news, regardless of how obtained, is presented impartially except in rare instances, is obviously absurd to believe. Hence, the reporter seeking to do a meaty objective job is handicapped. In no field of writing is the merely narrative more impotent in serving any public purpose nor absence of bias more difficult of attainment. Early in this book, the distinction was made between intentional color and honest interpretation. It should be the responsibility of readers to see that newspapers provide the latter.

In preparing himself to derive the most benefit from his experiences, the newspaper political reporter should: (1) know something about political philosophy, (2) be a student of public opinion, its nature and manipulation, (3) understand practical political organization and election machinery, and (4) be sufficiently on the "inside" to distinguish the bunkum from the realities of political phenomena.

POLITICAL PHILOSOPHY

Plato, in describing a highly disciplined perfect state in which philosophers would be kings, Aristotle, in advocating a balanced democratic government, and political theorists ever since, expressed points of view which the enlightened political reporter will detect in substance in the arguments of contemporary seekers for public office. Heaven forbid that the college-trained reporter should be a pedantic idealist passing judgment upon twentieth-century practical men of affairs in terms of his favorite thinker of the past. Nevertheless, historical perspective is indispensable in enabling one to "make sense" of modern affairs. Being conversant with the history of political thought, especially with how it has been affected by practical considerations, at least provides the political reporter with the tools for making his work personally instructive.

In the writings of many contemporaries, the aspiring political reporter will find plentiful interpretative analyses of the modern scene. A superabundant amount of material concerning democracy, communism and fascism, of course, exists. The average person may not be able to tell the difference between these and other political theories, but no political writer can be so ignorant. He should at least know when a demagogue is incorrect in branding an opponent as socialistic or fascistic, etc.

Political writers are a potent force in educating the public regarding the pros and cons of such matters as the two-party versus multiple-party systems, permanent registration, proportionate representation, the direct primary and the like. Nobody, however, can write on such subjects without deep understanding of them.

POLITICAL PUBLIC OPINION

Before formulating an opinion about the nature of public opinion, one must understand what is meant by each word. What is a public? And what is an opinion? Unless one knows the results of scholarly attempts to answer these questions, his own conclusions are invalid. Consequently, a minimum of training in sociology and psychology, or in the dual science, social psychology, is essential to the political writer. From a good course or textbook he will learn that few modern thinkers in the field share the faith formerly held in instincts or a group mind as the explanation of why men behave similarly. Instead, inspired by the revelations of the behaviorists, psychoanalysts, anthropologists and other specialists, they are tending toward placing the emphasis upon habits and attitudes as the answer.

The politician as a psychological phenomenon has been treated by Harold D. Lasswell in *Psychopathology and Politics*, by A. B. Wolfe in *Conservatism, Radicalism, and the Scientific Method* and by many other writers. Walter Lippmann's *Public Opinion* and *The Phantom Public* resulted from his observations as a newspaperman. Lincoln Steffens' momentous *Autobiography* was inspired similarly. There is a sizable library on modern propaganda, including political propaganda, and abundant reading material on all other phases of the subject.

Failure of the professional pollsters to predict correctly the outcome of the 1948 presidential election gave impetus to research into the motivations of voting behavior. Paul Lazarsfeld and associates at Columbia University stress the effects of group interrelationships (*The People's Choice*, *Voting*). Louis Bean emphasizes longtime economic trends (*How to Predict Elections*). Samuel Lubell thinks the effect of nationality and cultural background has been underestimated (*The Future of American Politics, The Revolt of the Moderates*). Angus Campbell and associates demonstrate in *The American Voter* that voting preferences are consistent with a person's total personal and cultural conditioning.

POLITICAL ORGANIZATION

LOCAL

Municipal political affairs in recent years generally have become dissociated from major party organizations. Candidates for mayor and other city offices run as independents but may be identified in state and national politics as members of established parties which tacitly lend them support. In smaller communities, the rival groups in a municipal campaign are more likely to cross established party lines and to be dissociated from all but strictly local issues.

Because of the nonpartisan character of municipal elections, it should be the newspaper's function properly to identify candidates by the interests of the persons or groups backing them. Local political groups may take names as the People's Party, but these have little or no meaning until party members have held office and given indication of what they represent. A local candidate's backing may be racial, religious, economic, geographic, or in some other way classifiable. In preparing slates of candidates, political parties try to have as many of the important elements as possible represented. Furthermore, it is customary to run a Catholic against a Catholic, a Jew against a Jew, someone of Swedish extraction against another with similar ancestry, and so on. In this way, awareness of nationality, racial and other backgrounds is kept alive as well as taken advantage of politically.

One way to label candidates is by the political factions to which they belong:

> Vernon County's primary races election got under way today as a free-for-all with the heaviest field of candidates that veteran observers can recall.
>
> Four distinct groups on the Democratic side filed candidates for almost every major position for which nominations will be made August 6.

Names for Every Post

> In the machine ranks, the Mayer and Van Dyke factions took no chances. Each tossed in an almost complete list, including names for party committee posts. Likewise, the United Democrats, Inc., bucking machine domination, and the Stevens group, which at times has sided with the machine, covered most of the major spots with their filings.
>
> The Republicans put in a list all the way up and down the line, with many of the names representing candidate committee recommendations. Several candidates for the major posts are unopposed. There were others who are apparently just taking a chance and going along for the ride. While there are many familiar names among the candidates, there also are many new faces in the primary field, with others difficult to identify from a political point of view.
>
> It was a close watch that was maintained by the representatives of the various groups which remained on the job in the county clerk's office in the courthouse until the deadline hour arrived last midnight. Among the watchers was Arthur L. Mayer, head of the faction.

Differ on Some Places

> It was said there was a lack of straight-out agreement within the machine factions on some of the major places. This was indicated by the covering of most of the positions at stake in August. The machine groups also played safe against illness, death or possible failure to later agree on a slate.
>
> Most of the machine faithful are certain that agreements will be worked out on a slate basis before the deadline for withdrawals on July 26. The machine hardly can afford a family showdown in the primaries in the light of the heavy listings and the opposition.
>
> If the expected straight-out machine ticket is set up, the big list will be materially reduced by withdrawals.
>
> The machine factions recognized each other in two or three places. One such case was for prosecutor, where the Mayer group filed Daniel O. Mazer for the position now held by Alonzo Timmerman, who is a candidate for a fourth term without Mayer backing. The Van Dyke following entered no one, as the office is considered a Mayer post.

Other Posts Appear Set

While others entered against Sam Graf of the Van Dyke faction for renomination for western judge of the county court, it is a foregone conclusion that he will be the machine selection. . . . The same is true in the case of . . .

PRECINCT AND WARD

To assist the party to power in elections involving established political parties, cities are organized by wards and their subdivisions, precincts. The lowest rung on the political organization ladder is that of precinct worker which carries the responsibility of ringing doorbells, talking to voters, handing out campaign literature, watching at the polls and assisting voters to and from polling places. Ambitious workers are conscious of their positions between elections and "talk up" the party or some of its prominent members on all occasions; intensive work, however, is only during the few weeks or months before an election.

Procedure for selecting precinct and ward captains differs, but ordinarily both are elected by registered members of the party in the sections. It may be, however, that only the ward or township captain or chairman is elected and given the responsibility of appointing precinct captains. A precinct, created by the election board, usually contains from 500 to 2,000 voters, and it is the precinct captain's job to carry his precinct in both primary and general elections.

Precinct workers are paid for their work during campaigns by the precinct captain who gets the money from the ward leader who gets it from the city or county committee which raises part of it and gets more from the state or national committee. Original sources of the millions spent annually to assist candidates to get elected are the candidates themselves, public office holders and others who have obtained employment with the assistance of the party and interested outsiders who believe they have more to gain by a certain candidate's being elected than if his opponent were to win. Some large donors, bidding for the friendship of whoever occupies an important political office, may contribute to the campaign funds of both major parties.

The precinct captain generally is credited with "controlling" at least fifty votes among his friends and relatives, the families of those whom he helps obtain positions on election day as judges and clerks at the polls and others for whom he has done political favors. Unlike the ordinary worker, the precinct captain is active between elections, obtaining minor favors for voters in his precinct such as assistance when they run foul of the law, financial help in case of illness or death, advice on how to obtain employment, and any other services which the strength and wealth of the organization permit. John Salter tells it well in *Boss Rule*.

Although the nonpolitically minded person doesn't realize it, if the power of a political party machine is to be broken it must be done in the primary. In the general election, the voter merely has a choice between two or more machine-picked slates. Under any circumstances, bucking the efficiently organized party is virtually impossible; so-called reform slates result from fusions of political cliques or parties out of office at the time and with no hope of victory without each others' cooperation. The history of such fusion movements is one of temporary successes only. The primary laws in many states, furthermore, make starting a third party difficult.

Most candidates for public office at the local level who receive regular party endorsement, earned the reward by hard work in the precincts. Not always, however, is this the case. Sometimes, a ward committeeman becomes jealous of the growing popularity of one of his subordinates and maneuvers to get him into a public office where he will be less of a personal power threat. Usually, this means a judgeship or some appointive job whose incumbent is required by the Hatch act or other laws, or by tradition, to minimize his politicking.

COUNTY

County chairmen usually are elected by ward and township leaders, some or all of whom constitute the county executive committee. No political leader whose concern is a unit smaller than the county merits the unofficial title of "boss." All bosses, furthermore, are not office holders or even party officials; they may be inflential dictators who prefer to operate in the background. By whatever type of person occupied, the political boss' office is the clearing house for finances and information. Reporters may obtain tips from underlings but seldom get anything official except directly from headquarters.

"Getting next" to a political boss is not impossible, as Lincoln Steffens discovered. How to do it, however, is an individual matter dependent upon the reporter's particular personality. Just as the boss must be cautious about making promises but scrupulous about keeping them once made, so must the political reporter become resigned to learning more "off the record" than on and to not learning anything about a great deal of important party business. Frank Kent has aptly defended newspapers for not giving more "inside political dope" by explaining that newspapers are unable to obtain such information. Furthermore, to get what he does, the reporter cannot incur the displeasure of his source. Instead, he often must report seriously what he knows to be the insincere remarks of some demagogue, overlook his personal foibles, correct his bad grammar and in general "cover up" for him. The alternative is openly to defy and fight the party machine; a newspaper finds it difficult to take that attitude against all political groups without discrimination.

STATE, NATIONAL

State and national committees nominally exist continuously but are quiescent most of the time, arousing from their lethargy about a year before an election. Most active are potential candidates who are "pulling strings" to obtain machine backing when nominating time comes around. With feigned modesty, the aspirant gets some friend or group of backers to "front" for him so that the suggestion that he run for office may seem to emanate from someone other than himself. To reporters, he is evasive and unambitious and is so quoted by a press which, of course, knows better. Until an official announcement is made, however, it is dangerous to go too far in surmising anyone's intentions.

PRE-CAMPAIGN ACTIVITIES

PETITIONS

To have his name placed on the printed ballot as a candidate for office, a person must obtain the signatures of a certain proportion of the voters on nominating petitions which must be filed before a certain date with the proper public official — city clerk, county clerk, secretary of state, etc. Because top positions usually are given to candidates filing their papers first, candidates stand in line waiting for the hour at which it is legal to file them.

It is news both when petitions are taken out and when they are filed. The candidate's name, address, occupation, political experience and general background are included in the first story about his intentions. Sometimes he already has prepared a statement or platform regarding his candidacy although generally that comes later. In city elections, the first petition stories should contain information as to the deadlines for filing, the number of signatures needed and possibly something about the position at stake. The names of prominent signers of a petition are newsworthy.

> The next clerk of the Milltown Municipal court will be either the incumbent, Andrew L. Ziegler, or Constable Eustace L. Cohen for whom nominating petitions, containing the required number of signatures, were filed yesterday, the deadline, in the office of City Clerk Jerome Z. Day.

Mr. Ziegler, who has been court clerk since establishment of the Municipal court three years ago, filed petitions containing 1,416 names, 11 fewer than the maximum permitted. Cohen's petitions contained 1,043 names. Minimum number of names required was 892, or 5 per cent of the vote cast at the last general election.

Graham R. Olson, 146 Arnold avenue, insurance man who took out petition forms last week, failed to file. His name appeared on one of Cohen's petitions. Feature of Ziegler's petitions was one sheet containing only the names of Milltown's 16 aldermen.

Until late yesterday, it was believed petitions would be filed for a candidate backed by the Milltown Democratic organization which took out blanks several days ago.

The election for Municipal court clerk will take place Nov. 3 at the same time as the state and national elections. There will be a separate ballot, however, for the office.

REGISTRATION

Eligibility to vote differs by states but some sort of registration usually is required. On certain specified days, all otherwise eligible voters (those who have resided in the state, county, and precinct a sufficient length of time, have paid certain taxes, given evidence of literacy, etc., as the case may be) appear at their polling places to have their names recorded. Such registration may be quadrennial, annual or permanent; for municipal elections no registration at all may be necessary. Voting by affidavit also may be permitted in case a voter is unable to register on the designated days. If there is permanent registration, the voter merely notifies election officials of a change of address.

The total number of voters registering is news. Knowing that only about 60 per cent of the nation's eligible voters take the trouble to register, crusading editors often investigate abnormally large registrations. Pulitzer prizes have been won by newspapers which checked registration lists to discover "ghost" votes from empty lots, abandoned buildings and transient hotels.

Despite the all-day rain, Saturday's registration of voters for the Nov. 3 election was slightly higher than normal for a first registration day when 21,678 Milltown voters registered, according to City Clerk J. M. Blackburn.

John A. Burgess, Republican township committeeman for Milltown, declared that this total should be 340 greater, to include additional registrants from the Seventh ward; the clerk's office, however, reports that its figure is accurate.

The 21,678 total represents about 70 per cent of the total vote cast in Milltown in 1962. A registration of 65 per cent of voters normally is expected on the first registration day. Final registration day this year will be Tuesday, Oct. 6, when the polling places again will be open from 6 A.M. to 9 P.M. Registration is essential in order to be eligible to vote in November; no affidavits will be accepted.

According to the city clerk's office, Milltown's registration by wards was as follows . . .

Ghosts also walk in the Eighth ward, at least on municipal election day.

To be specific, Tuesday, April 2, at least three nice spooks materialized in the southernmost ward of Milltown and helped the voters there select their aldermen and other city officials.

One of them called himself Hugh Hillis and gave 130 Elmwood avenue as the apartment building he haunts.

The second and third identified themselves as Thomas Long and Nicholas Reding and claimed to be neighbors in the closets of 333 Howard street, also an apartment building.

Thus it is seen that the ethereal denizens of the Eighth ward differ from those of the Fifth ward, where you will recall from my article of last Friday, the dusky unrealities preferred empty lots as their mundane habitats for the day.

This is not surprising, of course, when it is realized that the Eighth ward is predominately an apartment house section, whereas the Fifth ward is punctuated with wide open spaces.

Here is the dope on Spooks Hillis, Long, and Reding . . .

PRIMARIES

With the notable exception of the national tickets every four years, most candidates for important office are chosen by party primaries instead of by conventions as formerly. Any citizen may enter a primary election as a candidate for the nomination of any party. A voter, however, can participate in the primary of one party only. The names of only those candidates who have filed nominating petitions appear on the printed ballot, but the voter can add the name of anyone else. It is seldom, however, that a "write-in" candidate is elected.

In some southern states where the Democratic nomination is tantamount to election, run-off primaries are held of the two or three candidates receiving the most votes. In a majority of states which have primary laws, a plurality at a single primary is sufficient to nominate.

If there is little contest in his own party, in most states a voter may vote in the primary for another although he intends to vote for his own party candidate in the general election. If too many voters desert it in a general election, however, the party may not receive a large enough proportion of the total vote to receive a place on the ballot at the next election.

CONVENTIONS

Adoption of a direct primary law does not mean the end of state party conventions, but such conventions (or conferences) are held outside the law and for the purpose only of recommending and endorsing candidates to receive the party's nomination at a primary election. Often rival factions within a party hold separate conventions and endorse different "slates."

The news writer can estimate the strength of candidates at a state or national convention by comparing the instructions given to delegates. Delegations often support "favorite sons" from their localities and may deadlock a convention by refusing, after the early ballots, to change their votes to one of the leading candidates. Some delegations from states with open primaries are uninstructed.

A party convention is called to order by a temporary chairman who gives a prepared "keynote" speech. Then a permanent chairman is elected and he also gives a speech. Usually the committee's recommendation for permanent chairman is taken, but sometimes rival factions may nominate different candidates. The vote for permanent chairman then may be an indication of how delegates will vote later on other important matters.

The group in control of a state or national committee has the advantage of obtaining a personnel to its liking. Through its committee on credentials it determines which delegates are eligible for seats, if rival delegations from the same locality claim recognition.

Vote on the platform submitted by the committee on resolutions is conducted by a roll call of delegations. After the platform is adopted, with or without amendments, the next procedure is the election of candidates. Often, several ballots are necessary for a choice. When a deadlock continues after several ballots, a "dark horse," someone not among the leaders, may be elected as a compromise candidate.

A party convention frequently is interrupted by the demonstrations of different delegations. When the time to nominate candidates arrives, the roll call begins. Each delegation either nominates someone or passes its turn or permits some other delegation, whose turn normally would come later, to use its opportunity. In addition to the principal nominating speech there may be several other speeches to second a nomination. Each speech is the signal for an outburst of enthusiasm by supporters of the candidate.

A party *conference* is for the purpose of discussing an important matter. A party *caucus* differs from a conference because all who attend it, by their attendance, pledge themselves to support the opinion of the majority. Insurgent members may stay away from party caucuses, because they do not wish to commit themselves to the support of what the majority will favor.

CAMPAIGNS

SPEECHES

A campaign really gets underway with the first speech of the candidate. In the case of a presidential candidate this is the speech of acceptance of the nomination made at a formal notification ceremony. Although presidential candidates usually have fresh speeches for every important occasion thereafter, in the case of candidates for less important offices the opening or keynote speech may be the pattern for all others delivered during the campaign. The political reporter traveling with the candidate may be hard put to it to obtain a fresh angle in reporting the day's forensics, but the local news writers who hear the candidate only once are not so handicapped.

When candidates start calling each other names, hurling challenges, answering each other's arguments, and raising new issues, the political reporter's problem is easy. Otherwise, he may be forced to rely upon the press releases of political headquarters. If he travels with a candidate he tells of the crowds, the opinions of local leaders, the reception given the candidate, etc.

In reporting and writing up a political speech the reporter should observe the orthodox rules for such occasions as described in Chapter XII.

STRATEGY

Newspapermen have this in common with politicians: there are no two groups which come in for more indiscriminate damning than those to which they belong. Just as there are highly ethical editors and publishers, there also are politicians, in and out of office, who desire wholeheartedly to serve the public good. The "system," however, invariably demands that before he can be a statesman a man must be a politician and get himself elected to office. The process of becoming elected and of assuring oneself of reelection involves compromise, evasion, equivocation and other "expediencies" which are distasteful to the reputable public servant and shocking to the callow political reporter.

The plight of the high-minded man in politics, of the newspaperman and of the public may be inferred from the following summing up by Frank Kent in *The Great Game of Politics*:

No candidate and no campaign are exactly what they seem. The part that is open and above board is always less vital than the part that is secret. The voters see the performance but not the rehearsal. They completely lack information of the real movements by which the candidate becomes a candidate. They are in the dark as to how the issues are evolved and why, when and by whom. They see and know nothing until the curtain goes up and there before them is the smiling candidate, playing his part in complete makeup and wearing a full set of false whiskers. . . .

It is not a reflection upon many honest and sincere men who hold elective offices or who seek such offices. It is merely a statement of facts, and the point is that, under our system, complete frankness with the voters is not possible, because there is no way of obtaining complete frankness from both sides in a political fight. A downright, outspoken candidate, who honestly, openly and fearlessly expresses exactly what he believes to every group of voters on every issue, declining to dodge or evade, and refusing to appeal to prejudice or cater to class, would be overwhelmingly beaten by the candidate on the other side who would promptly take advantage of such honesty to gather for himself the large number of voters alienated by the other fellow.

To give voters the "feel" of a campaign a reporter interviews rival candidates and accompanies them as they "make the rounds."

BY *Mervin Block*

The westside state senator whispered to Dan Ward:

"Put on your brass knucks and start hitting . . . not with fancy talk like a professor. . . ."

Ward smiled nervously, then suggested that the reporter, who had overheard the remark, dress it up in more dignified tones.

The scene was Henrici's restaurant at lunch time. The state senator was Bernie Neistein, Democratic committeeman of the 29th ward, a friend of Ward and a fellow De Paul university alumnus.

Ward, on his way out, had spotted Neistein sitting near the door and detoured to give him a big hello and a handshake. The brass knuckles suggestion, which Neistein said was a message from Jim Denvir, the president of his ward organization, followed.

That Ward does talk like a professor was demonstrated a few minutes earlier when he addressed 120 lawyers in a private room of the restaurant.

Heads De Paul Law School

Ward, on leave as dean of the De Paul law school while running for state's attorney on the Democratic ticket, used such sesquipedalian words as denouement, discursively, obloquy, sacrosanct, plus a number of other big words not ordinarily used, especially by a man running for political office.

Altho Ward, 42, never was a politician — in the sense that he rang doorbells or harangued voters — he's now in politics up to his leonine head.

His speech at Henrici's was his second public appearance of the day, a day that began at 7 A.M. with the jarring ring of his alarm clock.

Despite only 5½ hours' sleep, Ward dutifully showered, shaved, breakfasted, reloaded his tan briefcase, and drove away from his home in La Grange Park for another long day of campaigning. (Driving his leased 1960 Ford station wagon was a former De Paul law student, who is helping out in the campaign.)

Ward paused in his headquarters at 69 W. Washington st., then went to the federal building to participate in a mock trial for the benefit of 50 railroad policemen.

Entering the courtroom, he greeted District Atty. Robert Tieken, who took the role of the judge, then went to the counsel table, where he simulated the defense of a boxcar thief.

Dissects Opponent's Record

At the outset, when the "prosecutor" jocularly mentioned Ward was a candidate "of the opposition party," Ward generated laughter by telling the audience:

"So there'll be no misunderstanding, that's the Democratic party."

He walked back to his headquarters, checked messages, returned several telephone calls, and then handshook his way to Henrici's.

Forty minutes late, he sat down at the head table and hastily disposed of salisbury steak (known as hamburger in Wimpy's, three doors away), and then was introduced to the junior bar section (under 36) of the Illinois State Bar association.

Ward informed the assemblage he would satisfy the ritual of reciting a joke before a lecture, then told about an overburdened British soldier who blurted, "Would to God that I were dead!" "Who said that?" demanded his sergeant major. "It was Shelley, I think," said the soldier.

Gesturing with his right hand and jingling coins in his pocket with his left, Ward then proceeded to dissect the record of his opponent, State's Atty. Adamowski. Ward was extremely displeased with it.

Touching intermittently on his topic — "The Prosecutor and Defense Attorney, Their Roles in Shaping Constitutional Rights" — he asserted:

"I can't think of a more important service rendered than that of a defense attorney."

Ward spoke 47 minutes, then headed toward the office. On the way, he encountered Si Murray, 22d ward Republican committeeman. There was a handshake, a brief exchange, and he soon was back at his desk.

Keeps Shirts in Office

The candidate's afternoon was occupied with making telephone calls, taking telephone calls, cogitating, planning, reading, talking with his press agent (John Drexler), and discussing strategy with his unofficial campaign manager (Atty. Robert C. Eardley).

At 6:45 P.M., when many men are sliding into their easy chair in the parlor, Ward started shaving and washing up in his office for the work that lay ahead. He put on a freshly laundered white shirt (but kept the same gray and black rep tie) then, escorted by Eardley, hurriedly downed a hamburger in a nearby restaurant. (Because of his 'round-the-clock routine, Ward keeps a supply of clean shirts in his office.)

Arriving at 2167 W. De Kalb st., site of a 25th Ward rally, Ward ran the gantlet of handshakers, shook hands with a candidate who was shaking his way out, and chatted confidentially with Rep. Roland Libonati.

Ald. Vito Marzullo, the ward committeeman, led the crowd of 300 in a standing ovation for Ward, then told them he knew they would support "this great humanitarian." Marzullo referred to Adamowski as "this monster."

Ward, without any quips, sailed right into his speech, telling the bi-racial, polyglot audience that "your ward has a great tradition of interest in government." He made some scathing comments about his opponent, and, after 12 minutes of politicking (not in professorial language), moved on, to the accompaniment of another standing ovation from the semi-captive audience.

On the way to his station wagon, he paused to shake hands and chat with a Democratic precinct captain, Andy Flando, a former Republican committeeman of the ward.

Seventeen miles and 50 minutes later, Ward was in the basement of Casimir Kogut's home at 12352 Carpenter St., Calumet Park, sitting next to another candidate, John S. Boyle.

Without any humorous observations, Ward told the 100 members of the Calumet Township Democrat club that he was honored to be there, that "victory or defeat will be determined in rooms such as this in the suburbs of Chicago," and, after 18 minutes of talking, "I regret I can't stay longer."

On the way out, Ward again ran into Township Committeeman Kogut's son, shook hands with him again and said, "Very nice meeting. Good night now." (Ward estimated that he shook about 100 hands during the day.)

Ward, 6 feet 2 inches and 200 pounds, eased himself into the front seat of his white station wagon, and Eardley drove off to distant La Grange Park.

About midnight, the station wagon — emblazoned with campaign slogans — pulled up to Ward's $35,000 Georgian home at 1143 Blanchan av. His three young children were asleep, but his wife, the former Marilyn Corleto, was up, waiting to serve him a glass of milk. (He had seen his children briefly at breakfast and, as the campaign progresses, he'll see them less and less.)

After an hour poring over his work in the recreation room, he got into bed. Six hours' sleep — and he was off and running again.

ROORBACKS

The word "roorback" entered the dictionary as a common noun following the presidential election of 1844 during which a last-minute attempt was made to defeat James K. Polk by newspaper publicity for a fictitious book by a nonexistent author named Roorback supposedly telling of Polk's having bought and branded a number of Negro slaves.

There is a difference between raising false issues and plain lying. The former is for the purpose of misdirecting attention from important to insignificant matters; the latter is sheer falsehood. Roorbacks generally appear as late as possible to be effective and yet permit the opposition insufficient time for an answer. The political reporter always should be wary of a new important issue raised late in a campaign unless it is one which couldn't have been brought up earlier.

May it be said to the credit of newspapermen that they generally have the intelligence to "see through" political humbug, but they are stymied as to what they say, for the reasons which have been enumerated in this chapter. The political reporter who is "taken in" by political bunk is inadequate for his job, which is one for seasoned and not callow men.

ISSUES

The interpretative reporter talks not only to candidates and political leaders, but also to representatives of civic, business, labor and other groups and with ordinary citizens in the attempt to determine the issues upon which the outcome of an election depends.

Nobody has developed this technique better than Samuel Lubell whose periodic series of articles on the political thinking of "the man in the street" are supplemented by his uncannily correct forecasts of election results. Lubell's methods confound the professional pollsters and academic political analysts who go to elaborate extremes to be certain those whom they interview represent a correct cross-sectional sample of the electorate as a whole.

Lubell studies election results. When he notes similar significant changes in voting behavior, even in precincts thousands of miles apart, he follows his nose for news to the areas to determine the cause. He has "pet" precincts and blocks and even residences in all parts of the country based on past experience of their value as political weathervanes, enabling him to make generalizations. Lubell's main interest is in discovering the reasons for voting behavior rather than merely straw voting. Too much political writing to explain the issues of a campaign derives from the writers' ideas or desires as to what they should be. Neither these pundits nor the politicians determine the issues. Rather, the voters do so, and they favor those candidates who they think hold views closest to their own.

Another and more conventional method of determining the issues of a campaign is by historical perspective. The following is typical of the way *The Christian Science Monitor* often handles such stories:

BY *Robert Blanchard*
Special to the Christian Science Monitor

Helena, Mont. Montanans, having witnessed one of the most vigorous state primary elections in recent times, are beginning to sense an equally active general election campaign is under way.

It has been said often here that in Montana "men are men, Democrats are Democrats, and Republicans are Republicans" — after the primary elections. If this ever was true, it was this year.

While the primary election was a "battle of the giants," or individuals — with "conservatives" and "liberals" within each party splintering the loyalties — the campaign which ends Nov. 8 is almost strictly the battle of the issues.

The intraparty splints have been mended, for the time being, and the historical divergent poles in Montana politics are tugging as never before for those magic "independent" votes around the political equator.

Deep Roots

Montana's extreme political polarization came to light as early as 1878 when the Butte Miners Union was formed to fight a threatened wage reduction for copper miners. It spread to the rural areas when Montana was singed by the post-World War I political prairie fire of discontent — the ultraliberal Nonpartisan League.

A farmers' organization founded in North Dakota, the league sponsored state ownership and operation of grain elevators, flour mills, packing plants, and utilities. It appealed to many eastern Montana wheat growers, suffering from low prices. Former Senator Burton K. Wheeler, a candidate for Vice-President on the Progressive Party ticket in 1924, was an early league representative in Washington.

The wedge between the two dominant political groups deepens more each year as automation increases in mines and on farms; as domestic copper production decreases; as the eastern half of the state grumbles over market conditions and as "family farms" disappear; as neighboring states bypass Montana in highway construction; as property taxes continue to rise, even though vital school bond issues are defeated and as teachers leave the state because its salaries stand 30th in the nation and next to last in the region; as the state's unemployment fund reaches rock bottom and small businesses pay more and more to keep it alive; and as the state's general fund pays day-to-day bills with paltry sums borrowed from other state funds with no letup in sight.

The major issues in this campaign include each side's solutions and blame for the problems . . .

There followed a series of paragraphs comparing the Democratic and Republican attitudes toward such issues as taxation, highway finance, right-to-work laws, education, finance, unemployment compensation funds and the like. The last section of the article compared the rival candidates.

ELECTIONS

PREDICTIONS

As election day approaches, reporters who have followed the campaign more objectively than candidates or party leaders, usually are better able to predict its outcome than they. It is customary for large newspapers which assign reporters to travel with candidates, to "switch assignments" at least once as the campaign progresses; that means, one writer will travel with Candidate A for a few weeks or months and then shift places with the reporter who has been covering Candidate B. Straw votes among political writers have shown them much better able to predict election outcomes than publishers, editors or editorial writers.

In 1956, the New York *Times* spent a huge sum of money to send more than thirty of its best reporters all over the country to see if they could correctly predict the outcome of the presidential election, state by state. The experiment was a success but some critics asked whether the main function of the press in such a campaign is prediction. Rather, some contended, it should be to clarify issues and put candidates "on the spot" regarding them.

ELECTION DAY

The size of the vote, violence at polling places, amusing anecdotes, the circumstances under which the candidates cast their ballots, last-minute statements and predictions, and methods used to get out the vote or persuade voters on their way to the polls furnish news on election day before the ballots are counted.

Ordinary newsroom routine is upset on election day as there are extras to get out and extra help to obtain to assist in collecting returns. A newspaper may use its news carriers or other employes to wait at polling places until the votes are counted or may receive its returns through campaign headquarters. Often, the police gather returns and release them to reporters.

As the results come in by isolated districts they are tabulated, and the political writer prepares a trend story for the first edition. Some outcomes can be predicted comparatively early; often, in a close race, the result is in doubt until the last vote is counted. When the result is apparent, campaign committees and candidates issue statements claiming victory or conceding defeat. Losers send messages of congratulations to winners, and everybody poses for pictures.

If an outcome is close, a loser may demand a recount. Some elections are protested by defeated candidates who charge fraud, stuffing or tampering with ballot boxes and other irregularities. All candidates are required to file statements of campaign expenditures. Investigations of alleged violations of the corrupt practices act during an election are not infrequent.

The mid-election day story should include the number voting and a comparison with previous elections.

Candidates were being nominated in today's statewide primary elections for United States Senator and Representatives in Congress, and for some state and local offices in St. Louis and St. Louis county. In the city and county, balloting was generally light, indicating one of the smallest off-year primary votes in years.

By 4 P.M., it was estimated 61,889 ballots had been cast in the city, following 10 hours of balloting in the 784 precincts. This was 18 per cent of the total registration of 343,830.

In the county, an estimated 9,936 ballots were cast by 4 P.M., nine hours after the 7 A.M. opening of the polls.The estimated vote was 7.9 per cent of the 125,782 registration.

St. Louis polling places will close at 7 P.M. Those in the county will close at 8:07 P.M. with the exception of those in University City, where the closing time is 8 P.M. The hours given are daylight saving time.

Special Watch on Two Wards

Special deputy election commissioners are on duty in all precincts of the Fifth and Sixth Wards, in which a recent recanvass of the registration indicated efforts to pad the lists. Chairman Frank L. Rammacciotti of the Election Board, said the deputies were stationed in the two downtown wards to guard against any election irregularities.

Ballots and registration lists for the two wards were not delivered to the polling places until early today. Rammacciotti said this was done because many of the election officials resided outside of the wards and they did not have adequate means to care for them. These were the only two wards where this was done, the ballots and voters' lists having been delivered to election officials in all other wards last night.

The special deputies in the Fifth and Sixth Wards were instructed specifically to guard against ballots being marked openly instead of in the regular voting booth, and to see that all ballots were counted by Republican and Democratic poll officials working together instead of dividing ballots for a separate tabulation by each party's officials.

Two Ballots in City

City voters received two ballots at the polls, a party primary ballot and one for the two amendments to the City Charter and the proposed $4,000,000 bond issue for rubbish collection facilities, each calling for a Yes or No vote.

Proposed amendment No. 1 would permit . . .

St. Louis *Post-Dispatch*

ELECTION RESULTS

When all or nearly all returns are in, so that the outcome is known, the news feature naturally is who won. The story also should emphasize: (1) by how much — in total votes and proportions, (2) areas in which different candidates were strongest and weakest, (3) upsets — incumbents with long services who were defeated, candidates on a party slate who lost whereas most of the others won, etc., (4) whether results coincide with predictions, (5) statements by winners, losers and party leaders, and similar matters.

''POST MORTEMS''

A great deal of post-election interpretative writing is of the "I told you so" or "We should have known it" type. By analyzing the vote in different sections where the electorate is predominantly of one type — workers, members of a particular racial, national, or religious group — it is possible to imagine which campaign issues or attitudes antedating the campaign were most effective. The skilled political writer analyzes results in the search for trends. Often, he has to compare local with state and national results to interpret correctly.

When a new office holder or party takes over a city hall, county building, state or national capitol, the citizenry expects that "there will be some changes made." Party platforms and campaign speeches provide clues as to what they will be, but voters have become suspicious of politicians' promises. Personality sketches and reviews of the past records of successful candidates are valuable.

BY *Leo Egan*

Mayor Wagner's upset primary victory was widely interpreted yesterday as a mandate for him to reorganize the Democratic party in the city and the state.

It was also interpreted as giving him a substantial advantage in the general election over Attorney General Louis J. Lefkowitz, the Republican candidate for Mayor, and any independent candidates such as City Controller Lawrence E. Gerosa.

A final unofficial tabulation of the vote in Thursday's primary showed that Mr. Wagner had won by a plurality of 159,786 votes, beating state Controller Arthur Levitt by a 3-to-2 margin.

Mr. Wagner received 451,458 votes to Mr. Levitt's 291,672. He carried all of the city's sixty-five Assembly districts except for one in Manhattan and five in Brooklyn.

No Haste Foreseen

The indications were that Mr. Wagner would refuse to be rushed into carrying out any reorganization mandate arising from his "anti-boss" victory. Instead, it appeared he would move with "all deliberate speed."

It also became evident that he would encounter serious opposition in replacing Representative Charles A. Buckley and Councilman Joseph T. Sharkey, the Democratic leaders of the Bronx and Brooklyn, respectively.

Carmine G. De Sapio, leader of Manhattan's Tammany organization and the prime target of Mr. Wagner's campaign, and Joseph A. McKinney, the Staten Island leader, are scheduled for replacement within the next three weeks when the New York and Richmond County committees meet to reorganize.

Buckley Impatient

Both suffered crushing defeats in the primary. The leadership posts in the three other boroughs were not at stake in the primary.

Mr. Buckley impatiently brushed aside last night a suggestion that he might retire voluntarily since he had been unable to carry a single Bronx district for Mr. Levitt.

"I've seen Mayors come and go," Mr. Buckley, a veteran of fifty years in politics, philosophized. "The county leadership doesn't mean a thing to me but I'm not going to let him push me out."

Mr. Buckley pointed out that none of the members of the Bronx executive committee had any public office controlled by the Mayor. The executive committee is the only group authorized to pick or replace a county leader. . . . New York *Times*

17

Government

I. City Government

   1. *Mayor*
   2. *City Council*
   3. *City Clerk*
   4. *Corporation Council*
   5. *Public Works*
   6. *Finances*
   7. *Other Offices and Boards*
   8. *Urban Renewal*

II. Schools and Education

   1. *Integration*
   2. *Religion*
   3. *Delinquency*
   4. *Exceptional Children*
   5. *Automation*
   6. *Academic Freedom*

III. County Government

   1. *County Board*
   2. *County Clerk*

IV. State Government

V. Federal Government

VI. The Weather

   1. *Elements of Interest*
   2. *Writing the Story*
   3. *Interpretations*
   4. *Definitions*

THE NEED TO KNOW

Thomas Jefferson once said: "A nation that expects to be ignorant and free . . . expects something that never was and never will be." I believe this applies with special force today. If our people cannot understand government, they will take little interest in it. In our state, we have a habit of submitting many things to the people in the form of constitutional amendments. The people don't understand them, and they stay away from the polls in droves. We have had state bond issues approved by as few as 8 per cent of the registered voters. With government at the state and national levels becoming more and more complex and having increasing impact on our daily lives, we must have an informed citizenry. Otherwise, a few people will take advantage of the national ignorance and take charge.

Edward W. Stagg in Nieman Reports

NO TIME TO LOSE

It is reported that one of the fastidious newly married ladies of this town kneads bread with her gloves on. This incident may be somewhat peculiar, but there are others. The editor of this paper needs bread with his shoes on; he needs bread with his shirt on; he needs bread with his pants on, and unless some of the delinquent subscribers to this "Old Rag of Freedom" pony up before long, he will need bread without a damn thing on, and Wisconsin is no Garden of Eden in the winter time.

Melrose (Wis.) Chronicle

As POPULATION INCREASES AND ALL PHASES OF LIFE BECOME more complex, "closing the gap" between governed and governors becomes a major problem in a democracy. The media of communication have a great opportunity and responsibility to stimulate interest and participation on the part of the citizenry in governmental affairs.

Journalism's first obligation is to report fully the activities of public agencies and officials. Since all public issues ultimately are decided by public opinion, the duty includes presentation of the pros and cons of all important matters and expert analysis of them. In other words, interpretative reporting and writing are essential in the field of governmental affairs.

To prepare himself for the role of expert in this field, the aspiring interpretative reporter must be thoroughly grounded in political history and theory. He must understand the nature and purpose of all governmental agencies and the political connections and motivations of public officials and their backers. No matter how public spirited or socially conscious they may be, office holders are candidates for reelection or reappointment; they do not cease to be politicians and become statesmen suddenly the day they take office.

The interpretative reporter who specializes in governmental news makes use of all of the devices of the interpretative reporter anywhere. To place an immediate occurrence in proper perspective, he may give its historical background. Even before legislators or administrators take action, he may describe the existence of a problem. When a proposal is pending, he explains its nature, the arguments pro and con and the political alignment as regards it. He describes the functions of various offices and officers and reviews the records of the representatives of the people.

CITY GOVERNMENT

Closest to the average newspaper and its readers is city government. On the next page is shown the outline of the government in a typical middle-sized American city having the mayor-council plan of government. If the city had the commission plan, instead of the aldermen there would be two, four or six commissioners, usually elected at large, and fewer appointive officers, the duties usually performed by them be-

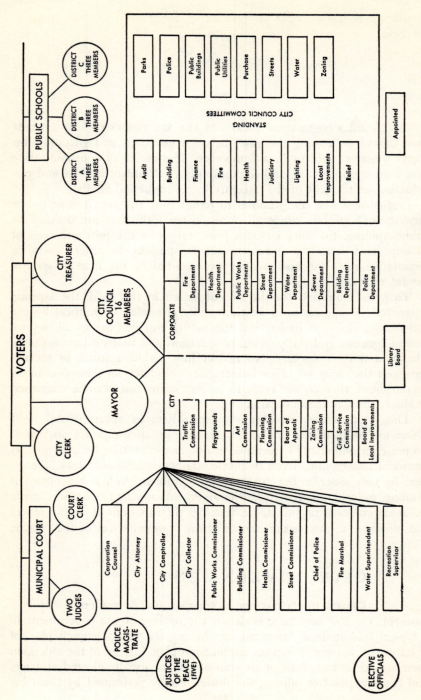

TYPICAL, MAYOR-COUNCIL CITY GOVERNMENT

ing assigned to the full-time commissioners. If the city had the city manager plan, the important officer would be not the mayor but the city manager who would perform the duties, in a small city, of many appointive officers under the mayor-council plan. Under the city manager plan, the office of the mayor, if it were retained at all, would be little more than that of presiding officer at council meetings. A city manager runs a city as a general superintendent operates a business or as a superintendent of schools directs a school system. He is chosen for his expert knowledge of municipal business affairs and is not necessarily a resident of the city at the time of his appointment.

MAYOR

Under the mayor-council plan, which still exists in a majority of American cities, the mayor is chosen as is a governor of a state or a president of the United States, by popular election every two or four years. A significant change has taken place in recent years, however, in that city politics has been divorced from state and national. Except in the larger cities, candidates for mayor generally do not run as Republicans, Democrats or Socialists but as independents, their backing crossing party lines.

As the executive head of the city, the mayor is the chief news source in the city hall. He should be aware of every important occurrence in all city departments, most of them headed by persons whom he has appointed with the approval of the city council. For details, the reporter should see the department heads themselves, or subordinates in closer touch with the news at hand.

Because the mayor is called upon to take part in most important nongovernmental activities in the city, he is a potent source of miscellaneous tips. He is visited by delegations of all sorts and receives letters of complaint and inquiry; he buys the first Red Cross button, proclaims special days and weeks, welcomes convention delegates, attends meetings and gives speeches.

If he is a strong mayor, he has a program for the city which he reveals in his reports, messages and remarks to the city council. Usually he is close to certain aldermen who introduce motions, resolutions and ordinances embodying his ideas. Unable to speak on legislative matters without leaving the presiding officer's chair, the mayor who is a leader has spokesmen in the council who present his point of view for him.

An alderman Wednesday proposed that Chicago, Evanston, Skokie and Lincolnwood join in development of a new recreation area.

The land involved is along both sides of the Sanitary District channel between Touhy and Howard.

* * *

Ald. Jack I. Sperling (50th) showed a tentative plan for building a fieldhouse, ball diamonds, playgrounds and tennis courts on the now vacant land.

In a resolution prepared for introduction to the council, Sperling asked Mayor Daley to call a meeting of officials involved.

These would include officials of the Sanitary District, present owner of the land, the city and the suburbs.

Sperling said his plan has the backing of Mayor Daley.

* * *

Recently the Sanitary District rejected a proposal that the land be leased at 7 cents a square foot for industrial purposes.

Sperling described the area as "ideally located" and "desperately needed" for recreational purposes.

The city boundary touches on the area. Details for acquisition of the land have not yet been explored fully, Sperling said.

Chicago *Daily News*

CITY COUNCIL

Councilmen or aldermen usually are elected by wards, geographical units into which the city is divided. They devote only part time to their official duties, possibly doing little more than attend weekly or semimonthly meetings. Committee meetings are held council night before the general session and may be closed to reporters. Chairmen of important committees, such as finance, streets, and relief, are compelled to give some attention to their aldermanic duties throughout the week, at times at least, and may be interviewed in case of important news. A typical order of business for a city council meeting follows:

Roll call by the city clerk
Minutes of the last meeting
Communications read by the city clerk
Standing committees (reports called for in alphabetical order)
Special committee reports
Call of wards (each alderman brings up any matter pertaining to his
     ward which needs council or executive attention)
Miscellaneous business, including mayoral reports
Adjournment

The rules for covering a city council meeting do not differ from those which apply to any other type of meeting. Because of the importance of council meetings, however, it frequently is necessary to write two or more stories adequately to play up different matters affecting the public. It is seldom that a reporter can write his story entirely from the notes he is able to take as motions are made and argued, matters referred to different committees, etc. Usually he must verify names, the wording of motions and resolutions, the outcome of votes, and other matters by consulting the city clerk or his stenographer at the end of a meeting.

In an advance story of a council meeting, the nature of business likely to come up should be emphasized. The experienced reporter usually can anticipate the nature of debate and the lineup of votes. He also should attempt to interpret the significance and possible aftermath of any controversial matter.

> The plan to build a $20,000,000 city airport at Pratt and Sumner will be disposed of by formal vote of the common council tonight.
>
> If the lineup of councilmen remains unchanged, the so-called southeast site will go down to defeat by a vote of 5 to 4.
>
> Councilmen Howard, Lane, Otis and Cade favor the northwest airport. Councilmen Moore, Kole, Blede, Masse and Walz are opposed.

Mayor Wants Action

> Mayor McCartney, who also favors the southeast site, has promised that he will try to get a final decision before Jan. 31 — the date on which the offer of a gift of 650 acres at the site expires.
>
> Regardless of the outcome, few observers had any hope that tonight's action would be final.
>
> Arthur Schuman, secretary of the Metropolitan Civic Airport Trust, today was on the verge of conceding defeat. He said the would-be donors of the $750,000 for land at the southeast site would have their money returned to them at once.
>
> "Nothing short of a miracle can save it now," Schuman declared.
>
> "They have kicked this around for ten years and now the airlines have moved to St. Martin. I'm all through.
>
> "If the city wants a modern airport now, let the city department heads get one. It's their job from here on. Apparently they don't want the aid of the industrial groups."

Will Seek Ballot

> Councilman Otis will attempt to keep the southeast site alive even though voted down tonight. He said he would seek a ballot proposition on the question at the next election, probably in June.
>
> If the northwest site is turned down tonight, St. Martin County Airport will remain as the city's "major interim airport," according to a council resolution already adopted.

Making reliable contacts and keeping friendships while reporting fearlessly is the main problem of the city hall reporter. Clerks and others like to give tips to favorite newsmen but often do so in confidence which must be respected. It frequently requires great reportorial ingenuity to wheedle information out of others while concealing the source of one's knowledge. Often it is best for the city editor to assign a special reporter to a particular story so that the regular man on the beat will not alienate his sources.

Strong papers, and state and national press associations have waged vigorous fights in the post-World War II years to end or prevent secret meetings of city councils, village boards, and similar groups from which reporters as well as the public are excluded. Some state legislatures have been persuaded to pass laws requiring open sessions. Then the problem becomes one of discovering and exposing the subterfuges which may be used, as informal and unofficial get-togethers, possibly at lunch or in a private home. The newspaper which fights secrecy is acting on the democratic principle that the public's business should not be transacted in private. If it persists it usually wins its campaign because of the public support it generates.

In reporting the outcome of a meeting the interpretative reporter explains the issues involved, the arguments of debaters and the political lineup on votes.

> The City Council confirmed the appointment of George L. Ramsey as the new city building commissioner, but after an uproarious debate.
>
> The Council also upheld the first veto by a mayor of Chicago in 24 years, and that was after a lot of argument, too.
>
> When quiet was restored Wednesday, it seemed that none of the protesters had any personal objection to Ramsey. They felt that such a nomination, no matter who the individual involved might be, should first be studied by a Council committee.
>
> Ramsey's nomination was approved 34 to 13 on a motion by Ald. P. J. Cullerton (38th), Mayor Daley's floor leader in the Council, to suspend the rules.
>
> Ramsey was nominated by the mayor to succeed Richard Smykal, who has been acting building commissioner since May 1, 1954.
>
> Smykal was nominated for city commissioner of conservation (of neighborhoods), and this was approved without a squabble.
>
> The mayor invoked his veto power to correct a clerical error growing out of the Zoning Committee's recommendation that a petition to change the land bounded by 44th, 45th, Hamlin and Springfield from manufacturing to industrial uses be turned down.
>
> Inadvertently, the committee clerk put the petition among those recommended for passage.
>
> **Not Attacking Mayor**
>
> John C. Melaniphy, acting corporation counsel, said a mayoral veto was the only way to correct the error.
>
> The Council upheld the veto, but only after confusion that resulted when Ald. Emil V. Pacini (10th), Zoning Committee chairman, moved to override the veto.
>
> Pacini's resolution was resoundingly voted down, in the belief that he was attacking the mayor. Later Pacini explained his action was purely a technical one to make sure that the veto would stand on the record.
>
> Chicago *Sun-Times*

CITY CLERK

This elective officer might be termed the city's secretary. He attends council meetings and takes minutes, receives communications addressed to the city, issues licenses (dog, beach, etc.), receives nominating petitions, supervises elections and preserves all city records.

CORPORATION COUNSEL

A lawyer, he is legal adviser to the city and its representative in court in major matters. In smaller communities his duties are performed by the *city attorney* who, in larger places, is the prosecuting attorney in criminal cases; much of his work relates to minor court cases. His title may be *city solicitor*.

PUBLIC WORKS

The tendency is toward consolidation, under a *commissioner of public works*, of the departments of streets, water, public buildings, local improvements and others. If the offices are not consolidated, the commissioner of public works has charge of new construction of streets, sewers, etc., whereas the *street commissioner* has the responsibility of seeing that the streets are kept clean and in repair and usually has charge of garbage collection. The *city engineer* works under the commissioner of public works.

The newspaper has it within its power to interpret the activities of these departments for tax-paying readers. One way is by an eyewitness description of their functionings.

BY *Charles B. Cleveland*

A uniformed policeman noted the pile of garbage strewn in the alley; walked around to the apartment with an arrest book in his hand.

This is a frequent scene in Chicago now as every ward has a policeman assigned to arrest garbage violators who litter alleys and who fail to employ refuse cans.

Let's walk along with Officer Peter Miller, a veteran of nine years at the Fillmore Station, as he enforces laws on refuse in the 29th Ward.

Here's an alley in back of 509 South Keller av., with rubbish and garbage piled alongside the building. There are no refuse cans.

"This alley was cleaned yesterday," Vito Marzullo, ward superintendent said, "now look at it — "

Miller knocked on the apartment door and Mrs. Yolanda Nania, a tenant, answered.

"I think it is a good thing you are doing, trying to keep the alleys

clean," she said. "But we have no cans. We had some before but somebody took them."

"Did you dump your garbage in the alley?" she was asked.

She shrugged. "Yes. What else can we do?"

"Notify the owner to get some cans for this building," Officer Miller
warned. "I'm going to check here on Saturday and if there are no cans,
I'm going to issue a summons and he'll have to go to court."

In back of 4101–03 W. Van Buren st., a pile of rubbish lay alongside
a half-filled can. The landlord, Daniel King, was brought down to look
at the litter.

"I don't know about it," he said. "That didn't come from our place.
Somebody must have come along and dumped it there."

A man came up to the reporter as he watched the scene. "You looking
at the alleys?" he asked. The reporter nodded. "How about telling that
landlord over there," he pointed across the street, "to get some cans. The
people have to dump in the alleys."

A youngster, Barney McCarville, of 4157 W. Van Buren st., also
watched the scene. "Our alley doesn't look like that," he said proudly.
"We've got cans and we use them and we keep the alley clean."

"We've got seven-day service," Marzullo said, "but if the people won't
help —"   Chicago *Daily News*

The nature of issues that are being debated by public officials can be
brought home to the ordinary citizen by emphasizing his stake in the
outcome.

BY *Marion Porter*

The man on the street doesn't know and doesn't care whether he is
riding on "batch-mix" or "continuous-process" asphalt.

But right now exponents of the two different schools of mixing are
having a dignified controversy on the subject.

Because J. W. "Bill" Goose of the Jefferson Construction Company is
a continuous-process man, he has not yet been awarded contracts on street
jobs on which he was low bidder. City specifications call for the batch-mix
method. The contracts are held up pending the arrival of Law Director
Gilbert Burnett, now on vacation, who will decide whether the city should,
or should not, let contracts to "a nonconforming" bidder, even though
he be low bidder.

May Get Court Decision

"I'm going to get a decision from the Court of Appeals, if necessary,
before I do anything," Goose said yesterday. "I'm going to find out if one
man can set up specifications as to method of mixing — if specifications of
the ingredients are all right, of course."

Works Director James B. Wilson said that the Jefferson Construction
Company probably won't get four of the street contracts it bid on, but
none of the other recent bidders will get them either, because the City
plans to do the work itself.

The company, however, may get two other street contracts on which it was low bidder because they involve street-construction work at property-owners' expense. Burnett will have to rule on this also.

Either method of making asphalt is acceptable to the State Highway Department, said Harry Eads, Anchorage, senior material laboratory aide for the Highway Department. The Jefferson Company now has a State contract for resurfacing sections of Broadway. The Highway Department inspects every carload of the material.

"It's just two different methods of reaching the same conclusion," said Eads. "We don't care how they make it as long as the results are right. If the sprockets and feed gates are set right the continuous-process is just as accurate as the batch-mix; and likewise, if the operators accurately weigh the ingredients in the batch-mix method, it is just as accurate as the continuous-process."

Weigh Ingredients First

To the layman, the chief difference in the two methods is in the preliminary steps. The batch-mix people weigh the ingredients first. Everything is done by machine in the continuous-process method. One side claims that the machine process is more accurate since it is not subject to the human element of skill, fatigue, and indifference. The batch-mix people lean toward placing trust in man rather than machine.

The Jefferson Construction Company's expensive, gigantic Barber-Green mixing plant on Crittenden Drive is flanked by piles of gravel, rocks and sand. The material is picked up in automatic containers with wickets on them, passed along through a series of conveyor belts; stewed, boiled, stirred, screened and sprayed and comes out as the finished product, untouched by human hands, at the rate of 6 tons in five minutes . . .

Louisville *Courier-Journal*

FINANCES

The three most frequently elected officials are the mayor, city clerk and city treasurer; other city officers also may be chosen by the voters but usually are appointed by the chief executive with the approval of the council. It is the duty of the *city treasurer*, of course, to collect taxes and other moneys due the city and to pay bills upon executive order. There also may be a *city auditor* who keeps detailed records of the city's financial setup and acts as financial advisor. Also there may be a *city collector*, who is chiefly a desk clerk to take in money and a *purchasing agent*, in charge of buying material authorized by the city council.

The financial setup of a city requires study to be understood. The reporter struggling to comprehend it has the consolation of knowing that many city officials don't know what it's all about. State law limits the taxing power of a municipality, usually by restricting the rate at which each $100 of assessed valuation of real and personal property can be taxed for each of several different purposes. The city's budget cannot call for expenditures beyond the total tax collection possible for a given purpose as streets, parks, libraries, etc. The financial operations of a city furthermore are limited by state laws, restricting the city's bonding power. A city, for instance, may be allowed to issue tax anticipation warrants to only 50 or 75 per cent of the total amount which would be realized from the collection of taxes if all were paid. Financial houses which purchase these warrants, however, may not be willing to approve the issuance of as many as the law would permit. In Illinois, a city's bonding power is limited to 2½ per cent of assessed valuation.

The reporter with a good grounding in economics and commerce courses has an advantage in comprehending municipal finance. Any reasonably intelligent reporter, however, can grasp it if it is explained clearly to him. He should not feel embarrassed to ask some city official qualified to do so — the city treasurer, auditor or chairman of the council finance committee perhaps — to give him an hour's time to outline the basic principles of the system. Once he has mastered the essentials himself he will be in a position to perform a valuable public service by making each story related to city finance a lesson in an important phase of government for tax-paying readers. With training, he may even be an authority on the finances of his own city at least.

At least three financial stories annually are of "sure fire" interest. They are: (1) announcement by the assessor of the assessed valuations of real property, (2) announcement of tax rates, (3) passage of the city budget.

The assessment story may not be an annual, as many places have new assessments biennially or quadrennially. There invariably follow interminable appeals to the board of tax appeals by property owners seeking reductions, and there always is at least one additional news story regarding the quantity of such suits. It is in the public interest that those who pay taxes understand the procedure by which they are levied.

The highest assessment roll in the city's history — a gross valuation of $878,370,697 on property — was reported yesterday by Assessor Ray Levin.

The assessments for the 1963–64 tax year represented an increase of $20,912,496 over last year's roll, but it was offset by a rise in exemptions for veterans and for hospital, charitable and religious organizations.

These exemptions reduced the net total to $858,323,458, but this is $11,700,582 greater than last year's figure.

Levin valued land at $297,014,769, an increase of $1,061,554. Building values were upped from $371,683,405 last year to $379,286,329 and tangible personal property (merchandise, equipment, furniture and fixtures) was appraised at $116,985,599, an increase of $10,768,098.

The State Board of Equalization valued private utility properties at $85,084,000, an increase of $1,479,920 over last year's appraisals.

"The $8,500,000 increase in the assessed value of buildings," said Levin, "was due mainly to equalization studies which resulted in increases on multiple-storied downtown building units.

"The balance of the increase is due to revised assessed values where alterations were made to existing structures and partial assessments on new construction, both residential and industrial."

The increase of a million dollars in land values, the assessor explained, resulted from equalization of values and increased values on newly developed subdivisions, including the Rose Division, Clear Valley and Copper Terrace.

Levin, however, refused to increase the assessed value of existing homes in exact proportion to inflated sales prices.

"In my opinion," he said, "the inflated replacement cost on existing homes should not represent the actual value of the homes."

But in his valuation on homes, Levin granted no reductions for depreciation because of the increase in the cost of labor and materials.

"Holding back reductions for depreciation is less painful to the home owner than increasing the assessed value to today's prices," the assessor said.

The raise in value of tangible personal property was declared due partially to the establishment of new businesses and by recent checks by the assessor's auditors on business inventories.

The report showed the number of veterans applying for the $1,000 property tax exemption increased from 16,645 to 22,095. The property exempted for veterans was valued at $14,423,239, an increase of 33 per cent over the amount exempted last year.

The result of the property tax exemption for hospital, charitable and religious organizations, voted last November, was reflected . . .

When he knows the valuation placed on his property and the legally adopted tax rate (the amount he will have to pay for each $100 worth of assessed valuation) the taxpayer can figure out his own tax bill. Taxpayers' suits to set aside a tax rate in whole or part on the basis that some item in the city budget is improper are frequent. Usual practice in such cases, and when appeals are pending from the assessor's valuations, is to pay the tax under protest. If the protest is allowed, often after an appellate court decision, refunds are made. To postpone tax collections until after all appeals are decided would be to deprive the city of revenue.

The following is an example of how a trained reporter can make other aspects of municipal finance comprehensible to laymen.

Although the city's bonded indebtedness will be reduced $99,000 in 1963 and $98,000 in 1964, no real "breathing spell" to permit a sizable addition to the total indebtedness will occur until after 1966, figures obtained today from E. M. Corbitt, city auditor, reveal.

It was because they felt that the city already is bonded too heavily that a majority of the city council this week voted down a proposal of Ald. Robert E. Jones, chairman of the streets committee, that a special bond issue election be held to raise $175,000 as the city's share in a new $300,000 state streets' improvement program.

Total bonded indebtedness of the city today is $980,000; the maximum permitted by law is $1,250,000. However, it is the feeling of many aldermen and some city officials that approval could not be obtained from Kerrigan & Cross, financial attorneys, for an increase in the bonded indebtedness at this time. It is pointed out that some difficulty has been encountered in obtaining approval of some of the recent bond issues.

To Retire Certain Bonds

May 1, 1963, general obligation bonds totalling $31,000 will be retired and June 1 another $63,000 will be paid off. Aug. 1, $5,000 will be retired. It is the feeling of some members of the council who favor a new streets' improvement bond issue that these reductions in the total bonded indebtedness would be sufficient to obtain approval next spring of their new bonds.

"Big" years for the retirement of Milltown city bonds will be in 1967 and 1968, in each of which $109,000 worth will be retired. In 1970 $101,000 of bonds will be retired. Thereafter, unless new bonds are issued in the meantime, the tax levies for bond retirement will be reduced greatly.

The following figures indicate the amount of bonds to be retired each year from 1963 to 1975 inclusive:

Year	Amount
1963	$99,000
1964	98,000
1965	94,000
1966	94,000
1967	109,000
1968	109,000
1969	70,000
1970	101,000
1971	50,000
1972	39,000
1973	39,000
1974	34,000
1975	33,000

For the years 1976 to 1981 inclusive the retirement will be $15,000. For 1982 it will be $25,000. The city at present is not bonded beyond that year.

OTHER OFFICES AND BOARDS

The police and fire departments and the courts already have been discussed and schools will be the subject of the next section. There remain the offices of the building commissioner, commissioner of health, superintendent of playgrounds and recreation, other minor officers (sealer, purchasing agent, etc.) and the numerous official and semi-official boards and commissions.

The first requisite of the city hall reporter is to be aware of the existence of these offices and boards and of their functions. In no two communities is the setup exactly alike, although generally to be found are the following: civil service commission, zoning board, park board, board of tax appeals, library board and planning commission. The number of land clearance commissions and housing authorities is increasing.

In some cities, these groups are active and newsworthy; in others they are dormant, their existence seeming to serve little purpose other than to provide the mayor with the opportunity to appoint minor political followers to prestige positions. A live chairman, however, can make any one of the groups a vital factor in municipal affairs. The civil service commission, for instance, can cease being the rubber stamp for political appointments that it is in many places and can become a real watchdog of the merit system by insisting that all jobs which should be filled by civil service examinations are so filled, that the spirit of civil service not be defeated through repeated temporary appointments in lieu of holding examinations to fill vacancies, that too much weight not be given in the final ratings of candidates to the "intangible" qualifications as contained in the recommendations of political friends, that dismissals from city employment be for valid reasons rather than as a result of trumped up charges, and that the conduct of examinations be absolutely honest.

Civil Service examinations for seven city positions now filled by temporary employes will be held next month. They will be given in the Board of Health building, 19 W. Market street, Ralph Williamson, secretary of the Civil Service commission, announced yesterday.

The highest paying position is that of deputy city treasurer with an annual salary of $7,750. The examination will be given at 9 A.M. April 2. The present deputy is John Cooper.

Examinations for three jobs as assistant supervisor of operations at Municipal Airport will be held at 9 A.M. April 12. The incumbents are Roy Brody, Mitchell Arnold and Herbert Small.

Dr. Peter Orthcott, president of the board of health, telegraphed 30 more hotels and restaurants yesterday, warning that those with unsanitary conditions must correct them immediately or be closed.

Nine restaurant operators were summoned before the board yesterday for unsanitary food conditions. Five agreed to close until corrections were made. Three others said corrections were being made and inspectors were sent to check.

The ninth, Joe's Grill, 90 East Wabash street, had cleaned up since Wednesday's inspection. The restaurant was allowed to remain open with a warning not to repeat the violations.

The five restaurants which closed voluntarily, and the violations reported by inspectors were as follows . . .

URBAN RENEWAL

No aspect of local governmental operations in the large cities has grown more in importance in recent years than slum clearance and urban renewal. Federal, state and local funds are involved and many metropolitan centers are undergoing wholesale renovations costing into the millions or billions of dollars. Whereas a generation ago the strength of a political machine was its ability to act as a welfare and relief organization — the Tammany Hall method — today municipal political leaders feel that their strength comes mostly from their ability to remake the appearance of their bailiwicks by tearing down and rebuilding. Mayors and their planning, housing and land clearance boards trot to Washington to seek approval of "workable plans," the first step in obtaining federal funds for any program. There follows an interminable number of steps, including legislative and administrative action at three levels of government, condemnation proceedings, letting of contracts, demolition, housing of dispossessed tenants, haggling over plans for buildings, streets, the location of parks, schools, and the like. Civil libertarians and human relations groups often are apprehensive over the futures of Negroes and members of other minority groups who are most frequently affected by slum clearance projects. The movement of whites to the suburbs means that the proportion of nonwhites within the big city limits is becoming greater. Political as well as social and economic "upheavals" often result.

So intricate and important has this field of activity become that large newspapers increasingly are hiring or training reportorial specialists to keep up with developments.

SCHOOLS AND EDUCATION

Routine coverage of school news is not too difficult. It consists of watching such items as enrollment figures, bond issues, faculty and curriculum changes, new buildings and equipment, commencement and other programs, student activities and the like. Such stories as the following are commonplace:

The Baltimore County Board of Education yesterday announced that construction on a new elementary school building, needed to serve several rapidly growing communities in the Lansdowne-Baltimore Highlands section, will begin this week.

To be known as the Riverview Elementary School, the structure will be erected on a site situated south of the proposed extention of Hollins Ferry road in the Lansdowne area. The low bid for the school was $744,-900.

Pupil Overflow

Need for the new school is evidenced by the fact that a 230-pupil overload already exists at the two elementary schools at Lansdowne and Baltimore Highlands that now serve this section of the county.

A pupil overflow at Lansdowne is housed in the school library and in two rented churchrooms. The Baltimore Highlands school utilizes a basement room as a temporary classroom. Regular classrooms are generally overcrowded at both schools.

The new facility is situated within a 1,200-unit housing development, only part of which is now completed.

The school will contain eighteen classrooms that will normally accommodate 630 pupils. It will also include a library, remedial instruction room, multipurpose room, cafeteria, health suite and administration office.

Grimm Comments

Preston L. Grimm, statistical and research expert for the county school system, explained that the new Riverview school is designed to offer only interim relief for enrollment gains in the Baltimore Highlands school district.

"Long range plans envision the construction, at some future date, of a new elementary school at Baltimore Highlands, for which a site has already been acquired," Mr. Grimm said.

"This is expected to occur when the area is sufficiently developed to justify its erection."   Baltimore *Sun*

Helping citizens — over 50 per cent of whose local tax dollar goes to maintain the public schools — understand what's going on educationally is a different matter. Since the children of World War II veterans began reaching school age in the early fifties, there has been hardly a school district in the United States which has not found it necessary to expand its educational facilities. Nevertheless, in many places there persist grave shortages in buildings, classrooms, equipment and teachers. As the total tax burden — federal, state, and local — has grown during the Cold War period, taxpayers have been increasingly reluctant to approve school bond issues and little progress has been made toward obtaining financial aid from the federal government. Whereas formerly school elections aroused only meager interest, by the mid-sixties exactly the opposite was coming to be the case in many places.

In addition to the basic problem of finances, other educational issues have become controversial and, consequently, newsworthy.

INTEGRATION

The court action and violence which followed the United States Supreme Court decision outlawing racial segregation have made headlines the world over. Since only token integration has taken place in most southern cities, this will continue to be so for some time to come. Outside the south, segregation exists *de facto* if not *de jure* in many places as a result of housing segregation. Some bond issues for the construction of new schools have been defeated in the suburbs in order to discourage migration of Negroes and other minority groups. The National Association for the Advancement of Colored People and other groups pressure school boards to redraw district lines so as to encourage integration. Other groups violently oppose such proposals.

RELIGION

Parochial schools, mostly Roman Catholic, have increased greatly in number and enrollment in the post-war years, disrupting public school attendance in some places and relieving congestion in others. Bitter local campaigns have resulted when Catholics have sought membership on public school boards. Defeat of bond issues for public schools sometimes has been blamed on Catholic voters. At the national level, the Catholic church has opposed federal aid to education unless its schools share in it. The parochial schools believe their children should benefit from free bus transportation and similar "fringe" benefits. Released time programs, whereby children are excused from school to take religious instruction elsewhere, may be highly debatable locally.

If there is one thing above others that the average newspaper wants to avoid it is stirring up religious controversy. Consequently, handling of such matters usually is "gingerly" and only when the circumstances compel any mention at all.

DELINQUENCY

From one standpoint, the history of public school education in America could be written to show how, step by step, the schools have assumed responsibilities formerly considered the prerogative of the home, factory or other institutions. Most of the broadening of the curriculum has resulted from outside pressure, including statutes requiring that this or that — American history, the dangers of dope addiction, automobile driving, and the like — be taught. As a consequence, the student's free choice is limited, especially if he is among the increasing number who seek to meet college entrance requirements. Were it not for compulsory attendance laws, the already serious "drop-out" problem would be greater. Problem children are mostly ones in revolt against regimentation, real or imagined. In the huge high schools of today, potentially disturbed adolescents develop intense feelings of revolt. Despite physical education and intramural athletic programs, participation in varsity sports is limited to an increasingly smaller proportion of the student body with resulting frustrations. The same is true of other school activities, with opportunities to become officers or star performers restricted to the minority. In several large cities, post-athletic contest riots between fans representing rival schools have become serious. The emphasis which rooting alumni insist colleges and universities place on sports, especially football, sets a nationwide pattern. Exposures of widespread professional gambling activities, which include attempts, successful and otherwise, to bribe players, occur frequently. Even if the schools solved all the problems suggested in this paragraph, of course, the problem of juvenile delinquency would continue to exist because its social and economic causes are mostly outside, not inside, the school walls.

EXCEPTIONAL CHILDREN

Counselors, psychologists, psychiatrists and other advisors deal with individual problems of disturbed and other children. Special classes or instructions exist for physically handicapped children — the deaf, dumb, blind, crippled and mentally retarded — and the gifted child is attracting more and more attention. Opinions differ as to whether children should be grouped according to potential ability, usually determined by intelligence or other tests, or achievement. On the one hand, the consciousness of being labeled superior, medium or inferior is considered disturbing to some children who will have to compete in a world of unequals. On the other hand, it is contended that fast learners are held back if instruction has to be kept at the level of the slowest. The pros and cons of this matter have been debated by educators and parents for a number of years in many parts of the country.

AUTOMATION

Related to this issue is the controversy over the extent to which instruction should be standardized in the interest of reducing teaching burdens. Under the influence of teachers' colleges during the past generation, testing of many kinds — intelligence, aptitude, achievement, etc. — has developed considerably. The results are used for placement of students in classes in the grades and high schools and by colleges and universities to determine admissions. Criticism is growing that if improperly used these tests result in "giving a student a number" at an early age and prejudice teachers' attitudes toward actual classroom work. Also and more seriously, it is contended that the tests do not measure a student's ability to organize his thoughts, his total understanding of a topic, imagination, ingenuity or originality. Devised for fast grading by machines, the tests require the student merely to put an x after which of three or four answers to a question is correct. University professors, especially in the professional schools such as law and medicine, complain that students are coming to lack the ability to express themselves and that automatized teaching makes for conformist robots. Teaching machines, airborne television programs, and the like ease the teacher problem, it is admitted, but stultify initiative and creativeness.

ACADEMIC FREEDOM

There is hardly an American community which has not had a "case" involving a teacher with allegedly heretical ideas, a reading list which someone does not like or a textbook or magazine under attack by a patriotic or other pressure group. This situation unquestionably has made teaching less attractive to many young men and women and has contributed to the development of the strong administrator type of school superintendent. As in all other aspects of contemporary complex society, rules and regulations and forms and reports have multiplied in the school system. Teachers often complain that they are left too little time to teach and that they have increasingly less to say about the determination of educational policy. In huge school systems, not only pupils but teachers as well run the risk of becoming merely numbers.

Lengthy as it may seem, the foregoing discussion has by no means exhausted the subject. Educational news by contrast with school news requires the attention of journalists with specialized knowledge and understanding. It is a great field for the interpretative reporter.

COUNTY GOVERNMENT

The county building is what ordinarily is known as the courthouse because the county court is the most important room in it. The same building probably also contains the circuit court and possibly the municipal court, if there is one, and the court of a police magistrate or justice of the peace. There also are other offices of county officials.

COUNTY BOARD

Corresponding to the city council (or *board of aldermen*) of a city, is the county board, also called *board of commissioners* or *board of supervisors*, which is the governing body of a county. Its president (or chairman) may either be elected by the voters or selected by the board members who are elected by townships or at large. In smaller places, the board may meet infrequently, as bimonthly or semi-annually; in large places it meets almost as frequently as the city council. Its powers are limited because the county is primarily an agent of the state in collecting taxes, enforcing laws, recording documents, constructing and maintaining highways, providing poor relief, administering rural schools, supervising nominations and elections, guarding public health and performing other functions. These duties are the responsibility of the elective county officers.

COUNTY CLERK

Secretary of the county board, the county clerk also issues licenses (wedding, hunting, etc.), accepts nominating papers, supervises the printing of ballots, receives election returns and keeps county records. If there is not a separate elective officer, *a register of deeds*, he also records articles of incorporation, receives applications for corporation charters, and keeps all other records and documents of private transactions. It is to him one writes for a copy of his birth certificate or to prove ownership of a piece of property.

Duties of the *sheriff, prosecuting attorney* and *coroner* and the operation of the county court already have been explained. The sheriff usually has his office in the county jail and the coroner may be a practicing physician or undertaker with a private office.

The *county treasurer* is an agent of the state, collecting taxes which he forwards to the state capital. He pays county employes out of funds reallocated to the county from the state and meets other obligations in similar fashion. The *county assessor* assesses the value of property in the county, prepares maps to show real estate ownership and reports his findings to the state.

The *county highway commissioner, county engineer, county surveyor, county superintendent of schools, county health officer, county agricultural agent* and other county officials perform duties suggested by their titles.

With the "population explosion" into the suburbs, county government has had to pay more attention to unincorporated areas because they inevitably are involved in problems related to water supply, transportation, recreation, policing and the like. Counties also operate poor farms, homes for the aged, jails, general hospitals, special hospitals for the tubercular, mentally ill and others, nursing homes and other institutions which cities and states also maintain. The awarding of contracts must be watched carefully as well as the quality of service performed. Illegal operations, as gambling, banned from the cities, may flourish in nearby areas.

An authoritative interpretative reporter may goad public officials to take action at the same time he enlightens readers regarding a governmental function.

BY *Len Kholos*

Erie County commissioners' refusal to enter into regional planning with the city is not only hampering efforts to attract new industry, it is actually costing Erie taxpayers extra thousands of dollars.

In an interview with The Erie Dispatch last week, J. Cal Callahan, of Morris Knowles Inc., disclosed that the federal government is willing to pay half the cost of developing a workable program when more than one community is involved.

"The federal government feels that regional planning is the only sensible vehicle for progress, not only to promote orderly growth of an area but to prevent mistakes that will be costly in future years," Callahan said.

* * *

How is refusal of the county leaders to cooperate costing Erie taxpayers money?

Before the government will forward funds for redevelopment, whether it be for industrial or residential purposes, the communities involved must prepare a workable program.

Erie has already spent $5,000 and has contracted to spend $25,000 more to prepare this program in order to become eligible for federal planning money.

Assuming that the cost of work within the city would cost the same amount in a regional planning setup, the federal government would then have paid $15,000 plus half the costs incurred outside the city limits.

* * *

Can the individual communities in the county do anything to protect their own futures?

County Solicitor Jacob Held has told county commissioners that they cannot spend any money for planning. This came as a surprise to local government observers.

Held may also claim that the boroughs and townships are not allowed to spend money to plan for themselves.

On the other hand, the government will pay half the costs of preparing a workable program for communities of less than 25,000 population or, if they join in the city's planning efforts, half of the cost of the joint project.

* * *

We have explained why the federal government wants communities to have a workable program before it will forward funds for redevelopment. Now, here is what a workable program includes:

1. Sound local housing and health codes, enforced; an end to tolerating illegal, degrading, unhealthy substandard structures and areas.

2. A general master plan for community development, an end to haphazard planning and growth, a road map for the future.

3. Basic analysis of neighborhoods and the kind of treatment needed, an inventory of blighted and threatened areas upon which a plan of treatment to stop blight in its tracks can be developed.

4. An effective administrative organization to run the program, co-ordinated activity toward a common purpose by all offices and arms of the local government.

5. Financial capacity to carry out the program, utilizing local revenues and resources to build a better community for the future instead of continuing to pay heavily for past mistakes.

6. Rehousing of displaced families; expanding the supply of good housing for all income groups, through new construction and rehabilitation, so that families paying premium prices for slums can be rehoused.

7. Full-fledged, community-wide citizen participation and support, public demand for a better community and public backing for the steps needed to get it.   Erie *Dispatch*

STATE GOVERNMENT

Unless he works in one of the 50 state capitals, the beginning reporter has little contact with state governmental offices. If he is ambitious to become the state capital correspondent for a metropolitan newspaper as a possible step toward a similar position in Washington, D.C., covering the city hall and local politics furnishes excellent training.

Although he does not attend legislative sessions or visit the offices of state officers, some member of the editorial staff of the small city newspaper follows what is happening at the state capital as the local community is certain to be affected. City officials, civic organizations, and other individuals and groups discuss state governmental matters and make known their opinions to their representatives in the legislature. Often it is necessary to obtain passage of a state law before it is possible for the city council to take some desired action; the corporation counsel may write such laws which members of the legislature from the district introduce and push to adoption.

The following are examples of how to localize what is happening at the state capital so as to emphasize its importance and the role played by local persons:

Mayor Walter E. Lewis today urged State Rep. Oscar R. Fall and State Sen. James L. Born to support the bill pending in the state legislature which would permit Milltown and other cities in the state between 25,000 and 100,000 population to establish a municipal court.

All doubt as to the legality of Milltown's compulsory automobile testing station was removed today when Gov. Dale O. Hart signed the enabling act prepared by Corporation Counsel V. K. Kenwood and passed unanimously last week by both houses of the legislature.

Representatives of The Crib, Milltown's foundling home, will go to the state capital tomorrow to join the lobby fighting passage of a bill which would establish a state department of public welfare. The bill is considered a threat to the local institution because it is believed a state department with power to direct all such establishments would insist upon regulations which The Crib could not meet and continue to exist.

Killing of the remaining state library appropriation in Springfield last night in the term-end jam by a legislature anxious to adjourn late tonight, will deprive Milltown of the purchase of books and periodicals to the amount of $6,000 during the next two years, Miss Edith Delancey, city librarian, revealed today.

Local newspapers use, often by rewriting to play up the local angle, press releases from state offices. State representatives often write weekly newsletters to summarize legislative activities. Press associations in state capitals handle special queries from newspaper clients regarding matters of special interest. Only the largest papers, however, can afford to maintain bureaus in the capitals, either while the legislatures are in session or at any other time. Such assignments almost invariably go to reporters with experience covering local politics and government.

FEDERAL GOVERNMENT

Of the major divisions of the executive department of the federal government — those represented in the president's cabinet — only one has a permanent peacetime representative in the city or small town. That is the post office department. In moderate-sized cities, at least for a few days before April 15 each year, representatives of the Internal Revenue division of the Treasury Department occupy space in the post office or federal building to assist local taxpayers in preparing their federal income tax returns and to collect taxes.

A record high in the number of federal income tax returns filed and payments received was reported yesterday at the office of the collector of internal revenue here.

The approach of the midnight deadline brought thousands of persons to the office and there was sufficient extra help to take care of taxpayers who needed assistance in filling out the forms. Extra cashiers were on hand to accept payments. Because taxpayers had familiarized themselves with their problems, comparatively few had to wait long in line.

The peak in the day's business came in the early afternoon, but there were long lines in the early evening. Early closing of offices and manufacturing establishemnts, as well as the complete shut-down for some for the entire day, also help make easier the trips of the last-minute visitors to the tax offices.

Payments in cash, money orders and checks totaling $150,000,000 were received yesterday. One check was for $1,000,000. In the two previous weeks $50,000,000 had been paid in person and through the mail.

In the internal revenue offices there were hundreds of bags of mail waiting to be opened. The opening of this mail, containing millions of dollars in checks and money orders, will begin tomorrow and will be finished by the end of the week.

With the exceptions noted, the federal government as a local news source in a small city hardly exists. As its power increases and that of the states declines, however, the lives of American citizens are more and more affected by it. Whereas the press associations and special column writers from Washington must be relied upon for interpretations of major current events in the national capital, intelligent handling of much local news requires an understanding of national political issues and events.

Work for the unemployed, for instance, in depression years was provided through funds supplied by the federal government. In wartime there was the Office of Price Administration. Financial assistance also has been obtained through such federal agencies as the Home Owners Loan corporation and the Federal Housing administration, and the bank deposits of most everyone today are insured through the Federal Deposit Insurance corporation. Most far reaching, perhaps, is the federal Social Security act which provides for old age pensions, unemployment insurance, aid for dependent children, widows, the blind, and other needy persons, and the Fair Labor Standards (wage and hour) act.

To write about how the local community is affected by these and other federal governmental activities without understanding them is not conducive to effectiveness.

It was the suburbs' turn today to absorb some criticism from the United States Public Health Service.

Milk sanitation conditions in several of them were found to be below a high standard set by Milltown, the federal agency said in a report released by the Advisory Committee of the Milltown-Wayne County Health survey.

Richmond had a rating of only 75.01 per cent for raw milk from 40 dairy farms under control of its health department and 73.15 per cent for three pasteurization plants, the report showed.

This compared with Milltown's rating of 91 per cent compliance with conditions set up in the recommended USPHS ordinance and code.

"The weighted rating for all milk sold in Richmond was 86.74 per cent," the surveyors declared, "the increase being due to the fact that 80 per cent of the milk sold in the city was being produced under the control of other agencies maintaining a more efficient control.

"It is advisable that Richmond adopt the standard ordinance and limit sale of milk to Grade A pasteurized in order to be in line with the state, Milltown, and other communities in the county."

Sanitation control of milk also was found to be "less than satisfactory" in Bluffs, Blytheville and Lakeside.

Milltown's milk control was praised by the surveyors, and the report commented, "there has been no communicable disease epidemic traced to the Milltown milk supply since 1936."

Nevertheless, the USPHS declared improvement in inspection services is needed immediately "if these high standards are to be protected."

The report also criticized an ordinance recently adopted by the county commissioners requiring all milk and milk products to be pasteurized, but not specifying grading.

THE WEATHER

Another important federal governmental office, purposely omitted from the preceding section because the news emanating from it is not classifiable as governmental, is the Weather Bureau, a part of the Department of Commerce. If, as is often the case in small places, there is no local representative of the Bureau to provide official information, the newspaper obtains the most reliable data available from other sources. Possibly a college or high school can provide it; if compelled to rely upon its own resources, the newspaper at least can make certain that its thermometer is properly set up. As any conversationalist knows, the weather is interesting even when there are no hurricanes, floods or droughts. Since man lived in caves his everyday life has been dependent to a large extent upon the behavior of the elements; the machine or power age has not reduced man's dependency in this respect. In fact, in many aspects of life, it has increased the dependency, as delicate machines may require certain atmospheric conditions for proper operation.

ELEMENTS OF INTEREST

It is not necessary to read a newspaper to know that it is abnormally hot or cold or that there has been a thunderstorm, but the reader does expect his newspaper to furnish authentic statistics about the weather, the widespread consequences of any unusual climatic condition and predictions as to a change in the situation.

To meet this reader demand, newspapers print weather reports and forecasts daily. The maximum and minimum temperatures for the preceding twenty-four hours and the next day's forecast frequently are printed on the first page with detailed hourly readings, reports from other cities, wind velocity, rainfall and other details on an inside page. If the weather becomes unusual in any way, a full-length news story is written.

When the weather becomes extreme, the reporter should seek information including the following:

    1. Statistics and Explanation

        a. Maximum and minimum for day

        b. Hourly readings

    c. Comparison with other days during the season

    d. Comparison with all-time records for the same date, month and season

    e. Comparison with situations in other localities

    f. Humidity, wind velocity, etc.

    g. Predictions: when relief expected

    h. Official description of nature of phenomenon

2. Casualties

    a. Illness and death directly caused by the weather

        (1) Heat prostrations

        (2) Freezing

        (3) Lightning

        (4) Tornadoes, cyclones and hurricanes

        (5) Floods

        (6) Sleet and hail

    b. Injuries and deaths of which the weather was a contributing cause

        (1) Drownings

        (2) Spoiled food

        (3) Accidents from slippery pavements, snow, wind, etc.

        (4) Fires

        (5) Heart disease from heat exhaustion

3. Property damage

    a. Telephone and telegraph wires

    b. Water craft sunk

    c. Bridges and highways, pavements buckling

    d. Farm buildings and animals

    e. Automobiles, buses, and other public conveyances

4. Interference with ordinary life

    a. Transportation

        (1) Railroads

        (2) Buslines and streetcars

        (3) Airlines

        (4) Highways and bridges

        (5) Private automobiles

    b. Communication

        (1) Mail service

        (2) Telephone

        (3) Telegraph

        (4) Cable

        (5) Radio

        (6) Stoppage of food and other supplies

    c. Public utilities

        (1) Electric lights

    (2) Gas pressure
    (3) Water supply
    (4) Fuel shortage
  5. Methods of seeking relief
   a. Increased demands on water supply
   b. Bathing beaches and parks
   c. Trips
   d. Sale of fans
   e. Children cooled by hydrants, hoses, etc.
  6. Methods of handling situation
   a. Police activity
   b. Volunteer groups: Boy Scouts, Legionnaires, etc.
   c. Red Cross and other relief agencies
   d. Use of ashes and other materials
   e. Public warnings on driving, diet, etc.
  7. Freaks
   a. Narrow escapes
   b. Undamaged property surrounded by desolation
   c. Unusual accidents

WRITING THE STORY

   Because the weather affects every reader in his daily activities, no matter what unusual features are included or how the story is written, the reporter must include in his account as many of the preceding elements as are pertinent. Emphasis should be on the effects of an unusual weather condition: casualties, damage, disrupted service, etc., and upon the basic statistics such as temperature, inches of rain or snowfall, wind velocity, etc.

   New Yorkers who prayed for rain to relieve the heat and humidity of the week end received their fill in varying degrees yesterday when Sunday's freak thunder showers were followed by a steady downpour.

   The chief sufferers were those in the suburbs, particularly in Westchester, where residents bailed out flooded cellars and were left for short periods without power in their homes. Motorists felt the weight of heavy rains in Westchester, where parts of the Bronx River, Hutchinson River, and Saw Mill River Parkways were washed out and detours outlined by state police.

   Those in the city escaped with only a wet day that recorded 1.58 inches of rain at the United States Weather Bureau atop the Whitehall Building at 17 Battery Place. But in Dobbs Ferry, N.Y., 20 miles up the Hudson River, a precipitation of 6.6 inches resulted in the 24 hours ended at 7 P.M. The New York Board of Water Supply reported that the Kensico Reservoir at Valhalla went up 5.24 inches.

   Flying conditions were also affected by the weather. Rain, fog, low ceilings and poor visibility forced 122 cancellations of flights at La Guardia Field during the day. They included fifty-nine in-bound and sixty-three out-bound flights.

When rain subsided at 6:40 last night, Benjamin Parry, chief meteorologist at the Weather Bureau here, predicted something better for today. He said it will be cloudy and cool, with intermittent rain until this afternoon, fresh northeasterly winds and a high temperature of 65 degrees. Yesterday's high was 68 at 3:15 A.M. with 66 prevailing between 10 A.M. and 3 P.M., a noteworthy drop from Sunday afternoon's 82.5.

The 1.58 precipitation here brought the month's total to 5.79 inches, which is 2.95 above normal, but still far below the May, 1908, record of 9.1. The year's total is 13.91, a deficiency of 3.28 below normal.

The storm, Mr. Parry reported, originated several days ago in the West, looped south to Oklahoma, then turned northeast. Thunderstorms within the parent storm, he pointed out, hit parts of New York and New Jersey between 4 P.M. and 7 P.M. on Sunday. He said it missed the weather station at the Battery completely, since his gauges there did not record any rainfall until 3 A.M. yesterday.

It hit Dobbs Ferry hard enough at 5:15 to record 2.78 inches in the first 30 minutes. Reports from Fairfield County in Connecticut also told of a heavy rainfall of four inches at 8 A.M.

The sections of highway washed out in Westchester were the Bronx River Parkway intersections at Palmer and DeWitt Avenues in White Plains, the Hutchinson River Parkway between Mamaroneck and Westchester Avenues in Mamaroneck, and the Saw Mill River Parkway north of the traffic circle at Hawthorne. New York *Herald Tribune*

The effects of weather often best can be explained by eyewitness descriptive accounts.

Tragedy struck in the little railroad village of Butler Tuesday night. Lightning struck the village baseball diamond, killing the manager of the Butler American Legion baseball team and two members and injuring five other team members.

The bolt hit at 6:45 P.M., out of an overcast sky. The blow made the entire village tremble. Window panes rattled. Children ran screaming to their mothers. The bolt hit like a broadside from a battleship, and there was a blinding flash. Then the rain came down in solid sheets, bent back and forth by hammering winds.

Several seconds later another bolt struck a transformer in the North Western road yards, throwing part of the village in darkness.

On the baseball diamond the victims of the bolt lay scattered in the dirt.

The bolt that hit the diamond struck at the shortstop position, tearing open a trench four inches deep and three feet long. The bolt ripped the clothing and shoes off the three victims. Peter Hillstrom, 14, was standing only a few feet from where the bolt hit.

William Simerlein, 16, was in left field, about 40 feet away. Raymond Phillips, 40, was about 50 feet away. The players who escaped with injuries were standing farther away. The only player who was not knocked down was Marvin Huberty, 17, who was batting out flies.

Two other Butler boys, Emil Wruck, 19, and James Murray, 16, were sitting in an automobile alongside the diamond. They were shaken up by the crash.

Wruck jumped out of the car and ran into a nearby tavern, yelling, "Get the fire department! Call an ambulance! Some guys are hurt on the baseball field."

The siren of the Butler volunteer fire department began wailing. Firemen ran in the rain for the firehouse. At nearby Hampton Heights the volunteer fire department also responded to the alarm.

On the baseball diamond, just east of N. 124th st., and two blocks south of W. Hampton av., the players who could move began picking themselves up.

Dazed, James Gundrum was one of the first to get up. His first thought was to give artificial respiration to the victims. He trotted over to Hillstrom. Patches of Hillstrom's hair had been burned off his head.

The back of his head was crushed. Gundrum realized that Hillstrom was dead. Gundrum walked over to Phillips and Simerlein. They lay in nude heaps. Gundrum knew that they, too, were dead. . . .

Milwaukee *Journal*

INTERPRETATIONS

Public curiosity concerning unusual weather conditions is a form of scientific interest. To satisfy it, the media of communication cannot be expected to define each meteorological term as it appears in a news account, as many of the most common must be used almost daily. When occasion seems to demand, however, parenthetical inserts, sidebars and longer feature articles can be used, mostly for the benefit of middle-aged readers who went to junior high school before its curriculum was enriched by elementary instruction in this field.

After many decades of stubborn refusal to popularize its vocabulary, the United States Weather Bureau has relented in recent years. It takes cognizance of popular usage now by permitting such phrases as "unusually fine weather" and "clear and bright" in its forecasts, and it no longer uses "alert" in official storm notices unless danger immediately threatens.

Explanations of natural phenomena can be given in scientifically accurate but easily understood language.

Washington — (UP) — A Weather Bureau spokesman said Wednesday that the mid-continent's scourge of tornadoes was "unusual" in scope but otherwise "typical."

He said the conditions that produced the wind barrage were "a classical arrangement" of warm and cold air masses. This occurs frequently in April and May.

Cold air masses from the Pacific and Canada tangled with masses of warm and moist air from the Gulf of Mexico. Tongues of cold air pushed out on top of lighter warm air.

Result: tornado-breeding turbulence along a line or "front" where the conflicting air masses ran afoul of each other.

* * *

Except for the great extent of the tornado area, the weather conditions were "typical for April and May."

When the turbulence is not too great, the result is thunderstorms. When it becomes "extraordinarily severe" tornadoes develop.

Radar observation of some of Tuesday's storm areas showed violent updrafts surging as high as 40,000 to 50,000 feet. When only thunderstorms develop, the updrafts usually go no higher than 20,000 or 30,000 feet.

* * *

Reports received here, the Bureau spokesman said, indicate the tornado warning system worked well except for a few storms.

The bureau's "severe local storm warning service" is headquartered at Kansas City.

It gets storm reports from thousands of volunteer and professional observers. When tornado conditions appear, the service issues warnings that may cover as many as four or five states.

It cannot pinpoint communities where tornadoes actually may appear. Tornado conditions may blanket an area of 10,000 square miles or larger.

* * *

The bureau pins its hope of perfecting tornado warning on radar. Radar can spot storm conditions for 150 miles in all directions.

Radar warning systems are operating in several Texas communities and a few others elsewhere, including Kansas City, Oklahoma City and Wichita, Kan.

There are none in Michigan, the worst-hit state in Tuesday's storms.

Eventually, the bureau hopes to have radar coverage from South Dakota to Mexico and east to the Allegheny Mountains.

Chicago *Daily News*

DEFINITIONS

In order to write weather accounts understandably, the reporter must know the meaning of the most important meteorological terms. The following list was prepared especially for this chapter by J. R. Fulks of the Chicago office of the United States Weather Bureau:

Barometer. An instrument for measuring atmospheric pressure. There are two types. In one, the mercury barometer, pressure is measured as the height (commonly expressed in the United States in inches) to which the atmosphere will lift mercury in a vacuum. An average height of the barometer at sea level is about 29.9 inches, and in the lowest several thousand feet 1 inch less for each thousand feet above sea level. The other type of barometer is the aneroid which measures air pressure by the expansion or contraction of one or more metal vacuum cells. Pressure is also measured in millimeters of mercury, but the international unit used by meteorological services is the millibar (1 millibar equals 1000 dynes; 30 inches of mercury equals 1015.92 millibars). An airplane altimeter is a high-precision aneroid barometer. Ordinarily, when the barometer is around 31 there will be good weather for 24 hours or more. When the barometer goes below 29, wind and rain are likely.

Ceiling. An aviation term used in the United States to designate the height above ground of the lowest opaque cloud layer which covers more than half the sky.

Cold wave. A sudden drop of temperature. Defined by the United States Weather Bureau for each region and season. A typical wintertime cold wave in the central United States is a drop of 20 degrees (from the temperature 24 hours earlier) to below 10°F.

Cyclone. Same as a *low.* The term cyclone refers to its system of rotating winds. It is a moving storm, usually accompanied by rain or snow.

Fog. A condition of lowered visibility caused by minute water droplets suspended in the air. It is a cloud resting on the ground.

Forecasts, weather. Statements of expected weather, prepared by specially trained professional meteorologists. They are based on weather data collected rapidly over a large portion of the world. To obtain the most probable expected weather, the forecaster makes physical computations, considers statistical factors, and applies judgment based on long experience. Specific forecasts are generally for periods of one to three days at the most, but the Weather Bureau issues both five-day and monthly forecasts of *average* conditions. Weather forecasts are of many types: public, aviation, marine, agricultural, forest fire weather, and others.

Front. A boundary between two different air masses, one colder than the other. A *cold front* moves toward the warmer air, a *warm front* toward the colder air. When a cold front overtakes a warm front, they form an *occluded* front.

Frost. A deposit of ice crystals on outside objects caused by condensation of moisture from the atmosphere on clear cold nights. Killing frost is defined as the first frost of autumn sufficient to kill essentially all vegetation in the area.

High. An area of high barometric pressure, usually several hundred to a thousand miles or more in diameter. In the Northern Hemisphere, winds blow clockwise about a high center. The approach of a high generally means improving weather — the ending of rain or snow, then clearing, colder, and finally somewhat warmer as a result of sunshine. The weather in highs, like lows, varies from one high to another and will differ depending on where the center passes. A slow-moving high may cause fog, and often accumulation of air pollution, in and near its center.

Humidity. A general term applying to any of various measures of the amount of moisture in the atmosphere. See *Relative humidity.*

Hurricane. The name applied in the Caribbean Region, Gulf of Mexico, North Atlantic, and eastern North Pacific (off Mexico) to a tropical cyclone in which the strongest winds are 75 miles per hour or greater. The same type of storm in the western Pacific is called a typhoon.

Lake breeze. A relatively cool breeze which frequently blows, on warm afternoons, from a cool lake onto adjacent warmer land. It may extend less than a mile, or as much as several miles inland.

Lake effect. A general term which applies to any effect of a lake on weather. Near the shores of the Great Lakes a sometimes spectacular effect is that of heavy snowfall over a small area (perhaps a county). It is caused by moisture-laden air in winter moving from the lake onto the land, the air having been originally very cold, probably much below 0°F, before it moved onto the lake.

Local storm. Any storm of small scale, such as a thunderstorm. *Severe local storms* are those likely to cause damage, including severe thunderstorms, damaging hail, and tornadoes.

Low. An area of low barometric pressure usually a few hundred miles in diameter. In the Northern Hemisphere, winds blow counterclockwise around a low center. Typically, the approach of a low means worsening weather — increasing cloudiness and finally, rain or snow, but the pattern of weather varies for different lows and will be different depending on how far away the center actually passes. The low may affect weather up to several hundred miles from its center. Usually, as a low approaches, the weather becomes warmer, then colder as the low passes; this is typical of a low that passes to the north, but there may be little or no warmer weather if the low passes to the south.

Mean temperature. The average temperature over any specified period of time, such as a day, month or year. The Weather Bureau uses the average of the lowest and highest temperature of each day as the mean temperature — an approximation that is very close to the true mean.

Mist. A condition intermediate between fog and haze — a thin fog. Also, in the United States, often applied to drizzle (fine rain).

Precipitation. Water droplets or frozen water particles falling to the ground. It includes rain, drizzle, freezing rain, freezing drizzle, snow, snow pellets, snow grains, hail, ice pellets (in the United States, sleet) and ice needles. The term *precipitation* is applied also to total measured depth of precipitation for which purpose any frozen form is first melted.

Relative humidity. A commonly used measure of atmospheric humidity. It is the percentage of moisture actually in the air compared to the amount it would hold if completely saturated at the given temperature. High humidity contributes to human discomfort at high temperatures but only slightly so if at all at low temperatures.

Shower. A rain of short duration, such as with a thunderstorm. Typically, showers begin abruptly and the intensity of precipitation varies considerably. There may be many separate showers on a day of showery weather. The term is also used with other than rain, for example, *snow shower* or *sleet shower.*

Smog. A contraction of the words "smoke" and "fog." It is however applied commonly in large cities or industrial areas when the pollutants may include other types in addition to smoke and fog.

Squall. A strong wind which begins suddenly and lasts a matter of minutes — somewhat longer than a gust. Also, especially in nautical usage, a sudden strong wind and an accompanying cloud mass that may produce precipitation, thunder and lightning. A *squall line* is a line or band of active thunderstorms.

Storm. Is a general term that may mean a cyclone, thunderstorm, wind storm, dust storm, snow storm, hail storm, tornado, hurricane, etc.

Storm warning. Can be a warning of any type of storm, but is applied more specifically to warnings for mariners. Marine storm warnings are of four types: *Small Craft* (less than 39 mph), *Gale* (39–54 mph), *Whole Gale* (55–73 mph), and *Hurricane* (74 mph and greater). The figures refer to wind speeds.

Temperature-humidity index. A measure of human discomfort in warm weather. It takes into account the effect of both temperature and humidity. Exactly, THI equals 0.4 times (air temperature plus wet bulb temperature) plus 15, all in degrees Fahrenheit. With a THI of 70, nearly everyone feels comfortable; at 75, at least half the people become uncomfortable and, at 79 or higher, nearly everyone is uncomfortable. Fewer people however are uncomfortable if there is a good breeze.

Thundershower. A thunderstorm accompanied by rain.

Tornado. A small, violently rotating storm, commonly a few hundred yards in diameter. It accompanies a thunderstorm, but only a very few thunderstorms have tornadoes. Direction of rotation is usually the same as a Low, and the strongest winds range generally 100 to 300 mph.

Water vapor. Water in gaseous form. The atmosphere always contains some water vapor, but the amount varies greatly. In hot humid conditions, it sometimes constitutes as much as 2 per cent (by weight) of the air. At low temperatures, the amount is much less. Water vapor is invisible, but when it condenses it forms water droplets that become visible as clouds or fog.

Wind direction. The direction *from* which wind blows.

18

Business, Finance, Labor

I. The Business Beat

1. *Routine News*
2. *Stressing the "Why"*
3. *Localization*
4. *Trends*

II. Financial News

1. *Stock Exchanges*
2. *Seeking Explanations*
3. *Definitions*

III. Problems and Policies

1. *Secrecy*
2. *"Puffery"*
3. *"Payola"*
4 *Codes*

IV. Labor

1. *Labor Laws*
2. *Covering Labor*
3. *Labor Problems*
4. *Stressing the Public Interest*
   a. Union Affairs
   b. Policy Statements
   c. Management Agreements
   d. Union Demands
   e. Strikes

BUSINESS IS ROMANTIC

Today's coverage is suggestive of the physician who appraises one's estate of health by merely taking the temperature and pulse, and looking at the patient's tongue. Of course Wall street and the investment markets are importantly newsworthy in their own right. So are the standard indices of commerce and industry such as freight car loadings, corporation earnings, brokers' loans, excess banking reserves, as well as those relating to production of electric power, steel, automobiles and so on. But much of the time they are essentially routine — except to the speculator — and are overemphasized.

This is pulse-feeling. The lay reader deserves more interpretation and background of trends and developments in the broad phases of business and industry. There are new products emerging, commercial markets expanding, manufacturing processes being improved and always new problems of competition are arising. . . .

There is just as much popular appeal, or "romance," in business and industry as there is to politics, stage, sports and high finance. The average businessman (and newspaper reader) thinks there is more. They are all businesses if you want to look at them that way.
                                        Howard Carswell, New York World-Telegram

NEWSPAPER OF THE FUTURE

The scene is in the general offices of a large metropolitan daily.

The city editor, an efficient, business-like lady, is seated at her desk. All the office force are women; the composing-room foreman is an Amazonian type female, and advertising, layout, circulation, all duties around the paper are handled by women.

Suddenly the door to the private office bursts open, and in rushes a young lady with a handful of copy in her hand. She lays it quickly on the editor's desk and stands at attention. The "editoress" glances at the copy, then at the girl reporter.

"When did this occur?" the editor asks.

"Thirty minutes ago," the girl replies.

"Too old," the editor snaps, and tosses the copy into the wastebasket.

Another snappy young lady enters soon after with her copy. After glancing at the editor queries, "When did this happen?"

"Fifteen minutes ago," the reporter replies.

"Too old for the street edition — we can use it only in the state edition," coldly barks the lady editor.

Suddenly there is a swish of skirts and a dapper, snappy little red-headed reporter slams a batch of copy on the editorial desk.

The editor picks it up, and once more the question, "When did this occur?"

The little red-head holds up her hand, and in quick, brisk voice says, "Listen! You'll hear the shot!"

                                        Texas Press Messenger

SINCE THE END OF WORLD WAR II, THE NUMBER OF SHARE-holders of publicly owned corporations in the United States has more than tripled. This does not mean that control of the management policies of American businesses and industries has passed into the hands of housewives, widows, factory workers and middle-class shopkeepers. In fact, in monetary terms, the total ownership of stocks and bonds by small investors still is but a minute fraction of the invested wealth of the nation. It does mean, however, that millions of newspaper readers who formerly ignored the financial and business pages now have a vested interest in them. As a result, such pages are being expanded and their contents geared to appeal to the average reader and not just to the broker or banker. The phenomenal increase in general readership of the *Wall Street Journal* and the popularity of some syndicated columns in this field have helped inspire many newspapers to give greater attention to business and financial news, and specializing in this kind of journalism has become much more attractive to active newspapermen, especially beginners.

Whereas a generation ago ability to read a financial ticker tape, bank statement and annual report of a corporation was about all that was required of him, today's business or financial page reporter must be able to explain as well as report what goes on in his field of activity. Several developments have made almost nonexistent the strictly local business news story. Among these have been the growth of retail chain stores which are parts of nationwide operations, the mushrooming of shopping centers serving more than one community, the specialization of factory production so that few products any more are manufactured all in one plant, the growth of dependency of small industries upon large ones for subcontracts and of large industries upon the federal government for orders, the increase in foreign trade and investments, government aid to underdeveloped countries, and other similar trends which add up to this: what happens almost anywhere else in the world today can affect the prosperity of the small town which is no longer self-sufficient economically as it may have been in grandfather's day.

THE BUSINESS BEAT

Despite the trend toward localization of as much as possible of what appears on the business-financial pages, there is no business beat as such. That is, the reporter's day is not spent making regular "stops" comparable to those which other newsgatherers make at police headquarters, city hall, etc. Rather, covering a story for the business page, means mostly investigating a tip or following up an idea, and each assignment may require making contacts with an entirely different set of news sources. Thus, the business page reporter must be fully conversant with the public and private agencies from which information of all kinds can be obtained.

ROUTINE NEWS

Publicity departments of businesses, industries, trade organizations and governmental agencies voluntarily supply the bulk of the routine news in this field: new advertising campaigns; new products; stock sales; production figures; expansion programs; comments on pending legislation, court decisions, or other events affecting business; big orders received; reports on dollar sales; new models; personnel changes in partnerships, corporation officials, managerial appointments, promotions, and the like; new building or other expansion plans; moves to new locations; public shows and exhibits, etc.

Trade associations and institutes make reports covering entire industries monthly, quarterly, semiannually and annually. The weekly reports on department store sales issued by the twelve Federal Reserve banks are regarded as a "holy index" even though they do not include suburban stores or discount houses. Federal Reserve bank monthly reports are an index to the state of the over-all economy and usually include profiles of particular industries. The monthly index of industrial production gives information regarding the outputs of mines, mills, etc. Even more up-to-date are the reports put out by some state agencies, the *Illinois Business Review*, a monthly summary published by the Bureau of Economic and Business Research of the College of Commerce of the University of Illinois, being a good example. Its summaries are made public from two to six weeks after the data are gathered whereas government figures may be two or three months old. Similar first-rate reports are put out in Indiana and Texas, among other states.

Other good over-all business and economic indicators are monthly and weekly reports on carloadings; reports of shipments of folding paper cartons; reports on shipments of collapsible metal tubes; weekly Edison Electric Institute reports on electrical production and percentage changes. Gross national product reports (dollar values of all goods and services produced) are widely used but price increases and inflation will affect this index and possibly give a false picture of the nation's real output.

Since so much of this news originates or at least is announced in New York or Washington, it first reaches local newspaper offices throughout the country via press association financial wires. The business page editor must be highly selective and naturally considers the particular interests of the readers in his circulation area. It is easy to clutter a page with indiscriminate use of commodity market reports — livestock market prices, dairy, poultry, produce, grains, prices of various futures, dividends and earning tables and the like.

Typical examples of how the business reporter obtains information would be the following: a railroad shipping clerk knew that a company which was close-mouthed was on the decline because its shippings had fallen off; a city assessor provided information on plans for a major shopping center with which the reporter confronted the developer who persuaded him to postpone publication in exchange for a promise of an exclusive story eventually; a department store official had an informed guess on the sales volume of a statewide chain which did not disclose sales or earnings; a paragraph in a routine quarterly report of a company indicated a major change in marketing plans; a union official confirmed rumors of a reduction in a plant's production as indicated by the laying off of a large number of employes. Frequently, a business reporter can persuade a company to talk even though it at first declares, "We don't want to say anything for competitive reasons," by pointing out that he can dig out the information he wants from Dun & Bradstreet reports or from other sources available to competitors as well as everyone else.

STRESSING THE "WHY"

Even in the case of a routine story, the explanation may be the feature. For example, businesses have been known to move to avoid the disturbance caused by jet airplanes. A concern once changed location because the vibrations from trucks on nearby highways interrupted the manufacture of delicate parts. More significantly, a major appliance store pulled out of a shopping center, saying that shopping habits had changed and customers did not care to hunt for major durable goods in the midst of other commodities.

A routine story could be written:

XYZ Cola reported lower earnings, etc.

More significant would be:

> The coldest weather in 79 years cut XYZ Cola sales to the lowest in 20 years, etc.

If stories are written in this way, one leading business and financial editor commented, "Aunt Jane with her 1½ shares of XYZ Cola stock won't be so prone to seek to oust the dumb bunny management."

The following is a typical *Wall Street Journal* lead which offers explanation as well as facts:

> Prices for most major commodity futures declined yesterday. July and October copper, "M" coffee, and all deliveries of corn, lard, and July oats at Chicago fell to new season lows.
>
> Continued selling of cash corn by the government was responsible for the decline in corn prices. It was the fifth session in the last six that prices dropped to new season lows. The government is selling corn to keep market prices low and penalize farmers who did not participate in the 1961 crop reduction program.
>
> The market price for corn declined despite news that a large export business is pending. Egypt yesterday was in the U.S. market for one million bushels of corn. From one million to two million bushels of corn are expected to be sold this week to European nations. The United Kingdom is also scheduled to buy U.S. corn.
>
> The price for scrap copper was reduced ¼ cent a pound yesterday. The London copper market also was down. Last week the smelters reduced their buying price for scrap copper ½ cent a pound.
>
> A lack of export buying and slow domestic consumer demand for lard brought active selling into the futures market. Declines ranged to ½ cent a pound.
>
> Livestock prices generally weakened because of a seasonal increase in marketings.

The reporter must not be so naïve as to accept uncritically whatever he is told. An electric plant once moved out of the state saying that the "labor climate" was unfavorable. Several months later it advertised its plant for sale, citing as an advantage, "skilled, stable labor." One Wisconsin business editor has this warning note:

> Business executives pressed for "why?" usually tell reporters that it's all due to high taxes, unreasonable wage demands by labor, too much government interference, not enough tariff protection and spiraling costs of goods and services. Never mentioned in public (it's been called the "conspiracy of silence") is the fact that other factors may have had a more important part in lower profits, salary cuts, layoffs, production cutbacks, plant moves and shutdowns, etc. The other factors include bad guesses by management on product acceptance, excessive production costs, poor scheduling, bad design, insufficient market research, lack of quality control and/or generally poor management.

LOCALIZATION

Famine in India, an earthquake in Japan, revolution in Venezuela or the peaceful overthrow of a government anywhere can affect local business conditions. This it may do directly if an industry sells or buys abroad, or indirectly if anyone with whom it does business is directly affected.

Local opinion should be sought whenever important new legislation is proposed, introduced, passed or tested in the courts. Always the desideratum should be, "How will this affect us locally?" The same is true of work stoppages from strikes or for other reasons. If the commodity is coal, oil, steel or some other basic which is used locally by manufacturers or the public, estimates of stockpiles should be obtained.

The direct relationship between the politics of a foreign nation and an American business was stressed by Donald K. White in the following column in the San Francisco *Chronicle*:

Gillette Co. looks sharp, feels sharp and is sharp as a result of the Tory victory in the British elections last month.

The company's stock was down to $66.37½ a share the day before the election and the prognosis was for a rough go if the voting went against the Tories.

But it didn't and investors took heart and brought the stock back up to $72.50 a share last week.

On the surface there doesn't seem to be much connection between elections in Britain and razor blades, the Friday night fights, VIV lipstick, Pamper shampoo and Toni home permanents. The last three items are also Gillette products.

The connection becomes clear when you realize Gillette got 43 per cent of its net profit from overseas sources last year. And the bulk of that profit came from the clean-shaven British, who voted back into office the party Gillette investors felt was better for their interests.

Similarly, in the Milwaukee *Journal*, Harry S. Watson explained the ramifications of a new congressional action as follows:

Business executives across the country Friday will start to wrestle with a new cost increase that for some will run into tens of thousands of dollars a year.

The boost in costs will come in the form of increased postal rates, which go into effect at midnight Thursday. The increase will amount to an estimated 33% in over-all postage costs.

For the individual person, the postage increase probably won't be too costly, but for companies that make extensive use of mail, the added expense will run up into sizable chunks of cash.

Some firms, such as utilities, banks and insurance companies, say they will just have to "take it." They use first class mail for bills, statements, premium notices, and invoices and see no way — at the moment — to avoid the added 1¢ postage charge.

Scramble to Trim List

For other firms, which depend heavily on bulk mailings for promotion, advertising and selling efforts, it means a scramble to prune mailing lists, revise promotional literature and catalogs and investigate other advertising media.

One Milwaukee manufacturer, who has depended almost entirely on direct mail advertising for sales, is planning to change back to a salesman-distributor setup, gradually eliminating the direct mail effort.

"The postage increase comes at a bad time," a direct mail advertising specialist said. "Business isn't good and that's just the time when you step up promotional literature and advertising. But now we're going to get hit with an increase in a fixed, uncontrollable cost."

Effects of the rate increase will be felt heavily next month by such firms here as Northwestern Mutual Life Insurance Co., the First Wisconsin National bank, the Wisconsin Telephone Co. and the Electric Co.

$230,000 on First Class

Northwestern Mutual mails from seven to nine million first class letters annually through its central mailing office. Last year, it spent $230,000 for first class postage. The Aug. 1 rate increase will add about $24,000 to the bill for the remainder of this year, and about $69,000 each year thereafter. . . .

TRENDS

Any old-timer knows that methods of doing business have changed considerably during his lifetime. It requires journalistic perception, however, to become aware of a new development when it is still new. In the early sixties it was apparent that speedier transportation, including "piggy backing" by trucks and railroads, had made it expedient for local businessmen to maintain smaller inventories than formerly. Both the Chicago stockyards and railroad passenger service were in decline, much more foodstuffs of all kinds were being rushed in refrigerator cars from place of origin to place of consumption, one-industry towns were disappearing, chambers of commerce were more intent on attracting diversification and other changes were occurring which affected the entire social as well as the economic life of communities.

Two of the most significant new businesses were retail discount houses and leasing companies. The former originated shortly after the end of World War II in New England in abandoned factory towns, most of them depleted as industries moved south, often as a result of strong state governmental inducement, to obtain cheaper, usually nonunion labor.

Some smart operators bought the distress merchandise of retailers who faced bankruptcy and made fortunes. Through their operations it was learned that customers take to self-service in department stores as well as in groceries and this type of merchandising spread, mostly in the suburbs where automobile parking was made available. Pegging his story to the remarks of an authority, the financial editor of the St. Louis *Globe-Democrat* told about discount selling as follows:

BY James A. Cockrell
Globe-Democrat Financial Editor

— Discount house selling, the shrill and beshambled dimly lit merchandising experiment of a few years ago, is growing.

— But discount selling no longer will be a fight between the "new merchants" and established stores. These latter figures are joining the discount evolution in force and are armed with their own merchandising skills.

— Discount selling techniques will affect all department store, supermarkets and chain drugstore selling in the future.

These predictions come from an expert on discount selling, Richard G. Zimmerman, publisher of Super Mart Merchandising. and The Discount Merchandiser. This week-end, Mr. Zimmerman was in St. Louis to address the Sales and Marketing Executives of St. Louis.

Many diverse interests are entering the expanding discount field, he pointed out, including department stores, mail order firms, Wall Street financiers, real estate men, soft goods manufacturers and others.

Among these new entries, he said, are Spartan Industries, a manufacturer of soft goods with sales of $43,000,000; Mangel's Stores, a specialty apparel chain with sales of $65,000,000; Interstate Department Store (which recently joined forces with Montgomery Ward), and Katz Drugs.

Discounters today, he continued, are "gaining increased prestige among the Wall Street fraternity."

And well they might: Mr. Zimmerman reports that "a return of 30 per cent after taxes is not exceptional" for some discount operations!

This, he added, is about three times what traditional retailers are getting.

And what is a discount house?

It goes, he explained, by many names, such as bargain store, closed-door shopping center, factory outlet, mill store, promotional or self-service department store, soft-goods super market, and others.

Mr. Zimmerman offered the description suggested by the Council on Consumer Information: "A retail store whose policy is to sell nationally advertised, trademarked, and branded goods below the suggested list price or fair trade price to all consumers on a continuing basis."

The discount formula in the beginning, he declared, seemed "temporary." To the retailing profession, discount operations looked a "shambles, with dimly-lit interiors, roughly handled merchandise, no service of any kind, barkers shouting bargains over the public address system and similar 'primitive' features," he continued:

But how big are discount operations in the totaling retailing scene?

In one sense, they are still quite small.

Last year, the nation's some 1985 discount centers had sales of $2,900,000,000, compared with super markets' $35,000,000,000; department stores' $14,000,000,000; drug stores' $7,000,000,000, and variety stores' $4,000,000,000.

But this year, some 2400 discount centers, it is estimated, will have a volume of about $4,100,000,000 — a sales increase in one year of 41 per cent.

Similarly, the Chicago *Daily News* ran a "round-up" piece to highlight the increasing importance of leasing:

BY *Dale Morrison*

A growing Chicago firm counts among its assets a fleet of airplanes, ocean-going vessels, a pickle washer, a fortune cookie machine and a hog farrower.

It will soon add a strudel dough machine to its holdings.

What's more, as its name indicates, Nationwide Leasing Co. doesn't use any of the diverse items it carries on its books — it leases them to people who do.

"Long-term leasing isn't new in itself," said Robert Sheridan, Nationwide's youthful president. "What's new is leasing as a business in its own right."

Sheridan's 4-year-old company was the first general leasing firm headquartered in Chicago. The first in the nation — U.S. Leasing Co. — was founded in San Francisco only nine years ago.

Nationwide now has offices at 11 S. LaSalle and in New York, Boston, Houston, Wichita, Kan., St. Louis and Dallas.

In essence, what Nationwide and similar firms do is put up money for expanding enterprises.

Take the case of a cooky cutter manufacturer who wants to set up a new plant. The company has land and buildings, but lacks equipment and capital.

The company doesn't want to tie up its commercial bank credit with a long-term loan for fixed assets.

By turning to a leasing company, the firm can order cooky cutters of the type it wants from the manufacturer it chooses. The leasing company foots the bill, then collects rent from the cooky cutter firm for use of the equipment.

A variation of the standard leasing arrangement is sometimes useful to companies that have all the equipment they need, but are hungry for working capital.

They can sell some of their equipment to the leasing company, pay rent on it and use the ready cash from the sale.

Nationwide currently leases about $25,000,000 in equipment to more than 2,000 firms.

"The big companies have seen the advantages in leasing," Sheridan said. "And the smaller companies sometimes haven't had anywhere else to turn."

"The middle-sized firms that we feel could really benefit from our service are just beginning to come around."

Among Nationwide's biggest lessees is RCA, which rents about $3,000,000 in defense and other equipment.

Most of Nationwide's leases run from five to 10 years, during which the equipment is amortized and Nationwide collects its markup (about 6 per cent a year), Sheridan said.

When the original lease is up, it can be extended on a year to year basis at reduced rentals.

Besides being a financing tool, Sheridan said leasing has become a potent aid to selling. About half Nationwide's business comes to it through manufacturers representatives who direct their sales prospects to the firm.

How big will leasing get?

"It's growing at 40 per cent a year now, and we're just getting started," Sheridan said.

Sheridan has been invited to speak Tuesday at a meeting of the American Gear Manufacturers Assn. in the Edgewater Beach to explain the merits of leasing as a way to beat equipment obsolescence.

FINANCIAL NEWS

Until they broadened their scope to include business news, most newspaper financial pages contained little more than listings of transactions on the New York and/or other stock exchanges. Such charts still are used and every editor must exercise judgment as to what items to include in the limited amount of space at his disposal. He does so by editing the listings transmitted by the press associations or obtained from local brokerage houses to include those securities in which his readers have the greatest interest, because they are those of outstanding nationally known companies or of companies which have plants or do business in the community.

STOCK EXCHANGES

Elementary is ability to read stock quotations. A typical line as follows:

High	Low	Stocks	Div.	Sales in 100's	High	Low	Close	Net Change
26⅞	18⅝	Jeff.	1	278	20¾	19⅛	20	—1¼

This means that the highest price for which one share of Jefferson company stock sold during the current year was $26⅞ and the lowest price was $18⅝ per share. The "1" means that the stock paid $1 per share in dividends last year. This day, 27,800 shares were sold on the exchange, at prices which ranged from $20¾ to $19⅛ per share. The day's last sale was for $20 which was $1¼ less than the closing sale the preceding day.

This is the raw material on the basis of which the financial reporter describes the "ups" and "downs" of the market. Since perhaps 90 per cent of all stock trading takes place in New York, what happens on the New York Stock Exchange is, of course, of primary importance. There are also, however, the American Stock Exchange, with about one-quarter the amount of trading as the New York Stock Exchange, the Midwest Stock Exchange in Chicago and numerous small exchanges in different cities throughout the country. Before its securities can be listed on an exchange, the corporation must register under the Securities and Exchange act of 1934 which means it must meet minimum standards of financial soundness. Then its application must be approved by the exchange's board of governors. This act does not guarantee the value of the stock but, because of the double scrutiny by federal government and exchange, listed stocks generally are considered more secure. "Over-the-counter" sales, however, more than double the accumulated total of sales on all the exchanges combined. They are sales made by their issuers either directly to the public or through some agents other than an exchange. The securities are mostly those of companies with less than $300,000 annual gross sales which means they are not registered with the S.E.C. The salesmen are supervised by their own self-regulatory agency, the National Association of Securities Dealers, which provides information to the press, as does the National Quotation bureau.

The advantages of a stock exchange are said to be: (1) to provide financial facilities for the convenient transaction of business, (2) to maintain high standards of commercial honor and integrity, and (3) to promote just and equitable principles of trade and business. This is decidedly not to say, however, that most other trading is unethical, dangerous or otherwise undesirable. As a matter of fact, the extent to which what happens on the large exchanges actually reflects the state of the nation's financial health is a matter of considerable dispute. Certain it is that the exchanges respond emotionally to political and other news and the prices of particular securities may fluctuate wildly within a matter of hours or minutes. Some skeptics say that a great deal of what goes on is just dignified or aristocratic gambling.

SEEKING EXPLANATIONS

Whatever the truth may be, the financial reporter has the responsibility to seek reasons for important fluctuations. He is aided in the first instance by the Dow Jones & Co. ticker-tape news service which continuously transmits selected stock quotations, late news on the grain, meat, and foreign markets, sometimes baseball scores, and top national and international news. Its most important function is reporting business news of all kinds and its averages of what stocks are doing in accumulated major categories — industrials, railroads, utilities — are widely accepted as indices of the financial market as a whole. How the averages operate was described for lay readers by the Chicago *Daily News* as follows:

BY *Joe Beckman*

Ask a broker, "How's the market?" and you'll usually hear him say something like, "The Dow Jones industrial average was up about 3 points the last hour."

Everyone connected with the securities market discusses the Dow Jones averages, but just what are they and how are they computed?

Dow Jones & Co., operator of the news service known to LaSalle Streeters as "the broad tape," compiles averages on several different types of investments.

Those watched by most market followers are the industrial, rail, utility and composite stock averages, reported each hour and at the close.

But while the averages have many followers, they also have many critics.

The critics charge that using an average of 30 or 65 stocks hardly can tell you what the more than 1,100 common stocks on the New York Exchange are doing.

Their criticism is well taken from one point of view, because occasionally the average will move in one direction while the bulk of stocks in the market will go the other way.

Even so, as Dow Jones itself says:

"The purpose of the averages is to give a general rather than precise idea of the fluctuations in the securities markets and to provide a basis of historical continuity of security price movements."

In a sense, the investor should use the averages as a doctor uses a thermometer. It is an important diagnostic tool, but certainly it is not the only one.

Of the stock averages compiled by Dow Jones, the industrial average is the one investors most carefully scrutinize.

The industrial average is made up of the stock prices of 30 industrial corporations, generally regarded as "blue chips."

These are: Allied Chemical, Aluminum Co., American Can, American Telephone, American Tobacco, Anaconda, Bethlehem Steel, Chrysler, Du

Pont, Eastman Kodak, General Electric, General Foods, General Motors, Goodyear, International Harvester and International Nickel.

Also included are International Paper, Johns-Manville, Owens-Illinois Glass, Proctor & Gamble, Sears, Roebuck, Standard Oil of Calif., Standard Oil of N.J., Swift, Texaco, Union Carbide, United Aircraft, U.S. Steel, Westinghouse Electric and Woolworth.

The average goes back to Jan. 2, 1897, when Dow Jones began publication of the daily average closing prices of 12 active stocks. This continued until 1916 when the list was increased to 20. This list was increased to 30 on Oct. 1, 1928.

The stocks in the average now and then are changed to stay modern. Otherwise, the average today might have a buggy whip manufacturer among its components. Substitutions also are made when a stock becomes too inactive or its price is too low.

To compute the average, you would think that Dow Jones would simply take the 30 stocks' prices, add them up and divide by 30.

Not so, though this is the way it was done in the beginning. When stocks were split or a stock dividend was declared, the divisor had to be changed.

Dow Jones at first multiplied the price of each split share by the amount of the split to get away from the distortion that would otherwise have been caused.

In 1928, it adopted the method still used. The night before a split is to take effect, the average is worked out in the usual way.

Then the stocks' prices are added up again, but with the stock that is about to be split included as if the split were already a fact. This total is divided by the average already calculated.

The result is the new divisor, which today is 3.09 for the industrial average. It won't be changed again until a component is split or a stock dividend is declared.

The history of the railroad average also dates back to Jan. 2, 1897. Originally it was comprised of 12 railroads, but this was increased to 20 on March 7, 1928.

The roads in the list now are the Santa Fe, Atlantic Coast Line, Baltimore & Ohio, Canadian Pacific, Chesapeake & Ohio, Chicago & North Western, Rock Island, Delaware & Hudson, Erie-Lackawanna, Great Northern, Illinois Central, Kansas City Southern, Louisville & Nashville, New York Central, Nickel Plate, Norfolk & Western, Pennsylvania, Southern Ry. and Union Pacific.

The rail divisor now is 5.34 and it is not changed if the stock split, stock dividend, or substitution causes a distortion of less than 2 points in the railroad average.

The Dow Jones utility average was started in late 1929 and was made up of 20 stocks, but five stocks were dropped from the list June 2, 1938.

It is comprised of American Electric Power, Cleveland Electric Illuminating, Columbia Gas System, Commonwealth Edison, Consolidated Natural Gas, Detroit Edison, Houston Light & Power, Niagara Mohawk Power, Pacific Gas & Electric, Panhandle Eastern Pipe Line, Peoples Gas,

Philadelphia Electric, Public Service Electric & Gas and Southern California Edison.

The utility average divisor currently is 7.91.

The composite average is an average of the 65 stocks making up the other three stock averages and its divisor is now 16.47. The average was begun No. 9, 1933.

Many people, both in and out of the market, err when they report an average "up $3." Correct terminology is in points, not dollars, since the changing divisors ruin direct dollar-point relations.

The following article by the same writer shows how this background information is utilized to make the day's news comprehensive:

BY *Joe Beckman*

"This type of market is the kind that separates the men from the boys."

That's a customer's man in one of Chicago's major brokerage houses talking about the Friday market. His comment also was applicable to other sessions this week and the way they've been going the last several weeks — since Labor Day, in fact.

In some ways the market seemed like a boat that had lost its rudder. It took directions from the latest news reports.

Tax selling in many stocks took its toll.

One LaSalle Streeter complained, "Is the tax-selling over with now in (a particular stock) and the 'smart money men' moving in? Or is the tax-selling still to hit?"

These cross-currents hurt.

But there was more to consider than just tax-selling.

International tension mounted, the business recovery was running behind the expectations of many observers and some third quarter earnings reports were less than exhilarating.

Chicago's Inland Steel nearly tripled its earnings from the year-ago period, as did Bethlehem Steel. But Jersey Standard Oil, General Motors and Chrysler all reported lower earnings, the last named showing a $4,800,000 loss.

Technically, the Dow Jones industrial average stayed in its narrow 690–710 trading range.

Will it break below 690? One analyst said there was a 50–50 chance. If it does, he felt the DJI might fall another 20 points or so.

For the week, the DJI was off 0.62 at 129.52 and 65 stocks off 2.24 at 241.28.

The more comprehensive Standard & Poor's 500-stock index slipped only 0.14, indicating the market was really better off than you might guess, looking only at the Dow Jones averages.

Volume rose to 16,990,958 shares from 16,801,760 the week before.

Jersey Standard was the week's most active issue, gaining 1⅜ to 46⅛ on 265,400 shares.

Of the 1,463 issues traded on the New York Exchange this week,

744 declined while 563 advanced. A total of 103 stocks touched new 1961 highs while 95 touched new lows.

Among Chicago stocks, Commonwealth Edison was off 1⅛, Fansteel, planning a stock split and dividend hike, off 1, Brunswick off 1¾, International Harvester off 1¼ and Admiral up 1¼. . . .

Tax selling occurs near the end of the year when investors get rid of securities to establish a loss for income tax purposes, which suggests the importance to the financial reporter of understanding the effect tax laws have on market operations. The layman often is mystified by sales of what from all indications are profitable businesses, for instance. Often they occur so that the seller can pay a capital gains tax of 25 per cent on the difference between the value of the property when he purchased it and its value at the time of his own sale. This, his financial advisers have figured out, means a greater long-run return on his investment than staying in business and paying the graduated corporation income tax. Put in laymen's language this means it sometimes is bad business to be too successful provided one wants to stay in the same line of work.

Many in the financial world consider the Standard & Poor ratings and analyses a better clue to the economy as a whole than the Dow Jones averages. The latter are based on a formula devised a long time ago and do not include electronics, airlines, and some other more recently developed industries. Standard & Poor uses a list of five hundred stocks which is more modern.

Another valuable source of business and financial news is Dun & Bradstreet which, among other things, issues a monthly report on business failures based on data from 25 large cities. The emphasis is on explanation as is also true of the Dun & Bradstreet annual and other reports.

The possible assignments for the business-financial page are interminable. The alert interpretative reporter constantly asks "why?" especially when any form of behavior seems to become widespread, as investing capital abroad, establishing branch banks, splitting stock, purchasing government bonds or shares of an investment club or mutual fund rather than investing directly in common stocks, and so forth. The following is a round-up article regarding the then-current trend:

BY *Richard Elden*

During the first six months of 1961 American private enterprise in record numbers went to the public to raise new capital.

And new offerings of bonds and stocks are continuing to appear at a sizzling pace.

In addition, hundreds of small and large privately-held companies are considering going public while closely held corporations are exploring the opportunities of secondary offerings.

New issues in registration include American Heritage Publishing Co., Cole Vending Industries Inc., Combined Insurance Co. of America, Cowles Magazines & Broadcasting Inc., Empire Fund Inc., Executive House Inc. and Playskool Manufacturing Co.

Companies reported to be considering the plunge include Barton Distilling Co., Harper & Brothers, Norton Co., Playboy Clubs International, Jos. Schlitz Brewing Co., Taylor Wine Co. and Venus Distributors Inc.

During the first six months of this year, 711 corporate securities came to market. This was more than five per business day.

By classes of securities, bonds accounted for nearly two-thirds of the dollar value of the offerings, following the pattern established over the years.

Out of an over-all total of $4.7 billion of underwritings in the first half of 1961, industrial common stock issues aggregated $1.3 billion against $703,000,000 in the like 1960 period.

"Going public for the first time is much like taking the plunge into matrimony," explained Frederick W. Straus, partner, Straus, Blosser & McDowell.

"You hesitate for a long time, you spend some sleepless nights wondering if you are doing the right thing. But once it is over with, you wonder why you waited so long."

Why does a company go public? Straus put the reasons in two classes, the company's problems and the owner's problems. Of the former, he said:

"The company may be expanding and may require additional working capital . . . or it may want to build a new plant or expand its present one . . . or it may be considering corporate acquisitions."

In addition to reasons, he continued, "there is the difficult problem that a closely held company has in attracting key management men." It may not be able to use that great personal lure — the stock option.

As to the owner, a prime reason may be "to put his estate into a more liquid position.

"Too many times men have died owning all or the majority of a privately held company and in order to pay the estate taxes the company must be sold at a price way below its fair market value."

A second reason is that it may be "prudent for him to diversify his assets" or, after years of ploughing profits back into the company, he "may want cash to spend."

If the company has resolved these questions, Straus said, it must next ask: Is this business ready to go public?

Is it operating profitably now and does it have a satisfactory record of profits? Does it have a suitable earnings outlook? Is its competitive position such that the company can grow? Is there management in depth? Is research adequate? Does the company maintain modern marketing programs? Does it have adequate financial controls?

"If the answers to these questions are mainly to the affirmative," said Straus, "then assuming favorable market conditions, the company is ready to go to the public with its securities."

Given the current market conditions, the rush to go public is expected to continue at a record pace in the months ahead.

Chicago *Sun-Times*

DEFINITIONS

Because of the injury that might otherwise result, the business-financial page reporter must be deadly accurate. Among other precautions he must observe is not to use business or financial terms unless he thoroughly understands their meaning. He should not hesitate to ask a news source to define and explain unfamiliar words and expressions. Among the fundamentals in his lexicon are the following:

Arbitration. Submitting a dispute to a third party to decide and agreeing to abide by his decision.

Articles of incorporation. The charter granted by the state permitting the organization of a corporation. It usually contains details relating to such matters as the purpose or purposes for which the corporation is formed, its principal place of business, the number of its directors and the amount of its capitilization.

Audit. Verification of records and accounts.

Balance sheet. The report of a company's assets and liabilities, profits and losses.

Bankruptcy. Abandonment of one's business and assignment of his assets to his creditors which discharges the debtor from future liability, enables the creditors to secure title to all the debtor's assets and provides a pro rata distribution of the assets among all creditors. A petition in bankruptcy may be voluntary if initiated by the debtor, or involuntary if initiated by the creditors.

Bear. (Stock or produce exchange.) One who believes the market will decline and contracts to sell securities or commodities at some future date at a certain price in the belief he will be able to buy them for resale at a lower one. In a bear market, the average price of all stocks drops because of widespread selling.

Bonds. A bond is a formal promise, always under seal, by the maker, usually a corporation, to pay a principal sum of money at a specified time and interest at a fixed rate at regular intervals. *Registered bonds* are paid only to the party named in the instrument and recorded on the corporation's books. A *coupon bond* is payable to bearer and may be transferred by mere delivery.

Broker. A financial agent who buys and sells securities for others, usually on a commission basis.

Bucket shop. A phony securities exchange which really engages in speculation or gambling on the ups and downs of the market.

Bull. (Stock or produce exchange.) One who expects, or tries to effect, a rise in prices. Sometimes a great number of people decide more or less at the same time to buy stocks. Such general buying action raises the average price of all stocks. If the price rise is big enough and lasts long enough, it is a bull market.

Call loans. Subject to payment upon demand.

Check off. Reduction from employe's paychecks of union dues which the employer then transmits to union officials.

Clearing house. A device to simplify and facilitate the daily exchange of checks and drafts and the settlement of balances among associated banks.

Collateral. Stocks, bonds and other evidences of property deposited by a borrower to secure a loan, as a pledge or guarantee that the loan will be repaid at maturity.

Collective bargaining. Bargaining between an organized group of workers and an employer instead of between each individual worker and an employer.

Conciliation. The attempt to settle a dispute by consultation with rival parties who do not pledge themselves to abide by any third person's decisions.

Controlling ownership. A controlling owner is one who owns sufficient shares to give him stockholder voting control which may sometimes be less than 50 per cent of the total stock.

Corporation. Any body consisting of one or more individuals treated by the law as a unit. The rights and liabilities of a business corporation are distinct from those of the individuals which comprise it.

Craft union. A labor organization of skilled workers doing similar work. Called a horizontal union because no one craft union would include all workers in any one large industry.

Credit. Postponed money payment; a promise to pay money or its equivalent at some future time.

Curb. A market for securities not listed on any regular exchange.

Debenture. Similar to a bond except that the security is the company's earnings only.

Deficit financing, debt management. Financial arrangements by United States treasury, companies operating at a loss to borrow new cash, consolidate debts, shift from short to long term loans, refinance, etc. The objective generally is to reduce interest charges, put loan repayments on regular basis, assure enough funds to meet payroll costs and bills for raw materials.

Depletion. Exhaustion or using up of assets, such as raw materials used for production.

Depreciation. Loss of value through use or disuse.

Discount. Receiving payment on an acceptance or note from bank for a consideration. The indorser still is responsible in case the maker of the note or acceptance defaults.

Discount rate. The interest charged for discounting a note.

Dividend. The share of the surplus distributed to a stockholder.

Dumping. The sale of products abroad at prices lower than those charged at home.

Escalator clause. A provision in a union contract whereby wages fluctuate with the cost of living.

Feather bedding. Union rules to slow up or reduce work and to prevent speed up so as to protect jobs and avoid unemployment.

Federal Reserve banks. Bankers' banks dealing only with member banks and the government, the purpose of which as set forth in the preamble of the act creating them is, "to furnish an elastic currency, to afford means of rediscounting commercial paper, to establish a more effective supervision of banking in the United States, and for other purposes."

Foreign exchange. A clearing house to adjust balances between countries.

Futures. A contract for future delivery.

Hedging. To sell or purchase a security or commodity to offset the purchase or sale of another security or commodity.

Holding company. A corporation which produces nothing for the market but merely invests in the securities of other corporations.

Income, earnings or profit. Must be used with modifiers: net, gross, operating, nonoperating, etc. Net profit is figure most people interested in. Gross profit is sales less cost of selling the goods. Operating profit is gross profit less operating expenses (overhead). Net profit is operating profit less income taxes, any other charges or extraordinary expenses.

Index numbers. An index number represents the price of a group of commodities, or the average price during a given period, which is used as a basis or standard with which to compare the prices of these commodities at other dates.

Industrial union. A labor organization in which membership is open to all workers, skilled or unskilled, within any industry. Called vertical instead of horizontal because of its inclusiveness.

Insolvent. Unable to pay one's debts.

Insurance. A contract whereby one party, for a consideration, promises to indemnify another party in the event a specified loss occurs.

Interest. The price paid for the use of capital.

Interlocking directors. Individuals who are on the boards of two or more corporations which do business with each other.

Investment club or house. Small investors pool their resources, usually by monthly payments, for the purpose of purchasing securities. They profit in proportion to their investment.

Jurisdictional strike. Members of one union refuse to work if those of another union are employed.

Liquidation. Conversion of available assets into cash.

Lockout. The wholesale exclusion of workers from a plant by an employer.

Maintenance of membership. Workers must remain union members during life of contract with employer.

Majority owner. One who owns 50.1 per cent or more of the stock of a company.

Margin. To buy securities on margin means to do so without putting up the full purchase price in cash, with a broker lending the rest.

Mediation. Third party attempts to end a dispute by persuasion.

Monopoly. That substantial unit of action on the part of one or more persons engaged in some kind of business which gives exclusive control, more particularly, though not solely, with respect to price.

Mutual fund. A corporation which invests members' capital in securities and pays dividends on the earnings.

Net income. See *Income.*

Nonprofit. No dividends or financial advantage to owners.

Odd-lot investor. A broker who combines small requests for sales or purchases by several customers to be able to make an adequately sized bid on the exchange.

Open and closed shop. An open shop is one in which both union and nonunion workers are employed. A closed shop is one in which either nonunion or union workers only are employed.

Option. The right to have first chance, as in the purchase of property, usually obtained by a money payment which is not returnable if the deal falls through.

Overhead. Expense of equipment, stock and maintenance which is relatively constant regardless of production.

Premium income. In insurance, the income of an insurance company from premiums paid by policy holders. Interest and dividends from investments are the other major source of revenue.

Prime rate. The interest rate charged by banks to customers — business firms and individuals — who have the best credit ratings and solid collateral. Prime rate generally is one percentage point higher than the discount rate — the interest rate which federal reserve banks charge on loans made by commercial banks from the reserve bank.

Profit and loss statement. It summarizes income and expenses of an organization or business, to show net profit or loss for the fiscal period covered.

Profit sharing. Sharing with workers the profits of good years; in effect, a bonus based on profits.

Proxy statement. A signed document to give another authority to act for the signer. Proxy fights develop at stockholders' meetings when rival groups solicit proxies from absent stockholders.

Receiver. A temporary court-appointed officer to conduct a bankrupt business in the interest of the creditors.

Receivership. Operation of a business by the creditors when the debtor otherwise would be bankrupt or in danger of bankruptcy.

Rediscounting. The purchasing by one bank of a note or bill of exchange held by another.

Rent. The price paid for the use of land or anything else.

Reserve. Lawful money or other liquid assets which a bank must keep on hand to insure prompt payment of its deposits and liabilities.

Revenue. Generally, the cash received in any fiscal period. It may include cash from sales of goods or services (operating revenue); cash from investments, sale or property or from other sources such as patent rights, royalties and license agreements (nonoperating revenue).

Right-to-work laws. Open shop laws.

Sabotage. A conscious or willful act on the part of workers intended to reduce the output of production or to restrict trade and reduce profits by the withdrawal of efficiency from work and by putting machinery out of order and producing as little as possible without getting dismissed from the job.

Scab. A strikebreaker.

Sell short. To contract to sell securities one does not own in the expectation of being able to buy them later more cheaply.

Speculation. Taking a risk when making a purchase in the hope future developments will make the deal profitable.

Stock certificates. A stock certificate represents one or more shares of the corporation's capital. Its price is determined by the market, usually a stock exchange, where securities are bought and sold. *Preferred stock* holders have a prior claim on the company's assets before the *common stock* holders in the event of bankruptcy. *Cumulative stock* arrears are paid before the common stock receives a dividend in case dividends are omitted at certain periods. *Participating preferred stock* entitles the holder to a share in the profits, in addition to the stated dividend.

Stock split. To increase the total number of shares of stock, usually by doubling the number and dividing the par value of each share. This has the same effect as a stock dividend but is treated differently for taxation purposes. It enables small investors to buy more easily.

Surplus. The equity of stockholders in a corporation above the par value of the capital stock.

Sweetheart contract. One between management and a labor leader which benefits them at the expense of the rank and file.

Trust. A company which deals in capital and handles funds that are principally inactive, thus conserving existing wealth.

Trustee in bankruptcy. Court-appointed officer who converts a bankrupt's assets into cash and pays the creditors.

Underwriting. To insure against loss, to guarantee to meet an obligation if the original party fails to do so.

Wildcat strike. One not authorized by union officials.

Yellow dog contract. A contract for labor in which the worker is required to promise not to join any labor union during the term of his employment.

PROBLEMS AND POLICIES

As the scope and consequently the readership of the business-financial page increases, so do the problems of the editor and the need for a strong sense of social responsibility. Tips are received from many sources — brokers, lawyers, union leaders, competitors, shipping agents, trade associations and the like — and some of the tipsters may be motivated by other than pure public-spiritedness. Misinformation or injudicious handling of news may be injurious to innocent persons. Premature disclosure regarding a pending real estate transaction, for example, may ruin a potential deal. And then there is the little old lady who reads a story about the profits being made by raisers of soybeans and wants to cash in her small savings to speculate on the grain market. She calls the editor for further information and advice.

SECRECY

Increasingly, the business reporter is likely to be stymied because of federal government security regulations which make it impossible for even the most cooperative official or public relations counsel to provide information. Often the editor suspects that there is too much "hush-hush" about what happens to be common knowledge in his community, so he may contact the Freedom of Information Committee of the American Society of Newspaper Editors or some such group to see what can be done about "knocking some sense" into the heads of some Washington bureaucrats. Seldom, however, does he dare defy requests from officials with proper credentials.

"PUFFERY"

Biggest perpetual problem is how to distinguish between legitimate news and free publicity. "Business Office Musts" from the advertising department are distasteful to any editor who wants to use only the yardstick of legitimate public interest. This means that he wishes to keep no blacklist of nonadvertisers whose news is to be ignored or played down and he resents any successful attempt to persuade him to use a spurious story whose only effect is to increase someone's sales.

Especially in the sections devoted to real estate and main business district news, the business-financial page may seem to be a booster page and its editor to be interested in promoting the best interests of the community — much as the sports editor usually promotes the success of the home-town team. Emphasis on innovation and progress, however, does not mean excessive "puffery" provided there is plenty of legitimate news available which almost always is the case. How to teach this lesson to business executives and their public relations representatives, however, is not often easy.

Businessmen who employ expensive public relations men want to be relieved of responsibility. They expect the highly paid help to maintain relations with the press and both boss and public relations men resent it when a journalist attempts to circumvent this line of authority. Often, however, it is imperative to do so. One of the best places is the cocktail party. This is a genteel type of "payola" to which many business enterprises are addicted. The business reporter may be as bored as the society reporter who attends a tea party a day, but he might otherwise not get the opportunity to rub elbows with top executives. More naïve than their public relations men, these officials often provide tips and information of importance, and possibly exclusive as far as the imbibing newsman is concerned. It is a constant source of amazement to newspapermen how ignorant those who make the news usually are as regards its reporting and editing. They do, however, understand that any business enterprise must operate in accordance with rules and, though not understanding, are often prone to accept the explanation, "That is not done," when a reporter diplomatically rejects a suggestion.

"PAYOLA"

How far the reporter should go in accepting favors from news sources is a stickler. Many of them can afford expensive gifts at Christmas or on other occasions and may be offended if a friendly newspaperman refuses to accept their largess. Most editors wish there were an easy rule applicable to all occasions. Some forbid their staff members to accept any presents, even passes to public entertainments and certainly not expensive junkets by airplane to be present at the dedication of a new plant or on some similar occasion. Others are willing to accept anything which does not cost more than a fifth of whisky. Still others will take whatever a news source is handing out to other friends. Whatever rule is adopted, difficulty arises in enforcing it without making exceptions.

CODES

What follows are extracts from a memorandum on "Business News Policy," issued to the staff by Creed C. Black, executive editor of the Wilmington (Delaware) *News-Journal.*

One of the traditional and thorny problems of newspapers is distinguishing between legitimate news of the business world and free advertising. Wilmington has its share of both legitimate business news stories and space-grabbers. The aim of our newspapers is to get the legitimate news in and keep the puffs out.

Our policy is based on the premise that the decision on whether an item will be published will rest with the news departments.

Advertising salesmen have been instructed to explain that they have no connection with the news departments, and advertisers are being requested to deal directly with our city desks when they have stories they consider newsworthy.

Our decisions will be based solely on news value. If it's news, no amount of advertising will keep it out of the paper; if it isn't news, no amount of advertising will get it in.

To follow such a policy successfully, consistency is absolutely essential. If we slip up in one instance, we're putting ourselves in a position that's hard to explain the next time somebody wants similar treatment and wants to know why we won't do thus-and-so for him when we did it for so-and-so . . .

There will be no attempt here to set down a comprehensive list of hard-and-fast rules, for that's obviously impractical. But here are some general guidelines on various types of items we encounter:

Personnel Changes. Appointments, promotions, resignations, etc., are news up — or down — to a point, depending on how important the job is. Obviously we can't cover all personnel changes in the business and industrial community, so we must be selective.

Probably the biggest problem here, just because of the sheer weight of numbers, is with the Du Pont Company. I am told that the public relations department there does a good bit of screening in its releases. But if you are in doubt about the importance of a Du Pont position, consult the PR people. Ditto for Hercules, Atlas, etc.

New Businesses. A new business or a change in ownership is news. So is a major expansion of an established firm, or a major remodeling project. Let's not get sucked in, however, by somebody who's just added another showcase or finally put a badly needed coat of paint on the walls.

And when pictures are justified, let's strive for something besides ground-breakings and ribbon-cuttings.

Giveaways. Everybody who's giving something away seems to think we should provide full coverage, including photos of the jubilant winners. We shouldn't and we won't.

Our first consideration here is the lottery laws. If anything must be bought to make one eligible for the prize, the drawing is legally a lottery and we can't touch the story.

Beyond that, our general policy is that we aren't interested in give-aways unless there's something unusual enough to give the story an angle that will enable it to stand on its own as a readable human interest feature. And even when a story is justified, the name of the firm giving away the prize should be only an incidental part of the story.

Business Anniversaries.   The fact that a firm has been in business for *x* number of years hardly excites our readers, even though some businessmen have the idea this qualifies as big news every 12 months. We will not report such anniversaries except on special occasions — such as a 50th, 75th, or 100th anniversary.

Dealerships.   It is not news when a men's clothing store adds a new line of shirts; it is news when an auto dealer takes on a new car. The distinction (and it can be applied generally) depends on both the nature of the product and the type of business. A clothing store, for example, handles scores of products; an auto dealer handles only one or two lines, and usually he is the exclusive dealer for these.

Company Awards.   If a company could get newspaper coverage of awards it makes or prizes it gives its own employees, there would be no limit on the number of plaques, scrolls, certificates and gold keys gathering dust in Wilmington households. So let's help fight the dust menace by covering only very special awards within a company — a recognition of 50 years of service, for example — or genuine honors bestowed by professional organizations embracing more than a single company.

Special Sections.   Special sections are somewhat of a case apart, since their aim is frankly promotional. Even so, no editorial content will be devoted to a special section event unless participation in it is broad enough to give it general interest. And in *all* special sections, remember, the editorial content is as good — or as bad — as *we* make it. If it sounds like advertising, that's our fault.

Trade Names.   Strictly apart from the question of what is and what is not a legitimate business news story, there's the problem of whether to use commercial names of businesses or products in other news stories.

No pat rule is possible here. A good general guide is to use commercial names only when the story would be incomplete without them. You don't have to say, for instance, that thieves looted a Buick parked in front of the Wilmington Dry Goods; a car parked on Market Street would do. But if an elevator falls in a store, name the store; if a man jumped out of a hotel window, name the hotel.

There has been a tendency in our papers to go out of the way not only to describe a car as a compact car but to name the make as well. Only if the size of the car is an important element of the story is it necessary to designate it as a compact, and the make is almost never relevant. . . .

We will not use stories on the sale of individual homes unless historic interest or something similar makes them especially newsworthy. The sale of such a home or of commercial property should be reported immediately and not saved for the real estate pages. Prices are permissible if known.

Stories and photos on the real estate pages should be confined to developments or general trends instead of to individual homes for sale. That is, a picture of one home in a new development would be permissible, but we would want to avoid using a single home that's come on the market in an established neighborhood. Price ranges of homes in a development are permissible.

Let's be sure we don't use repeated pictures or stories on the same development and let's also avoid follow-up stories on crowd turnouts at individual developments and stick to general roundups on the state of the real estate market.

Several years ago, the Atlanta newspapers got together to draw up a statement as to how to reduce the "puff" evil to a minimum. In part, the agreement read as follows:

The following items are specific types of publicity which we will NOT carry in the future:

a. Fashion shows, cooking schools, garden schools or any similar promotion of any kind originated by or which has any commercial connection with any business.

b. Beauty specialists.

c. Pictures of salesmen or managers who change jobs or pictures of new members of organizations.

d. Pictures of buyers.

e. Pictures of either the exterior or interior of stores except in those cases which might be considered in the light of real estate news.

f. Interiors of buildings.

g. Special promotions such as the "Bell Ringers," "Hour Glass" teasers, etc.

h. Luncheons or store promotions.

i. Entertainment of prominent people by stores.

j. Receptions for authors in book departments.

k. Pictures of merchandise. It is understood that this not only includes retail but distributors' publicity; as, for example, pictures of distributors holding a can of beer, etc.

l. Pictures of grocery chain new members.

m. Santa Claus promotions.

n. Robots and trick automobiles disguised as locomotives, etc.

o. All promotions on the part of stores which feature the Junior League, the debutantes or other social celebrities.

p. All commercial promotions such as state fairs, carnivals, auto races, flower shows, etc. This does not apply to civic enterprises or those enterprises which are operated strictly for charity, as for example, Scottish Rite hospital, but it is understood that where publicity is given these promotions the names of no retail or commercial organizations are to be used.

q. Photograph contests, dancing schools, insurance stories, stories and pictures of used car lots.

r. Elimination of travel, resort publicity.

s. Any paid local ads simulating news matter must take the word "Advertisement" spelled out in 8-point black.

t. No automobile publicity will be carried in daily paper. All must go Sundays.

u. All special sections for advertisers cannot carry over 30 per cent publicity.

Special: Photographs of meetings of business organizations, which hold conventions in Atlanta; pictures will be used of men of prominence who attend. These will be run in one column cuts only.

Publicity on wrestling matches will be limited to 3 inches on week days and 3 inches on Sunday before the match, but story after the match will be based on news value as determined by sports department.

Advertisers should not be given preference over any other teams in soft ball leagues. No requests will come from business office on soft ball stories.

In addition, according to *Editor & Publisher*, unwritten understandings between news executives on the papers included, in substance, the following:

Mention of meeting places (such as restaurants and department stores) is to be considered part of the story in advance material, but not to be used in stories appearing following the event.

Stories about airlines, railroads, bus lines and other transportation services are "out," except in cases of change of regular schedules, when brief stories are permitted, or of revolutionary changes in services offered the public. (Air-conditioning not included in the latter category.)

No definite rule promulgated on bowling. The commercial angle, however, should be subordinated as much as possible and individuals rather than commercial teams played up.

In stories of skeet shooting events, names of powder companies, cartridge and shot gun manufacturers and hardware stores eliminated.

Stories about lectures, concerts, recitals, football and baseball games and other musical, educational and sports events shall not contain location of the place where tickets may be purchased, nor the price of tickets.

No publicity shall be given music or dancing teachers, except, perhaps, in the case of annual concerts.

Stories having to do with the arrival of athletic teams or so-called notables shall not mention the hotel at which they are stopping.

In stories about benefit dances by organizations, the name of the orchestra shall not be used, except in the rare cases when nationally-known orchestras are brought to the city.

Identification of persons in stories of all types to be eliminated as far as possible where identification mentions name of some commercial organization.

Brief stories about merchants' associations and similar business-promoting organizations excepted, provided commercial affiliation of members is eliminated.

In stories about changes in price of gasoline, names of all companies must be eliminated.

Stories about changes in law firms and changes of location are "out." Changes which affect the titles of prominent firms are approved, however.

Names of undertakers shall not be used in connection with ambulance calls to accident or crime scenes. Use of undertakers' names in death stories left to the individual editors, but the consensus is that names of funeral directors should be used prior to the funeral and not after it has been held.

LABOR

The history of the American labor movement is as much that of a struggle of different ideologies for supremacy within the ranks of labor itself as it is that of a fight between capital and labor for a share of the national wealth and income. In its early stages, organized labor was handicapped because of its control by leaders of foreign birth or influence and by native born intellectuals who lacked experience as workers and were discredited further because of their known unorthodoxy in other fields.

In the middle half of the nineteenth century, labor was too prone to espouse every new economic or political theory that offered a possible step upward on the economic scale. Agrarianism, idealistic cooperative plans, greenbackism, the single tax, free silver and syndicalism were among the ideologies with sizable followings within the ranks of labor. Until the American Federation of Labor emerged as powerful under the leadership of Samuel Gompers late in the nineteenth century, organized labor hardly was an important permanent factor in American economic and political life.

The A.F.L.'s triumph over the Knights of Labor represented a victory for the craft union idea as opposed to industrial unionism. Gompers and his followers believed in working within the existent capitalistic system, seeking through unions of craftsmen organized horizontally throughout industry as a whole, to obtain the maximum benefits for the workers. The Knights of Labor had admitted unskilled as well as skilled workers.

Craft unionism remained dominant until 1936, when, under the leadership of John L. Lewis, the Committee (later called Congress) for Industrial Organization began to organize many large basic industries, such as the mining, motor and steel industries, in which large masses of unskilled workers were not eligible for membership in craft unions. C.I.O. unions were industrial or vertical unions because membership in them was all-inclusive within a given plant in which there might conceivably be numerous craft unions.

In December 1955, the two big organizations reunited as the A.F.L.-C.I.O. but a decade later many old units of each, at all levels from international to local, still operated with virtually unchanged autonomy. Also, still independent were the railway brotherhoods and a number of other large groups, as the miners and teamsters and several mavericks which were expelled as left-wing by the C.I.O. in 1949.

Despite the comparative contemporary strength of the labor movement as a whole, not more than one-fourth of the entire labor force belong to unions. Little progress ever has been made among white-collar (professional) workers whose proportion of the total labor force continues to grow with the expanding service industries and as mechanical automation reduces the ranks of the blue-collar workers.

In the United States, with its rugged individualistic frontier tradition and its democratic open class social system, there never has developed strong class consciousness at any social or economic level. Despite considerable demogoguery to the contrary, socialistic and communistic ideas never have attracted any appreciable number of rank-and-file working people. There is no political labor party as in many other parts of the world, and organized political activity by labor always has been condemned by the rest of the populace. Because of the absence of class consciousness as a welding force, there has developed a strong type of labor leader in the United States. Whoever happens to be the leading labor figure at any time is bound to be considered a "public enemy" by anti-laborites. Regardless of the justice involved, this has been true of such widely different labor leaders as Samuel Gompers, Eugene V. Debs, John L. Lewis, Sidney Hillman, Walter Reuther, James Petrillo, Harry Bridges and James Hoffa.

Because it never has enjoyed the confidence of an appreciable proportion of the American people, organized labor has been faced with the problem of avoiding mistakes which are more costly to it than similar ones are to any other segment of the population.

LABOR LAWS

The National Labor Relations (Wagner) act of 1935 was called labor's *magna carta* because it gave federal protection to the right to organize and bargain collectively and to maintain closed shops. It was mostly under its protection that the C.I.O. became established in the mass production industries, using the Gandhi-inspired sit-down strikes strategy. The Taft-Hartley act of 1947 and the Landrum-Griffin act of 1959 considerably weakened the basic law from the standpoint of labor. Among other things the former outlawed jurisdictional strikes (one union against another), secondary boycotts, strikes for union recognition and the closed shop except by majority vote of eligible employes. It also stipulated penalties for breaches of contract and boycotts by unions, forbade union contributions and expenditures for political purposes, forbade the services of the National Labor Relations board to unions which had not registered financial information and filed anticommunist affidavits for all its officers, allowed employers greater freedom to campaign against unionization of workers, gave the federal government the power to use injunctions to compel an eighty-day "cooling-off" period before a strike could be called.

The Labor-Management Reporting and Disclosures act (Landrum-Griffin) of 1959 was aimed at racketeering labor officials. Among other things it required annual reports from all unions, gave the F.B.I. power to enter cases of suspected violations, forbade "hot cargo" pacts in which a trucker, for example, refused to handle cargo from another trucker if the union labeled it forbidden, outlawed extortion or blackmail publicity, outlawed "sweetheart" contracts between unscrupulous employers and labor leaders, and provided for secret ballots in union elections, machinery for ousting crooked union officials and a ban against arbitrary raising of union dues or assessments without a secret ballot vote of the members.

In the 1950s, several states adopted "right-to-work" laws. These were a misnomer for open shop as they guaranteed nobody a job and were intended to forbid closed union shops under any circumstance. In its behalf, organized labor increased agitation for the guaranteed annual wage, shorter work week and strengthening or recovery of old protections as maintenance of membership clauses, seniority rights, check-off systems for the collection of dues, pensions, longer vacations, profit sharing plans and the like.

COVERING LABOR

Important as all these other factors indisputably are, the basic issue involved in most contract disputes is wages. As in the case of business, there is no regular labor beat. The smart labor reporter notes in his futures book the dates of expirations of contracts between important unions and industries and, weeks or months in advance, starts interviewing both management and labor officials to determine what exactly will be at stake when the new contracts are up for negotiation.

Newspaper headlines naturally emphasize conflict, especially when it leads to strikes and lockouts. It is easy to overlook the fact that the overwhelming majority of labor-management affairs are conducted harmoniously and that there are numerous companies and even entire industries in which there has been little or no trouble for decades or longer. Labor leaders have traditionally charged that when matters do come to a point of conflict, the press underplays its side of the story. During the day-by-day account of a strike, the issues causing it often become lost because of the emphasis given incidents of violence, hot-headed statements by leaders and human interest accounts.

LABOR PROBLEMS

Understandable today is the contention that any major or protracted shutdown in any part of the American economy would be catastrophic throughout the entire economy, so interrelated have all parts of it become. How to preserve the dignity and freedom to work or not to work guaranteed all Americans in the Thirteenth amendment to the Constitution and at the same time protect the innocent masses from the repercussions of a strike or lockout is a major social and political issue. Through its Mediation and Conciliation service, the federal government investigates and provides leadership in bringing about peaceful settlements of most disputes. During periods of comparatively full production and high prosperity, as during a Cold War with huge government expenditures to keep industry going, its successes far outnumber its failures. Organized labor has been a strong supporter of American foreign policy and local unions prod employers to be diligent in seeking good government contracts to maintain full employment. If such a condition continues, organized labor may be expected to devote more of its energy to worker education programs and to plans to assist workers to participate in community affairs.

Greatest obstacle to such activities continues to be the matter of racial integration. A.F.L. unions were discriminatory against Negroes and the unskilled foreign born. The C.I.O. forbade such discrimination, but unions must share with management the blame for the slowness with which Negroes and members of other minority groups obtain equal job opportunities, are upgraded, and are given seniority rights, not to mention managerial positions.

STRESSING THE PUBLIC'S INTEREST

In covering many aspects of labor news, the reporter should consider the public interest as paramount.

UNION AFFAIRS

Aside from the same reader interest that exists regarding the activities of any large organization, in the cases of unions there is the additional public interest as regards their control and policies.

POLICY STATEMENTS

Organized labor is a political force. Consequently, it is significant news when a large union or prominent labor leaders comment upon some current matter of widespread interest.

MANAGEMENT AGREEMENTS

In the field of labor, as in all others, it is conflict that attracts attention although, as in other fields, such as marital relations and law observance, strife is the exception rather than the rule. Nevertheless, changes in wages and hours and working conditions of thousands of employes affect a whole community.

> With increases of $15,000 in appropriations ($10,000 from the city and $5,000 from the county), the Chattanooga Public Library has prepared a schedule of salary increases for its overworked staff.
>
> In an administrative committee report to the board of trustees yesterday, Mrs. Griffin Martin, chairman, said, "The completion of a salary scale and scheme of service by the staff association (members of the library staff) and the adoption of this by the board of trustees is an outstanding accomplishment of the year."
>
> The increases will leave the public library here below other comparable libraries in salaries, but the new scale is expected to help the library fill several vacancies for which competent librarians could not be secured at the salaries previously within the scope of the library budget. . . .
>
> Chattanooga *Times*

> Higher retail meat prices faced housewives today as butcher shops prepared to hike pay for their workmen $10 a week.
>
> The agreement providing for the pay increase, which is retroactive to Oct. 1, was accepted last night at a meeting of 4,000 members of the A.F.L. Amalgamated Meat Cutters and Butcher Workmen in Carmen's Hall.
>
> The session was called by Emmet Kelly, international vice-president of the union and secretary-treasurer of the Chicago local. . . .
>
> Chicago *Daily News*

UNION DEMANDS

When management balks at union demands, a strike is always a potential threat. State and federal conciliators may step in to attempt mediation; one side may offer to arbitrate. In all such cases, the reporter should seek the versions of both union and management as to the issues: what the union asks and what management offers. This involves comparing the new conditions sought with existing ones. A résumé of the past history of relations between the particular company and the union may suggest the possibility of peaceful settlement in the current situation.

STRIKES

Unless it is a "wildcat," a strike is preceded by a strike vote of the membership. Maybe this vote may be taken long in advance of the actual walkout and may consist in authorizing the officers to use their own discretion. In states with "cooling off" periods it may be necessary to file notices of intention of strike weeks or months in advance. One result of such laws may be that a union keeps an industry under almost perpetual notice, as was the case frequently under the wartime Smith-Connally act.

After a strike begins, the reporter describes factually what happens: (1) how many members of what unions walk out, when and where, (2) what is the status of picketing — number engaged, location and activities, (3) police handling of the situation and comment by both union and management on the handling, (4) violence or threats of violence, (5) the effect upon the public because of curtailed production or services, (6) efforts to settle the strike. A fair treatment of labor disputes requires constant contact with both sides and equal space to comments. Also, good reporting consists in frequent reminders as to the issues involved; that is, the union's demands and the company's counter proposals. Too often tempers become so inflamed that by the time a strike ends, nobody remembers what it was all about in the first place. The newspaper which never forgets that nobody, including the participants, really wants a strike, contributes toward peaceful settlement by not contributing to the incipient ill will.

If the nationwide telephone strike begins as scheduled at 6 A.M. today, here's how the Chicago and Illinois telephone subscriber will be affected:

1. Service on Chicago local calls, either dial or manual operation, will probably continue as usual. The 8,400 local operators in Chicago belong to a nonstriking union.

2. Long distance and suburban toll calls will be limited to emergency use only. Long-distance and toll operators are members of the striking union, but emergency calls can be handled by the supervisory employes of the telephone company.

3. Local service outside Chicago will be normal in those Illinois cities which have dial phones, such as Aurora, Joliet, Evanston, Zion, Alton, Peoria, Champaign, Urbana, Decatur and Springfield.

4. Local service outside Chicago will be limited to emergency use only in Illinois cities which have manual telephones.

5. Branch telephone offices will be open, but only partly manned, for

visitors who want to order a phone installed, make a complaint, pay a bill or transact other business with the company.

The Illinois Bell Telephone Co. yesterday advised that no long distance or toll call be attempted unless the emergency is acute. But if you need a doctor or wish to report a death in the family to kin in another city, here's what to do:

Pick up the phone and wait. If a local operator answers, ask for long distance or your toll number.

The operator will tell you what to do next. If, instead of the local operator you hear a recorded message that a telephone strike is in progress, flash your receiver slowly until an emergency operator answers your signal.

Be prepared to describe briefly and clearly the emergency that necessitates your call.

The strike has been called on a national basis by the National Federation of Telephone Workers. There are seven unions of Illinois Bell Telephone Co. employes, of which three are affiliated with the N.F.T.W. . . .

Chicago *Sun*

19

Religion, Science

I. Religion

   1. *Promoting Understanding*

   2. *Church and Politics*

   3. *Religious Group Pressures*

   4. *Religious Controversy*

   5. *Correct Nomenclature*

II. Science

   1. *Changing Attitudes*

   2. *Space Age Glossary*

   3. *The Newspaper's Responsibility*

     a. *Don't's for Writers*
     b. *Hints for Editors*
     c. *Some Ethical Problems*

   4. *Reaching the Reader*

     a. *Elements of Interest*
     b. *Humanizing the Copy*

A NEWSPAPERMAN'S PRAYER

Teach me that 60 minutes make an hour, 16 ounces one pound and 100 cents a dollar.

Help me to live so that I can lie down at night with a clear conscience, without a gun under my pillow, and unhaunted by the faces of those to whom I have brought pain.

Grant that I may earn my meal ticket on the square, and that in earning it I may not stick the gaff in where it does not belong.

Deafen me to the jingle of tainted money and the rustle of unholy skirts.

Blind me to the faults of the other fellow but reveal to me my own.

Keep me young enough to laugh with my children.

And when comes the smell of flowers, the tread of soft steps and the crunching of wheels out in front, make the ceremony short and the epitaph simple — "Here lies a man."

Syracuse Post-Standard

CHARLES A. DANA'S CODE OF ETHICS

1. Get the news, get all the news and nothing but the news.
2. Copy nothing from another publication without perfect credit.
3. Never print an interview without the knowledge and consent of the party interviewed.
4. Never print a paid advertisement as news matter. Let every advertisement appear as an advertisement.
5. Never attack the weak or the defenseless, either by argument, by invective, or by ridicule, unless there is some absolute public necessity for so doing.
6. Fight for your opinions, but do not believe that they contain the whole truth or the only truth.
7. Support your party, if you have one, but do not think all the good men are in it and all the bad ones outside it.
8. Above all, know and believe that humanity is advancing; that there is progress in human life and human affairs; and that as sure as God lives, the future will be greater and better than the present or the past.
9. Never be in a hurry.
10. Hold fast to the Constitution.
11. Stand by the Stars and Stripes. Above all, stand for Liberty, whatever else happens.
12. A word that is not spoken never does any mischief.
13. All the goodness of a good egg cannot make up for the badness of a bad one.
14. If you find you have done wrong, don't fear to say so.

A REGULAR FRIDAY OR SATURDAY FEATURE IN MOST NEWS-papers is a column or page of church notices, listing the times of Sunday services and possibly sermon subjects and announcements of meetings of church organizations throughout the week. Special events, such as installation of a new pastor or dedication of a new building, are written up on either the church page or in the regular news sections, often with pictures. Meetings of missionary societies, weekday Bible classes and similar activities receive attention on club pages or in other parts of the paper.

RELIGION

Handling all of this routine church news is time-consuming and easy to the extent that church authorities cooperate in preparing material adequately and on time. Personal acquaintances between reporter and news sources are important so that ill will does not result from mistaken ideas regarding deadlines and space limitations.

Covering all of the sermons delivered any Sunday in any place of any size is impossible. Some papers ignore them all. Others "take turns," reporting a minimum but different sample each week. Still others run "A Reporter Goes to Church" piece written by a staff member who attends a different church each week. Sometimes these pieces are more than accounts of particular services and include historical background regarding the church and possibly an explanation of the major tenets of the denomination. Always, however, great care is taken not to offend, to explain dogma and ritual sympathetically from the standpoint of the believer.

PROMOTING UNDERSTANDING

This practice accentuates the fact that religious controversy is mostly a hush-hush matter, journalistically as well as among friends. As Gustavus A. Myers details in A History of Bigotry, religious intolerance has been severe throughout American history, with virtually every one of the 260-plus denominations which exist in this country having suffered from some sort of discrimination at one time or another. On the whole, however, freedom of religion and separation of church and state, as guaranteed by the Constitution, have worked well for over a century and three-fourths and nobody, least of all the press, wants to stir up trouble.

Most people know little about religions other than their own. Helping them understand the faith of others, however, never has been considered to be a function of periodical journalism. About the only occasion on which this rule is broken is on a religious holiday.

BY *Edward H. Eulenberg*

Symbolism at many levels attends the celebration of Passover, the Jewish holiday that will begin at sunset next Friday.

Some of the symbols are visible, touched, and tasted — the matzoth, bitter herbs, and red wine.

Others are in the spoken word in home and synagog services.

Some are expressed, others implied, denoting a tie with the past, responsibility to the future, regeneration, hope.

Though the eight-day holiday is marked by synagog services on the first two and last two days, the central service is the seder (pronounced sayder) held in Jewish homes on the first two nights.

(Only seven days and a first-night seder are observed by Reform Judaism and by Jews in Israel.)

The holiday and its services are based on the Biblical story (in Exodus) of the Israelites' liberation from Egyptian slavery.

The seder, often with two or three generations of a family present, portrays much of the symbolism.

The service starts with blessing of the wine — traditionally red — the first of four cups served during the seder in commemoration of God's four promises of freedom to Israel.

A fifth cup of wine — to which no lips are touched — is set on the table. This is dedicated to Israel's most beloved prophet, Elijah, who according to legend will herald the Messiah — symbol of hope for a world of peace and righteousness.

Other visible symbols, displayed on an ornamented tray, are explained. Some are tasted.

These include the roasted lamb's shankbone (symbol of the paschal lamb); vegetable greens (symbols of the holiday's origin in an earlier spring festival); and bitter herbs (recalling the bitterness of slavery).

Best known is the matzoh, or unleavened bread (recalling the hastily baked bread prepared by the Israelites as they fled into the desert).

Matzoth are eaten during the entire Passover period, instead of bread.

The youngest member of the household prompts recital of the Passover story by asking the four questions — starting, "Why is this night different from all other nights?"

In response, the story is read from the Haggadah (the book of the seder service).

The narrative fulfills the commandment of Exodus that "in every generation it is man's duty to regard himself as if he had gone forth from Egypt," and for every man to "tell his son" the story.

Thus is symbolized the sweep of history that links every Jew to his past and obligates him to transmit his heritage to future generations.

At the final synagog service, renewal of life is represented in the reading of the Song of Songs with its hopeful note:

"For, lo, the winter is past; the rain is over and gone; the flowers appear on the earth. . . ."

This Biblical book is still as well-beloved as when the revered Rabbi Akiba, centuries ago, called it the "holy of holies" of the holy writings.

Chicago *Daily News*

CHURCH AND POLITICS

As any political or journalistic insider knows, religious peace is more apparent — because of the hush-hush policy — than real. For more than a century, religious controversy was at a minimum because the United States was predominantly a Protestant nation. Split into 267 sects, Protestants could proselyte each other but, except for the Know Nothings just before the Civil War and the Ku Klux Klan immediately afterward, few felt great alarm over Roman Catholicism. In the mid-twentieth century, however, there is visible evidence of the extent to which the two major divisions of Christianity are pulling even. Church statistics of all sorts are extremely unreliable, because of different methods of counting communicants. The best available, however, as recounted by Ora Spaid, religious editor of the Louisville *Courier-Journal*, indicates that between the two campaigns, 1928 and 1960, in which Catholics were nominees for the presidency, the American Roman Catholic population increased from 19,000,000 to 40,000,000. In most large cities, today Catholic parochial school attendance almost equals that in public schools and the religious affiliations of candidates for public office are considered important by political parties.

Because the Republicans were entrenched among the upper economic classes, during the second half of the nineteenth century, the Democrats made strong appeals to the immigrants who came in waves and settled in the large urban centers to do the most menial work. The social welfare services, developed by Tammany Hall in New York and by other urban Democratic organizations, resulted in the recruitment of most of these new citizens into the Democratic party. They were predominantly from southern Europe and Roman Catholics. Today, their grandchildren run the city governments of virtually every large city in the United States, although the exodus of the older white elements to the suburbs is increasing the importance of the urban Negro voter. The relationship that exists between parishioners and their church is suggested by the appellation usually given the local Catholic archdiocese office. It is Powerhouse, and its opposition to any important public issue jeopardizes its success. Public health commissioners do well to clear promotional matter related to venereal diseases, birth control, and some other matters so as not to risk public chastisement. The hierarchy is concerned over assignment of judges to such courts as Juvenile, Divorce, Domestic Relations and Family, and with the attitudes of social welfare workers, hospital administrators, and others.

RELIGIOUS GROUP PRESSURES

At all levels of government, the activities of religious groups interested in censoring motion pictures, plays, magazines, books, and the like are opposed by civil libertarians, most strongly represented by the American Civil Liberties Union. A generation ago it was Protestant groups which were most active, censoring books in Boston and fostering laws forbidding the teaching of Darwinism in the South. Today, Catholic groups, as the Legion of Decency and the National Organization for Decent Literature, bring pressure on motion picture theaters, libraries, and bookstores and advocate the establishment of official censorship boards. The revival of Sunday blue laws, forbidding certain commercial operations, as the sale of used automobiles, is more economic than religious in origin. Such groups as the Jews and Seventh Day Adventists, however, are in opposition for religious reasons.

The schools probably are the battleground for more religious controversies than any other institution. In the late forties the United States Supreme Court ruled that school properties cannot be used for religious instruction but that so-called released time programs, whereby children are excused from school to go elsewhere for religious instruction, are legal. Originally supported by Protestants who feared the effect of the decline in Sunday School attendance, released time programs now are also approved by Catholics, especially in areas where there are no parochial schools. Jews are unalterably opposed.

Although the state and federal governments already contribute considerable sums to local boards of education, through such programs as those which provide hot lunches and through the National Defense act and similar legislation, "federal aid to education" is a controversial phrase whenever a bill is before Congress to provide large-scale federal expenditures for school building construction, teachers' salaries or other services. Catholics oppose such federal aid unless it is provided parochial as well as public schools and have succeeded in blocking several proposals, even when they were endorsed by the nation's first Roman Catholic president.

Whether children of certain sects, chiefly the Jehovah's Witnesses, shall be required to salute the flag; how much and what kind of Bible reading there should be in the public schools; what "fringe" benefits, as free transportation, should be available to parochial school students;

whether Catholics have the right to serve on public school boards, especially if they send their children to parochial schools; what religious emphasis should be given to Christmas observances; and other issues often become important at the local level. Most editors would prefer to ignore them, but such is difficult to do when large groups rally, parade, petition and go to court. In such cases, the only choice is to "bring it all into the open" where it is going to have to be decided ultimately.

RELIGIOUS CONTROVERSY

No matter how hard-boiled they may be otherwise, editors and reporters handle both church and religious news reverently. To do the opposite doubtless would be to commit commercial suicide. Nevertheless, many newspapers run daily horoscopes despite the protest of those who say astrology, in addition to bring made obsolete by astronomy, involves fatalistic concepts inimical to religious ideas of free will and individual responsibility. Some papers also like to play up claims of visions, revelations and apparently miraculous escapes. Journalistic critics assert that when someone says that the "Man Upstairs" heard his prayers and was responsible for his escape from death, the implication is that others who prayed in vain deserved the fate that befell them and is a blasphemous assumption. Nevertheless, some newspapers feature such claims and may be prone to inquire of anyone who confronts disaster or experiences sorrow whether he or others involved had premonitions. Superstition may be perpetuated by the treatment given Friday the 13th, Ground Hog day, and similar occasions. A frequent problem is how to handle the remarks of a public speaker who insists that God is on his side and condemns others as irreligious, sacrilegious or atheistic. So many prominent men of affairs take this line that it is difficult to edit their remarks to delete all such unfounded, unfair and unprovable expressions.

CORRECT NOMENCLATURE

BY *James W. Carty Jr.*
Religious News Editor, the Nashville Tennessean *

Incorrect use of titles in the reporting of church news discourages reader interest, but correct use helps build confidence in the reliability of the news, feature and interpretative articles.

In fact, the wrong designations can draw some hot protests. The appropriate bring grateful letters or phone calls.

* Now professor of journalism, Bethany (West Virginia) college.

A reporter has to be cautious lest he use the wrong synonym for the sake of variety.

An example concerns the different designations for the spiritual heads of the church. Many terms are available. They include the Reverend, Rabbi, priest, minister, pastor, evangelist clergyman, father, brother. Actually, these concepts have different meanings. Some are interchangeable with different denominations; others are not.

A Catholic priest would be called the Reverend or Father and lives in the rectory. A Monsignor is the Rt. Rev.; a bishop, the Most Reverend; a nun, Sister.

Christian Science has practitioners, lecturers, readers. A title would be Reader John Jones.

The words reverend, pastor, doctor, or clergyman would not be used for the Church of Christ minister or evangelist. Two other correct terms for addressing them are preacher or brother.

An Episcopal clergyman, a deacon or priest, would be called the Reverend, and lives in the rectory. A dean is the Very Reverend. A bishop is the Right Reverend; an archbishop, of which there are none in the United States, would be called the Most Reverend.

A Jewish clergyman would be called Rabbi or Doctor if he holds that degree.

The Lutheran designation would be Pastor John Jones or the Reverend.

A Methodist pastor, minister or preacher also would be called the Reverend. The episcopal head is Bishop John Jones, never the Right or Most Reverend.

Seventh-day Adventist pastors are addressed as Elder.

Presbyterian ministers also are called the Reverend Mister. Their residence is the manse.

Groups also are concerned about their title. Most resent being called a sect.

America's two largest indigenous groups, the Christian Church (Disciples of Christ), and Church of Christ do not want to be called denominations. They prefer brotherhood or religious movement.

Other groups are careful about stating the power of conventions. For example, Southern Baptists and Christian churches (Disciples of Christ) are careful to point out that the convention resolutions are not binding on congregations, which are autonomous. Both groups use the title the Reverend for pastors, preachers, ministers.

And editors, remember also not to displease women. Don't call their presbyterial a presbytery.

Since Paul Blanshard's *Catholic Power and American Freedom* appeared in 1949 and the Vatican became more vocal in international affairs, the convictions of many who are concerned over possible serious religious strife in America perhaps have deepened, even though the majority remain indifferent. In that year, the American Catholic Trade Union movement was mainly responsible for a purge of left-wing unions in the Congress of Industrial Organizations and President Truman had to accede to Protestant protest and abandon plans to name an ambassador to the Vatican. During the fifties, as usually happens during a period of insecurity following war or depression, there was a wave of revivalism, led by Billy Graham, and church attendance boomed. Protestants and Other Americans United for Separation of Church and State also increased in membership and activity, and the National Conference of Christians and Jews did little more than persuade some white congregations to listen to Negro preachers during annual Brotherhood Week. Any lessening of anti-Catholicism in the United States probably resulted from the outspoken opposition of the Vatican to the spread of Communism, despite the fact that outside the Soviet Union — in such nations as Italy, Hungary and Poland — the majority of Communists were also Catholics. During this period the American Catholic church became the principal financial support of worldwide Catholic missionary efforts and contributed heavily to other causes operated from headquarters in Rome. In all this, many fundamentalist Protestants and others saw cause for alarm. Newspapers in general leave it for magazine and book authors to discuss the ideological issues involved.

Holidays, such as Christmas, Easter and Thanksgiving, provide opportunity for writing which catches the religious atmosphere without revealing denominational basis. Such stories emphasize the attendance at commemorative ceremonies, the extent and nature of charitable activities, possibly extracts from sermons or statements by church leaders, anecdotes of moral or ethical behavior, specific incidents to promote peace and/or good will among men.

SCIENCE

As the awful power of science to make the planet uninhabitable became apparent, the absolute necessity for everyone's understanding something of the implications of scientific progress (?) became recognized.

Even before the atom bomb and sputniks, newspapers had awakened to their social responsibility as regards science. The remarkable improvement, in completeness of coverage, in accuracy, and clarity of writing and, in general, social purpose followed years of misunderstanding and consequent inadequate cooperation between scientific writers and scientists. Out of the name-calling came a mutual decision to "get together" in a common program to protect the public against false science and to assist it in obtaining the maximum benefit from what the experimental laboratories and the scholars' studies are revealing daily, almost hourly.

CHANGING ATTITUDES

The change in emphasis from the spectacular in science to the practical was inevitable in an age in which the average man tinkers with his radio, automobile and household electrical equipment, takes motion pictures, dreams of owning his own airplane and uses scientific language unknown to his grandfathers.

Professor Hillier Krieghbaum, chairman of the Department of Journalism at New York University, has said:

> The public reads science news and wants more. A survey for the National Association of Science Writers and New York University, financed by the Rockefeller Foundation, dramatically demonstrated this recently. This survey of 1,919 American adults, conducted by the Survey Research Center at the University of Michigan in the spring of 1957, showed that 37 per cent of the respondents read *all* of the newspaper items dealing with medical news and 28 per cent read *all* of the nonmedical science news stories. This is an over-all average of one out of every three adults reading *all* the science news that gets into print.

On the other hand, Dr. Frank Fremont-Smith, of the Josiah Macy Jr. Foundation, expressed the views of a growing number of scientists as follows:

> It seems to me that the medical profession, the universities, and hospitals have ignored too long the fact that they can be successful only with genuine public support and they are going to get genuine public support only if their story, their very dramatic and thrilling story, is appropriately told to the public. There is no better group to tell this to the public in terms that the public can understand — because, God knows, we cannot make ourselves understood to the public — than the intelligent, thoughtful science writers.

SPACE AGE GLOSSARY

One paper, the Atlanta *Journal* used this United Press International piece under the heading, "Fallout of Words Follows Orbiting," in its issue of March 7, 1962.

Washington, March 7 (UPI) — The bird, fueled by lox, roared off its pad at Mach 4. At T plus four, the astronaut began to fly by wire but by the time it reached the Van Allen radiation belt, the bird's sun-seeker took over and directed it toward the moon.

A passage from some weird new "Alice in Wonderland"? Not at all. It's a sample of the massive fallout of strange words resulting from man's conquest of space and the rockets he uses to get him there.

Translated it means:

The rocket, fueled by liquid oxygen, took off from its launching site at four times the speed of sound. Four minutes later, the space pilot took manual control. By the time the vehicle reached a belt of high-energy particles trapped by earth's magnetic field, a navigation device keyed to the sun assumed control and steered the rocket toward the moon.

All of this has been a bonanza for the word experts. They have come up with a variety of glossaries. Most are being published by the government or scientific societies for the benefit of persons working in space or related fields.

Ablation — Melting of nose cone materials during reentry of a spacecraft into the earth's atmosphere.

Abort — Failure of a space vehicle to accomplish its purposes for any reason other than enemy action.

Aeropause — An upper region of the atmosphere in which the air ceases to function for manned or unmanned flight.

Agravic — Weightlessness.

Apogee — The point or position at which a satellite in its orbit is farthest from the earth.

Barber Chair — An adjustable seat that can quickly position the occupant to increase his tolerance to high acceleration.

Beta Rays — Electrons given off by radioactive atoms.

Ferret — A vehicle equipped for detection, location, recording and analyzing electromagnetic radiation.

Hot Configuration — A test missile equipped and ready for firing.

Moon — A man-made satellite.

Node — Either of two points at which an orbiting body intersects the orbit of the earth.

Pad Deluge — Water sprayed on launch pads during launch to reduce temperatures.

Perigee — The point at which a satellite in orbit is closest to earth.

Rad — A unit of an absorbed dose of radiation. It amounts to 100 ergs of energy per gram of the affected material.

Scrub — To cancel a scheduled test firing.

Silo — A missile shelter consisting of a hardened verticle hole in the ground with facilities for launching.

Spatiography — The geography of space.

Terrella — A self-contained, manned spaceship in which crew life is maintained during flight by a closed-cycle breathing system.

X — Symbol for experimental.

Y — Symbol for prototype.

By assigning to scientific news, men with sufficient training to talk the language of those whom they must interview, newspapers have broken down much of the reluctance of inventors, medical men and theoretical scientists to give information to the press. Whatever hesitancy to cooperate remains results from several factors: fear of being considered a publicity seeker, fear of revealing the nature of an experiment before absolute proof has been obtained, a feeling that one's fellow scientists deserve to hear of a new scientific fact or theory for the first time at a learned gathering, fear of being misquoted, doubt of the reporter's ability to translate a technical matter into popular terms, fear that improper emphasis will be given to sensational, unimportant aspects of a news item.

On the other hand, partly through the pressure of well-intentioned journalists, many leading scientists have come to realize the value to them of sharing their findings with the public, of their social obligation to do so, and of the sincerity of a vast majority of present-day newspapermen in attempting to do a completely honest and creditable job. Scientists and writers cooperate to combat "quacks."

The two leading press associations and most large newspapers today have science editors. Several of them were among the few who knew the real nature of the "Manhattan Project" before the atom bomb tests in New Mexico. Not only did they keep the great confidence placed in them, but they also produced an amazing amount of brilliant writing which made it possible for the ordinary newspaper reader to understand fission, isotopes, electrons, plutonium and many other terms which he considered recondite or boresome when encountered in classes at school. The newspaper handling given atomic energy, radar, and other recent scientific topics makes it difficult to recall that newspapers of the past virtually ignored Robert Fulton, Samuel F. B. Morse, Charles Darwin and the Wright brothers.

Professor Krieghbaum reports:

A poll of several hundred newspaper editors a year ago, on the first anniversary of Sputnik I, showed that three editors out of every four reported their dailies were giving at least half again as much space to science developments as before the Russians launched their first satellite. Almost half of this group indicated that their papers were using twice as much space. Not a single editor reported that his daily was using less space for science news during the first year of the Space Age.

THE NEWSPAPER'S RESPONSIBILITY

In the stories of sufferers from virulent diseases who have been given pathetic false hope because of premature announcements of new cures, of lives and fortunes which have been lost because of misplaced confidence in inventions, and of persecution and injustice resulting from unscientific superstition, are implied the social responsibility of the news-paper as regards scientific news. Likewise, for that matter, is implied the duty that the reputable scientist has not only to maintain proper caution himself but to discipline his fellows as well.

The rise of science, since primitive man thought the sun was alive, moving across the sky each day, and attempted to cajole the unseen forces to his own gain, has been one of overcoming the obstacles which ignorance and tradition have put in the way of knowledge. The present, however, truly is a scientific age and a major theory or discovery in any branch of science may have tremendous effect upon man's way of living and his manner of thinking.

DON'T'S FOR WRITERS

To the late Dr. Edwin E. Slosson, first director of Science Service, a news agency dealing only in scientific news, goes much of the credit for having made American newspapers scientific-minded. The following are extracts from a list of "Don'ts for Would-Be Writers of Scientific Articles for the Public Press" compiled by Dr. Slosson. They emphasize the news-paper's responsibility:

> Don't overestimate the reader's knowledge and don't underestimate the reader's intelligence. He may not know as much as you about this par-ticular thing — let's hope not anyway — but otherwise he may be as bright as you are — let's hope so anyway.
>
> Don't try to tell all you know in 500 words. Leave some over for another time. The clean plate rule does not apply here.
>
> Don't think that because a thing is old to you it is known to the public. Many of your readers are still living in the nineteenth century; some of them in the eighteenth. Anything new to your readers is "news" to them if hung on a timely peg.
>
> Don't leave out the human interest. Your reader is a human being even if you are only a scientist.
>
> Don't forget that your reader is interrupting you every ten lines to ask, "Why?" "What for?" or "Well, what of it?" and if you don't answer his tacit questions he will soon stop reading. . . .
>
> Don't say "this discovery is interesting" unless you can prove that it is, and if you can prove it, you don't have to say it. . . .
>
> Don't define a hard word by a harder word. Vladivostok is a hard word, but when a press correspondent arrives at Vladivostok he goes right on in-land without stopping to explain that "this is a city south of Khabarovsk and east of Tsitsikhar." So, if you want to say "calorie," say it, but don't make it worse by "explaining" it as "the quantity of heat necessary to effect a rise of temperature of one degree Centigrade of a cube of water each dimension of which is one tenth part of the length of a bar of platinum and iridium alloy lying in the observatory of St. Cloud." If you think you must define the calorie say casually something like this, that 100 calories of energy can be derived from three cubes of sugar or from

a small pat of butter, or explain that a man needs to expend 100 calories an hour to keep his body running, and 160 calories if he is working hard.

Don't think you must leave out all the technical terms. Use them whenever necessary without apology, and if possible without formal definition. People are not so easily scared by strange words as you may think. They rather like 'em. . . .

When the Great war broke out everybody had to learn a new language for which there was no dictionary. But the war correspondent wrote without hesitation: "At zero hour the barrage was raised and the poilu and the doughboy sprang over the top, sticking their bayonets into the boche." And the man in the street read it without batting an eye, although the sentence contained a half-dozen words not to be found in his vocabulary before. But if this sentence were being written by one of our conscientious scientists he would word it in this fashion:

"At zero hour — to use the military term for the time set for the beginning of an offensive — the barrage — that is to say the line on which the artillery fire is directed — was raised and the poilu — this is a French slang term for soldier, meaning 'hairy' and corresponding to our 'rough-neck' — and the doughboy, this is an American slang term for infantryman derived from the round buttons worn in the Civil War or the 'dobe' huts inhabited in the Mexican War or the pipe-clayed belts of the Revolutionary War or because the secretary of war was named Baker — sprang over the top — that is to say surmounted the parapet of the entrenchments — sticking their bayonets — a weapon invented at Bayonne, France, in 1650 — into the boche — a contemptuous term referring to the Germans, probably an abbreviation of *caboche* or *blockhead* originally applied to Alsatians."

HINTS FOR EDITORS

Watson Davis, successor to Dr. Slosson, has compiled a list of "Stories to Be Careful Of." It follows, together with Dr. Davis' introductory paragraph:

Stories on this list should, in general, *not* be used, at least until they are thoroughly checked and investigated by several competent specialists in the subject. These are not forbidden stories for some of the impossible things of today may become possible tomorrow, but scientific discoveries rarely come nowadays from accident or inspiration. They are usually the result of systematic research of many investigators.

General

Any "secret" scientific or technical process

Any process or preparation, where the essential element is not disclosed, bearing a coined name

Announcement of the sudden achievement of "what scientists have long sought for in vain," and rediscoveries of "lost arts"

Complaints of "a conspiracy of silence" against the inventor or other evidence of a persecution complex

Sweeping claims of any sort

"Supernatural" Stuff

Telepathy and mind reading

Spirit manifestations of any sort

"*Supernatural*" *Stuff* (*Contd.*)

Long range weather forecasts in general

Long range weather forecasts based on animal habits

Astrologists and horoscopes

End of the world predictions for the near future

Evil or beneficial influence of the number 13

Evil or beneficial influence of the number 7

Evil or beneficial influence of any number

Stars affecting human events or destinies

Phrenology

Numerology

Predictions based on lines of hand, shape of nose or bumps on head

Intelligence or character reading based on size and shape of features, handwriting or hands

Charms, amulets, lucky coins and other such survivals of savagery

Rediscoveries of lost prophetic books

Animals that "think," "read minds," etc.

Medical

Universal germ killers

Any absolute cure of any disease

Unauthenticated treatments of cancer, tuberculosis, colds and such diseases

Cancer "cures"

Cures of deafness, blindness or baldness

Doctors who advertise

Cures for "male and female weakness"

Drugs for curing obesity and underweight

Rejuvenation

Electrical treatments for serious disorders

Electric belts

Electronic treatments by the Abrams or other such methods

Spinal adjustments

Whiskey as an antidote for snake bite

Mad stones for snake bite

"Marking" of children by experiences of mother before birth

Determining or controlling sex before birth

Mineral waters as cures for disease

Cure of rabies by a stone or by shooting the dog

Physics and Mechanics

Perpetual motion

Machines that produce more energy than they use

Fuelless motors

Chemicals that greatly increase gasoline mileage

Fluids that recharge storage batteries

Methods of burning water or ashes

Chemicals that make coal burn hotter

Rediscovery of supposed lost arts, such as hardening of copper

Death rays

Engine stopping rays

Divining rods

Intuitive methods of discovering water, oil and minerals

Transmutation of metals

Animal and Plant World

Creation of life

Spontaneous generation of life

Sea serpents

Seeds that grow after more than 300 years, especially that old chestnut about wheat in mummy cases

Superhuman intelligence in animals

Prehistoric and gigantic animals living today

Gigantic snakes in temperate zones

"Hearts," "nerves" or other animal-like organs in plants

Record-breaking new species of rubber plants

Inheritance of acquired characters

Animal and Plant World (Contd.)

Absolute proof or disproof of evolution

Hybrids between unlike plants or animals: e.g., goat and pig, or carrot and beet

Toads or frogs enclosed for many years in stones or rocks

Living "Missing Links"

Man-eating trees

Miscellaneous

Discovery of prehistoric men of gigantic or dwarfed size

Ozone in seaside, mountain or prairie air; radium water

Messages from or to Mars or other planets; inhabitants of other planets

"Moron" as synonym for "sex offender"

People living to extreme ages, as 115 or 120 years

Skeletons or mummies of "giants" (more than 7 feet tall)

"Squaring" the circle; trisecting the angle

Moon's influence on weather, crops or people

Influence of sunspots on animal propagation, death rate, etc.

Children "brighter than Einstein"

Discovery of the secret of the pyramids, sphinx or other ancient monuments

Discovery and interpretation of ciphers in old books or manuscripts

Lost continents, such as Atlantis and Mu

Equinoctial storms

Earthquakes are necessarily accompanied by volcanic eruptions

Mound-builders as a "mysterious lost race" (they were just plain Indians)

SOME ETHICAL PROBLEMS

What scientists deplore is reporting which they consider "shallow, inept and totally lacking in scope and understanding," to use the phraseology which Dr. Jonathan Karas of the Lowell Technological Institute applied to the radio and television handling of the first manned Soviet orbital space flight. Dr. Karas said:

Apparently, most networks and local stations had done little background scientific research in preparing for an event that was inevitable and sent anyone available to interview local scientists. Consequently, the public, eager to learn the details of what had happened, was subjected to answers to shop-worn questions such as: "Is this significant?" "When will the Russians land on Mars?" "Does this mean that the United States is behind in space travel?" Such questions, to which obvious answers are apparent, left some of the scientists being interviewed staring in amazement.

The reason was obvious. Newscasters well qualified to report on fires or conduct man-on-the-street interviews were suddenly asked by their stations to interview scientists about a scientific feat — they found themselves good reporters caught in the wrong league so they pulled out the standard questions — nondefinitive and lackluster. . . .

Since 1957, radio and television stations have been informing the public about lack of a definitive educational plan, lack of American understanding, and other changes which must be made. Yet these same stations have made no moves to obtain scientific counsel in preparing to report scientific news to the public. They should learn a lesson from the progressive newspapers and periodicals who recognize the value of science writers and editors to cover and report on scientific news.

The greatest post-war force in improving science reporting has been the National Association of Science Writers whose membership approximates 500 and whose annual conventions attract more than 1,000. Its bi-monthly *News Letter* is a forum for discussion of problems of scientific newsgathering.

In many fields today, the science writer is faced with the problem of government-imposed secrecy. Also, government publicity men can make the science writer's task difficult by extravagant announcements of innovations in the nation's missile and other programs. Many launchings at Cape Canaveral have been conducted in a carnival atmosphere. Hundreds of journalists, seated in bleachers, have had less opportunity to observe details than television watchers. The reporter must be on the alert to distinguish between a publicity or political propaganda stunt and a genuinely important event.

Noting a trend among magazine advertisers to hire newspapermen, including science writers, to compose endorsements or what amounts to endorsements of their products, the National Association of Science Writers passed a resolution that:

1. A science writer shall take all necessary measures to insure that the information he purveys to the public is accurate, truthful and impartial.

2. A science writer should not for any remuneration by a commercial organization permit his name to be used to promote a commercial service, a commercial product or a commercial organization. Such activity shall be considered prejudicial to the best interest of this association.

REACHING THE READER

With both scientist and reporter realizing the necessity of "writing down" so that scientific news will be effective, and realizing also that, although familiar to a scholar, some item of scientific interest may seem new and even startling to most average readers, the first problem of scientific news writing concerns the elements of reader interest involved.

ELEMENTS OF INTEREST

An item of scientific news seldom appeals to the nonscientific reader because it happens to relate to geology, astronomy or psychiatry but because of its emotional value to him as an individual. This value may be: (1) purely personal, to the extent that the revelations of the laboratory are utilized to increase human comfort, improve health, extend the life-span, increase productivity and affect ways of thinking, (2) the result of curiosity, either ordinary or scholarly, concerning the nature of the past, of the universe and of man himself, (3) because of an interest in progress and the future, regarding which scientists in all fields issue warnings and make predictions, or (4) romantic, interest in the doctor who risks his life in his experimentations, the explorer who braves danger to become a popular hero, etc.

To elaborate on each of these interests and to classify the news which satisfies each longing:

1. Personal interest
   a. Comfort
      (1) Communication: telephone, telegraph, radio, etc.
      (2) Transportation: automobile, airplane, etc.
      (3) Entertainment: motion pictures, mechanical toys, ferris wheel
      (4) Machine-made products: furniture, homes, etc.
      (5) Power: electricity, water, etc.
   b. Health
      (1) Infant and maternal mortality
      (2) Preventive medicine
      (3) Research into the cause of disease
      (4) Sanitation, smoke control, etc.
      (5) Noise abatement
      (6) Birth control
      (7) Eugenics, sterilization, etc.
      (8) Mental hygiene
      (9) Safety devices in industry
      (10) X-ray, vitamins, violet rays, sun baths, etc.
      (11) Synthetic food and diets
      (12) Difficult operations and cures
   c. Productivity
      (1) Machinery to increase production
      (2) Robots and labor-saving devices
      (3) Scientific agriculture
      (4) Scientific business methods
   d. Ways of thinking
      (1) Darwinism and Mendelism, etc.
      (2) Relativity
      (3) Reconciliation of science and religion
      (4) New metaphysical and philosophical creeds and theories
      (5) Psychoanalysis and psychiatry
2. Curiosity
   a. Nature of the past
      (1) Excavations of evidences of former civilizations

        (2) Fossils and remains of prehistoric animals and men

        (3) Research among primitive tribes of today

        (4) Proof or disproof of biblical stories

        (5) Origin of the white race, American Indian, Negro, etc.

  b. Nature of the universe

        (1) Eclipses, comets, meteors, etc.

        (2) Theories concerning life on Mars, the moon, etc.

        (3) Nature of the atom and electron

        (4) Speed of light, curved space, quanta

        (5) Discovery of new planets, stars, universes

        (6) Discovery of new elements, mutation of elements

  c. Nature of man

        (1) Evidences of evolution

        (2) Search for the "missing link"

        (3) Origin of life and the age of man

        (4) Mental tests, inferiority complexes, etc.

        (5) Glands and personality

3. Progress

  a. Warnings of science

        (1) Race suicide

        (2) Overpopulation

        (3) Necessity of birth control

        (4) Susceptibility to disease

        (5) Waste of natural resources

        (6) Ascendancy of insects

  b. Predictions and theories

        (1) Elimination of manual labor

        (2) Improved aviation, television, etc.

        (3) Exploration of other planets

        (4) Skyscrapers and city planning

        (5) Constructive use of nuclear energy

        (6) Control of elements, weather, etc.

        (7) Scientific criminology and penology

        (8) Selective breeding

        (9) Electrogenesis

     (10) Scientific government

4. Romantic

  a. Heroism

        (1) Sacrifices to research

        (2) Exploration

        (3) Bravery in adversity, bad health, etc.

        (4) Struggle to save life

  c. Adventure

        (1) Hardship at the poles, in the jungle, etc.

        (2) Stratosphere flights
        (3) Deep sea diving
    d. Unusual
        (1) Theories concerning other worlds
        (2) New inventions
        (3) Animal and plant freaks

HUMANIZING THE COPY

A point the scientists have conceded, in the face of evidence, is that dramatizing an item of scientific news does not destroy its educational value. Austin H. Clark, eminent biologist, for instance, once confessed that he would not object to a newspaper article beginning:

> Those unfeeling mothers who leave their babies on the doorsteps of prosperous people's houses have their counterparts among the birds, etc.

as a popular translation of a scientific paper in which he might declare:

> Most cuckoos, the honey-guides of Africa, the weaver finches, some hang-nests, our cow birds, the rice-grackle, a south American duck, and, according to recent information, one of the paradise birds, lay their eggs in nests of the other birds which hatch these eggs and raise the young.

Dr. Dael Wolfle, executive officer of the American Association for the Advancement of Science, has lamented: "The chief thing wrong with science news writing is the audience. The average reader does not know enough about science to let the reporter do his best job."

That is the challenge. That is the opportunity.

20

Sports; Reviewing and Criticism; Features

I. Sports
  1. *The Sports Reporter*
    a. *Remaining Cool*
    b. *Following Plays*
    c. *Knowing the Rules*
    d. *Knowing the Records*
    e. *Talking the Language*
  2. *Writing Sports News*

II. Reviewing and Criticism
  1. *The Reporter-Critic*
    a. *Essayists*
    b. *Formulas*
    c. *Reviewing*
    d. *Criticism*
  2. *Handling the Assignment*
    a. *Motion Pictures*
    b. *The Stage*
    c. *Books*
    d. *Music*
    e. *The Dance*
    f. *The Fine Arts*

III. Features
  1. *Featurized News*
    a. *Oddities*
    b. *Converted Assignment*
    c. *Situations*
    d. *Events*
  2. *Straight Features*
    a. *Familiar Places*
    b. *Obscure Places*
    c. *Familiar Persons*
    d. *Obscure Persons*
    e. *Occupational Types*
    f. *Historical*
    g. *Stunts*
    h. *Situations*

FREEDOM TO COMMENT

Sport news comes nearer than anything else I know of to the common denominator of news. There is probably more universal reader interest in the sports pages than in any of the other parts of the modern newspaper.

W. P. Beazell, formerly of the New York World

The sporting columns in many newspapers have fallen to a degrading level as a result of direct and indirect bribery. There is little truth in them. The dear public is being stuffed to the gills with paid publicity. There is a remedy for this rotten situation, and only one. That is for sports promoters to treat their enterprises as business undertakings and to advertise them at paid rates.

E. H. Gauvreau, formerly managing editor, New York Graphic

The gentlemen who take to themselves the title of critic, or have had it conferred upon them by the editors of newspapers, and who are gladly acclaimed by the public as leaders of opinion, observed, studied, and followed (or else denounced and declared incompetent by dissidents) may properly be regarded, and in many cases would regard themselves, merely as contributors to the general mass of opinion, not as dictators. They may be very sure they are right, and properly so. They may be leaders, and often are, of somebody. They may have enthusiastic followers who dare not express an opinion till they have read the next morning's paper, a well-known cohort and practice condemned, at least publicly, by the leaders themselves. But what they say is not the last word always. Is there a last word? . . .

Even the most authoritative and the ablest of these gentlemen have been known to change their minds. Indeed, some would be disposed to say that those who do not find it necessary or inevitable to change their minds or to modify their opinions in some degree, in the course of a lifetime, have very little mind to change. A change of mind is not a sign of weakness but of strength. How many are there of those who have practiced writing for the daily press in a lifetime who do not congratulate themselves secretly that their opinions of years ago are buried in dusty newspaper files which few or none except in an access of malignity, care to overhaul and note!

Some will deny that there are fixed principles in art, maintaining that art is a man-made thing and that what man has decreed, man may change. Modernist thinkers may hold fast to his idea. But if there are immutable laws that govern art, there are undoubtedly areas of doubt, questionable fringes, areas open to dispute. The Constitution of the United States has to be interpreted. In how many thousand cases has the Supreme Court not had to adjudicate what was the law? And, still more disturbing, how many times has that august tribunal completely reversed itself?

Shall musical critics of the highest flight have a greater immunity from change?

Richard Aldrich, one time music critic, New York Times

THE COUNTRY CLUBS WITH THEIR GOLF COURSES, TENNIS COURTS swimming pools and other athletic facilities have proved to be fascinating places. Churches, boys' clubs and other organizations engaged in social service work have discovered the value of sports in character building. Schools have acquiesced to criticism and pressure and are developing intramural as well as interscholastic or intercollegiate sports programs. As a result of these and other influences, Americans — men, women, and children — are playing games much more than they did a decade ago, and even metropolitan newspapers are devoting more space to amateur athletics than formerly.

SPORTS

Knowledge of the fine points of a game which comes from having played it oneself increases a person's interest in the skill of experts at the sport. Baseball became established as the national sport at a time when it was the most common sandlot pastime; in later years, the boys who played it vicariously relived the thrills of their adolescence through the achievements of Christy Mathewson, Babe Ruth, Ted Williams and others. Today, with young and old enjoying golf, tennis, bowling, swimming and other sports, interest in professional experts in these fields is growing.

With all professional sports and many amateur sports, such as college football, conducted for profit, the miles and miles of space devoted annually to sports news in the nation's newspapers is actually unpaid for advertising. It is free publicity, however, which newspapers are not reluctant to give because, for a large number of readers, the sports page is the most interesting in the paper. A few editors have experimented in reducing the space devoted to sports news but have been forced, by reader pressure, to abandon the attempt to make those who profit from sports pay for their advertising.

THE SPORTS REPORTER

High value is put upon the experience gained in writing sports, generally for two reasons: (1) only the critics and reviewers have anywhere near comparable freedom as to both what they say and the manner of saying it, (2) there is no audience more critical than that which consists of sports fans who demand of a writer absolute accuracy and soundness of critical judgment.

REMAINING COOL

Everyone who attends an athletic event does so in quest of pleasure — that is, everyone except the sports reporters. This does not mean that sports reporters do not enjoy their work; it does mean that they cannot permit their enthusiasm to approach that which the fan displays. The press box is not a cheering section because its inhabitants have all they can do to follow closely what is happening so as to explain the difficult plays and decisions for fans who were too busy spurring on alma mater to notice exactly what happened. It is pleasant for the reporter to view sports events from the best seats and without paying admission, but he never is able to assume the carefree attitude of the casual fan.

FOLLOWING PLAYS

From his superior vantage point, the sports reporter should be expected to observe accurately. In many sports, the action is so fast that spectators cannot always follow it. The news story should let the bleacherite know what kind of pitch went for a home run or should tell the fans in the cheap seats how the knockout blow was struck. At major sports events, the work of newspapermen is facilitated by the assistance of an official scorer who decides whether a hit or error is to be scored. There also will be statisticians to prepare details in addition to those going into the official score book. At minor events, however, the reporter usually has to compile most of his own statistics. If, in addition to a general story of an event, a play-by-play account is desired, customary practice is to assign two reporters. An indispensable part of any featured sports story is a summary or box score, as the particular sport requires, which is run separately or at the end of the story proper. To the fan, the summary or box score is a complete account in itself.

KNOWING THE RULES

The sports fan not only attends contests but receives considerable pleasure from discussing the past performances and future chances of players and teams. A favorite pastime is to second-guess the coach or manager and to pass judgment upon the abilities of referees and umpires. Just as popular among fans is criticism of the writeups of sports reporters. In other words, the sports writer has to "know his stuff" just as much as do players and officials. It is inconceivable that a reporter not understand the rules of the game he is covering. Writers of business news can make mistakes which only economists recognize; sports writers produce copy for readers who think they know as much as they.

KNOWING THE RECORDS

To keep up with what is expected of him, the sports reporter not only must understand the rule book but also must know the record book containing the statistics of what players and teams have done in the past. Otherwise, he will not know whether a particular achievement is unusual. The reporter whose mind is a storehouse of information regarding the history of sports is in a position to enrich his copy considerably. He can compare players of today with those of yesterday and frequently may remember "way back when" something, recalled by an immediate event, occurred. At his disposal, in case his memory is weak, are numerous sports record books in the newspaper's morgue.

TALKING THE LANGUAGE

A New York sports writer of a generation ago, Charles Dryden, is given credit for having been the first to introduce on the sports page an informality and originality of language which would scandalize readers if found in the regular news sections. The credit for genius due Dryden has been dimmed because of the banal depths to which thousands of imitators, consciously or unconsciously, have sunk since then. Stanley Walker has been quoted as saying: "If it is true, and it appears to be, that Dryden was the father of whimsical baseball reporting, then the man has a great deal to answer for. He may have freed some reporters and afforded them the chance to do their gorgeous word-painting with a bold and lavish hand, but for every one he liberated he set demons to work in the brains of a dozen others — demons which made American sports writing the most horrendous mess of gibberish ever set before the eyes of a reader."

Today the desideratum in effective sports writing is informality and originality without triteness. Expressions which fans use in discussing a game cannot be considered hackneyed, but overuse of any word weakens any news story, sports or otherwise. For every sport there is a vernacular used by players and fans, familiar examples being "love" in tennis and "fore" in golf, with which the sports writer must be thoroughly familiar. It is in his use of shopworn synonyms to describe typical plays that he must be cautious. The following is a list of expressions which must be used with considerable discrimination or not at all.

bingle	concentrated practice	flipper
brand of ball	concerted effort	fork hand
brilliant rally	crush	forms the nucleus
cagers	department of play	fracas
charges	flash	functioned smoothly

466 HANDLING IMPORTANT ASSIGNMENTS

466 HANDLING IMPORTANT ASSIGNMENTS

got off on wrong foot	much heralded	seasoned team
gridders	netted a gain	sent to the showers
homer	old platter	show up well
horsehide	pellet	slam
hot corner	performed well	sock
in the thick of action	pigskin	strong bidders
it augurs well	pile up a total	superb guarding
keen battle	pilfered sacks	tap the apple
keystone hassock	pill	tidal wave of enthusiasm
looms	populated bases	tough going
lost its stride	prospects are bright	triple threat
made his debut	run riot	usual brilliant playing
many surprises are	run roughshod	vanquished
in store for —	rung up a victory	warriors
mermen	salary arm	wealth of material
moundsman	scintillating play	*win* as a noun

WRITING SPORTS NEWS

One advantage the sports writer has over the reporter who specializes in political, governmental, business, scientific or any other type of news: the rules are definite and, despite minor occasional changes, remain the same year after year in all parts of the country. This situation, which contributes to the ease of sports reporting, also may lead to monotony. It is the belief of many successful writers that the opportunity to develop an individual writing style which sports reporting affords more than any other kind of newspaper work, exists up to a certain point only, after which the sports reporter should do the more serious writing for which his work has trained him. On the other hand, however, there are scores of first-rate sports writers whose copy seems just as fresh as ever after years of writing. Outstanding is Walter (Red) Smith, whose syndicated column originates with the New York *Herald Tribune*.

In reporting amateur or local sports, the sports reporter almost invariably supports the home team. Any criticism of local heroes is constructive and usually is consistent with what a large number of fans believes. The tendency to "build up" local players may be overdone to the detriment of both the players and writer when performances do not square with predictions. The sports writer has a friendly attitude and makes it clear that he, as well as his readers, wants the home team to win. On the other hand, he must never forget that he is writing for readers and must not act as a virtual public relations man for a coach or manager who may wish to use him to send up deceptive trial balloons to confuse opponents, or to promote his own interests.

Although all contests of a particular sport are played according to the same rules, the major news interest of an individual game might be any one of a number of potential elements. In determining the feature of a game, the sports reporter considers the following:

1. Significance
   a. Is a championship at stake?
   b. Effect of the result on the all-time records of the contestants
   c. Effect of the result on the season's records of the contestants
   d. Are the contestants old rivals?
   e. Are they resuming relations after a long period?
   f. Will the outcome suggest either contestant's probable strength against future opponents?
2. Probable outcome
   a. Relative weight and experience of contestants
   b. Ability as demonstrated against other opponents, especially common ones
   c. Improvement during the season
   d. New plays, tactics, etc.
   e. New players, return of injured players, strength of substitutes, etc.
   f. Former contests between the two contestants
   g. Weather conditions favorable to either contestant
   h. Lack of practice, injuries and other handicaps
   i. Tradition of not being able to win away from home
   j. Recent record, slumps, etc.
3. How victory was won
   a. The winning play, if score was close
   b. The style of play of both winner and loser
   c. Costly errors and mistakes of judgment
   d. Spurts which overcame opponent's lead
4. Important plays
   a. How each score was made
   b. Spectacular catches, strokes, etc.
   c. The result of "hunches"
   d. Penalties, fouls, etc.
   e. Disputed decisions of umpire or referee
5. Individual records, stars, etc.
   a. Records broken
   b. High scores
   c. Players who "delivered" in pinches
   d. Teamwork
   e. Players not up to usual form
6. Injuries
7. The occasion or crowd
   a. Size of crowd; a record?

    b. An annual event?

    c. Enthusiasm, riots, demonstrations, etc.

8. The weather

    a. Condition of track or playing field

    b. Effect of heat or cold

    c. Effect of sun on fielders, etc.

    d. Which side was more handicapped? Why?

    e. Delays because of rain, etc.

9. Box score, summary, and statistics

REVIEWING & CRITICISM

If he is not ambitious to become a foreign correspondent or a sports columnist, the college-trained cub reporter is likely to want to be a critic — motion picture, dramatic, musical, literary or other forms of art. Unfortunately for the youngster with talent which might lead to success in such writing, the average small newspaper offers him inadequate opportunities either for experience or editorial guidance. As a result, many — including some of the best that the schools of journalism turn out — redirect their energies into other channels.

This section is intended both for the few who create opportunities for themselves, perhaps by developing a column of motion picture or book criticism in addition to their other work, and for the regular staff members who draw the assignments to cover the annual high school play, the local art club's exhibits, the occasional Broadway cast which makes a one-night stop, and the home talent Gilbert and Sullivan light opera.

THE REPORTER-CRITIC

ESSAYISTS

The lure of critical reviewing, in addition to free tickets, probably is the opportunity it seems to offer for self-expression. The great critics, including Matthew Arnold, Stuart Sherman and George Bernard Shaw, also have been creative artists and social philosophers. In addition to explaining to their readers how some muralist, playwright or composer regarded life, they have chronicled their own reactions.

To prevent his "spouting off" too much on the basis of only textbook knowledge and classroom discussions, it is perhaps fortunate that the beginning reporter is hampered in his critical writing. Before he can be a competent critic he must first serve an apprenticeship as a reviewer. When he covers a dramatic, musical or any other kind of aesthetic event, he does well to accept the assignment as one in straight news reporting. That is, while he is learning.

The purpose of the average member of a small town audience at a motion picture, play or concert is pleasure seeking. A safe guide for the tyro in criticism, therefore, is the reaction of audiences; no matter how high he rises in critical writing, it supplies an element of news interest of which he always must take cognizance. What got applause? What evoked laughs? Regardless of what the reporter thinks of the audience's taste, to make a fair report of the occasion, he must mention what indisputably were its high points from the standpoint of those for whom it was presented.

This advice is not tantamount to condoning the practice of building a review upon fatuous sentences or short paragraphs lauding each performer, but it is intended as a brake for those who might be tempted to use a night at the opera merely as an inspiration for an essay upon the fallacies of hedonism as demonstrated by "Faust" or a dissertation on the evidence regarding Hamlet's insanity.

The following is an example of a straight-forward, objective report:

BY *Olin Downes*

Lenox, Mass., Aug. 6 — "Peter Grimes," the opera by the librettist, Montagu Slater, and the composer, Benjamin Britten, designated by Serge Koussevitzky before the curtain as the opera that came "first after Carmen," was given its American premiere by the students' orchestra, chorus and soloists of the Berkshire Music Center this evening in the Opera Concert Theatre at Tanglewood.

The performance was conducted by Leonard Bernstein, who had as collaborators Eric Crozier and Frederick Cohen, stage directors; Richard Rychtarik, stage designer; Hugh Ross, choral director, and Boris Goldowsky, director of the opera department. Mr. Britten had come from London to attend this production, supervised dramatically by Mr. Crozier, who had directed the world premiere of the work at Sadlers Wells on June 7.

It is known that this score had been commissioned of Mr. Britten by Dr. Koussevitzky, representing the Koussevitzky Musical Foundation which he established in memory of his late wife, Natalie Koussevitzky, to whom the opera is dedicated. Mr. Britten had said to Dr. Koussevitzky: "This opera is yours." Dr. Koussevitzky related his reply: "No, this opera belongs to the world." He said finally that he had been asked to remind the audience that the performers at this premiere were students. . . .

New York *Times*

FORMULAS

The critic with a bias is as dangerous as the political or labor reporter whose prejudices forbid his interpreting fairly the activities or viewpoints of more than one side in a controversy. In criticism, application of a formula as to what an artistic form should be often results in conclusions as grotesque as condemning a cow for not being a horse.

An example of a critic with a formula is one who believes art should exist for art's sake only and that no artistic form ever should be utilized for propagandic purposes. As a result, if the hero of a motion picture or play happens to be identified with a particular racial, nationality, economic or other type or group, the critic is likely stupidly to condemn the entire production as propaganda even though it be an honest and perhaps brilliant attempt to describe sympathetically a certain segment of life.

Even worse than the opponent of propaganda is the exponent of it who is sympathetic only when a certain theory is promulgated by the particular art form under review. Such critics dismiss books, plays or other artistic creations with (to them) derisive adjectives, as "romantic" or "too realistic" etc., with a condescension which, in the small community at least, cannot but brand them as supercilious or, as the critics' critics may put it, "half-baked high brows."

The critic with a formula is bound to be mostly a negative, carping, constantly dissatisfied one. Because a Hollywood production does not square with his conception of what the Old Globe players would have done, he sees no good in the result. Regretting that some artistic hero of his did not execute the idea, he is likely to make absurd comparisons between what is and what might have been.

The essence of competent reviewing of any kind is understanding an artist's purpose so as to interpret it to others. Any art form — painting, drama, the novel, music, etc. — is a medium of communication. No artistic creation should be condemned merely because of inability to understand its language although those who hold that the artist should use a vocabulary which it is possible for others to learn have a valid point.

The duty of the reviewer or critic, in addition to that of describing a piece of art or an artistic event, should be to assist his readers in an understanding of the artist's motives to enhance their enjoyment of it. This obligation is prerequisite to that of passing expert judgment upon the artist's success in his undertaking; the role of evaluator is one which the critic-reporter should postpone until he has reached maturity himself in objective understanding, and not even then if his public consists largely of laymen. The greatest service the newspaper which gives space to artistic news can perform for both artists and spectators or auditors is to interpret the former to the latter. The educational background that such service requires easily may be imagined.

The writer of the following example attempted to explain motives without passing judgment:

> Under the auspices of the Adult Education council and the cooperation of the Greek people and the Greek Orthodox churches of Chicago, Vassos and Tanagra Kanellos, directors of the Institute of Hellenic Chorodrama at Athens, presented in Orchestra hall last night a program of

music, dance and drama drawn in great part from ancient Attic sources.

The performance brought the Chicago observance of the Greek Orthodox Easter week to a climax and was intended also as a tribute to the
University of Athens, which is now celebrating its centennial.

From a purely cultural standpoint the prime purpose of the program
was to reproduce, as accurately as possible, the blend of the arts which distinguished ancient Greek drama. To this end excerpts from Aeschylos'
"Prometheus Bound" and Euripides' "The Trojan Woman" were presented in what was announced as a close approximation of their original
form. A vast amount of scholarship has gone into the process of determining just what that form was.   Chicago *Daily Tribune*

REVIEWING

The difference between reviewing and criticism has been implied in
the discussions under both previous headings. No matter how critical he
may become with experience and expert judgment, no writer of the arts
can overlook his duty to supply the answer to the question, "What is it
like?" to the reader who has not read the book, attended the play or
viewed the exhibit in question.

Is it a book about Russia or about how to raise puppies? A farce or
a tragedy? A painting in imitation of Cezanne or one suggestive of
Paul Cadmus? The reader who must select the books he reads, the motion
pictures, plays and musical events he attends, expects the newspaper to
tell him the answers. He wants, furthermore, an honest, fair statement,
not an advertiser's blurb; and he doesn't want his pleasure spoiled by
being told too much. That is, if the success of the playwright or novelist
depends upon an unusual plot incident, it is unfair to both the artist and
his audience for the writer to reveal its nature. How to convey an adequate impression of the nature of an artistic creation without spoiling
one's fun demands only that quality known as common sense.

THE JEWISH PEOPLE: PAST AND PRESENT. Jewish Encyclopedia
        Handbooks. 430 pp., $10.

To acquaint American Jews with the cultural legacy with which Hitler
unwittingly endowed them is the purpose of a three-volume encyclopedia
of Jewish history, religion, culture, and sociology, the first volume of which
has just been published, under the editorship of a group of European
scholars.

Basically, the work is a translation of part of the 20-volume General
Encyclopedia in Yiddish, one-third of which had been published in Paris
before the outbreak of the war in 1939. Included, however, are new and
additional articles by eminent American and English specialists.

The first volume comprises monographs on Jewish anthropology,
archaeology, ancient and modern history, and the origin and growth of
Jewish religion, philosophy and mysticism.

The contributors are noted in their respective fields. . . .

                    New York *Post*

CRITICISM

To pass judgment upon the merits of a book, play, painting, musical number, motion picture, or any other attempt at art demands expert judgment. To be an expert, one must have a specialist's education and training. This does not mean necessarily that the newspaper critic must be able to produce masterpieces himself to be qualified to pass judgment upon the efforts of another, but it does mean that he must have a thorough-going understanding of the field about which he writes.

It is not peculiar that supposedly expert critics often do not agree. Neither do political theorists, economists or scientists. A difference of opinion among specialists, however, is based upon sound principles whereas philistines have as their premises only stereotypes.

The critic who wins the respect of readers usually is one who has proved his ability to report correctly an artistic event and to review fairly the nature of a piece of art. If he can observe correctly and interpret with understanding, he also may be trusted as an artistic "tipster." If he lacks either of the other qualities, however, his starred selections will be ignored.

These, then, are the three responsibilities of the finished critic, which the ambitious beginner would do well to master one at a time in order: (1) to describe objectively an artistic object or event, (2) to explain what the artist intends it to convey, (3) to pass expert judgment on the artist's success in achieving his purpose.

Note in the following example how the writer, although passing critical judgments, remained aware of his role as reporter:

> **ROSE MARIE:** At the Fair Park Casino. A musical play in three acts by Rudolf Friml. Book and lyrics by Otto Harbach and Oscar Hammerstein II. Staged by José Ruben. Musical direction of Giuseppe Bamboschek. Chorus and ensembles directed by Carl Randall. Scenery by Karl Koeck and August Meyer. The cast:

Emile La Flamme	George Young	Hard-Boiled Herman	Johnny Silver
Sergeant Malone	Carlton Gauld	Jim Kenyon	Walter Cassel
Black Eagle	Craig Timberlake	Rose Marie	
Lady Jane	Nina Olivette	La Flamme	Christina Carroll
Edward Hawley	Rolin Bauer	Nutsie	Chris Robinson
Wanda	Elizabeth Houston	Ethel Brander	Evelyn Daw
		Conductor, Giuseppe Bamboschek.	

BY JOHN ROSENFIELD

No matter what happens in between, the first and last weeks of a Starlight Operetta season at the Fair Park Casino are dependable. "Rose Marie," which opened the tenth and final week Monday night, is in the tradition, a good show. Four solid song hits, a quantity of good singing, the best totem dance yet for the Casino, and some miscellaneous comedy that the large crowd enjoyed determinedly, made a respectable sum of diversion for the 2,900 patrons.

"Rose Marie" is the third Friml opus of the summer although Herman Stothart, now of the MGM studios, deserves an assist. Not a little of the score is his or of his fashioning. Anyhow the title song which goes "Rose Marie, I Love You" was the first show-stopper, especially as Walter Cassel sang it.

Christina Carroll, with a slightly full-blown beauty with an excellent voice and much tempermental warmth, ululated the "Indian Love Call" to everybody's satisfaction, every time she sang it, which was often. She also salvaged "Lak Jemm," a fairish piece that most of us had forgotten.

For the "Totem Tom-Tom" number Carl Randall sent the tout ensemble on stage as vivid as the Indians they were supposed to be. They negotiated impressive serpentines in quick-step, a few pinwheels, a linear collapse and some ritualistic semaphore movements. The number worked up to a high pitch of excitement. This was good going, especially on a strangely cramped stage. We don't know why the wood wings were brought in so far.

Mr. Cassel and Miss Carroll transacted the Canadian love affair with communicative ardor. Not even the first-act black-out could break their betrothal clinch. Here, too, were splendid young American voices of Metropolitan Opera caliber as well as record and such vocalism cannot be improved on these days. . . .   Dallas *Morning News*

HANDLING THE ASSIGNMENT

Two factors which the reviewer-critic must bear in mind are: (1) are those upon whose work he is to pass judgment professionals or amateurs? (2) is the performance (dramatic or musical), production, presentation, or object of art an original creation or a copy or imitation?

It is unfair to judge an amateur by professional standards. The home talent cast usually gets as much fun out of rehearsing and acting as do the relatives and friends who witness the result. Generally, amateur events should be reported objectively with the audience's reactions as the guide.

Whereas Broadway first-nighters are as interested in the work of a playwright as in the excellence of actors, when the local dramatic club puts on something by Oscar Wilde or Somerset Maugham, it is stupid to place the emphasis in the review upon the familiar plot or problem with which the dramatist was concerned. Rather, it is the acting and staging which should command attention.

The broader the critic's background, the better able he is to make comparisons between immediate and past events. If he has seen several actresses play the same part, he can explain the differences in interpretations. When a motion picture is adapted from a novel, short story, or stage play, he can point out the changes made in plot and artistic emphasis. The same orchestra under different conductors behaves differently in rendering the same musical masterpiece; two authors handling the same subject may have little in common as to either method or conclusions.

MOTION PICTURES

There are few places large enough to support a newspaper which do not also have a motion picture theater. For the assistance of small-town editors, motion picture producers issue publicity material descriptive of their films and performers. Obviously, however, much to be preferred is the locally written review or criticism composed from the standpoint of the audience rather than that of the advertiser; fearlessness is a quality without which motion picture reviewing is likely to be jejune.

THE STAGE

What has been said about the motion picture applies also to the legitimate stage. If the play is a much-acted one, the reviewer should not devote any appreciable amount of space to relating the story of the plot or to describing the general motive. Rather, he should perform the difficult task of distinguishing between the acting and the actor's role and should consider stage management and direction. Obviously, to criticize effectively he must have some acquaintance with the technique of play production.

If the play is a production, the critic rightfully evaluates the playwright's success in achieving his purpose. Is there proper congruity in settings, costumes, language and plot? Is the action logical or is the happy ending arrived at by a series of unnatural coincidences? Are exits and entrances merely artificial devices to get characters on and off the stage?

If the production deals with a problem, is it met squarely or is it falsely simplified? Are the characters truly representative of the types they portray or are they superficial or caricatures? Is the play propaganda? If it points a moral, is the playwright sincere or naïve or bigoted? Is anything risque just smut for smut's sake or is it essential for dramatic completeness?

These are just a few of the questions the critic must ask himself. For whatever conclusions he reaches he must give sound reasons.

BOOKS

The first task of the editor of a book review page is one of selection of those few of the thousands of volumes published annually which are to receive mention. Harry Hanson, veteran newspaper and magazine book reviewer, told an *Editor & Publisher* interviewer:

> The daily book review lifts a book from an overtowering mass of printed material and makes it an integral part of life. It often becomes

news of the first order. Between the covers of all these volumes there may be an authoritative voice touching on our vital problems, and if this is true, that voice certainly deserves a hearing. The book reviewer's job, it seems to me, is to sort this flood of titles, find the one that fits in the day's news, and then write about it as news.

That the first duty of the writer about books is to assist readers to select those they wish to read also is the viewpoint of another leading reviewer, Joseph Wood Krutch, who said:

> The best review is not the one which is trying to be something else. It is not an independent essay on the subject of the book in hand and not an aesthetic discourse upon one of the literary genres. The best book review is the best review of the book in question, and the better it is the closer it sticks to its ostensible subject. . . . However penetrating a piece of writing may be, it is not a good review if it leaves the reader wondering what the book itself is like as a whole or it is concerned with only some aspects of the book's quality.

On the other hand, that the book review also may be an opportunity for good writing is recognized by Mrs. Irita Van Doren, editor of one of the most successful newspaper book reviewing departments in this country, *Books*, Sunday supplement of the New York *Herald Tribune*. Mrs. Van Doren told *Editor & Publisher*:

> Book reviews generally fall into two classes. The strictly reportorial, which just gives an account of what the book is about or merely outlines its plot, and the strictly critical, which is usually dull and dissertative. It has been our aim to choose a middle course. We try to give an account of the book and a critical opinion. We try to make the reviews not only authoritative but interesting in their own right. That is the reason we try to find the best writers to write about the best books.

As to the style of book reviewing or criticizing there is no formula. The writer is free to use virtually any method he chooses, the only test being the effectiveness of the style used. Somewhere in the review or criticism the writer should be expected to classify the book as to type — fiction, philosophy, biography, etc. — to describe its contents, communicate something of its quality, and pass judgment upon it.

The writer should be warned against misuse of clichés and omnibus words, especially adjectives such as "vigorous," "amazing," "haunting," "powerful," "gripping," "exciting," "thrilling," and the like.

MUSIC

The reporter who is timid about covering a musical event because he lacks technical training in music, at least has the consolation that by far a majority of his readers, both those who attended the event under review and those who didn't, know no more than he. The superior musical review, of course, is written for both the professor of music and the music-lover. The qualities demanded of the musical critic were summarized as follows by the late Lawrence Gilman, long music critic for the New York *Herald Tribune* in an interview in *Editor & Publisher:*

> The best music critic is a good newspaperman. Of course, he must know music, deeply and thoroughly and exactly; he must know what he is talking about. But the first and indispensable requirement of any article written for a newspaper, no matter on what subject, is that it must be readable — it must be interesting as well as clearly intelligible to the lay reader of average education. A professional musician might be able to write a competent, technical account of a composition or a musical performance. But his review would probably be interesting only to other musicians.
>
> The chief aim of a newspaper critic must be to interest the general reader. And if he can interest those readers who have not heard the performance, as well as those who have, he is entitled to call it a day. Quite apart from its value as a report and estimate of a musical performance, his criticism must be able to stand alone as an interesting, readable story.

It is the musician with whom the musical critic primarily is interested because only occasionally, even in the large cities, is he required to pass judgment upon a new symphony, opera or other musical creation. Thus, if the audience includes musically trained auditors, he may well take his cue from their reactions as to the merits of the performance. If he is woefully lacking in musical training, he can make his entire story descriptive of the audience or the personalities of the musicians.

THE DANCE

Whereas music is written with complete directions by the composer to guide the virtuoso, and whereas rules for the playwright, novelist, painter and sculptor may be found in textbooks, no way as yet has been devised to score the movements which characterize what, historical evidence proves, was one of the first if not the original form of art. Motion picture recording may prove the way out for future teachers of the dance who wish to convey the qualities of the work of a Harald Kreutzberg or Ruth St. Denis.

The medium of the dance is motion, but motion may be either abstract or pantomimic, rhythmic or natural. Folk dancing, being pantomimic, reflects the customs of the people participating in it. Natural dancing consists in such normal movements as running, walking, skipping, leaping, etc., without studied posing. What is called the German school of dancing emphasizes strength, endurance and precision of movement. The ballet is rhythmic and repetitious. Greek or classical dancing, revived since World War I by the late Isadora Duncan, is symbolic and involves the entire body, not just the head, arms, and legs. Miss Duncan considered her art interpretative of poetry, music, the movements of nature and of moods and emotions; as such, it defied analysis.

To review a dancing entertainment with any intelligence, the reporter must understand the principles superficially sketched in the preceding two paragraphs. A sympathetic attitude perhaps is more essential than in reviewing any other form of art, if for no other reason than that it is the form with which the average person has the least everyday contact.

THE FINE ARTS

The camera was to a large extent the cause of the contemporary "war" in the field of painting which has repercussions among the sculptors and architects as well. Dadaism, futurism, surrealism and other recent "schools" of art are revolts against the formal, and a popular explanation given laymen is that the day of the portrait painter is gone and with it a theory as to the purpose of art. It is argued that the role of the twentieth century artist is to communicate an idea or an emotion; the extremes to which some go in upsetting tradition is dumfounding to laymen. In the works of such painters as Grant Wood and Thomas Benton, who call themselves "regional" artists, is found an abandonment of the photographic purpose but the models still are recognizable.

Current tendencies in painting, sculpturing and architecture are not new. The history of art reveals that throughout the centuries every conceivable theory has been tired out. Likewise, the search for a definition of art is as old as artistic criticism; upon his answer to the question depends largely the nature of what an artist produces.

Through reading and fraternizing with artistic people the reporter can become educated in the meaning of art to the different "schools," the work of whose representatives he is called upon to review. In no other field is the responsibility for interpreting the artist to his public greater than in that of the manual arts. In fact, such interpretation is about all there is to this kind of criticism.

FEATURES

The difference between news and feature stories is largely one of intention. Numerous examples in preceding chapters have illustrated how unorthodox journalistic rhetorical methods, customarily associated with feature writing, may be used to improve ordinary news stories in which the writer's purpose is to be informative about overt happenings. On the other hand, a feature article emphasizing human interest may be composed according to the standard rules for formal news writing.

In addition to designating those stories of events which might have been written up in straight news style, the term "feature" also is used to include human interest stories related to or suggested by news events, a quantity of different types of articles only slightly or not at all connected with any news item, and a growing number of special informative articles and regular columns of advice and instructions.

FEATURIZED NEWS

"Make it into a feature," the reporter says to himself or is told by the city editor when he has a schedule of facts about something which actually has happened of little public importance but of considerable potential reader interest.

ODDITIES

One of the milestones in the evolution of the modern newspaper was when the James Gordon Bennetts began printing accounts of happenings which previously had been considered too trivial to merit attention. Today, without consciousness of the loss of any dignity, the average newspaper balances its offering of serious matter by a liberal sprinkling of "brighteners," usually brief, cleverly written feature items of relatively unimportant happenings. Some papers group a number of such shorts each day in a column headed, "Oddities in the News," "Strange as It May Seem," or by some similar title.

Columbus, Ohio — (UP) — Exasperated by the endless questions of 3-year-old Harold Thompson, a neighbor who was painting his house painted the child red "from head to foot" and sent him home.

The child's mother, Mrs. Lester Thompson, scrubbed him clean — except for a few red splotches — and sent him out to play again.

A few minutes later, she charged in a police complaint, the child returned. This time he was painted a battleship gray.

It was her last day in Williamsville, and Mrs. Mary McLain, who has lived 50 years there, was saddened at the thought.

But she was willing to leave. Her husband, James, 75-year-old city employe retired, wanted to go back to St. Louis, the home town he had left more than 50 years before.

He had retired a year ago, and his old home had been in his thoughts ever since.

And so they were leaving. The house at 678 Thorn ave., had been sold a week ago. The moving van, loaded with their furniture, was in front, ready to take their goods and their life to St. Louis.

Only one piece of furniture — Mrs. McLain's old worn rocking chair — had been left out.

It remained on the porch, where she had rocked contentedly in it ever since a stroke five years earlier had paralyzed her legs. There, on the porch, she would rock quietly, exchanging greetings with her neighbors. But now she was leaving.

"I'm going to sit down in my good old chair for the last time," Mrs. McLain told her husband, and her voice was sad.

"We've been very happy, haven't we, James?" she murmured as she closed her eyes to fix forever in her mind the sight of the street she was leaving.

After a few moments her husband shook her gently.

"It's time to be going, dear," he warned.

Mrs. McLain did not answer. She had gone on already.

The doctor who examined her said that Mrs. McLain had died of a heart attack.

CONVERTED ASSIGNMENT

Often a reporter goes out on what he believes to be a serious assignment and encounters a situation lending itself much more readily to feature than straight news treatment. Or he may be instructed, "If it isn't worth a news story, write a feature about it," such an order implying what every city editor believes — that a competent reporter should be able to write a feature story about anything. Decision to give feature treatment to what otherwise might be a regular news story may be influenced by another newspaper's having published an earlier account in orthodox style. This happens frequently when the article is of an evening event for an afternoon newspaper and a morning newspaper already has had a story about it.

This is the story of the conversion of a newspaper reporter.

Traditionally he's a hard nut to crack anyway, but when religion is concerned, he's doubly so. Last night he entered the Salvation Army building at Sherman avenue and Greenwood street with a cuss word in his eye and leering sarcasm on his face.

Inside was a big tent, staked out in the regular canvas oval camp-meeting style. The reporter could hear the evangelistic exordium coming from the female in the pulpit.

Pushing back the tent flap, he trod down the sawdust aisle. The female was leading a hymn. He snorted in contempt and looked disdainfully at the weaklings all around him who had religion. The girl in the pulpit attracted his eye — he wasn't an old reporter. She was dressed in the Army's trim uniform and wore the black-ribboned bonnet. There was an aura of something almost celestial around her. It quieted the reporter's disbelief.

Looks Around Him

He looked around him. A carnival procession of lights were stretched over a bar nailed across the tent pole in the rude semblance of a cross. Overhead the canvas top was billowing in a draft, almost as though a prairie wind had struck it. Late visitors came in, like shades of Gypsy Smith and Billy Sunday. They shuffled down the sawdust aisle, stirring up a smell of fresh pine shavings.

The varnished seats down in front that resembled the dismantled rows of some ancient nickelodeon were filling with other shades. There were Adam Goa and his congregation from the holy thinking plains of Kansas. From somewhere came the dulcimer tones of a piano and the muffled percussion of a drum. The reporter wanted to join in the inspired hymn. The tent was billowing above again, and down in front Adam Goa's shades had risen and were whooping up an old chantey. . . .

The reporter, with a bursting chest, seized the hymn book. It was titled "Fralsnings — Armens Sangbok." It wasn't enough to erase the vision of Adam Goa down there in front. Then came the sounds of creaking wagon wheels and grandfather Jewel lived again. He was straight and stalwart and was handing down Miss Mary Ann, with an arm around her waist.

Other late-arriving rustics were gathering outside making noises, and the prairie wind was blowing over groves of trees wherein the young folk paid homage to Eros.

The reporter strove to shut out all this. It was religion, that of his old home state, and it wasn't becoming to his profession. Uncle Jimmy, another famed Kansas exhorter, was stumping up to the pulpit preparatory to the revival meetin' rogations. And there was the shade of Beulah Woolson, the soul who had been inside the gates of heaven. Oh Lord!

The reporter, half blinded, broke suddenly up the sawdust aisle. They were singing a hymn behind him.

> O neighbors have you seen old Rummy,
> With a scowl upon his face?
> I saw him on the street this morning,
> And he's going to leave the place!
> He's going to leave the place!
> Old Rummy's going to pack his baggage,
> For it's getting mighty warm!

The reporter dashed past the poster advertising the Army's sunshine brigade. In the street again, he shook his head clear.

"Cripes," he muttered, "that old-time religion in Evanston, and it almost got me, too!" Evanston (Illinois) *News-Index*

SITUATIONS

Not a single event but a series of them may suggest a featurized situation story to a reporter or editor. Such articles have a strong element of news interest as they summarize and possibly explain what "everybody" is doing or talking about. They are not concocted features but are based upon recent events. In their *Pathways to Print* the late Harry F. Harrington and Lawrence Martin explained the difference between the situation feature and the interpretative article as follows:

The situation feature differs from the strictly interpretative story mainly in that it is content to assemble the evidence pro and con — or at most to offer a symposium of opinion, leaving the interpretation largely to the individual reader. This type of feature article creates nothing essentially new; it simply analyzes and coordinates, smoothing out difficulties and hazy impressions which waylay a reader who is not in a position to understand all of the hidden implications of a series of events. In its fullest expression, the situation story is a fusion of the past, present and future.

A situation story explains the "atmosphere" in which an immediate incident or series of incidents must be understood. It may be known as a "round-up" story.

BY *Ruth Dunbar*

Chicago's first inhabitants — the Indians — are moving back.

Chippewas, Sioux, Potawatomis and members of some 60 other tribes are migrating here at the rate of 100 a month. A controversial relocation program of the federal government has pushed the city's Indian population to nearly 5,000.

During the last year, the migration rate has doubled. Most of the new residents come from reservations in Wisconsin, Minnesota, and Dakotas, Oklahoma, Mississippi and the Southwest — in that order.

The Bureau of Indian Affairs, which administers the program under which Indians are transplanted to Chicago and three other cities, calls it "an opportunity plan."

Kurt Freifuss, director of the Chicago office of the bureau, said it "provides opportunities lacking on reservations, speeds up the integration of the Indian and breaks down a vicious pattern of isolation perpetuated by the reservations."

Others, including some Indian leaders, regard the relocation program as an unfortunate and sometimes forced uprooting.

The most common objections are that too much pressure is put on the Indian to relocate and that he is not prepared for abrupt transition to city life. Some contend the program is another attempt to deprive Indians of their diminishing land holdings.

Why do Indians come to Chicago and what do they dream of finding here?

The Snowball family, full-blooded Winnebagos, arrived a few weeks ago from northern Wisconsin. They discussed their hopes and fears in the waiting room of the Indian Bureau office at 608 S. Dearborn. . . .

Chicago *Sun-Times*

EVENTS

"Go out and see what is going on at — " the city editor may say. His purpose is not investigation, certainly not exposé; rather, he wants a news feature on an organization or activity not lending itself to straight news treatment but of public interest or importance.

BY *Emery Hutchison*

Forty children who know prejudice only as a big word were frolicking in the spray arching from a fire hose.

The sight, a typical one at Camp Reinberg, near Palatine, is a recommended antidote to anyone who has been reading the lynch news from Georgia.

The skins of half the children were dark.

The experiment in inter-racial summer camping is one of the first of its kind.

Ninety-six youngsters, 48 of them Negroes, are enjoying a 10-day outing at the camp under the auspices of two Chicago community houses.

They are the fifth of seven groups from low income families who are taking turns in sharing the fun of outdoor life at the camp.

Watching the bathing youngsters from the shade of a tree was William Brueckner, 47, the outing supervisor and head resident of Emerson House, 645 N. Wood st.

"'The children mix well," he said with satisfaction. "Even the smallest, and we have them as young as 5, discuss their differences in color, but that's all it is to them.

"And we hope that's all it ever will be."

A barefoot Negro boy about 10, stepping as gingerly as a tight-rope walker on the rough grass, headed for his cottage, then stopped with a grimace.

"Mr. Brueckner!" he cried, "How'm I gonna walk in these old sickleburrs?"

Brueckner lifted the boy to one shoulder and carried him on his way.

A 5-year-old Negro boy, slightly envious, decided he also wanted to play "horsie," and an 8-year-old white youngster obliged.

"I got lost today — twice," the "horsie" boasted to his rider.

Henry Cameron, 26, one of the counselors from Parkway Community House, 5120 South Park Way, looked on with a grin.

Cameron, a Negro, is a visiting student from Georgetown, British Guiana.

"They play like brothers," said the lanky youth. "Whatever we cultivate in them here," he added, his face becoming serious, "will be to their advantage later in life." Chicago *Daily News*

STRAIGHT FEATURES

Not related to any current news event, the straight newspaper feature article originates as an idea with a reporter or editor. In gathering material for it, the feature writer may stumble upon newsworthy information which lends weight to his story; the origin of his quest, however, was a desire to supplement rather than expand upon the day's regular news budget.

FAMILIAR PLACES

To make the commonplace attractive is a popular feature assignment. Although the average citizen uses the public parks and beaches, knows the names of the city's leading industries and the locations of important buildings, monuments and other landmarks, he may not be acquainted with the "inside" regarding them — their origin, history, laborious upkeep, etc. The skilled feature writer should be able to find a new interesting angle about the city's most widely known institutions.

BY *Herb Owens*

Milo, Ia. — Seventy-five years ago, in the late years of Pope Pius IX, "some of the boys" in a German Catholic farm settlement about seven miles southeast of here were celebrating the Fourth of July — and they decided the community needed a church.

Enthusiasm sprouted up immediately. Anthony Keller hauled stone out of the hills for a foundation. Michael Ripperger had a tract of good timber. Someone else had a sawmill outfit. All got together and built a church on the brow of a hill, opposite the Rosemount postoffice.

That spirit of enthusiasm and co-operation, carried down through the years by families of the original builders, still thrives around the Church of St. Mary's of Perpetual Help, more widely known as "Rosemount church."

Anniversary

The diamond anniversary will be celebrated on the church grounds next Thursday starting with a mass and continuing through a schedule of games and entertainment. It will end with a dance at night. Last year, approximately 3,500 persons, many coming "home" from many miles away, were at the celebration.

The church now has only one member who was alive when the original Rosemount church was constructed. He is Hubert Keller, 84, son of the farmer who hauled stone for the foundation. . . . Des Moines *Tribune*

OBSCURE PLACES

Straying off the beaten path, the roving reporter finds sections of his own community which neither he nor the "other half" realized exist. Such a reporter is able to make the "ole home town" much more interesting than heretofore.

We visited two nudist camps in New Jersey recently to see just what happens there and what kind of people nudists are.

Both camps — Goodland, a mile and a half from Hackettstown, and Sunshine Park, three miles from Mays Landing on the main road from Philadelphia to Ocean City — are affiliated with the American Sunbathing Association, the leading nudist organization in the country with 35 clubs in 15 states. Two states, New York and Ohio, have anti-nudism laws, though there are some nudist camps in upstate New York.

Both camps are strict about admitting visitors. Starers are thrown out on their ears, and single men are allowed at Sunshine Park only if accompanied by a woman member of their families, or by their fiancees. No liquor or beer is permitted at either of the two camps.

Both Goodland and Sunshine Park are small resort **communities** where members may own or rent small cottages. Accommodations are also available for transients. As at ordinary resorts, the main activities at nudist camps are outdoor sports: swimming, volleyball, boating, sunbathing, etc. — and in the evening games like bridge or ping-pong. The only difference is that at nudist camps you do most or all these things naked.

Going without clothes is not required, but at Sunshine Park almost everyone wears nothing at all, or at most shoes and a sunhat, from getting up time in the morning until retiring at night. At Goodland, clothes are worn at meals.

Before visiting a nudist camp, we were worried about what our reactions might be. We needn't have been. After a few minutes, going without clothes seemed the most natural thing in the world. Our experience, and one of the old hands said it had been his too, was that at first we were conscious only that everyone else was not wearing clothes. Later we remembered we didn't have any on either. . . .   PM

FAMILIAR PERSONS

When a person enters the public limelight for the first time he is worthy of a write-up to satisfy curiosity regarding him. Thereafter, as long as he continues successful or interesting, he is the potential subject of innumerable articles. What is he like? How did he do it? To what does he accredit his success? If he had it to do over again, how would he behave differently? These questions suggest only a few of the many angles from which a widely known citizen may be re-introduced to readers. Frequent practice is to run a series of "who's who" articles on the community's leading figures.

BY *M. W. Newman*

Master builder Ludwig Mies van der Rohe is a modest man, but quite sure of himself — as he has reason to be.

When he sees one of his famous buildings, he puffs up a storm on his cigar and says to himself:

"Well, it still looks pretty good."

The world-famous and much-honored architect, one of the great creative spirits of Chicago, will be 75 Monday.

He is widely regarded as one of the three giants of modern architecture. The other two are the Swiss master, Charles-Edouard Le Corbusier, and the late Frank Lloyd Wright.

To architects everywhere, the German-born Mies van der Rohe is known simply as "Mies" (pronounced Meece).

His skin-and-bones, glass-house style of design first came to full realization in the celebrated apartment buildings at 860–880 Lake Shore Dr.

Those elegant twin towers went up in 1951. They set a style for present-day design that quickly became standard.

Almost everyone imitates the Miesian manner now, usually for the worse. Few seem able to capture the sophistication and purity of style that are Mies' trademark.

His masterly manner is sure to distinguish the 30-story federal courthouse he has designed for the Loop — the first of three buildings that will make up the new federal center at Adams and Dearborn.

Three other architectural firms are associated with Mies in the project, he is quick to point out. But it is no secret who is doing the designing.

"Everything we do is done by reason," he says of his work, considered cold and unfeeling by some persons.

Architecture depends on its time, and this is an unemotional age.

"I do not want to be interesting. I want to be good."

The flamboyant Frank Lloyd Wright, once an admirer of Mies van der Rohe, later took potshots at Mies' unromantic styling. Mies shrugged it off in his quiet way.

Mies is a dapper, friendly man of great courtesy.

He suffers painfully from arthritis, but insisted on arising to greet a visitor in his high-ceilinged, white-walled apartment at 200 E. Pearson.

Mies Van Der Rohe, a widower and grandfather, never has bothered to move into one of his own glass-house buildings.

He likes the way the space flows freely in his roomy apartment. There is little furniture — bearing out Mies' dictum, "Less is more."

On the walls hang paintings by the modern master, Paul Klee.

The best-known Miesian building in the world probably is the $43,000,000 Seagram tower on New York's Park Avenue.

In Chicago, Mies is responsible for 13 luxurious lake front apartment buildings. He often was associated with the late Herbert Greenwald, a dynamic developer.

Mies also created many of the world-renowned buildings on the Illinois Tech campus, including its jewel, Crown Hall.

But Mies never got the chance to finish the campus. He obviously regrets it. Other designers have been given the job.

Unbuilt buildings are nothing new to Mies. One writer called his design for the Chicago exposition hall "the greatest unbuilt building of the 20th century."

Mies also has had other disappointments here. They do not dampen his feelings for Chicago. This was the place, after all, that took him in after he left Hitler Germany, and gave him the chance to build.

"I don't know if 860 (Lake Shore Dr.) could have or would have been built anywhere else," he said.

That, of course was the building that put Mies in the direct line of great Chicago architects —Louis Sullivan, John Wellborn Root, and Frank Lloyd Wright.

"Yes," Mies said with a slow smile, "I like Chicago."

Chicago *Daily News*

OBSCURE PERSONS

Likewise in every community are scores or hundreds of persons, not so much in the limelight, who nevertheless have had picturesque lives or unique experiences. In fact, there probably is nobody about whom an interesting feature article could not be written by a skillful interviewer.

by *Marjorie Lipkin*

When she was just a young girl, Agnes Lucas Wirth's father taught her the importance of protecting a family with life insurance. She was so impressed that she often asked him to have her dolls insured.

Today, Mrs. Lucas, as she is known professionally, has seven children and three grandchildren, and she is one of Cleveland's leading figures in the life insurance field. She, too, teaches children the importance of insurance.

Mrs. Lucas has been in the insurance field 13 years. Before that she was a nurse for 23 years, caring for patients and teaching, mainly at Huron Road Hospital. Some of the nurses she taught served overseas in World War I with the famous Lakeside Unit.

She entered insurance sales work in 1933 when she was left a widow with four children. She since has remarried.

"The children had to eat," she said. "I chose insurance because I wanted to save other women the trouble and hard work I'd had to endure. For 10 years I worked 16 to 18 hours every day, went to school twice a week, and managed a large household, doing all my cleaning, shopping, cooking, baking, mending, washing and ironing. It was hard work, putting four children through school!"

That hard work will be shared from now on, for her son, Robert Lucas, recently returned from five years in the Army, has joined her in the insurance business and shares her small office at the Equitable Life Assurance Society of the United States in the Union Commerce Building. Mrs. Lucas is a special agent for the firm and also conducts her own general insurance business.

"I love it, and it's a wonderful field for a woman," she said. "There are great opportunities for women in the insurance world. They can see some family problems better than most men."

Although she has not practiced nursing officially since her first marriage, Mrs. Lucas says she has been called in to help at nearly every sickness, birth, and death in the neighborhood of her home at 419 Eddy Rd.

Cleveland *Press*

OCCUPATIONAL TYPES

In addition to whatever news interest he may have as an individual, everyone is the potential source of a feature article because of the way in which he earns a living. When hard put to it to find a personality easily worked up into a story, the reporter can seek out someone engaged in a job about which what he has to say can be used effectively.

So you think that certain streetcar conductor is a pretty nice looking girl, eh? So you wink slyly and snap your sleeve garters at her when you think nobody is looking, eh? Here, then, is some good advice:

Next time you feel in a flirtatious mood on that streetcar, it might be prudent to look to the front of the trolley, where the mirror reflects the motorman's face. If he has fastened a baleful eye on you, get off the streetcar and transfer to one going in the opposite direction.

Now hold your seat for just a moment and we'll explain this advice. During the war many motormen were in service and their wives, needing supplementary earnings, were given jobs by the Cleveland Transit System. And even when the landlords were not in service, help was sometimes so badly needed that wives were persuaded to go to work on the streetcars.

Many of these women have retired to domestic life, but others are still working — and doing a fine job, C.T.S. officials aver.

Six Man-and-Wife Teams

In some cases, the husbands and their mates preferred to work on different cars. But from the Denison Avenue-W. 73d station alone there are six couples who prefer to work on the same streetcar.

"I hardly ever saw my husband before I went to work as a conductorette," said one of the wives. "Now we can go to work together and I can talk intelligently about his work and sympathize with his problems. It's a dandy arrangement." . . . Cleveland *Plain Dealer*

HISTORICAL

The familiar or unusual place or person feature quite frequently is historical, as there is no community without a building or citizen associated with some important event of the past. Old-timers like to recall events of yesterday. If possible, the historical feature should be illustrated with pictures taken at the time of the event being recalled.

The mystery of an old sign painted on the upper portion of the west wall of a four-story building at 414–18 Market street, was partly solved today by two St. Louisans who are keenly interested in the history and architecture of the city's oldest buildings. They are John A. Bryan, research architect at the Jefferson National Expansion Memorial, and Dr. William G. Swekosky, a dentist whose hobby is the history of old buildings.

The sign which caused them to delve into old city directories advertises "Crow & Farrell, Dry Goods." Who Crow and Farrell were and the years when they did business have perplexed many persons. Recently, however, Bryan and Swekosky, working independently, decided to find out for themselves.

Bryan, using an old city directory, said he found that the dry goods establishment occupied the ground floor at 418 Market about 1864, but he was unable to identify either Mr. Farrell or Mr. Crow. The latter, he says, is not the Wayman Crow who was a former member of the legislature and a leader in the establishment of Elliott Seminary, now Washington University. Wayman Crow's dry goods firm was on Main (now First) street, Bryan said.

Dr. Swekosky said the firm of Crow and Farrell was in the wholesale and retail dry goods business and rented space at the Market street address from 1868 to 1876. The firm was headed by William F. Crow and

John Farrell, he said, and later was at the northwest corner of Fourth street and Washington avenue, but he was unable to identify the two men any further.

The sign is in black letters on a white background painted on the rough brick wall. It was uncovered when the adjoining five-story commercial structure, on the southeast corner of Market street and Broadway, was torn down last year. The site today is a parking lot. . . .

St. Louis *Post-Dispatch*

STUNTS

The stunt reporter courts adventure and finds it in submarines, airplanes, ambulances, breadlines, slums, morgues, police patrols and all sorts of out-of-the-way places. Reporters impersonate beggars, unemployed persons, street-corner Santa Clauses and criminals to obtain feature stories about the reactions of others and an insight into how certain types of individuals exist.

Riding alongside a milkman on his early morning route. It sounds calm enough, yet if the precautions a dairy owner takes are any indication, it is more hazardous than sailing aloft thousands of feet in the air or clanging through the city to a fire on a hook and ladder.

After producing a signed statement to the effect that in case of some dire mishap the company would be absolved from all blame and responsibility, I was allowed to climb up on the high narrow seat next to Joseph Plenn.

"I've never had an accident," Mr. Plenn assured me, "in the 12 years I've been with the company."

Nevertheless, one wagon a week meets with some accident, sometimes while it is standing still. Motorists are notably reckless in the wee small hours.

"Besides, you might get pneumonia," I was warned, "with ice and water under your seat."

By three o'clock yesterday morning, Mr. Plenn had Fanny hitched and our wagon loaded with great piles of cases holding icy quarts and pints and half-pints.

In the eerie blackness that enveloped the city, there was something cheery about the bright little white wagon with its gleaming candle light, something comforting about the stinging swish of Fanny's tail over my foot. Even the rattling of hundreds of milk bottles as we jogged down deserted streets was pleasant in the deep and sinister silence.

Drowsy householders don't care so much about the clatter of milk bottles or the whistle of a milkman. And occasionally when he calls on his second trip of the day, which starts about eight o'clock, he is severely scolded for his noise.

Sometimes he is scolded for lack of noise. Many families use the milk-wagon in place of an alarm clock and if the wagon is too quiet or is late, their whole day's schedule is thrown out of whack. . . .

Philadelphia *Bulletin*

SITUATIONS

Differing from the round-up story of a series of current news events, the straight situation feature article is "trumped up" by an investigating reporter. What happens to discarded automobiles? What name appears most frequently in the city directory? How do college students earn their tuitions? What pets are most popular in the community? Do men and women differ in what they look for in apartments? These questions suggest the types of assignment which originate as "hunches." Factual, even statistical in content, the written stories nevertheless, were "manufactured."

BY *Dale Morrison*

As you mull over your income tax forms this weekend in a last minute rush to meet the April 17 deadline, you may wonder where it all goes.

Not the money, everybody knows where that goes.

But what about Form 1040 or 1040A or 1040W or Schedule G, or the other monuments to documented confusion that Americans use to keep their government in the green?

When John Q. Taxpayer drops his tax return in the corner mailbox he launches it on a seven-year trip to oblivion with a few interesting way points.

Before it's forgotten, it's processed, probed and purged by a small army of experts.

The government's first processing step, naturally enough, is to remove returns from their envelopes.

It may not sound like much but it's a big job.

This week the Chicago office of the Internal Revenue Service has 140 employes doing nothing but opening envelopes, taking out forms, and noting on the return the amount of money sent in.

Harold R. All, district director of the I.R.S. here, said his office is expected to receive about 600,000 pieces of mail a day early next week.

From Jan. 1 to the week of the tax deadline it receives an average of 80,000 returns a day.

Once the envelope is opened, returns and money — in the form of checks, currency or money order — part company.

At the end of each working day the receipts from the 26 northern Illinois counties served by the Chicago office are deposited in the I.R.S. account of the Federal Reserve Bank of Chicago.

Deposits from personal income tax payments average $11,000,000 a day during the height of the season and total about $2 billion a year.

Uncle Sam can tap the I.R.S. account to meet current expenses the minute the money is in the bank.

Meanwhile, the incoming returns are broken down into more than 20 categories.

Mailing lists are made up from each category — wage-earner, small businessman, farmer, etc. — so that next year each taxpayer receives the same series of forms he filed this year.

At this stage, raw material for statistical surveys is drawn from the forms.

In the next processing step, the arithmetic in each return is checked.

I.R.S. auditors say that of the 2,800,000 taxpayers who file in the Chicago area, many have divergent views on the sum of 2 and 2.

About two-thirds of the returns are checked by hand and eye.

A skilled Comptometer operator can work through 35 returns an hour.

The other third — returns filed on punched card (Form 1040A) — are shipped to the I.R.S.'s service center in Kansas City, Mo.

There, electronics data processing machines check addition hundreds of times faster than flesh and blood processors.

Next comes the check for what revenue men delicately call "irregularities."

Highly trained agents scan each return, looking for those little apparent inconsistencies that frequently send poor John Q. scurrying for his records and sometimes send tax cheats to jail.

More often an agent's curiosity is aroused by what appear to be exorbitant business or medical expenses. The taxpayer is then asked to come in and give documentary proof of his claims.

Occasionally agents pick a return at random and ask the taxpayer to justify it.

Once over the checking hurdles returns are divided into two classes: those that will cost the government money and those that need a bill for the taxpayer.

Of late, the I.R.S. has gone to some pains to get out refunds before it sends out bills.

If a refund is due, the government must pay before June 1 or face 6 per cent interest charges. Interest from taxpayers who owe money starts the day the return is due.

Once accounts are squared the returns are confined to filing cabinets covering some 25,000 square feet of the main Chicago I.R.S. office.

After three years of dust-gathering there, they are moved to the two-square block federal records building at 78th St. and Deamington, where they gather more dust for another four years.

With the expiration of the statute of limitations at the end of seven years, the returns are just so much scrap to the government, just as well forgotten.

The forms are bundled and either sold to scrap dealers or burned.

Chicago *Daily News*

Becoming proficient as a feature writer is excellent preparation for interpretative reporting and writing of more significant happenings in city, state, nation and the world.

APPENDICES

THE REPORTER'S GUIDE

In the opinion of many a newspaper editor, the typical reporter is a near illiterate who is dedicated to the proposition that the preposition is to end sentences with. To help the reporter overcome his ignorance, most newspapers provide him with a style book — and in their very diversity, newspaper style books make some of the most entertaining reading to be found anywhere.

The style books do not always agree on usage. The Indianapolis Star spells it "clew," the Indianapolis News "clue." Most papers capitalize Pope, but the Miami Herald does not. In most papers, rape is rape, but in the Memphis Commercial Appeal it is usually criminal attack. The Minneapolis Star and Tribune permit partial decommissioning of generals ("If it's Lt. Gen. John A. Jones in the first reference, plain Jones will suffice in later references"), but in the New York Times, once a general always a general. And no paper cares to folo the trail blazed by the Chicago Tribune into a virgin land of simplified spelling: altho, thru, sirup, burocracy.

All Women Aren't Ladies. Disagreements multiply in the areas of race and religion. The Miami Herald draws a careful distinction between white cops, who are always "policemen," and Negro cops, who are always "patrolmen." In the Memphis Commercial Appeal if a minister is white, he is "the Rev.," if Negro he is simply "Rev." The Denver Post is explicit on Roman Catholic ritual: "Mass is celebrated, said or read. High Mass is sung, never held. The Rosary is recited or said, never read." But the Miami News takes the easy way out: "Write it 'the mass (or rosary) will be at 7 P.M.' rather than having it sung, read, held, recited, given or said."

Matters of taste and the social amenities come under close style-book scrutiny. The Buffalo Evening News avoids "mention of hideous creatures or gruesome circumstances" and substitutes "glamorous" for "sexy"; the Commercial Appeal warns its reporters to "write nothing that will spoil the appetite." The Chicago Tribune permits "s.o.b.," but defines it as a "Trumanism." The Los Angeles Times, concluding that all women aren't ladies, ungallantly applies its conclusion: "A salesgirl or a saleswoman is not a saleslady, and a washerwoman is not a washlady, so a scrubwoman cannot be a scrublady." In Detroit, the News withholds the title of "Mr." from all males who are not Protestant clergy, dead, or the President of the United States. "However," cautions the News, "other cases may arise in which a tone of respect is desirable; in such cases Mr. may be used."

No One Loses Legs. Some style books draw exquisitely fine beads on proper form. The Salt Lake City Tribune explains the distinction between three cupfuls of sugar and three cups full of sugar, and softly suggests the typographical peril in such words as "shot, suit, short, shift, skit, etc." The Detroit News confidently calls a girl a girl until she reached 21, when she becomes a woman; at 17 a boy becomes a youth, at 21 a man. "Beware of such relative descriptions as elderly, aged or old," says the Washington Post and Times Herald. "Few men under 70 would appreciate those adjectives, and few women this side of the morgue." On Denver's Rocky Mountain News, "animals may speak only with the special permission of the city editor." "Look out for people who lose legs or arms," say the Minneapolis Star and Tribune. "They really don't."

Too often the style books merely belabor the obvious and the picayune. Rare is the reporter anywhere who is not advised that cars do not run into trees (they crash against them). The Commercial Appeal demands that kerosene be identified as coal oil the first time the term is used; the Washington Post style book devotes 450 words to discussing the difference between optometrists, ophthalmologists, oculists, and opticians.

The Jewel. Are newspaper style books necessary? Some newspapers — and possibly thousands of newspaper reporters — think not. The New York Herald Tribune, the Boston Record and American, the Manchester, N.H., Union Leader and many other dailies don't have a style book. But the majority of United States dailies apparently agree with the Washington Post, which holds that consistency of style in a newspaper "is more than a jewel; it is a necessity."

Time Magazine

Appendix **A**

Style

Newspaper style is arbitrary and inconsistent. It differs from paper to paper. In the examples given in this book, the styles of the newspapers from which they were taken have been preserved. The style of the text proper is a compromise between orthodox newspaper style and that recommended in such works as the University of Chicago and Government Printing Office manuals. What follows is a sample style book which has internal consistency.

PREPARATION OF COPY

1. Typewrite all copy. Double or triple space. See that the keys are clean.

2. In the upper left-hand corner of each sheet, write: (a) your name, (b) a "slug" line to indicate the nature of the story, (c) the number of the page. For example:

JONES, HENRY
Watson murder
Page 3

3. Begin the first page half-way down from the top. Leave an inch and a half at the top of each succeeding page.

4. Leave a margin of at least an inch on both sides of the page.

5. Write on only one side of the paper.

6. Never write perpendicularly in the margin.

7. Indicate the end of each article by use of a double cross sign (#) or by the figure "30."

8. Do not write more than one article on a sheet, unless they are to be run under the same head.

9. In case you have a series of short items or personals, list them in paragraph form and indicate their nature in the "slug" line.

10. If you must make corrections in pencil, do so legibly, printing if

necessary. Be particularly careful of proper nouns. To be absolutely certain underscore all *a's, u's* and *w's,* and overscore all *o's, n's* and *m's.*

11. A cross (x) is better than a period in written work.

12. Never divide a word between pages. Avoid dividing between lines. Always end each page with a paragraph.

13. In case you have crossed out something and wish it restored, write "stet" on the side of the page.

14. Designate paragraphs by the symbol L.

15. If you intentionally misspell a word or use slang or an expression which you wish printed, write "Folo Copy" in the margin.

16. Read your own copy before handing it in.

PUNCTUATION

The rules of punctuation are the same as for any other kind of composition. This section, therefore, is merely precautionary and explanatory regarding some difficult and disputed usages:

THE PERIOD:

1. Omit the period after headings, captions, figure and paragraph numbers, subheadings, single-line heads, trigonometric abbreviations, roman numerals, letters not used as abbreviations (in mathematical expressions), and chemical symbols.

2. Use no periods in tabulated matter or in lists set in half-measure.

3. Use no periods after nicknames, as *Joe, Ed, Dan,* etc.

4. Use a series of periods to indicate quoted matter that has been omitted.

5. Omit the period after *per cent.*

6. Use a period between dollars and cents: $5.67.

7. Use a period with abbreviations: *Mr., Mich., Prof.*

THE COMMA:

1. Set off participial phrases by commas, as: *Seeing the man make a move toward the door, he drew his gun and fired.*

2. Use a comma after *to wit, namely, viz., i.e., whereas, resolved,* etc.

3. When two numbers occur together, separate them by commas rather than by dashes.

4. In athletic summaries, separate name of player and abbreviation of position by commas, as *Davidson, qb; Lohr, fb.*

5. Use a comma before a direct quotation.

6. Do not use a comma before "and" in a list: *red, white and blue.*

7. Use a comma when adjectives are coordinate but omit when each is dependent upon what follows, as *a bright young fellow.*

8. Use no comma in *5 hours 25 minutes 13 seconds,* or in *6 feet 1 inch tall.*

9. Punctuate lists of names with cities or states thus: *Harold Black, Pittsburgh; Joseph Mason, Cleveland.*

10. In recording elections use this form: *George Washington, president; John Adams, vice president; Thomas Jefferson, secretary; James Madison, treasurer.*

11. Use a comma in general to indicate a break in the sense. In doubtful cases the decision should be for clearness, even without regard to grammatical construction.

12. Do not use a comma between a man's name and *Jr.* or *Sr.*

13. In sports news punctuate thus: Harvard 10, Yale 5.

14. Observe common grammatical rules regarding uses of commas in parenthetic expressions, words in apposition, with contrasted words and phrases, with introductory words and phrases, in direct address, in phrases indicating residence, position, or title, in large numbers, with restrictive and nonrestrictive clauses, etc.

THE COLON:

1. Use a colon before a quotation of more than one sentence.

2. Use a colon in writing the time of day, as *4:15 o'clock.*

3. Note the use of the colon after the subtitles of this section on punctuation.

4. Use a colon to introduce a series of results, as *The following officers were elected: George Washington, president, etc.*

5. Use a colon to introduce a resolution, as *Resolved: That the government should own the railroads.*

6. Use a colon between chapter and verse in scriptural references, as *Genesis 6:15–20.*

THE SEMICOLON:

1. Use a semicolon to separate coordinate clauses of the same sentence, when they are not separated by a coordinate conjunction, as *This is not the right road; we should have turned left at the cross-roads.*

2. Use a semicolon in a series of names and addresses, as *Maurice Bogart, Brooklyn; Bruce Burnham, Scranton; John Winslow, Easton.*

3. Use a semicolon between coordinate clauses which are joined by a conjunctive adverb such as *therefore, however, so, hence, nevertheless,*

etc., as *We started earlier than we expected; nevertheless, we did not arrive on time.*

4. Punctuate results of balloting thus: *yeas 5; nays 3.*

5. The semicolon rapidly is being replaced by the comma but sometimes is required for clearness in long involved sentences.

THE DASH:

1. Avoid the dash in punctuation, using instead either commas or parentheses.

2. Use a dash after *First — , Second — , Third —.*

3. Use a dash in cases as *Table 2 — Continued: Note —.*

4. Use a dash after a man's name at the beginning of an interview, as *Arthur Griswold — I have no statement to make.* (Use no quotation marks for this form.)

5. Use a dash after Q. and A. in verbatim testimony, as *Q. — Where were you born? A. — Tokio.*

6. Use a dash for emphatic pause, as *He drew his sword and killed — a mosquito.*

7. Use a dash for unfinished sentences, putting quotation marks, if any, outside the dash, as *Well, if I were —*

8. In announcing texts of sermons use the form: *First Corinthians* 15:1–10.

9. Use a dash in summaries of track meets, as *100 yard dash — Haber, Arizona, first; George, New Mexico, second; Nelson, Texas, third. Time* 10:1–5.

10. The only other mark of punctuation to be used with a dash is a period.

THE APOSTROPHE:

1. Use an apostrophe to mark an omission in contractions of words, as *I've, can't, don't, '95.*

2. Omit the apostrophe in such words, as *phone, varsity, bus.*

3. Use an apostrophe in making plurals of letters, but not plurals of figures, as *four A's, early '90s.*

4. Use an apostrophe for possessives except of pronouns, as *the girl's shoes, Burns' poems;* but *its, ours, yours, his.*

5. In referring to more than one member of the Jones family write *Joneses* instead of *Jones'.*

6. Write *state prison, state rights,* etc., not *state's prison.*

7. Omit the apostrophe in such names as *Merchants and Farmers bank* if the concern itself omits it.

8. Use one apostrophe only to indicate common possession, as *Bucknell and Swarthmore's goat.*

QUOTATION MARKS:

1. Quote the subjects of lectures, articles in periodicals, names of books, etc., names of plays, but not characters.
2. Place marks of punctuation inside quotation marks; use double or regular quotation marks on the outside and single quotation marks within.
3. If a quotation is to have more than one paragraph in it, use quotation marks at the beginning of each paragraph, but at the end of the last one only.
4. Use quotation marks to set off a word of unusual meaning, or an unfamiliar or coined word. If the word is repeated several times, it is not necessary to repeat the quotation marks.
5. Do not use quotation marks for common nicknames, as *Bobo Olson, Kid Gavilan, Yogi Berra,* except when used with the name, as *Carl "Bobo" Olson.*
6. Do not quote names of newspapers or magazines.
7. Extracts from other papers when followed by a dash and the name of the paper need no quotation marks. Example: . . . . — The *Milwaukee Journal.*
8. Matter that is centered or set in smaller type than the context does not need quotation marks.
9. Do not quote a communication carrying date and signature.

PARENTHESES:

1. Avoid parentheses as much as possible in news copy.
2. When parentheses are used, punctuate the rest of the sentence as if the parentheses and the enclosed words were not there.
3. If any mark is required after the portion of the sentence preceding the parentheses, put it after the second curve.
4. When the name of the state, though not a part of the title of a newspaper, is given with the title, use this form: The Madison (Wis.) *Capital-Times.* Omit the name of the state after large cities, as The Denver *Post.*

THE INTERROGATION POINT:

Use the interrogation point at the end of all expressions containing a question, rhetorical or otherwise.

THE HYPHEN:

1. Use a hyphen with prefixes to proper names, as *un-American, anti-Catholic.*

2. Use a hyphen in writing figures, as *thirty-five, ninety-ninth, one-seventh.*

3. Omit the hyphen in titles, as *vice president, managing editor, editor in chief, attorney general.* But: *captain-elect, all-college.*

4. Use a hyphen in measures only if used as adjectives, as *3-in. valve, 7-ft. plank;* but *3 in. long.*

5. Write as one word: *baseball, basketball, football, today, tonight, yesterday, homecoming, cheerleader, textbook, thunderstorm, anyone, cannot, bookcase, downstate, upstate, snowstorm, lineup, writeup, makeup.*

6. Words compounded of the following prefixes and suffixes are generally written solid: *a-, after-, ante-, auto-, bi-, demi-, -ever, grand-, -holder, in-, inter-, intra-, -less, mid-, mis-, off-, on-, over-, post-, re-, -some, sub-, super-, tri-, un-, up-, -ward, -wise, -with.*

7. Words compounded with the following prefixes and suffixes generally are hyphenated: *able-, brother-, by-, cross-, -elect, ex-, father-, great-, half-, -hand, mother-, open-, public-, quarter-, -rate, self-.*

8. Write as separate words: *post office, mass meeting, proof reader, copy reader, per cent, pro temp, some way, half nelson, half dozen, half dollar, all right, any time, back yards, every time, ex officio, fellow man, no one, police court, squeeze play, freshman cabinet, fire department.*

9. The tendency is toward combining such words and toward the elimination of the hyphen with prefixes and suffixes.

10. Use a hyphen in scores, as *Kentucky won 8-5.*

WORD DIVISION:

1. Avoid dividing words between lines.

2. Always divide words by syllables.

3. Do not divide short words or monosyllables.

4. Do not separate a consonant from a vowel that affects its pronunciation, as *nec-essity* for *ne-cessity.*

5. Do not divide a diphthong or separate two successive vowels, one of which is silent, as *bo-wing, pe-ople,* for *bow-ing, peo-ple.*

6. Do not separate a syllable that has been added to a word by the addition of an *s,* as *financ-es.*

7. Do not divide hyphenated words except at the syllable where the regular hyphen comes.

8. Do not begin a line with a hyphen.

9. Do not divide words between pages.

CAPITALIZATION

CAPITALIZE:

1. All proper nouns, names of the months and days of the week.

2. Names of political parties and organizations, as *Republican, Democratic, Bolsheviki, Fascist, the Republic of France, the British Empire, the Kingdom of Norway.*

3. All titles preceding names, as *Prof. R. L. Strong, Editor in Chief Paul Gilmore;* but *Dr. C. R. Richards, president; George Fearnside, managing editor.*

4. Names of sections of the country, as *East, Middlewest, Orient.* Do not capitalize points of the compass, as *east, west, south, north,* or *oriental, occidental,* etc.

5. Names of religious denominations and nouns and pronouns referring to a deity, as *the Koran, the Old Testament, Psalms, Book of Job.*

6. Principal words in the titles of books, plays, articles, poems, pictures, newspapers, lectures, etc., including the initial *A* or *The,* as *The Los Angeles Times,* "*The Grandmothers*" by *Glenway Wescott.*

7. Abbreviations of college degrees, as *B.A., Ph.D., M.A.*

8. Names of races, nationalities and localities, as *Yankee, Negro, Creole, Hoosier.*

9. Nicknames of cities, states, athletic organizations, etc., as the *Leopards, the Giants, the Spring City five.*

10. Distinguishing names of holidays and festivals, as *Fourth of July, Labor Day, New Year's Day, Easter.*

11. Chemical compounds, as $NaCl$, H_2O.

12. Names of national and state legislative bodies when specific ones are meant, as *Congress, House of Representatives* or *House, Parliament, General Assembly.*

13. *Cabinet, University, Council, Library, Faculty, Varsity,* etc., when standing alone for particular organizations, as *He made the Varsity his second year; The Library will be open today.*

14. *Union, Republic, the States* when referring to the United States, but do not capitalize adjectives such as *national, federal,* etc.

15. *Stars and Stripes, Old Glory, Union Jack,* etc.

16. Epithets affixed to proper names, as *Alexander the Great.*

17. The first word of a direct or indirect quotation which would make a complete sentence by itself, as *John said,* "*We must go.*"

18. *No., Fig., Chapter, Room, Hotel, Gulf, Lake,* etc., when followed by a number or letter or name, as *No. 24, Fig. 6, Chapter IV, Parlor A, Room 61, Hotel Walcott, Gulf of Mexico, Highway 12, Lake Geneva.*

19. The distinguishing words, but *not* the general terms in names of clubs, societies, companies, corporations, etc., as *Good Fellowship society, American Mathematical society, Federation of German clubs, Freshman cabinet, Public Speaking forum,* etc.

20. The distinguishing words, but *not* the general terms in names of streets, buildings, hotels, stations, wards, districts, universities, colleges, high schools, academies, gymnasiums, libraries, etc., as *Broad street, Union station, Coxe laboratory, Packer hall, Ninth ward, Red river, Princeton university, Lawrence college, Baylor high school, St. Peter's church, Taylor gymnasium, Packard laboratory.*

DO NOT CAPITALIZE:

1. Titles of any kind when used after names.
2. Names as classes as, *freshman, sophomore,* etc.
3. Names of studies or departments except when names of languages, as *English, Latin,* but *mathematics, chemistry, botany,* etc. And: *the department of physics, the biology department.*
4. College degrees when spelled out, as *bachelor of arts.*
5. Points of the compass, as *north, southwest.*
6. Scientific names of plants, animals and birds.
7. *Government, administration, state* or *nation.*
8. The subject of a debate, as *Resolved: That capital punishment should be abolished.*
9. Write *northern Africa, central Europe,* etc.
10. *High school, college, university,* etc., when used indefinitely, as *he attends high school, and she goes to college.*
11. *Fraternity, faculty, undergraduate, graduate, alumni.*
12. Seasons of the year, as *spring, autumn, winter, summer.*
13. Common religious terms, as *heaven, hell, devil, angelic, scriptures, gospel, biblical.*
14. Common nouns that were originally proper nouns, as *prussian blue, india rubber, plaster of paris, bessemer steel.*
15. *a.m.* and *p.m.,* but *M.*
16. The prefixes *von, de, di, le, la,* etc., except when they begin sentences.
17. *Club, society, association, company, army, navy,* etc.
18. *Spring show, alma mater, tariff act, chapel, post office, north pole, fatherland, fire ordinance, middle ages, varsity wrestlers, freshmen swimmers, athletic teams, trophy room,* etc.
19. Boards and committees, as *board of publications, executive committee, decorations committee, board of trustees.*
20. Political and legislative bodies, bureaus, offices, departments, legal bodies, etc., when standing alone, as *school board, weather bureau, health*

department, nominating committee, assembly, city council, senate, congress, parliament.

21. When in doubt, do NOT capitalize.

ABBREVIATIONS

ABBREVIATE:

1. Titles before names, as *Mr., Mrs., Dr., Gen., Mme., the Rev.,* military terms, etc.

2. Write *Prof. M. A. Johnson,* but *Professor Johnson.*

3. Names of states only when they follow names of cities, as *Nashville, Tenn.* Never write, *He lives in Tenn.*

4. Names of months that contain more than five letters, but only in dates and date lines, as *Sept. 15, Trenton, N.J.*

5. *Number* before figures, as *No. 17.*

6. Units of measure when preceded by numerals, as *7 ft. 2 in.*

7. Common designations of weights and measures in the singular only, as *lb.* but not *lbs., in.* but not *ins.* Exceptions: *Figs. 1 and 2, Vols. 3 and 4, Nos. 5 and 6.*

8. *Master of arts* to *M.A., bachelor of arts* to *B.A., doctor of philosophy* to *Ph.D.* and other academic titles used with names, as *John Dollard, Ph.D.* NEVER *Dr. John Dollard, Ph.D.*

9. *Saint* and *Mount* in proper names, but not *Fort,* as *St. John, Mt. Wilson,* but *Fort Wayne.*

10. *Morning* to *a.m.,* and *afternoon* to *p.m.* Never let the hour stand alone. It is *7:30 p.m. yesterday,* or *7:30 o'clock last evening.*

11. Widely-known organizations, as *D.A.R., I.O.O.F., A.E.F., R.O.TC, B.P.O.E., G.A.R., L.O.O.M.,* etc.

12. *North, South,* etc., in addresses, as *751 W. Cherry street.*

DO NOT ABBREVIATE:

1. Christian names, as *Robert, Thomas, Alexander,* except in sports stories.

2. *University, street, avenue, railway, institute, boulevard,* etc.

3. The *United States of America,* except *U.S.A.* or *U.S.N.* written after names of army and navy men; also *U.S.S. Texas; Utica, N.Y., U.S.A.*

4. Names of days of the week, or those of months of the year, except in datelines.

5. *Christmas* to *Xmas, Brothers* to *Bros.*

6. The title *Senator, Representative, Congressman, Chaplain, Sec-*

retary, Treasurer, Vice President, President, Historian, Sergeant at Arms,
when used either before or after a name.

7. *Per cent* to %; *cents* to *cts.* or *c.* or *¢.*

8. Avoid *etc.* in a news story.

9. Never begin a sentence with an abbreviation or an Arabic numeral
unless the abbreviation is part of a title.

10. *Company, corporation, association, society,* etc.

11. *Department* to *dept., mathematics* to *math., building* to *bldg.,*
and to *&* except in names of companies.

TITLES

1. Give first names or initials of persons the first time they are
mentioned in a news story. Use the first name or initials, as *John R. Jones*
or *J. R. Jones,* but NEVER *Mr. John R. Jones* or *Mr. J. R. Jones.* The title
Mr. replaces the first name or initials.

2. Give the first name of an unmarried woman, not the initials only:
Miss Mary Sweet, not *Miss M. A. Sweet.*

3. The correct form is: *The Rev. John R. Jones* or *The Rev. Mr.*
Jones. Do not omit the *The.*

4. Never say *Mrs. Doctor* or *Mrs. Professor.* The title belongs to the
husband only.

5. Titles usually are better placed after names and then in small
letters, as *Herbert Weeks, superintendent of the water works.*

6. Get the correct titles for faculty members: *coach, president, dean,*
professor, instructor, director.

7. Titles used before a name always should be capitalized.

8. In reporting the results of an election this form is preferable:
Officers-elect were: Jacob Potts, president; Adellon Hogan, vice president;
Clayton Bentley, secretary; Coleman Gunderson, treasurer. Consistency
is the rule. DO NOT capitalize some and not others, or abbreviate some and
write out others.

9. Write *Mr. and Mrs. A. R. Filbey,* not *A. R. Filbey and wife.*

10. Write *Prof. and Mrs. H. L. Flynn,* not *Mr. and Mrs. Prof. H. L.*
Flynn.

11. Never use *Honorable* or *Hon.*

FIGURES

1. Spell out figures from one to ten; eleven and above should be
used as figures. Note exceptions below.

2. Use 9 *p.m.; 3:45 o'clock this afternoon.*

3. Use *Sept. 30, 1961.* Omit the *st., th., rd.,* etc. after dates.

4. Use figures for sums of money, as *$5, $76.23;* not *$5.00.*

5. Use figures for street numbers, as *1187 Monroe street.*

6. Use figures for scores, degrees of temperature, telephone numbers, automobile licenses, latitudes and longitudes, distances, times in races, betting odds, votes, percentages, prices, dimensions, etc. as *90 degrees, 65 per cent, 90 × 125 feet, 60-foot beam,* etc.

7. The form *60th* is optional with *sixtieth.*

8. Avoid beginning a sentence with a figure. If you do, the figure must be spelled out, as *Seventy members of the club.*

9. In sentences requiring more than one numeral, one below and the other above ten, spell out both, as *from five to fifteen years.*

10. Use figures for sports records, as *Ohio State 6, Purdue 0.*

11. Use figures for ages, as *He was 74 years old; 2-year-old Kenneth.*

12. Spell out phrases, as *one case in a thousand, ninety-nine men out of a hundred.*

13. Express a series of two or more years thus: *1961–62.*

14. In football matters use figures to enumerate yard lines, as *9-yard line.* Likewise, in track accounts use *100-yard dash, 16-pound hammer throw.*

Copy Reader's Symbols

ⓢ
si̠ter

Circling an inserted letter is an extra precaution to assure its being placed correctly.

(of the league)
championship⟋by winning

When a number of words are inserted, lines should be used to indicate their position.

b⟋o⟋r⟋ther

Letter order should be corrected by a curved line.

⌒
semiannual

Parentheses may be used to set off an inserted mark of punctuation.

he (only⟋won

Word order should be corrected by a single curved line.

Chicago ~~on last~~ Monday

When a word is crossed out, the sentence should be "closed up."

Hershey said that, ~~he saw the three enter~~ and ~~that~~ (the three were looking....

When more than a line is crossed out, sentence continuity should be indicated by a continuity line.

another⟋man

A slanting line should be used to separate words run together.

an‿other

If the typewriter "stutters," words should be closed up.

america
‗

Two short lines under a letter mean that the letter should be capitalized.

Man

A slanting line through a capital letter means letter should be small.

⑤

Circling a figure means that it should be spelled out.

(forty-nine)

Circling a spelled-out figure means that the numeral should be used.

(General)

Circling a word that is spelled out means that the word should be abbreviated.

(Pres.)

Circling an abbreviation means that the word should be spelled out.

show. ⌐Of general...

A new paragraph should be indicated by a right-angle line.

not

A straight line under a word means that the word should be set in italics.

not

A wavy line under a word means that the word should be in bold face.

found
WARM
ocean

In written copy u's, w's, and a's should be underscored, and n's, m's, and o's overscored.

#-30-

A double-cross mark or the figure "30" should be used to indicate the end of an article.

Proof Reader's Symbols

⊔ Four score and seven yearsago our fathers brought ⊔
forth on this continent a new nation, conceived in
liberty, and dedicated to the

⌒proposition that all men are created equal. Now we ＝
are engaged in a great civil war, testing whether that
∧ nation‸or any nation so conceived and so dedicated,
can⎵long endure. We are met on a great battlefield ⌒
of that war. We have come to ‾dedicate a portion of ⊙
that field as a final resting-place‾ for those who here
𝒮 here gave their lives that that Ńation might live. it *l.c./ cap*
is altogether fitting and proper that we should do this.

⊙ But, in a large sense‸we cannot dedicate—we can-
not consecrate—we cannot hallow‸this ground⎵ The |—|⊙
brave men, living and dead, who struggled here, have
consecrated it far above our poor power to add or detract. The world will little not‸nor long remember
𝓉𝓇. what we� here⎰say⎱ but it can never forget wh⌒at they ⊂
did here.

It is for us, the living, rather, to be here dedẟicated 𝒮
w.f. to the unfi̲nished work which they who fought here
have thus far so nobly advanced. It is rather for us
to be here dedicated to the great task remaining before
us—that from these honored dead we take increased
devotion to that cause for which they gave the las̲t full
;/ measure of devotion‸that we here highly resolve that
these dead shall not have died in vain; that this nation,
under ǵod, shall have a new birth of freedom; and that *cap.*
government of the people, by the people, for the people,
shall not perish from the earth.

(Address at the dedication of the Gettysburg Na- *ital.*
𝓉 Ńional Cemetery, Nov. 19, 1863. Reprint from‸Abra- ⋎
ham Lincoln Complete Works," by Nicholay and Hay).

507

PUNCTUATION

⊙	Insert period.
⸴/	Insert comma.
;/	Insert semicolon.
⊙	Insert colon.
⩗	Insert apostrophe.
⩗⩗	Insert double quotation marks.
⩗	Insert single quotation marks.
⊢¹⊣	Put in one-em dash.
⊢²⊣	Put in two-em dash.
=/	Put in hyphen.
?/	Put in question mark.
!/	Put in exclamation mark.

INSERTION AND OMISSION

⋀	Put in element indicated in margin in place shown by caret.
⸿	Take out element indicated.
stet	Don't make change indicated; let it stand as it is.
~~loan~~	A line of dots is placed under the element that is to remain as it is.

KIND OF TYPE

Rom.   Change to Roman type.

Ital.   Change to Italic type.

cap.   Change to capital letter.

s.c.   Change to small capital letter.

l.c.   Change to lower case, or small letter.

b.f.   Change to black, or bold face, type.

w.f.   Substitute type from regular font for that of wrong font.

X   Substitute perfect for imperfect type.

PARAGRAPHING

¶   Begin a new paragraph.

no ¶   Don't begin a new paragraph.

SPACING

vvv   Correct uneven spacing between words.

Put in space.

⌒   Close up by taking out all spacing.

⊕   Close up but leave some space.

⌒   Reduce the space.

ⱴ   Push down a slug that prints.

////   Put in thin space between letters, *i.e.,* "letter space."

POSITION

⊏   Move to the left.

⊐   Move to the right.

⊓   Move up.

⊔   Move down.

□   Indent one em.

‖   Make lines parallel.

=   Make letters align.

ǝ   Turn over element that is upside down.

tr.   Transpose order of words, letters, or figures.

UNCERTAINTY

Qu?   Look this up to see whether or not it is correct.

See copy (out)   See what has been omitted in proof by comparing with copy.

Newspaper Terms

Ad — Abbreviation for advertisement.

Add — Fresh copy to be added to a story already written.

Advance — A preliminary story.

Agate — A very small type, usually used for advertising copy only.

Alive — Copy or type still usable.

A.M.s. — Morning newspapers.

Angle — A phase or part of a story.

A.N.P.A. — American Newspaper Publishers association.

AP — Associated Press.

Art — All newspaper illustrations are called art.

Assignment — A reportorial task.

A.S.N.E. — American Society of Newspaper Editors.

Bank — A part of a headline. Also called "deck."

Banner — A headline extending across the entire page. Also called "streamer."

Beat — A reporter's regular run. Also means a "scoop" or exclusive story.

B.F. — Bold face.

Boil — Reduce in size.

Boiler plate — Stereotyped material ready for mounting.

Bold face — Darker type.

Box — A story, usually short, enclosed in rules.

Break — The point at which a story must be continued to another page. Also refers to the availability of news.

Bug — A Morse telegraph operator's sending apparatus.

Bull dog — The early edition of a newspaper.

Bulletin — A short lead of important or last minute information, usually to be printed at the head of another story related to the same event.

By-line — The author's name at the top of a story.

Canned copy — Publicity.

Caps — Capital letters. Also called "upper case" to distinguish them from small letters or "lower case."

Caption — The headline above a piece of art.

Chase — Form in which columns of type are locked to make a page.

Clip — A clipped newspaper article.

Copy — All written material.

Cover — Be responsible for a story of an event.

Credit line — Acknowledgment of indebtedness to someone, as for loan of a cut, etc.

Cropping — Reducing the size of an illustration by trimming.

Cub — A beginning reporter.

Cut — A zinc etching or halftone engraving.

Cutlines — Identification of the subjects of a piece of art, printed below the illustration.

Dateline — The city from which a news dispatch comes and the date of the dispatch.

Deadline — The last moment at which copy can be accepted for an issue.

Deck — See "bank."

Dingbat — A decorative bit of type.

Double truck — Two adjacent pages made up as one.

DPR, NPR — Day press rates; night press rates. Used on telegrams.

Drop — A smaller head to continue after a streamer or banner.

Dummy — Drawn plan for a news page makeup.

Ear — A small box in the upper corner of the front page.

Electro — Electrotype.

Em — A unit for measuring line lengths and column widths.

En — Half a quad em.

File — In press association bureaus it means arrange copy for sending over the wire.

Filler — Short items for use in rectifying a page.

Flag — The newspaper's name on the editorial page.

Flash — A short press association notice of an important event.

Flimsy — Thin paper used in making carbon copies.

Flush — Even with a margin.

Folio — Page number.

Font — A complete assortment of type of a particular design.

Form — A page of type locked in a chase.

Fudge — A detachable part of a page plate which may be replaced by another to make possible the printing of last-minute news.

FYI — For your information.

Galley — A metal tray to hold type.

Guide — A word or words at the top of a reporter's copy to indicate the nature of the story. Also called "slug."

Halftone — Ordinary cut printed from plate consisting of small dots.

Handout — Publicity release.

Head — Headline.

Hell box — Box in which discarded type is thrown.

Hold — Delay publication until further orders.

HTK — Head to come. Used when story is sent to composing room before headline is prepared.

Insert — A paragraph or paragraphs to be inserted in copy already written.

Jump — Break a story from one page to another.

Justify — Filling out a line of type by spacing so that it will be even on each side.

Kill — Do not use.

Layout — Arrangement of pictures or other art work from which a single cut is to be made.

Letterpress printing — Printing from a raised or relief surface, like a rubber stamp.

l.c. — Lower case or small type.

Linage — The total number of lines of an advertisement or number of advertisements, computed in agate lines of which there are 14 to a column inch.

Line — Also called "banner" or "streamer."

Linotype — Type setting machine.

Lobster shift — Working hours after an edition is out.

Lockup — Tightening up type matter in a chase to make page ready for stereotyping.

Log or Logotype — Trade name of advertiser, masthead of newspaper, etc.

Make over — Change the nature of a page already set in type and make a new stereotype of it.

Makeup — Placing articles in position for printing in a page.

Masthead — Statement of ownership, membership in associations, etc., on the editorial page.

Matrix — Papier mâché material on which impression of form is made for the purpose of casting a plate.

Media Records — A national organization which measures advertising in newspapers.

Mill — Typewriter.

Offset — Method of lithographing printing whereby the impression is transferred to a rubber blanket which in turn transfers it to paper.

Overset — Additional type for which there was no room in edition.

Pad — Make longer.

Pi — Mixed type.

Pica — Twelve-point type.

Pick up — Continue with copy already set.

Pix — Picture.

Play up — Emphasize or feature.

P.M.'s — Afternoon newspapers.

Point — One-twelfth of a pica (about $\frac{1}{72}$ of an inch), a unit of type measurement.

Precede — Material to be printed ahead of copy already set.

Presses — Machines which print, cut and fold newspapers.

Printer — Automatic printer telegraph machine which types a story as it comes in over wire.

Proof — First impression of set type on which corrections are made.

Quads—Blank pieces of metal used to fill out lines when type does not do so.

Query — Brief statement by a correspondent of a story which he can send if it is wanted.

Quoin — Lock used to tighten lead in form.

Release — Advanced copy held for publication at a certain time.

Replate — Make over an edition when important news arrives after the presses have started.

Retouching — Correcting or improving art work.

Ribbon — A smaller streamer headline run beneath a larger.

Rim — Outer edge of a central copy desk.

Roto — Rotogravure.

Rule — Written on copy this means that a lead or insert or add is still to come.

Run — A beat.

Runover — Part of a story which continues on a second page.

Sacred cow — Subject always receiving favorable mention.

Schedule — List of day's assignments.

Scoop — An exclusive story.

Shirttail — A short related article run at the end of a longer one.

Sidebar — A complete article on one phase of a longer story, run separately.

Slant — Emphasize a particular point in writing.

Slot — Inside of a semi-circular copy reading desk.

Slug — Guideline to indicate nature of copy. Also a line of type.

Spread — Playing up an important story, usually with art work.

Stereotyping — Process of converting a flat newspaper page form into a cylindrical metal plate to fit rotary presses.

Stet — Restore struck part of news copy.

Stick — A small amount of type, usually about two inches, or 150 words of copy.

Stone — The table on which chases are placed.

Streamer — See "banner."

String — A correspondent's clippings pasted together and sent in for measurement to determine pay due him.

Subhead — Small headline inserted in the body of a story.

Take — A portion of copy of a long story.

Thirty — End of a news story.

Tight — Not much room for news material.

Trim — Reduce in size.

Type face — The design of a type letter.

UPI — United Press International.

Wide open — Considerable room for news material.

INDEX

Index

Abbreviations, 501–502
Academic freedom, 388
Academic preparation, 21–22
Accidents, 278–283
Accuracy, 133–138
Achievement, individuals, 162; organizations, 163
Actions, civil, 334–336
Active voice, 109–110
Address, 160
Adjectives, 126–127
Admitting to probate, 338–339
Adverbs, 127–128
Adverse criticism, public relations, 42
Age, 160–161
A History of Bigotry, 443
Aldrich, Richard, 462
American and English Encyclopedia of Law, 148
American Bar association, 320
American Newspaper Publishers association, 44
American Society of Newspaper Editors, 9–10; 27–29; 44; 146; 186; 427
Analysis, 199–200
Anecdotes, gossip, 230–231
"A Newspaperman's Prayer," 442
Appeals, legal, 342–343
Appellate courts, 324
Arraignment, 303
Associated Press, 15; 179; 189; 249; vs International News, 147
Associated Press Managing Editors, 16; 19; 21; 51; 53–54; 99; 101; 129; 165
Astonisher lead, 80
Atlanta business code, 431–433

Atlanta *Journal*, 450
Attractive, making it, 84–95; 164
Authority in news, 138–142
Automation and schools, 387–388
Avoiding banality, 111–113

Backgrounding the News, 259; 316
Baltimore *Sun*, 191; 282; 320
Banality, avoiding, 111–113
Bankruptcy, 336
"Banquets," 236
Bean, Louis, 350
Beazell, S. P., 462
Beinhorn, Sherman, 142–145
Best evidence, 342
Biographical sidebars, 116–167
Black Creed, 429
Blanshard, Paul, 449
Block paragraphing, 58–59
Blotter, police, 294–296
Board, county, 388–389
Body of news story, 56–61; speech, 250–253
Book reviews, 474–475
Boosts, 125
Boss Rule, 353
Boxes, 82
"Break That Cliché," 98
Brevities, sources of, 213–214
Bromides, 112
Brown, Rep. Clarence, 171
Brown, Maynard, 15
Buffalo *Evening News*, 205
Burden of proof, 340
Buried feature, 180
Business, 407–415
"Business is Romantic," 406

Campaigns, political, 358–363
Campbell, Angus, 350
Canham, Erwin D., 86
Capitalization, 499–501
Capone, Al, 325
Carswell, Howard, 406
Cartridge lead, 80
Carty, James W., Jr., 447–448
Case, Sen. Francis, 129
Catholic Power and American Freedom, 449
Causes and motives, 198–199
Certiorari, 337
Chall, Mrs. Jeanne S., 103
Changing attitudes, science, 450
Charnley, Mitchell, 133
Chicago *Daily News,* 102; 122; 171; 205; 414; 417–420
Chicago *Sun,* 230; 236
Chicago *Sun-Times,* 317
Children, exceptional, 387
Childs, Marquis W., 17
Christian Science Monitor, 86; 315
Chronological writing, 60–61
Church and politics, 445–446
Circumstances of death, 261–262
Circumstantial evidence, 341
City clerk, 377
City council, 193–197; 374–376
City government, 371–388
Civil actions, 334–336
Civil law, 326–337
Civil service, 383
Civil trials, 332–333
Clark, Austin H., 460
Clauses, superfluous, 108
Clerk, city, 377; county, 389
Clichés, 98; 111
Closing statements, criminal, 309
Cockrell, James A., 413
Code of ethics, 27–29; 442
Codes, business, 429–433
Coincidences, 171
Combined stories, 183
Coming-out parties, 225
Comparisons, 200–201
Completing the account, 187–197
Comprehensive lead, 170; 182
Conciseness, 104–110
Condemnation suits, 335
Conditional clause lead, 78
Confidence, winning reader, 131–155

Connotation, 124–125
Consequence, 70–71
Conservatism, Radicalism and the Scientific Method, 350
Contemporary trends, 51
Contesting a will, 339
Contrast lead, 88
Controversy, religious, 447
Conventions, 241–245; political, 337–338
Converted assignment, 479–480
Cony, Edward R., 204
Copy, preparation of, 493–494
Copy reader's symbols, 505–506
Copyright, 146–148
Corporation counsel, 377
Correct nomenclature, church, 447–448
Correct usage, 113–119
Costume, bride's, 228
County courts, 323; government, 388–391; politics, 353–354
Court system, 322–326
Cowlitz County Advocate, 132
Credo, newspaperman's, 2
Crime news, 291–296; ethics, 314–318; statistics, 299–300
Criminal procedure, 302–307; trials, 307–314
Criticism, 468–473
Cross, Harold L., 146
Crowded lead, 81
Cub reporting, 22–23
Cumulative interest, 92–93

Dale, Edgar, 103
Damage suits, 334
Damages, libel, 152
Dana, Charles, 442
Dance, 476–477
Dangerous words, 150–152
Dangers of public relations, 43–44
Dates, 228
David, Judge Joseph B., 320
Davis, Elmer, 129–130
Davis, Richard Harding, 8
Davis, Watson, 454
Decision making, reportorial, 26
Decorations, society, 224
"Deep Thinking," 86
Defending an action, law, 330–332
Defense of public relations, 42–43
Defenses against libel, 152–154

Definitions, financial, 422–427; semantics, 123–124; weather, 399–403
Delayed identification, 166
Denials, interviews, 39
Description, 163–164
Descriptive lead, 88–89
Des Moines *Register*, 286
Details, superfluous, 105
Dialogue lead, 92
Direct address, 94–95
Disasters, 278–283
Divorce, 334–335
Double identification, 165
Dow Jones & Co., 417; 420
Dun and Bradstreet, 420

Edison Electric institute, 409
Editor & Publisher, 2; 40; 66; 256
Editorializing, 124–125
Education, 384–388
Eisenhower, Dwight D., 146; 161
Elections, 364–367
Elements of interest, accidents, 278–289; science, 457–460; society, 224; weather, 394–396
Elliott, Jackson S., 249
Emphasis, proper, 110
Employment, 219–220
Enforcing civil law, 333–334
Engagements, 225
Entertainment places, 231–232
Epigram lead, 90
Erlandson, Erling H., 105–106; 107
Ernst, Morris L., 149
Essayists, 468–469
Ethics, 24–29; code, 442; crime, 314–318; science, 456–457; society, 234
Evaluating a career, 264–265
Evaluative words, 126–128
Evanston *Review*, 191
Events, feature, 481–482; identification, 169
Evictions, 335
Evidence, court, 308–309; rules of, 340–342
Exceptional children, 387
Explanation, financial, 417–422
Extraordinary remedies, legal, 336–337
Eyewitness accounts, 188–190

Facts, organizing the, 49–63
Factual background, 187–188
Faherty, Robert, 102
Fair comment, 153
Familiar persons, 484–485; places, 482–483
Faults, brevities, 214–216; grammatical, 113–114
Features, 477–490; follow-up, 173–174; playing up, 64–83; society, 228–229
Federal Bureau of Investigation, 299; 325
Federal courts, 324–325; government, 392–394
Figures, 502–503
Figures of speech, 111
Filing a will, 338
Finances, city, 379–382
Financial news, 415–433
Finley, Dr. John H., 9
Fine arts, 477
First day story, convention, 242–245
Fitzgerald, Stephen E., 102
Five w's and the H, 74–77
Flesch, Rudolf, 99–100; 103
Follow-up, 172–178; conventions, 245; features, 181–182; meetings, 239–241; obituaries, 273; speeches, 247–253
Following plays, sports, 464
Forecasts, 201
Foreclosures, 335
Formal interviews, 38–39
Formulas, readability, 99–104; reviewing, 469–471
Freaks, 95
Freedom of the press, 27–29
Freedom to comment, 462
Fremont-Smith, Frank, 450
Friendships on beats, 36–37
Fulks, J. R., 399
Funerals, 270–273

Garst, Robert E., 202
Gauvreau, E. H., 462
Gilman, Lawrence, 476
Giving it substance, 185–208
Gone With the Wind, 233
Gossip, 213–216; columns, 230–232
Government, 369–403; secrecy, 44–45; 146

Graham, Billy, 449
Grammatical faults, 113–114
Grand jury, 304–305
Growth of interpretation, 15–17
Guests, 218–219
Gunning, Robert, 99–101

Handling important assignments, 209–490
Hanson, Harry, 474
Harrington, Harry F., 480
Harris, Sydney J., 4; 122
"Hath Difficulties? Behold the Editor," 132
Hearsay evidence, 341
Historical features, 487–488
Holidays, 449
Hold Your Tongue, 149
How, the, 77
How to Lie With Statistics, 19
How to prepare, reporter, 18–24
How to Predict Elections, 350
Huff, Darrell, 19
Human interest, 71–74; crime, 298–299

Identification, 159–171
Illinois Business Review, 408
Illness, 257–258
Impressionistic reporting, 128–130
"In a Couple of Years," 256
Indefinite who, 166
Indirect reference, 140–141
Inferior courts, 323
Informational background, 18–21
Injunctions, 336
Inquests, 278
Insinuations, 152
Integration, schools, 385–386
International Association of Chiefs of Police, 299
Interpretation, 14–17; 45–48; 197–201; weather, 398–399
Interviews, 33–41; personality, 232–233
Invasion of privacy, 26
Inverted pyramid form, 52–54
Investigations, 177–178; 203–205
Issues, political, 362–363
"It Happens Every Day," 212

Journalism, today and tomorrow, 5–6
"Journalism's Adolescence," 32

John, Dr. Otto, 189–190
Judicial notice, 340
Judicial opinions, 320
Jury, picking the, 308
Juveniles, 298

Karas, Dr. Jonathan, 456
Keeping up-to-date, 157–184
Kent, Frank, 353; 358
Kinsley, Philip, 158
Kiplinger, Willard M., 346
Kobre, Sidney, 47–48; 259; 315–316
Kole, John W., 193
Krieghbaum, Hillier, 450; 452
Krutch, Joseph Wood, 475

Labor, 433–439
LaGuardia, Fiorello, 346
Language, sports, 465–466
Lasswell, Harold D., 350
Laws, kinds, 321–322; labor, 434–435; obeying them, 145–146
Lazarsfeld, Paul, 350
Leading questions, law, 341
Leads, 55–56; speech, 248–250
Learning the ropes, police, 288–294
Lee, Ivy, 43
Leigh, Vivien, 233
Lerner, Max, 2
Libel, 148–155
Life span, 162
Library Trends, 42
Lindey, Alexander, 149
Lindstrom, Carl, 189
Lippmann, Walter, 350
Literary allusion lead, 90–91
Localization, 175; 191; business, 411–412; obituaries, 266–267; rewrite, 183–184
Louisville Courier-Journal, 171; 206–208; 445
Lubell, Samuel, 350; 362

Making it attractive, 84–95; 164
Making it readable, 96–119
Malice, absence of, 153–154
Mallon, Paul, 140
Mandamus, 337
Markel, Lester, 17; 103; 186
Martin, Lawrence, 480
Martin, Robert G., 107
May, Edgar, 205

Mayor, 373–374
McBride, Mary Margaret, 129
McCarthy, Joseph R., 128–129; 141; 192
McCormick, Robert, 189
Mead, Margaret, 252–253
Meetings, 237–241
Melrose (Wis.) *Chronicle*, 370
Memphis *Press-Scimitar*, 191–192
Mencken, Henry L., 264; 269
Mental health, 259–260
Method, suicide, 276–277
Milwaukee *Journal*, 193; 205; 411–412
Mindszenty, Cardinal, 21
"Mirrors of Life," 286
Modern newsgatherer, 3–29
Mollenhoff, Clark, 146
"More Antics With Semantics," 122
More than one feature, 81–83
Morgue stories, 266–267
Morrison, John L., 21
Moss, Rep. John E., 44; 146
Motion pictures, 474
Motions, criminal, 305–306
Motives, suicide, 276
Music, 475–476
Myers, Gustavus A., 443

Name, society, 224
Nashville *Tennessean*, 447
National Association for the Advancement of Colored People, 386
National Association of Science Writers, 457
National Broadcasting company, 189
Nationality, 161–162
Nature of newspaper work, 6–9
Need for interpretation, 14–15
New York *Times*, 364
New Yorker, 233
Newcomers, 219
News, definition, 139; featurized, 478–480; past, 162; peg, 87–88; values, 67–74
Newsgathering, problems of, 30–48
Newspaper policy, 25–26; terms, 511–514
"Newspaperman's Credo," 2
Newsweek, 15
Nieman Reports, 192; 202; 370

Night life, 231
"No Time to Lose," 370
Nomenclature, religion, 447–448
Nose for news, 11–13
Notes, reporter's, 62–63
Nouns, 126
Noyes, Newbold, Jr., 32; 128

Obeying the law, 145–146
Obituaries, 260–275
Obscure persons, 485–486; places, 483–484
Occasions, 164; 167; society, 224
Occupation, 160; types, 486–487
Occupational aids, reporter, 23–24
Officers, court, 325–326
"One Big Happy Family," 4
1–2–3–4 lead, 83
Opening statement, trials, 318
Opinion evidence, 341
Organizing the facts, 49–63
Organizations, identification, 167–168; meetings, 238
Osborn, Henry Fairfield, 315

Paine, Robert, 19
Paragraphing, block, 58–59
Parochial schools, 386
Parody lead, 91
Parts of speech, 114
Passive voice, 109–110
Pathways to Print, 480
Payola, 428
Peoria newspapers, 188
Perseverance, 34–36
Persistence, 142–145
Personal element, 213
Personality interviews, 232–244
Personifications, shopworn, 112
Persons and personalities, 211–234; familiar, 484–485; obscure, 485–486
Perspective, 201–208; accidents, 282–283
Peru *Tribune*, 298
Philosophy, political, 349
Phrases, 128; leads, 79; superfluous, 107–108
Picking the feature, 179–180; accidents, 280; crime, 297–302; society, 228–229
Picking the identification, 164–165

Places, 168–169; familiar, 482–483;
    meetings, 238; obscure, 483–484;
    weddings, 228
Playing safe, libel, 154–155
Playing up the feature, 64–83
Pleas, criminal, 305–306
Politics, 345–363; church, 445–446;
    finances, 427–433; organization,
    350–354; philosophy, 349; "post
    mortems," 366–367; public opin-
    ion, 349–350
"Politics is Serious Business," 346
Police, 288–294
Policy, newspaper, 25–26
Polk, James K., 361
Pre-campaign activities, 354–358
Precautions, accidents, 280–281
Precincts, 352–353
Predictions, 170
Preliminary hearing, 303–304
Preliminary story, conventions, 242;
    meetings, 237–239; speeches, 246–
    247
President's press conference, 141
Press conferences, 141
Pressures, religion, 446–447
Presumptions, legal, 340
Primaries, 356
Principles of news writing, 1–208
Pringle, Henry F., 40
Privacy, invasion of, 26
Privilege, 153; legal, 341
Probate courts, 323; proceedings,
    337–339
Problems, financial, 427–433; labor,
    436; newsgathering, 30–48
Program, meetings, 238–239
Prohibition, law, 337
Prominence, 70
Proof reader's symbols, 507–510
Proper emphasis, 110
Protestants and Other Americans
    United for Separation of Church
    and State, 449
Providing perspective, 201–208
Proximity, 68–70
Psychopathology and Politics, 350
Public Opinion, 350
Public opinion, political, 349–350
Public relations, 41–44
Public works, 377–378
Publicity seekers, 37–38
Publishers' Auxiliary, 86

Puffery, 125; 427–428
Pulitzer, Joseph, 9
Punch lead, 80
Punctuation, 494–498
Punishments, 314

Qualification, 136
Question lead, 88
Questions, leading, 341
Quill, 210
Quo warranto, 337
Quotation lead, 91–92

Race, 161–162
Ramsey, Claude, 141
Rayburn, Sam, 270–273
Rea, Wayne, 210
Readable, making it, 96–119
Readability formulas, 99–104
Reader's Digest, 15
Real evidence, 341
Receiverships, 335–336
Receptions, 225
Records, sports, 465
Reece, B. Carroll, 192
Refreshments, society, 224
Registration, voters, 355–356
Relationship, 163; weddings, 228–
    229
Religion, 443–449; and schools, 386
Remaining cool, sports, 464
Reminiscences, 175–176
Reporter, decision-making, 20; notes,
    62–63; prerogatives, 24–25; quali-
    fications, 9–17
Reputation, individuals, 163; organ-
    izations, 167–168
Resourcefulness, 33–34
Resurrected story, 178
Résumés, 202
Responsibility in science, 452–456
Retractions, 154
Reviewing, 468–477
Reviewing a life, 262–263
Revived story, 176–177
Rewrite, 178–184
Rhetorical devices, 78–80
Roman Catholic schools, 386
Romance, 228
Roorbacks, 361–362
Roosevelt, F. D., 315

Rules, sports, 464–465
Running story, 176

Sackett, H. W., 151
St. Louis *Globe-Democrat*, 413
Salter, John, 353
San Francisco *Chronicle*, 411
Sancton, Thomas, 128
Saying it right, 121–130
Schools, 384–388
Science, 449–460
Science Service, 453; 454
Second-day story, 171–173; comment, 174–175; obituary, 268–270
Second-hand information, 134–135
Secondary feature, 180–181
Secrecy in government, 44–45; 146; 227
Sentences, criminal, 313–314
Separate stories, 81
Sequence, 74
Shirttail method, 81
Shopworn personifications, 112
Shorthand, 23
Showers, 225
Sibley, Bob, 256
Side features, 267–268
Sidebars, 190–191; biographical, 166–167
Siebert, Frederick S., 148–149
Sigma Delta Chi on secrecy, 44
Significance, 199
Simplicity, 108–109
Simpson, Kirke L., 270
Situations, crime, 300–302; features, 480–482, 489–490; and trends, 205–208
Slosson, Dr. Edwin E., 453
Smart, Ted, 205
Smith, Walter "Red," 466
Society news, 224–230; gossip, 232; page, 222–224
Sources of brevities, 213–214
Space age glossary, 450–451
Spaid, Ora, 206; 445
Speech, figures of, 111
Speech, parts of, 114
Speeches, 246–253; political, 388
Spiraling, 57
Sports, 463–468
"Spot News is Not Enough," 86
Staccato lead, 89

"Staff Meeting," 50
Stage, 474
Stagg, Edward W., 370
Standard & Poor, 420
State government, 391–392; politics, 359
Statements, closing, 309; opening, 308
Statistics, 19; crime, 299–300
Staunton, Helen M., 212
Steffens, Lincoln, 350
Stern, J. David, 166
Stock exchanges, 415–416
Strategy, political, 358–359
Strikes, 438–439
Stunts, 205; 488
Style, 104; meetings, 241; obituaries, 275; sheets, 493–503; society, 224–225; wedding, 229–230
Substantive clause lead, 78–79
Suicides, 275–278
Summary statement lead, 78
Superfluous clauses, 108; details, 105; phrases, 107–108; words, 105–107
Superstition, 447
Supreme Court, 147; 191; 321; 385
Surveys, 203
Suspended interest, 93–94
Sylvester, B. F., 50; 66
Synonyms, 165
Syracuse *Post-Standard*, 442

Terms, newspaper, 511–514
Terral, Rufus, 282
Texas Press Messenger, 406
The American Voter, 350
"The Case for Interpretation," 186
"The City Editor at Home," 66
The Fading American Newspaper, 189
The Future of American Politics, 350
The Great Game of Politics, 358
The Law of Libel, 151
"The Mission of the Press," 210
"The Need to Know," 370
The People's Choice, 350
The People's Right to Know, 146
The Phantom Public, 350
"The Reporter's Guide," 492
The Revolt of the Moderates, 350

"The Rewards of a Reporter," 159
The Rights and Privileges of the Press, 148
Themes, news stories, 60
Tie-back, 170
Time, meetings, 238
Time, 15; 492
Timeliness, 68
Titles, 161; 502
Total effect, 136–138
Trends, business, 412–415; contemporary, 518
Trials, civil, 332–333; criminal, 307–314
Trips, 220–221
Troublesome words, 115–119
Truman, Harry S., 146; 171; 449
Truth as a defense, 152–153
Types of personal news, 216–222; of society news, 223–224

Unfamiliar words, 124
Uniform Crime Reports, 300
United Press International, 179; 189; 191; 450–451
United States News & World Report, 20
Unity in news stories, 57–58
Urban renewal, 384
Usage, correct, 113–119

Vacations, 221–222
Valuable traits, reporter, 11
Van Doren, Mrs. Irita, 475
Verbs, 127
Verdict, criminal, 312–313
Verification, 135
Voice, passive and active, 109–110

Voting, 350

Wall Street Journal, 204; 407
War record, 162
Wards, 352–353
Washington Cover-up, 146
Watson, Harry S., 411
Weather, 394–403
Weddings, 226–228
Welch, Joseph N., 128
What, the, 75
What is news? 13
Wheeling (W. Va.) *News*, 320
When, the, 76–77
Where, the, 76
White, David Manning, 137
Who, the, 74
White, Donald K., 411
Why, the, 75; in business, 409–410
Wiggins, J. Russell, 141
Williams. Edward, 205
Wills, 338–339
Wilmington *News-Journal*, 429
Wilson, Earl, 231
Winchell, Walter, 216
Winn, Marcia, 98
Winning reader confidence, 131–155
Witnesses, qualifications, 340
Wolfe, A. B., 350
Wilfle, Dr. Dael, 460
Words, 171; dangerous, 150–152; evaluative, 126–128; superfluous, 105–107; troublesome, 115–119; unfamiliar, 125

Yankwich, Judge Leon R., 320

Zangara, Giuseppe, 315